50 Essays

A Portable Anthology

50
Essays

A Portable Anthology

Third Edition

Edited by

SAMUEL COHEN

University of Missouri

Bedford/St. Martin's BOSTON ◆ NEW YORK

For Bedford/St. Martin's

Developmental Editor: Amy Gershman
Editorial Assistant: Kate Mayhew
Production Associate: Ashley Chalmers
Marketing Manager: Adrienne Petsick
Text Design: Sandra Rigney
Project Management: DeMasi Design and Publishing Service
Cover Design: Marine Bouvier Miller
Cover Photo: *Elevated View of Books in a Circle.* Dimitri Vervitsiotis/ Digital Vision/Getty Images, Inc.
Composition: Jeff Miller Book Design
Printing and Binding: RR Donnelley & Sons, Inc.

President: Joan E. Feinberg
Editorial Director: Denise B. Wydra
Editor in Chief: Karen S. Henry
Director of Marketing: Karen R. Soeltz
Director of Production: Susan W. Brown
Associate Director of Editorial Production: Elise S. Kaiser
Manager, Publishing Services: Emily Berleth

Library of Congress Control Number: 2010906346

Manufactured in the United States of America.

5 4 3 2 1 0
f e d c b a

For information, write: Bedford/St. Martin's, 75 Arlington Street, Boston, MA 02116 (617-399-4000)

ISBN-10: 0-312-60965-5
ISBN-13: 978-0-312-60965-8

Acknowledgments
Acknowledgments and copyrights are continued at the back of the book on pages 467–70, which constitute an extension of the copyright page.

Preface for Instructors

50 Essays: A Portable Anthology is a compact, inexpensive collection of classic and contemporary essays, most of which have already proven popular in hundreds of classrooms and with thousands of students. Learning how to read good writing effectively is crucial to learning how to write and think critically — and *50 Essays* is full of exceptional prose and many opportunities to practice reading, thinking, and writing about it.

50 Essays includes a core of classic essays such as Maya Angelou's "Graduation," E. B. White's "Once More to the Lake," and Malcolm X's "Learning to Read," accompanied by fresh, recent selections such as Eric Schlosser's "Kid Kustomers" and Michael Pollan's "What's Eating America." For such a compact volume, *50 Essays* represents an extraordinary diversity of voices and genres — from polemical exhortations to personal narratives, from speeches to meditations, from nuanced arguments to humorous articles. Of varied length and complexity, the essays should stimulate ideas for students' own writing as they provide sound models for rhetorical analysis.

But *50 Essays* is more than just a selection of good readings: It is a versatile and practical collection designed to prompt critical thinking and writing in the composition classroom. For maximum flexibility and ease of navigation, the essays are arranged alphabetically by author, while alternate tables of contents are provided to help instructors shape courses that meet their teaching preferences. For example, one table of contents is organized by theme (ethics, gender, identity, pop culture, science and nature, among others); another by rhetorical mode (narration, description, comparison, and so forth); another by rhetorical purpose (personal, expository, argumentative writing); another by pairs and clusters of readings (Zora Neale Hurston and Audre Lorde on "Women

Speaking to Racism," Nancy Mairs and David Sedaris on "Coping with Disabilities," Stephen Jay Gould and Michael Pollan on "Shaping Our Future in Science," and more); and a final table lists the selections chronologically by the date of the essay's composition.

For students, an introduction provides advice on the key skills of active reading, critical thinking, and writing. Terms in bold throughout the introduction refer to a glossary at the back of the book — which defines important writing terms, such as *audience, evidence*, and *plagiarism*. An annotated model paper shows students how to work with and analyze multiple sources. Headnotes contextualize each reading in its writer's own place and time. As an aid to comprehension, the essays themselves are lightly glossed. Several types of assignments follow each reading and provide multiple avenues into it: questions on content, on rhetorical strategy, on connections between and among selections, and on ideas for further analysis and research.

NEW TO THIS EDITION

Seventeen readings are new to this edition, including texts by Rachel Carson, Bill McKibben, Michael Pollan, Scott Russell Sanders, Eric Schlosser, and Alice Walker. A number of argument essays, as well as more readings on contemporary topics (such as media and pop culture and science, nature, and the environment) have been added in response to instructors' requests for such selections.

New editorial features introduce even greater teaching flexibility: There are more topically linked essays throughout the book; a new alternate table of contents highlights possible pairings and clusters; and each selection is followed by questions that make connections to other selections.

Students are also offered more help with the kinds of reading, writing, and thinking they will do throughout college. A new model paper in the Introduction is annotated to demonstrate how students can work with and synthesize multiple sources and develop and support a thesis. An updated appendix on MLA-style documentation helps students write their own source-based papers.

YOU GET MORE DIGITAL CHOICES FOR *50 ESSAYS*

50 Essays doesn't stop with a book. Online, you'll discover both free and affordable premium resources to help students get even more out of the book and your course. You'll also find convenient instructor resources, such as downloadable sample syllabi, classroom activities, and even a nationwide community of teachers. To learn more about or order any of the products below, contact your Bedford/St. Martin's sales representative, e-mail sales support (sales_support@bfwpub.com), or visit the Web site at bedfordstmartins.com/50essays/catalog.

Student Resources

Send students to free and open resources, upgrade to an expanding collection of innovative digital content, or package a standalone CD-ROM for free with *50 Essays*.

Re:Writing, the best free collection of online resources for the writing class, offers clear advice on citing sources in *Research and Documentation Online* by Diana Hacker, 30 sample papers and designed documents, and more than 9,000 writing and grammar exercises with immediate feedback and reporting in *Exercise Central*. Updated and redesigned, *Re:Writing* also features five free videos from *VideoCentral* and three new visual tutorials from our popular *ix visual exercises* by Cheryl Ball and Kristin Arola. *Re:Writing* is completely free and open (no codes required) to ensure access to all students. Visit bedfordstmartins.com/rewriting.

VideoCentral is a growing collection of videos for the writing class that captures real-world, academic, and student writers talking about how and why they write. Writer and teacher Peter Berkow interviewed hundreds of people — from Michael Moore to Cynthia Selfe — to produce fifty brief videos about topics such as revising and getting feedback. *VideoCentral* can be packaged with *50 Essays* at a significant discount. An activation code is required. To learn more, visit bedfordstmartins.com/videocentral. To order *VideoCentral* packaged with the print book, use ISBN 0-312-56354-X or 978-0-312-56354-7.

Re:Writing Plus gathers all of Bedford/St. Martin's premium digital content for composition into one online collection. It includes hundreds of model documents, the first ever peer review game, and *VideoCentral*. *Re:Writing Plus* can be purchased separately or packaged with the print book at a significant discount. An activation code is required. To learn more, visit bedfordstmartins.com/rewriting. To order *Re:Writing Plus* packaged with the print book, use ISBN 0-312-56353-1 or 978-0-312-56353-0.

i-series on CD-ROM presents multimedia tutorials in a flexible format — because there are things you can't do in a book:

- *ix visual exercises* help students put into practice key rhetorical and visual concepts. To order *ix visual exercises* packaged with the print book, use ISBN 0-312-56352-3 or 978-0-312-56352-3.
- *i-claim: visualizing argument* offers a new way to see argument — with six tutorials, an illustrated glossary, and over seventy multimedia arguments. To order *i-claim: visualizing argument* packaged with the print book, use ISBN 0-312-56351-5 or 978-0-312-56351-6.
- *i-cite: visualizing sources* bring research to life through an animated introduction, four tutorials, and hands-on source practice. To order *i-claim: visualizing argument* packaged with the print book, use ISBN 0-312-56369-8 or 978-0-312-56369-1.

To learn more, visit bedfordstmartins.com/50essays/catalog.

Instructor Resources

You have a lot to do in your course. Bedford/St. Martin's wants to make it easy for you to find the support you need — and to get it quickly. To find everything available with *50 Essays*, visit bedfordstmartins.com/50essays/catalog.

The Instructor's Manual for *50 Essays*, *Resources for Teaching* 50 Essays, is bound into the instructor's edition of the book, offering sample syllabi and notes on the questions that follow each essay in the book. The manual is also available in a PDF that can be downloaded from the Bedford/St. Martin's online catalog.

Teaching Central offers the entire list of Bedford/St. Martin's print and online professional resources in one place. You'll find landmark reference works, sourcebooks on pedagogical issues, award-winning collections, and practical advice for the classroom — all free for instructors.

Bits collects creative ideas for teaching a range of composition topics in an easily searchable blog. A community of teachers — leading scholars, authors, and editors — discuss revision, research, grammar and style, technology, peer review, and much more. Take, use, adapt, and pass the ideas around. Then, come back to the site to comment or share your own suggestion.

Content cartridges for the most common course management systems — Blackboard, WebCT, Angel, and Desire2Learn — allow you to easily download digital materials from Bedford/St. Martin's for your course.

ACKNOWLEDGMENTS

Many thanks go to the instructors who helped shape this edition of *50 Essays*: Sandy Borel, Battle Mountain High School; Patricia Cain, Pasadena Memorial High School; Anne Ducote, James Madison High School; Susan Edwards, Greenwood Community High School; Christine Ethier, Community College of Philadelphia; Linda Fracek, Grove High School; Racquel Goodison, Borough of Manhattan Community College; Loren Gruber, Missouri Valley College; Jane Jacques, Keyano College; Jill Jessen, Rochester High School; Jennifer Kleckner, C. E. Jordan High School; Janis Krell, Bob Jones High School; Michael Lee, Columbia Basin College; Vern Lindquist, Sullivan County Community College; Matthew Logsdon, Henry Clay High School; Sam Lusk, Southeastern Oklahoma State University; Jennifer McAdams, Upland High School; Barbara McClure, Santa Rosa Junior College; Tanya Millner-Harlee, Manchester Community College; Carol Morrow, Westminster College; Jennifer Poness, Winston Churchill High School; David Putnam, Crest Senior High School; Carrie Riley, Avon High School; Rob Roensch, Towson University; Tim Sadenwasser, Augusta State University; Heather Sargent, Johnson High School; Stephanie Schleicher, Auburn Senior High School; Jessica Shepherd, Fishers High School; Susan Smith, Spaulding High School; Eileen Thompson, Edison State Community College; Harry Thorne, College of Staten Island; and Katie Tiller, Boyle County High School.

I would also like to thank the people at Bedford/St. Martin's who made this book possible, particularly Joan Feinberg, Denise Wydra, Karen Henry, Steve Scipione, and Elizabeth Schaaf. I would especially like to recognize the work of John Sullivan and Karin Halbert, whose vision, experience, and support made the first and second editions possible, and Amy Gershman, whose hard work, good ideas, and patience are responsible for the improvements in the third. Thanks also to Kate Mayhew who ably assisted Amy. I would also like to acknowledge the help of Emily Berleth, who guided the book through production; Leslie Connor, for her careful copyediting; Elaine Kosta for clearing permissions; and Molly Parke for her marketing insights. I would like to thank the teachers from whom I was lucky to learn how to read and write, and teach. I would like to thank my Spring 2003 Writing I students, who were taught this book in its early stages and who had a great deal of unflinchingly honest advice for how to put it together, and the students I have had the pleasure to teach since then. I would like to thank the English Department at the University of Missouri for the job, the office, and the opportunity to work with great students, and my colleagues in Columbia, especially the graduate students in the department who have taught the book and taught me about how it works and how hard they work. Most of all, I would like to thank Kristin Bowen for everything she's taught me about textbooks and much, much more; our boys, Ben and Henry, who have grown up with this book and are now both much taller than it; and our dog Nilla who, although she cannot read, as far as we know, seems to feel warmly toward the book because a batch of manuscript always arrives with a biscuit from the delivery person.

Contents

Preface for Instructors v

Alternate Tables of Contents

By Theme xix

By Pairs and Clusters xxii

By Rhetorical Mode xxv

By Purpose xxvii

By Chronological Order xxix

Introduction for Students: Active Reading, Critical Thinking, and the Writing Process 1

SHERMAN ALEXIE, *The Joy of Reading and Writing: Superman and Me* 15

"I read anything that had words and paragraphs. I read with equal parts joy and desperation. I loved those books, but I also knew that love had only one purpose. I was trying to save my life."

MAYA ANGELOU, *Graduation* 20

"I was no longer simply a member of the proud graduating class of 1940; I was a proud member of the wonderful, beautiful Negro race."

GLORIA ANZALDÚA, *How to Tame a Wild Tongue* 33

"Ethnic identity is twin skin to linguistic identity — I am my language. Until I can take pride in my language, I cannot take pride in myself."

BARBARA LAZEAR ASCHER, *On Compassion* 46

"Compassion is not a character trait like a sunny disposition. It must be learned, and it is learned by having adversity at our windows. . . ."

JAMES BALDWIN, *Notes of a Native Son* 50

". . . I had had time to become aware of the meaning of all my father's bitter warnings, had discovered the secret of his proudly pursed lips and rigid carriage: I had discovered the weight of white people in the world."

DAVE BARRY, *Turkeys in the Kitchen* 72

"Men are still basically scum when it comes to helping out in the kitchen."

WILLIAM F. BUCKLEY JR., *Why Don't We Complain?* 76

"I think the observable reluctance of the majority of Americans to assert themselves in minor matters is related to our increased sense of helplessness in an age of technology and centralized political and economic power."

RACHEL CARSON, *The Obligation to Endure* 83

"Can anyone believe it is possible to lay down such a barrage of poisons on the surface of the earth without making it unfit for all life? They should not be called 'insecticides,' but 'biocides.' "

JUDITH ORTIZ COFER, *The Myth of the Latin Woman: I Just Met a Girl Named María* 91

". . . You can leave the Island, master the English language, and travel as far as you can, but if you are a Latina . . . the Island travels with you."

JARED DIAMOND, *The Ends of the World as We Know Them* 98

"To save ourselves, we don't need new technology: we just need the political will to face up to our problems of population and the environment."

JOAN DIDION, *On Morality* 106

"For better or worse, we are what we learned as children: my own childhood was illuminated by graphic litanies of the grief awaiting those who failed in their own loyalties to each other."

ANNIE DILLARD, *Seeing* 112

"It's all a matter of keeping my eyes open. Nature is like one of those line drawings that are puzzles for children: Can you find hidden in the tree a duck, a house, a boy, a bucket, a zebra, and a boot?"

FREDERICK DOUGLASS, *Learning to Read and Write* 129

". . . I would at times feel that learning to read had been a curse rather than a blessing. It had given me a view of my wretched condition, without the remedy."

BARBARA EHRENREICH, *Serving in Florida* 136

"You might imagine, from a comfortable distance, that people who live, year in and year out, on $6 to $10 an hour have discovered some survival stratagems unknown to the middle class. But no."

LARS EIGHNER, *On Dumpster Diving* 146

"I am a scavenger. I think it a sound and honorable niche, although if I could I would naturally prefer to live the comfortable consumer life, perhaps — and only perhaps — as a slightly less wasteful consumer owing to what I have learned as a scavenger."

STEPHANIE ERICSSON, *The Ways We Lie* 159

". . . [I]t's not easy to entirely eliminate lies from our lives. No matter how pious we may try to be, we will still embellish, hedge, and omit to lubricate the daily machinery of living."

STEPHEN JAY GOULD, *Sex, Drugs, Disasters, and the Extinction of Dinosaurs* 169

". . . A recognition of the very phenomenon that made our evolution possible by exterminating the previously dominant dinosaurs . . . might actually help to save us from joining those magnificent beasts in contorted poses among the strata of the earth."

LANGSTON HUGHES, *Salvation* 179

" 'Langston, why don't you come? Why don't you come and be saved? Oh, Lamb of God! Why don't you come?' "

ZORA NEALE HURSTON, *How It Feels to Be Colored Me* 182

"I have no separate feeling about being an American citizen and colored. I am merely a fragment of the Great Soul that surges within the boundaries. My country, right or wrong."

THOMAS JEFFERSON, *The Declaration of Independence* 187

"We hold these truths to be self-evident, that all men are created equal, that they are endowed by their Creator with certain unalienable Rights, that among these are Life, Liberty, and the pursuit of Happiness."

STEVEN JOHNSON, *Games* 196

". . . [E]ven the most avid reader in this culture is invariably going to spend his or her time with other media. . . . And these other forms of culture have intellectual or cognitive virtues in their own right."

MARTIN LUTHER KING JR., *Letter from Birmingham Jail* 203

"I submit that an individual who breaks a law that conscience tells him is unjust, and who willingly accepts the penalty of imprisonment in order to arouse the conscience of the community over its injustice, is in reality expressing the highest respect for law."

MAXINE HONG KINGSTON, *No Name Woman* 221

"Those of us in the first American generations have had to figure out how the invisible world the emigrant built around our childhoods fit in solid America."

VERLYN KLINKENBORG, *Our Vanishing Night* 234

"Living in a glare of our own making, we have cut ourselves off from our evolutionary and cultural patrimony — the light of the stars and the rhythms of day and night."

AUDRE LORDE, *The Fourth of July* 239

"My mother and father believed that they could best protect their children from the realities of race in American and the fact of American racism by never giving them name, much less discussing their nature."

NANCY MAIRS, *On Being a Cripple* 244

"People — crippled or not — wince at the word 'cripple,' as they do not at 'handicapped' or 'disabled.' Perhaps I want them to wince."

MALCOLM X, *Learning to Read* 257

". . . [T]he ability to read awoke inside me some long dormant craving to be mentally alive. I certainly wasn't seeking any degree, the way a college confers a status symbol upon its students."

BILL McKIBBEN, *Curbing Nature's Paparazzi* 267

"After a lifetime of exposure to nature shows and magazine photos, we arrive at the woods conditioned to expect splendor and are surprised when the parking lot does not contain a snarl of animals mating and killing one another."

N. SCOTT MOMADAY, *The Way to Rainy Mountain* 273

"A single knoll rises out of the plain in Oklahoma, north and west of the Wichita Range. For my people, the Kiowas, it is an old landmark, and they gave it the name Rainy Mountain."

BHARATI MUKHERJEE, *Two Ways to Belong in America* 280

"This is a tale of two sisters from Calcutta, Mira and Bharati, who have lived in the United States for some 35 years, but who find themselves on different sides in the current debate over the status of immigrants."

GEORGE ORWELL, *Shooting an Elephant* 284

"It was a tiny incident in itself, but it gave me a better glimpse than I had had before of the real nature of imperialism — the real motives for which despotic governments act."

PLATO, *The Allegory of the Cave* 292

"And now, I said, let me show in a figure how far our nature is enlightened or unenlightened. . . ."

MICHAEL POLLAN, *What's Eating America* 300

"It's not just sweetening the soft drinks or lending a shine to the magazine cover over by the checkout. The supermarket itself — the wallboard and joint compound, the linoleum and fiberglass and adhesives out of which the building itself has been built — is in no small measure a manifestation of corn."

RICHARD RODRIGUEZ, *Aria: Memoir of a Bilingual Childhood* 307

"Because I wrongly imagined that English was intrinsically a public language and Spanish an intrinsically private one, I easily noted the difference between classroom language and the language of home."

MIKE ROSE, *"I Just Wanna Be Average"* 331

"Students will float to the mark you set. I and the others in the vocational classes were bobbing in pretty shallow water."

SCOTT RUSSELL SANDERS, *The Men We Carry in Our Minds* 346

". . . I was baffled when the women at college accused me and my sex of having cornered the world's pleasures. I think something of my bafflement has been felt by other boys (and by girls as well) who have grown up in dirt-poor farm country. . . ."

ERIC SCHLOSSER, *Kid Kustomers* 353

"Indeed, market research has found that children often recognize a brand logo before they can recognize their own name."

DAVID SEDARIS, *A Plague of Tics* 359

"It wasn't that I enjoyed pressing my nose against the scalding hood of a parked car — pleasure had nothing to do with it. A person *had* to do these things because nothing was worse than the anguish of not doing them."

SUSAN SONTAG, *Regarding the Pain of Others* 373

"Still, there are pictures whose power does not abate, in part because one cannot look at them. Pictures of the ruined faces that will always testify to a great inequity survived, at a cost. . . ."

ELIZABETH CADY STANTON, *Declaration of Sentiments and Resolutions* 379

"We hold these truths to be self-evident: that all men and women are created equal. . . ."

BRENT STAPLES, *Just Walk on By: Black Men and Public Space* 383

"Over the years, I learned to smother the rage I felt at so often being taken for a criminal. Not to do so would surely have led to madness."

JONATHAN SWIFT, *A Modest Proposal* 387

". . . I propose to provide for [poor infants] in such a manner as instead of being a charge upon their parents or the parish, or wanting food and raiment for the rest of their lives, they shall on the contrary contribute to the feeding, and partly to the clothing, of many thousands."

AMY TAN, *Mother Tongue* 396

"I am fascinated by language in daily life. I spend a great deal of my time thinking about the power of language — the way it can evoke an emotion, a visual image, a complex idea, or a simple truth. Language is the tool of my trade. And I use them all — all the Englishes I grew up with."

HENRY DAVID THOREAU, *Where I Lived, and What I Lived For* 403

"When we are unhurried and wise, we perceive that only great and worthy things have any permanent and absolute existence, that petty fears and petty pleasures are but the shadow of the reality."

SOJOURNER TRUTH, *Ain't I a Woman?* 410

"I have ploughed, and planted, and gathered into barns, and no man could head me. And ain't I a woman?"

SARAH VOWELL, *Shooting Dad* 412

"We're older now, my dad and I. The older I get, the more I'm interested in becoming a better daughter. First on my list: Figure out the whole gun thing."

ALICE WALKER, *In Search of Our Mothers' Gardens* 420

"And so our mothers and grandmothers have, more often than not anonymously, handed on the creative spark, the seed of the flower they themselves never hoped to see: or like a sealed letter they could not plainly read."

E. B. WHITE, *Once More to the Lake* 431

"Summertime, oh, summertime, pattern of life indelible, the fade-proof lake, the woods unshatterable, the pasture with the sweetfern and the juniper forever and ever, summer without end. . . ."

MARIE WINN, *Television: The Plug-In Drug* 438

". . . Isn't there a better family life available than this dismal, mechanized arrangement of children watching television for however long is allowed them, evening after evening?"

VIRGINIA WOOLF, *The Death of the Moth* 448

"It was as if someone had taken a tiny bead of pure life and decking it as lightly as possible with down and feathers, had set it dancing and zig-zagging to show us the true nature of life."

Documentation Guide 453

Glossary of Writing Terms 459

Index of Authors and Titles 471

Table of Contents by Theme

Education

Sherman Alexie, *The Joy of Reading and Writing: Superman and Me* 15
Maya Angelou, *Graduation* 20
Gloria Anzaldúa, *How to Tame a Wild Tongue* 33
Frederick Douglass, *Learning to Read and Write* 129
Audre Lorde, *The Fourth of July* 239
Malcolm X, *Learning to Read* 257
Richard Rodriguez, *Aria: Memoir of a Bilingual Childhood* 307

Ethics

William F. Buckley Jr., *Why Don't We Complain?* 76
Joan Didion, *On Morality* 106
Annie Dillard, *Seeing* 112
Stephanie Ericsson, *The Ways We Lie* 159
Martin Luther King Jr., *Letter from Birmingham Jail* 203
Nancy Mairs, *On Being a Cripple* 244
George Orwell, *Shooting an Elephant* 284
Plato, *The Allegory of the Cave* 292
Susan Sontag, *Regarding the Pain of Others* 373
Jonathan Swift, *A Modest Proposal* 387
Virginia Woolf, *The Death of the Moth* 448

Family

Dave Barry, *Lost in the Kitchen* 72
Langston Hughes, *Salvation* 179
Maxine Hong Kingston, *No Name Woman* 221
N. Scott Momaday, *The Way to Rainy Mountain* 273
Bharati Mukherjee, *Two Ways to Belong in America* 280
Richard Rodriguez, *Aria: Memoir of a Bilingual Childhood* 307
David Sedaris, *A Plague of Tics* 359
Amy Tan, *Mother Tongue* 396
Sarah Vowell, *Shooting Dad* 412
Alice Walker, *In Search of Our Mothers' Gardens* 420
E. B. White, *Once More to the Lake* 431
Marie Winn, *Television: The Plug-In Drug* 438

Gender

Dave Barry, *Turkeys in the Kitchen* 72
Maxine Hong Kingston, *No Name Woman* 221
Scott Russell Sanders, *The Men We Carry in Our Minds* 346
Elizabeth Cady Stanton, *Declaration of Sentiments and Resolutions* 379
Brent Staples, *Just Walk on By: Black Men and Public Space* 383
Sojourner Truth, *Ain't I a Woman?* 410
Alice Walker, *In Search of Our Mothers' Gardens* 420

History and Politics

Jared Diamond, *The Ends of the World as We Know Them* 98
Thomas Jefferson, *The Declaration of Independence* 187
Martin Luther King Jr., *Letter from Birmingham Jail* 203
Bharati Mukherjee, *Two Ways to Belong in America* 280
George Orwell, *Shooting an Elephant* 284
Michael Pollan, *What's Eating America* 300
Elizabeth Cady Stanton, *Declaration of Sentiments and Resolutions* 379
Jonathan Swift, *A Modest Proposal* 387

Identity

Maya Angelou, *Graduation* 20
Gloria Anzaldúa, *How to Tame a Wild Tongue* 33
James Baldwin, *Notes of a Native Son* 50
Judith Ortiz Cofer, *The Myth of the Latin Woman: I Just Met a Girl Named María* 91
Nancy Mairs, *On Being a Cripple* 244
N. Scott Momaday, *The Way to Rainy Mountain* 273
David Sedaris, *A Plague of Tics* 359
Brent Staples, *Just Walk on By: Black Men and Public Space* 383
Sarah Vowell, *Shooting Dad* 412
Alice Walker, *In Search of Our Mothers' Gardens* 420

Media and Pop Culture

Steven Johnson, *Games* 196
Bill McKibben, *Curbing Nature's Paparazzi* 267
Michael Pollan, *What's Eating America* 300
Eric Schlosser, *Kid Kustomers* 353
Marie Winn, *Television: The Plug-In Drug* 438

Race and Culture

Gloria Anzaldúa, *How to Tame a Wild Tongue* 33
James Baldwin, *Notes of a Native Son* 50
Judith Ortiz Cofer, *The Myth of the Latin Woman: I Just Met a Girl Named María* 91

Zora Neale Hurston, *How It Feels to Be Colored Me* 182
Martin Luther King Jr., *Letter from Birmingham Jail* 203
Maxine Hong Kingston, *No Name Woman* 221
Audre Lorde, *The Fourth of July* 239
Alice Walker, *In Search of Our Mothers' Gardens* 420

Reading, Writing, and Speaking

Sherman Alexie, *The Joy of Reading and Writing: Superman and Me* 15
Gloria Anzaldúa, *How to Tame a Wild Tongue* 33
Frederick Douglass, *Learning to Read and Write* 129
Stephanie Ericsson, *The Ways We Lie* 159
Malcolm X, *Learning to Read* 257
Richard Rodriguez, *Aria: Memoir of a Bilingual Childhood* 307
Amy Tan, *Mother Tongue* 396

Science, Nature, and the Environment

Rachel Carson, *The Obligation to Endure* 83
Jared Diamond, *The Ends of the World as We Know Them* 98
Annie Dillard, *Seeing* 112
Stephen Jay Gould, *Sex, Drugs, Disasters, and the Extinction of Dinosaurs* 169
Verlyn Klinkenborg, *Our Vanishing Night* 234
Bill McKibben, *Curbing Nature's Paparazzi* 267
N. Scott Momaday, *The Way to Rainy Mountain* 273
Michael Pollan, *What's Eating America* 300
Henry David Thoreau, *Where I Lived, and What I Lived For* 403
E. B. White, *Once More to the Lake* 431
Virginia Woolf, *The Death of the Moth* 448

Work and Class

Barbara Lazear Ascher, *On Compassion* 46
Barbara Ehrenreich, *Serving in Florida* 136
Lars Eighner, *On Dumpster Diving* 146
Scott Russell Sanders, *The Men We Carry in Our Minds* 346

Table of Contents by Pairs and Clusters

The following pairs and clusters of three and four essays engage with each other on a topic. The list is not exhaustive, but it may serve as a useful starting point for ideas for class discussion or writing assignments. Note that every selection in this book is followed by a "connections" question inviting comparison and contrast with another essay, and some of those questions suggest additional pairings that are not indicated here.

Language and Identity

Gloria Anzaldúa, *How to Tame a Wild Tongue* 33
Richard Rodriguez, *Aria: Memoir of a Bilingual Childhood* 307
Amy Tan, *Mother Tongue* 396

Immigrant Tales

Judith Ortiz Cofer, *The Myth of the Latin Woman: I Just Met a Girl Named María* 91
Bharati Mukherjee, *Two Ways to Belong in America* 280

Ancestors and Legacies

Maxine Hong Kingston, *No Name Woman* 221
N. Scott Momaday, *The Way to Rainy Mountain* 273
Sarah Vowell, *Shooting Dad* 412
Alice Walker, *In Search of Our Mothers' Gardens* 420

Miseducational Systems

Maya Angelou, *Graduation* 20
Mike Rose, *"I Just Wanna Be Average"* 331

Saved by Reading

Sherman Alexie, *The Joy of Reading and Writing: Superman and Me* 15
Frederick Douglass, *Learning to Read and Write* 129
Malcolm X, *Learning to Read* 257

Men Encountering Racism

James Baldwin, *Notes of a Native Son* 50
Brent Staples, *Just Walk on By: Black Men and Public Space* 383

Women Speaking to Racism

Zora Neale Hurston, *How It Feels to Be Colored Me* 182
Audre Lorde, *The Fourth of July* 239

Exclaiming Gender Stereotypes

Dave Barry, *Turkeys in the Kitchen* 72
Judith Ortiz Cofer, *The Myth of the Latin Woman: I Just Met a Girl Named María* 91
Scott Russell Sanders, *The Men We Carry in Our Minds* 346

Proclaiming Women's Rights

Elizabeth Cady Stanton, *Declaration of Sentiments and Resolutions* 379
Sojourner Truth, *Ain't I a Woman?* 410

Living Poor

Barbara Lazear Ascher, *On Compassion* 46
Barbara Ehrenreich, *Serving in Florida* 136
Lars Eighner, *On Dumpster Diving* 146

Coping with Disabilities

Nancy Mairs, *On Being a Cripple* 244
David Sedaris, *A Plague of Tics* 359

Seeing and Reality

Annie Dillard, *Seeing* 112
Plato, *The Allegory of the Cave* 292
Susan Sontag, *Regarding the Pain of Others* 373

Media Messages

Steven Johnson, *Games* 196
Eric Schlosser, *Kid Kustomers* 353
Marie Winn, *Television: The Plug-In Drug* 438

Looking at Nature

Annie Dillard, *Seeing* 112
Verlyn Klinkenborg, *Our Vanishing Night* 234
Bill McKibben, *Curbing Nature's Paparazzi* 267

Saving Ourselves and the Earth

Rachel Carson, *The Obligation to Endure* 83
Jared Diamond, *The Ends of the World as We Know Them* 98
Stephen Jay Gould, *Sex, Drugs, Disasters, and the Extinction of Dinosaurs* 169

Shaping Our Future in Science

Stephen Jay Gould, *Sex, Drugs, Disasters, and the Extinction of Dinosaurs* 169
Michael Pollan, *What's Eating America* 300

Nature and Morality

E. B. White, *Once More to the Lake* 431
Virginia Woolf, *The Death of the Moth* 448

Defining Independence

Thomas Jefferson, *The Declaration of Independence* 187
Elizabeth Cady Stanton, *Declaration of Sentiments and Resolutions* 379
Henry David Thoreau, *Where I Lived, and What I Lived For* 403

Moral Choices

Joan Didion, *On Morality* 106
George Orwell, *Shooting an Elephant* 284

Avoiding the Truth

Stephanie Ericsson, *The Ways We Lie* 159
Langston Hughes, *Salvation* 179

Consequences of Conformity

William F. Buckley Jr., *Why Don't We Complain?* 76
George Orwell, *Shooting an Elephant* 284

Arguing Against Injustice

Thomas Jefferson, *The Declaration of Independence* 187
Martin Luther King Jr., *Letter from Birmingham Jail* 203
Jonathan Swift, *A Modest Proposal* 387

Table of Contents by Rhetorical Mode

Narration

Maya Angelou, *Graduation* 20
Langston Hughes, *Salvation* 179
Maxine Hong Kingston, *No Name Woman* 221
Audre Lorde, *The Fourth of July* 239
N. Scott Momaday, *The Way to Rainy Mountain* 273
George Orwell, *Shooting an Elephant* 284
David Sedaris, *A Plague of Tics* 359
Alice Walker, *In Search of Our Mothers' Gardens* 420

Description

Annie Dillard, *Seeing* 112
Zora Neale Hurston, *How It Feels to Be Colored Me* 182
Sarah Vowell, *Shooting Dad* 412
E. B. White, *Once More to the Lake* 431
Virginia Woolf, *Death of the Moth* 448

Process Analysis

Sherman Alexie, *The Joy of Reading and Writing: Superman and Me* 15
Frederick Douglass, *Learning to Read and Write* 129
Lars Eighner, *On Dumpster Diving* 146
Malcolm X, *Learning to Read* 257

Example

Barbara Lazear Ascher, *On Compassion* 46
Jared Diamond, *The Ends of the World as We Know Them* 98
Barbara Ehrenreich, *Serving in Florida* 136
Thomas Jefferson, *The Declaration of Independence* 187
Scott Russell Sanders, *The Men We Carry in Our Minds* 346
Eric Schlosser, *Kid Kustomers* 353
Sojourner Truth, *Ain't I a Woman?* 410
Alice Walker, *In Search of Our Mothers' Gardens* 420

Definition

Gloria Anzaldúa, *How to Tame a Wild Tongue* 33
Joan Didion, *On Morality* 106
Stephen Jay Gould, *Sex, Drugs, Disasters, and the Extinction of Dinosaurs* 169
Nancy Mairs, *On Being a Cripple* 244
Scott Russell Sanders, *The Men We Carry in Our Minds* 346

Classification

Judith Ortiz Cofer, *The Myth of the Latin Woman: I Just Met a Girl Named María* 91
Jared Diamond, *The Ends of the World as We Know Them* 98
Stephanie Ericsson, *The Ways We Lie* 159
Mike Rose, *"I Just Wanna Be Average"* 331
Scott Russell Sanders, *The Men We Carry in Our Minds* 346
Amy Tan, *Mother Tongue* 396

Comparison/Contrast

James Baldwin, *Notes of a Native Son* 50
Dave Barry, *Turkeys in the Kitchen* 72
Annie Dillard, *Seeing* 112
Bharati Mukherjee, *Two Ways to Belong in America* 280
Richard Rodriguez, *Aria: Memoir of a Bilingual Childhood* 307
Henry David Thoreau, *Where I Lived, and What I Lived For* 403

Cause/Effect

William F. Buckley Jr., *Why Don't We Complain?* 76
Rachel Carson, *The Obligation to Endure* 83
Verlyn Klinkenborg, *Our Vanishing Night* 234
Michael Pollan, *What's Eating America* 300
Eric Schlosser, *Kid Kustomers* 353
Brent Staples, *Just Walk on By: Black Men and Public Space* 383
Marie Winn, *Television: The Plug-In Drug* 438

Argument/Persuasion

Rachel Carson, *The Obligation to Endure* 83
Stephen Jay Gould, *Sex, Drugs, Disasters, and the Extinction of Dinosaurs* 169
Steven Johnson, *Games* 196
Martin Luther King Jr., *Letter from Birmingham Jail* 203
Verlyn Klinkenborg, *Our Vanishing Night* 234
Bill McKibben, *Curbing Nature's Paparazzi* 267
Plato, *The Allegory of the Cave* 292
Susan Sontag, *Regarding the Pain of Others* 373
Elizabeth Cady Stanton, *Declaration of Sentiments and Resolutions* 379
Jonathan Swift, *A Modest Proposal* 387
Alice Walker, *In Search of Our Mothers' Gardens* 420

Table of Contents by Purpose

Personal

Sherman Alexie, *The Joy of Reading and Writing: Superman and Me* 15
Maya Angelou, *Graduation* 20
Gloria Anzaldúa, *How to Tame a Wild Tongue* 33
James Baldwin, *Notes of a Native Son* 50
Judith Ortiz Cofer, *The Myth of the Latin Woman: I Just Met a Girl Named María* 91
Frederick Douglass, *Learning to Read and Write* 129
Langston Hughes, *Salvation* 179
Zora Neale Hurston, *How It Feels to Be Colored Me* 182
Maxine Hong Kingston, *No Name Woman* 221
Audre Lorde, *The Fourth of July* 239
Nancy Mairs, *On Being a Cripple* 244
Malcolm X, *Learning to Read* 257
N. Scott Momaday, *The Way to Rainy Mountain* 273
Richard Rodriguez, *Aria: Memoir of a Bilingual Childhood* 307
Mike Rose, *"I Just Wanna Be Average"* 331
Scott Russell Sanders, *The Men We Carry in Our Minds* 346
David Sedaris, *A Plague of Tics* 359
Amy Tan, *Mother Tongue* 396
Sarah Vowell, *Shooting Dad* 412
Alice Walker, *In Search of Our Mothers' Gardens* 420
E. B. White, *Once More to the Lake* 431

Expository

Barbara Lazear Ascher, *On Compassion* 46
Dave Barry, *Turkeys in the Kitchen* 72
William F. Buckley Jr., *Why Don't We Complain?* 76
Jared Diamond, *The Ends of the World as We Know Them* 98
Joan Didion, *On Morality* 106
Annie Dillard, *Seeing* 112
Lars Eighner, *On Dumpster Diving* 146
Bharati Mukherjee, *Two Ways to Belong in America* 280

George Orwell, *Shooting an Elephant* 284
Michael Pollan, *What's Eating America* 300
Eric Schlosser, *Kid Kustomers* 353
Brent Staples, *Just Walk on By: Black Men and Public Space* 383
Virginia Woolf, *The Death of the Moth* 448

Argumentative

Rachel Carson, *The Obligation to Endure* 83
Barbara Ehrenreich, *Serving in Florida* 136
Stephanie Ericsson, *The Ways We Lie* 159
Stephen Jay Gould, *Sex, Drugs, Disasters, and the Extinction of Dinosaurs* 169
Thomas Jefferson, *The Declaration of Independence* 187
Steven Johnson, *Games* 196
Martin Luther King Jr., *Letter from Birmingham Jail* 203
Verlyn Klinkenborg, *Our Vanishing Night* 234
Bill McKibben, *Curbing Nature's Paparazzi* 267
Plato, *The Allegory of the Cave* 292
Susan Sontag, *Regarding the Pain of Others* 373
Elizabeth Cady Stanton, *Declaration of Sentiments and Resolutions* 379
Jonathan Swift, *A Modest Proposal* 387
Henry David Thoreau, *Where I Lived, and What I Lived For* 403
Sojourner Truth, *Ain't I a Woman?* 410
Marie Winn, *Television: The Plug-In Drug* 438

Table of Contents by Chronological Order

Plato, *The Allegory of the Cave* **360 B.C.E.** 292
Jonathan Swift, *A Modest Proposal* **1729** 387
Thomas Jefferson, *The Declaration of Independence* **1776** 187
Frederick Douglass, *Learning to Read and Write* **1845** 129
Elizabeth Cady Stanton, *Declaration of Sentiments and Resolutions* **1848** 379
Sojourner Truth, *Ain't I a Woman?* **1851** 410
Henry David Thoreau, *Where I Lived, and What I Lived For* **1854** 403
Zora Neale Hurston, *How It Feels to Be Colored Me* **1928** 182
George Orwell, *Shooting an Elephant* **1936** 284
Langston Hughes, *Salvation* **1940** 179
E. B. White, *Once More to the Lake* **1941** 431
Virginia Woolf, *The Death of the Moth* **1942** 448
James Baldwin, *Notes of a Native Son* **1955** 50
William F. Buckley Jr., *Why Don't We Complain?* **1960** 76
Rachel Carson, *The Obligation to Endure* **1962** 83
Martin Luther King Jr., *Letter from Birmingham Jail* **1963** 203
Malcolm X, *Learning to Read* **1965** 257
Joan Didion, *On Morality* **1968** 106
Maya Angelou, *Graduation* **1969** 20
N. Scott Momaday, *The Way to Rainy Mountain* **1969** 273
Annie Dillard, *Seeing* **1974** 112
Maxine Hong Kingston, *No Name Woman* **1976** 221
Marie Winn, *Television: The Plug-In Drug* **1977; revised 2002** 438
Audre Lorde, *The Fourth of July* **1982** 239
Richard Rodriguez, *Aria: Memoir of a Bilingual Childhood* **1982** 307
Stephen Jay Gould, *Sex, Drugs, Disasters, and the Extinction of Dinosaurs* **1984** 169
Barbara Lazear Ascher, *On Compassion* **1986** 46
Dave Barry, *Turkeys in the Kitchen* **1986** 72
Nancy Mairs, *On Being a Cripple* **1986** 244
Brent Staples, *Just Walk on By: Black Men and Public Space* **1986** 383
Gloria Anzaldúa, *How to Tame a Wild Tongue* **1987** 33
Mike Rose, *"I Just Wanna Be Average"* **1989** 331

Amy Tan, *Mother Tongue* **1990** 396
Stephanie Ericsson, *The Ways We Lie* **1992** 159
Judith Ortiz Cofer, *The Myth of the Latin Woman: I Just Met a Girl Named María* **1993** 91
Lars Eighner, *On Dumpster Diving* **1993** 146
Bharati Mukherjee, *Two Ways to Belong in America* **1996** 280
Sherman Alexie, *The Joy of Reading and Writing: Superman and Me* **1997** 15
Bill McKibben, *Curbing Nature's Paparazzi* **1997** 267
David Sedaris, *A Plague of Tics* **1997** 359
Sarah Vowell, *Shooting Dad* **2000** 412
Barbara Ehrenreich, *Serving in Florida* **2001** 136
Eric Schlosser, *Kid Kustomers* **2001** 353
Alice Walker, *In Search of Our Mothers' Gardens* **2002** 420
Susan Sontag, *Regarding the Pain of Others* **2003** 373
Jared Diamond, *The Ends of the World as We Know Them* **2005** 98
Steven Johnson, *Games* **2005** 196
Michael Pollan, *What's Eating America* **2006** 300
Verlyn Klinkenborg, *Our Vanishing Night* **2008** 234
Scott Russell Sanders, *The Men We Carry in Our Minds* **2008** 346

50 Essays

A Portable Anthology

Introduction for Students: Active Reading, Critical Thinking, and the Writing Process

READING, WRITING, 'RITHMETIC

Hard work, preparation, and lots of reading can add up to good writing. That is the arithmetic of writing. We become active, critical, intelligent readers and writers by carefully reading the writing that others have done and then applying what we have learned to our own writing. Reading and writing are most of what you will do in your college courses. The strongest readers and writers have learned to see these activities as inextricably intertwined. You read, you write, then you read some more, then you write again. And this pattern applies in nearly all of your classes, not just those in English and history and other disciplines that come to mind as reading and writing heavy. Math, biology, and engineering classes require the same skills. Acquiring and strengthening them at the start of your college career will help you all the way to graduation and beyond, as reading and writing are central to so many of the careers you might find yourself in a few years down the road.

This introduction will briefly consider the best ways to approach the kinds of assignments you will encounter in your college writing courses. As you read it, think about the ways you read and write now. Do you do some of these things already? Have you tried them before? Be open to the advice, but remember, it is only the advice of one teacher. Your teacher may have different ideas, just as you may, and these ideas may change. Here's an example: in the first edition of this book, I argued against reading while lying down, saying it was better to sit up so you could pay better attention and stay awake. Students, teachers, and my editor disagreed. I decided they were right. The point? As the introduction will explain, the best thing you can do with the texts you encounter in school and in the world is try both to understand them and to evaluate them, and be open to having your mind changed by them. And if you want, do so while stretched out on a nice comfortable couch.

ACTIVE READING

We read for a number of reasons. We want the news, we want information, we want to be entertained. We want to hear other people thinking. We want to be taken out of ourselves and live other lives. We also read because it is crucial to learning how to write. The poet Jane Kenyon gave this advice on becoming a better writer: "Have good sentences in your ears." To write well — to express your ideas efficiently and clearly — you need to observe how others do it. You need to see examples of the ways writers write, the techniques and forms they use. Because good writing is about more than correctness, though, you also have to observe the ways writers think. Working with ideas — handling the ideas of others and presenting your own — is the most important thing writers do, and so the most important thing for writers to learn. Since it is so important, of course, it is difficult. Life is like that. But reading examples of good writing gives you access to models: it shows writers engaging with ideas, holding them up to the light, turning them this way and that, and maybe modifying them in some way, adding something, taking something away, taking them apart entirely, offering their own instead.

To learn to do the same, however, you need to do more than simply mimic what good writers do. You need to treat their writing the same way they treat ideas. Hold their writing up to the light, turn it this way and that, figure out how it works and also how it doesn't, think about how it might be wrong — how you might think differently about their subjects. This activity is sometimes called active or critical reading.

The essays in this collection are here to be studied as models; they are also here to be read critically. While you might learn something from every essay, they are not chapters in a chemistry textbook. Your job is not to take what they say as the gospel truth. Instead, you should evaluate what you read. This doesn't mean you should treat these essays as movie critics treat movies or restaurant critics treat food: These essays aren't here for you to simply judge, to give a thumbs up or down to, to savor or spit out. Instead, you should evaluate their ideas and the way they present them as if in conversation with them. Ask questions of them, argue with their assumptions, examine how they connect their ideas, and test these connections. In learning to think this way about what writers create, you will learn to think like a writer.

There are many techniques that can help you read this way. What they boil down to is reading actively rather than passively. Think of passive reading as like watching television. While there are some good, thoughtful programs on TV, most of us watch TV passively — sitting on a couch, maybe eating, maybe doing something else simultaneously (but not our schoolwork, of course), and letting television wash over us. Active reading, in contrast, requires full attention. Posture aside, your mind needs to be sitting up straight, concentrating on the page, ready to reach down into the page and grab the words. Here are some tips to ensure that you get the most out of what you read.

WAYS TO READ ACTIVELY

Read consciously. In addition to being awake, it is important to be conscious of the situation you are in. Why are you reading? Merely for comprehension, or for observation of the writing itself, or for argument about the ideas? What are you reading? For what purpose or occasion or publication was the piece written, and by whom? Is it a selection from someone's autobiography? Is it an article from a newspaper or an editorial? How has it been contextualized — is it in a chapter on a certain kind of writing or on a certain idea or theme? Keeping these questions in mind as you read makes you notice more, think harder, and make connections among ideas.

Read critically. Always ask yourself what you think about the writer's arguments. Although doing this does not require you to take issue with every or any single thing an author writes, it does ask you to think of reading as conversation: The writer is talking to you, telling you what she thinks about something, and you are free to answer back.

Read with a pencil in hand. This is the best, easiest way to answer back. Many students leave their books untouched, thinking that they will remember what they read or that it is wrong to write in books or that they won't be able to sell them back at the end of the semester if they write in them. These are common objections, but consider this: You won't recall everything (nobody remembers everything he or she reads, and memorizing isn't the only or even the most important thing we do when we read); it's not wrong to write in a book (books don't have feelings, but if they did, they'd like the attention); and bookstores will buy back marked-up books (go check out the used books in the bookstore). Making marks on the page — annotating — is the surest way to read actively. Underline important passages, circle words you haven't heard of, scribble furious rants in the margin, jot down questions about content or writing strategy, use exclamation points and question marks and arrows and Xs. Grab the text with your bare hands. Reading with a highlighter is the passive version of marking your book because it is less suited to annotating and more suited to identifying chunks of text. The result of marking with a highlighter is that you haven't engaged with your reading so much as prioritized parts of it a little bit — used fluorescent yellow or pink or green to say, "Hey, there's something important here." While a highlighter might be more appropriate in your chemistry textbook, even there it can be dangerous: While checking out the used books in the bookstore, notice how often entire paragraphs and even pages are afloat in seas of highlighter ink, and ask yourself how that helped the students whose books these used to be. Pencils are also good for chewing, sticking in your hair to hold your bun together, and sliding behind your ear to make you look smart and industrious.

Use a notebook or computer. Many readers like to take notes in a notebook or computer. Although there are disadvantages to this kind of note taking relative to annotation — your marks are not right in the text and so are less immediately accessible and less immediately tied to the lines on the page — there are also advantages. You can make lengthy notes. You can copy important and well-phrased sentences (making sure to enclose them in quotation marks and to note where they came from). You can **paraphrase**[1] ideas, you can **summarize**, you can note your reactions as you read. Doing these things can make you think more about what you're reading. Some readers use a double-entry system in which they draw a line down the middle of the page, note or reproduce particular passages from the reading in the left column, and respond to those passages in the right column. Many variations on this kind of note taking are possible (and all of them, of course, can be reproduced on a computer).

An Example of Annotation and Note Taking from Virginia Woolf, "The Death of the Moth" (p. 448)

What is she looking for?

The legs agitated themselves once more. I looked as if for the enemy against which he struggled. I looked out of doors. What had happened there? Presumably it was midday, and work in the fields had stopped. Stillness and quiet had replaced the previous animation. The birds had taken themselves off to feed in the brooks. The horses stood still. Yet the power was there all the same, massed outside indifferent, impersonal, not attending to anything in particular. Somehow it was opposed to the little hay-colored moth. It was useless to try to do anything. One could only watch the extraordinary efforts made by those tiny legs against an oncoming doom which could, had it chosen, have submerged an entire city, not merely a city, but masses of human beings; nothing, I knew, had any chance against death. Nevertheless after a pause of exhaustion the legs fluttered again. It was superb this last protest, and so frantic that he succeeded at last in righting himself. One's sympathies, of course, were all on the side of life. Also, when there was nobody to care or to know, this gigantic effort on the part of an insignificant little moth, against a power of such magnitude, to retain what no one else valued or desired to keep, moved one strangely. Again, somehow, one saw life, a pure bead. I lifted the pencil again, useless though I knew it to be. But even as I did so, the unmistakable tokens of death showed themselves. The body

It's like "power" is a person

Odd word choice

Shift from "I" to "one" — and use of "of course" — as if everyone would feel this way

So why does she do it?

1. Words in **boldface** are treated in the glossary of writing terms, which starts on page 459.

Says "yes" but not to life — seems like it should be "no" somehow

relaxed, and instantly grew stiff. The struggle was over. The insignificant little creature now knew death. As I looked at the dead moth, this minute wayside triumph of so great a force over so mean an antagonist filled me with wonder. Just as life had been strange a few minutes before, so death was now as strange. The moth having righted himself now lay most decently and uncomplainingly composed. O yes, he seemed to say, death is stronger than I am.

Interesting way to put it

Is he OK with being dead?

Notes

At first, I couldn't figure what the big deal was about the moth, but by the end you can see that it's about more than a moth

I like when she describes the moth's final effort as "superb"

I wonder if there's anything to Woolf using a pencil to try to save the moth. If the moth living would somehow mean that life can triumph over death, and Woolf was a writer, does her trying to save the moth with the pencil have anything to do in her mind with the power of writing? Maybe she just has a pencil in her hand because she's a writer

Hard not to think about Woolf's suicide when you read the last line, "death is stronger than I am." I know it's the moth talking, but she does use "I" . . .

Note the different kinds of entries here. The first is about the reader's changing thoughts as she reads. The second is a moment of appreciation. The third and fourth are trains of thought that start from small parts of the essay. None of these sum up the reading, though that is a good thing to do also. Instead, these entries record reactions and thoughts inspired by the essay, and — like the notes made alongside the excerpt — could serve as ways back into the essay when it is time to write about it. See page 7 for a checklist of things you can annotate and make notes about as you read.

CRITICAL THINKING/CRITICAL READING

The sample of annotation above shows how active reading is much more than reading to understand. Summarizing what has been read is important; moving beyond summary to active engagement is something else, and it is crucial to really making use of what you've read. One name for this something else is critical thinking.

A CHECKLIST FOR ANNOTATING A READING

As you read, consider marking or taking notes on the following:

- ☐ Main topics
- ☐ Secondary topics
- ☐ Main points
- ☐ Supporting points
- ☐ Examples, **evidence**, or other support
- ☐ Ideas or ways of saying things that you like
- ☐ Ideas or ways of saying things that you don't like
- ☐ Ideas you want to think more about later
- ☐ References or words with which you are not familiar

Critical thinking doesn't mean being critical in the everyday sense, that is, being negative. It means being inquisitive, evaluative, even skeptical. When reading, it means thinking not just about what someone says but about the unspoken assumptions that lay behind what she says, the unnamed implications of what she says, and the way she says it. It also means evaluating — asking if you agree with a writer's implicit and explicit **conclusions**, even asking if you agree with the framing of the question asked or the topic addressed, and judging the eloquence and/or effectiveness of the writing. Critical thinking is a catchall term for a number of activities that add up to active, thoughtful engagement with a subject. For many, it is the single most important skill higher education makes possible: it allows people to actively judge and process the things they read and hear rather than passively accept them. For others, it has an arguably more powerful aspect: that of allowing individuals to accept or reject the common wisdom that is all around them, in everyday life, at work, in politics.

When applied to reading, critical thinking might be called critical reading. See page 8 for a checklist of critical reading questions, with follow-up questions, that you can ask yourself when reading critically (that is, always). While they will not all be applicable for every occasion, most will be helpful as you try to understand and evaluate others' writing.

A CHECKLIST FOR CRITICAL READING

- ☐ What is the writing situation? Where did the text originally appear?
- ☐ What is the writer's subject?
  - ☐ Is she choosing to focus or not to focus on something important? Is she leaving something out?
- ☐ What is the writer's main point about her subject?
  - ☐ Do you agree? Do you disagree? Why?
- ☐ What is the writer's purpose in making that point?
  - ☐ What do you think of that purpose? Do you think that she achieves it?
- ☐ To what sort of audience does the writer seem to be addressing herself?
  - ☐ Are you part of that audience? Who is, and who is left out?
- ☐ What are the assumptions behind the writer's treatment of her subject?
  - ☐ Do you agree with them? Do you disagree? Why?
- ☐ What further conclusions could be drawn from the writer's point?
  - ☐ Do you agree with them? Do you disagree? Why?
- ☐ What do you think of the way the writer makes her argument?
  - ☐ Is it convincing? Logical? Does she fight fair?
- ☐ What can you borrow (without plagiarizing)?
  - ☐ Are there particular techniques the writer uses to argue, describe, narrate, or just shape a sentence that you want to remember and use in your own writing?

THE WRITING PROCESS

As the last critical reading question indicates, writers get better by paying attention to how the writing they like works and trying to duplicate those effects in their own work. This is not the same thing as **plagiarism**: you know not to take another's work and pretend it's your own. The very best writers got so good not by copying words and ideas without giving proper credit, but by imitating other writers — their **styles**, their **tones**, their patterns of organization — and using these as starting points for developing their own voices.

Reading actively, critically, and with an eye toward borrowing helps you to become a better writer. However, nothing helps you learn to write like writing itself. While there will be a number of occasions in your academic career when you will be required to hand in formal, typed, proofread essays, take advantage of the times when you have to write informally — in class, in journals, online. Think of times when you don't have to write but could — sitting on the bus, waiting for your computer to boot up — and get out a notebook and write. Like strengthening a muscle through repeated exercise, the more you use your writing skills the stronger they will become.

This strength will help you when it is time to write formal, academic essays, and it can help to lessen anxiety about writing. Every writer, when faced with more demanding assignments, feels some form of dread, trepidation, or nervous excitement. In other words, it is far from rare for writers of all levels of experience to freeze up, space out, or throw in the towel. Many of the best ways writers have found to get past the difficulty of getting started involve recognizing that writing is a process. People often imagine a typical scene when they think of writing: They see the writer, hunched over the blank pad or in front of the blank screen, waiting for inspiration to strike, then, having been struck, finding the exact words to express this inspiration, and then, finishing, leaning back with a sigh of contentment at a job well done. Very few people actually write this way.

Rather than thinking that you must sit down and create a polished piece of work out of thin air, remember that writers can go through many stages when they write and that each stage can help produce a final product. Before you begin to write a first **draft**, try a number of **prewriting** activities, which can help you brainstorm or come up with ideas. You can work up notes or a formal or informal outline before you draft. At this point you can also make use of comments you wrote in the margins of your text. After taking a first stab at a draft, you can **revise**. As important as recognizing that you can break down the writing process into these stages is knowing that they don't have to be followed. After producing a draft, you may return to outlining and brainstorming. You can even do this as you draft: as you see your main point (your **thesis**) changing or your **argument** taking a different course, go back to your notes or outline and modify accordingly. When you get to the revision stage, when you think you might be focusing on correctness and style, you may find not only that you need to rewrite what you wrote in the drafting stage but also that you need to rethink the ideas you came up with during the prewriting stage. While smoothing out the **transitions** between your **paragraphs**, you may find they are rough because the connections among your ideas are also rough, and so you will need to smooth out your ideas before you can smooth out your expression of them.

This may all sound daunting. It shouldn't. Thinking about writing as a recursive process — one in which you loop back to the starting point as you revise and build on your work — means you don't have to try to get everything perfect the first time. It allows you to get your ideas down on paper as they come to you because you know you can always go back and change them. It allows you to think critically about your work because it never feels like it's too late to improve any aspect of it. Read as a writer reads — critically, actively — and write as a writer writes — in stages, recursively — and pretty soon (that is, before you even know it) you will be a thoughtful, fluid writer who enjoys practicing her craft. There is no complicated mathematical formula to explain the interrelation of critical reading, creative brainstorming, careful revision, and all of the other elements that are part of what makes good writing, but the basic arithmetic — reading + hard work = good writing — holds up.

I hope that you enjoy reading the essays in this book, and that you find that they help you with your writing. At the end of this introduction you'll find an example of an essay written in response to readings in *50 Essays*. Annotations have been added to highlight important parts of the essay — elements like the **thesis statement**, transitions, and a **conclusion**. Read it over for ideas about how to put together sentences and paragraphs, how to construct an argument, and how to document sources. This essay is also a good example of **synthesis** — the process of considering a number of different readings, putting them in conversation with each other, and forming your own **claim** or thesis, making your own statement. Remember, though, that there's no one model you should follow, no one way to write about anything. Examples are good, but you need to find your own voice, your own way to say what you want to say.

Schaff 1

Jonathon Schaff
Professor Cohen
English 101
17 February 2010

Dangerous Duality: How Racism Splits Us in Two
By Jonathon Schaff

I have never been told that I am a problem. I have been told that my behavior is problematic, but no one has ever told me that there was something wrong with me just for being me. What's more, I've never been avoided on the street or denied a meal because of my skin color. But I am not an African American. I am a member of the white majority in America, and I can only try to understand the African American experience of living in this country by submerging myself in the words and ideas of black writers.

*Author discusses his own **point of view***

Something can happen to the human mind when it is informed that it is a problem. The mind splits, somehow, and part of us begins to believe that we might be in the wrong. African Americans who have been victimized by racism oftentimes see themselves in two different, irreconcilable ways.

Thesis statement makes the author's claim

The idea that multiple identities form as a product of racism may have been first introduced by W. E. B. Du Bois in his important 1903 essay, "Of Our Spiritual Strivings," in which he refers to a state of "double-consciousness." By this he meant that blacks felt, forty years after being legally freed, that they were black and American at the same time, and yet not both at once. Du Bois wrote:

> It is a peculiar sensation, this double-consciousness, this sense of always looking at one's self through the eyes of others, of measuring one's worth by the tape of a world that looks on in amused contempt and pity. One ever feels his twoness, — an American, a Negro; two souls, two thoughts, two unreconciled strivings; two warring ideals in one dark body, whose dogged strength alone keeps it from being torn asunder. (45)

Du Bois could not fully separate his own identity from the way he was perceived by other people, and he did not think that other blacks could either. He saw himself through the eyes of the white majority. Living like that, it is easy to understand how his double-consciousness formed. People make shallow judgments about others; because these judgments happened to him so often, Du Bois let them register as facts. He suggests that being both black and American, at least in 1903, was impossible; that to be an authentic American required something other than what he had.

Du Bois's essay continues to echo in the work of black authors. One reason for the persistence of his ideas is that African Americans continued to suffer indignities long after slavery was abolished. Jim

Schaff 2

Crow laws prevented blacks from having access to the same quality of life that whites enjoyed by means of segregation. Barred from white swimming pools and restaurants, Jim Crow had a corrosive effect on the African American psyche. In his essay, "Notes of a Native Son," published in 1955, James Baldwin writes about the death of his father. A severe man, the son of a slave, and feared by his children, Baldwin's father taught him to hate and mistrust whites because they would inevitably do blacks harm. Of his father's hatred, Baldwin wrote:

> It had something to do with his blackness, I think — he was very black — with his blackness and his beauty, and with the fact that he knew that he was black but did not know that he was beautiful. He claimed to be proud of his blackness but it had also been the cause of much humiliation and it had fixed bleak boundaries to his life. (52)

*Use of **quotation** conveys a sense of the original author*

Perhaps Baldwin's father couldn't see his own beauty because he knew himself as black first and foremost, beyond anything else. Perhaps, like Du Bois, he constantly saw himself through the eyes of others. As the son of a slave, how could he not? Baldwin's father lived as an allegedly free man who experienced a lot of injustice. Would he feel the same way if he were alive today?

Messages of inferiority are routinely delivered to African Americans even in today's society. Blacks make less money than whites do across the board. A report out of the University of Dayton claims, "Whites with high school diplomas, college degrees or Master's Degrees all earn approximately twenty percent more than their black counterparts. Even more striking, whites with professional degrees (such as medicine or law) earn, on average, thirty-one percent more than blacks with comparable educations" (Apr. 2009). These statistics represent not just individual wage earners but the way African Americans are perceived, and the way they perceive themselves; if a white doctor is making more than his black coworker, that black coworker seems worth less than his counterpart. And a black doctor who knows about the discrepancy between his wages and his white colleague's might not only feel slighted; he might even feel accountable for his smaller paycheck, despite his abilities as a practitioner. Double-consciousness exists today, though it may have become more complicated.

***Topic sentence** states the paragraph's main idea*

Author uses evidence from an outside source to support his claim

Beyond messages of economic inferiority, today's society arguably continues to inform blacks that they are dangerous and frightening. Brent Staples's essay, "Just Walk on By: Black Men and Public Space," offers a series of poignant anecdotes about his life as a graduate student and an adult. Staples recalls the fear he inspired in others as a habitual nighttime walker. He recollects crossing the street and hearing people in the cars he walked in front of lock their doors.

Use of transition connects two ideas

Schaff 3

He also remembers the way other people would cross the street if they were on course to pass him on the sidewalk (384). Americans' fear of black men at night prevented people from ever getting to know Brent Staples. He was judged so quickly, from such a distance, that he never even had a chance.

As a white person, I find it hard to imagine the world reflexively avoiding me. How could Staples *not* feel as though he were contributing to his own misfortune? How could he *not* feel as though there was something scary locked up inside of him? How does a person who has been made to feel so ugly convince himself that he is beautiful? Baldwin's father could not do it. I don't know that I could, either.

Staples, an intelligent man, a writer for the *New York Times*, seems to be able to keep a healthy sense of who he is, but it is not easy. He remarks that he feels like he travels through "bear country," late at night on the streets (386). People take on the ferociousness of animals when they see him coming around a corner. Ironically, it is the scared strangers who are the real threat in these scenarios. They imagine Staples to be dangerous when, in actuality, they are the ones capable of doing harm. So, Staples whistles traditionally white classical music, by Beethoven and Vivaldi, to alert and pacify the scared strangers. This means that he has looked at himself through white eyes and discovered a way to avoid causing trouble. But walking down the street without whistling the Moonlight Sonata should not instigate an attack. Yet this is the reality for many black Americans. Pressure is put upon them from the white majority to behave a certain way, even if that way is senseless and the consequences for failing to conform to it are barbaric. Staples, not so long ago, was made to feel the confusing shame of being both instigator and victim, when he deserved better.

Author uses summary to make a point in his own words

If blacks throughout our nation's history have suffered from racism, is it realistic to think that there is an end in sight? Circumstances have changed — slavery has given way to Jim Crow, which has given way to more subtle forms of discrimination, which coexist with the same old-fashioned, street-level racism Du Bois, Baldwin, and Staples have all felt — but the underlying duality remains, and remains dangerous. As Baldwin put it, "I imagine that one of the reasons people cling to their hates so stubbornly is because they sense, once hate is gone, that they will be forced to deal with pain" (69). Even though the United States elected an African American president, is the country truly post-racial? There is a lot of pain that this country will have to deal with if and when it lets go of its hate. But if the era of healing lasts half as long as the epoch of prejudice, then we could be in for a better way of living, a way that prefers empathy to ignorance and unity to division.

***Conclusion** sums up main point and extends the author's ideas*

*Author uses expressive **diction** and **tone** in concluding paragraph*

Schaff 4

Works Cited

Baldwin, James. "Notes of a Native Son." *50 Essays.* 3rd Edition. Ed. Samuel Cohen. Boston: Bedford, 2011. 50–78. Print.

Du Bois, W. E. B. *The Souls of Black Folk.* 1903. Introd. Randall Kenan. New York: Signet, 1995. Print.

Randall, Vernellia. "Institutional Racism in America." *Race, Racism and the Law.* The University of Dayton School of Law, 23 Nov. 2009. Web. 25 Nov. 2009.

Staples, Brent. "Just Walk on By: Black Men and Public Spaces." Cohen 383–86. Print.

SHERMAN ALEXIE

The Joy of Reading and Writing: Superman and Me

Born in 1966 and raised on the Spokane Indian Reservation in Wellpinit, Washington, Sherman Alexie is one of the foremost Native American writers and the recipient of the Native Writers' Circle of the Americas 2010 Lifetime Achievement Award. He is best known for his fiction, from his first collection of stories, The Lone Ranger and Tonto Fistfight in Heaven *(1993), which won the PEN/Hemingway Award for Best First Book of Fiction, to three novels,* Reservation Blues *(1995),* Indian Killer *(1996), and* Flight *(2007), and the young adult novel* The Absolutely True Diary of a Part-Time Indian *(2007). He has also written twelve books of poems, including "The Business of Fancydancing" (1991) and his latest,* Face *(2009); screenplays, including that for the movie* Smoke Signals *(1999), with Chris Eyre; and an album, with Jim Boyd, made of songs from the book* Reservation Blues.

"The Joy of Reading and Writing: Superman and Me" displays Alexie's characteristic mix of popular culture reference and reflection on what it means to be an Indian in today's America. As you read, note how carefully Alexie crafts what at first glance might seem to be a slight essay. Note especially the way images and phrases are repeated and the effect he constructs from these repetitions.

I learned to read with a Superman comic book. Simple enough, I suppose. I cannot recall which particular Superman comic book I read, nor can I remember which villain he fought in that issue. I cannot remember the plot, nor the means by which I obtained the comic book. What I can remember is this: I was 3 years old, a Spokane Indian boy living with his family on the Spokane Indian Reservation in eastern Washington state. We were poor by most standards, but one of my parents usually managed to find some minimum-wage job or another, which made us middle-class by reservation standards. I had a brother and three sisters. We lived on a combination of irregular paychecks, hope, fear, and government surplus food.

My father, who is one of the few Indians who went to Catholic school on purpose, was an avid reader of westerns, spy thrillers, murder mysteries, gangster epics, basketball player biographies, and anything else he could find. He bought his books by the pound at Dutch's Pawn Shop, Goodwill, Salvation Army, and Value Village. When he had extra money, he bought new novels at supermarkets, convenience stores, and hospital gift shops. Our house was filled with books. They were stacked in crazy piles in the bathroom, bedrooms, and living room. In a fit of unemployment-inspired creative energy, my father built a set of bookshelves and soon filled them with a random assortment of books about the Kennedy assassination, Watergate, the Vietnam War, and the entire 23-book series of the Apache westerns. My father loved books, and since I loved my father with an aching devotion, I decided to love books as well.

I can remember picking up my father's books before I could read. The words themselves were mostly foreign, but I still remember the exact moment when I first understood, with a sudden clarity, the purpose of a paragraph. I didn't have the vocabulary to say "paragraph," but I realized that a paragraph was a fence that held words. The words inside a paragraph worked together for a common purpose. They had some specific reason for being inside the same fence. This knowledge delighted me. I began to think of everything in terms of paragraphs. Our reservation was a small paragraph within the United States. My family's house was a paragraph, distinct from the other paragraphs of the LeBrets to the north, the Fords to our south, and the Tribal School to the west. Inside our house, each family member existed as a separate paragraph but still had genetics and common experiences to link us. Now, using this logic, I can see my changed family as an essay of seven paragraphs: mother, father, older brother, the deceased sister, my younger twin sisters, and our adopted little brother.

At the same time I was seeing the world in paragraphs, I also picked up that Superman comic book. Each panel, complete with picture, dialogue, and narrative was a three-dimensional paragraph. In one panel, Superman breaks through a door. His suit is red, blue, and yellow. The brown door shatters into many pieces.

I look at the narrative above the picture. I cannot read the words, but I assume it tells me that “Superman is breaking down the door.” Aloud, I pretend to read the words and say, “Superman is breaking down the door.” Words, dialogue, also float out of Superman’s mouth. Because he is breaking down the door, I assume he says, “I am breaking down the door.” Once again, I pretend to read the words and say aloud, “I am breaking down the door.” In this way, I learned to read.

5 This might be an interesting story all by itself. A little Indian boy teaches himself to read at an early age and advances quickly. He reads “Grapes of Wrath” in kindergarten when other children are struggling through “Dick and Jane.” If he’d been anything but an Indian boy living on the reservation, he might have been called a prodigy. But he is an Indian boy living on the reservation and is simply an oddity. He grows into a man who often speaks of his childhood in the third person, as if it will somehow dull the pain and make him sound more modest about his talents.

A smart Indian is a dangerous person, widely feared and ridiculed by Indians and non-Indians alike. I fought with my classmates on a daily basis. They wanted me to stay quiet when the non-Indian teacher asked for answers, for volunteers, for help. We were Indian children who were expected to be stupid. Most lived up to those expectations inside the classroom but subverted them on the outside. They struggled with basic reading in school but could remember how to sing a few dozen powwow songs. They were monosyllabic in front of their non-Indian teachers but could tell complicated stories and jokes at the dinner table. They submissively ducked their heads when confronted by a non-Indian adult but would slug it out with the Indian bully who was 10 years older. As Indian children, we were expected to fail in the non-Indian world. Those who failed were ceremonially accepted by other Indians and appropriately pitied by non-Indians.

I refused to fail. I was smart. I was arrogant. I was lucky. I read books late into the night, until I could barely keep my eyes open. I read books at recess, then during lunch, and in the few minutes left after I had finished my classroom assignments. I read books in the car when my family traveled to powwows or basketball games. In shopping malls, I ran to the bookstores and read bits and pieces of as many books as I could. I read the books my father brought home from the pawnshops and secondhand. I read the books I borrowed from the library. I read the backs of cereal boxes. I read the newspaper. I read the bulletins posted on the walls of the school, the clinic, the tribal offices, the post office. I read junk mail. I read auto-repair manuals. I read magazines. I read anything that had words and paragraphs. I read with equal parts joy and desperation. I loved those books, but I also knew that love had only one purpose. I was trying to save my life.

Despite all the books I read, I am still surprised I became a writer. I was going to be a pediatrician. These days, I write novels, short stories, and poems. I visit schools and teach creative writing to Indian kids. In all my years in the reservation school system, I was never taught how to write poetry, short stories, or novels. I was certainly never taught that Indians wrote poetry, short stories, and novels. Writing was something beyond Indians. I cannot recall a single time that a guest teacher visited the reservation. There must have been visiting teachers. Who were they? Where are they now? Do they exist? I visit the schools as often as possible. The Indian kids crowd the classroom. Many are writing their own poems, short stories, and novels. They have read my books. They have read many other books. They look at me with bright eyes and arrogant wonder. They are trying to save their lives. Then there are the sullen and already defeated Indian kids who sit in the back rows and ignore me with theatrical precision. The pages of their notebooks are empty. They carry neither pencil nor pen. They stare out the window. They refuse and resist. "Books," I say to them. "Books," I say. I throw my weight against their locked doors. The door holds. I am smart. I am arrogant. I am lucky. I am trying to save our lives.

For Discussion and Writing

1. What is Superman doing in the comic book panel Alexie remembers? Why is it important to remember this detail at the very end of the essay?
2. In paragraph 7, Alexie repeats a certain verb fourteen times. What is this verb, and what effect does this repetition have? What might Alexie be trying to say about the process of his coming to literacy, in terms of both the effort required and the height of the obstacles encountered (or, given the metaphor introduced in paragraph 4, the thickness of the doors that must be broken through)?

3. **connections** In "Learning to Read and Write" (p. 129), Frederick Douglass writes, "In moments of agony, I envied my fellow-slaves for their stupidity" (par. 6). Compare this sentiment to Alexie's feelings about his fellow classmates on the reservation (par. 6). Do you think that Alexie envied his classmates? Why, or why not? How were his difficulties different from those faced by other Indians?
4. In paragraph 5, Alexie writes about himself in the third person, in effect dramatizing what happens when one writes the story of one's life. Using the third person, write about a particularly important moment or aspect of your life. Afterward, write a short reflection on the distancing effect of referring to yourself as "he" or "she." How does this type of writing help you learn about yourself?

MAYA ANGELOU

Graduation

Born Marguerite Johnson in St. Louis, Missouri, in 1928, Maya Angelou has been a successful dancer, actor, poet, playwright, fiction writer, producer, director, newspaper editor, civil rights leader, and academic, among other accomplishments. Her autobiographical book I Know Why the Caged Bird Sings *(1969) was nominated for a National Book Award. In 1993 she delivered her poem, "On the Pulse of Morning," at the inauguration of President Clinton.*

"Graduation," from I Know Why the Caged Bird Sings, *tells the story of Angelou's high school graduation in Stamps, Arkansas. Of that day, she writes, "Oh, it was important, all right" (par. 5); as she tells the story, the importance of this day for Angelou grows beyond that of the typical graduation. As you read, note the way she carefully brings the reader along with her as she re-creates the excitement and disappointment of that day and as she reflects on the significance of the moment that allowed her to say, "We were on top again. As always, again. We survived" (par. 61).*

The children in Stamps trembled visibly with anticipation. Some adults were excited too, but to be certain the whole young population had come down with graduation epidemic. Large classes were graduating from both the grammar school and the high school. Even those who were years removed from their own day of glorious release were anxious to help with preparations as a kind of dry run. The junior students who were moving into the vacating classes' chairs were tradition-bound to show their talents for leadership and management. They strutted through the school and around the campus exerting pressure on the lower grades. Their authority was so new that occasionally if they pressed a little too hard it had to be overlooked. After all, next term was coming, and it never hurt a sixth grader to have a play sister in the eighth grade, or a tenth-year student to be able to call a twelfth grader Bubba. So all was endured in a spirit of shared understanding. But the graduating classes themselves were the nobility. Like travelers with exotic destinations on their minds, the graduates were remarkably forgetful. They came to school without their books, or tablets, or even pencils. Volunteers fell over themselves to secure replacements for the missing equipment. When accepted, the willing workers might or might not be thanked, and it was of no importance to the pregraduation rites. Even teachers were respectful of the now quiet and aging seniors, and tended to speak to them, if not as equals, as beings only slightly lower than themselves. After tests were returned and grades given, the student body, which acted like an extended family, knew who did well, who excelled, and what piteous ones had failed.

Unlike the white high school, Lafayette County Training School distinguished itself by having neither lawn, nor hedges, nor tennis court, nor climbing ivy. Its two buildings (main classrooms, the grade school, and home economics) were set on a dirt hill with no fence to limit either its boundaries or those of bordering farms. There was a large expanse to the left of the school which was used alternately as a baseball diamond or basketball court. Rusty hoops on swaying poles represented the permanent recreational equipment, although bats and balls could be borrowed from the P.E. teacher if the borrower was qualified and if the diamond wasn't occupied.

Over this rocky area relieved by a few shady tall persimmon trees the graduating class walked. The girls often held hands and no longer bothered to speak to the lower students. There was a sadness about them, as if this old world was not their home and they were bound for higher ground. The boys, on the other hand, had become more friendly, more outgoing. A decided change from the closed attitude they projected while studying for finals. Now they seemed not ready to give up the old school, the familiar paths, and classrooms. Only a small percentage would be continuing on to college — one of the South's A & M (agricultural and mechanical) schools, which trained Negro youths to be carpenters, farmers, handymen, masons, maids, cooks, and baby nurses. Their future rode heavily on their shoulders, and blinded them to the collective joy that had pervaded the lives of the boys and girls in the grammar school graduating class.

Parents who could afford it had ordered new shoes and ready-made clothes for themselves from Sears and Roebuck or Montgomery Ward. They also engaged the best seamstresses to make the floating graduating dresses and to cut down secondhand pants which would be pressed to a military slickness for the important event.

Oh, it was important, all right. Whitefolks would attend the 5
ceremony, and two or three would speak of God and home, and the Southern way of life, and Mrs. Parsons, the principal's wife, would play the graduation march while the lower-grade graduates paraded down the aisles and took their seats below the platform. The high school seniors would wait in empty classrooms to make their dramatic entrance.

In the Store I was the person of the moment. The birthday girl. The center. Bailey had graduated the year before, although to do so he had had to forfeit all pleasures to make up for his time lost in Baton Rouge.

My class was wearing butter-yellow piqué dresses, and Momma launched out on mine. She smocked the yoke into tiny crisscrossing puckers, then shirred the rest of the bodice. Her dark fingers ducked in and out of the lemony cloth as she embroidered raised daisies around the hem. Before she considered herself finished she had added a crocheted cuff on the puff sleeves, and a pointy crocheted collar.

I was going to be lovely. A walking model of all the various styles of fine hand sewing and it didn't worry me that I was only twelve years old and merely graduating from the eighth grade. Besides, many teachers in Arkansas Negro schools had only that diploma and were licensed to impart wisdom.

The days had become longer and more noticeable. The faded beige of former times had been replaced with strong and sure colors. I began to see my classmates' clothes, their skin tones, and the dust that waved off pussy willows. Clouds that lazed across the sky were objects of great concern to me. Their shiftier shapes might have held a message that in my new happiness and with a little bit of time I'd soon decipher. During that period I looked at the arch of heaven so religiously my neck kept a steady ache. I had taken to smiling more often, and my jaws hurt from the unaccustomed activity. Between the two physical sore spots, I suppose

I could have been uncomfortable, but that was not the case. As a member of the winning team (the graduating class of 1940) I had outdistanced unpleasant sensations by miles. I was headed for the freedom of open fields.

Youth and social approval allied themselves with me and we 10
trammeled memories of slights and insults. The wind of our swift passage remodeled my features. Lost tears were pounded to mud and then to dust. Years of withdrawal were brushed aside and left behind, as hanging ropes of parasitic moss.

My work alone had awarded me a top place and I was going to be one of the first called in the graduating ceremonies. On the classroom blackboard, as well as on the bulletin board in the auditorium, there were blue stars and white stars and red stars. No absences, no tardinesses, and my academic work was among the best of the year. I could say the preamble to the Constitution even faster than Bailey. We timed ourselves often: "We the people of the United States in order to form a more perfect union . . ." I had memorized the Presidents of the United States from Washington to Roosevelt in chronological as well as alphabetical order.

My hair pleased me too. Gradually the black mass had lengthened and thickened, so that it kept at last to its braided pattern, and I didn't have to yank my scalp off when I tried to comb it.

Louise and I had rehearsed the exercises until we tired out ourselves. Henry Reed was class valedictorian. He was a small, very black boy with hooded eyes, a long, broad nose and an oddly shaped head. I had admired him for years because each term he and I vied for the best grades in our class. Most often he bested me, but instead of being disappointed I was pleased that we shared top places between us. Like many Southern Black children, he lived with his grandmother, who was as strict as Momma and as kind as she knew how to be. He was courteous, respectful, and soft-spoken to elders, but on the playground he chose to play the roughest games. I admired him. Anyone, I reckoned, sufficiently afraid or sufficiently dull could be polite. But to be able to operate at a top level with both adults and children was admirable.

His valedictory speech was entitled "To Be or Not to Be." The rigid tenth-grade teacher had helped him write it. He'd been working on the dramatic stresses for months.

15 The weeks until graduation were filled with heady activities. A group of small children were to be presented in a play about buttercups and daisies and bunny rabbits. They could be heard throughout the building practicing their hops and their little songs that sounded like silver bells. The older girls (nongraduates, of course) were assigned the task of making refreshments for the night's festivities. A tangy scent of ginger, cinnamon, nutmeg, and chocolate wafted around the home economics building as the budding cooks made samples for themselves and their teachers.

In every corner of the workshop, axes and saws split fresh timber as the woodshop boys made sets and stage scenery. Only the graduates were left out of the general bustle. We were free to sit in the library at the back of the building or look in quite detachedly, naturally, on the measures being taken for our event.

Even the minister preached on graduation the Sunday before. His subject was, "Let your light so shine that men will see your good works and praise your Father, Who is in Heaven." Although the sermon was purported to be addressed to us, he used the occasion to speak to backsliders, gamblers, and general ne'er-do-wells. But since he had called our names at the beginning of the service we were mollified.

Among Negroes the tradition was to give presents to children going only from one grade to another. How much more important this was when the person was graduating at the top of the class. Uncle Willie and Momma had sent away for a Mickey Mouse watch like Bailey's. Louise gave me four embroidered handkerchiefs. (I gave her crocheted doilies.) Mrs. Sneed, the minister's wife, made me an undershirt to wear for graduation, and nearly every customer gave me a nickel or maybe even a dime with the instruction "Keep on moving to higher ground," or some such encouragement.

Amazingly the great day finally dawned and I was out of bed before I knew it. I threw open the back door to see it more clearly, but Momma said, "Sister, come away from that door and put your robe on."

20 I hoped the memory of that morning would never leave me. Sunlight was itself young, and the day had none of the insistence maturity would bring it in a few hours. In my robe and barefoot in the backyard, under cover of going to see about my new beans, I gave myself up to the gentle warmth and thanked God that no

matter what evil I had done in my life He had allowed me to live to see this day. Somewhere in my fatalism I had expected to die, accidentally, and never have the chance to walk up the stairs in the auditorium and gracefully receive my hard-earned diploma. Out of God's merciful bosom I had won reprieve.

Bailey came out in his robe and gave me a box wrapped in Christmas paper. He said he had saved his money for months to pay for it. It felt like a box of chocolates, but I knew Bailey wouldn't save money to buy candy when we had all we could want under our noses.

He was as proud of the gift as I. It was a soft-leather-bound copy of a collection of poems by Edgar Allan Poe, or, as Bailey and I called him, "Eap." I turned to "Annabel Lee" and we walked up and down the garden rows, the cool dirt between our toes, reciting the beautifully sad lines.

Momma made a Sunday breakfast although it was only Friday. After we finished the blessing, I opened my eyes to find the watch on my plate. It was a dream of a day. Everything went smoothly and to my credit, I didn't have to be reminded or scolded for anything. Near evening I was too jittery to attend to chores, so Bailey volunteered to do all before his bath.

Days before, we had made a sign for the Store, and as we turned out the lights Momma hung the cardboard over the doorknob. It read clearly: CLOSED, GRADUATION.

My dress fitted perfectly and everyone said that I looked like a 25
sunbeam in it. On the hill, going toward the school, Bailey walked behind with Uncle Willie, who muttered, "Go on, Ju." He wanted him to walk ahead with us because it embarrassed him to have to walk so slowly. Bailey said he'd let the ladies walk together, and the men would bring up the rear. We all laughed, nicely.

Little children dashed by out of the dark like fireflies. Their crepe-paper dresses and butterfly wings were not made for running and we heard more than one rip, dryly, and the regretful "uh uh" that followed.

The school blazed without gaiety. The windows seemed cold and unfriendly from the lower hill. A sense of ill-fated timing crept over me, and if Momma hadn't reached for my hand I would have drifted back to Bailey and Uncle Willie, and possibly beyond. She made a few slow jokes about my feet getting cold, and tugged me along to the now-strange building.

Around the front steps, assurance came back. There were my fellow "greats," the graduating class. Hair brushed back, legs oiled, new dresses and pressed pleats, fresh pocket handkerchiefs and little handbags, all homesewn. Oh, we were up to snuff, all right. I joined my comrades and didn't even see my family go in to find seats in the crowded auditorium.

The school band struck up a march and all classes filed in as had been rehearsed. We stood in front of our seats, as assigned, and on a signal from the choir director, we sat. No sooner had this been accomplished than the band started to play the national anthem. We rose again and sang the song, after which we recited the pledge of allegiance. We remained standing for a brief minute before the choir director and the principal signaled to us, rather desperately I thought, to take our seats. The command was so unusual that our carefully rehearsed and smooth-running machine was thrown off. For a full minute we fumbled for our chairs and bumped into each other awkwardly. Habits change or solidify under pressure, so in our state of nervous tension we had been ready to follow our usual assembly pattern: the American national anthem, then the pledge of allegiance, then the song every Black person I knew called the Negro National Anthem. All done in the same key, with the same passion and most often standing on the same foot.

Finding my seat at last, I was overcome with a presentiment of 30
worse things to come. Something unrehearsed, unplanned, was going to happen, and we were going to be made to look bad. I distinctly remember being explicit in the choice of pronoun. It was "we," the graduating class, the unit, that concerned me then.

The principal welcomed "parents and friends" and asked the Baptist minister to lead us in prayer. His invocation was brief and punchy, and for a second I thought we were getting on the high road to right action. When the principal came back to the dais, however, his voice had changed. Sounds always affected me profoundly and the principal's voice was one of my favorites. During assembly it melted and lowed weakly into the audience. It had not been in my plan to listen to him, but my curiosity was piqued and I straightened up to give him my attention.

He was talking about Booker T. Washington, our "late great leader," who said we can be as close as the fingers on the hand, etc. . . . Then he said a few vague things about friendship and the friendship of kindly people to those less fortunate than themselves. With that his voice nearly faded, thin, away. Like a river diminishing to a stream and then to a trickle. But he cleared his throat and said, “Our speaker tonight, who is also our friend, came from Texarkana to deliver the commencement address, but due to the irregularity of the train schedule, he's going to, as they say, ‘speak and run.’ ” He said that we understood and wanted the man to know that we were most grateful for the time he was able to give us and then something about how we were willing always to adjust to another's program, and without more ado — “I give you Mr. Edward Donleavy.”

Not one but two white men came through the door off-stage. The shorter one walked to the speaker's platform, and the tall one moved to the center seat and sat down. But that was our principal's seat, and already occupied. The dislodged gentleman bounced around for a long breath or two before the Baptist minister gave him his chair, then with more dignity than the situation deserved, the minister walked off the stage.

Donleavy looked at the audience once (on reflection, I'm sure that he wanted only to reassure himself that we were really there), adjusted his glasses and began to read from a sheaf of papers.

He was glad “to be here and to see the work going on just as it 35
was in the other schools.”

At the first “Amen” from the audience I willed the offender to immediate death by choking on the word. But Amens and Yes, sir's began to fall around the room like rain through a ragged umbrella.

He told us of the wonderful changes we children in Stamps had in store. The Central School (naturally, the white school was Central) had already been granted improvements that would be in use in the fall. A well-known artist was coming from Little Rock to teach art to them. They were going to have the newest microscopes and chemistry equipment for their laboratory. Mr. Donleavy didn't leave us long in the dark over who made these improvements available to Central High. Nor were we to be ignored in the general betterment scheme he had in mind.

He said that he had pointed out to people at a very high level that one of the first-line football tacklers at Arkansas Agricultural and Mechanical College had graduated from good old Lafayette County Training School. Here fewer Amen's were heard. Those few that did break through lay dully in the air with the heaviness of habit.

He went on to praise us. He went on to say how he had bragged that "one of the best basketball players at Fisk sank his first ball right here at Lafayette County Training School."

The white kids were going to have a chance to become Galileos 40
and Madame Curies and Edisons and Gauguins, and our boys (the girls weren't even in on it) would try to be Jesse Owenses and Joe Louises.

Owens and the Brown Bomber were great heroes in our world, but what school official in the white-goddom of Little Rock had the right to decide that those two men must be our only heroes? Who decided that for Henry Reed to become a scientist he had to work like George Washington Carver, as a bootblack, to buy a lousy microscope? Bailey was obviously always going to be too small to be an athlete, so which concrete angel glued to what country seat had decided that if my brother wanted to become a lawyer he had to first pay penance for his skin by picking cotton and hoeing corn and studying correspondence books at night for twenty years?

The man's dead words fell like bricks around the auditorium and too many settled in my belly. Constrained by hard-learned manners I couldn't look behind me, but to my left and right the proud graduating class of 1940 had dropped their heads. Every girl in my row had found something new to do with her handkerchief. Some folded the tiny squares into love knots, some into triangles, but most were wadding them, then pressing them flat on their yellow laps.

On the dais, the ancient tragedy was being replayed. Professor Parsons sat, a sculptor's reject, rigid. His large, heavy body seemed devoid of will or willingness, and his eyes said he was no longer with us. The other teachers examined the flag (which was draped stage right) or their notes, or the windows which opened on our now-famous playing diamond.

Graduation, the hush-hush magic time of frills and gifts and congratulations and diplomas, was finished for me before my name was called. The accomplishment was nothing. The meticulous maps, drawn in three colors of ink, learning and spelling decasyllabic words, memorizing the whole of *The Rape of Lucrece* — it was for nothing. Donleavy had exposed us.

We were maids and farmers, handymen and washerwomen, 45
and anything higher that we aspired to was farcical and presumptuous.

Then I wished that Gabriel Prosser and Nat Turner had killed all whitefolks in their beds and that Abraham Lincoln had been assassinated before the signing of the Emancipation Proclamation, and that Harriet Tubman had been killed by that blow on her head and Christopher Columbus had drowned in the *Santa Maria*.

It was awful to be a Negro and have no control over my life. It was brutal to be young and already trained to sit quietly and listen to charges brought against my color with no chance of defense. We should all be dead. I thought I should like to see us all dead, one on top of the other. A pyramid of flesh with the whitefolks on the bottom, as the broad base, then the Indians with their silly tomahawks and teepees and wigwams and treaties, the Negroes with their mops and recipes and cotton sacks and spirituals sticking out of their mouths. The Dutch children should all stumble in their wooden shoes and break their necks. The French should choke to death on the Louisiana Purchase (1803) while silkworms ate all the Chinese with their stupid pigtails. As a species, we were an abomination. All of us.

Donleavy was running for election, and assured our parents that if he won we could count on having the only colored paved playing field in that part of Arkansas. Also — he never looked up to acknowledge the grunts of acceptance — also, we were bound to get some new equipment for the home economics building and the workshop.

He finished, and since there was no need to give any more than the most perfunctory thank-you's, he nodded to the men on the stage, and the tall white man who was never introduced joined him at the door. They left with the attitude that now they were off to something really important. (The graduation ceremonies at Lafayette County Training School had been a mere preliminary.)

The ugliness they left was palpable. An uninvited guest who 50
wouldn't leave. The choir was summoned and sang a modern arrangement of "Onward, Christian Soldiers," with new words pertaining to graduates seeking their place in the world. But it didn't work. Elouise, the daughter of the Baptist minister, recited

"Invictus," and I could have cried at the impertinence of "I am the master of my fate, I am the captain of my soul."

My name had lost its ring of familiarity and I had to be nudged to go and receive my diploma. All my preparations had fled. I neither marched up to the stage like a conquering Amazon, nor did I look in the audience for Bailey's nod of approval. Marguerite Johnson, I heard the name again, my honors were read, there were noises in the audience of appreciation, and I took my place on the stage as rehearsed.

I thought about colors I hated: ecru, puce, lavender, beige, and black.

There was shuffling and rustling around me, then Henry Reed was giving his valedictory address, "To Be or Not to Be." Hadn't he heard the whitefolks? We couldn't *be*, so the question was a waste of time. Henry's voice came out clear and strong. I feared to look at him. Hadn't he got the message? There was no "nobler in the mind" for Negroes because the world didn't think we had minds, and they let us know it. "Outrageous fortune"? Now, that was a joke. When the ceremony was over I had to tell Henry Reed some things. That is, if I still cared. Not "rub," Henry, "erase." "Ah, there's the erase." Us.

Henry had been a good student in elocution. His voice rose on tides of promise and fell on waves of warnings. The English teacher had helped him to create a sermon winging through Hamlet's soliloquy. To be a man, a doer, a builder, a leader, or to be a tool, an unfunny joke, a crusher of funky toadstools. I marveled that Henry could go through with the speech as if we had a choice.

55 I had been listening and silently rebutting each sentence with my eyes closed; then there was a hush, which in an audience warns that something unplanned is happening. I looked up and saw Henry Reed, the conservative, the proper, the A student, turn his back to the audience and turn to us (the proud graduating class of 1940) and sing, nearly speaking,

> "Lift ev'ry voice and sing
> Till earth and heaven ring
> Ring with the harmonies of Liberty . . ."

It was the poem written by James Weldon Johnson. It was the music composed by J. Rosamond Johnson. It was the Negro national anthem. Out of habit we were singing it.

Our mothers and fathers stood in the dark hall and joined the hymn of encouragement. A kindergarten teacher led the small children onto the stage and the buttercups and daisies and bunny rabbits marked time and tried to follow:

> "Stony the road we trod
> Bitter the chastening rod
> Felt in the days when hope, unborn, had died.
> Yet with a steady beat
> Have not our weary feet
> Come to the place for which our fathers sighed?"

Each child I knew had learned that song with his ABC's and along with "Jesus Loves Me This I Know." But I personally had never heard it before. Never heard the words, despite the thousands of times I had sung them. Never thought they had anything to do with me.

On the other hand, the words of Patrick Henry had made such an impression on me that I had been able to stretch myself tall and trembling and say, "I know not what course others may take, but as for me, give me liberty or give me death."

And now I heard, really for the first time:

> "We have come over a way that with tears
> has been watered,
> We have come, treading our path through
> the blood of the slaughtered."

While echoes of the song shivered in the air, Henry Reed bowed 60
his head, said "Thank you," and returned to his place in the line. The tears that slipped down many faces were not wiped away in shame.

We were on top again. As always, again. We survived. The depths had been icy and dark, but now a bright sun spoke to our souls. I was no longer simply a member of the proud graduating class of 1940; I was a proud member of the wonderful, beautiful Negro race.

Oh, Black known and unknown poets, how often have your auctioned pains sustained us? Who will compute the lonely nights made less lonely by your songs, or the empty pots made less tragic by your tales?

If we were a people much given to revealing secrets, we might raise monuments and sacrifice to the memories of our poets, but slavery cured us of that weakness. It may be enough, however, to have it said that we survive in exact relationship to the dedication of our poets (include preachers, musicians, and blues singers).

For Discussion and Writing

1. How do the achievements for which the graduation speaker praises recent graduates from the narrator's school differ from the narrator's hopes for herself and her classmates?
2. How does Angelou use the order in which she relates the background information and events of her story to manipulate the reader's emotions? Why do you think she does this?
3. **connections** Compare the importance of literature in "Graduation" and in Gloria Anzaldúa's "How to Tame a Wild Tongue" (p. 33). What does poetry mean to Angelou here, and what does it mean to Anzaldúa?
4. Write about a time in your life when expectations and reality didn't match up. What was the situation? How did you react? Did you adjust your expectations? Or were you able to maintain them?

GLORIA ANZALDÚA

How to Tame a Wild Tongue

Gloria Anzaldúa was born in 1942 in the Rio Grande Valley of South Texas. At age eleven she began working in the fields as a migrant worker and then on her family's land after the death of her father. Working her way through school, she eventually became a schoolteacher and then an academic, speaking and writing about feminist, lesbian, and Chicana issues and about autobiography. She is best known for This Bridge Called My Back: Writings by Radical Women of Color *(1981), which she edited with Cherríe Moraga, and* Borderlands/La Frontera: The New Mestiza *(1987). Anzaldúa died in 2004.*

"How to Tame a Wild Tongue" is from Borderlands/La Frontera. *In it, Anzaldúa is concerned with many kinds of borders — between nations, cultures, classes, genders, languages. When she writes, "So, if you want to really hurt me, talk badly about my language" (par. 27), Anzaldúa is arguing for the ways in which identity is intertwined with the way we speak and for the ways in which people can be made to feel ashamed of their own tongues. Keeping hers wild — ignoring the closing of linguistic borders — is Anzaldúa's way of asserting her identity.*

"We're going to have to control your tongue," the dentist says, pulling out all the metal from my mouth. Silver bits plop and tinkle into the basin. My mouth is a motherlode.

The dentist is cleaning out my roots. I get a whiff of the stench when I gasp. "I can't cap that tooth yet, you're still draining," he says.

"We're going to have to do something about your tongue," I hear the anger rising in his voice. My tongue keeps pushing out the wads of cotton, pushing back the drills, the long thin needles. "I've never seen anything as strong or as stubborn," he says. And I think, how do you tame a wild tongue, train it to be quiet, how do you bridle and saddle it? How do you make it lie down?

> "Who is to say that robbing a people of
> its language is less violent than war?"
>
> — RAY GWYN SMITH[1]

I remember being caught speaking Spanish at recess — that was good for three licks on the knuckles with a sharp ruler. I remember being sent to the corner of the classroom for "talking back" to the Anglo teacher when all I was trying to do was tell her how to pronounce my name. "If you want to be American, speak 'American.' If you don't like it, go back to Mexico where you belong."

"I want you to speak English. *Pa' hallar buen trabajo tienes que* 5
saber hablar el inglés bien. Qué vale toda tu educación si todavía hablas inglés con un 'accent,'" my mother would say, mortified that I spoke English like a Mexican. At Pan American University, I and all Chicano students were required to take two speech classes. Their purpose: to get rid of our accents.

Attacks on one's form of expression with the intent to censor are a violation of the First Amendment. *El Anglo con cara de inocente nos arrancó la lengua.* Wild tongues can't be tamed, they can only be cut out.

OVERCOMING THE TRADITION OF SILENCE

> *Ahogadas, escupimos el oscuro.*
> *Peleando con nuestra propia sombra*
> *el silencio nos sepulta.*

En boca cerrada no entran moscas. "Flies don't enter a closed mouth" is a saying I kept hearing when I was a child. *Ser habladora* was to be a gossip and a liar, to talk too much. *Muchachitas bien criadas*, well-bred girls don't answer back. *Es una falta de respeto* to talk back to one's mother or father. I remember one of the sins I'd recite to the priest in the confession box the few times I went to confession: talking back to my mother, *hablar pa' 'tras, repelar. Hocicona, repelona, chismosa,* having a big mouth, questioning, carrying tales are all signs of being *mal criada*. In my culture they are all words that are derogatory if applied to women — I've never heard them applied to men.

The first time I heard two women, a Puerto Rican and a Cuban, say the word *"nosotras,"* I was shocked. I had not known the word existed. Chicanas use *nosotros* whether we're male or female. We are robbed of our female being by the masculine plural. Language is a male discourse.

> And our tongues have become
> dry   the wilderness has
> dried out our tongues   and
> we have forgotten speech.
>
> — IRENA KLEPFISZ[2]

Even our own people, other Spanish speakers *nos quieren poner candados en la boca*. They would hold us back with their bag of *reglas de academia*.

Oyé como ladra: el lenguaje de la frontera

> *Quien tiene boca se equivoca.*
>
> — MEXICAN SAYING

10 "*Pocho*, cultural traitor, you're speaking the oppressor's language by speaking English, you're ruining the Spanish language," I have been accused by various Latinos and Latinas. Chicano Spanish is considered by the purist and by most Latinos deficient, a mutilation of Spanish.

But Chicano Spanish is a border tongue which developed naturally. Change, *evolución, enriquecimiento de palabras nuevas por invención o adopción* have created variants of Chicano Spanish, *un nuevo lenguaje. Un lenguaje que corresponde a un modo de vivir.* Chicano Spanish is not incorrect, it is a living language.

For a people who are neither Spanish nor live in a country in which Spanish is the first language; for a people who live in a country in which English is the reigning tongue but who are not Anglo; for a people who cannot entirely identify with either standard (formal, Castillian) Spanish nor standard English, what recourse is left to them but to create their own language? A language which they can connect their identity to, one capable of communicating the realities and values true to themselves — a language with terms that are neither *español ni inglés*, but both. We speak a patois, a forked tongue, a variation of two languages.

Chicano Spanish sprang out of the Chicanos' need to identify ourselves as a distinct people. We needed a language with which we could communicate with ourselves, a secret language. For some of us, language is a homeland closer than the Southwest — for many Chicanos today live in the Midwest and the East. And because we are a complex, heterogeneous people, we speak many languages. Some of the languages we speak are:

1. Standard English
2. Working class and slang English
3. Standard Spanish
4. Standard Mexican Spanish
5. North Mexican Spanish dialect
6. Chicano Spanish (Texas, New Mexico, Arizona, and California have regional variations)
7. Tex-Mex
8. *Pachuco* (called *caló*)

My "home" tongues are the languages I speak with my sister and brothers, with my friends. They are the last five listed, with 6 and 7 being closest to my heart. From school, the media, and job situations, I've picked up standard and working class English. From Mamagrande Locha and from reading Spanish and Mexican literature, I've picked up Standard Spanish and Standard Mexican Spanish. From *los recién llegados*, Mexican immigrants, and *braceros*, I learned the North Mexican dialect. With Mexicans I'll try to speak either Standard Mexican Spanish or the North Mexican dialect. From my parents and Chicanos living in the Valley, I picked up Chicano Texas Spanish, and I speak it with my mom, younger brother (who married a Mexican and who rarely mixes Spanish with English), aunts, and older relatives.

With Chicanas from *Nuevo México* or *Arizona* I will speak Chi- 15
cano Spanish a little, but often they don't understand what I'm saying. With most California Chicanas I speak entirely in English (unless I forget). When I first moved to San Francisco, I'd rattle off something in Spanish, unintentionally embarrassing them. Often it is only with another Chicana *tejana* that I can talk freely.

Words distorted by English are known as anglicisms or *pochismos*. The *pocho* is an anglicized Mexican or American of Mexican origin who speaks Spanish with an accent characteristic of North Americans and who distorts and reconstructs the language according to the influence of English.[3] Tex-Mex, or Spanglish, comes most naturally to me. I may switch back and forth from English to Spanish in the same sentence or in the same word. With my sister and my brother Nune and with Chicano *tejano* contemporaries I speak in Tex-Mex.

From kids and people my own age I picked up *Pachuco*. *Pachuco* (the language of the zoot suiters) is a language of rebellion, both against Standard Spanish and Standard English. It is a secret language. Adults of the culture and outsiders cannot understand it. It is made up of slang words from both English and Spanish. *Ruca* means girl or woman, *vato* means guy or dude, *chale* means no, *simón* means yes, *churro* is sure, talk is *periquiar, pigionear* means petting, *que gacho* means how nerdy, *ponte águila* means watch out, death is called *la pelona*. Through lack of practice and not having others who can speak it, I've lost most of the *Pachuco* tongue.

CHICANO SPANISH

Chicanos, after 250 years of Spanish/Anglo colonization, have developed significant differences in the Spanish we speak. We collapse two adjacent vowels into a single syllable and sometimes shift the stress in certain words such as *maíz/maiz, cohete/cuete*. We leave out certain consonants when they appear between vowels: *lado/lao, mojado/mojao*. Chicanos from South Texas pronounce *f* as *j* as in *jue (fue)*. Chicanos use "archaisms," words that are no longer in the Spanish language, words that have been evolved out. We say *semos, truje, haiga, ansina,* and *naiden*. We retain the "archaic" *j*, as in *jalar,* that derives from an earlier *h*, (the French *halar* or the Germanic *halon* which was lost to standard Spanish in the 16th century), but which is still found in several regional dialects such as the one spoken in South Texas. (Due to geography, Chicanos from the Valley of South Texas were cut off linguistically from other Spanish speakers. We tend to use words that the Spaniards brought over from Medieval Spain. The majority of the Spanish colonizers in Mexico and the Southwest came from Extremadura — Hernán Cortés was one of them —

and Andalucía. Andalucians pronounce *ll* like a *y*, and their *d*'s tend to be absorbed by adjacent vowels: *tirado* becomes *tirao*. They brought *el lenguaje popular, dialectos y regionalismos*.[4])

Chicanos and other Spanish speakers also shift *ll* to *y* and *z* to *s*.[5] We leave out initial syllables, saying *tar* for *estar, toy* for *estoy, hora* for *ahora* (*cubanos* and *puertorriqueños* also leave out initial letters of some words). We also leave out the final syllable such as *pa* for *para*. The intervocalic *y*, the *ll* as in *tortilla, ella, botella*, gets replaced by *tortia* or *tortiya, ea, botea*. We add an additional syllable at the beginning of certain words: *atocar* for *tocar, agastar* for *gastar*. Sometimes we'll say *lavaste las vacijas*, other times *lavates* (substituting the *ates* verb endings for the *aste*).

We use anglicisms, words borrowed from English: *bola* from 20
ball, *carpeta* from carpet, *máchina de lavar* (instead of *lavadora*) from washing machine. Tex-Mex argot, created by adding a Spanish sound at the beginning or end of an English word such as *cookiar* for cook, *watchar* for watch, *parkiar* for park, and *rapiar* for rape, is the result of the pressures on Spanish speakers to adapt to English.

We don't use the word *vosotros/as* or its accompanying verb form. We don't say *claro* (to mean yes), *imagínate*, or *me emociona*, unless we picked up Spanish from Latinas, out of a book, or in a classroom. Other Spanish-speaking groups are going through the same, or similar, development in their Spanish.

LINGUISTIC TERRORISM

> *Deslenguadas. Somos los del español deficiente.* We are your linguistic nightmare, your linguistic aberration, your linguistic *mestisaje*, the subject of your *burla*. Because we speak with tongues of fire we are culturally crucified. Racially, culturally, and linguistically *somos huérfanos* — we speak an orphan tongue.

Chicanas who grew up speaking Chicano Spanish have internalized the belief that we speak poor Spanish. It is illegitimate, a bastard language. And because we internalize how our language has been used against us by the dominant culture, we use our language differences against each other.

Chicana feminists often skirt around each other with suspicion and hesitation. For the longest time I couldn't figure it out. Then it dawned on me. To be close to another Chicana is like looking into the mirror. We are afraid of what we'll see there. *Pena.* Shame. Low estimation of self. In childhood we are told that our language is wrong. Repeated attacks on our native tongue diminish our sense of self. The attacks continue throughout our lives.

Chicanas feel uncomfortable talking in Spanish to Latinas, afraid of their censure. Their language was not outlawed in their countries. They had a whole lifetime of being immersed in their native tongue; generations, centuries in which Spanish was a first language, taught in school, heard on radio and TV, and read in the newspaper.

25 If a person, Chicana or Latina, has a low estimation of my native tongue, she also has a low estimation of me. Often with *mexicanas y latinas* we'll speak English as a neutral language. Even among Chicanas we tend to speak English at parties or conferences. Yet, at the same time, we're afraid the other will think we're *agringadas* because we don't speak Chicano Spanish. We oppress each other trying to out-Chicano each other, vying to be the "real" Chicanas, to speak like Chicanos. There is no one Chicano language just as there is no one Chicano experience. A monolingual Chicana whose first language is English or Spanish is just as much a Chicana as one who speaks several variants of Spanish. A Chicana from Michigan or Chicago or Detroit is just as much a Chicana as one from the Southwest. Chicano Spanish is as diverse linguistically as it is regionally.

By the end of this century, Spanish speakers will comprise the biggest minority group in the U.S., a country where students in high schools and colleges are encouraged to take French classes because French is considered more "cultured." But for a language to remain alive it must be used.[6] By the end of this century English, and not Spanish, will be the mother tongue of most Chicanos and Latinos.

So, if you want to really hurt me, talk badly about my language. Ethnic identity is twin skin to linguistic identity — I am my language. Until I can take pride in my language, I cannot take pride in myself. Until I can accept as legitimate Chicano Texas Spanish, Tex-Mex, and all the other languages I speak, I cannot accept the legitimacy of myself. Until I am free to write bilingually and to switch codes without having always to translate, while I still have to speak English or Spanish when I would rather speak Spanglish, and as long as I have to accommodate the English speakers rather than having them accommodate me, my tongue will be illegitimate.

I will no longer be made to feel ashamed of existing. I will have my voice: Indian, Spanish, white. I will have my serpent's tongue — my woman's voice, my sexual voice, my poet's voice. I will overcome the tradition of silence.

> My fingers
> move sly against your palm
> Like women everywhere, we speak in code. . . .
>
> — MELANIE KAYE/KANTROWITZ[7]

"Vistas," corridos, y comida: My Native Tongue

In the 1960s, I read my first Chicano novel. It was *City of Night* by John Rechy, a gay Texan, son of a Scottish father and a Mexican mother. For days I walked around in stunned amazement that a Chicano could write and could get published. When I read *I Am Joaquín*[8] I was surprised to see a bilingual book by a Chicano in print. When I saw poetry written in Tex-Mex for the first time, a feeling of pure joy flashed through me. I felt like we really existed as a people. In 1971, when I started teaching High School English to Chicano students, I tried to supplement the required texts with works by Chicanos, only to be reprimanded and forbidden to do so by the principal. He claimed that I was supposed to teach "American" and English literature. At the risk of being fired, I swore my students to secrecy and slipped in Chicano short stories, poems, a play. In graduate school, while working toward a Ph.D., I had to "argue" with one advisor after the other, semester after semester, before I was allowed to make Chicano literature an area of focus.

30 Even before I read books by Chicanos or Mexicans, it was the Mexican movies I saw at the drive-in — the Thursday night special of $1.00 a carload — that gave me a sense of belonging. *"Vámonos a las vistas,"* my mother would call out and we'd all — grandmother, brothers, sister, and cousins — squeeze into the car. We'd wolf down cheese and bologna white bread sandwiches while watching Pedro Infante in melodramatic tearjerkers like *Nosotros*

los pobres, the first "real" Mexican movie (that was not an imitation of European movies). I remember seeing *Cuando los hijos se van* and surmising that all Mexican movies played up the love a mother has for her children and what ungrateful sons and daughters suffer when they are not devoted to their mothers. I remember the singing-type "westerns" of Jorge Negrete and Miquel Aceves Mejía. When watching Mexican movies, I felt a sense of homecoming as well as alienation. People who were to amount to something didn't go to Mexican movies, or *bailes*, or tune their radios to *bolero*, *rancherita*, and *corrido* music.

The whole time I was growing up, there was *norteño* music sometimes called North Mexican border music, or Tex-Mex music, or Chicano music, or *cantina* (bar) music. I grew up listening to *conjuntos*, three- or four-piece bands made up of folk musicians playing guitar, *bajo sexto*, drums, and button accordion, which Chicanos had borrowed from the German immigrants who had come to Central Texas and Mexico to farm and build breweries. In the Rio Grande Valley, Steve Jordan and Little Joe Hernández were popular, and Flaco Jiménez was the accordion king. The rhythms of Tex-Mex music are those of the polka, also adapted from the Germans, who in turn had borrowed the polka from the Czechs and Bohemians.

I remember the hot, sultry evenings when *corridos* — songs of love and death on the Texas-Mexican borderlands — reverberated out of cheap amplifiers from the local *cantinas* and wafted in through my bedroom window.

Corridos first became widely used along the South Texas/Mexican border during the early conflict between Chicanos and Anglos. The *corridos* are usually about Mexican heroes who do valiant deeds against the Anglo oppressors. Pancho Villa's song, *"La cucaracha,"* is the most famous one. *Corridos* of John F. Kennedy and his death are still very popular in the Valley. Older Chicanos remember Lydia Mendoza, one of the great border *corrido* singers who was called *la Gloria de Tejas*. Her *"El tango negro,"* sung during the Great Depression, made her a singer of the people. The everpresent *corridos* narrated one hundred years of border history, bringing news of events as well as entertaining. These folk musicians and folk songs are our chief cultural mythmakers, and they made our hard lives seem bearable.

I grew up feeling ambivalent about our music. Country-western and rock-and-roll had more status. In the 50s and 60s, for the slightly educated and *agringado* Chicanos, there existed a sense of shame at being caught listening to our music. Yet I couldn't stop my feet from thumping to the music, could not stop humming the words, nor hide from myself the exhilaration I felt when I heard it.

There are more subtle ways that we internalize identification, 35
especially in the forms of images and emotions. For me food and certain smells are tied to my identity, to my homeland. Woodsmoke curling up to an immense blue sky; woodsmoke perfuming my grandmother's clothes, her skin. The stench of cow manure and the yellow patches on the ground; the crack of a .22 rifle and the reek of cordite. Homemade white cheese sizzling in a pan, melting inside a folded *tortilla*. My sister Hilda's hot, spicy *menudo, chile colorado* making it deep red, pieces of *panza* and hominy floating on top. My brother Carito barbequing *fajitas* in the backyard. Even now and 3,000 miles away, I can see my mother spicing the ground beef, pork, and venison with *chile*. My mouth salivates at the thought of the hot steaming *tamales* I would be eating if I were home.

Si le preguntas a mi mamá, "¿Qué eres?"

> "Identity is the essential core of who we are as individuals, the conscious experience of the self inside."
>
> — GERSHEN KAUFMAN[9]

Nosotros los Chicanos straddle the borderlands. On one side of us, we are constantly exposed to the Spanish of the Mexicans, on the other side we hear the Anglos' incessant clamoring so that we forget our language. Among ourselves we don't say *nosotros los americanos, o nosotros los españoles, o nosotros los hispanos*. We say *nosotros los mexicanos* (by *mexicanos* we do not mean citizens of Mexico; we do not mean a national identity, but a racial one). We distinguish between *mexicanos del otro lado* and *mexicanos de este lado*. Deep in our hearts we believe that being Mexican has nothing to do with which country one lives in. Being Mexican is a state of soul — not one of mind, not one of citizenship. Neither eagle nor serpent, but both. And like the ocean, neither animal respects borders.

> *Dime con quien andas y te diré quien eres.*
> (Tell me who your friends are and I'll tell you who you are.)
>
> — MEXICAN SAYING

Si le preguntas a mi mamá, "¿Qué eres?" te dirá, "Soy mexicana." My brothers and sister say the same. I sometimes will answer *"soy mexicana"* and at others will say *"soy Chicana" o "soy tejana."* But I identified as *"Raza"* before I ever identified as *"mexicana"* or "Chicana."

As a culture, we call ourselves Spanish when referring to ourselves as a linguistic group and when copping out. It is then that we forget our predominant Indian genes. We are 70–80 percent Indian.[10] We call ourselves Hispanic[11] or Spanish-American or Latin American or Latin when linking ourselves to other Spanish-speaking peoples of the Western hemisphere and when copping out. We call ourselves Mexican-American[12] to signify we are neither Mexican nor American, but more the noun "American" than the adjective "Mexican" (and when copping out).

Chicanos and other people of color suffer economically for not acculturating. This voluntary (yet forced) alienation makes for psychological conflict, a kind of dual identity — we don't identify with the Anglo-American cultural values and we don't totally identify with the Mexican cultural values. We are a synergy of two cultures with various degrees of Mexicanness or Angloness. I have so internalized the borderland conflict that sometimes I feel like one cancels out the other and we are zero, nothing, no one. *A veces no soy nada ni nadie. Pero hasta cuando no lo soy, lo soy.*

When not copping out, when we know we are more than noth- 40
ing, we call ourselves Mexican, referring to race and ancestry; *mestizo* when affirming both our Indian and Spanish (but we hardly ever own our Black ancestory); Chicano when referring to a politically aware people born and/or raised in the U.S.; *Raza* when referring to Chicanos; *tejanos* when we are Chicanos from Texas.

Chicanos did not know we were a people until 1965 when Ceasar Chavez and the farmworkers united and *I Am Joaquín* was published and *la Raza Unida* party was formed in Texas. With that recognition, we became a distinct people. Something momentous happened to the Chicano soul — we became aware of our reality and acquired a name and a language (Chicano Spanish) that reflected that reality. Now that we had a name, some of the fragmented pieces began to fall together — who we were, what we were, how we had evolved. We began to get glimpses of what we might eventually become.

Yet the struggle of identities continues, the struggle of borders is our reality still. One day the inner struggle will cease and a true integration take place. In the meantime, *tenémos que hacer la lucha. ¿Quién está protegiendo los ranchos de mi gente? ¿Quién está tratando de cerrar la fisura entre la india y el blanco en nuestra sangre? El Chicano, si, el Chicano que anda como un ladrón en su propia casa.*

Los Chicanos, how patient we seem, how very patient. There is the quiet of the Indian about us.[13] We know how to survive. When other races have given up their tongue, we've kept ours. We know what it is to live under the hammer blow of the dominant *norteamericano* culture. But more than we count the blows, we count the days the weeks the years the centuries the eons until the white laws and commerce and customs will rot in the deserts they've created, lie bleached. *Humildes* yet proud, *quietos* yet wild, *nosotros losmexicanos-Chicanos* will walk by the crumbling ashes as we go about our business. Stubborn, persevering, impenetrable as stone, yet possessing a malleability that renders us unbreakable, we, the *mestizas* and *mestizos*, will remain.

Notes

1. Ray Gwyn Smith, *Moorland Is Cold Country*, unpublished book.

2. Irena Klepfisz, "*Di rayze aheym*/The Journey Home," in *The Tribe of Dina: A Jewish Women's Anthology*, Melanie Kaye/Kantrowitz and Irena Klepfisz, eds. (Montpelier, VT: Sinister Wisdom Books, 1986), 49.

3. R. C. Ortega, *Dialectología Del Barrio*, trans. Hortencia S. Alwan (Los Angeles, CA: R. C. Ortega Publisher & Bookseller, 1977), 132.

4. Eduardo Hernandéz-Chávez, Andrew D. Cohen, and Anthony F. Beltramo, *El Lenguaje de los Chicanos: Regional and Social Characteristics of Language Used by Mexican Americans* (Arlington, VA: Center for Applied Linguistics, 1975), 39.

5. Hernandéz-Chávez, xvii.

6. Irena Klepfisz, "Secular Jewish Identity: Yidishkayt in America," in *The Tribe of Dina*, Kaye/Kantrowitz and Klepfisz, eds., 43.

7. Melanie Kaye/Kantrowitz, "Sign," in *We Speak in Code: Poems and Other Writings* (Pittsburgh, PA: Motheroot Publications, Inc., 1980), 85.

8. Rodolfo Gonzales, *I Am Joaquín/Yo Soy Joaquín* (New York, NY: Bantam Books, 1972). It was first published in 1967.

9. Gershen Kaufman, *Shame: The Power of Caring* (Cambridge, MA: Schenkman Books, Inc., 1980), 68.

10. John R. Chávez, *The Lost Land: The Chicago Images of the Southwest* (Albuquerque, NM: University of New Mexico Press, 1984), 88–90.

11. "Hispanic" is derived from *Hispanis* (*España*, a name given to the Iberian Peninsula in ancient times when it was a part of the Roman Empire) and is a term designated by the U.S. government to make it easier to handle us on paper.

12. The Treaty of Guadalupe Hidalgo created the Mexican-American in 1848.

13. Anglos, in order to alleviate their guilt for dispossessing the Chicano, stressed the Spanish part of us and perpetrated the myth of the Spanish Southwest. We have accepted the fiction that we are Hispanic, that is Spanish, in order to accommodate ourselves to the dominant culture and its abhorrence of Indians. Chávez, 88–91.

For Discussion and Writing

1. List the different kinds of languages Anzaldúa says she speaks and organize them according to a principle of your own selection. Explain that principle and what the list it produces tells us about the Chicano/a experience with language.
2. How does Anzaldúa use definition to discuss her experience with language, and to what effect?
3. **connections** Compare Anzaldúa's sense of herself as an American to Audre Lorde's in "The Fourth of July" (p. 239). In what way does each woman feel American? In what way does each not?
4. In her discussion of moving back and forth between the varieties of languages she speaks, Anzaldúa uses the term "switch codes" (par. 27). Define that term and write about situations in your life in which you switch codes.

BARBARA LAZEAR ASCHER

On Compassion

Barbara Lazear Ascher, born in 1946, worked as a lawyer for two years before she became a full-time writer. Her essays, which have appeared in newspapers and magazines, have been collected in Playing after Dark *(1986) and* The Habit of Loving *(1989). She has also written books about her brother's death from AIDS (*Landscape without Gravity: A Memoir of Grief, *1993) and romance (*Dancing in the Dark: Romance, Yearning, and the Search for the Sublime, *1999).*

A New Yorker, Ascher draws her examples for "On Compassion" from life in that city. The brief scenes she describes — the encounter on the street corner, the moment in the café — allow the reader to imagine the thoughts and feelings of the participants. As you read, take note of how the specific details of the city enliven her examples and the way that specificity helps the examples to illustrate her argument.

The man's grin is less the result of circumstance than dreams or madness. His buttonless shirt, with one sleeve missing, hangs outside the waist of his baggy trousers. Carefully plaited dreadlocks bespeak a better time, long ago. As he crosses Manhattan's Seventy-ninth Street, his gait is the shuffle of the forgotten ones held in place by gravity rather than plans. On the corner of Madison Avenue, he stops before a blond baby in an Aprica stroller. The baby's mother waits for the light to change and her hands close tighter on the stroller's handle as she sees the man approach.

The others on the corner, five men and women waiting for the crosstown bus, look away. They daydream a bit and gaze into the weak rays of November light. A man with a briefcase lifts and lowers the shiny toe of his right shoe, watching the light reflect, trying to catch and balance it, as if he could hold and make it his, to ease the heavy gray of coming January, February, and March. The winter months that will send snow around the feet, calves, and knees of the grinning man as he heads for the shelter of Grand Central or Pennsylvania Station.

But for now, in this last gasp of autumn warmth, he is still. His eyes fix on the baby. The mother removes her purse from her shoulder and rummages through its contents: lipstick, a lace handkerchief, an address book. She finds what she's looking for and passes a folded dollar over her child's head to the man who stands and stares even though the light has changed and traffic navigates about his hips.

His hands continue to dangle at his sides. He does not know his part. He does not know that acceptance of the gift and gratitude are what make this transaction complete. The baby, weary of the unwavering stare, pulls its blanket over its head. The man does not look away. Like a bridegroom waiting at the altar, his eyes pierce the white veil.

5 The mother grows impatient and pushes the stroller before her, bearing the dollar like a cross. Finally, a black hand rises and closes around green.

Was it fear or compassion that motivated the gift?

Up the avenue, at Ninety-first Street, there is a small French bread shop where you can sit and eat a buttery, overpriced croissant and wash it down with rich cappuccino. Twice when I have stopped here to stave hunger or stay the cold, twice as I have sat and read and felt the warm rush of hot coffee and milk, an old man has wandered in and stood inside the entrance. He wears a stained blanket pulled up to his chin, and a woolen hood pulled down to his gray, bushy eyebrows. As he stands, the scent of stale cigarettes and urine fills the small, overheated room.

The owner of the shop, a moody French woman, emerges from the kitchen with steaming coffee in a Styrofoam cup, and a small paper bag of . . . of what? Yesterday's bread? Today's croissant? He accepts the offering as silently as he came, and is gone.

Twice I have witnessed this, and twice I have wondered, what compels this woman to feed this man? Pity? Care? Compassion? Or does she simply want to rid her shop of his troublesome presence? If expulsion were her motivation she would not reward his arrival with gifts of food. Most proprietors do not. They chase the homeless from their midst with expletives and threats.

10 As winter approaches, the mayor of New York City is moving the homeless off the streets and into Bellevue Hospital. The New

York Civil Liberties Union is watchful. They question whether the rights of these people who live in our parks and doorways are being violated by involuntary hospitalization.

I think the mayor's notion is humane, but I fear it is something else as well. Raw humanity offends our sensibilities. We want to protect ourselves from an awareness of rags with voices that make no sense and scream forth in inarticulate rage. We do not wish to be reminded of the tentative state of our own well-being and sanity. And so, the troublesome presence is removed from the awareness of the electorate.

Like other cities, there is much about Manhattan now that resembles Dickensian London. Ladies in high-heeled shoes pick their way through poverty and madness. You hear more cocktail party complaints than usual, "I just can't take New York anymore." Our citizens dream of the open spaces of Wyoming, the manicured exclusivity of Hobe Sound.

And yet, it may be that these are the conditions that finally give birth to empathy, the mother of compassion. We cannot deny the existence of the helpless as their presence grows. It is impossible to insulate ourselves against what is at our very doorstep. I don't believe that one is born compassionate. Compassion is not a character trait like a sunny disposition. It must be learned, and it is learned by having adversity at our windows, coming through the gates of our yards, the walls of our towns, adversity that becomes so familiar that we begin to identify and empathize with it.

For the ancient Greeks, drama taught and reinforced compassion within a society. The object of Greek tragedy was to inspire empathy in the audience so that the common response to the hero's fall was: "There, but for the grace of God, go I." Could it be that this was the response of the mother who offered the dollar, the French woman who gave the food? Could it be that the homeless, like those ancients, are reminding us of our common humanity? Of course, there is a difference. This play doesn't end — and the players can't go home.

For Discussion and Writing

1. What examples of encounters with the homeless does Ascher offer?
2. Imagine and list alternative examples of encounters with the homeless that Ascher might have used. How might they have changed her essay?

3. **connections** Both Ascher and Lars Eighner in "On Dumpster Diving" (p. 146) write about people who are down on their luck: Eighner as one who has been down on his luck himself, Ascher from the perspective of the more fortunate. How do their differing perspectives inform their essays?
4. Where does Ascher believe compassion comes from? Do you agree or disagree? Why? Can you illustrate your argument with an example from your own experience?

JAMES BALDWIN

Notes of a Native Son

Born in Harlem in 1924, a preacher and a published writer of reviews and essays at a young age, James Baldwin became a noted writer of American prose. Though he lived abroad for much of his adult life, in Paris, Switzerland, and Istanbul, Baldwin wrote incisively and passionately about the experience of being black in America. His first novel, Go Tell It on the Mountain *(1953), drew on his youth in the church and on his relationship with his preacher father as well as on the rolling, repetitive, swelling language of the sermon. His essay collection* Notes of a Native Son *(1955) reflected further on his own life and on African American experience as well as on the literary and cultural products that have come out of that experience. Baldwin's next novels,* Giovanni's Room *(1956) and* Another Country *(1962), delved into the issue of homosexuality. In his open explorations in fiction and nonfiction of taboo subjects and often hidden but sometimes quite open prejudices, Baldwin became a model of a writer practicing thoughtful yet always heartfelt engagement with the world.*

"Notes of a Native Son" considers the hatred at the heart of race relations in midcentury America and at the heart of Baldwin's relationship with his father. That Baldwin accepts that hate as neither the totality nor the final destination of these relationships is testament to his sensibility and strength as a writer and as a man.

I

On the 29th of July, in 1943, my father died. On the same day, a few hours later, his last child was born. Over a month before this, while all our energies were concentrated in waiting for these events, there had been, in Detroit, one of the bloodiest race riots of the century. A few hours after my father's funeral, while he lay in state in the undertaker's chapel, a race riot broke out in Harlem. On the morning of the 3rd of August, we drove my father to the graveyard through a wilderness of smashed plate glass.

The day of my father's funeral had also been my nineteenth birthday. As we drove him to the graveyard, the spoils of injustice, anarchy, discontent, and hatred were all around us. It seemed to me that God himself had devised, to mark my father's end, the most sustained and brutally dissonant of codas. And it seemed to me, too, that the violence which rose all about us as my father left the world had been devised as a corrective for the pride of his eldest son. I had declined to believe in that apocalypse which had been central to my father's vision; very well, life seemed to be saying, here is something that will certainly pass for an apocalypse until the real thing comes along. I had inclined to be contemptuous of my father for the conditions of his life, for the conditions of our lives. When his life had ended I began to wonder about that life and also, in a new way, to be apprehensive about my own.

I had not known my father very well. We had got on badly, partly because we shared, in our different fashions, the vice of stubborn pride. When he was dead I realized that I had hardly ever spoken to him. When he had been dead a long time I began to wish I had. It seems to be typical of life in America, where opportunities, real and fancied, are thicker than anywhere else on the globe, that the second generation has no time to talk to the first. No one, including my father, seems to have known exactly how old he was, but his mother had been born during slavery. He was of the first generation of free men. He, along with thousands of other Negroes, came North after 1919 and I was part of that generation which had never seen the landscape of what Negroes sometimes call the Old Country.

He had been born in New Orleans and had been a quite young man there during the time that Louis Armstrong, a boy, was running errands for the dives and honky-tonks of what was always presented to me as one of the most wicked of cities — to this day, whenever I think of New Orleans, I also helplessly think of Sodom and Gomorrah. My father never mentioned Louis Armstrong, except to forbid us to play his records; but there was a picture of him on our wall for a long time. One of my father's strong-willed female relatives had placed it there and forbade my father to take it down. He never did, but he eventually maneuvered her out of the house and when, some years later, she was in trouble and near death, he refused to do anything to help her.

5 He was, I think, very handsome. I gather this from photographs and from my own memories of him, dressed in his Sunday best and on his way to preach a sermon somewhere, when I was little. Handsome, proud, and ingrown, "like a toe-nail," somebody said. But he looked to me, as I grew older, like pictures I had seen of African tribal chieftains: he really should have been naked, with war-paint on and barbaric mementos, standing among spears. He could be chilling in the pulpit and indescribably cruel in his personal life and he was certainly the most bitter man I have ever met; yet it must be said that there was something else in him, buried in him, which lent him his tremendous power and, even, a rather crushing charm. It had something to do with his blackness, I think — he was very black — with his blackness and his beauty, and with the fact that he knew that he was black but did not know that he was beautiful. He claimed to be proud of his blackness but it had also been the cause of much humiliation and it had fixed bleak boundaries to his life. He was not a young man when we were growing up and he had already suffered many kinds of ruin; in his outrageously demanding and protective way he loved his children, who were black like him and menaced, like him; and all these things sometimes showed in his face when he tried, never to my knowledge with any success, to establish contact with any of us. When he took one of his children on his knee to play, the child always became fretful and began to cry; when he tried to help one of us with our homework the absolutely unabating tension which emanated from him caused our minds and our tongues to become paralyzed, so that he, scarcely knowing why, flew into a rage and the child, not knowing why, was punished. If it ever entered his head to bring a surprise home for his children, it was, almost unfailingly, the wrong surprise and even the big watermelons he often brought home on his back in the summertime led to the most appalling scenes. I do not remember, in all those years, that one of his children was ever glad to see him come home. From what I was able to gather of his early life, it seemed that this inability to establish contact with other people had always marked him and had been one of the things which had driven him out of New Orleans. There was something in him, therefore, groping and tentative, which was never expressed and which was buried with him. One saw it most clearly when he was facing new people and hoping to impress them. But he never did,

not for long. We went from church to smaller and more improbable church, he found himself in less and less demand as a minister, and by the time he died none of his friends had come to see him for a long time. He had lived and died in an intolerable bitterness of spirit and it frightened me, as we drove him to the graveyard through those unquiet, ruined streets, to see how powerful and overflowing this bitterness could be and to realize that this bitterness now was mine.

When he died I had been away from home for a little over a year. In that year I had had time to become aware of the meaning of all my father's bitter warnings, had discovered the secret of his proudly pursed lips and rigid carriage: I had discovered the weight of white people in the world. I saw that this had been for my ancestors and now would be for me an awful thing to live with and that the bitterness which had helped to kill my father could also kill me.

He had been ill a long time — in the mind, as we now realized, reliving instances of his fantastic intransigence in the new light of his affliction and endeavoring to feel a sorrow for him which never, quite, came true. We had not known that he was being eaten up by paranoia, and the discovery that his cruelty, to our bodies and our minds, had been one of the symptoms of his illness was not, then, enough to enable us to forgive him. The younger children felt, quite simply, relief that he would not be coming home anymore. My mother's observation that it was he, after all, who had kept them alive all these years meant nothing because the problems of keeping children alive are not real for children. The older children felt, with my father gone, that they could invite their friends to the house without fear that their friends would be insulted or, as had sometimes happened with me, being told that their friends were in league with the devil and intended to rob our family of everything we owned. (I didn't fail to wonder, and it made me hate him, what on earth we owned that anybody else would want.)

His illness was beyond all hope of healing before anyone realized that he was ill. He had always been so strange and had lived, like a prophet, in such unimaginably close communion with the Lord that his long silences which were punctuated by moans and hallelujahs and snatches of old songs while he sat at the living-room window never seemed odd to us. It was not until he refused to eat because, he said, his family was trying to poison him that my mother was forced to accept as a fact what had, until then, been only an unwilling suspicion. When he was committed, it was discovered that he had tuberculosis and, as it turned out, the disease of his mind allowed the disease of his body to destroy him. For the doctors could not force him to eat, either, and, though he was fed intravenously, it was clear from the beginning that there was no hope for him.

In my mind's eye I could see him, sitting at the window, locked up in his terrors; hating and fearing every living soul including his children who had betrayed him, too, by reaching towards the world which had despised him. There were nine of us. I began to wonder what it could have felt like for such a man to have had nine children whom he could barely feed. He used to make little jokes about our poverty, which never, of course, seemed very funny to us; they could not have seemed very funny to him, either, or else our all too feeble response to them would never have caused such rages. He spent great energy and achieved, to our chagrin, no small amount of success in keeping us away from the people who surrounded us, people who had all-night rent parties to which we listened when we should have been sleeping, people who cursed and drank and flashed razor blades on Lenox Avenue. He could not understand why, if they had so much energy to spare, they could not use it to make their lives better. He treated almost everybody on our block with a most uncharitable asperity and neither they, nor, of course, their children were slow to reciprocate.

The only white people who came to our house were welfare 10
workers and bill collectors. It was almost always my mother who dealt with them, for my father's temper, which was at the mercy of his pride, was never to be trusted. It was clear that he felt their very presence in his home to be a violation: this was conveyed by his carriage, almost ludicrously stiff, and by his voice, harsh and vindictively polite. When I was around nine or ten I wrote a play which was directed by a young, white schoolteacher, a woman, who then took an interest in me, and gave me books to read and, in order to corroborate my theatrical bent, decided to take me to see what she somewhat tactlessly referred to as "real" plays. Theatergoing was forbidden in our house, but, with the really

cruel intuitiveness of a child, I suspected that the color of this woman's skin would carry the day for me. When, at school, she suggested taking me to the theater, I did not, as I might have done if she had been a Negro, find a way of discouraging her, but agreed that she should pick me up at my house one evening. I then, very cleverly, left all the rest to my mother, who suggested to my father, as I knew she would, that it would not be very nice to let such a kind woman make the trip for nothing. Also, since it was a schoolteacher, I imagine that my mother countered the idea of sin with the idea of "education," which word, even with my father, carried a kind of bitter weight.

Before the teacher came my father took me aside to ask *why* she was coming, what *interest* she could possibly have in our house, in a boy like me. I said I didn't know but I, too, suggested that it had something to do with education. And I understood that my father was waiting for me to say something — I didn't quite know what; perhaps that I wanted his protection against this teacher and her "education." I said none of these things and the teacher came and we went out. It was clear, during the brief interview in our living room, that my father was agreeing very much against his will and that he would have refused permission if he had dared. The fact that he did not dare caused me to despise him: I had no way of knowing that he was facing in that living room a wholly unprecedented and frightening situation.

Later, when my father had been laid off from his job, this woman became very important to us. She was really a very sweet and generous woman and went to a great deal of trouble to be of help to us, particularly during one awful winter. My mother called her by the highest name she knew. She said she was a "christian." My father could scarcely disagree but during the four or five years of our relatively close association he never trusted her and was always trying to surprise in her open, Midwestern face the genuine, cunningly hidden, and hideous motivation. In later years, particularly when it began to be clear that this "education" of mine was going to lead me to perdition, he became more explicit and warned me that my white friends in high school were not really my friends and that I would see, when I was older, how white people would do anything to keep a Negro down. Some of them could be nice, he admitted, but none of them were to be trusted and most of them were not even nice. The best thing was to have as little to do with them as possible. I did not feel this way and I was certain, in my innocence, that I never would.

But the year which preceded my father's death had made a great change in my life. I had been living in New Jersey, working in defense plants, working and living among southerners, white and black. I knew about the south, of course, and about how southerners treated Negroes and how they expected them to behave, but it had never entered my mind that anyone would look at me and expect *me* to behave that way. I learned in New Jersey that to be a Negro meant, precisely, that one was never looked at but was simply at the mercy of the reflexes the color of one's skin caused in other people. I acted in New Jersey as I had always acted, that is as though I thought a great deal of myself — I had to *act* that way — with results that were, simply, unbelievable. I had scarcely arrived before I had earned the enmity, which was extraordinarily ingenious, of all my superiors and nearly all my coworkers. In the beginning, to make matters worse, I simply did not know what was happening. I did not know what I had done, and I shortly began to wonder what *anyone* could possibly do, to bring about such unanimous, active, and unbearably vocal hostility. I knew about jim-crow but I had never experienced it. I went to the same self-service restaurant three times and stood with all the Princeton boys before the counter, waiting for a hamburger and coffee; it was always an extraordinarily long time before anything was set before me; but it was not until the fourth visit that I learned that, in fact, nothing had ever been set before me: I had simply picked something up. Negroes were not served there, I was told, and they had been waiting for me to realize that I was always the only Negro present. Once I was told this, I determined to go there all the time. But now they were ready for me and, though some dreadful scenes were subsequently enacted in that restaurant, I never ate there again.

It was the same story all over New Jersey, in bars, bowling alleys, diners, places to live. I was always being forced to leave, silently, or with mutual imprecations. I very shortly became notorious and children giggled behind me when I passed and their elders whispered or shouted — they really believed that I was mad. And it did begin to work on my mind, of course; I began to be afraid to go anywhere and to compensate for this I went places to which I really should not have gone and where, God knows, I had no desire to be. My reputation in town naturally enhanced my reputation at work and my working day became one long series of acrobatics designed to keep me out of trouble. I cannot say that these acrobatics succeeded. It began to seem that the machinery of the organization I worked for was turning over, day and night, with but one aim: to eject me. I was fired once, and contrived, with the aid of a friend from New York, to get back on the payroll; was fired again, and bounced back again. It took a while to fire me for the third time, but the third time took. There were no loopholes anywhere. There was not even any way of getting back inside the gates.

That year in New Jersey lives in my mind as though it were the 15
year during which, having an unsuspected predilection for it, I first contracted some dread, chronic disease, the unfailing symptom of which is a kind of blind fever, a pounding in the skull and fire in the bowels. Once this disease is contracted, one can never be really carefree again, for the fever, without an instant's warning, can recur at any moment. It can wreck more important things than race relations. There is not a Negro alive who does not have this rage in his blood — one has the choice, merely, of living with it consciously or surrendering to it. As for me, this fever has recurred in me, and does, and will until the day I die.

My last night in New Jersey, a white friend from New York took me to the nearest big town, Trenton, to go to the movies and have a few drinks. As it turned out, he also saved me from, at the very least, a violent whipping. Almost every detail of that night stands out very clearly in my memory. I even remember the name of the movie we saw because its title impressed me as being so patly ironical. It was a movie about the German occupation of France, starring Maureen O'Hara and Charles Laughton and called *This Land Is Mine*. I remember the name of the diner we walked into when the movie ended: it was the "American Diner." When we walked in the counterman asked what we wanted and I remember answering with the casual sharpness which had become my habit: "We want a hamburger and a cup of coffee, what do you think we want?" I do not know why, after a year of such rebuffs, I so completely failed to anticipate his answer, which was, of course, "We don't serve Negroes here." This reply failed to discompose me, at least for the moment. I made some sardonic comment about the name of the diner and we walked out into the streets.

This was the time of what was called the "brown-out," when the lights in all American cities were very dim. When we re-entered the streets something happened to me which had the force of an optical illusion, or a nightmare. The streets were very crowded and I was facing north. People were moving in every direction but it seemed to me, in that instant, that all of the people I could see, and many more than that, were moving toward me, against me, and that everyone was white. I remember how their faces gleamed. And I felt, like a physical sensation, a *click* at the nape of my neck as though some interior string connecting my head to my body had been cut. I began to walk. I heard my friend call after me, but I ignored him. Heaven only knows what was going on in his mind, but he had the good sense not to touch me — I don't know what would have happened if he had — and to keep me in sight. I don't know what was going on in my mind, either; I certainly had no conscious plan. I wanted to do something to crush these white faces, which were crushing me. I walked for perhaps a block or two until I came to an enormous, glittering, and fashionable restaurant in which I knew not even the intercession of the Virgin would cause me to be served. I pushed through the doors and took the first vacant seat I saw, at a table for two, and waited.

I do not know how long I waited and I rather wonder, until today, what I could possibly have looked like. Whatever I looked like, I frightened the waitress who shortly appeared, and the moment she appeared all of my fury flowed towards her. I hated her for her white face, and for her great, astounded, frightened eyes. I felt that if she found a black man so frightening I would make her fright worthwhile.

She did not ask me what I wanted, but repeated, as though she had learned it somewhere, "We don't serve Negroes here." She did not say it with the blunt, derisive hostility to which I had grown so accustomed, but, rather, with a note of apology in her voice, and fear. This made me colder and more murderous than ever. I felt I had to do something with my hands. I wanted her to come close enough for me to get her neck between my hands.

So I pretended not to have understood her, hoping to draw her 20
closer. And she did step a very short step closer, with her pencil

poised incongruously over her pad, and repeated the formula: ". . . don't serve Negroes here."

Somehow, with the repetition of that phrase, which was already ringing in my head like a thousand bells of a nightmare, I realized that she would never come any closer and that I would have to strike from a distance. There was nothing on the table but an ordinary water-mug half full of water, and I picked this up and hurled it with all my strength at her. She ducked and it missed her and shattered against the mirror behind the bar. And, with that sound, my frozen blood abruptly thawed, I returned from wherever I had been, I *saw*, for the first time, the restaurant, the people with their mouths open, already, as it seemed to me, rising as one man, and I realized what I had done, and where I was, and I was frightened. I rose and began running for the door. A round, potbellied man grabbed me by the nape of the neck just as I reached the doors and began to beat me about the face. I kicked him and got loose and ran into the streets. My friend whispered, *"Run!"* and I ran.

My friend stayed outside the restaurant long enough to misdirect my pursuers and the police, who arrived, he told me, at once. I do not know what I said to him when he came to my room that night. I could not have said much. I felt, in the oddest, most awful way, that I had somehow betrayed him. I lived it over and over and over again, the way one relives an automobile accident after it has happened and one finds oneself alone and safe. I could not get over two facts, both equally difficult for the imagination to grasp, and one was that I could have been murdered. But the other was that I had been ready to commit murder. I saw nothing very clearly but I did see this: that my life, my *real* life, was in danger, and not from anything other people might do but from the hatred I carried in my own heart.

II

I had returned home around the second week in June — in great haste because it seemed that my father's death and my mother's confinement were both but a matter of hours. In the case of my mother, it soon became clear that she had simply made a miscalculation. This had always been her tendency and I don't believe that a single one of us arrived in the world, or has since arrived anywhere else, on time. But none of us dawdled so intolerably about the business of being born as did my baby sister. We sometimes amused ourselves, during those endless, stifling weeks, by picturing the baby sitting within in the safe, warm dark, bitterly regretting the necessity of becoming a part of our chaos and stubbornly putting it off as long as possible. I understood her perfectly and congratulated her on showing such good sense so soon. Death, however, sat as purposefully at my father's bedside as life stirred within my mother's womb and it was harder to understand why he so lingered in that long shadow. It seemed that he had bent, and for a long time, too, all of his energies towards dying. Now death was ready for him but my father held back.

All of Harlem, indeed, seemed to be infected by waiting. I had never before known it to be so violently still. Racial tensions throughout this country were exacerbated during the early years of the war, partly because the labor market brought together hundreds of thousands of ill-prepared people and partly because Negro soldiers, regardless of where they were born, received their military training in the south. What happened in defense plants and army camps had repercussions, naturally, in every Negro ghetto. The situation in Harlem had grown bad enough for clergymen, policemen, educators, politicians, and social workers to assert in one breath that there was no "crime wave" and to offer, in the very next breath, suggestions as to how to combat it. These suggestions always seemed to involve playgrounds, despite the fact that racial skirmishes were occurring in the playgrounds, too. Playground or not, crime wave or not, the Harlem police force had been augmented in March, and the unrest grew — perhaps, in fact, partly as a result of the ghetto's instinctive hatred of policemen. Perhaps the most revealing news item, out of the steady parade of reports of muggings, stabbings, shootings, assaults, gang wars, and accusations of police brutality is the item concerning six Negro girls who set upon a white girl in the subway because, as they all too accurately put it, she was stepping on their toes. Indeed she was, all over the nation.

I had never before been so aware of policemen, on foot, on 25
horseback, on corners, everywhere, always two by two. Nor had I ever been so aware of small knots of people. They were on stoops and on corners and in doorways, and what was striking about

them, I think, was that they did not seem to be talking. Never, when I passed these groups, did the usual sound of a curse or a laugh ring out and neither did there seem to be any hum of gossip. There was certainly, on the other hand, occurring between them communication extraordinarily intense. Another thing that was striking was the unexpected diversity of the people who made up these groups. Usually, for example, one would see a group of sharpies standing on the street corner, jiving the passing chicks; or a group of older men, usually, for some reason, in the vicinity of a barber shop, discussing baseball scores, or the numbers or making rather chilling observations about women they had known. Women, in a general way, tended to be seen less often together — unless they were church women, or very young girls, or prostitutes met together for an unprofessional instant. But that summer I saw the strangest combinations: large, respectable, churchly matrons standing on the stoops or the corners with their hair tied up, together with a girl in sleazy satin whose face bore the marks of gin and the razor, or heavy-set, abrupt, no-nonsense older men, in company with the most disreputable and fanatical "race" men, or these same "race" men with the sharpies, or these sharpies with the churchly women. Seventh Day Adventists and Methodists and Spiritualists seemed to be hobnobbing with Holy-rollers and they were all, alike, entangled with the most flagrant disbelievers; something heavy in their stance seemed to indicate that they had all, incredibly, seen a common vision, and on each face there seemed to be the same strange, bitter shadow.

The churchly women and the matter-of-fact, no-nonsense men had children in the Army. The sleazy girls they talked to had lovers there, the sharpies and the "race" men had friends and brothers there. It would have demanded an unquestioning patriotism, happily as uncommon in this country as it is undesirable, for these people not to have been disturbed by the bitter letters they received, by the newspaper stories they read, not to have been enraged by the posters, then to be found all over New York, which described the Japanese as "yellow-bellied Japs." It was only the "race" men, to be sure, who spoke ceaselessly of being revenged — how this vengeance was to be exacted was not clear — for the indignities and dangers suffered by Negro boys in uniform; but everybody felt a directionless, hopeless bitterness, as well as that panic which can scarcely be suppressed when one knows that a human being one loves is beyond one's reach, and in danger. This helplessness and this gnawing uneasiness does something, at length, to even the toughest mind. Perhaps the best way to sum all this up is to say that the people I knew felt, mainly, a peculiar kind of relief when they knew that their boys were being shipped out of the south, to do battle overseas. It was, perhaps, like feeling that the most dangerous part of a dangerous journey had been passed and that now, even if death should come, it would come with honor and without the complicity of their countrymen. Such a death would be, in short, a fact with which one could hope to live.

It was on the 28th of July, which I believe was a Wednesday, that I visited my father for the first time during his illness and for the last time in his life. The moment I saw him I knew why I had put off this visit so long. I had told my mother that I did not want to see him because I hated him. But this was not true. It was only that I *had* hated him and I wanted to hold on to this hatred. I did not want to look on him as a ruin: it was not a ruin I had hated. I imagine that one of the reasons people cling to their hates so stubbornly is because they sense, once hate is gone, that they will be forced to deal with pain.

We traveled out to him, his older sister and myself, to what seemed to be the very end of a very Long Island. It was hot and dusty and we wrangled, my aunt and I, all the way out, over the fact that I had recently begun to smoke and, as she said, to give myself airs. But I knew that she wrangled with me because she could not bear to face the fact of her brother's dying. Neither could I endure the reality of her despair, her unstated bafflement as to what had happened to her brother's life, and her own. So we wrangled and I smoked and from time to time she fell into a heavy reverie. Covertly, I watched her face, which was the face of an old woman; it had fallen in, the eyes were sunken and lightless; soon she would be dying, too.

In my childhood — it had not been so long ago — I had thought her beautiful. She had been quick-witted and quick-moving and very generous with all the children, and each of her visits had been an event. At one time one of my brothers and myself had thought of running away to live with her. Now she could no longer produce out of her handbag some unexpected and yet familiar delight. She made me feel pity and revulsion and fear. It was awful to realize that she no longer caused me to feel affection. The closer we came to the hospital the more querulous she became and at the same time, naturally, grew more dependent on me. Between pity and guilt and fear I began to feel that there was another me trapped in my skull like a jack-in-the-box who might escape my control at any moment and fill the air with screaming.

She began to cry the moment we entered the room and she saw 30
him lying there, all shriveled and still, like a little black monkey. The great, gleaming apparatus which fed him and would have compelled him to be still even if he had been able to move brought to mind, not beneficence, but torture; the tubes entering his arm made me think of pictures I had seen when a child, of Gulliver, tied down by the pygmies on that island. My aunt wept and wept; there was a whistling sound in my father's throat; nothing was said; he could not speak. I wanted to take his hand, to say something. But I do not know what I could have said, even if he could have heard me. He was not really in that room with us, he had at last really embarked on his journey; and though my aunt told me that he said he was going to meet Jesus, I did not hear anything except that whistling in his throat. The doctor came back and we left, into that unbearable train again, and home. In the morning came the telegram saying that he was dead. Then the house was suddenly full of relatives, friends, hysteria, and confusion and I quickly left my mother and the children to the care of those impressive women, who, in Negro communities at least, automatically appear at times of bereavement armed with lotions, proverbs, and patience, and an ability to cook. I went downtown. By the time I returned, later the same day, my mother had been carried to the hospital and the baby had been born.

III

For my father's funeral I had nothing black to wear and this posed a nagging problem all day long. It was one of those problems, simple, or impossible of solution, to which the mind insanely clings in order to avoid the mind's real trouble. I spent most of that day at the downtown apartment of a girl I knew, celebrating my birthday with whiskey and wondering what to wear that night. When planning a birthday celebration one naturally does not expect that it will be up against competition from a funeral and this girl had anticipated taking me out that night, for a big dinner and a night club afterwards. Sometime during the course of that long day we decided that we would go out anyway, when my father's funeral service was over. I imagine *I* decided it, since, as the funeral hour approached, it became clearer and clearer to me that I would not know what to do with myself when it was over. The girl, stifling her very lively concern as to the possible effects of the whiskey on one of my father's chief mourners, concentrated on being conciliatory and practically helpful. She found a black shirt for me somewhere and ironed it and, dressed in the darkest pants and jacket I owned, and slightly drunk, I made my way to my father's funeral.

The chapel was full, but not packed, and very quiet. There were, mainly, my father's relatives, and his children, and here and there I saw faces I had not seen since childhood, the faces of my father's one-time friends. They were very dark and solemn now, seeming somehow to suggest that they had known all along that something like this would happen. Chief among the mourners was my aunt, who had quarreled with my father all his life; by which I do not mean to suggest that her mourning was insincere or that she had not loved him. I suppose that she was one of the few people in the world who had, and their incessant quarreling proved precisely the strength of the tie that bound them. The only other person in the world, as far as I knew, whose relationship to my father rivaled my aunt's in depth was my mother, who was not there.

It seemed to me, of course, that it was a very long funeral. But it was, if anything, a rather shorter funeral than most, nor, since there were no overwhelming, uncontrollable expressions of grief, could it be called — if I dare to use the word — successful. The minister who preached my father's funeral sermon was one of the few my father had still been seeing as he neared his end. He presented to us in his sermon a man whom none of us had ever seen — a man thoughtful, patient, and forbearing, a Christian inspiration to all who knew him, and a model for his children. And no doubt the children, in their disturbed and guilty state, were almost ready to believe this; he had been remote enough to be anything and, anyway, the shock of the incontrovertible, that it was really our father lying up there in that casket, prepared the mind for anything. His sister moaned and this grief-stricken moaning was taken as corroboration. The other faces held a dark, non-committal thoughtfulness. This was not the man they had known, but they had scarcely expected to be confronted with *him*; this was, in a sense deeper than questions of fact, the man they had not known, and the man they had not known may have been the real one. The real man, whoever he had been, had suffered and now he was dead: this was all that was sure and all that mattered now. Every man in the chapel hoped that when his hour came he, too, would be eulogized, which is to say forgiven, and that all of his lapses, greeds, errors, and strayings from the truth would be invested with coherence and looked upon with charity. This was perhaps the last thing human beings could give each other and it was what they demanded, after all, of the Lord. Only the Lord saw the midnight tears, only He was present when one of His children, moaning and wringing hands, paced up and down the room. When one slapped one's child in anger the recoil in the heart reverberated through heaven and became part of the pain of the universe. And when the children were hungry and sullen and distrustful and one watched them, daily, growing wilder, and further away, and running headlong into danger, it was the Lord who knew what the charged heart endured as the strap was laid to the backside; the Lord alone who knew what one *would* have said if one had had, like the Lord, the gift of the living word. It was the Lord who knew of the impossibility every parent in that room faced: how to prepare the child for the day when the child would be despised and how to *create* in the child — by what means? — a stronger antidote to this poison than one had found for oneself. The avenues, side streets, bars, billiard halls, hospitals, police stations, and even the playgrounds of Harlem — not to mention the houses of correction, the jails, and the morgue — testified to the potency of the poison while remaining silent as to the efficacy of whatever antidote, irresistibly raising the question of whether or not such an antidote existed; raising, which was worse, the question of whether or not an antidote was desirable; perhaps poison should be fought with poison. With these several schisms in the mind and with more terrors in the heart than could be named, it was better not to judge the man who had gone down under an impossible burden. It was better to remember. *Thou knowest this man's fall; but thou knowest not his wrassling.*

While the preacher talked and I watched the children — years of changing their diapers, scrubbing them, slapping them, taking them to school, and scolding them had had the perhaps inevitable result of making me love them, though I am not sure I knew this then — my mind was busily breaking out with a rash of disconnected impressions. Snatches of popular songs, indecent jokes, bits of books I had read, movie sequences, faces, voices, political issues — I thought I was going mad; all these impressions suspended, as it were, in the solution of the faint nausea produced in me by the heat and liquor. For a moment I had the impression that my alcoholic breath, inefficiently disguised with chewing gum, filled the entire chapel. Then someone began singing one of my father's favorite songs and, abruptly, I was with him, sitting on his knee, in the hot, enormous, crowded church which was the first church we attended. It was the Abyssinia Baptist Church on 138th Street. We had not gone there long. With this image, a host of others came. I had forgotten, in the rage of my growing up, how proud my father had been of me when I was little. Apparently, I had had a voice and my father had liked to show me off before the members of the church. I had forgotten what he had looked like when he was pleased but now I remembered that he had always been grinning with pleasure when my solos ended. I even remembered certain expressions on his face when he teased my mother — had he loved her? I would never know. And when had it all begun to change? For now it seemed that he had not always been cruel. I remembered being taken for a haircut and scraping my knee on the footrest of the barber's chair and I remembered my father's face as he soothed my crying and applied the stinging iodine. Then I remembered our fights, fights which had been of the worst possible kind because my technique had been silence.

I remembered the one time in all our life together when we had 35
really spoken to each other.

It was on a Sunday and it must have been shortly before I left home. We were walking, just the two of us, in our usual silence, to or from church. I was in high school and had been doing a lot of writing and I was, at about this time, the editor of the high school magazine. But I had also been a Young Minister and had been preaching from the pulpit. Lately, I had been taking fewer engagements and preached as rarely as possible. It was said in the church, quite truthfully, that I was "cooling off."

My father asked me abruptly, "You'd rather write than preach, wouldn't you?"

I was astonished at his question — because it was a real question. I answered, "Yes."

That was all we said. It was awful to remember that that was all we had *ever* said.

The casket now was opened and mourners were being led up 40
the aisle to look for the last time on the deceased. The assumption was that the family was too overcome with grief to be allowed to make this journey alone and I watched while my aunt was led to the casket and, muffled in black, and shaking, led back to her seat. I disapproved of forcing the children to look on their dead father, considering that the shock of his death, or, more truthfully, the shock of death as a reality, was already a little more than a child could bear, but my judgment in this matter had been overruled and there they were, bewildered and frightened and very small, being led, one by one, to the casket. But there is also something very gallant about children at such moments. It has something to do with their silence and gravity and with the fact that one cannot help them. Their legs, somehow, seem *exposed*, so that it is at once incredible and terribly clear that their legs are all they have to hold them up.

I had not wanted to go to the casket myself and I certainly had not wished to be led there, but there was no way of avoiding either of these forms. One of the deacons led me up and I looked on my father's face. I cannot say that it looked like him at all. His blackness had been equivocated by powder and there was no suggestion in that casket of what his power had or could have been. He was simply an old man dead, and it was hard to believe that he had ever given anyone either joy or pain. Yet, his life filled that room. Further up the avenue his wife was holding his newborn child. Life and death so close together, and love and hatred, and right and wrong, said something to me which I did not want to hear concerning man, concerning the life of man.

After the funeral, while I was downtown desperately celebrating my birthday, a Negro soldier, in the lobby of the Hotel Braddock, got into a fight with a white policeman over a Negro girl. Negro girls, white policemen, in or out of uniform, and Negro males — in or out of uniform — were part of the furniture of the lobby of the Hotel Braddock and this was certainly not the first time such an incident had occurred. It was destined, however, to receive an unprecedented publicity, for the fight between the policeman and the soldier ended with the shooting of the soldier. Rumor, flowing immediately to the streets outside, stated that the soldier had been shot in the back, an instantaneous and revealing invention, and that the soldier had died protecting a Negro woman. The facts were somewhat different — for example, the soldier had not been shot in the back, and was not dead, and the girl seems to have been as dubious a symbol of womanhood as her white counterpart in Georgia usually is, but no one was interested in the facts. They preferred the invention because this invention expressed and corroborated their hates and fears so perfectly. It is just as well to remember that people are always doing this. Perhaps many of those legends, including Christianity, to which the world clings began their conquest of the world with just some such concerted surrender to distortion. The effect, in Harlem, of this particular legend was like the effect of a lit match in a tin of gasoline. The mob gathered before the doors of the Hotel Braddock simply began to swell and to spread in every direction, and Harlem exploded.

The mob did not cross the ghetto lines. It would have been easy, for example, to have gone over Morningside Park on the west side or to have crossed the Grand Central railroad tracks at 125th Street on the east side, to wreak havoc in white neighborhoods. The mob seems to have been mainly interested in something more potent and real than the white face, that is, in white power, and the principal damage done during the riot of the summer of 1943 was to white business establishments in Harlem. It might have been a far bloodier story, of course, if, at the hour the riot began, these establishments had still been open. From the Hotel Braddock the mob fanned out, east and west along 125th Street, and for the entire length of Lenox, Seventh, and Eighth avenues. Along each of these avenues, and along each major side street — 116th, 125th, 135th, and so on — bars, stores, pawnshops, restaurants, even little luncheonettes had been smashed open and entered and looted — looted, it might be added, with more haste than efficiency. The shelves really looked as though a bomb had struck them. Cans of beans and soup and dog food, along with toilet paper, corn flakes, sardines and milk tumbled every which way, and abandoned cash registers and cases of beer leaned crazily out of the splintered windows and were strewn along the avenues. Sheets, blankets, and clothing of every description formed a kind of path, as though people had dropped them while running. I truly had not realized that Harlem *had* so many stores until I saw them all smashed open; the first time the word *wealth* ever entered my mind in relation to Harlem was when I saw it scattered in the streets. But one's first, incongruous impression of plenty was countered immediately by an impression of waste. None of this was doing anybody any good. It would have been better to have left the plate glass as it had been and the goods lying in the stores.

It would have been better, but it would also have been intolerable, for Harlem had needed something to smash. To smash something is the ghetto's chronic need. Most of the time it is the members of the ghetto who smash each other, and themselves. But as long as the ghetto walls are standing there will always come a moment when these outlets do not work. That summer, for example, it was not enough to get into a fight on Lenox Avenue, or curse out one's cronies in the barber shops. If ever, indeed, the violence which fills Harlem's churches, pool halls, and bars erupts outward in a more direct fashion, Harlem and its citizens are likely to vanish in an apocalyptic flood. That this is not likely to happen is due to a great many reasons, most hidden and powerful among them the Negro's real relation to the white American. This relation prohibits, simply, anything as uncomplicated and satisfactory as pure hatred. In order really to hate white people, one has to blot so much out of the mind — and the heart — that this hatred itself becomes an exhausting and self-destructive pose. But this does not mean, on the other hand, that love comes easily: the white world is too powerful, too complacent, too ready with gratuitous humiliation, and, above all, too ignorant and too innocent for that. One is absolutely forced to make perpetual qualifications and one's own reactions are always canceling each other out. It is this, really, which has driven so many people mad, both white and black. One is always in the position of having to decide between amputation and gangrene. Amputation is swift but time may prove that the amputation was not necessary — or one may delay the amputation too long. Gangrene is slow, but it is impossible to be sure that one is reading one's symptoms right. The idea of going through life as a cripple is more than one can bear, and equally unbearable is the risk of swelling up slowly, in agony, with poison. And the trouble, finally, is that the risks are real even if the choices do not exist.

"But as for me and my house," my father had said, "we will 45
serve the Lord." I wondered, as we drove him to his resting place, what this line had meant for him. I had heard him preach it many times. I had preached it once myself, proudly giving it an interpretation different from my father's. Now the whole thing came back to me, as though my father and I were on our way to Sunday school and I were memorizing the golden text: *And if it seem evil unto you to serve the Lord, choose you this day whom you will serve; whether the gods which your fathers served that were on the other side of the flood, or the gods of the Amorites, in whose land ye dwell: but as for me and my house, we will serve the Lord.* I suspected in these familiar lines a meaning which had never been there for me before. All of my father's texts and songs, which I had decided were meaningless, were arranged before me at his death like empty bottles, waiting to hold the meaning which life would give them for me. This was his legacy: nothing is ever escaped. That bleakly memorable morning I hated the unbelievable streets and the Negroes and whites who had, equally, made them that way. But I knew that it was folly, as my father would have said, this bitterness was folly. It was necessary to hold on to the things that mattered. The dead man mattered, the new life mattered; blackness and whiteness did not matter; to believe that they did was to acquiesce in one's own destruction. Hatred, which could destroy so much, never failed to destroy the man who hated and this was an immutable law.

It began to seem that one would have to hold in the mind forever two ideas which seemed to be in opposition. The first idea was acceptance, the acceptance, totally without rancor, of life as it is, and men as they are: in the light of this idea, it goes without saying that injustice is a commonplace. But this did not mean that one could be complacent, for the second idea was of equal power: that one must never, in one's own life, accept these injustices as commonplace but must fight them with all one's strength. This fight begins, however, in the heart and it now had been laid to my charge to keep my own heart free of hatred and despair. This intimation made my heart heavy and, now that my father was irrecoverable, I wished that he had been beside me so that I could have searched his face for the answers which only the future would give me now.

For Discussion and Writing

1. Identify all of the different stories Baldwin tells in "Notes of a Native Son."
2. How does Baldwin relate the story of his relationship with his father to the story of the relationship between black and white America?
3. **connections** Compare Baldwin's prose style to that of Martin Luther King Jr., in "Letter from Birmingham Jail" (p. 203). There are certain obvious similarities; what are they, and what are some differences?
4. Write about a moment in your life when you were extremely angry. How did you handle it, and what does the experience tell you about yourself now?

DAVE BARRY

Turkeys in the Kitchen

A nationally syndicated columnist based at the Miami Herald, *Dave Barry was born in Armonk, New York, in 1947. He came to his present career as a humorist after working as a reporter and business writing consultant. He has won the Pulitzer Prize for commentary and published a number of humor collections.*

As do many of his pieces, "Turkeys in the Kitchen" depends for its humor and its insights on observation of everyday life and the stereotypical behavior observed therein. Much of the humor in this piece comes at the expense of Barry and his fellow men, who behave abominably but, at least in Barry's case, realize it. "I realize this is awful," Barry candidly admits of his behavior and turns self-knowledge into self-mocking humor.

Men are still basically scum when it comes to helping out in the kitchen. This is one of two insights I had last Thanksgiving, the other one being that Thanksgiving night must be the slowest night of the year in terms of human sexual activity. Nobody wants to engage in human sexual activity with somebody who smells vaguely like yams and is covered with a thin layer of turkey grease, which describes pretty much everybody in the United States on Thanksgiving except the Detroit Lions, who traditionally play football that day and would therefore be too tired.

But that, as far as I can tell, is not my point. My point is that despite all that has been said in the past 20 years or so about sexual equality, most men make themselves as useful around the kitchen as ill-trained Labrador retrievers. This is not just my opinion: It is a scientific finding based on an exhaustive study of what happened last Thanksgiving when my family had dinner at the home of friends named Arlene and Gene. Picture a typical Thanksgiving scene: On the floor, three small children and a dog who long ago had her brain eaten by fleas are running as fast as they can directly into things, trying to injure themselves. On the television, the Detroit Lions are doing pretty much the same thing. In the kitchen, Arlene, a prosecuting attorney responsible for a large staff, is doing something with those repulsive organs that are placed in little surprise packets inside turkeys, apparently as a joke. Surrounding Arlene are thousands of steaming cooking containers. I would no more enter that kitchen than I would attempt to park a nuclear aircraft carrier, but my wife, who runs her own business, glides in very casually and picks up *exactly* the right kitchen implement and starts doing *exactly* the right thing without receiving any instructions whatsoever. She quickly becomes enshrouded in steam.

So Gene and I, feeling like the scum we are, finally bumble over and ask what we can do to help, and from behind the steam comes Arlene's patient voice asking us to please keep an eye on the children. Which we try to do. But there is a famous law of physics that goes: "You cannot watch small children and the Detroit Lions at the same time, and let's face it, the Detroit Lions are more interesting." So we would start out watching the children, and then one of us would sneak a peek at the TV and say, "Hey! Look at this tackle!" And then we'd have to watch for a while to see the replay and find out whether the tackled person was dead or just permanently disabled. By then the children would have succeeded in injuring themselves or the dog, and this voice from behind the kitchen steam would call, *very* patiently, "Gene, *please* watch the children."

I realize this is awful. I realize this sounds just like Ozzie and Harriet. I also realize that there are some males out there, with hyphenated last names, who have advanced much farther than Gene and I have, who are not afraid to stay home full time and get coated with baby vomit while their wives work as test pilots, and who go into the kitchen on a daily basis to prepare food for other people, as opposed to going in there to get a beer and maybe some peanut butter on a spoon. But I think Gene and I are fairly typical. I think most males rarely prepare food for others, and when they do, they have their one specialty dish (spaghetti, in my case) that they prepare maybe twice a year in a very elaborate production, for which they expect to be praised as if they had developed, right there in the kitchen, a cure for heart disease.

In defense of men, let me say this: Women do not make it easy 5
to learn. Let's say a woman is in the kitchen, working away after

having been at her job all day, and the man, feeling guilty, finally shuffles in and offers to help. So the woman says something like: "Well, you can cut up the turnips." Now to the *woman*, who had all this sexist Home Economics training back in the pre-feminism era, this is a very simple instruction. It is the absolute simplest thing she can think of. But to the man, who got his training in Shop Class, learning things he would never ever need to know for the rest of his life, such as how to make "dado" joints, this instruction raises many troubling questions:

1. Which ones are the turnips?
2. Do you have to wash them first?
3. Do you have to peel them? (Then why did you just wash them!?) What do you peel them with?
4. Do you cut them into strips? Cubes? Little round pieces? Do you use the same thing you peeled them with?

This is just a partial list of the questions that I, for one, would have if somebody asked me to "cut up the turnips." So what the man does is he sort of fumbles around for a while and finally he picks up something (which is later identified as a zucchini) and approaches the sink with it, and the woman snatches it from his hands and says, very patiently (much too patiently), "That's all right. I'll do it." And off he slinks.

One more example: If I ever, for any reason, attempt to heat water in a pot, my wife will saunter by, and, very quietly, without making a fuss, she'll change the water to some other size pot. It makes no difference what size pot I start with: she will change it, based on her thousands of hours of kitchen experiences and sexist training, and I will continue to feel like the Kitchen Bozo.

I asked my wife to read this and tell me what she thought. This is what she said: She said before Women's Liberation, men took care of the cars and women took care of the kitchen, whereas now that we have Women's Liberation, men no longer feel obligated to take care of the cars. This seemed pretty accurate to me, so I thought I'd just tack it on to the end here, while she makes waffles.

For Discussion and Writing

1. Identify the stereotypes about the genders to which Barry refers.
2. Barry's tone here is comic. How does his use of humor relate to his comparison of men and women? Does he refute stereotypes about the differences between men and women or confirm them?

3. **connections** Compare Barry's use of humor to that of David Sedaris in "A Plague of Tics" (p. 359). How is their humor similar and different, and how does each use humor to make his point?
4. Think of different kinds of behavior you've noticed people engaging in at holiday gatherings. Can you, as Barry does, make general points about people from your specific observations of these behaviors?

WILLIAM F. BUCKLEY JR.

Why Don't We Complain?

William F. Buckley Jr. (1925–2008), born in New York City, was one of the leading voices of conservative politics. Best known as founder and longtime editor of the opinion journal National Review *and host of the PBS political talk show* Firing Line, *Buckley also wrote a syndicated column, contributed to many magazines, and authored over forty fiction and nonfiction books.*

"Why Don't We Complain?" originally appeared in Esquire *in 1960. Buckley's connection of political apathy to failures to act in other parts of life is still timely today. As you read, though, think about all that has happened in America since the writing of this article.*

It was the very last coach and the only empty seat on the entire train, so there was no turning back. The problem was to breathe. Outside the temperature was below freezing. Inside the railroad car, the temperature must have been about 85 degrees. I took off my overcoat, and a few minutes later my jacket, and noticed that the car was flecked with the white shirts of passengers. I soon found my hand moving to loosen my tie. From one end of the car to the other, as we rattled through Westchester County, we sweated; but we did not moan.

I watched the train conductor appear at the head of the car. "Tickets, all tickets, please!" In a more virile age, I thought, the passengers would seize the conductor and strap him down on a seat over the radiator to share the fate of his patrons. He shuffled down the aisle, picking up tickets, punching commutation cards. *No one addressed a word to him.* He approached my seat, and I drew a deep breath of resolution. "Conductor," I began with a considerable edge to my voice. . . . Instantly the doleful eyes of my seatmate turned tiredly from his newspaper to fix me with a resentful stare: what question could be so important as to justify my sibilant intrusion into his stupor? I was shaken by those eyes.

I am incapable of making a discreet fuss, so I mumbled a question about what time were we due in Stamford (I didn't even ask whether it would be before or after dehydration could be expected to set in), got my reply, and went back to my newspaper and to wiping my brow.

The conductor had nonchalantly walked down the gauntlet of eighty sweating American freemen, and not one of them had asked him to explain why the passengers in that car had been consigned to suffer. There is nothing to be done when the temperature *outdoors* is 85 degrees, and indoors the air conditioner has broken down; obviously when that happens there is nothing to do, except perhaps curse the day that one was born. But when the temperature outdoors is below freezing, it takes a positive act of will on somebody's part to set the temperature *indoors* at 85. Somewhere a valve was turned too far, a furnace overstoked, a thermostat maladjusted: something that could easily be remedied by turning off the heat and allowing the great outdoors to come indoors. All this is so obvious. What is not obvious is what has happened to the American people.

It isn't just the commuters, whom we have come to visualize as a supine breed who have got onto the trick of suspending their sensory faculties twice a day while they submit to the creeping dissolution of the railroad industry. It isn't just they who have given up trying to rectify irrational vexations. It is the American people everywhere.

5 A few weeks ago at a large movie theatre I turned to my wife and said, "The picture is out of focus." "Be quiet," she answered. I obeyed. But a few minutes later I raised the point again, with mounting impatience. "It will be all right in a minute," she said apprehensively. (She would rather lose her eyesight than be around when I make one of my infrequent scenes.) I waited. It was *just* out of focus — not glaringly out, but out. My vision is 20–20, and I assume that is the vision, adjusted, of most people in the movie house. So, after hectoring my wife throughout the first reel, I finally prevailed upon her to admit that it *was* off, and very annoying. We then settled down, coming to rest on the presumption that: a) someone connected with the management of the theatre must soon notice the blur and make the correction; or b) that someone seated near the rear of the house would make the complaint in behalf of those of us up front; or c) that — any minute

now — the entire house would explode into catcalls and foot stamping, calling dramatic attention to the irksome distortion.

What happened was nothing. The movie ended, as it had begun, just out of focus, and as we trooped out, we stretched our faces in a variety of contortions to accustom the eye to the shock of normal focus.

I think it is safe to say that everybody suffered on that occasion. And I think it is safe to assume that everyone was expecting someone else to take the initiative in going back to speak to the manager. And it is probably true even that if we had supposed the movie would run right through with the blurred image, someone surely would have summoned up the purposive indignation to get up out of his seat and file his complaint.

But notice that no one did. And the reason no one did is because we are all increasingly anxious in America to be unobtrusive, we are reluctant to make our voices heard, hesitant about claiming our rights; we are afraid that our cause is unjust, or that if it is not unjust, that it is ambiguous; or if not even that, that it is too trivial to justify the horrors of a confrontation with Authority; we will sit in an oven or endure a racking headache before undertaking a head-on, I'm-here-to-tell-you complaint. That tendency to passive compliance, to a heedless endurance is something to keep one's eyes on — in sharp focus.

I myself can occasionally summon the courage to complain, but I cannot, as I have intimated, complain softly. My own instinct is so strong to let the thing ride, to forget about it — to expect that someone will take the matter up, when the grievance is collective, in my behalf — that it is only when the provocation is at a very special key, whose vibrations touch simultaneously a complexus of nerves, allergies, and passions, that I catch fire and find the reserves of courage and assertiveness to speak up. When that happens, I get quite carried away. My blood gets hot, my brow wet, I become unbearably and unconscionably sarcastic and bellicose: I am girded for a total showdown.

Why should that be? Why could not I (or anyone else) on 10
that railroad coach have said simply to the conductor, "Sir," — I take that back: that sounds sarcastic — "Conductor, would you be good enough to turn down the heat? I am extremely hot. In fact, I tend to get hot every time the temperature reaches 85 degr —" Strike that last sentence. Just end it with the simple

statement that you are extremely hot, and let the conductor infer the cause.

Every New Year's Eve I resolve to do something about the Milquetoast in me and vow to speak up, calmly, for my rights, and for the betterment of our society, on every appropriate occasion. Entering last New Year's Eve I was fortified in my resolve because that morning at breakfast I had had to ask the waitress three times for a glass of milk. She finally brought it — after I had finished my eggs, which is when I don't want it any more. I did not have the manliness to order her to take the milk back, but settled instead for a cowardly sulk, and ostentatiously refused to drink the milk — though I later paid for it — rather than state plainly to the hostess, as I should have, why I had not drunk it, and would not pay for it.

So by the time the New Year ushered out the Old, riding in on my morning's indignation and stimulated by the gastric juices of resolution that flow so faithfully on New Year's Eve, I rendered my vow. Henceforward I would conquer my shyness, my despicable disposition to supineness. I would speak out like a man against the unnecessary annoyances of our time.

Forty-eight hours later, I was standing in line at the ski-repair store in Pico Peak, Vermont. All I needed, to get on with my skiing, was the loan, for one minute, of a small screwdriver, to tighten a loose binding. Behind the counter in the workshop were two men. One was industriously engaged in servicing the complicated requirements of a young lady at the head of the line, and obviously he would be tied up for quite a while. The other — "Jiggs," his workmate called him — was a middle-aged man, who sat in a chair puffing a pipe, exchanging small talk with his working partner. My pulse began its telltale acceleration. The minutes ticked on. I stared at the idle shopkeeper, hoping to shame him into action, but he was impervious to my telepathic reproof and continued his small talk with his friend, brazenly insensitive to the nervous demands of six good men who were raring to ski.

Suddenly my New Year's Eve resolution struck me. It was now or never. I broke from my place in line and marched to the counter. I was going to control myself. I dug my nails into my palms. My effort was only partially successful:

"If you are not too busy," I said icily, "would you mind handing 15
me a screwdriver?"

Work stopped and everyone turned his eyes on me, and I experienced that mortification I always feel when I am the center of centripetal shafts of curiosity, resentment, perplexity.

But the worst was yet to come. "I am sorry, sir," said Jiggs deferentially, moving the pipe from his mouth. "I am not supposed to move. I have just had a heart attack." That was the signal for a great whirring noise that descended from heaven. We looked, stricken, out the window, and it appeared as though a cyclone had suddenly focused on the snowy courtyard between the shop and the ski lift. Suddenly a gigantic Army helicopter materialized, and hovered down to a landing. Two men jumped out of the plane carrying a stretcher, tore into the ski shop, and lifted the shopkeeper onto the stretcher. Jiggs bade his companion good-by, was whisked out the door, into the plane, up to the heavens, down — we learned — to a nearby Army hospital. I looked up manfully — into a score of man-eating eyes. I put the experience down as a reversal.

As I write this, on an airplane, I have run out of paper and need to reach into my briefcase under my legs for more. I cannot do this until my empty lunch tray is removed from my lap. I arrested the stewardess as she passed empty-handed down the aisle on the way to the kitchen to fetch the lunch trays for the passengers up forward who haven't been served yet. "Would you please take my tray?" "Just a *moment*, sir," she said, and marched on sternly. Shall I tell her that since she is headed for the kitchen *anyway*, it cannot delay the feeding of the other passengers by the two seconds necessary to stash away my empty tray? Or remind her that not fifteen minutes ago she spoke unctuously into the loudspeaker the words undoubtedly devised by the airline's highly paid public-relations counselor: "If there is anything I or Miss French can do for you to make your trip more enjoyable, *please* let us —" I have run out of paper.

I think the observable reluctance of the majority of Americans to assert themselves in minor matters is related to our increased sense of helplessness in an age of technology and centralized political and economic power. For generations, Americans who were too hot, or too cold, got up and did something about it. Now we call the plumber, or the electrician, or the furnace man. The habit of looking after our own needs obviously had something to do with the assertiveness that characterized the American family familiar to readers of American literature. With the technification of life goes our direct responsibility for our material environment, and we are conditioned to adopt a position of helplessness not only as regards the broken air conditioner, but as regards the overheated train. It takes an expert to fix the former, but not the latter: yet these distinctions, as we withdrew into helplessness, tend to fade away.

20 Our notorious political apathy is a related phenomenon. Every year, whether the Republican or the Democratic Party is in office, more and more power drains away from the individual to feed vast reservoirs in far-off places; and we have less and less say about the shape of events which shape our future. From this aberration of personal power comes the sense of resignation with which we accept the political dispensations of a powerful government whose hold upon us continues to increase.

An editor of a national weekly news magazine told me a few years ago that as few as a dozen letters of protest against an editorial stance of his magazine was enough to convene a plenipotentiary meeting of the board of editors to review policy. "So few people complain, or make their voices heard," he explained to me, "that we assume a dozen letters represent the inarticulated views of thousands of readers." In the past ten years, he said, the volume of mail has noticeably decreased, even though the circulation of his magazine has risen.

When our voices are finally mute, when we have finally suppressed the natural instinct to complain, whether the vexation is trivial or grave, we shall have become automatons, incapable of feeling. When Premier Khrushchev first came to this country late in 1959 he was primed, we are informed, to experience the bitter resentment of the American people against his tyranny, against his persecutions, against the movement which is responsible for the then great number of American deaths in Korea, for billions in taxes every year, and for life everlasting on the brink of disasters; but Khrushchev was pleasantly surprised, and reported back to the Russian people that he had been met with overwhelming cordiality (read: apathy), except, to be sure, for "a few fascists who followed me around with their wretched posters, and should be . . . horsewhipped."

I may be crazy, but I say there would have been lots more posters in a society where train temperatures in the dead of winter are not allowed to climb up to 85 degrees without complaint.

For Discussion and Writing

1. What are Buckley's three examples of situations in which one might complain?
2. What does Buckley argue is the relationship between our failure to complain and our failure to care about politics? How does he attempt to convince us of that relationship?
3. **connections** Compare Buckley's argument about our behavior as citizens with Barbara Lazear Ascher's in "On Compassion" (p. 46). Do they focus on the same kinds of behaviors? How do their differences in subject relate to the differences in their essays?
4. Write an essay in which you reflect on your own political feelings and orientation. What do you care about, and why? How do you demonstrate your beliefs?

RACHEL CARSON

The Obligation to Endure

Rachel Carson (1907–1964) studied biology at the Marine Biological Laboratory at Woods Hole, Massachusetts, and the U.S. Fish and Wildlife Service and received her MA in zoology from Johns Hopkins University, before becoming a full-time nature writer in the 1950s. Her early books were Under the Sea-Wind *(1941),* The Sea Around Us *(1951), and* The Edge of the Sea *(1955). In the late 1950s she turned her attention to environmental issues, and the result was* Silent Spring *(1962), a book that brought environmental issues to the American public in a way they had never before been raised and led to the banning of the dangerous pesticide DDT. Carson is considered by many to be the mother of the modern American environmental movement.*

Our reading, which comes from that incredibly influential book, shows Carson's gift for turning technical knowledge into something not just understandable by the layperson but intellectually compelling and emotionally affecting — and so, capable of motivating change. As you read, watch for evidence of this gift: when Carson writes, "The history of life on earth has been a history of interaction between living things and their surroundings," she is not simply making a generalization, but rather is laying simple but solid groundwork on which to build her readers' understanding of complex scientific issues.

THE OBLIGATION TO ENDURE

The history of life on earth has been a history of interaction between living things and their surroundings. To a large extent, the physical form and the habits of the earth's vegetation and its animal life have been molded by the environment. Considering the whole span of earthly time, the opposite effect, in which life actually modifies its surroundings, has been relatively slight. Only within the moment of time represented by the present century has one species — man — acquired significant power to alter the nature of his world.

During the past quarter century this power has not only increased to one of disturbing magnitude but it has changed in character. The most alarming of all man's assaults upon the environment is the contamination of air, earth, rivers, and sea with dangerous and even lethal materials. This pollution is for the most part irrecoverable; the chain of evil it initiates not only in the world that must support life but in living tissues is for the most part irreversible. In this now universal contamination of the environment, chemicals are the sinister and little-recognized partners of radiation in changing the very nature of the world — the very nature of its life. Strontium 90, released through nuclear explosions into the air, comes to earth in rain or drifts down as fallout, lodges in soil, enters into the grass or corn or wheat grown there, and in time takes up its abode in the bones of a human being, there to remain until his death. Similarly, chemicals sprayed on croplands or forests or gardens lie long in soil, entering into living organisms, passing from one to another in a chain of poisoning and death. Or they pass mysteriously by underground streams until they emerge and, through the alchemy of air and sunlight, combine into new forms that kill vegetation, sicken cattle, and work unknown harm on those who drink from once pure wells. As Albert Schweitzer has said, "Man can hardly even recognize the devils of his own creation."

It took hundreds of millions of years to produce the life that now inhabits the earth — eons of time in which that developing and evolving and diversifying life reached a state of adjustment and balance with its surroundings. The environment, rigorously shaping and directing the life it supported, contained elements that were hostile as well as supporting. Certain rocks gave out dangerous radiation; even within the light of the sun, from which all life draws its energy, there were short-wave radiations with power to injure. Given time — time not in years but in millennia — life adjusts, and a balance has been reached. For time is the essential ingredient; but in the modern world there is no time.

The rapidity of change and the speed with which new situations are created follow the impetuous and heedless pace of man rather than the deliberate pace of nature. Radiation is no longer merely the background radiation of rocks, the bombardment of cosmic rays, the ultraviolet of the sun that have existed before there was any life on earth; radiation is now the unnatural creation of man's tampering with the atom. The chemicals to which life is asked to make its adjustment are no longer merely the calcium and silica and copper and all the rest of the minerals washed out of the rocks and carried in rivers to the sea; they are the synthetic creations of man's inventive mind, brewed in his laboratories, and having no counterparts in nature.

5 To adjust to these chemicals would require time on the scale that is nature's; it would require not merely the years of a man's life but the life of generations. And even this, were it by some miracle possible, would be futile, for the new chemicals come from our laboratories in an endless stream; almost five hundred annually find their way into actual use in the United States alone. The figure is staggering and its implications are not easily grasped — 500 new chemicals to which the bodies of men and animals are required somehow to adapt each year, chemicals totally outside the limits of biologic experience.

Among them are many that are used in man's war against nature. Since the mid-1940s over 200 basic chemicals have been created for use in killing insects, weeds, rodents, and other organisms described in the modern vernacular as "pests"; and they are sold under several thousand different brand names.

These sprays, dusts, and aerosols are now applied almost universally to farms, gardens, forests, and homes — nonselective chemicals that have the power to kill every insect, the "good" and the "bad," to still the song of birds and the leaping of fish in the streams, to coat the leaves with a deadly film, and to linger on in soil — all this though the intended target may be only a few weeds or insects. Can anyone believe it is possible to lay down such a barrage of poisons on the surface of the earth without making it unfit for all life? They should not be called "insecticides," but "biocides."

The whole process of spraying seems caught up in an endless spiral. Since DDT was released for civilian use, a process of escalation has been going on in which ever more toxic materials must be found. This has happened because insects, in a triumphant vindication of Darwin's principle of the survival of the fittest, have evolved super races immune to the particular insecticide used, hence a deadlier one has always to be developed — and then a deadlier one than that. It has happened also because, for reasons to be described later, destructive insects often undergo a "flareback," or resurgence, after spraying, in numbers greater than before. Thus the chemical war is never won, and all life is caught in its violent crossfire.

Along with the possibility of the extinction of mankind by nuclear war, the central problem of our age has therefore become the contamination of man's total environment with such substances of incredible potential for harm — substances that accumulate in the tissues of plants and animals and even penetrate the germ cells to shatter or alter the very material of heredity upon which the shape of the future depends.

10 Some would-be architects of our future look toward a time when it will be possible to alter the human germ plasm by design. But we may easily be doing so now by inadvertence, for many chemicals, like radiation, bring about gene mutations. It is ironic to think that man might determine his own future by something so seemingly trivial as the choice of an insect spray.

All this has been risked — for what? Future historians may well be amazed by our distorted sense of proportion. How could intelligent beings seek to control a few unwanted species by a method that contaminated the entire environment and brought the threat of disease and death even to their own kind? Yet this is precisely what we have done. We have done it, moreover, for reasons that collapse the moment we examine them. We are told that the enormous and expanding use of pesticides is necessary to maintain farm production. Yet is our real problem not one of *overproduction*? Our farms, despite measures to remove acreages from production and to pay farmers *not* to produce, have yielded such a staggering excess of crops that the American taxpayer in 1962 is paying out more than one billion dollars a year as the total carrying cost of the surplus-food storage program. And is the situation helped when one branch of the Agriculture Department tries to reduce production while another states, as it did in 1958, "It is believed generally that reduction of crop acreages under provisions of the Soil Bank will stimulate interest in use of chemicals to obtain maximum production on the land retained in crops."

All this is not to say there is no insect problem and no need of control. I am saying, rather, that control must be geared to realities, not to mythical situations, and that the methods employed must be such that they do not destroy us along with the insects.

* * *

The problem whose attempted solution has brought such a train of disaster in its wake is an accompaniment of our modern way of life. Long before the age of man, insects inhabited the earth — a group of extraordinarily varied and adaptable beings. Over the course of time since man's advent, a small percentage of the more than half a million species of insects have come into conflict with human welfare in two principal ways: as competitors for the food supply and as carriers of human disease.

Disease-carrying insects become important where human beings are crowded together, especially under conditions where sanitation is poor, as in time of natural disaster or war or in situations of extreme poverty and deprivation. Then control of some sort becomes necessary. It is a sobering fact, however, as we shall presently see, that the method of massive chemical control has had only limited success, and also threatens to worsen the very conditions it is intended to curb.

Under primitive agricultural conditions the farmer had few insect problems. These arose with the intensification of agriculture — the devotion of immense acreages to a single crop. Such a system set the stage for explosive increases in specific insect populations. Single-crop farming does not take advantage of the principles by which nature works; it is agriculture as an engineer might conceive it to be. Nature has introduced great variety into the landscape, but man has displayed a passion for simplifying it. Thus he undoes the built-in checks and balances by which nature holds the species within bounds. One important natural check is a limit on the amount of suitable habitat for each species. Obviously then, an insect that lives on wheat can build up its population to much higher levels on a farm devoted to wheat than on one in which wheat is intermingled with other crops to which the insect is not adapted.

The same thing happens in other situations. A generation or more ago, the towns of large areas of the United States lined their streets with the noble elm tree. Now the beauty they hopefully created is threatened with complete destruction as disease sweeps through the elms, carried by a beetle that would have only limited chance to build up large populations and to spread from tree to tree if the elms were only occasional trees in a richly diversified planting.

Another factor in the modern insect problem is one that must be viewed against a background of geologic and human history: the spreading of thousands of different kinds of organisms from their native homes to invade new territories. This worldwide migration has been studied and graphically described by the British ecologist Charles Elton in his recent book *The Ecology of Invasions*. During the Cretaceous Period, some hundred million years ago, flooding seas cut many land bridges between continents and living things found themselves confined in what Elton calls "colossal separate nature reserves." There, isolated from others of their kind, they developed many new species. When some of the land masses were joined again, about 15 million years ago, these species began to move out into new territories — a movement that is not only still in progress but is now receiving considerable assistance from man.

The importation of plants is the primary agent in the modern spread of species, for animals have almost invariably gone along with the plants, quarantine being a comparatively recent and not completely effective innovation. The United States Office of Plant Introduction alone has introduced almost 200,000 species and varieties of plants from all over the world. Nearly half of the 180 or so major insect enemies of plants in the United States are accidental imports from abroad, and most of them have come as hitchhikers on plants.

In new territory, out of reach of the restraining hand of the natural enemies that kept down its numbers in its native land, an invading plant or animal is able to become enormously abundant. Thus it is no accident that our most troublesome insects are introduced species.

These invasions, both the naturally occurring and those depen- 20
dent on human assistance, are likely to continue indefinitely. Quarantine and massive chemical campaigns are only extremely expensive ways of buying time. We are faced, according to Dr. Elton, "with a life-and-death need not just to find new technological means of suppressing this plant or that animal"; instead we need the basic knowledge of animal populations and their relations to their surroundings that will "promote an even balance and damp down the explosive power of outbreaks and new invasions."

Much of the necessary knowledge is now available but we do not use it. We train ecologists in our universities and even employ them in our governmental agencies but we seldom take their advice. We allow the chemical death rain to fall as though there were no alternative, whereas in fact there are many, and our ingenuity could soon discover many more if given opportunity.

Have we fallen into a mesmerized state that makes us accept as inevitable that which is inferior or detrimental, as though having lost the will or the vision to demand that which is good? Such thinking, in the words of the ecologist Paul Shepard, "idealizes life with only its head out of water, inches above the limits of toleration of the corruption of its own environment. . . . Why should we tolerate a diet of weak poisons, a home in insipid surroundings, a circle of acquaintances who are not quite our enemies, the noise of motors with just enough relief to prevent insanity? Who would want to live in a world which is just not quite fatal?"

Yet such a world is pressed upon us. The crusade to create a chemically sterile, insect-free world seems to have engendered a fanatic zeal on the part of many specialists and most of the so-called control agencies. On every hand there is evidence that those engaged in spraying operations exercise a ruthless power. "The regulatory entomologists . . . function as prosecutor, judge and jury, tax assessor and collector and sheriff to enforce their own orders," said Connecticut entomologist Neely Turner. The most flagrant abuses go unchecked in both state and federal agencies.

It is not my contention that chemical insecticides must never be used. I do contend that we have put poisonous and biologically potent chemicals indiscriminately into the hands of persons largely or wholly ignorant of their potentials for harm. We have subjected enormous numbers of people to contact with these poisons, without their consent and often without their knowledge. If the Bill of Rights contains no guarantee that a citizen shall be secure against lethal poisons distributed either by private individuals or by public officials, it is surely only because our forefathers, despite their considerable wisdom and foresight, could conceive of no such problem.

I contend, furthermore, that we have allowed these chemicals 25
to be used with little or no advance investigation of their effect on soil, water, wildlife, and man himself. Future generations are

unlikely to condone our lack of prudent concern for the integrity of the natural world that supports all life.

There is still very limited awareness of the nature of the threat. This is an era of specialists, each of whom sees his own problem and is unaware of or intolerant of the larger frame into which it fits. It is also an era dominated by industry, in which the right to make a dollar at whatever cost is seldom challenged. When the public protests, confronted with some obvious evidence of damaging results of pesticide applications, it is fed little tranquilizing pills of half truth. We urgently need an end to these false assurances, to the sugar coating of unpalatable facts. It is the public that is being asked to assume the risks that the insect controllers calculate. The public must decide whether it wishes to continue on the present road, and it can do so only when in full possession of the facts. In the words of Jean Rostand, "The obligation to endure gives us the right to know."

For Discussion and Writing

1. When Carson cites Albert Schweitzer's "Man can hardly even recognize the devils of his own creation" (par. 2), what devils is she thinking of? What point is she trying to make?
2. Carson writes, "Much of the necessary knowledge is now available but we do not use it" (par. 21). How does Carson use scientific and historical facts in her argument? How does she make the available knowledge more usable?
3. **connections** Compare this essay to Verlyn Klinkenborg's "Our Vanishing Night" (p. 234). How does each write about the unintended consequences of the developments that comprise what Carson calls "our modern way of life" (par. 13)?
4. Organic farming has become more popular since Carson wrote *Silent Spring*; many supermarkets now have sections of organic produce and other products. Unfortunately, these products are often more expensive than their chemically farmed counterparts, leaving people with a decision to make about whether to spend extra money for food that many people think is better for them and better for the environment. Do you think the extra expense is worth it? Why or why not?

JUDITH ORTIZ COFER

The Myth of the Latin Woman: I Just Met a Girl Named María

Judith Ortiz Cofer was born in Puerto Rico in 1952 and grew up there and in New Jersey. She is a poet, fiction writer, and autobiographer, and teaches literature and writing at the University of Georgia. In 2010, Cofer was inducted into the Georgia Writers Hall of Fame. Much of her work, such as her novel The Line of the Sun *(1989) and* The Latin Deli: Prose and Poetry *(1993), explores her experiences as a Puerto Rican émigré and a Latina. Her most recent book is* A Love Story Beginning in Spanish: Poems *(2005).*

"The Myth of the Latin Woman: I Just Met a Girl Named María" considers the stereotypes Americans hold about Latinas, and it does so through narrative and reflection. At the end of one of the stories she tells in her essay, dealing with an offensive man, Cofer writes, "My friend complimented me on my cool handling of the situation" (par. 10), then notes that what she really wanted to do was push the man into the pool. Notice, as you read, the ways in which Cofer is able in this essay, as in that incident, to strike a balance between anger and analysis.

On a bus trip to London from Oxford University where I was earning some graduate credits one summer, a young man, obviously fresh from a pub, spotted me and as if struck by inspiration went down on his knees in the aisle. With both hands over his heart he broke into an Irish tenor's rendition of "María" from *West Side Story*. My politely amused fellow passengers gave his lovely voice the round of gentle applause it deserved. Though I was not quite as amused, I managed my version of an English smile: no show of teeth, no extreme contortions of the facial muscles — I was at this time of my life practicing reserve and cool. Oh, that British control, how I coveted it. But María had followed me to London, reminding me of a prime fact of my life: you can leave the Island, master the English language, and travel as far as you can, but if you are a Latina, especially one like me who so obviously belongs to Rita Moreno's gene pool, the Island travels with you.

This is sometimes a very good thing — it may win you that extra minute of someone's attention. But with some people, the same things can make *you* an island — not so much a tropical paradise as an Alcatraz, a place nobody wants to visit. As a Puerto Rican girl growing up in the United States and wanting like most children to "belong," I resented the stereotype that my Hispanic appearance called forth from many people I met.

Our family lived in a large urban center in New Jersey during the sixties, where life was designed as a microcosm of my parents' casas on the island. We spoke in Spanish, we ate Puerto Rican food bought at the bodega, and we practiced strict Catholicism complete with Saturday confession and Sunday mass at a church where our parents were accommodated into a one-hour Spanish mass slot, performed by a Chinese priest trained as a missionary for Latin America.

As a girl I was kept under strict surveillance, since virtue and modesty were, by cultural equation, the same as family honor. As a teenager I was instructed on how to behave as a proper señorita. But it was a conflicting message girls got, since the Puerto Rican mothers also encouraged their daughters to look and act like women and to dress in clothes our Anglo friends and their mothers found too "mature" for our age. It was, and is, cultural, yet I often felt humiliated when I appeared at an American friend's party wearing a dress more suitable to a semiformal than to a playroom birthday celebration. At Puerto Rican festivities, neither the music nor the colors we wore could be too loud. I still experience a vague sense of letdown when I'm invited to a "party" and it turns out to be a marathon conversation in hushed tones rather than a fiesta with salsa, laughter, and dancing — the kind of celebration I remember from my childhood.

I remember Career Day in our high school, when teachers told 5
us to come dressed as if for a job interview. It quickly became obvious that to the barrio girls, "dressing up" sometimes meant wearing ornate jewelry and clothing that would be more appropriate (by mainstream standards) for the company Christmas party than as daily office attire. That morning I had agonized in front of my closet, trying to figure out what a "career girl" would

wear because, essentially, except for Marlo Thomas on TV, I had no models on which to base my decision. I knew how to dress for school: at the Catholic school I attended we all wore uniforms; I knew how to dress for Sunday mass, and I knew what dresses to wear for parties at my relatives' homes. Though I do not recall the precise details of my Career Day outfit, it must have been a composite of the above choices. But I remember a comment my friend (an Italian-American) made in later years that coalesced my impressions of that day. She said that at the business school she was attending the Puerto Rican girls always stood out for wearing "everything at once." She meant, of course, too much jewelry, too many accessories. On that day at school, we were simply made the negative models by the nuns who were themselves not credible fashion experts to any of us. But it was painfully obvious to me that to the others, in their tailored skirts and silk blouses, we must have seemed "hopeless" and "vulgar." Though I now know that most adolescents feel out of step much of the time, I also know that for the Puerto Rican girls of my generation that sense was intensified. The way our teachers and classmates looked at us that day in school was just a taste of the culture clash that awaited us in the real world, where prospective employers and men on the street would often misinterpret our tight skirts and jingling bracelets as a come-on.

Mixed cultural signals have perpetuated certain stereotypes — for example, that of the Hispanic woman as the "Hot Tamale" or sexual firebrand. It is a one-dimensional view that the media have found easy to promote. In their special vocabulary, advertisers have designated "sizzling" and "smoldering" as the adjectives of choice for describing not only the foods but also the women of Latin America. From conversations in my house I recall hearing about the harassment that Puerto Rican women endured in factories where the "boss men" talked to them as if sexual innuendo was all they understood and, worse, often gave them the choice of submitting to advances or being fired.

It is custom, however, not chromosomes, that leads us to choose scarlet over pale pink. As young girls, we were influenced in our decisions about clothes and colors by the women — older sisters and mothers who had grown up on a tropical island where the natural environment was a riot of primary colors, where showing your skin was one way to keep cool as well as to look sexy. Most important of all, on the island, women perhaps felt freer to dress and move more provocatively, since, in most cases, they were protected by the traditions, mores, and laws of a Spanish/Catholic system of morality and machismo whose main rule was: *You may look at my sister, but if you touch her I will kill you.* The extended family and church structure could provide a young woman with a circle of safety in her small pueblo on the island; if a man "wronged" a girl, everyone would close in to save her family honor.

This is what I have gleaned from my discussions as an adult with older Puerto Rican women. They have told me about dressing in their best party clothes on Saturday nights and going to the town's plaza to promenade with their girlfriends in front of the boys they liked. The males were thus given an opportunity to admire the women and to express their admiration in the form of *piropos:* erotically charged street poems they composed on the spot. I have been subjected to a few piropos while visiting the Island, and they can be outrageous, although custom dictates that they must never cross into obscenity. This ritual, as I understand it, also entails a show of studied indifference on the woman's part; if she is "decent," she must not acknowledge the man's impassioned words. So I do understand how things can be lost in translation. When a Puerto Rican girl dressed in her idea of what is attractive meets a man from the mainstream culture who has been trained to react to certain types of clothing as a sexual signal, a clash is likely to take place. The line I first heard based on this aspect of the myth happened when the boy who took me to my first formal dance leaned over to plant a sloppy overeager kiss painfully on my mouth, and when I didn't respond with sufficient passion said in a resentful tone: "I thought you Latin girls were supposed to mature early" — my first instance of being thought of as a fruit or vegetable — I was supposed to *ripen*, not just grow into womanhood like other girls.

It is surprising to some of my professional friends that some people, including those who should know better, still put others "in their place." Though rarer, these incidents are still commonplace in my life. It happened to me most recently during a stay at a very classy metropolitan hotel favored by young professional couples for their weddings. Late one evening after the theater, as I walked toward my room with my new colleague (a woman with whom I was coordinating an arts program), a middle-aged man in a tuxedo, a young girl in satin and lace on his arm, stepped directly into our path. With his champagne glass extended toward me, he exclaimed, "Evita!"

Our way blocked, my companion and I listened as the man 10
half-recited, half-bellowed "Don't Cry for Me, Argentina." When he finished, the young girl said: "How about a round of applause for my daddy?" We complied, hoping this would bring the silly spectacle to a close. I was becoming aware that our little group was attracting the attention of the other guests. "Daddy" must have perceived this too, and he once more barred the way as we tried to walk past him. He began to shout-sing a ditty to the tune of "La Bamba" — except the lyrics were about a girl named María whose exploits all rhymed with her name and gonorrhea. The girl kept saying "Oh, Daddy" and looking at me with pleading eyes. She wanted me to laugh along with the others. My companion and I stood silently waiting for the man to end his offensive song. When he finished, I looked not at him but at his daughter. I advised her calmly never to ask her father what he had done in the army. Then I walked between them and to my room. My friend complimented me on my cool handling of the situation. I confessed to her that I really had wanted to push the jerk into the swimming pool. I knew that this same man — probably a corporate executive, well educated, even worldly by most standards — would not have been likely to regale a white woman with a dirty song in public. He would perhaps have checked his impulse by assuming that she could be somebody's wife or mother, or at least *somebody* who might take offense. But to him, I was just an Evita or a María: merely a character in his cartoon-populated universe.

Because of my education and my proficiency with the English language, I have acquired many mechanisms for dealing with the anger I experience. This was not true for my parents, nor is it true for the many Latin women working at menial jobs who must put up with stereotypes about our ethnic group such as: "They make good domestics." This is another facet of the myth of the Latin woman in the United States. Its origin is simple to deduce. Work as domestics, waitressing, and factory jobs are all that's available to women with little English and few skills. The myth of the Hispanic menial has been sustained by the same media phenomenon that made "Mammy" from *Gone with the Wind* America's idea of the black woman for generations: María, the housemaid or counter girl, is now indelibly etched into the national psyche. The big and the little screens have presented us with the picture of the funny Hispanic maid, mispronouncing words and cooking up a spicy storm in a shiny California kitchen.

This media-engendered image of the Latina in the United States has been documented by feminist Hispanic scholars, who claim that such portrayals are partially responsible for the denial of opportunities for upward mobility among Latinas in the professions. I have a Chicana friend working on a Ph.D. in philosophy at a major university. She says her doctor still shakes his head in puzzled amazement at all the "big words" she uses. Since I do not wear my diplomas around my neck for all to see, I too have on occasion been sent to that "kitchen," where some think I obviously belong.

One such incident that has stayed with me, though I recognize it as a minor offense, happened on the day of my first public poetry reading. It took place in Miami in a boat-restaurant where we were having lunch before the event. I was nervous and excited as I walked in with my notebook in my hand. An older woman motioned me to her table. Thinking (foolish me) that she wanted me to autograph a copy of my brand-new slender volume of verse, I went over. She ordered a cup of coffee from me, assuming that I was the waitress. Easy enough to mistake my poems for menus, I suppose. I know that it wasn't an intentional act of cruelty, yet of all the good things that happened that day, I remember that scene most clearly, because it reminded me of what I had to overcome before anyone would take me seriously. In retrospect I understand that my anger gave my reading fire, that I have almost always taken doubts in my abilities as a challenge — and that the result is, most times, a feeling of satisfaction at having won a convert when I see the cold, appraising eyes warm to my words, the body language change, the smile that indicates that I have opened some avenue for communication. That day I read to that woman and her lowered eyes told me that she was embarrassed at her little faux pas, and when I willed her to look up at me, it was my victory, and she graciously allowed me to punish her with my full attention. We shook hands at the end of the reading, and I never saw her again. She has probably forgotten the whole thing but maybe not.

Yet I am one of the lucky ones. My parents made it possible for me to acquire a stronger footing in the mainstream culture by giving me the chance at an education. And books and art have saved me from the harsher forms of ethnic and racial prejudice that many of my Hispanic *compañeras* have had to endure. I travel a lot around the United States, reading from my books of poetry and my novel, and the reception I most often receive is one of positive interest by people who want to know more about my culture. There are, however, thousands of Latinas without the privilege of an education or the entrée into society that I have. For them life is a struggle against the misconceptions perpetuated by the myth of the Latina as whore, domestic, or criminal. We cannot change this by legislating the way people look at us. The transformation, as I see it, has to occur at a much more individual level. My personal goal in my public life is to try to replace the old pervasive stereotypes and myths about Latinas with a much more interesting set of realities. Every time I give a reading, I hope the stories I tell, the dreams and fears I examine in my work, can achieve some universal truth which will get my audience past the particulars of my skin color, my accent, or my clothes.

I once wrote a poem in which I called us Latinas “God’s brown 15
daughters.” This poem is really a prayer of sorts, offered upward, but also, through the human-to-human channel of art, outward. It is a prayer for communication, and for respect. In it, Latin women pray “in Spanish to an Anglo God / with a Jewish heritage,” and they are “fervently hoping / that if not omnipotent, / at least He be bilingual.”

For Discussion and Writing

1. What do the incidents on the bus, in the hotel, and at the poetry reading have in common?
2. What are the different kinds of Latinas Cofer says are recognized in mainstream Anglo-American culture? By making explicit her observations of how others classify people like her, what point does she make about classification in general?
3. **connections** Compare Cofer’s thoughts on being a Latina writer to Alice Walker’s attention to the creativity of African American women in “In Search of Our Mothers’ Gardens” (p. 420). Which aspects of their experience do Cofer and Walker share? Which are different? How do the ways they connect their experience to their heritage compare?
4. Write about how you perceive others in certain ways because of something about them — how they look, where they live, what they do for a living. Can we live without these kinds of snap judgments? Can we live with them? Be sure to use specific examples as you write.

JARED DIAMOND

The Ends of the World as We Know Them

Born in Boston, Massachusetts, in 1937, Jared Diamond was for many years a professor of physiology at the UCLA School of Medicine. In addition to his ornithological research in New Guinea, Diamond has become an environmental historian and is now a professor of geography at UCLA. In addition to his scholarly work in these fields, Diamond has written a number of successful popular books, including The Third Chimpanzee: The Evolution and Future of the Human Animal *(1991),* Why Is Sex Fun? *(1997),* Guns, Germs, and Steel: The Fates of Human Societies *(1997), and* Collapse: How Societies Choose to Fail or Succeed *(2005).*

People have many motivations for writing about the past, but a common one is worry about the present. Another is hope for the future. Diamond asks, "What lessons can we draw from history?" (par. 20). The answers depend in part on what kind of questions you ask of it. As you follow Diamond's arguments about the past, keep in mind both of these motivations, and think about the kinds of questions Diamond is asking and the kind of answers he finds.

Los Angeles — New Year's weekend traditionally is a time for us to reflect, and to make resolutions based on our reflections. In this fresh year, with the United States seemingly at the height of its power and at the start of a new presidential term, Americans are increasingly concerned and divided about where we are going. How long can America remain ascendant? Where will we stand 10 years from now, or even next year?

Such questions seem especially appropriate this year. History warns us that when once-powerful societies collapse, they tend to do so quickly and unexpectedly. That shouldn't come as much of a surprise: peak power usually means peak population, peak needs, and hence peak vulnerability. What can be learned from history that could help us avoid joining the ranks of those who declined swiftly? We must expect the answers to be complex, because historical reality is complex: while some societies did indeed collapse spectacularly, others have managed to thrive for thousands of years without major reversal.

When it comes to historical collapses, five groups of interacting factors have been especially important: the damage that people have inflicted on their environment; climate change; enemies; changes in friendly trading partners; and the society's political, economic, and social responses to these shifts. That's not to say that all five causes play a role in every case. Instead, think of this as a useful checklist of factors that should be examined, but whose relative importance varies from case to case.

For instance, in the collapse of the Polynesian society on Easter Island three centuries ago, environmental problems were dominant, and climate change, enemies, and trade were insignificant; however, the latter three factors played big roles in the disappearance of the medieval Norse colonies on Greenland. Let's consider two examples of declines stemming from different mixes of causes: the falls of classic Maya civilization and of Polynesian settlements on the Pitcairn Islands.

Maya Native Americans of the Yucatan Peninsula and adjacent 5
parts of Central America developed the New World's most advanced civilization before Columbus. They were innovators in writing, astronomy, architecture, and art. From local origins around 2,500 years ago, Maya societies rose especially after the year A.D. 250, reaching peaks of population and sophistication in the late 8th century.

Thereafter, societies in the most densely populated areas of the southern Yucatan underwent a steep political and cultural collapse: between 760 and 910, kings were overthrown, large areas were abandoned, and at least 90 percent of the population disappeared, leaving cities to become overgrown by jungle. The last known date recorded on a Maya monument by their so-called Long Count calendar corresponds to the year 909. What happened?

A major factor was environmental degradation by people: deforestation, soil erosion, and water management problems, all of which resulted in less food. Those problems were exacerbated by droughts, which may have been partly caused by humans themselves through deforestation. Chronic warfare made matters worse, as more and more people fought over less and less land and resources.

Why weren't these problems obvious to the Maya kings, who could surely see their forests vanishing and their hills becoming eroded? Part of the reason was that the kings were able to insulate themselves from problems afflicting the rest of society. By extracting wealth from commoners, they could remain well fed while everyone else was slowly starving.

What's more, the kings were preoccupied with their own power struggles. They had to concentrate on fighting one another and keeping up their images through ostentatious displays of wealth. By insulating themselves in the short run from the problems of society, the elite merely bought themselves the privilege of being among the last to starve.

Whereas Maya societies were undone by problems of their own 10
making, Polynesian societies on Pitcairn and Henderson Islands in the tropical Pacific Ocean were undone largely by other people's mistakes. Pitcairn, the uninhabited island settled in 1790 by the H.M.S. Bounty mutineers, had actually been populated by Polynesians 800 years earlier. That society, which left behind temple platforms, stone and shell tools, and huge garbage piles of fish and bird and turtle bones as evidence of its existence, survived for several centuries and then vanished. Why?

In many respects, Pitcairn and Henderson are tropical paradises, rich in some food sources and essential raw materials. Pitcairn is home to Southeast Polynesia's largest quarry of stone suited for making adzes, while Henderson has the region's largest breeding seabird colony and its only nesting beach for sea turtles. Yet the islanders depended on imports from Mangareva Island, hundreds of miles away, for canoes, crops, livestock, and oyster shells for making tools.

Unfortunately for the inhabitants of Pitcairn and Henderson, their Mangarevan trading partner collapsed for reasons similar to those underlying the Maya decline: deforestation, erosion, and warfare. Deprived of essential imports in a Polynesian equivalent of the 1973 oil crisis, the Pitcairn and Henderson societies declined until everybody had died or fled.

The Maya and the Henderson and Pitcairn Islanders are not alone, of course. Over the centuries, many other societies have declined, collapsed, or died out. Famous victims include the Anasazi in the American Southwest, who abandoned their cities in the 12th century because of environmental problems and climate change, and the Greenland Norse, who disappeared in the 15th century because of all five interacting factors on the checklist. There were also the ancient Fertile Crescent societies, the Khmer at Angkor Wat, the Moche society of Peru — the list goes on.

But before we let ourselves get depressed, we should also remember that there is another long list of cultures that have managed to prosper for lengthy periods of time. Societies in Japan, Tonga, Tikopia, the New Guinea Highlands, and Central and Northwest Europe, for example, have all found ways to sustain themselves. What separates the lost cultures from those that survived? Why did the Maya fail and the shogun succeed?

15 Half of the answer involves environmental differences: geography deals worse cards to some societies than to others. Many of the societies that collapsed had the misfortune to occupy dry, cold, or otherwise fragile environments, while many of the long-term survivors enjoyed more robust and fertile surroundings. But it's not the case that a congenial environment guarantees success: some societies (like the Maya) managed to ruin lush environments, while other societies — like the Incas, the Inuit, Icelanders, and desert Australian Aborigines — have managed to carry on in some of the earth's most daunting environments.

The other half of the answer involves differences in a society's responses to problems. Ninth-century New Guinea Highland villagers, 16th-century German landowners, and the Tokugawa shoguns of 17th-century Japan all recognized the deforestation spreading around them and solved the problem, either by developing scientific reforestation (Japan and Germany) or by transplanting tree seedlings (New Guinea). Conversely, the Maya, Mangarevans, and Easter Islanders failed to address their forestry problems and so collapsed.

Consider Japan. In the 1600s, the country faced its own crisis of deforestation, paradoxically brought on by the peace and prosperity following the Tokugawa shoguns' military triumph that ended 150 years of civil war. The subsequent explosion of Japan's population and economy set off rampant logging for construction of palaces and cities, and for fuel and fertilizer.

The shoguns responded with both negative and positive measures. They reduced wood consumption by turning to light-timbered construction, to fuel-efficient stoves and heaters, and to coal as a source of energy. At the same time, they increased wood production by developing and carefully managing plantation forests. Both the shoguns and the Japanese peasants took a long-term view: the former expected to pass on their power to their children, and the latter expected to pass on their land. In addition, Japan's isolation at the time made it obvious that the country would have to depend on its own resources and couldn't meet its needs by pillaging other countries. Today, despite having the highest human population density of any large developed country, Japan is more than 70 percent forested.

There is a similar story from Iceland. When the island was first settled by the Norse around 870, its light volcanic soils presented colonists with unfamiliar challenges. They proceeded to cut down trees and stock sheep as if they were still in Norway, with its robust soils. Significant erosion ensued, carrying half of Iceland's topsoil into the ocean within a century or two. Icelanders became the poorest people in Europe. But they gradually learned from their mistakes, over time instituting stocking limits on sheep and other strict controls, and establishing an entire government department charged with landscape management. Today, Iceland boasts the sixth-highest per-capita income in the world.

20 What lessons can we draw from history? The most straightforward: take environmental problems seriously. They destroyed societies in the past, and they are even more likely to do so now. If 6,000 Polynesians with stone tools were able to destroy Mangareva Island, consider what six billion people with metal tools and bulldozers are doing today. Moreover, while the Maya collapse affected just a few neighboring societies in Central America, globalization now means that any society's problems have the potential to affect anyone else. Just think how crises in Somalia, Afghanistan, and Iraq have shaped the United States today.

Other lessons involve failures of group decision making. There are many reasons why past societies made bad decisions, and thereby failed to solve or even to perceive the problems that would eventually destroy them. One reason involves conflicts of interest, whereby one group within a society (for instance, the pig farmers who caused the worst erosion in medieval Greenland and Iceland) can profit by engaging in practices that damage the rest of society. Another is the pursuit of short-term gains at the expense of long-term survival, as when fishermen overfish the stocks on which their livelihoods ultimately depend.

History also teaches us two deeper lessons about what separates successful societies from those heading toward failure. A society contains a built-in blueprint for failure if the elite insulates itself from the consequences of its actions. That's why Maya kings, Norse Greenlanders, and Easter Island chiefs made choices that eventually undermined their societies. They themselves did not begin to feel deprived until they had irreversibly destroyed their landscape.

Could this happen in the United States? It's a thought that often occurs to me here in Los Angeles, when I drive by gated communities, guarded by private security patrols, and filled with people who drink bottled water, depend on private pensions, and send their children to private schools. By doing these things, they lose the motivation to support the police force, the municipal water supply, Social Security, and public schools. If conditions deteriorate too much for poorer people, gates will not keep the rioters out. Rioters eventually burned the palaces of Maya kings and tore down the statues of Easter Island chiefs; they have also already threatened wealthy districts in Los Angeles twice in recent decades.

In contrast, the elite in 17th-century Japan, as in modern Scandinavia and the Netherlands, could not ignore or insulate themselves from broad societal problems. For instance, the Dutch upper class for hundreds of years has been unable to insulate itself from the Netherlands' water management problems for a simple reason: the rich live in the same drained lands below sea level as the poor. If the dikes and pumps keeping out the sea fail, the well-off Dutch know that they will drown along with everybody else, which is precisely what happened during the floods of 1953.

The other deep lesson involves a willingness to re-examine long-held core values, when conditions change and those values no longer make sense. The medieval Greenland Norse lacked such a willingness: they continued to view themselves as transplanted Norwegian pastoralists, and to despise the Inuit as pagan hunters, even after Norway stopped sending trading ships and the climate had grown too cold for a pastoral existence. They died off as a result, leaving Greenland to the Inuit. On the other hand, the

British in the 1950s faced up to the need for a painful reappraisal of their former status as rulers of a world empire set apart from Europe. They are now finding a different avenue to wealth and power, as part of a united Europe.

In this New Year, we Americans have our own painful reappraisals to face. Historically, we viewed the United States as a land of unlimited plenty, and so we practiced unrestrained consumerism, but that's no longer viable in a world of finite resources. We can't continue to deplete our own resources as well as those of much of the rest of the world.

Historically, oceans protected us from external threats; we stepped back from our isolationism only temporarily during the crises of two world wars. Now, technology and global interconnectedness have robbed us of our protection. In recent years, we have responded to foreign threats largely by seeking short-term military solutions at the last minute.

But how long can we keep this up? Though we are the richest nation on earth, there's simply no way we can afford (or muster the troops) to intervene in the dozens of countries where emerging threats lurk — particularly when each intervention these days can cost more than $100 billion and require more than 100,000 troops.

A genuine reappraisal would require us to recognize that it will be far less expensive and far more effective to address the underlying problems of public health, population, and environment that ultimately cause threats to us to emerge in poor countries. In the past, we have regarded foreign aid as either charity or as buying support; now, it's an act of self-interest to preserve our own economy and protect American lives.

Do we have cause for hope? Many of my friends are pessimis- 30
tic when they contemplate the world's growing population and human demands colliding with shrinking resources. But I draw hope from the knowledge that humanity's biggest problems today are ones entirely of our own making. Asteroids hurtling at us beyond our control don't figure high on our list of imminent dangers. To save ourselves, we don't need new technology: we just need the political will to face up to our problems of population and the environment.

I also draw hope from a unique advantage that we enjoy. Unlike any previous society in history, our global society today is the first with the opportunity to learn from the mistakes of societies remote from us in space and in time. When the Maya and Mangarevans were cutting down their trees, there were no historians or archaeologists, no newspapers or television, to warn them of the consequences of their actions. We, on the other hand, have a detailed chronicle of human successes and failures at our disposal. Will we choose to use it?

For Discussion and Writing

1. What are the five leading factors that Diamond says have led to the collapse of societies?
2. This essay was originally published on New Year's Day, and Diamond begins by making reference to the idea of New Year's resolutions. How does he build the essay from this opening? How does the essay use the idea to strengthen its argument?
3. **connections** In "The Obligation to Endure" (p. 83), Rachel Carson writes about the history of life on earth, what she calls "the whole span of earthly time" (par. 1). Compare Carson's historical frame to Diamond's. Do the differences in the length of their historical frames — the amount of time they look at — have any effect on their arguments?
4. Diamond says he draws hope from the idea that today we have access to a historical record from which we can learn what to do and not to do in order to avoid collapse. However, he ends his essay by asking, "Will we choose to use it?" Do you have hope for the future of American society? Humanity? If so, why? If not, why not?

JOAN DIDION

On Morality

Joan Didion, a fifth-generation Californian born in 1934, has been an essayist since her undergraduate days. Known for a reflexive, self-conscious yet cool style, and a sharp political eye, Didion has, in essays and novels, carved out a unique place in American letters. Best known for her essay collections Slouching Towards Bethlehem *(1968) and* The White Album *(1979), her novels, including* Play It as It Lays *(1970) and* The Last Thing He Wanted *(1996), are also widely read. Her latest book,* The Year of Magical Thinking *(2005), chronicles her grief after her husband's sudden death.*

In "On Morality," from Slouching Towards Bethlehem, *Didion questions the idea of ideal "good." She believes that we are individuals, products of our childhood, and that the "cautionary tales" we are told in our youth represent the values we learn to live by.*

As it happens I am in Death Valley, in a room at the Enterprise Motel and Trailer Park, and it is July, and it is hot. In fact it is 119°. I cannot seem to make the air conditioner work, but there is a small refrigerator, and I can wrap ice cubes in a towel and hold them against the small of my back. With the help of the ice cubes I have been trying to think, because *The American Scholar*[1] asked me to, in some abstract way about "morality," a word I distrust more every day, but my mind veers inflexibly toward the particular.

Here are some particulars. At midnight last night, on the road in from Las Vegas to Death Valley Junction, a car hit a shoulder and turned over. The driver, very young and apparently drunk, was killed instantly. His girl was found alive but bleeding internally, deep in shock. I talked this afternoon to the nurse who had driven the girl to the nearest doctor, 185 miles across the floor of the Valley and three ranges of lethal mountain road. The nurse

1. A general-interest journal published by the Phi Beta Kappa Society.

explained that her husband, a talc miner, had stayed on the highway with the boy's body until the coroner could get over the mountains from Bishop, at dawn today. "You can't just leave a body on the highway," she said. "It's immoral."

It was one instance in which I did not distrust the word, because she meant something quite specific. She meant that if a body is left alone for even a few minutes on the desert, the coyotes close in and eat the flesh. Whether or not a corpse is torn apart by coyotes may seem only a sentimental consideration, but of course it is more: one of the promises we make to one another is that we will try to retrieve our casualties, try not to abandon our dead to the coyotes. If we have been taught to keep our promises — if, in the simplest terms, our upbringing is good enough — we stay with the body, or have bad dreams.

I am talking, of course, about the kind of social code that is sometimes called, usually pejoratively, "wagon-train morality." In fact that is precisely what it is. For better or worse, we are what we learned as children: my own childhood was illuminated by graphic litanies of the grief awaiting those who failed in their loyalties to each other. The Donner-Reed Party,[2] starving in the Sierra snows, all the ephemera of civilization gone save that one vestigial taboo, the provision that no one should eat his own blood kin. The Jayhawkers, who quarreled and separated not far from where I am tonight. Some of them died in the Funerals[3] and some of them died down near Badwater and most of the rest of them died in the Panamints. A woman who got through gave the Valley its name. Some might say that the Jayhawkers were killed by the desert summer, and the Donner Party by the mountain winter, by circumstances beyond control; we were taught instead that they had somewhere abdicated their responsibilities, somehow breached their primary loyalties, or they would not have found themselves helpless in the mountain winter or the desert summer, would not have given way to acrimony, would not have deserted one another, would not have *failed*. In brief, we heard such stories as cautionary tales, and they still suggest the only kind of "morality"

2. A group of eighty-seven people who tried to cross the mountains into California during the stormy winter of 1846. The forty-seven who survived the ordeal ate the flesh of those who died.
3. The Funerals and the Panamints are mountain ranges close to Death Valley.

that seems to me to have any but the most potentially mendacious meaning.

You are quite possibly impatient with me by now; I am talking, you want to say, about a "morality" so primitive that it scarcely deserves the name, a code that has as its point only survival, not the attainment of the ideal good. Exactly. Particularly out here tonight, in this country so ominous and terrible that to live in it is to live with antimatter, it is difficult to believe that "the good" is a knowable quantity. Let me tell you what it is like out here tonight. Stories travel at night on the desert. Someone gets in his pickup and drives a couple of hundred miles for a beer, and he carries news of what is happening, back wherever he came from. Then he drives another hundred miles for another beer, and passes along stories from the last place as well as from the one before; it is a network kept alive by people whose instincts tell them that if they do not keep moving at night on the desert they will lose all reason. Here is a story that is going around the desert tonight: over across the Nevada line, sheriff's deputies are diving in some underground pools, trying to retrieve a couple of bodies known to be in the hole. The widow of one of the drowned boys is over there; she is eighteen, and pregnant, and is said not to leave the hole. The divers go down and come up, and she just stands there and stares into the water. They have been diving for ten days but have found no bottom to the caves, no bodies and no trace of them, only the black 90° water going down and down and down, and a single translucent fish, not classified. The story tonight is that one of the divers has been hauled up incoherent, out of his head, shouting — until they got him out of there so that the widow could not hear — about water that got hotter instead of cooler as he went down, about light flickering through the water, about magma, about underground nuclear testing.

That is the tone stories take out here, and there are quite a few of them tonight. And it is more than the stories alone. Across the road at the Faith Community Church a couple of dozen old people, come here to live in trailers and die in the sun, are holding a prayer sing. I cannot hear them and do not want to. What I can hear are occasional coyotes and a constant chorus of "Baby the Rain Must Fall" from the jukebox in the Snake Room next door, and if I were also to hear those dying voices, those Midwestern voices drawn to this lunar country for some unimaginable atavistic rites, *rock of ages cleft for me,* I think I would lose my own reason. Every now and then I imagine I hear a rattlesnake, but my husband says that it is a faucet, a paper rustling, the wind. Then he stands by a window, and plays a flashlight over the dry wash outside.

What does it mean? It means nothing manageable. There is some sinister hysteria in the air out here tonight, some hint of the monstrous perversion to which any human idea can come. "I followed my own conscience." "I did what I thought was right." How many madmen have said it and meant it? How many murderers? Klaus Fuchs said it, and the men who committed the Mountain Meadows Massacre said it, and Alfred Rosenberg[4] said it. And, as we are rotely and rather presumptuously reminded by those who would say it now, Jesus said it. Maybe we have all said it, and maybe we have been wrong. Except on that most primitive level — our loyalties to those we love — what could be more arrogant than to claim the primacy of personal conscience? ("Tell me," a rabbi asked Daniel Bell when he said, as a child, that he did not believe in God. "Do you think God cares?") At least some of the time, the world appears to me as a painting by Hieronymus Bosch;[5] were I to follow my conscience then, it would lead me out onto the desert with Marion Faye, out to where he stood in *The Deer Park*[6] looking east to Los Alamos and praying, as if for rain, that it would happen: *". . . let it come and clear the rot and the stench and the stink, let it come for all of everywhere, just so it comes and the world stands clear in the white dead dawn."*

4. Klaus Fuchs fled Germany to the United States, where he worked on the development of the atomic bomb during World War II. He moved to Great Britain to assume an important position at the British atomic energy center. He was convicted and imprisoned for providing atomic energy secrets to the Soviet Union. The Mountain Meadows Massacre occurred in September 1857 in Utah. A group of 130 to 140 emigrants heading for California were attacked by Indians incited and joined by Mormons angry at the treatment they had received during their earlier trek across the continent. All but seventeen children were massacred. Alfred Rosenberg was a Nazi leader often called "The Grand Inquisitor of the Third Reich." He was hanged for war crimes in 1946.

5. Hieronymus Bosch (ca. 1450–ca. 1516), a Dutch painter of fantastic and hellish images.

6. A novel by Norman Mailer.

* * *

Of course you will say that I do not have the right, even if I had the power, to inflict that unreasonable conscience upon you; nor do I want you to inflict your conscience, however reasonable, however enlightened, upon me. ("We must be aware of the dangers which lie in our most generous wishes," Lionel Trilling[7] once wrote. "Some paradox of our nature leads us, when once we have made our fellow men the objects of our enlightened interest, to go on to make them the objects of our pity, then of our wisdom, ultimately of our coercion.") That the ethic of conscience is intrinsically insidious seems scarcely a revelatory point, but it is one raised with increasing infrequency; even those who do raise it tend to *segue* with troubling readiness into the quite contradictory position that the ethic of conscience is dangerous when it is "wrong," and admirable when it is "right."

You see I want to be quite obstinate about insisting that we have no way of knowing — beyond that fundamental loyalty to the social code — what is "right" and what is "wrong," what is "good" and what "evil." I dwell so upon this because the most disturbing aspect of "morality" seems to me to be the frequency with which the word now appears; in the press, on television, in the most perfunctory kinds of conversation. Questions of straightforward power (or survival) politics, questions of quite indifferent public policy, questions of almost anything: they are all assigned these factitious moral burdens. There is something facile going on, some self-indulgence at work. Of course we would all like to "believe" in something, like to assuage our private guilts in public causes, like to lose our tiresome selves; like, perhaps, to transform the white flag of defeat at home into the brave white banner of battle away from home. And of course it is all right to do that; that is how, immemorially, things have gotten done. But I think it is all right only so long as we do not delude ourselves about what we are doing, and why. It is all right only so long as we remember that all the *ad hoc* committees, all the picket lines, all the brave signatures in *The New York Times,* all the tools of agitprop straight across the spectrum, do not confer upon anyone any *ipso facto* virtue. It is all right only so long as we recognize that the end may

7. Lionel Trilling (1905–1975), an eminent critic of literature and modern culture.

or may not be expedient, may or may not be a good idea, but in any case has nothing to do with "morality." Because when we start deceiving ourselves into thinking not that we want something or need something, not that it is a pragmatic necessity for us to have it, but that it is a *moral imperative* that we have it, then is when we join the fashionable madmen, and then is when the thin whine of hysteria is heard in the land, and then is when we are in bad trouble. And I suspect we are already there.

For Discussion and Writing

1. How does Didion feel about the claim people make that there can be a "moral imperative" to do something?
2. How does Didion define morality? Does she say what it is, or what it isn't, or both? Why do you think she approaches the task of defining in this way?
3. **connections** Compare the way Didion treats the general question of right and wrong in "On Morality" to the way Swift handles a specific moral question in "A Modest Proposal" (p. 387). While these essays in some ways could not be more different, both are concerned with knowing what is the right thing to do. What does each essay have to say about this shared question? How does each say it?
4. This essay was first published under the title "The Insidious Ethic of Conscience." Do you agree with Didion that claims of (and belief in) the dictates of conscience can be insidious? Why or why not? Can you support your answer with contemporary or historical examples of appeals to conscience?

ANNIE DILLARD

Seeing

Born in 1945 in Pittsburgh, Annie Dillard is best known as a nature writer. Pilgrim at Tinker Creek *(1974) won a Pulitzer Prize and established her as a writer whose nature walks lead not just into the woods but also upward, to spiritual considerations. In her nonfiction, fiction, and poetry, including her autobiographical* An American Childhood *(1987), she has continued to describe the world around her in close detail and then to leap off into the metaphysical. Dillard is professor emeritus at Wesleyan University in Connecticut.*

"Seeing" has appeared in both Harper's *and* Pilgrim at Tinker Creek*; the later version appears here. As you read, keep an eye out for Dillard's famous use of description as she marvels at the wonder of vision, how it shapes our view of the world, and how, wielded correctly, our eyes can be used as tools to surprise and enchant.*

When I was six or seven years old, growing up in Pittsburgh, I used to take a precious penny of my own and hide it for someone else to find. It was a curious compulsion; sadly, I've never been seized by it since. For some reason I always "hid" the penny along the same stretch of sidewalk up the street. I would cradle it at the roots of a sycamore, say, or in a hole left by a chipped-off piece of sidewalk. Then I would take a piece of chalk, and, starting at either end of the block, draw huge arrows leading up to the penny from both directions. After I learned to write I labeled the arrows: SURPRISE AHEAD or MONEY THIS WAY. I was greatly excited, during all this arrowdrawing, at the thought of the first lucky passer-by who would receive in this way, regardless of merit, a free gift from the universe. But I never lurked about. I would go straight home and not give the matter another thought, until, some months later, I would be gripped again by the impulse to hide another penny.

* * *

It is still the first week in January, and I've got great plans. I've been thinking about seeing. There are lots of things to see, unwrapped gifts and free surprises. The world is fairly studded and strewn with pennies cast broadside from a generous hand. But — and this is the point — who gets excited by a mere penny? If you follow one arrow, if you crouch motionless on a bank to watch a tremulous ripple thrill on the water and are rewarded by the sight of a muskrat kit paddling from its den, will you count that sight a chip of copper only, and go your rueful way? It is dire poverty indeed when a man is so malnourished and fatigued that he won't stoop to pick up a penny. But if you cultivate a healthy poverty and simplicity, so that finding a penny will literally make your day, then, since the world is in fact planted in pennies, you have with your poverty bought a lifetime of days. It is that simple. What you see is what you get.

I used to be able to see flying insects in the air. I'd look ahead and see, not the row of hemlocks across the road, but the air in front of it. My eyes would focus along that column of air, picking out flying insects. But I lost interest, I guess, for I dropped the habit. Now I can see birds. Probably some people can look at the grass at their feet and discover all the crawling creatures. I would like to know grasses and sedges — and care. Then my least journey into the world would be a field trip, a series of happy recognitions. Thoreau, in an expansive mood, exulted, "What a rich book might be made about buds, including, perhaps, sprouts!" It would be nice to think so. I cherish mental images I have of three perfectly happy people. One collects stones. Another — an Englishman, say — watches clouds. The third lives on a coast and collects drops of seawater which he examines microscopically and mounts. But I don't see what the specialist sees, and so I cut myself off, not only from the total picture, but from the various forms of happiness.

Unfortunately, nature is very much a now-you-see-it, now-you-don't affair. A fish flashes, then dissolves in the water before my eyes like so much salt. Deer apparently ascend bodily into heaven; the brightest oriole fades into leaves. These disappearances stun me into stillness and concentration; they say of nature that it conceals with a grand nonchalance, and they say of vision that it is a deliberate gift, the revelation of a dancer who for my eyes only flings away her seven veils. For nature does reveal as well as conceal: now-you-don't-see-it, now-you-do. For a week last September migrating red-winged blackbirds were feeding heavily down by the creek at the back of the house. One day I went out to investigate the racket; I walked up to a tree, an Osage orange, and a hundred birds flew away. They simply materialized out of the tree. I saw a tree, then a whisk of color, then a tree again. I walked closer and another hundred blackbirds took flight. Not a branch, not a twig budged: the birds were apparently weightless as well as invisible. Or, it was as if the leaves of the Osage orange had been freed from a spell in the form of red-winged blackbirds; they flew from the tree, caught my eye in the sky, and vanished. When I looked again at the tree the leaves had reassembled as if nothing had happened. Finally I walked directly to the trunk of the tree and a final hundred, the real diehards, appeared, spread, and vanished. How could so many hide in the tree without my seeing them? The Osage orange, unruffled, looked just as it had looked from the house, when three hundred red-winged blackbirds cried from its crown. I looked downstream where they flew, and they were gone. Searching, I couldn't spot one. I wandered downstream to force them to play their hand, but they'd crossed the creek and scattered. One show to a customer. These appearances catch at my throat; they are the free gifts, the bright coppers at the roots of trees.

It's all a matter of keeping my eyes open. Nature is like one of 5
those line drawings of a tree that are puzzles for children: Can you find hidden in the leaves a duck, a house, a boy, a bucket, a zebra, and a boot? Specialists can find the most incredibly well-hidden things. A book I read when I was young recommended an easy way to find caterpillars to rear: you simply find some fresh caterpillar droppings, look up, and there's your caterpillar. More recently an author advised me to set my mind at ease about those piles of cut stems on the ground in grassy fields. Field mice make them; they cut the grass down by degrees to reach the seeds at the head. It seems that when the grass is tightly packed, as in a field of ripe grain, the blade won't topple at a single cut through the stem; instead, the cut stem simply drops vertically, held in the crush of grain. The mouse severs the bottom again and again, the stem keeps dropping an inch at a time, and finally the head is low enough for the mouse to reach the seeds. Meanwhile, the

mouse is positively littering the field with its little piles of cut stems into which, presumably, the author of the book is constantly stumbling.

If I can't see these minutiae, I still try to keep my eyes open. I'm always on the lookout for antlion traps in sandy soil, monarch pupae near milkweed, skipper larvae in locust leaves. These things are utterly common, and I've not seen one. I bang on hollow trees near water, but so far no flying squirrels have appeared. In flat country I watch every sunset in hopes of seeing the green ray. The green ray is a seldom-seen streak of light that rises from the sun like a spurting fountain at the moment of sunset; it throbs into the sky for two seconds and disappears. One more reason to keep my eyes open. A photography professor at the University of Florida just happened to see a bird die in midflight; it jerked, died, dropped, and smashed on the ground. I squint at the wind because I read Stewart Edward White: "I have always maintained that if you looked closely enough you could *see* the wind — the dim, hardly-made-out, fine débris fleeing high in the air." White was an excellent observer, and devoted an entire chapter of *The Mountains* to the subject of seeing deer: "As soon as you can forget the naturally obvious and construct an artificial obvious, then you too will see deer."

But the artificial obvious is hard to see. My eyes account for less than one percent of the weight of my head; I'm bony and dense; I see what I expect. I once spent a full three minutes looking at a bullfrog that was so unexpectedly large I couldn't see it even though a dozen enthusiastic campers were shouting directions. Finally I asked, "What color am I looking for?" and a fellow said, "Green." When at last I picked out the frog, I saw what painters are up against: the thing wasn't green at all, but the color of wet hickory bark.

The lover can see, and the knowledgeable. I visited an aunt and uncle at a quarter-horse ranch in Cody, Wyoming. I couldn't do much of anything useful, but I could, I thought, draw. So, as we all sat around the kitchen table after supper, I produced a sheet of paper and drew a horse. "That's one lame horse," my aunt volunteered. The rest of the family joined in: "Only place to saddle that one is his neck"; "Looks like we better shoot the poor thing, on account of those terrible growths." Meekly, I slid the pencil and paper down the table. Everyone in that family, including my three young cousins, could draw a horse. Beautifully. When the paper came back it looked as though five shining, real quarter horses had been corralled by mistake with a papier-mâché moose; the real horses seemed to gaze at the monster with a steady, puzzled air. I stay away from horses now, but I can do a creditable goldfish. The point is that I just don't know what the lover knows; I just can't see the artificial obvious that those in the know construct. The herpetologist asks the native, "Are there snakes in that ravine?" "Nosir." And the herpetologist comes home with, yessir, three bags full. Are there butterflies on that mountain? Are the bluets in bloom, are there arrowheads here, or fossil shells in the shale?

Peeping through my keyhole I see within the range of only about thirty percent of the light that comes from the sun; the rest is infrared and some little ultraviolet, perfectly apparent to many animals, but invisible to me. A nightmare network of ganglia, charged and firing without my knowledge, cuts and splices what I do see, editing it for my brain. Donald E. Carr points out that the sense impressions of one-celled animals are *not* edited for the brain: "This is philosophically interesting in a rather mournful way, since it means that only the simplest animals perceive the universe as it is."

A fog that won't burn away drifts and flows across my field of 10
vision. When you see fog move against a backdrop of deep pines, you don't see the fog itself, but streaks of clearness floating across the air in dark shreds. So I see only tatters of clearness through a pervading obscurity. I can't distinguish the fog from the overcast sky; I can't be sure if the light is direct or reflected. Everywhere darkness and the presence of the unseen appalls. We estimate now that only one atom dances alone in every cubic meter of intergalactic space. I blink and squint. What planet or power yanks Halley's Comet out of orbit? We haven't seen that force yet; it's a question of distance, density, and the pallor of reflected light. We rock, cradled in the swaddling band of darkness. Even the simple darkness of night whispers suggestions to the mind. Last summer, in August, I stayed at the creek too late.

Where Tinker Creek flows under the sycamore log bridge to the tear-shaped island, it is slow and shallow, fringed thinly in cattail marsh. At this spot an astonishing bloom of life supports vast breeding populations of insects, fish, reptiles, birds, and mammals. On windless summer evenings I stalk along the creek bank or straddle the sycamore log in absolute stillness, watching for muskrats. The night I stayed too late I was hunched on the log staring spellbound at spreading, reflected stains of lilac on the water. A cloud in the sky suddenly lighted as if turned on by a switch; its reflection just as suddenly materialized on the water upstream, flat and floating, so that I couldn't see the creek bottom, or life in the water under the cloud. Downstream, away from the cloud on the water, water turtles smooth as beans were gliding down with the current in a series of easy, weightless push-offs, as men bound on the moon. I didn't know whether to trace the progress of one turtle I was sure of, risking sticking my face in one of the bridge's spiderwebs made invisible by the gathering dark, or take a chance on seeing the carp, or scan the mud bank in hope of seeing a muskrat, or follow the last of the swallows who caught at my heart and trailed it after them like streamers as they appeared from directly below, under the log, flying upstream with their tails forked, so fast.

But shadows spread, and deepened, and stayed. After thousands of years we're still strangers to darkness, fearful aliens in an enemy camp with our arms crossed over our chests. I stirred. A land turtle on the bank, startled, hissed the air from its lungs and withdrew into its shell. An uneasy pink here, an unfathomable blue there, gave great suggestion of lurking beings. Things were going on. I couldn't see whether that sere rustle I heard was a distant rattlesnake, slit-eyed, or a nearby sparrow kicking in the dry flood debris slung at the foot of a willow. Tremendous action roiled the water everywhere I looked, big action, inexplicable. A tremor welled up beside a gaping muskrat burrow in the bank and I caught my breath, but no muskrat appeared. The ripples continued to fan upstream with a steady, powerful thrust. Night was knitting over my face an eyeless mask, and I still sat transfixed. A distant airplane, a delta wing out of nightmare, made a gliding shadow on the creek's bottom that looked like a stingray cruising upstream. At once a black fin slit the pink cloud on the water, shearing it in two. The two halves merged together and seemed to dissolve before my eyes. Darkness pooled in the cleft of the creek and rose, as water collects in a well. Untamed, dreaming lights flickered over the sky. I saw hints of hulking underwater shadows, two pale splashes out of the water, and round ripples rolling close together from a blackened center.

At last I stared upstream where only the deepest violet remained of the cloud, a cloud so high its underbelly still glowed feeble color reflected from a hidden sky lighted in turn by a sun halfway to China. And out of that violet, a sudden enormous black body arced over the water. I saw only a cylindrical sleekness. Head and tail, if there was a head and tail, were both submerged in cloud. I saw only one ebony fling, a headlong dive to darkness; then the waters closed, and the lights went out.

I walked home in a shivering daze, up hill and down. Later I lay open-mouthed in bed, my arms flung wide at my sides to steady the whirling darkness. At this latitude I'm spinning 836 miles an hour round the earth's axis; I often fancy I feel my sweeping fall as a breakneck arc like the dive of dolphins, and the hollow rushing of wind raises hair on my neck and the side of my face. In orbit around the sun I'm moving 64,800 miles an hour. The solar system as a whole, like a merry-go-round unhinged, spins, bobs, and blinks at the speed of 43,200 miles an hour along a course set east of Hercules. Someone has piped, and we are dancing a tarantella until the sweat pours. I open my eyes and I see dark, muscled forms curl out of water, with flapping gills and flattened eyes. I close my eyes and I see stars, deep stars giving way to deeper stars, deeper stars bowing to deepest stars at the crown of an infinite cone.

"Still," wrote van Gogh in a letter, "a great deal of light falls on 15
everything." If we are blinded by darkness, we are also blinded by light. When too much light falls on everything, a special terror results. Peter Freuchen describes the notorious kayak sickness to which Greenland Eskimos are prone. "The Greenland fjords are peculiar for the spells of completely quiet weather, when there is not enough wind to blow out a match and the water is like a sheet of glass. The kayak hunter must sit in his boat without stirring a finger so as not to scare the shy seals away. . . . The sun, low in the sky, sends a glare into his eyes, and the landscape around moves into the realm of the unreal. The reflex from the mirrorlike water hypnotizes him, he seems to be unable to move, and all of a sudden it is as if he were floating in a bottomless void, sinking, sinking, and sinking. . . . Horror-stricken, he tries to stir, to cry out, but he cannot, he is completely paralyzed, he just falls and falls."

Some hunters are especially cursed with this panic, and bring ruin and sometimes starvation to their families.

Sometimes here in Virginia at sunset low clouds on the southern or northern horizon are completely invisible in the lighted sky. I only know one is there because I can see its reflection in still water. The first time I discovered this mystery I looked from cloud to no-cloud in bewilderment, checking my bearings over and over, thinking maybe the ark of the covenant was just passing by south of Dead Man Mountain. Only much later did I read the explanation: polarized light from the sky is very much weakened by reflection, but the light in clouds isn't polarized. So invisible clouds pass among visible clouds, till all slide over the mountains; so a greater light extinguishes a lesser as though it didn't exist.

In the great meteor shower of August, the Perseid, I wail all day for the shooting stars I miss. They're out there showering down, committing hara-kiri in a flame of fatal attraction, and hissing perhaps at last into the ocean. But at dawn what looks like a blue dome clamps down over me like a lid on a pot. The stars and planets could smash and I'd never know. Only a piece of ashen moon occasionally climbs up or down the inside of the dome, and our local star without surcease explodes on our heads. We have really only that one light, one source for all power, and yet we must turn away from it by universal decree. Nobody here on the planet seems aware of this strange, powerful taboo, that we all walk about carefully averting our faces, this way and that, lest our eyes be blasted forever.

Darkness appalls and light dazzles; the scrap of visible light that doesn't hurt my eyes hurts my brain. What I see sets me swaying. Size and distance and the sudden swelling of meanings confuse me, bowl me over. I straddle the sycamore log bridge over Tinker Creek in the summer. I look at the lighted creek bottom: snail tracks tunnel the mud in quavering curves. A crayfish jerks, but by the time I absorb what has happened, he's gone in a billowing smokescreen of silt. I look at the water: minnows and shiners. If I'm thinking minnows, a carp will fill my brain till I scream. I look at the water's surface: skaters, bubbles, and leaves sliding down. Suddenly, my own face, reflected, startles me witless. Those snails have been tracking my face! Finally, with a shuddering wrench of the will, I see clouds, cirrus clouds. I'm dizzy, I fall in. This looking business is risky.

Once I stood on a humped rock on nearby Purgatory Mountain, watching through binoculars the great autumn hawk migration below, until I discovered that I was in danger of joining the hawks on a vertical migration of my own. I was used to binoculars, but not, apparently, to balancing on humped rocks while looking through them. I staggered. Everything advanced and receded by turns; the world was full of unexplained foreshortenings and depths. A distant huge tan object, a hawk the size of an elephant, turned out to be the browned bough of a nearby loblolly pine. I followed a sharp-shinned hawk against a featureless sky, rotating my head unawares as it flew, and when I lowered the glass a glimpse of my own looming shoulder sent me staggering. What prevents the men on Palomar from falling, voiceless and blinded, from their tiny, vaulted chairs?

I reel in confusion; I don't understand what I see. With the 20
naked eye I can see two million light-years to the Andromeda galaxy. Often I slop some creek water in a jar and when I get home I dump it in a white china bowl. After the silt settles I return and see tracings of minute snails on the bottom, a planarian or two winding round the rim of water, roundworms shimmying frantically, and finally, when my eyes have adjusted to these dimensions, amoebae. At first the amoebae look like muscae volitantes, those curled moving spots you seem to see in your eyes when you stare at a distant wall. Then I see the amoebae as drops of water congealed, bluish, translucent, like chips of sky in the bowl. At length I choose one individual and give myself over to its idea of an evening. I see it dribble a grainy foot before it on its wet, unfathomable way. Do its unedited sense impressions include the fierce focus of my eyes? Shall I take it outside and show it Andromeda, and blow its little endoplasm? I stir the water with a finger, in case it's running out of oxygen. Maybe I should get a tropical aquarium with motorized bubblers and lights, and keep this one for a pet. Yes, it would tell its fissioned descendants, the universe is two feet by five, and if you listen closely you can hear the buzzing music of the spheres.

Oh, it's mysterious lamplit evenings, here in the galaxy, one after the other. It's one of those nights when I wander from window to window, looking for a sign. But I can't see. Terror and a beauty insoluble are a ribband of blue woven into the fringes of garments of things both great and small. No culture explains, no bivouac offers real haven or rest. But it could be that we are not seeing something. Galileo thought comets were an optical illusion. This is fertile ground: since we are certain that they're not, we can look at what our scientists have been saying with fresh hope. What if there are *really* gleaming, castellated cities hung upside-down over the desert sand? What limpid lakes and cool date palms have our caravans always passed untried? Until, one by one, by the blindest of leaps, we light on the road to these places, we must stumble in darkness and hunger. I turn from the window. I'm blind as a bat, sensing only from every direction the echo of my own thin cries.

I chanced on a wonderful book by Marius von Senden, called *Space and Sight*. When Western surgeons discovered how to perform safe cataract operations, they ranged across Europe and America operating on dozens of men and women of all ages who had been blinded by cataracts since birth. Von Senden collected accounts of such cases; the histories are fascinating. Many doctors had tested their patients' sense perceptions and ideas of space both before and after the operations. The vast majority of patients, of both sexes and all ages, had, in von Senden's opinion, no idea of space whatsoever. Form, distance, and size were so many meaningless syllables. A patient "had no idea of depth, confusing it with roundness." Before the operation a doctor would give a blind patient a cube and a sphere; the patient would tongue it or feel it with his hands, and name it correctly. After the operation the doctor would show the same objects to the patient without letting him touch them; now he had no clue whatsoever what he was seeing. One patient called lemonade "square" because it pricked on his tongue as a square shape pricked on the touch of his hands. Of another postoperative patient, the doctor writes, "I have found in her no notion of size, for example, not even within the narrow limits which she might have encompassed with the aid of touch. Thus when I asked her to show me how big her mother was, she did not stretch out her hands, but set her two index fingers a few inches apart." Other doctors reported their patients' own statements to similar effect. "The room he was in . . . he knew to be but part of the house, yet he could not conceive that the whole house could look bigger"; "Those who are blind from birth . . . have no real conception of height or distance.

A house that is a mile away is thought of as nearby, but requiring the taking of a lot of steps. . . . The elevator that whizzes him up and down gives no more sense of vertical distance than does the train of horizontal."

For the newly sighted, vision is pure sensation unencumbered by meaning: "The girl went through the experience that we all go through and forget, the moment we are born. She saw, but it did not mean anything but a lot of different kinds of brightness." Again, "I asked the patient what he could see; he answered that he saw an extensive field of light, in which everything appeared dull, confused, and in motion. He could not distinguish objects." Another patient saw "nothing but a confusion of forms and colors." When a newly sighted girl saw photographs and paintings, she asked, " 'Why do they put those dark marks all over them?' 'Those aren't dark marks,' her mother explained, 'those are shadows. That is one of the ways the eye knows that things have shape. If it were not for shadows many things would look flat.' 'Well, that's how things do look,' Joan answered. 'Everything looks flat with dark patches.' "

But it is the patients' concepts of space that are most revealing. One patient, according to his doctor, "practiced his vision in a strange fashion; thus he takes off one of his boots, throws it some way off in front of him, and then attempts to gauge the distance at which it lies; he takes a few steps towards the boot and tries to grasp it; on failing to reach it, he moves on a step or two and gropes for the boot until he finally gets hold of it." "But even at this stage, after three weeks' experience of seeing," von Senden goes on, " 'space,' as he conceives it, ends with visual space, i.e. with color-patches that happen to bound his view. He does not yet have the notion that a larger object (a chair) can mask a smaller one (a dog), or that the latter can still be present even though it is not directly seen."

25 In general the newly sighted see the world as a dazzle of color-patches. They are pleased by the sensation of color, and learn quickly to name the colors, but the rest of seeing is tormentingly difficult. Soon after his operation a patient "generally bumps into one of these color-patches and observes them to be substantial, since they resist him as tactual objects do. In walking about it also strikes him — or can if he pays attention — that he is continually passing in between the colors he sees, that he can go past a

visual object, that a part of it then steadily disappears from view; and that in spite of this, however he twists and turns — whether entering the room from the door, for example, or returning back to it — he always has a visual space in front of him. Thus he gradually comes to realize that there is also a space behind him, which he does not see."

The mental effort involved in these reasonings proves overwhelming for many patients. It oppresses them to realize, if they ever do at all, the tremendous size of the world, which they had previously conceived of as something touchingly manageable. It oppresses them to realize that they have been visible to people all along, perhaps unattractively so, without their knowledge or consent. A disheartening number of them refuse to use their new vision, continuing to go over objects with their tongues, and lapsing into apathy and despair. "The child can see, but will not make use of his sight. Only when pressed can he with difficulty be brought to look at objects in his neighborhood; but more than a foot away it is impossible to bestir him to the necessary effort." Of a twenty-one-year-old girl, the doctor relates, "Her unfortunate father, who had hoped for so much from this operation, wrote that his daughter carefully shuts her eyes whenever she wishes to go about the house, especially when she comes to a staircase, and that she is never happier or more at ease than when, by closing her eyelids, she relapses into her former state of total blindness." A fifteen-year-old boy, who was also in love with a girl at the asylum for the blind, finally blurted out, "No, really, I can't stand it anymore; I want to be sent back to the asylum again. If things aren't altered, I'll tear my eyes out."

Some do learn to see, especially the young ones. But it changes their lives. One doctor comments on "the rapid and complete loss of that striking and wonderful serenity which is characteristic only of those who have never yet seen." A blind man who learns to see is ashamed of his old habits. He dresses up, grooms himself, and tries to make a good impression. While he was blind he was indifferent to objects unless they were edible; now, "a sifting of values sets in . . . his thoughts and wishes are mightily stirred and some few of the patients are thereby led into dissimulation, envy, theft and fraud."

On the other hand, many newly sighted people speak well of the world, and teach us how dull is our own vision. To one patient, a human hand, unrecognized, is "something bright and then holes." Shown a bunch of grapes, a boy calls out, "It is dark, blue and shiny. . . . It isn't smooth, it has bumps and hollows." A little girl visits a garden. "She is greatly astonished, and can scarcely be persuaded to answer, stands speechless in front of the tree, which she only names on taking hold of it, and then as 'the tree with the lights in it.' " Some delight in their sight and give themselves over to the visual world. Of a patient just after her bandages were removed, her doctor writes, "The first things to attract her attention were her own hands; she looked at them very closely, moved them repeatedly to and fro, bent and stretched the fingers, and seemed greatly astonished at the sight." One girl was eager to tell her blind friend that "men do not really look like trees at all," and astounded to discover that her every visitor had an utterly different face. Finally, a twenty-two-year-old girl was dazzled by the world's brightness and kept her eyes shut for two weeks. When at the end of that time she opened her eyes again, she did not recognize any objects, but, "the more she now directed her gaze upon everything about her, the more it could be seen how an expression of gratification and astonishment overspread her features; she repeatedly exclaimed: 'Oh God! How beautiful!' "

I saw color-patches for weeks after I read this wonderful book. It was summer; the peaches were ripe in the valley orchards. When I woke in the morning, color-patches wrapped round my eyes, intricately, leaving not one unfilled spot. All day long I walked among shifting color-patches that parted before me like the Red Sea and closed again in silence, transfigured, wherever I looked back. Some patches swelled and loomed, while others vanished utterly, and dark marks flitted at random over the whole dazzling sweep. But I couldn't sustain the illusion of flatness. I've been around for too long. Form is condemned to an eternal danse macabre with meaning: I couldn't unpeach the peaches. Nor can I remember ever having seen without understanding; the color-patches of infancy are lost. My brain then must have been smooth as any balloon. I'm told I reached for the moon; many babies do. But the color-patches of infancy swelled as meaning filled them; they arrayed themselves in solemn ranks down distance which unrolled and stretched before me like a plain. The moon rocketed away. I live now in a world of shadows that shape and distance color, a world where space makes a kind of terrible sense. What gnosticism is this, and what physics? The fluttering patch I saw in my nursery window — silver and green and shape-shifting blue — is gone; a row of Lombardy poplars takes its place, mute, across the distant lawn. That humming oblong creature pale as light that stole along the walls of my room at night, stretching exhilaratingly around the corners, is gone, too, gone the night I ate of the bittersweet fruit, put two and two together and puckered forever my brain. Martin Buber tells this tale: "Rabbi Mendel once boasted to his teacher Rabbi Elimelekh that evenings he saw the angel who rolls away the light before the darkness, and mornings the angel who rolls away the darkness before the light. 'Yes,' said Rabbi Elimelekh, 'in my youth I saw that too. Later on you don't see these things anymore.' "

Why didn't someone hand those newly sighted people paints 30
and brushes from the start, when they still didn't know what anything was? Then maybe we all could see color-patches too, the world unraveled from reason, Eden before Adam gave names. The scales would drop from my eyes; I'd see trees like men walking; I'd run down the road against all orders, hallooing and leaping.

Seeing is of course very much a matter of verbalization. Unless I call my attention to what passes before my eyes, I simply won't see it. It is, as Ruskin says, "not merely unnoticed, but in the full, clear sense of the word, unseen." My eyes alone can't solve analogy tests using figures, the ones which show, with increasing elaborations, a big square, then a small square in a big square, then a big triangle, and expect me to find a small triangle in a big triangle. I have to say the words, describe what I'm seeing. If Tinker Mountain erupted, I'd be likely to notice. But if I want to notice the lesser cataclysms of valley life, I have to maintain in my head a running description of the present. It's not that I'm observant; it's just that I talk too much. Otherwise, especially in a strange place, I'll never know what's happening. Like a blind man at the ball game, I need a radio.

When I see this way I analyze and pry. I hurl over logs and roll away stones; I study the bank a square foot at a time, probing and tilting my head. Some days when a mist covers the mountains, when the muskrats won't show and the microscope's mirror shatters, I want to climb up the blank blue dome as a man would storm the inside of a circus tent, wildly, dangling, and with a steel knife claw a rent in the top, peep, and, if I must, fall.

But there is another kind of seeing that involves a letting go. When I see this way I sway transfixed and emptied. The difference between the two ways of seeing is the difference between walking with and without a camera. When I walk with a camera I walk from shot to shot, reading the light on a calibrated meter. When I walk without a camera, my own shutter opens, and the moment's light prints on my own silver gut. When I see this second way I am above all an unscrupulous observer.

It was sunny one evening last summer at Tinker Creek; the sun was low in the sky, upstream. I was sitting on the sycamore log bridge with the sunset at my back, watching the shiners the size of minnows who were feeding over the muddy sand in skittery schools. Again and again, one fish, then another, turned for a split second across the current and flash! the sun shot out from its silver side. I couldn't watch for it. It was always just happening somewhere else, and it drew my vision just as it disappeared: flash, like a sudden dazzle of the thinnest blade, a sparking over a dun and olive ground at chance intervals from every direction. Then I noticed white specks, some sort of pale petals, small, floating from under my feet on the creek's surface, very slow and steady. So I blurred my eyes and gazed towards the brim of my hat and saw a new world. I saw the pale white circles roll up, roll up, like the world's turning, mute and perfect, and I saw the linear flashes, gleaming silver, like stars being born at random down a rolling scroll of time. Something broke and something opened. I filled up like a new wineskin. I breathed an air like light; I saw a light like water. I was the lip of a fountain the creek filled forever; I was ether, the leaf in the zephyr; I was flesh-flake, feather, bone.

When I see this way I see truly. As Thoreau says, I return to my 35
senses. I am the man who watches the baseball game in silence in an empty stadium. I see the game purely; I'm abstracted and dazed. When it's all over and the white-suited players lope off the green field to their shadowed dugouts, I leap to my feet; I cheer and cheer.

* * *

But I can't go out and try to see this way. I'll fail, I'll go mad. All I can do is try to gag the commentator, to hush the noise of useless interior babble that keeps me from seeing just as surely as a newspaper dangled before my eyes. The effort is really a discipline requiring a lifetime of dedicated struggle; it marks the literature of saints and monks of every order East and West, under every rule and no rule, discalced and shod. The world's spiritual geniuses seem to discover universally that the mind's muddy river, this ceaseless flow of trivia and trash, cannot be dammed, and that trying to dam it is a waste of effort that might lead to madness. Instead you must allow the muddy river to flow unheeded in the dim channels of consciousness; you raise your sights; you look along it, mildly, acknowledging its presence without interest and gazing beyond it into the realm of the real where subjects and objects act and rest purely, without utterance. "Launch into the deep," says Jacques Ellul, "and you shall see."

The secret of seeing is, then, the pearl of great price. If I thought he could teach me to find it and keep it forever I would stagger barefoot across a hundred deserts after any lunatic at all. But although the pearl may be found, it may not be sought. The literature of illumination reveals this above all: although it comes to those who wait for it, it is always, even to the most practiced and adept, a gift and a total surprise. I return from one walk knowing where the killdeer nests in the field by the creek and the hour the laurel blooms. I return from the same walk a day later scarcely knowing my own name. Litanies hum in my ears; my tongue flaps in my mouth Ailinon, alleluia! I cannot cause light; the most I can do is try to put myself in the path of its beam. It is possible, in deep space, to sail on solar wind. Light, be it particle or wave, has force: you rig a giant sail and go. The secret of seeing is to sail on solar wind. Hone and spread your spirit till you yourself are a sail, whetted, translucent, broadside to the merest puff.

When her doctor took her bandages off and led her into the garden, the girl who was no longer blind saw "the tree with the lights in it." It was for this tree I searched through the peach orchards of summer, in the forests of fall and down winter and spring for years. Then one day I was walking along Tinker Creek thinking of nothing at all and I saw the tree with the lights in it. I saw the backyard cedar where the mourning doves roost charged and transfigured, each cell buzzing with flame. I stood on the grass with the lights in it, grass that was wholly fire, utterly focused and utterly dreamed. It was less like seeing than like being for the first time seen, knocked breathless by a powerful glance. The flood of fire abated, but I'm still spending the power. Gradually the lights went out in the cedar, the colors died, the cells unflamed and disappeared. I was still ringing. I had been my whole life a bell, and never knew it until at that moment I was lifted and struck. I have since only very rarely seen the tree with the lights in it. The vision comes and goes, mostly goes, but I live for it, for the moment when the mountains open and a new light roars in spate through the crack, and the mountains slam.

For Discussion and Writing

1. Dillard writes, "For the newly sighted, vision is a pure sensation unencumbered by meaning" (par. 23). What does vision mean for Dillard? What makes seeing so important to her?
2. Description is both a valued component of good writing and a trap — the merely descriptive, or description that serves more as filler than as central element, can be a mark of ineffective writing too. How does Dillard make her descriptions central to this essay? How do they work on their own as description — what kind of details does she use, how does she draw readers' attention to these details, from how close or how far, from what angle does she see the things she describes? And how do these descriptions work in the essay — what work do they do for Dillard?
3. **connections** Compare Dillard on seeing to Susan Sontag's discussion in "Regarding the Pain of Others" (p. 373). Though the two essays focus on different kinds of visual phenomena, both consider the way individuals see things. How do these reflections on seeing themselves see the action of seeing — that is, how do they understand the ways in which people see? Does one author conceptualize the act of seeing as effected more by the person seeing? Does one see it effected more by the object seen?
4. Dillard writes, "I see what I expect" (par. 7). In what ways beyond the visual do we see what we expect? Are there ways in which our perceptions of the world — of how it works and what it is made — the product of our preconceived and inherited notions? Can you think of a time when you misunderstood a situation or event because you at first saw and thought what you expected? Where do these expectations come from?

FREDERICK DOUGLASS

Learning to Read and Write

Frederick Douglass was born a slave in 1818 in Maryland. He learned to read and write, escaped to New York, and became a leader in the abolitionist movement. He engaged in speaking tours and edited North Star, *a newspaper named for the one guide escaping southern slaves could rely on to find their way to freedom. Douglass is best known for his autobiography,* Narrative of the Life of Frederick Douglass *(1845), from which "Learning to Read and Write" is excerpted. In this selection, Douglass tells the story of his coming to literacy. As you read, keep your eye on the ways in which Douglass describes the world opening up for him as he learns his letters and the range of emotions this process evokes in him.*

I lived in Master Hugh's family about seven years. During this time, I succeeded in learning to read and write. In accomplishing this, I was compelled to resort to various stratagems. I had no regular teacher. My mistress, who had kindly commenced to instruct me, had, in compliance with the advice and direction of her husband, not only ceased to instruct, but had set her face against my being instructed by any one else. It is due, however, to my mistress to say of her, that she did not adopt this course of treatment immediately. She at first lacked the depravity indispensable to shutting me up in mental darkness. It was at least necessary for her to have some training in the exercise of irresponsible power, to make her equal to the task of treating me as though I were a brute.

My mistress was, as I have said, a kind and tender-hearted woman; and in the simplicity of her soul she commenced, when I first went to live with her, to treat me as she supposed one human being ought to treat another. In entering upon the duties of a slaveholder, she did not seem to perceive that I sustained to her the relation of a mere chattel, and that for her to treat me as a human being was not only wrong, but dangerously so. Slavery proved as injurious to her as it did to me. When I went there, she was a pious, warm, and tender-hearted woman. There was no sorrow or suffering for which she had not a tear. She had bread for the hungry, clothes for the naked, and comfort for every mourner that came within her reach. Slavery soon proved its ability to divest her of these heavenly qualities. Under its influence, the tender heart became stone, and the lamb-like disposition gave way to one of tiger-like fierceness. The first step in her downward course was in her ceasing to instruct me. She now commenced to practice her husband's precepts. She finally became even more violent in her opposition than her husband himself. She was not satisfied with simply doing as well as he had commanded; she seemed anxious to do better. Nothing seemed to make her more angry than to see me with a newspaper. She seemed to think that here lay the danger. I have had her rush at me with a face made all up of fury, and snatch from me a newspaper, in a manner that fully revealed her apprehension. She was an apt woman; and a little experience soon demonstrated, to her satisfaction, that education and slavery were incompatible with each other.

From this time I was most narrowly watched. If I was in a separate room any considerable length of time, I was sure to be suspected of having a book, and was at once called to give an account of myself. All this, however, was too late. The first step had been taken. Mistress, in teaching me the alphabet, had given me the *inch*, and no precaution could prevent me from taking the *ell*.

The plan which I adopted, and the one by which I was most successful, was that of making friends of all the little white boys whom I met in the street. As many of these as I could, I converted into teachers. With their kindly aid, obtained at different times and in different places, I finally succeeded in learning to read. When I was sent of errands, I always took my book with me, and by going one part of my errand quickly, I found time to get a lesson before my return. I used also to carry bread with me, enough of which was always in the house, and to which I was always welcome; for I was much better off in this regard than many of the poor white children in our neighborhood. This bread I used to bestow upon the hungry little urchins, who, in return, would give me that more valuable bread of knowledge. I am strongly tempted to give the names of two or three of those little boys, as a testimonial of the gratitude and affection I bear them; but prudence forbids: — not that it would injure me, but it might embarrass them; for it is almost an unpardonable offence to teach slaves to read in this Christian country. It is enough to say of the dear little fellows, that they lived on Philpot Street, very near Durgin and Bailey's ship-yard. I used to talk this matter of slavery over with them. I would sometimes say to them, I wished I could be as free as they would be when they got to be men. "You will be free as soon as you are twenty-one, *but I am a slave for life!* Have not I as good a right to be free as you have?" These words used to trouble them; they would express for me the liveliest sympathy, and console me with the hope that something would occur by which I might be free.

I was now about twelve years old, and the thought of being *a* 5
slave for life began to bear heavily upon my heart. Just about this time, I got hold of a book entitled "The Columbian Orator." Every opportunity I got, I used to read this book. Among much of other interesting matter, I found in it a dialogue between a master and his slave. The slave was represented as having run away from his master three times. The dialogue represented the conversation which took place between them, when the slave was retaken the third time. In this dialogue, the whole argument in behalf of slavery was brought forward by the master, all of which was disposed of by the slave. The slave was made to say some very smart as well as impressive things in reply to his master — things which had the desired though unexpected effect; for the conversation resulted in the voluntary emancipation of the slave on the part of the master.

In the same book, I met with one of Sheridan's mighty speeches on and in behalf of Catholic emancipation. These were choice documents to me. I read them over and over again with unabated interest. They gave tongue to interesting thoughts of my own soul, which had frequently lashed through my mind, and died away for want of utterance. The moral which I gained from the dialogue was the power of truth over the conscience of even a slaveholder. What I got from Sheridan was a bold denunciation of slavery, and a powerful vindication of human rights. The reading of these documents enabled me to utter my thoughts, and to meet the arguments brought forward to sustain slavery; but while they relieved me of one difficulty, they brought on another even more painful than the one of which I was relieved. The more I read, the more I was led to abhor and detest my enslavers. I could regard them in no other light than a band of successful robbers, who had left their homes, and gone to Africa, and stolen us from our homes, and in a strange land reduced us to slavery. I loathed them as being the meanest as well as the most wicked of men. As I read and contemplated the subject, behold! that very discontentment which Master Hugh had predicted would follow my learning to read had already come, to torment and sting my soul to unutterable anguish. As I writhed under it, I would at times feel that learning to read had been a curse rather than a blessing. It had given me a view of my wretched condition, without the remedy. It opened my eyes to the horrible pit, but to no ladder upon which to get out. In moments of agony, I envied my fellow-slaves for their stupidity. I have often wished myself a beast. I preferred the condition of the meanest reptile to my own. Any thing, no matter what, to get rid of thinking! It was this everlasting thinking of my condition that tormented me. There was no getting rid of it. It was pressed upon me by every object within sight or hearing, animate or inanimate. The silver trump of freedom had roused my soul to eternal wakefulness. Freedom now appeared, to disappear no more forever. It was heard in every sound, and seen in every thing. It was ever present to torment me with a sense of my wretched condition. I saw nothing without seeing it, I heard nothing without hearing it, and felt nothing without feeling it. It looked from every star, it smiled in every calm, breathed in every wind, and moved in every storm.

I often found myself regretting my own existence, and wishing myself dead; and but for the hope of being free, I have no doubt but that I should have killed myself, or done something for which I should have been killed. While in this state of mind, I was eager to hear any one speak of slavery. I was a ready listener. Every little while, I could hear something about the abolitionists. It was some time before I found what the word meant. It was always used in such connections as to make it an interesting word to me. If a slave ran away and succeeded in getting clear, or if a slave killed his master, set fire to a barn, or did any thing very wrong in the mind of a slaveholder, it was spoken of as the fruit of *abolition*. Hearing the word in this connection very often, I set about learning what it meant. The dictionary afforded me little or no help. I found it was "the act of abolishing"; but then I did not know what was to be abolished. Here I was perplexed. I did not dare to ask any one about its meaning, for I was satisfied that it was something they wanted me to know very little about. After a patient waiting, I got one of our city papers, containing an account of the number of petitions from the north, praying for the abolition of slavery in the District of Columbia, and of the slave trade between the States. From this time I understood the words *abolition* and *abolitionist*, and always drew near when that word was spoken, expecting to hear something of importance to myself and fellow-slaves. The light broke in upon me by degrees. I went one day down on the wharf of Mr. Waters; and seeing two Irishmen unloading a scow of stone, I went, unasked, and helped them. When we had finished, one of them came to me and asked me if I were a slave. I told him I was. He asked, "Are ye a slave for life?" I told him that I was. The good Irishman seemed to be deeply affected by the statement. He said to the other that it was a pity so fine a little fellow as myself should be a slave for life. He said it was a shame to hold me. They both advised me to run away to the north; that I should find friends there, and that I should be free. I pretended not to be interested in what they said, and treated them as if I did not understand them; for I feared they might be treacherous. White men have been known to encourage slaves to escape, and then, to get the reward, catch them and return them to their masters. I was afraid that these seemingly good men might use me so; but I nevertheless remembered their advice, and from that time I resolved to run away. I looked forward to a time at which it would be safe for me to escape. I was too young to think of doing so immediately; besides, I wished to learn how to write, as I might have occasion to write my own pass. I consoled myself with the hope that I should one day find a good chance. Meanwhile, I would learn to write.

The idea as to how I might learn to write was suggested to me by being in Durgin and Bailey's ship-yard, and frequently seeing the ship carpenters, after hewing, and getting a piece of timber ready for use, write on the timber the name of that part of the ship for which it was intended. When a piece of timber was intended for the larboard side, it would be marked thus — "L." When a piece was for the starboard side, it would be marked thus — "S." A piece for the larboard side forward, would be marked thus — "L. F." When a piece was for starboard side forward, it would be marked thus — "S. F." For larboard aft, it would be marked thus — "L. A." For starboard aft, it would be marked thus — "S. A." I soon learned the names of these letters, and for what they were intended when placed upon a piece of timber in the ship-yard. I immediately commenced copying them, and in a short time was able to make the four letters named. After that, when I met with any boy who I knew could write, I would tell him I could write as well as he. The next word would be, "I don't believe you. Let me see you try it." I would then make the letters which I had been so fortunate as to learn, and ask him to beat that. In this way I got a good many lessons in writing, which it is quite possible I should never have gotten in any other way. During this time, my copy-book was the board fence, brick wall, and pavement; my pen and ink was a lump of chalk. With these, I learned mainly how to write. I then commenced and continued copying the Italics in Webster's Spelling Book, until I could make them all without looking on the book. By this time, my little Master Thomas had gone to school, and learned how to write, and had written over a number of copy-books. These had been brought home, and shown to some of our near neighbors, and then laid aside. My mistress used to go to class meeting at the Wilk Street meetinghouse every Monday afternoon, and leave me to take care of the house. When left thus, I used to spend the time in writing in the spaces left in Master Thomas's copy-book, copying what he had written. I continued to do this until I could write a hand very similar to that of Master Thomas. Thus, after a long, tedious effort for years, I finally succeeded in learning how to write.

For Discussion and Writing

1. List the different ways Douglass taught himself to read and write. List also some other things he learns.
2. The main focus of this passage is the process by which Douglass began to become literate. Who else in the passage undergoes a "learning" process, and what are the results?
3. **connections** Douglass teaches himself to read and write in a society that condemns literacy for people like him; the education and the society Malcolm X describes in "Learning to Read" (p. 257) are very different. How are they similar?

4. Douglass's education is presented as both pleasurable and painful, opening up new worlds to him at the same time as it helps him to understand painful facts. Describe something you have learned — a new subject, a new fact about the world — that has been similarly double-edged for you.

BARBARA EHRENREICH

Serving in Florida

Born in 1941 and raised in Butte, Montana, Barbara Ehrenreich earned a doctorate in biology before devoting herself to writing about culture and politics. She has written extensively on social class, work, gender, and politics in columns and in books, including The Worst Years of Our Lives: Irreverent Notes on a Decade of Greed *(1990),* Blood Rites: The Origins and History of the Passions for War *(1997),* Nickel and Dimed: On (Not) Getting By in America *(2001),* Bait and Switch: The (Futile) Pursuit of the American Dream *(2005), and her newest book* Bright-Sided: How the Relentless Promotion of Positive Thinking Has Undermined America *(2009).*

"Serving in Florida" comes from Nickel and Dimed. *In the book, Ehrenreich recounts her experiences trying to live on the income earned working a number of low-paying jobs. While these stories are engrossing, that is not the only reason they are in the book. As you read the stories in "Serving in Florida," keep an eye out for the ways in which Ehrenreich uses these stories to make a number of points about contemporary American life.*

I could drift along like this, in some dreamy proletarian idyll, except for two things. One is management. If I have kept this subject to the margins so far it is because I still flinch to think that I spent all those weeks under the surveillance of men (and later women) whose job it was to monitor my behavior for signs of sloth, theft, drug abuse, or worse. Not that managers and especially "assistant managers" in low-wage settings like this are exactly the class enemy. Mostly, in the restaurant business, they are former cooks still capable of pinch-hitting in the kitchen, just as in hotels they are likely to be former clerks, and paid a salary of only about $400 a week. But everyone knows they have crossed over to the other side, which is, crudely put, corporate as opposed to human. Cooks want to prepare tasty meals, servers want to serve them graciously, but managers are there for only one reason — to make sure that money is made for some theoretical entity, the corporation, which exists far away in Chicago or New York, if a corporation can be said to have a physical existence at all. Reflecting on her career, Gail tells me ruefully that she swore, years ago, never to work for a corporation again. "They don't cut you no slack. You give and you give and they take."

Managers can sit — for hours at a time if they want — but it's their job to see that no one else ever does, even when there's nothing to do, and this is why, for servers, slow times can be as exhausting as rushes. You start dragging out each little chore because if the manager on duty catches you in an idle moment he will give you something far nastier to do. So I wipe, I clean, I consolidate catsup bottles and recheck the cheesecake supply, even tour the tables to make sure the customer evaluation forms are all standing perkily in their places — wondering all the time how many calories I burn in these strictly theatrical exercises. In desperation, I even take the desserts out of their glass display case and freshen them up with whipped cream and bright new maraschino cherries; anything to look busy. When, on a particularly dead afternoon, Stu finds me glancing at a *USA Today* a customer has left behind, he assigns me to vacuum the entire floor with the broken vacuum cleaner, which has a handle only two feet long, and the only way to do that without incurring orthopedic damage is to proceed from spot to spot on your knees.

On my first Friday at Hearthside there is a "mandatory meeting for all restaurant employees," which I attend, eager for insight into our overall marketing strategy and the niche (your basic Ohio cuisine with a tropical twist?) we aim to inhabit. But there is no "we" at this meeting. Phillip, our top manager except for an occasional "consultant" sent out by corporate headquarters, opens it with a sneer: "The break room — it's disgusting. Butts in the ashtrays, newspapers lying around, crumbs." This windowless little room, which also houses the time clock for the entire hotel, is where we stash our bags and civilian clothes and take our half-hour meal breaks. But a break room is not a right, he tells us, it can be taken away. We should also know that the lockers in the break room and whatever is in them can be searched at any time. Then comes gossip; there has been gossip; gossip (which seems to mean employees talking among themselves) must stop. Off-duty employees are henceforth barred from eating at the restaurant, because "other servers gather around them and gossip." When Phillip has exhausted his agenda of rebukes, Joan complains about the condition of the ladies' room and I throw in my two bits about the vacuum cleaner. But I don't see any backup coming from my fellow servers, each of whom has slipped into her own personal funk; Gail, my role model, stares sorrowfully at a point six inches from her nose. The meeting ends when Andy, one of the cooks, gets up, muttering about breaking up his day off for this almighty bullshit.

Just four days later we are suddenly summoned into the kitchen at 3:30 P.M., even though there are live tables on the floor. We all — about ten of us — stand around Phillip, who announces grimly that there has been a report of some "drug activity" on the night shift and that, as a result, we are now to be a "drug-free" workplace, meaning that all new hires will be tested and possibly also current employees on a random basis. I am glad that this part of the kitchen is so dark because I find myself blushing as hard as if I had been caught toking up in the ladies' room myself: I haven't been treated this way — lined up in the corridor, threatened with locker searches, peppered with carelessly aimed accusations — since at least junior high school. Back on the floor, Joan cracks, "Next they'll be telling us we can't have *sex* on the job." When I ask Stu what happened to inspire the crackdown, he just mutters about "management decisions" and takes the opportunity to upbraid Gail and me for being too generous with the rolls. From now on there's to be only one per customer and it goes out with the dinner, not with the salad. He's also been riding the cooks, prompting Andy to come out of the kitchen and observe — with the serenity of a man whose customary implement is a butcher knife — that "Stu has a death wish today."

Later in the evening, the gossip crystallizes around the theory 5
that Stu is himself the drug culprit, that he uses the restaurant phone to order up marijuana and sends one of the late servers out to fetch it for him. The server was caught and she may have ratted out Stu, at least enough to cast some suspicion on him, thus accounting for his pissy behavior. Who knows? Personally, I'm ready to believe anything bad about Stu, who serves no evident function and presumes too much on our common ethnicity,

sidling up to me one night to engage in a little nativism directed at the Haitian immigrants: "I feel like I'm the foreigner here. They're taking over the country." Still later that evening, the drug in question escalates to crack. Lionel, the busboy, entertains us for the rest of the shift by standing just behind Stu's back and sucking deliriously on a imaginary joint or maybe a pipe.

The other problem, in addition to the less-than-nurturing management style, is that this job shows no sign of being financially viable. You might imagine, from a comfortable distance, that people who live, year in and year out, on $6 to $10 an hour have discovered some survival stratagems unknown to the middle class. But no. It's not hard to get my coworkers talking about their living situations, because housing, in almost every case, is the principal source of disruption in their lives, the first thing they fill you in on when they arrive for their shifts. After a week, I have compiled the following survey:

Gail is sharing a room in a well-known downtown flophouse for $250 a week. Her roommate, a male friend, has begun hitting on her, driving her nuts, but the rent would be impossible alone.

Claude, the Haitian cook, is desperate to get out of the two-room apartment he shares with his girlfriend and two other, unrelated people. As far as I can determine, the other Haitian men live in similarly crowded situations.

Annette, a twenty-year-old server who is six months pregnant and abandoned by her boyfriend, lives with her mother, a postal clerk.

Marianne, who is a breakfast server, and her boyfriend are paying $170 a week for a one-person trailer.

Billy, who at $10 an hour is the wealthiest of us, lives in the trailer he owns, paying only the $400-a-month lot fee.

The other white cook, Andy, lives on his dry-docked boat, which, as far as I can tell from his loving descriptions, can't be more than twenty feet long. He offers to take me out on it once it's repaired, but the offer comes with inquiries as to my marital status, so I do not follow up on it.

Tina, another server, and her husband are paying $60 a night for a room in the Days Inn. This is because they have no car and the Days Inn is in walking distance of the Hearthside. When Marianne is tossed out of her trailer for subletting (which is against trailer park rules), she leaves her boyfriend and moves in with Tina and her husband.

Joan, who had fooled me with her numerous and tasteful outfits (hostesses wear their own clothes), lives in a van parked behind a shopping center at night and showers in Tina's motel room. The clothes are from thrift shops.[1]

It strikes me, in my middle-class solipsism, that there is gross improvidence in some of these arrangements. When Gail and I are wrapping silverware in napkins — the only task for which we are permitted to sit — she tells me she is thinking of escaping from her roommate by moving into the Days Inn herself. I am astounded: how she can even think of paying $40 to $60 a day? But if I was afraid of sounding like a social worker, I have come out just sounding like a fool. She squints at me in disbelief: "And where am I supposed to get a month's rent and a month's deposit for an apartment?" I'd been feeling pretty smug about my $500 efficiency, but of course it was made possible only by the $1,300 I had allotted myself for start-up costs when I began my low-wage life: $1,000 for the first month's rent and deposit, $100 for initial groceries and cash in my pocket, $200 stuffed away for emergencies. In poverty, as in certain propositions in physics, starting conditions are everything.

There are no secret economies that nourish the poor; on the contrary, there are a host of special costs. If you can't put up the two months' rent you need to secure an apartment, you end up paying through the nose for a room by the week. If you have only a room, with a hot plate at best, you can't save by cooking up huge lentil stews that can be frozen for the week ahead. You eat fast food or the hot dogs and Styrofoam cups of soup that can be microwaved in a convenience store. If you have no money for health insurance — and the Hearthside's niggardly plan kicks in only after three months — you go without routine care or prescription drugs and end up paying the price. Gail, for example, was doing fine, healthwise anyway, until she ran out of money for estrogen pills. She is supposed to be on the company health plan by now, but they claim to have lost her application form and to be beginning the paperwork all over again. So she spends $9 a pop

1. I could find no statistics on the number of employed people living in cars or vans, but according to a 1997 report of the National Coalition for the Homeless, "Myths and Facts about Homelessness," nearly one-fifth of all homeless people (in twenty-nine cities across the nation) are employed in full- or part-time jobs. [Ehrenreich's note.]

for pills to control the migraines she wouldn't have, she insists, if her estrogen supplements were covered. Similarly, Marianne's boyfriend lost his job as a roofer because he missed so much time after getting a cut on his foot for which he couldn't afford the prescribed antibiotic.

My own situation, when I sit down to assess it after two weeks of work, would not be much better if this were my actual life. The seductive thing about waitressing is that you don't have to wait for payday to feel a few bills in your pocket, and my tips usually cover meals and gas, plus something left over to stuff into the kitchen drawer I use as a bank. But as the tourist business slows in the summer heat, I sometimes leave work with only $20 in tips (the gross is higher, but servers share about 15 percent of their tips with the busboys and bartenders). With wages included, this amounts to about the minimum wage of $5.15 an hour. The sum in the drawer is piling up but at the present rate of accumulation will be more than $100 short of my rent when the end of the month comes around. Nor can I see any expenses to cut. True, I haven't gone the lentil stew route yet, but that's because I don't have a large cooking pot, potholders, or a ladle to stir with (which would cost a total of about $30 at Kmart, somewhat less at a thrift store), not to mention onions, carrots, and the indispensable bay leaf. I do make my lunch almost every day — usually some slow-burning, high-protein combo like frozen chicken patties with melted cheese on top and canned pinto beans on the side. Dinner is at the Hearthside, which offers its employees a choice of BLT, fish sandwich, or hamburger for only $2. The burger lasts longest, especially if it's heaped with gut-puckering jalapeños, but by midnight my stomach is growling again.

So unless I want to start using my car as a residence, I have to 10
find a second or an alternative job. I call all the hotels I'd filled out housekeeping applications at weeks ago — the Hyatt, Holiday Inn, Econo Lodge, HoJo's, Best Western, plus a half dozen locally run guest houses. Nothing. Then I start making the rounds again, wasting whole mornings waiting for some assistant manger to show up, even dipping into places so creepy that the front-desk clerk greets you from behind bullet-proof glass and sells pints of liquor over the counter. But either someone has exposed my real-life housekeeping habits — which are, shall we say, mellow — or I am at the wrong end of some infallible ethnic equation: most, but

by no means all, of the working housekeepers I see on my job searches are African Americans, Spanish-speaking, or refugees from the Central European post-Communist world, while servers are almost invariably white and monolingually English-speaking. When I finally get a positive response, I have been identified once again as server material. Jerry's — again, not the real name — which is part of a well-known national chain and physically attached here to another budget hotel, is ready to use me at once. The prospect is both exciting and terrifying because, with about the same number of tables and counter seats, Jerry's attracts three or four times the volume of customers as the gloomy old Hearthside.

Picture a fat person's hell, and I don't mean a place with no food. Instead there is everything you might eat if eating had no bodily consequences — the cheese fries, the chicken-fried steaks, the fudge-laden desserts — only here every bit must be paid for, one way or another, in human discomfort. The kitchen is a cavern, a stomach leading to the lower intestine that is the garbage and dishwashing area, from which issue bizarre smells combining the edible and the offal: creamy carrion, pizza barf, and that unique and enigmatic Jerry's scent, citrus fart. The floor is slick with spills, forcing us to walk through the kitchen with tiny steps, like Susan McDougal in leg irons. Sinks everywhere are clogged with scraps of lettuce, decomposing lemon wedges, water-logged toast crusts. Put your hand down on any counter and you risk being stuck to it by the film of ancient syrup spills, and this is unfortunate because hands are utensils here, used for scooping up lettuce onto the salad plates, lifting out pie slices, and even moving hash browns from one plate to another. The regulation poster in the single unisex rest room admonishes us to wash our hands thoroughly, and even offers instructions for doing so, but there is always some vital substance missing — soap, paper towels, toilet paper — and I never found all three at once. You learn to stuff your pockets with napkins before going in there, and too bad about the customers, who must eat, although they don't realize it, almost literally out of our hands.

The break room summarizes the whole situation: there is none, because there are no breaks at Jerry's. For six to eight hours in a row, you never sit except to pee. Actually, there are three folding chairs at a table immediately adjacent to the bathroom, but hardly anyone ever sits in this, the very rectum of the gastroarchitectural system. Rather, the function of the peri-toilet area is to house the ashtrays in which servers and dishwashers leave their cigarettes burning at all times, like votive candles, so they don't have to waste time lighting up again when they dash back here for a puff. Almost everyone smokes as if their pulmonary well-being depended on it — the multinational mélange of cooks; the dishwashers, who are all Czechs here; the servers, who are American natives — creating an atmosphere in which oxygen is only an occasional pollutant. My first morning at Jerry's, when the hypoglycemic shakes set in, I complain to one of my fellow servers that I don't understand how she can go so long without food. "Well, I don't understand how *you* can go so long without a cigarette," she responds in a tone of reproach. Because work is what you do for others; smoking is what you do for yourself. I don't know why the antismoking crusaders have never grasped the element of defiant self-nurturance that makes the habit so endearing to its victims — as if, in the American workplace, the only thing people have to call their own is the tumors they are nourishing and the spare moments they devote to feeding them.

Now, the Industrial Revolution is not an easy transition, especially, in my experience, when you have to zip through it in just a couple of days. I have gone from craft work straight into the factory, from the air-conditioned morgue of the Hearthside directly into the flames. Customers arrive in human waves, sometimes disgorged fifty at a time from their tour buses, puckish and whiny. Instead of two "girls" on the floor at once, there can be as many as six of us running around in our brilliant pink-and-orange Hawaiian shirts. Conversations, either with customers or with fellow employees, seldom last more than twenty seconds at a time. On my first day, in fact, I am hurt by my sister servers' coldness. My mentor for the day is a supremely competent, emotionally uninflected twenty-three-year-old, and the others, who gossip a little among themselves about the real reason someone is out sick today and the size of the bail bond someone else has had to pay, ignore me completely. On my second day, I find out why. "Well, it's good to see *you* again," one of them says in greeting. "Hardly anyone comes back after the first day." I feel powerfully vindicated — a survivor — but it would take a long time, probably months, before I could hope to be accepted into this sorority.

I start out with the beautiful, heroic idea of handling the two jobs at once, and for two days I almost do it: working the breakfast/lunch shift at Jerry's from 8:00 till 2:00, arriving at the Hearthside a few minutes late, at 2:10, and attempting to hold out until 10:00. In the few minutes I have between jobs, I pick up a spicy chicken sandwich at the Wendy's drive-through window, gobble it down in the car, and change from khaki slacks to black, from Hawaiian to rust-colored polo. There is a problem, though. When, during the 3:00–4:00 o'clock dead time, I finally sit down to wrap silver, my flesh seems to bond to the seat. I try to refuel with a purloined cup of clam chowder, as I've seen Gail and Joan do dozens of times, but Stu catches me and hisses "No *eating!*" although there's not a customer around to be offended by the sight of food making contact with a server's lips. So I tell Gail I'm going to quit, and she hugs me and says she might just follow me to Jerry's herself.

15 But the chances of this are minuscule. She has left the flophouse and her annoying roommate and is back to living in her truck. But, guess what, she reports to me excitedly later that evening. Phillip has given her permission to park overnight in the hotel parking lot, as long as she keeps out of sight, and the parking lot should be totally safe since it's patrolled by a hotel security guard! With the Hearthside offering benefits like that, how could anyone think of leaving? This must be Phillip's theory, anyway. He accepts my resignation with a shrug, his main concern being that I return my two polo shirts and aprons.

Gail would have triumphed at Jerry's, I'm sure, but for me it's a crash course in exhaustion management. Years ago, the kindly fry cook who trained me to waitress at a Los Angeles truck stop used to say: Never make an unnecessary trip; if you don't have to walk fast, walk slow; if you don't have to walk, stand. But at Jerry's the effort of distinguishing necessary from unnecessary and urgent from whenever would itself be too much of an energy drain. The only thing to do is to treat each shift as a one-time-only emergency: you've got fifty starving people out there, lying scattered on the battlefield, so get out there and feed them! Forget that you will have to do this again tomorrow, forget that you will have to be alert enough to dodge the drunks on the drive home tonight — just burn, burn, burn! Ideally, at some point you enter what servers call a "rhythm" and psychologists term a "flow state," where signals pass from the sense organs directly to the muscles, bypassing the cerebral cortex, and a Zen-like emptiness sets in. I'm on a 2:00–10:00 P.M. shift now, and a male server from the morning shift tells me about the time he "pulled a triple" — three shifts in a row, all the way around the clock — and then got off and had a drink and met this girl, and maybe he shouldn't tell me this, but they had sex right then and there and it was like *beautiful*. . . .

For Discussion and Writing

1. Why is Ehrenreich working as a waitress?
2. Ehrenreich builds her argument about the difficulties of living on minimum or near-minimum wage through her use of examples. Her argument is well-constructed and her examples plentiful, but the effectiveness of many of her examples comes from their being part of a story. By looking closely at one of the stories she tells about her experiences and the experiences of the men and women she works with, describe how Ehrenreich embeds examples in stories about individuals.
3. **connections** Lars Eighner's "On Dumpster Diving" (p. 146) makes most of its readers rethink homelessness. Similarly, Ehrenreich's piece makes us rethink employment: contrary to what many comfortable middle- or upper-class people might think, it is clear from "Serving in Florida" that employed people can be homeless or at least in a precarious financial position. With regard to the way in which these pieces make us rethink ways of life, how are Ehrenreich's and Eighner's pieces similar? How are they different?
4. One of the key points of comparison between "Serving in Florida" and Lars Eighner's "On Dumpster Diving" (p. 146) is the position of the writer in relation to the life he or she is describing. It is also a point of contrast, as Eighner was homeless when he wrote his book, while Ehrenreich was only living as a wage worker in order to write her book. Write a dialogue between the two writers in which they discuss this difference. Might Eighner challenge Ehrenreich? Or praise her? How might she defend herself?

LARS EIGHNER

On Dumpster Diving

Born in Texas in 1948, Lars Eighner became famous with the publication of his memoir Travels with Lizbeth: Three Years on the Road and on the Streets *(1993). The memoir of his (and his dog's) homelessness,* Travels with Lizbeth *was a great success but was not enough to keep Eighner and Lizbeth off the streets. Eventually with the support of friends, new housing was found for them, but Lizbeth died in 1998. Eighner continues to write fiction, essays, and erotica, and has a new dog named Wilma.*

"On Dumpster Diving" is the essay that led to the writing of what was to become the rest of Travels with Lizbeth. *In it Eighner explains one aspect of his life during the three hard years that are the subject of his memoir — the process of feeding himself from the refuse of others. The clear-eyed way in which he describes this process and the manner in which he situates it in the larger culture make this essay worthy of careful reading.*

Long before I began Dumpster diving I was impressed with Dumpsters, enough so that I wrote the Merriam-Webster research service to discover what I could about the word "Dumpster." I learned from them that "Dumpster" is a proprietary word belonging to the Dempster Dumpster company.

Since then I have dutifully capitalized the word although it was lowercased in almost all of the citations Merriam-Webster photocopied for me. Dempster's word is too apt. I have never heard these things called anything but Dumpsters. I do not know anyone who knows the generic name for these objects. From time to time, however, I hear a wino or hobo give some corrupted credit to the original and call them Dipsy Dumpsters.

I began Dumpster diving about a year before I became homeless.

I prefer the term "scavenging" and use the word "scrounging" when I mean to be obscure. I have heard people, evidently meaning to be polite, using the word "foraging," but I prefer to reserve that word for gathering nuts and berries and such which I do also according to the season and the opportunity. "Dumpster diving" seems to me to be a little too cute and, in my case, inaccurate because I lack the athletic ability to lower myself into the Dumpsters as the true divers do, much to their increased profit.

5 I like the frankness of the word "scavenging," which I can hardly think of without picturing a big black snail on an aquarium wall. I live from the refuse of others. I am a scavenger. I think it a sound and honorable niche, although if I could I would naturally prefer to live the comfortable consumer life, perhaps — and only perhaps — as a slightly less wasteful consumer owing to what I have learned as a scavenger.

While my dog Lizbeth and I were still living in the house on Avenue B in Austin, as my savings ran out, I put almost all my sporadic income into rent. The necessities of daily life I began to extract from Dumpsters. Yes, we ate from Dumpsters. Except for jeans, all my clothes came from Dumpsters. Boom boxes, candles, bedding, toilet paper, medicine, books, a typewriter, a virgin male love doll, change sometimes amounting to many dollars: I acquired many things from the Dumpsters.

I have learned much as a scavenger. I mean to put some of what I have learned down here, beginning with the practical art of Dumpster diving and proceeding to the abstract.

What is safe to eat?

After all, the finding of objects is becoming something of an urban art. Even respectable employed people will sometimes find something tempting sticking out of a Dumpster or standing beside one. Quite a number of people, not all of them of the bohemian type, are willing to brag that they found this or that piece in the trash. But eating from Dumpsters is the thing that separates the dilettanti from the professionals.

10 Eating safely from the Dumpsters involves three principles: using the senses and common sense to evaluate the condition of the found materials, knowing the Dumpsters of a given area and checking them regularly, and seeking always to answer the question "Why was this discarded?"

Perhaps everyone who has a kitchen and a regular supply of groceries has, at one time or another, made a sandwich and eaten half of it before discovering mold on the bread or got a mouthful of milk before realizing the milk had turned. Nothing of the sort is likely to happen to a Dumpster diver because he is constantly reminded that most food is discarded for a reason. Yet a lot of perfectly good food can be found in Dumpsters.

Canned goods, for example, turn up fairly often in the Dumpsters I frequent. All except the most phobic people would be willing to eat from a can even if it came from a Dumpster. Canned goods are among the safest of foods to be found in Dumpsters, but are not utterly foolproof.

Although very rare with modern canning methods, botulism is a possibility. Most other forms of food poisoning seldom do lasting harm to a healthy person. But botulism is almost certainly fatal and often the first symptom is death. Except for carbonated beverages, all canned goods should contain a slight vacuum and suck air when first punctured. Bulging, rusty, dented cans and cans that spew when punctured should be avoided, especially when the contents are not very acidic or syrupy.

Heat can break down the botulin, but this requires much more cooking than most people do to canned goods. To the extent that botulism occurs at all, of course, it can occur in cans on pantry shelves as well as in cans from Dumpsters. Need I say that home-canned goods found in Dumpsters are simply too risky to be recommended.

From time to time one of my companions, aware of the source 15
of my provisions, will ask, "Do you think these crackers are really safe to eat?" For some reason it is most often the crackers they ask about.

This question always makes me angry. Of course I would not offer my companion anything I had doubts about. But more than that I wonder why he cannot evaluate the condition of the crackers for himself. I have no special knowledge and I have been wrong before. Since he knows where the food comes from, it seems to me he ought to assume some of the responsibility for deciding what he will put in his mouth.

For myself I have few qualms about dry foods such as crackers, cookies, cereal, chips, and pasta if they are free of visible contaminates and still dry and crisp. Most often such things are found in the original packaging, which is not so much a positive sign as it is the absence of a negative one.

Raw fruits and vegetables with intact skins seem perfectly safe to me, excluding of course the obviously rotten. Many are discarded for minor imperfections which can be pared away. Leafy vegetables, grapes, cauliflower, broccoli, and similar things may be contaminated by liquids and may be impractical to wash.

Candy, especially hard candy, is usually safe if it has not drawn ants. Chocolate is often discarded only because it has become discolored as the cocoa butter de-emulsified. Candying after all is one method of food preservation because pathogens do not like very sugary substances.

20 All of these foods might be found in any Dumpster and can be evaluated with some confidence largely on the basis of appearance. Beyond these are foods which cannot be correctly evaluated without additional information.

I began scavenging by pulling pizzas out of the Dumpster behind a pizza delivery shop. In general prepared food requires caution, but in this case I knew when the shop closed and went to the Dumpster as soon as the last of the help left.

Such shops often get prank orders, called "bogus." Because help seldom stays long at these places pizzas are often made with the wrong topping, refused on delivery for being cold, or baked incorrectly. The products to be discarded are boxed up because inventory is kept by counting boxes: A boxed pizza can be written off; an unboxed pizza does not exist.

I never placed a bogus order to increase the supply of pizzas and I believe no one else was scavenging in this Dumpster. But the people in the shop became suspicious and began to retain their garbage in the shop overnight.

While it lasted I had a steady supply of fresh, sometimes warm pizza. Because I knew the Dumpster I knew the source of the pizza, and because I visited the Dumpster regularly I knew what was fresh and what was yesterday's.

25 The area I frequent is inhabited by many affluent college students. I am not here by chance; the Dumpsters in this area are very rich. Students throw out many good things, including food. In particular they tend to throw everything out when they move at the end of a semester, before and after breaks, and around midterm when many of them despair of college. So I find it advantageous to keep an eye on the academic calendar.

The students throw food away around the breaks because they do not know whether it has spoiled or will spoil before they return. A typical discard is a half jar of peanut butter. In fact nonorganic peanut butter does not require refrigeration and is unlikely to spoil in any reasonable time. The student does not know that, and since it is Daddy's money, the student decides not to take a chance.

Opened containers require caution and some attention to the question "Why was this discarded?" But in the case of discards from student apartments, the answer may be that the item was discarded through carelessness, ignorance, or wastefulness. This can sometimes be deduced when the item is found with many others, including some that are obviously perfectly good.

Some students, and others, approach defrosting a freezer by chucking out the whole lot. Not only do the circumstances of such a find tell the story, but also the mass of frozen goods stays cold for a long time and items may be found still frozen or freshly thawed.

Yogurt, cheese, and sour cream are items that are often thrown out while they are still good. Occasionally I find a cheese with a spot of mold, which of course I just pare off, and because it is obvious why such a cheese was discarded, I treat it with less suspicion than an apparently perfect cheese found in similar circumstances. Yogurt is often discarded, still sealed, only because the expiration date on the carton had passed. This is one of my favorite finds because yogurt will keep for several days, even in warm weather.

Students throw out canned goods and staples at the end of 30
semesters and when they give up college at midterm. Drugs, pornography, spirits, and the like are often discarded when parents are expected — Dad's day, for example. And spirits also turn up after big party weekends, presumably discarded by the newly reformed. Wine and spirits, of course, keep perfectly well even once opened.

My test for carbonated soft drinks is whether they still fizz vigorously. Many juices or other beverages are too acid or too syrupy to cause much concern provided they are not visibly contaminated. Liquids, however, require some care.

One hot day I found a large jug of Pat O'Brien's Hurricane mix. The jug had been opened, but it was still ice cold. I drank three large glasses before it became apparent to me that someone had added the rum to the mix, and not a little rum. I never tasted the rum and by the time I began to feel the effects I had already ingested a very large quantity of the beverage. Some divers would have considered this a boon, but being suddenly and thoroughly intoxicated in a public place in the early afternoon is not my idea of a good time.

I have heard of people maliciously contaminating discarded food and even handouts, but mostly I have heard of this from people with vivid imaginations who have had no experience with the Dumpsters themselves. Just before the pizza shop stopped discarding its garbage at night, jalapeños began showing up on most of the discarded pizzas. If indeed this was meant to discourage me it was a wasted effort because I am native Texan.

For myself, I avoid game, poultry, pork, and egg-based foods whether I find them raw or cooked. I seldom have the means to cook what I find, but when I do I avail myself of plentiful supplies of beef which is often in very good condition. I suppose fish becomes disagreeable before it becomes dangerous. The dog is happy to have any such thing that is past its prime and, in fact, does not recognize fish as food until it is quite strong.

Home leftovers, as opposed to surpluses from restaurants, are 35
very often bad. Evidently, especially among students, there is a common type of personality that carefully wraps up even the smallest leftover and shoves it into the back of the refrigerator for six months or so before discarding it. Characteristic of this type are the reused jars and margarine tubs which house the remains.

I avoid ethnic foods I am unfamiliar with. If I do not know what it is supposed to look like when it is good, I cannot be certain I will be able to tell if it is bad.

No matter how careful I am I still get dysentery at least once a month, oftener in warm weather. I do not want to paint too romantic a picture. Dumpster diving has serious drawbacks as a way of life.

I learned to scavenge gradually, on my own. Since then I have initiated several companions into the trade. I have learned that there is a predictable series of stages a person goes through in learning to scavenge.

At first the new scavenger is filled with disgust and self-loathing. He is ashamed of being seen and may lurk around, trying to duck behind things, or he may try to dive at night.

(In fact, most people instinctively look away from a scavenger. 40
By skulking around, the novice calls attention to himself and

arouses suspicion. Diving at night is ineffective and needlessly messy.)

Every grain of rice seems to be a maggot. Everything seems to stink. He can wipe the egg yolk off the found can, but he cannot erase the stigma of eating garbage out of his mind.

That stage passes with experience. The scavenger finds a pair of running shoes that fit and look and smell brand new. He finds a pocket calculator in perfect working order. He finds pristine ice cream, still frozen, more than he can eat or keep. He begins to understand: People do throw away perfectly good stuff, a lot of perfectly good stuff.

At this stage, Dumpster shyness begins to dissipate. The diver, after all, has the last laugh. He is finding all manner of good things which are his for the taking. Those who disparage his profession are the fools, not he.

He may begin to hang onto some perfectly good things for which he has neither a use nor a market. Then he begins to take note of the things which are not perfectly good but are nearly so. He mates a Walkman with broken earphones and one that is missing a battery cover. He picks up things which he can repair.

At this stage he may become lost and never recover. Dumpsters 45
are full of things of some potential value to someone and also of things which never have much intrinsic value but are interesting. All the Dumpster divers I have known come to the point of trying to acquire everything they touch. Why not take it, they reason, since it is all free.

This is, of course, hopeless. Most divers come to realize that they must restrict themselves to items of relatively immediate utility. But in some cases the diver simply cannot control himself. I have met several of these pack-rat types. Their ideas of the values of various pieces of junk verge on the psychotic. Every bit of glass may be a diamond, they think, and all that glistens, gold.

I tend to gain weight when I am scavenging. Partly this is because I always find far more pizza and doughnuts than water-packed tuna, nonfat yogurt, and fresh vegetables. Also I have not developed much faith in the reliability of Dumpsters as a food source, although it has been proven to me many times. I tend to eat as if I have no idea where my next meal is coming from. But mostly I just hate to see food go to waste and so I eat much more than I should. Something like this drives the obsession to collect junk.

As for collecting objects, I usually restrict myself to collecting one kind of small object at a time, such as pocket calculators, sunglasses, or campaign buttons. To live on the street I must anticipate my needs to a certain extent: I must pick up and save warm bedding I find in August because it will not be found in Dumpsters in November. But even if I had a home with extensive storage space I could not save everything that might be valuable in some contingency.

I have proprietary feelings about my Dumpsters. As I have suggested, it is no accident that I scavenge from Dumpsters where good finds are common. But my limited experience with Dumpsters in other areas suggests to me that it is the population of competitors rather than the affluence of the dumpers that most affects the feasibility of survival by scavenging. The large number of competitors is what puts me off the idea of trying to scavenge in places like Los Angeles.

50 Curiously, I do not mind my direct competition, other scavengers, so much as I hate the can scroungers.

People scrounge cans because they have to have a little cash. I have tried scrounging cans with an able-bodied companion. Afoot a can scrounger simply cannot make more than a few dollars a day. One can extract the necessities of life from the Dumpsters directly with far less effort than would be required to accumulate the equivalent value in cans.

Can scroungers, then, are people who *must* have small amounts of cash. These are drug addicts and winos, mostly the latter because the amounts of cash are so small.

Spirits and drugs do, like all other commodities, turn up in Dumpsters and the scavenger will from time to time have a half bottle of a rather good wine with his dinner. But the wino cannot survive on these occasional finds; he must have his daily dose to stave off the DTs. All the cans he can carry will buy about three bottles of Wild Irish Rose.

I do not begrudge them the cans, but can scroungers tend to tear up the Dumpsters, mixing the contents and littering the area. They become so specialized that they can see only cans. They earn my contempt by passing up change, canned goods, and readily hockable items.

55 There are precious few courtesies among scavengers. But it is a common practice to set aside surplus items: pairs of shoes, clothing, canned goods, and such. A true scavenger hates to see good

stuff go to waste and what he cannot use he leaves in good condition in plain sight.

Can scroungers lay waste to everything in their path and will stir one of a pair of good shoes to the bottom of a Dumpster, to be lost or ruined in the muck. Can scroungers will even go through individual garbage cans, something I have never seen a scavenger do.

Individual garbage cans are set out on the public easement only on garbage days. On other days going through them requires trespassing close to a dwelling. Going through individual garbage cans without scattering litter is almost impossible. Litter is likely to reduce the public's tolerance of scavenging. Individual garbage cans are simply not as productive as Dumpsters; people in houses and duplexes do not move as often and for some reason do not tend to discard as much useful material. Moreover, the time required to go through one garbage can that serves one household is not much less than the time required to go through a Dumpster that contains the refuse of twenty apartments.

But my strongest reservation about going through individual garbage cans is that this seems to me a very personal kind of invasion to which I would object if I were a householder. Although many things in Dumpsters are obviously meant never to come to light, a Dumpster is somehow less personal.

I avoid trying to draw conclusions about the people who dump in the Dumpsters I frequent. I think it would be unethical to do so, although I know many people will find the idea of scavenger ethics too funny for words.

Dumpsters contain bank statements, bills, correspondence, 60
and other documents, just as anyone might expect. But there are also less obvious sources of information. Pill bottles, for example. The labels on pill bottles contain the name of the patient, the name of the doctor, and the name of the drug. AIDS drugs and antipsychotic medicines, to name but two groups, are specific and are seldom prescribed for any other disorders. The plastic compacts for birth control pills usually have complete label information.

Despite all of this sensitive information, I have had only one apartment resident object to my going through the Dumpster. In that case it turned out the resident was a university athlete who was taking bets and who was afraid I would turn up his wager slips.

Occasionally a find tells a story. I once found a small paper bag containing some unused condoms, several partial tubes of flavored sexual lubricant, a partially used compact of birth control pills, and the torn pieces of a picture of a young man. Clearly she was through with him and planning to give up sex altogether.

Dumpster things are often sad — abandoned teddy bears, shredded wedding books, despaired-of sales kits. I find many pets lying in state in Dumpsters. Although I hope to get off the streets so that Lizbeth can have a long and comfortable old age, I know this hope is not very realistic. So I suppose when her time comes she too will go into a Dumpster. I will have no better place for her. And after all, for most of her life her livelihood has come from the Dumpster. When she finds something I think is safe that has been spilled from the Dumpster I let her have it. She already knows the route around the best Dumpsters. I like to think that if she survives me she will have a chance of evading the dog catcher and of finding her sustenance on the route.

Silly vanities also come to rest in the Dumpsters. I am a rather accomplished needleworker. I get a lot of materials from the Dumpsters. Evidently sorority girls, hoping to impress someone, perhaps themselves, with their mastery of a womanly art, buy a lot of embroider-by-number kits, work a few stitches horribly, and eventually discard the whole mess. I pull out their stitches, turn the canvas over, and work an original design. Do not think I refrain from chuckling as I make original gifts from these kits.

65 I find diaries and journals. I have often thought of compiling a book of literary found objects. And perhaps I will one day. But what I find is hopelessly commonplace and bad without being, even unconsciously, camp. College students also discard their papers. I am horrified to discover the kind of paper which now merits an A in an undergraduate course. I am grateful, however, for the number of good books and magazines the students throw out.

In the area I know best I have never discovered vermin in the Dumpsters, but there are two kinds of kitty surprise. One is alley cats which I meet as they leap, claws first, out of Dumpsters. This is especially thrilling when I have Lizbeth in tow. The other kind of kitty surprise is a plastic garbage bag filled with some ponderous, amorphous mass. This always proves to be used cat litter.

City bees harvest doughnut glaze and this makes the Dumpster at the doughnut shop more interesting. My faith in the instinctive wisdom of animals is always shaken whenever I see Lizbeth attempt to catch a bee in her mouth, which she does whenever bees are present. Evidently some birds find Dumpsters profitable, for birdie surprise is almost as common as kitty surprise of the first kind. In hunting season all kinds of small game turn up in Dumpsters, some of it, sadly, not entirely dead. Curiously, summer and winter, maggots are uncommon.

The worst of the living and near-living hazards of the Dumpsters are the fire ants. The food that they claim is not much of a loss, but they are vicious and aggressive. It is very easy to brush against some surface of the Dumpster and pick up half a dozen or more fire ants, usually in some sensitive area such as the underarm. One advantage of bringing Lizbeth along as I make Dumpster rounds is that, for obvious reasons, she is very alert to ground-based fire ants. When Lizbeth recognizes the signs of fire ant infestation around our feet she does the Dance of the Zillion Fire Ants. I have learned not to ignore this warning from Lizbeth, whether I perceive the tiny ants or not, but to remove ourselves at Lizbeth's first pas de bourrée.° All the more so because the ants are the worst in the months I wear flip-flops, if I have them.

(Perhaps someone will misunderstand the above. Lizbeth does the Dance of the Zillion Fire Ants when she recognizes more fire ants than she cares to eat, not when she is being bitten. Since I have learned to react promptly, she does not get bitten at all. It is the isolated patrol of fire ants that falls in Lizbeth's range that deserves pity. Lizbeth finds them quite tasty.)

By far the best way to go through a Dumpster is to lower your- 70
self into it. Most of the good stuff tends to settle at the bottom because it is usually weightier than the rubbish. My more athletic companions have often demonstrated to me that they can extract much good material from a Dumpster I have already been over.

To those psychologically or physically unprepared to enter a Dumpster, I recommend a stout stick, preferably with some barb or hook at one end. The hook can be used to grab plastic garbage bags. When I find canned goods or other objects loose at the bottom of a Dumpster I usually can roll them into a small bag that I

pas de bourrée: A ballet step (French). [Ed.]

can then hoist up. Much Dumpster diving is a matter of experience for which nothing will do except practice.

Dumpster diving is outdoor work, often surprisingly pleasant. It is not entirely predictable; things of interest turn up every day and some days there are finds of great value. I am always very pleased when I can turn up exactly the thing I most wanted to find. Yet in spite of the element of change, scavenging more than most other pursuits tends to yield returns in some proportion to the effort and intelligence brought to bear. It is very sweet to turn up a few dollars in change from a Dumpster that has just been gone over by a wino.

The land is now covered with cities. The cities are full of Dumpsters. I think of scavenging as a modern form of self-reliance. In any event, after ten years of government service, where everything is geared to the lowest common denominator, I find work that rewards initiative and effort refreshing. Certainly I would be happy to have a sinecure again, but I am not heartbroken not to have one anymore.

I find from the experience of scavenging two rather deep lessons. The first is to take what I can use and let the rest go by. I have come to think that there is no value in the abstract. A thing I cannot use or make useful, perhaps by trading, has no value however fine or rare it may be. I mean useful in a broad sense — so, for example, some art I would think useful and valuable, but other art might be otherwise for me.

I was shocked to realize that some things are not worth acquir- 75
ing, but now I think it is so. Some material things are white elephants that eat up the possessor's substance.

The second lesson is of the transience of material being. This has not quite converted me to a dualist, but it has made some headway in that direction. I do not suppose that ideas are immortal, but certainly mental things are longer-lived than other material things.

Once I was the sort of person who invests material objects with sentimental value. Now I no longer have those things, but I have the sentiments yet.

Many times in my travels I have lost everything but the clothes I was wearing and Lizbeth. The things I find in Dumpsters, the love letters and ragdolls of so many lives, remind me of this lesson. Now I hardly pick up a thing without envisioning the time I will cast it away. This I think is a healthy state of mind. Almost everything I have now has already been cast out at least once, proving that what I own is valueless to someone.

Anyway, I find my desire to grab for the gaudy bauble has been largely sated. I think this is an attitude I share with the very wealthy — we both know there is plenty more where what we have came from. Between us are the rat-race millions who have confounded their selves with the objects they grasp and who nightly scavenge the cable channels looking for they know not what.

I am sorry for them. 80

For Discussion and Writing

1. Eighner is careful to offer definitions of the key terms he uses. List those key terms and their definitions.
2. Summarize Eighner's analysis of the practical stages through which a beginning Dumpster diver goes. What does his analysis tell us about the larger experience of having to scavenge for food? What does his writing style tell you about his views on his way of life?
3. **connections** Compare the "deep lessons" (par. 74) Eighner finds in scavenging to those found in living in the woods by Henry David Thoreau, as explained in "Where I Lived, and What I Lived For" (p. 403). How do their views of what Eighner calls "the rat-race millions" (par. 79) differ, and how could that difference be explained by the course each took to the way of life each describes?
4. How does reading Eighner make you feel about your own material values? How do you relate to Dumpster diving and to what he calls the "grab for the gaudy bauble" (par. 79)?

STEPHANIE ERICSSON

The Ways We Lie

A screenwriter and advertising copywriter, Stephanie Ericsson, born in 1953 and raised in San Francisco, is also an author of self-help books, including Companion through the Darkness: Inner Dialogues on Grief *(1993). "The Ways We Lie" originally appeared in the* Utne Reader. *Consider, as you read, how Ericsson breaks down the activity of lying into the different kinds of lies we tell but also manages to pull together the different sections of her essay to make a larger point about the role lying plays in our lives and our culture.*

The bank called today and I told them my deposit was in the mail, even though I hadn't written a check yet. It'd been a rough day. The baby I'm pregnant with decided to do aerobics on my lungs for two hours, our three-year-old daughter painted the living-room couch with lipstick, the IRS put me on hold for an hour, and I was late to a business meeting because I was tired.

I told my client that traffic had been bad. When my partner came home, his haggard face told me his day hadn't gone any better than mine, so when he asked, "How was your day?" I said, "Oh, fine," knowing that one more straw might break his back. A friend called and wanted to take me to lunch. I said I was busy. Four lies in the course of a day, none of which I felt the least bit guilty about.

We lie. We all do. We exaggerate, we minimize, we avoid confrontation, we spare people's feelings, we conveniently forget, we keep secrets, we justify lying to the big-guy institutions. Like most people, I indulge in small falsehoods and still think of myself as an honest person. Sure I lie, but it doesn't hurt anything. Or does it?

I once tried going a whole week without telling a lie, and it was paralyzing. I discovered that telling the truth all the time is nearly impossible. It means living with some serious consequences: The bank charges me $60 in overdraft fees, my partner keels over when I tell him about my travails, my client fires me for telling her I didn't feel like being on time, and my friend takes it personally when I say I'm not hungry. There must be some merit to lying.

5 But if I justify lying, what makes me any different from slick politicians or the corporate robbers who raided the S&L industry? Saying it's okay to lie one way and not another is hedging. I cannot seem to escape the voice deep inside me that tells me: When someone lies, someone loses.

What far-reaching consequences will I, or others, pay as a result of my lie? Will someone's trust be destroyed? Will someone else pay *my* penance because I ducked out? We must consider the *meaning of our actions*. Deception, lies, capital crimes, and misdemeanors all carry meanings. *Webster's* definition of *lie* is specific:

1. a false statement or action especially made with the intent to deceive;
2. anything that gives or is meant to give a false impression.

A definition like this implies that there are many, many ways to tell a lie. Here are just a few.

THE WHITE LIE

> *A man who won't lie to a woman has very little consideration for her feelings.* — BERGEN EVANS

The white lie assumes that the truth will cause more damage than a simple, harmless untruth. Telling a friend he looks great when he looks like hell can be based on a decision that the friend needs a compliment more than a frank opinion. But, in effect, it is the liar deciding what is best for the lied to. Ultimately, it is a vote of no confidence. It is an act of subtle arrogance for anyone to decide what is best for someone else.

Yet not all circumstances are quite so cut-and-dried. Take, for instance, the sergeant in Vietnam who knew one of his men was killed in action but listed him as missing so that the man's family would receive indefinite compensation instead of the lump-sum pittance the military gives widows and children. His intent was honorable. Yet for twenty years this family kept their hopes alive, unable to move on to a new life.

FAÇADES

Et tu, Brute? — CAESAR

We all put up façades to one degree or another. When I put on a 10
suit to go to see a client, I feel as though I am putting on another face, obeying the expectation that serious businesspeople wear suits rather than sweatpants. But I'm a writer. Normally, I get up, get the kid off to school, and sit at my computer in my pajamas until four in the afternoon. When I answer the phone, the caller thinks I'm wearing a suit (though the UPS man knows better).

But façades can be destructive because they are used to seduce others into an illusion. For instance, I recently realized that a former friend was a liar. He presented himself with all the right looks and the right words and offered lots of new consciousness theories, fabulous books to read, and fascinating insights. Then I did some business with him, and the time came for him to pay me. He turned out to be all talk and no walk. I heard a plethora of reasonable excuses, including in-depth descriptions of the big break around the corner. In six months of work, I saw less than a hundred bucks. When I confronted him, he raised both eyebrows and tried to convince me that I'd heard him wrong, that he'd made no commitment to me. A simple investigation into his past revealed a crowded graveyard of disenchanted former friends.

IGNORING THE PLAIN FACTS

Well, you must understand that Father Porter is only human.
— A MASSACHUSETTS PRIEST

In the '60s, the Catholic Church in Massachusetts began hearing complaints that Father James Porter was sexually molesting children. Rather than relieving him of his duties, the ecclesiastical authorities simply moved him from one parish to another between 1960 and 1967, actually providing him with a fresh supply of unsuspecting families and innocent children to abuse. After treatment in 1967 for pedophilia, he went back to work, this time in Minnesota. The new diocese was aware of Father Porter's obsession with children, but they needed priests and recklessly believed treatment had cured him. More children were abused until he was relieved of his duties a year later. By his own admission, Porter may have abused as many as a hundred children.

Ignoring the facts may not in and of itself be a form of lying, but consider the context of this situation. If a lie is *a false action done with the intent to deceive,* then the Catholic Church's conscious covering for Porter created irreparable consequences. The church became a co-perpetrator with Porter.

DEFLECTING

> *When you have no basis for an argument, abuse the plaintiff.*
>
> — CICERO

I've discovered that I can keep anyone from seeing the true me by being selectively blatant. I set a precedent of being up-front about intimate issues, but I never bring up the things I truly want to hide; I just let people assume I'm revealing everything. It's an effective way of hiding.

Any good liar knows that the way to perpetuate an untruth is to 15
deflect attention from it. When Clarence Thomas exploded with accusations that the Senate hearings were a "high-tech lynching," he simply switched the focus from a highly charged subject to a radioactive subject. Rather than defending himself, he took the offensive and accused the country of racism. It was a brilliant maneuver. Racism is now politically incorrect in official circles — unlike sexual harassment, which still rewards those who can get away with it.

Some of the most skilled deflectors are passive-aggressive people who, when accused of inappropriate behavior, refuse to respond to the accusations. This you-don't-exist stance infuriates the accuser, who, understandably, screams something obscene out of frustration. The trap is sprung and the act of deflection successful, because now the passive-aggressive person can indignantly say, "Who can talk to someone as unreasonable as you?" The real issue is forgotten and the sins of the original victim become the focus. Feeling guilty of name-calling, the victim is fully tamed and crawls into a hole, ashamed. I have watched this fighting technique work thousands of times in disputes between men and women, and what I've learned is that the real culprit is not necessarily the one who swears the loudest.

OMISSION

The cruelest lies are often told in silence. — R. L. STEVENSON

Omission involves telling most of the truth minus one or two key facts whose absence changes the story completely. You break a pair of glasses that are guaranteed under normal use and get a new pair, without mentioning that the first pair broke during a rowdy game of basketball. Who hasn't tried something like that? But what about omission of information that could make a difference in how a person lives his or her life?

For instance, one day I found out that rabbinical legends tell of another woman in the Garden of Eden before Eve. I was stunned. The omission of the Sumerian goddess Lilith from Genesis — as well as her demonization by ancient misogynists as an embodiment of female evil — felt like spiritual robbery. I felt like I'd just found out my mother was really my stepmother. To take seriously the tradition that Adam was created out of the same mud as his equal counterpart, Lilith, redefines all of Judeo-Christian history.

Some renegade Catholic feminists introduced me to a view of Lilith that had been suppressed during the many centuries when this strong goddess was seen only as a spirit of evil. Lilith was a proud goddess who defied Adam's need to control her, attempted negotiations, and when this failed, said adios and left the Garden of Eden.

This omission of Lilith from the Bible was a patriarchal strat- 20
egy to keep women weak. Omitting the strong-woman archetype of Lilith from Western religions and starting the story with Eve the Rib has helped keep Christian and Jewish women believing they were the lesser sex for thousands of years.

STEREOTYPES AND CLICHÉS

Where opinion does not exist, the status quo becomes stereotyped and all originality is discouraged. — BERTRAND RUSSELL

Stereotype and cliché serve a purpose as a form of shorthand. Our need for vast amounts of information in nanoseconds has made the stereotype vital to modern communication. Unfortunately, it often shuts down original thinking, giving those hungry for the truth a candy bar of misinformation instead of a balanced meal. The stereotype explains a situation with just enough truth to seem unquestionable.

All the "isms" — racism, sexism, ageism, et al. — are founded on and fueled by the stereotype and the cliché, which are lies of exaggeration, omission, and ignorance. They are always dangerous. They take a single tree and make it a landscape. They destroy curiosity. They close minds and separate people. The single mother on welfare is assumed to be cheating. Any black male could tell you how much of his identity is obliterated daily by stereotypes. Fat people, ugly people, beautiful people, old people, large-breasted women, short men, the mentally ill, and the homeless all could tell you how much more they are like us than we want to think. I once admitted to a group of people that I had a mouth like a truck driver. Much to my surprise, a man stood up and said, "I'm a truck driver, and I never cuss." Needless to say, I was humbled.

GROUPTHINK

Who is more foolish, the child afraid of the dark, or the man afraid of the light? — MAURICE FREEHILL

Irving Janis, in *Victims of Group Think*, defines this sort of lie as a psychological phenomenon within decision-making groups in which loyalty to the group has become more important than any other value, with the result that dissent and the appraisal of alternatives are suppressed. If you've ever worked on a committee or in a corporation, you've encountered groupthink. It requires a combination of other forms of lying — ignoring facts, selective memory, omission, and denial, to name a few.

The textbook example of groupthink came on December 7, 1941. From as early as the fall of 1941, the warnings came in, one after another, that Japan was preparing for a massive military operation. The navy command in Hawaii assumed Pearl Harbor was invulnerable — the Japanese weren't stupid enough to attack the United States' most important base. On the other hand, racist stereotypes said the Japanese weren't smart enough to invent a torpedo effective in less than 60 feet of water (the fleet was docked in 30 feet); after all, US technology hadn't been able to do it.

On Friday, December 5, normal weekend leave was granted to 25
all the commanders at Pearl Harbor, even though the Japanese consulate in Hawaii was busy burning papers. Within the tight, good-ole-boy cohesiveness of the US command in Hawaii, the myth of invulnerability stayed well entrenched. No one in the group considered the alternatives. The rest is history.

OUT-AND-OUT LIES

> *The only form of lying that is beyond reproach is lying for its own sake.* — OSCAR WILDE

Of all the ways to lie, I like this one the best, probably because I get tired of trying to figure out the real meanings behind things. At least I can trust the bald-faced lie. I once asked my five-year-old nephew, "Who broke the fence?" (I had seen him do it.) He answered, "The murderers." Who could argue?

At least when this sort of lie is told it can be easily confronted. As the person who is lied to, I know where I stand. The bald-faced lie doesn't toy with my perceptions — it argues with them. It doesn't try to refashion reality, it tries to refute it. *Read my lips. . . .* No sleight of hand. No guessing. If this were the only form of lying, there would be no such things as floating anxiety or the adult-children-of-alcoholics movement.

DISMISSAL

> *Pay no attention to that man behind the curtain!*
> *I am the Great Oz!* — THE WIZARD OF OZ

Dismissal is perhaps the slipperiest of all lies. Dismissing feelings, perceptions, or even the raw facts of a situation ranks as a kind of lie that can do as much damage to a person as any other kind of lie.

The roots of many mental disorders can be traced back to the dismissal of reality. Imagine that a person is told from the time she is a tot that her perceptions are inaccurate. *"Mommy, I'm scared."* "No you're not, darling." *"I don't like that man next door, he makes me feel icky."* "Johnny, that's a terrible thing to say, of course you like him. You go over there right now and be nice to him."

I've often mused over the idea that madness is actually a sane 30
reaction to an insane world. Psychologist R. D. Laing supports this hypothesis in *Sanity, Madness and the Family*, an account of his investigation into the families of schizophrenics. The common thread that ran through all of the families he studied was a deliberate, staunch dismissal of the patient's perceptions from a very early age. Each of the patients started out with an accurate grasp of reality, which, through meticulous and methodical dismissal, was demolished until the only reality the patient could trust was catatonia.

Dismissal runs the gamut. Mild dismissal can be quite handy for forgiving the foibles of others in our day-to-day lives. Toddlers who have just learned to manipulate their parents' attention sometimes are dismissed out of necessity. Absolute attention from the parents would require so much energy that no one would get to eat dinner. But we must be careful and attentive about how far we take our "necessary" dismissals. Dismissal is a dangerous tool, because it's nothing less than a lie.

DELUSION

We lie loudest when we lie to ourselves. — ERIC HOFFER

I could write the book on this one. Delusion, a cousin of dismissal, is the tendency to see excuses as facts. It's a powerful lying tool because it filters out information that contradicts what we want to believe. Alcoholics who believe that the problems in their lives are legitimate reasons for drinking rather than results of the drinking offer the classic example of deluded thinking. Delusion uses the mind's ability to see things in myriad ways to support what it wants to be the truth.

But delusion is also a survival mechanism we all use. If we were to fully contemplate the consequences of our stockpiles of nuclear weapons or global warming, we could hardly function on a day-to-day level. We don't want to incorporate that much reality into our lives because to do so would be paralyzing.

Delusion acts as an adhesive to keep the status quo intact. It shamelessly employs dismissal, omission, and amnesia, among other sorts of lies. Its most cunning defense is that it cannot see itself.

The liar's punishment [. . .] is that he cannot believe anyone else.
— GEORGE BERNARD SHAW

35 These are only a few of the ways we lie. Or are lied to. As I said earlier, it's not easy to entirely eliminate lies from our lives. No matter how pious we may try to be, we will still embellish, hedge, and omit to lubricate the daily machinery of living. But there is a world of difference between telling functional lies and living a lie. Martin Buber once said, "The lie is the spirit committing treason against itself." Our acceptance of lies becomes a cultural cancer that eventually shrouds and reorders reality until moral garbage becomes as invisible to us as water is to a fish.

How much do we tolerate before we become sick and tired of being sick and tired? When will we stand up and declare our *right* to trust? When do we stop accepting that the real truth is in the fine print? Whose lips do we read this year when we vote for president? When will we stop being so reticent about making judgments? When do we stop turning over our personal power and responsibility to liars?

Maybe if I don't tell the bank the check's in the mail I'll be less tolerant of the lies told me every day. A country song I once heard said it all for me: "You've got to stand for something or you'll fall for anything."

For Discussion and Writing

1. What are the different kinds of lies Ericsson catalogs?
2. How many kinds of lies does Ericsson describe? How does the number of kinds of lies help her make her larger point about lying?
3. **connections** What might Ericsson have to say about what William F. Buckley Jr. describes in "Why Don't We Complain?" (p. 76).
4. Imagine a day in which you told no lies of any kind. Write a narrative telling the story of that day and the consequences of your total honesty.

STEPHEN JAY GOULD

Sex, Drugs, Disasters, and the Extinction of Dinosaurs

Born in 1941 and raised in New York City, Stephen Jay Gould was a foremost paleontologist and evolutionary biologist. His theory of punctuated equilibrium — which draws on Darwin's explanation of evolution — constitutes his major mark on science, but his popular science essays have made their own mark on the culture. Essays from his long-running column in Natural History *magazine were gathered into collections from* Ever Since Darwin: Reflections in Natural History *(1977) to* I Have Landed: The End of a Beginning in Natural History *(2002), and he wrote essays on a wide range of topics outside of science, including art, literature, music, and even baseball. His contribution to the art of the essay is reflected in his editorship of the 2002 volume of* Best American Essays. *His final contribution to evolutionary biology, published shortly before his death in 2002, was the massive overview of the field and a final argument for punctuated equilibrium,* The Structure of Evolutionary Theory *(2002), and in 2008, he was posthumously awarded the Darwin-Wallace Medal for advances in evolutionary biology.*

In "Sex, Drugs, Disasters, and the Extinction of Dinosaurs," Gould uses one of life's great unsolved mysteries — the extinction of dinosaurs — to demonstrate the brilliance of science as a discipline founded not on answers, but on questions.

Science, in its most fundamental definition, is a fruitful mode of inquiry, not a list of enticing conclusions. The conclusions are the consequence, not the essence.

My greatest unhappiness with most popular presentations of science concerns their failure to separate fascinating claims from the methods that scientists use to establish the facts of nature. Journalists, and the public, thrive on controversial and stunning statements. But science is, basically, a way of knowing — in P. B.

Medawar's apt words, "the art of the soluble." If the growing corps of popular science writers would focus on how scientists develop and defend those fascinating claims, they would make their greatest possible contribution to public understanding.

Consider three ideas, proposed in perfect seriousness to explain that greatest of all titillating puzzles — the extinction of dinosaurs. Since these three notions invoke the primally fascinating themes of our culture — sex, drugs, and violence — they surely reside in the category of fascinating claims. I want to show why two of them rank as silly speculation, while the other represents science at its grandest and most useful.

Science works with testable proposals. If, after much compilation and scrutiny of data, new information continues to affirm a hypothesis, we may accept it provisionally and gain confidence as further evidence mounts. We can never be completely sure that a hypothesis is right, though we may be able to show with confidence that it is wrong. The best scientific hypotheses are also generous and expansive; they suggest extensions and implications that enlighten related, and even far distance, subjects. Simply consider how the idea of evolution has influenced virtually every intellectual field.

5 Useless speculation, on the other hand, is restrictive. It generates no testable hypothesis, and offers no way to obtain potentially refuting evidence. Please note that I am not speaking of truth or falsity. The speculation may well be true; still, if it provides, in principle, no material for affirmation or rejection, we can make nothing of it. It must simply stand forever as an intriguing idea. Useless speculation turns in on itself and leads nowhere; good science, containing both seeds for its potential refutation and implications for more and different testable knowledge, reaches out. But, enough preaching. Let's move on to the dinosaurs, and the three proposals for their extinction.

1. **Sex:** Testes function only in a narrow range of temperature. (Those of mammals hang externally in a scrotal sac because internal body temperatures are too high for their proper function.) A worldwide rise in temperature at the close of the Cretaceous period caused the testes of dinosaurs to stop functioning and led to their extinction by sterilization of males.
2. **Drugs:** Angiosperms (flowering plants) first evolved toward the end of the dinosaurs' reign. Many of these plants contain psychoactive

agents, avoided by mammals today as a result of their bitter taste. Dinosaurs had neither means to taste the bitterness nor livers effective enough to detoxify the substances. They died of massive overdoses.

3. **Disasters:** A large comet or asteroid struck the earth some 65 million years ago, lofting a cloud of dust into the sky and blocking sunlight, thereby suppressing photosynthesis and so drastically lowering world temperatures that dinosaurs and hosts of other creatures became extinct.

Before analyzing these three tantalizing statements, we must establish a basic ground rule often violated in proposals for the dinosaurs' demise. *There is no separate problem of the extinction of the dinosaurs.* Too often we divorce specific events from their wider contexts and systems of cause and effect. The fundamental fact of dinosaur extinction is its synchrony with the demise of so many other groups across a wide range of habitats, from terrestrial to marine.

The history of life has been punctuated by brief episodes of mass extinction. A recent analysis by University of Chicago paleontologists Jack Sepkoski and Dave Raup, based on the best and most exhaustive tabulation of data ever assembled, shows clearly that five episodes of mass dying stand well above the "background" extinctions of normal times (when we consider all mass extinctions, large and small, they seem to fall in a regular 26-million-year cycle . . .). The Cretaceous debacle, occurring 65 million years ago and separating the Mesozoic and Cenozoic eras of our geological time scale, ranks prominently among the five. Nearly all the marine plankton (single-celled floating creatures) died with geological suddenness; among marine invertebrates, nearly 15 percent of all families perished, including many previously dominant groups, especially the ammonites (relatives of squids in coiled shells). On land, the dinosaurs disappeared after more than 100 million years of unchallenged domination.

In this context, speculations limited to dinosaurs alone ignore the larger phenomenon. We need a coordinated explanation for a system of events that includes the extinction of dinosaurs as one component. Thus it makes little sense, though it may fuel our desire to view mammals as inevitable inheritors of the earth, to guess that dinosaurs died because small mammals ate their eggs (a perennial favorite among untestable speculations). It seems most unlikely that some disaster peculiar to dinosaurs befell these massive beasts — and that the debacle happened to strike just when one of history's five great dyings had enveloped the earth for completely different reasons.

The testicular theory, an old favorite from the 1940s, had its root in an interesting and thoroughly respectable study of temperature tolerances in the American alligator, published in the staid *Bulletin of the American Museum of Natural History* in 1946 by three experts on living and fossil reptiles — E. H. Colbert, my own first teacher in paleontology; R. B. Cowles; and C. M. Bogert.

The first sentence of their summary reveals a purpose beyond 10
alligators: "This report describes an attempt to infer the reactions of extinct reptiles, especially the dinosaurs, to high temperatures as based upon reactions observed in the modern alligator." They studied, by rectal thermometry, the body temperatures of alligators under changing conditions of heating and cooling. (Well let's face it, you wouldn't want to try sticking a thermometer under a 'gator's tongue.) The predictions under test go way back to an old theory first stated by Galileo in the 1630s — the unequal scaling of surfaces and volumes. As an animal, or any object, grows (provided its shape doesn't change), surface areas must increase more slowly than volumes — since surfaces get larger as length squared, while volumes increase much more rapidly, as length cubed. Therefore, small animals have high ratios of surface to volume, while large animals cover themselves with relatively little surface.

Among cold-blooded animals lacking any physiological mechanism for keeping their temperatures constant, small creatures have a hell of a time keeping warm — because they lose so much heat through their relatively large surfaces. On the other hand, large animals, with their relatively small surfaces, may lose heat so slowly that, once warm, they may maintain effectively constant temperatures against ordinary fluctuations of climate. In fact, the resolution of the "hot-blooded dinosaur" controversy that burned so brightly a few years back may simply be that, while large dinosaurs possessed no physiological mechanism for constant temperature, and were not therefore warm-blooded in the technical sense, their large size and relatively small surface area kept them warm.

Colbert, Cowles, and Bogert compared the warming rates of small and large alligators. As predicted, the small fellows heated up (and cooled down) more quickly. When exposed to a warm sun, a tiny 50-gram (1.76 ounce) alligator heated up one degree Celsius every minute and a half, while a large alligator, 260 times bigger at 13,000 grams (28.7 pounds), took seven and a half minutes to gain a degree. Extrapolating up to an adult 10-ton dinosaur, they concluded that a one-degree rise in body temperature would take eighty-six hours. If large animals absorb heat so slowly (through their relatively small surfaces), they will also be able to shed any excess heat gained when temperatures rise above a favorable level.

The authors then guessed that large dinosaurs lived at or near their optimum temperatures. Cowles suggested that a rise in global temperatures just before the Cretaceous extinction caused the dinosaurs to heat up beyond their optimal tolerance — and, being so large, they couldn't shed the unwanted heat. (In a most unusual statement within a scientific paper, Colbert and Bogert then explicitly disavowed this speculative extension of their empirical work on alligators.) Cowles conceded that this excess heat probably wasn't enough to kill or even to enervate the great beasts, but since testes often function within a narrow range of temperature, he proposed that this global rise might have sterilized all the males, causing extinction by natural contraception.

The overdose theory has recently been supported by UCLA psychiatrist Ronald K. Siegel. Siegel has gathered, he claims, more than 2,000 records of animals who, when given access, administer various drugs to themselves — from a mere swig of alcohol to massive doses of the big H. Elephants will swill the equivalent of twenty beers at a time, but do not like alcohol in concentrations greater than 7 percent. In a silly bit of anthropocentric speculation, Siegel states that "elephants drink, perhaps, to forget . . . the anxiety produced by shrinking rangeland and the competition for food."

Since fertile imaginations can apply almost any hot idea to the 15
extinction of dinosaurs, Siegel found a way. Flowering plants did not evolve until late in the dinosaurs' reign. These plants also produced an array of aromatic, amino-acid-based alkaloids — the major group of psychoactive agents. Most mammals are "smart" enough to avoid these potential poisons. The alkaloids simply don't taste good (they are bitter); in any case, we mammals have livers happily supplied with the capacity to detoxify them. But,

Siegel speculates, perhaps dinosaurs could neither taste the bitterness nor detoxify the substances once ingested. He recently told members of the American Psychological Association: "I'm not suggesting that all dinosaurs OD'd on plant drugs, but it certainly was a factor." He also argued that death by overdose may help explain why so many dinosaur fossils are found in contorted positions. (Do not go gentle into that good night.)

Extraterrestrial catastrophes have long pedigrees in the popular literature of extinction, but the subject exploded again in 1979, after a long lull, when the father-son, physicist-geologist team of Luis and Walter Alvarez proposed that an asteroid, some 10 km in diameter, struck the earth 65 million years ago.

The force of such a collision would be immense, greater by far than the megatonnage of all the world's nuclear weapons. In trying to reconstruct a scenario that would explain the simultaneous dying of dinosaurs on land and so many creatures in the sea, the Alvarezes proposed that a gigantic dust cloud, generated by particles blown aloft in the impact, would so darken the earth that photosynthesis would cease and temperatures drop precipitously. (Rage, rage against the dying of the light.) The single-celled photosynthetic oceanic plankton, with life cycles measured in weeks, would perish outright, but land plants might survive through the dormancy of their seeds (land plants were not much affected by the Cretaceous extinction, and any adequate theory must account for the curious pattern of differential survival). Dinosaurs would die by starvation and freezing; small, warm-blooded mammals, with more modest requirements for food and better regulation of body temperature, would squeak through. "Let the bastards freeze in the dark," as bumper stickers of our chauvinistic neighbors in Sun Belt states proclaimed several years ago during the Northeast's winter oil crisis.

All three theories, testicular malfunction, psychoactive overdosing, and asteroidal zapping, grab our attention mightily. As pure phenomenology, they rank about equally high on the hit parade of primal fascination. Yet one represents expansive science, the others restrictive and untestable speculation. The proper criterion lies in evidence and methodology; we must probe behind the superficial fascination of particular claims.

How could we possibly decide whether the hypothesis of testicular frying is right or wrong? We would have to know things that the fossil record cannot provide. What temperatures were optimal for dinosaurs? Could they avoid the absorption of excess heat by staying in the shade, or in caves? At what temperatures did their testicles cease to function? Were late Cretaceous climates ever warm enough to drive the internal temperatures of dinosaurs close to this ceiling? Testicles simply don't fossilize, and how could we infer their temperature tolerances even if they did? In short, Cowles's hypothesis is only an intriguing speculation leading nowhere. The most damning statement against it appeared right at the conclusion of Colbert, Cowles, and Bogert's paper, when they admitted: "It is difficult to advance any definite arguments against this hypothesis." My statement may seem paradoxical — isn't a hypothesis really good if you can't devise any arguments against it? Quite the contrary. It is untestable and unusable.

Siegel's overdosing has even less going for it. At least Cowles 20
extrapolated his conclusion from some good data on alligators. And he didn't completely violate the primary guideline of siting dinosaur extinction in the context of a general mass dying — for rise in temperature could be the root cause of a general catastrophe, zapping dinosaurs by testicular malfunction and different groups for other reasons. But Siegel's speculation cannot touch the extinction of ammonites or oceanic plankton (diatoms make their own food with good sweet sunlight; they don't OD on the chemicals of terrestrial plants). It is simply a gratuitous, attention-grabbing guess. It cannot be tested, for how can we know what dinosaurs tasted and what their livers could do? Livers don't fossilize any better than testicles.

The hypothesis doesn't even make any sense in its own context. Angiosperms were in full flower ten million years before dinosaurs went the way of all flesh. Why did it take so long? As for the pains of a chemical death recorded in contortions of fossils, I regret to say (or rather I'm pleased to note for the dinosaurs' sake) that Siegel's knowledge of geology must be a bit deficient; muscles contract after death and geological strata rise and fall with motions of the earth's crust after burial — more than enough reason to distort a fossil's pristine appearance.

The impact story, on the other hand, has a sound basis in evidence. It can be tested, extended, refined and, if wrong, disproved. The Alvarezes did not just construct an arresting guess for public consumption. They proposed their hypothesis after laborious geochemical studies with Frank Asaro and Helen Michel had revealed a massive increase of iridium in rocks deposited right at the time of the extinction. Iridium, a rare metal of the platinum group, is virtually absent from indigenous rocks of the earth's crust; most of our iridium arrives on extraterrestrial objects that strike the earth.

The Alvarez hypothesis bore immediate fruit. Based originally on evidence from two European localities, it led geochemists throughout the world to examine other sediments of the same age. They found abnormally high amounts of iridium everywhere — from continental rocks of the western United States to deep sea cores from the South Atlantic.

Cowles proposed his testicular hypothesis in the mid-1940s. Where has it gone since then? Absolutely nowhere, because scientists can do nothing with it. The hypothesis must stand as a curious appendage to a solid study of alligators. Siegel's overdose scenario will also win a few press notices and fade into oblivion. The Alvarezes' asteroid falls into a different category altogether, and much of the popular commentary has missed this essential distinction by focusing on the impact and its attendant results, and forgetting what really matters to a scientist — the iridium. If you talk just about asteroids, dust and darkness, you tell stories no better and no more entertaining than fried testicles or terminal trips. It is the iridium — the source of testable evidence — that counts and forges the crucial distinction between speculation and science.

The proof, to twist a phrase, lies in the doing. Cowles's hypoth- 25
esis has generated nothing in thirty-five years. Since its proposal in 1979, the Alvarez hypothesis has spawned hundreds of studies, a major conference, and attendant publications. Geologists are fired up. They are looking for iridium at all other extinction boundaries. Every week exposes a new wrinkle in the scientific press. Further evidence that the Cretaceous iridium represents extraterrestrial impact and not indigenous volcanism continues to accumulate. As I revise this essay in November 1984, new data include chemical "signatures" of other isotopes indicating unearthly provenance, glass spherules of a size and sort produced by impact and not by volcanic eruptions, and high-pressure varieties of silica formed (so far as we know) only under the tremendous shock of impact.

My point is simply this: Whatever the eventual outcome (I suspect it will be positive), the Alvarez hypothesis is exciting, fruitful science because it generates tests, provides us with things to do, and expands outward. We are having fun, battling back and forth, moving toward a resolution, and extending the hypothesis beyond its original scope (see "The Cosmic Dance of Siva" for some truly wondrous extensions).

As just one example of the unexpected, distant cross-fertilization that good science engenders, the Alvarez hypothesis made a major contribution to a theme that has riveted public attention in the past few months — so-called nuclear winter. In a speech delivered in April 1982, Luis Alvarez calculated the energy that a ten-kilometer asteroid would release on impact. He compared such an explosion with a full nuclear exchange and implied that all-out nuclear war might unleash similar consequences.

The theme of impact leading to massive dust clouds and falling temperatures formed an important input to the decision of Carl Sagan and a group of colleagues to model the climatic consequences of nuclear holocaust. Full nuclear exchange would probably generate the same kind of dust cloud and darkening that may have wiped out the dinosaurs. Temperatures would drop precipitously and agriculture might become impossible. Avoidance of nuclear war is fundamentally an ethical and political imperative, but we must know the factual consequences to make firm judgments. I am heartened by a final link across disciplines and deep concerns — another criterion, by the way, of science at its best: A recognition of the very phenomenon that made our evolution possible by exterminating the previously dominant dinosaurs and clearing a way for the evolution of large mammals, including us, might actually help to save us from joining those magnificent beasts in contorted poses among the strata of the earth.

For Discussion and Writing

1. What are the three different ideas for the cause of the extinction of the dinosaurs that Gould considers?
2. At one point early in "Sex, Drugs, Disasters, and the Extinction of the Dinosaurs," Gould writes, "But, enough preaching" (par. 5). This essay is about competing scientific hypotheses, not religion, so in what way is Gould "preaching"? What is the message of his sermon?

3. **connections** Gould, Carson (in "The Obligation to Endure" [p. 83]), Klinkenborg (in "Our Vanishing Night" [p. 234]), and Diamond (in "The Ends of the World as We Know Them" [p. 98]) can all be seen to be combining science and "preaching." Compare the way Gould's essay and one of these three essays do this. Are there different kinds of language involved? How do they connect their science and their preaching?
4. Gould's essay is less about the physical world that is science's object of study than it is about the way science pursues its object; that is, it is less about the physical world than it is about how to think about the physical world. Have you read works in other classes that have been less about the object of study than how to study it? Have you read (or seen, or heard) nonacademic "texts" or creations that are as much about "how to" as they are about "what"? How do they explore this aspect?

LANGSTON HUGHES

Salvation

Born in 1902 in Joplin, Missouri, Langston Hughes became a major figure in the Harlem Renaissance, a flowering of African American literature, art, music, and scholarship in the 1920s and 1930s. He was first and foremost a poet, incorporating the vernacular of the streets and the rhythms of the jazz clubs into his voice. He was also a playwright, a fiction writer, an essayist, and an autobiographer. In "Salvation" we can see the skills with which Hughes created imaginative literature; here, in nonfiction, he both tells the story of an important point in his life and makes his readers think about significant ideas, doing so poetically and with great economy and expressiveness.

I was saved from sin when I was going on thirteen. But not really saved. It happened like this. There was a big revival at my Auntie Reed's church. Every night for weeks there had been much preaching, singing, praying, and shouting, and some very hardened sinners had been brought to Christ, and the membership of the church had grown by leaps and bounds. Then just before the revival ended, they held a special meeting for children, "to bring the young lambs to the fold." My aunt spoke of it for days ahead. That night I was escorted to the front row and placed on the mourners' bench with all the other young sinners, who had not yet been brought to Jesus.

My aunt told me that when you were saved you saw a light, and something happened to you inside! And Jesus came into your life! And God was with you from then on! She said you could see and hear and feel Jesus in your soul. I believed her. I had heard a great many old people say the same thing and it seemed to me they ought to know. So I sat there calmly in the hot, crowded church, waiting for Jesus to come to me.

The preacher preached a wonderful rhythmical sermon, all moans and shouts and lonely cries and dire pictures of hell, and then he sang a song about the ninety and nine safe in the fold, but one little lamb was left out in the cold. Then he said: "Won't you come? Won't you come to Jesus? Young lambs, won't you come?" And he held out his arms to all us young sinners there on the mourners' bench. And the little girls cried. And some of them jumped up and went to Jesus right away. But most of us just sat there.

A great many old people came and knelt around us and prayed, old women with jet-black faces and braided hair, old men with work-gnarled hands. And the church sang a song about the lower lights are burning, some poor sinners to be saved. And the whole building rocked with prayer and song.

Still I kept waiting to *see* Jesus. 5

Finally all the young people had gone to the altar and were saved, but one boy and me. He was a rounder's son named Westley. Westley and I were surrounded by sisters and deacons praying. It was very hot in the church, and getting late now. Finally Westley said to me in a whisper: "God damn! I'm tired o' sitting here. Let's get up and be saved." So he got up and was saved.

Then I was left all alone on the mourners' bench. My aunt came and knelt at my knees and cried, while prayers and songs swirled all around me in the little church. The whole congregation prayed for me alone, in a mighty wail of moans and voices. And I kept waiting serenely for Jesus, waiting, waiting — but he didn't come. I wanted to see him, but nothing happened to me. Nothing! I wanted something to happen to me, but nothing happened.

I heard the songs and the minister saying: "Why don't you come? My dear child, why don't you come to Jesus? Jesus is waiting for you. He wants you. Why don't you come? Sister Reed, what is this child's name?"

"Langston," my aunt sobbed.

"Langston, why don't you come? Why don't you come and be 10
saved? Oh, Lamb of God! Why don't you come?"

Now it was really getting late. I began to be ashamed of myself, holding everything up so long. I began to wonder what God thought about Westley, who certainly hadn't seen Jesus either, but who was now sitting proudly on the platform, swinging his knickerbockered legs and grinning down at me, surrounded by deacons and old women on their knees praying. God had not struck Westley dead for taking his name in vain or for lying in the temple. So

I decided that maybe to save further trouble, I'd better lie, too, and say that Jesus had come, and get up and be saved.

So I got up.

Suddenly the whole room broke into a sea of shouting, as they saw me rise. Waves of rejoicing swept the place. Women leaped in the air. My aunt threw her arms around me. The minister took me by the hand and led me to the platform.

When things quieted down, in a hushed silence, punctuated by a few ecstatic "Amens," all the new young lambs were blessed in the name of God. Then joyous singing filled the room.

15 That night, for the last time in my life but one — for I was a big boy twelve years old — I cried. I cried, in bed alone, and couldn't stop. I buried my head under the quilts, but my aunt heard me. She woke up and told my uncle I was crying because the Holy Ghost had come into my life, and because I had seen Jesus. But I was really crying because I couldn't bear to tell her that I had lied, that I had deceived everybody in the church, and I hadn't seen Jesus, and that now I didn't believe there was a Jesus any more, since he didn't come to help me.

For Discussion and Writing

1. Why does Hughes cry that night?
2. Hughes's story is told very briefly; how does that brevity make it more powerful? How might a longer version have been less affecting?
3. **connections** Compare the feeling the young Hughes has when he is the last child on the bench to the feeling George Orwell has when the crowd follows him in "Shooting an Elephant" (p. 284). What are the effects of being watched on each?
4. Write about a time when you felt your family held certain expectations for you. Was it a positive experience, a negative one, or both? Why?

ZORA NEALE HURSTON

How It Feels to Be Colored Me

Born in 1891 in rural Alabama and raised in Florida, Zora Neale Hurston arrived in New York at the height of the Harlem Renaissance, a flowering of African American literature, art, music, and scholarship in the 1920s and 1930s, and became an active participant, writing stories and coauthoring a play with Langston Hughes. Her interest in the folk culture of the South, influenced by her studies with noted anthropologist Franz Boas, led to her return to Florida to study her native community and, eventually, to the work for which she is best known, the novel Their Eyes Were Watching God *(1937). When reading "How It Feels to Be Colored Me," it is interesting to think about Hurston's statements about race and identity — such as her image of people of different races as different-colored bags stuffed with similar contents — in the context of this anthropological training.*

I am colored but I offer nothing in the way of extenuating circumstances except the fact that I am the only Negro in the United States whose grandfather on the mother's side was *not* an Indian chief.

I remember the very day that I became colored. Up to my thirteenth year I lived in the little Negro town of Eatonville, Florida. It is exclusively a colored town. The only white people I knew passed through the town going to or coming from Orlando. The native whites rode dusty horses, the Northern tourists chugged down the sandy village road in automobiles. The town knew the Southerners and never stopped cane chewing when they passed. But the Northerners were something else again. They were peered at cautiously from behind curtains by the timid. The more venturesome would come out on the porch to watch them go past and got just as much pleasure out of the tourists as the tourists got out of the village.

The front porch might seem a daring place for the rest of the town, but it was a gallery seat for me. My favorite place was atop the gate-post. Proscenium box for a born first-nighter. Not only did I enjoy the show, but I didn't mind the actors knowing that I liked it. I usually spoke to them in passing. I'd wave at them and when they returned my salute, I would say something like this: "Howdy-do-well-I-thank-you-where-you-goin'?" Usually automobile or the horse paused at this, and after a queer exchange of compliments, I would probably "go a piece of the way" with them, as we say in farthest Florida. If one of my family happened to come to the front in time to see me, of course negotiations would be rudely broken off. But even so, it is clear that I was the first "welcome-to-our-state" Floridian, and I hope the Miami Chamber of Commerce will please take notice.

During this period, white people differed from colored to me only in that they rode through town and never lived there. They liked to hear me "speak pieces" and sing and wanted to see me dance the parse-me-la, and gave me generously of their small silver for doing these things, which seemed strange to me for I wanted to do them so much that I needed bribing to stop. Only they didn't know it. The colored people gave no dimes. They deplored any joyful tendencies in me, but I was their Zora nevertheless. I belonged to them, to the nearby hotels, to the county — everybody's Zora.

But changes came in the family when I was thirteen, and I was 5
sent to school in Jacksonville. I left Eatonville, the town of the oleanders, as Zora. When I disembarked from the river-boat at Jacksonville, she was no more. It seemed that I had suffered a sea change. I was not Zora of Orange County any more, I was now a little colored girl. I found it out in certain ways. In my heart as well as in the mirror, I became a fast brown — warranted not to rub nor run.

But I am not tragically colored. There is no great sorrow dammed up in my soul, nor lurking behind my eyes. I do not mind at all. I do not belong to the sobbing school of Negrohood who hold that nature somehow has given them a lowdown dirty deal and whose feelings are all hurt about it. Even in the helter-skelter skirmish that is my life, I have seen that the world is to the strong regardless of a little pigmentation more or less. No, I do not weep at the world — I am too busy sharpening my oyster knife.

Someone is always at my elbow reminding me that I am the granddaughter of slaves. It fails to register depression with me. Slavery is sixty years in the past. The operation was successful and the patient is doing well, thank you. The terrible struggle that made me an American out of a potential slave said "On the line!" The Reconstruction said "Get set!"; and the generation before said "Go!" I am off to a flying start and I must not halt in the stretch to look behind and weep. Slavery is the price I paid for civilization, and the choice was not with me. It is a bully adventure and worth all that I have paid through my ancestors for it. No one on earth ever had a greater chance for glory. The world to be won and nothing to be lost. It is thrilling to think — to know that for any act of mine, I shall get twice as much praise or twice as much blame. It is quite exciting to hold the center of the national stage, with the spectators not knowing whether to laugh or to weep.

The position of my white neighbor is much more difficult. No brown specter pulls up a chair beside me when I sit down to eat. No dark ghost thrusts its leg against mine in bed. The game of keeping what one has is never so exciting as the game of getting.

I do not always feel colored. Even now I often achieve the unconscious Zora of Eatonville before the Hegira.° I feel most colored when I am thrown against a sharp white background.

For instance at Barnard. "Beside the waters of the Hudson" I 10
feel my race. Among the thousand white persons, I am a dark rock surged upon, and overswept, but through it all, I remain myself. When covered by the waters, I am; and the ebb but reveals me again.

Sometimes it is the other way around. A white person is set down in our midst, but the contrast is just as sharp for me. For instance, when I sit in the drafty basement that is The New World Cabaret with a white person, my color comes. We enter chatting about any little nothing that we have in common and are seated by the jazz waiters. In the abrupt way that jazz orchestras have, this one plunges into a number. It loses no time in circumlocutions, but gets right down to business. It constricts the thorax and splits the heart with its tempo and narcotic harmonies. This

Hegira: A flight to escape danger. [Ed.]

orchestra grows rambunctious, rears on its hind legs and attacks the tonal veil with primitive fury, rending it, clawing it until it breaks through to the jungle beyond. I follow those heathen — follow them exultingly. I dance wildly inside myself; I yell within, I whoop; I shake my assegai° above my head, I hurl it true to the mark *yeeeeooww!* I am in the jungle and living in the jungle way. My face is painted red and yellow and my body is painted blue. My pulse is throbbing like a war drum. I want to slaughter something — give pain, give death to what, I do not know. But the piece ends. The men of the orchestra wipe their lips and rest their fingers. I creep back slowly to the veneer we call civilization with the last tone and find the white friend sitting motionless in his seat, smoking calmly.

"Good music they have here," he remarks, drumming the table with his fingertips.

Music. The great blobs of purple and red emotion have not touched him. He has only heard what I felt. He is far away and I see him but dimly across the ocean and the continent that have fallen between us. He is so pale with his whiteness then and I am *so* colored.

At certain times I have no race, I am *me*. When I set my hat at a certain angle and saunter down Seventh Avenue, Harlem City, feeling as snooty as the lions in front of the Forty-Second Street Library, for instance. So far as my feelings are concerned, Peggy Hopkins Joyce on the Boule Mich with her gorgeous raiment, stately carriage, knees knocking together in a most aristocratic manner, has nothing on me. The cosmic Zora emerges. I belong to no race nor time. I am the eternal feminine with its string of beads.

15 I have no separate feeling about being an American citizen and colored. I am merely a fragment of the Great Soul that surges within the boundaries. My country, right or wrong.

Sometimes, I feel discriminated against, but it does not make me angry. It merely astonishes me. How *can* any deny themselves the pleasure of my company? It's beyond me.

But in the main, I feel like a brown bag of miscellany propped against a wall. Against a wall in company with other bags, white,

assegai: A spear. [Ed.]

red, and yellow. Pour out the contents, and there is discovered a jumble of small things priceless and worthless. A first-water diamond, an empty spool, bits of broken glass, lengths of string, a key to a door long since crumbled away, a rusty knife-blade, old shoes saved for a road that never was and never will be, a nail bent under the weight of things too heavy for any nail, a dried flower or two still a little fragrant. In your hand is the brown bag. On the ground before you is the jumble it held — so much like the jumble in the bags, could they be emptied, that all might be dumped in a single heap and the bags refilled without altering the content of any greatly. A bit of colored glass more or less would not matter. Perhaps that is how the Great Stuffer of Bags filled them in the first place — who knows?

For Discussion and Writing

1. What point is Hurston trying to make in her first paragraph? *Is* she "the only Negro in the United States whose grandfather on the mother's side was *not* an Indian chief"?
2. Consider Hurston's use of imagination in her descriptions of the white neighbor, her experience at the jazz club, and in the final paragraph. How does she use specific details to ground these flights of imagination? How does she use these imaginative moments to make her points?
3. **connections** Name an African American writer in this book whom you think Hurston might include in what she calls "the sobbing school of Negrohood" (par. 6). How might he or she answer Hurston's criticism?
4. How do you respond to the conception of race with which Hurston ends her essay? Does it agree with how you understand race?

THOMAS JEFFERSON

The Declaration of Independence

Born in 1743 in the British colony that is now the state of Virginia, Thomas Jefferson, descendant of one of the first families of Virginia, went on to become a founding father of the nation born out of thirteen united colonies. In addition to being the primary writer of the Declaration of Independence, Jefferson was governor of Virginia, vice president, president (from 1801 to 1809), and founder of the University of Virginia.

The Declaration is more than a historical document. It is a clear and effective piece of writing. We present both an early version and the final document. As you read, note the choices that were made in its writing, in particular the revisions evident in the final draft.

DRAFT OF THE DECLARATION OF INDEPENDENCE

A Declaration of the Representatives of the UNITED STATES OF AMERICA, in General Congress Assembled.

When in the course of human events it becomes necessary for a people to advance from that subordination in which they have hitherto remained, & to assume among the powers of the earth the equal & independant station to which the laws of nature & of nature's god entitle them, a decent respect to the opinions of mankind requires that they should declare the causes which impel them to the change.

We hold these truths to be sacred & undeniable; that all men are created equal & independant, that from that equal creation they derive rights inherent & inalienable, among which are the preservation of life, & liberty, & the spirit of happiness; that to secure these ends, governments are instituted among men, deriving their just powers from the consent of the governed; that whenever any form of government shall become destructive of these ends, it is the right of the people to alter or to abolish it, & to institute new government, laying its foundation on such principles & organizing its powers in such form, as to them shall seem most likely to effect their safety & happiness. prudence indeed will dictate that governments long established should not be changed for light & transient causes: and accordingly all experience hath shewn that mankind are more disposed to suffer while evils are sufferable, than to right themselves by abolishing the forms to which they are accustomed. but when a long train of abuses & usurpations, begun at a distinguished period, & pursuing invariably the same object, evinces a design to subject them to arbitrary power, it is their right, it is their duty, to throw off such government & to provide new guards for their future security. such has been the patient sufferance of these colonies; & such is now the necessity which constrains them to expunge their former systems of government. The history of his present majesty, is a history of unremitting injuries and usurpations, among which no one fact stands single or solitary to contradict the uniform tenor of the rest, all of which have in direct object the establishment of an absolute tyranny over these states. to prove this, let facts be submitted to a candid world, for the truth of which we pledge a faith yet unsullied by falsehood.

> he has refused his assent to laws the most wholesome and necessary for the public good:
>
> he has forbidden his governors to pass laws of immediate & pressing importance, unless suspended in their operation till his assent should be obtained: and when so suspended, he has neglected utterly to attend to them:
>
> he has refused to pass other laws for the accommodation of large districts of people unless those people would relinquish the right of representation, a right inestimable to them, & formidable to tyrants alone:
>
> he has dissolved Representative houses repeatedly & continually, for opposing with manly firmness his invasions on the rights of the people:
>
> he has refused for a long space of time to cause others to be elected, whereby the legislative powers, incapable of annihilation, have returned to the people at large for their exercise, the state remaining in the mean time exposed to all the dangers of invasion from without, &, convulsions within:
>
> he has suffered the administration of justice totally to cease in some of these colonies, refusing his assent to laws for establishing judiciary powers:

he has made our judges dependant on his will alone, for the tenure of their offices, and amount of their salaries:

he has erected a multitude of new offices by a self-assumed power, & sent hither swarms of officers to harrass our people & eat out their substance: he has kept among us in times of peace standing armies & ships of war:

he has affected to render the military, independent of & superior to the civil power:

he has combined with others to subject us to a jurisdiction foreign to our constitutions and unacknowledged by our laws; giving his assent to their pretended acts of legislation, for quartering large bodies of armed troops among us:

for protecting them by a mock-trial from punishment for any murders they should commit on the inhabitants of these states;

for cutting off our trade with all parts of the world;

for imposing taxes on us without our consent;

for depriving us of the benefits of trial by jury

he has endeavored to prevent the population of these states; for that purpose obstructing the laws for naturalization of foreigners; refusing to pass others to encourage their migrations hither; & raising the conditions of new appropriations of lands;

for transporting us beyond seas to be tried for pretended offences;

for taking away our charters & altering fundamentally the forms of our governments;

for suspending our own legislatures & declaring themselves invested with power to legislate for us in all cases whatsoever;

he has abdicated government here, withdrawing his governors, & declaring us out of his allegiance & protection:

he has plundered our seas, ravaged our coasts, burnt our towns & destroyed the lives of our people:

he is at this time transporting large armies of foreign mercenaries to compleat the works of death, desolation & tyranny, already begun with circumstances of cruelty & perfidy unworthy the head of a civilized nation:

he has endeavored to bring on the inhabitants of our frontiers the merciless Indian savages, whose known rule of warfare is an undistinguished destruction of all ages, sexes, & conditions of existence:

he has incited treasonable insurrections of our fellow-citizens, with the allurements of forfeiture & confiscation of our property:

he has waged cruel war against human nature itself, violating its most sacred rights of life & liberty in the persons of a distant people who never offended him, captivating & carrying them into slavery in another hemisphere, or to incur miserable death in their transportation thither. this piratical warfare, the opprobrium of *infidel* powers, is the warfare of the CHRISTIAN king of Great Britain, determined to keep open a market where MEN should be bought & sold; he has prostituted his negative for

> suppressing every legislative attempt to prohibit or to restrain this execrable commerce: and that this assemblage of horrors might want no fact of distinguished die, he is now exciting those very people to rise in arms among us, and to purchase that liberty of which *he* has deprived them, by murdering the people upon whom *he* also obtruded them; thus paying off former crimes committed against the *liberties* of one people, with crimes which he urges them to commit against the *lives* of another.

in every stage of these oppressions we have petitioned for redress in the most humble terms; our repeated petitions have been answered by repeated injury. a prince whose character is thus marked by every act which may define a tyrant, is unfit to be the ruler of a people who mean to be free. future ages will scarce believe that the hardiness of one man, adventured within the short compass of twelve years only, on so many acts of tyranny without a mask, over a people fostered & fixed in principles of liberty.

Nor have we been wanting in attentions to our British brethren. we have warned them from time to time of attempts by their legislature to extend a jurisdiction over these our states. we have reminded them of the circumstances of our emigration & settlement here, no one of which could warrant so strange a pretension: that these were effected at the expence of our own blood & treasure, unassisted by the wealth or the strength of Great Britain: that in constituting indeed our several forms of government, we had adopted one common king, thereby laying a foundation for perpetual league & amity with them; but that submission to their [Parliament, was no Part of our Constitution, nor ever in Idea, if History may be] credited: and we appealed to their native justice & magnanimity, as to the ties of our common kindred to disavow these usurpations which were likely to interrupt our correspondence & connection. they too have been deaf to the voice of justice & of consanguinity, & when occasions have been given them, by the regular course of their laws, of removing from their councils the disturbers of our harmony, they have by their free election re-established them in power. at this very time too they are permitting their chief magistrate to send over not only soldiers of our common blood, but Scotch & foreign mercenaries to invade & deluge us in blood. these facts have given the last stab to agonizing affection, and manly spirit bids us to renounce for ever these unfeeling brethren. we must endeavor to forget our former love for them, and to hold them as we hold the rest of mankind, enemies in war, in peace friends. we might have been a free & a great people together; but a communication of grandeur & of freedom it seems is below their dignity. be it so, since they will have it: the road to glory & happiness is open to us too; we will climb it in a separate state, and acquiesce in the necessity which pronounces our everlasting Adieu!

We therefore the representatives of the United States of America in General Congress assembled do, in the name & by authority of the good people of these states, reject and renounce all allegiance & subjection to the kings of Great Britain & all others who may hereafter claim by, through, or under them; we utterly dissolve & break off all political connection which may have heretofore subsisted between us & the people or parliament of Great Britain; and finally we do assert and declare these colonies to be free and independant states, and that as free & independant states they shall hereafter have power to levy war, conclude peace, contract alliances, establish commerce, & to do all other acts and things which independant states may of right do. And for the support of this declaration we mutually pledge to each other our lives, our fortunes, & our sacred honor.

THE DECLARATION OF INDEPENDENCE

In Congress, July 4, 1776
The Unanimous Declaration of the
Thirteen United States of America

When in the Course of human events it becomes necessary for one people to dissolve the political bands which have connected them with another, and to assume among the powers of the earth, the separate and equal station to which the Laws of Nature and of Nature's God entitle them, a decent respect to the opinions of mankind requires that they should declare the causes which impel them to the separation.

We hold these truths to be self-evident, that all men are created equal, that they are endowed by their Creator with certain unalienable Rights, that among these are Life, Liberty, and the pursuit of Happiness. That to secure these rights, Governments are instituted among Men, deriving their just powers from the consent of the governed. That whenever any Form of Government becomes destructive of these ends, it is the Right of the People to alter or to abolish it, and to institute new Government, laying its foundation on such principles and organizing its powers in such form, as to them shall seem most likely to effect their Safety and Happiness. Prudence, indeed, will dictate that Governments long established should not be changed for light and transient causes; and accordingly all experience hath shewn that mankind are more disposed to suffer, while evils are sufferable, than right themselves by abolishing the forms to which they are accustomed. But when a long train of abuses and usurpations, pursuing invariably the same Object evinces a design to reduce them under absolute Despotism, it is their right, it is their duty, to throw off such Government, and to provide new Guards for their future security. Such has been the patient sufferance of these Colonies; and such is now the necessity which constrains them to alter their former Systems of Government. The history of the present King of Great Britain is a history of repeated injuries and usurpations, all having in direct object the establishment of an absolute Tyranny over these States. To prove this, let Facts be submitted to a candid world.

He has refused his Assent to Laws, the most wholesome and necessary for the public good.

He has forbidden his Government to pass laws of immediate and pressing importance, unless suspended in their operation till his Assent should be obtained; and when so suspended, he has utterly neglected to attend to them.

He has refused to pass other Laws for the accommodation of large districts of people, unless those people would relinquish the right of Representation in the Legislature, a right inestimable to them and formidable to tyrants only.

He has called together legislative bodies at places unusual, 10
uncomfortable, and distant from the depository of their Public Records, for the sole purpose of fatiguing them into compliance with his measures.

He has dissolved Representative Houses repeatedly, for opposing with manly firmness his invasions on the rights of the people.

He has refused for a long time, after such dissolutions, to cause others to be elected; whereby the Legislative Powers, incapable of

Annihilation, have returned to the People at large for their exercise; the State remaining in the mean time exposed to all the dangers of invasion from without, and convulsions within.

He has endeavored to prevent the population of these States; for that purpose obstructing the Laws for Naturalization of Foreigners; refusing to pass others to encourage their migration hither, and raising the conditions of new Appropriations of Lands.

He has obstructed the Administration of Justice, by refusing his Assent to Laws for establishing Judiciary Powers.

He has made Judges dependent on his Will alone, for the tenure 15
of their offices, and the amount and payment of their salaries.

He has erected a multitude of New Offices, and sent hither swarms of Officers to harass our people, and eat out their substance.

He has kept among us, in times of peace, Standing Armies without the Consent of our legislatures.

He has affected to render the Military independent of and superior to the Civil Power.

He has combined with others to subject us to a jurisdiction foreign to our constitution, and unacknowledged by our laws; giving his Assent to their Acts of pretended Legislation: For quartering large bodies of armed troops among us: For protecting them, by a mock Trial, from punishment for any Murders which they should commit on the Inhabitants of these States: For cutting off our Trade with all parts of the world: For imposing Taxes on us without our Consent: For depriving us in many cases, of the benefits of Trial by Jury: For transporting us beyond Seas to be tried for pretended offenses: for abolishing the free System of English Laws in a neighboring Province, establishing therein an Arbitrary government, and enlarging its Boundaries so as to render it at once an example and fit instrument for introducing the same absolute rule into these Colonies: For taking away our Charters, abolishing our most valuable Laws and altering fundamentally the Forms of our Governments: For suspending our own Legislatures, and declaring themselves invested with power to legislate for us in all cases whatsoever.

He has abdicated Government here, by declaring us out of his 20
Protection and waging War against us.

He has plundered our seas, ravaged our Coasts, burnt our towns, and destroyed the lives of our people.

He is at this time transporting large Armies of foreign Mercenaries to complete the works of death, desolation and tyranny, already begun with circumstances of Cruelty & Perfidy scarcely paralleled in the most barbarous ages, and totally unworthy the Head of a civilized nation.

He has constrained our fellow Citizens taken Captive on the high Seas to bear Arms against their Country, to become the executioners of their friends and Brethren, or to fall themselves by their Hands.

He has excited domestic insurrections amongst us, and has endeavored to bring on the inhabitants of our frontiers, the merciless Indian Savages, whose known rule of warfare, is an undistinguished destruction of all ages, sexes, and conditions.

In every stage of these Oppressions We have Petitioned for 25
Redress in the most humble terms: Our repeated Petitions have been answered only by repeated injury. A Prince, whose character is thus marked by every act which may define a Tyrant, is unfit to be the ruler of a free people.

Nor have We been wanting in attention to our British brethren. We have warned them from time to time of attempts by their legislature to extend an unwarrantable jurisdiction over us. We have reminded them of the circumstances of our emigration and settlement here. We have appealed to their native justice and magnanimity, and we have conjured them by the ties of our common kindred to disavow these usurpations, which would inevitably interrupt our connections and correspondence. They too have been deaf to the voice of justice and of consanguinity. We must, therefore, acquiesce in the necessity, which denounces our Separation, and hold them, as we hold the rest of mankind, Enemies in War, in Peace Friends.

We, THEREFORE the Representatives of the UNITED STATES OF AMERICA, in General Congress, Assembled, appealing to the Supreme Judge of the world for the rectitude of our intentions, do, in the Name, and by Authority of the good People of these Colonies, solemnly publish and declare, That these United Colonies are, and of Right ought to be FREE AND INDEPENDENT STATES; that they are Absolved from all Allegiance to the British Crown, and that all political connection between them and the State of Great Britain, is and ought to be totally dissolved; and that as Free and Independent States, they have full Power to levy War, conclude Peace, contract Alliances, establish Commerce, and to do all other Acts and Things which Independent States may of right do. And for the support of this Declaration, with a firm reliance on the protection of Divine Providence, we mutually pledge to each other our Lives, our Fortunes, and our sacred Honor.

For Discussion and Writing

1. How many examples of wrongs done by the Crown to the colonies are offered here? What is the effect of this list?
2. In small groups, compile lists of all of the differences between the first and second drafts of the Declaration. Write up a summary of these changes and an analysis of how they make the final document more effective.
3. **connections** Compare the Declaration and George Orwell's "Shooting an Elephant" (p. 284). How do these two condemnations of the British Empire differ?
4. Think about America today. From your personal experience and observations, discuss how it meets the promise of the opening of the Declaration's second paragraph, and how it does not.

STEVEN JOHNSON

Games

Steven Johnson (b. 1968), an innovative presence on the Internet, has written about science, culture, and computers for popular science magazines and other print and online magazines such as Discover, Wired, *and* Slate. *His books, with long and informative subtitles, include* Interface Culture: How New Technology Transforms the Way We Create and Communicate *(1997);* Emergence: The Connected Lives of Ants, Brains, Cities, and Software *(2001);* Mind Wide Open: Your Brain and the Neuroscience of Everyday Life *(2004);* Everything Bad Is Good for You: How Today's Popular Culture Is Actually Making Us Smarter *(2005);* The Ghost Map: The Story of London's Most Terrifying Epidemic — and How It Changed Science, Cities, and the Modern World *(2006); and* The Invention of Air: A Story of Science, Faith, Revolution, and the Birth of America *(2008).*

As you read this excerpt from Everything Bad Is Good for You, *think about the ways in which Johnson blends his interests in scientific innovation and in culture; the interconnection of the way people think and communicate and the technology they use — and here, the games they play — allows for some opportunities to draw interesting connections and question received wisdom about both technology and human beings.*

You can't get much more conventional than the conventional wisdom that kids today would be better off spending more time reading books, and less time zoning out in front of their video games. The latest edition of *Dr. Spock* — "revised and fully expanded for a new century" as the cover reports — has this to say of video games: "The best that can be said of them is that they may help promote eye-hand coordination in children. The worst that can be said is that they sanction, and even promote aggression and violent responses to conflict. But what can be said with much greater certainty is this: most computer games are a colossal waste of time." But where reading is concerned, the advice is quite different: "I suggest you begin to foster in your children a love of reading and the printed word from the start. . . . What is important is that your child be an avid reader."

In the middle of 2004, the National Endowment for the Arts released a study that showed that reading for pleasure had declined steadily among all major American demographic groups. The writer Andrew Solomon analyzed the consequences of this shift: "People who read for pleasure are many times more likely than those who don't to visit museums and attend musical performances, almost three times as likely to perform volunteer and charity work, and almost twice as likely to attend sporting events. Readers, in other words, are active, while nonreaders — more than half the population — have settled into apathy. There is a basic social divide between those for whom life is an accrual of fresh experience and knowledge, and those for whom maturity is a process of mental atrophy. The shift toward the latter category is frightening."

The intellectual nourishment of reading books is so deeply ingrained in our assumptions that it's hard to contemplate a different viewpoint. But as McLuhan famously observed, the problem with judging new cultural systems on their own terms is that the presence of the recent past inevitably colors your vision of the emerging form, highlighting the flaws and imperfections. Games have historically suffered from this syndrome, largely because they have been contrasted with the older conventions of reading. To get around these prejudices, try this thought experiment. Imagine an alternate world identical to ours, save one techno-historical change: video games were invented and popularized *before* books. In this parallel universe, kids have been playing games for centuries — and then these page-bound texts come along and suddenly they're all the rage. What would the teachers, and the parents, and the cultural authorities have to say about this frenzy of reading? I suspect it would sound something like this:

> Reading books chronically understimulates the senses. Unlike the long-standing tradition of gameplaying — which engages the child in a vivid, three-dimensional world filled with moving images and musical soundscapes, navigated and controlled with complex muscular movements — books are simply a barren string of words on the page. Only a small portion of the brain devoted to processing written language is

> activated during reading, while games engage the full range of the sensory and motor cortices.
>
> Books are also tragically isolating. While games have, for many years engaged the young in complex social relationships with their peers, building and exploring worlds together, books force the child to sequester him- or herself in a quiet space, shut off from interaction with other children. These new "libraries" that have arisen in recent years to facilitate reading activities are a frightening sight: dozens of young children, normally so vivacious and socially interactive, sitting alone in cubicles, reading silently, oblivious to their peers.
>
> Many children enjoy reading books, of course, and no doubt some of the flights of fancy conveyed by reading have their escapist merits. But for a sizable percentage of the population, books are downright discriminatory. The reading craze of recent years cruelly taunts the 10 million Americans who suffer from dyslexia — a condition that didn't even exist as a condition until printed text came along to stigmatize its sufferers.
>
> But perhaps the most dangerous property of these books is the fact that they follow a fixed linear path. You can't control their narratives in any fashion — you simply sit back and have the story dictated to you. For those of us raised on interactive narratives, this property may seem astonishing. Why would anyone want to embark on an adventure utterly choreographed by another person? But today's generation embarks on such adventures millions of times a day. This risks instilling a general passivity in our children, making them feel as though they're powerless to change their circumstances. Reading is not an active, participatory process; it's a submissive one. The book readers of the younger generation are learning to "follow the plot" instead of learning to lead.

It should probably go without saying, but it probably goes better with saying, that I don't agree with this argument. But neither is it exactly right to say that its contentions are untrue. The argument relies on a kind of amplified selectivity: it foregrounds certain isolated properties of books, and then projects worst-case scenarios based on these properties and their potential effects on the "younger generation." But it doesn't bring up any of the clear benefits of reading: the complexity of argument and storytelling offered by the book form; the stretching of the imagination triggered by reading words on a page; the shared experience you get when everyone is reading the same story.

A comparable sleight of hand is at work anytime you hear some- 5
one bemoaning today's video game obsessions, and their stupefying effects on tomorrow's generations. Games are not novels, and the ways in which they harbor novelistic aspirations are invari-

ably the least interesting thing about them. You can judge games by the criteria designed to evaluate novels: Are the characters believable? Is the dialogue complex? But inevitably, the games will come up wanting. Games are good at novelistic storytelling the way Michael Jordan was good at playing baseball. Both could probably make a living at it, but their world-class talents lie elsewhere.

Before we get to those talents, let me say a few words about the virtues of reading books. For the record, I think those virtues are immense ones — and not just because I make a living writing books. We should all encourage our kids to read more, to develop a comfort with and an appetite for reading. But even the most avid reader in this culture is invariably going to spend his or her time with other media — with games, television, movies, or the Internet. And these other forms of culture have intellectual or cognitive virtues in their own right — different from, but comparable to, the rewards of reading.

What are the rewards of reading, exactly? Broadly speaking, they fall into two categories: the information conveyed by the book, and the mental work you have to do to process and store that information. Think of this as the difference between acquiring information and exercising the mind. When we encourage kids to read for pleasure, we're generally doing so because of the mental exercise involved. In Andrew Solomon's words: "[Reading] requires effort, concentration, attention. In exchange, it offers the stimulus to and the fruit of thought and feeling." Spock says: "Unlike most amusements, reading is an activity requiring active participation: We must do the reading ourselves — actively scan the letters, make sense of the words, and follow the thread of the story." Most tributes to the mental benefits of reading also invoke the power of imagination; reading books forces you to concoct entire worlds in your head, rather than simply ingest a series of prepackaged images. And then there is the slightly circular — though undoubtedly true — argument for the long-term career benefits: being an avid reader is good for you because the educational system and the job market put a high premium on reading skills.

To summarize, the cognitive benefits of reading involve these faculties: effort, concentration, attention, the ability to make sense of words, to follow narrative threads, to sculpt imagined worlds out of mere sentences on the page. Those benefits are themselves amplified by the fact that society places a substantial emphasis on precisely this set of skills.

The very fact that I am presenting this argument to you in the form of a book and not a television drama or a video game should make it clear that I believe the printed word remains the most powerful vehicle for conveying complicated information — though the *electronic* word is starting to give printed books a run for their money. The argument that follows is centered squarely on the side of mental exercise — and not content. I aim to persuade you of two things:

1. By almost all the standards we use to measure reading's cognitive benefits — attention, memory, following threads, and so on — the nonliterary popular culture has been steadily growing more challenging over the past thirty years.
2. Increasingly, the nonliterary popular culture is honing *different* mental skills that are just as important as the ones exercised by reading books.

Despite the warnings of Dr. Spock, the most powerful examples 10
of both these trends are found in the world of video games. Over the past few years, you may have noticed the appearance of a certain type of story about gaming culture in mainstream newspapers and periodicals. The message of that story ultimately reduces down to: Playing video games may not actually be a *complete* waste of time. Invariably these stories point to some new study focused on a minor side effect of gameplaying — often manual dexterity or visual memory — and explain that heavy gamers show improved skills compared to non-gamers. (The other common let's-take-games-seriously story is financial, usually pointing to the fact that the gaming industry now pulls in more money than Hollywood.)

Now, I have no doubt that playing today's games does in fact improve your visual intelligence and your manual dexterity, but the virtues of gaming run far deeper than hand-eye coordination. When I read these ostensibly positive accounts of video games, they strike me as the equivalent of writing a story about the merits of the great novels and focusing on how reading them can improve your spelling. It's true enough, I suppose, but it doesn't do justice to the rich, textured experience of novel reading. There's a comparable blindness at work in the way games have been covered to date. For all the discussion of gaming culture that you see, the actual experience of playing games has been strangely misrepresented. We hear a lot about the content of games: the carnage and drive-by killings and adolescent fantasies. But we rarely hear accurate descriptions about what it actually *feels like* to spend time in these virtual worlds. I worry about the experiential gap between people who have immersed themselves in games, and people who have only heard secondhand reports, because the gap makes it difficult to discuss the meaning of games in a coherent way. It reminds me of the way the social critic Jane Jacobs felt about the thriving urban neighborhoods she documented in the sixties: "People who know well such animated city streets will know how it is. People who do not will always have it a little wrong in their heads — like the old prints of rhinoceroses made from travelers' descriptions of the rhinoceroses."

So what does the rhinoceros actually look like? The first and last thing that should be said about the experience of playing today's video games, the thing you almost never hear in the mainstream coverage, is, that games are fiendishly, sometimes maddeningly, *hard*.

For Discussion and Writing

1. Why do many people think video games are bad for children? Why does Johnson think they're good?
2. Johnson writes that an important reason for the bad reputation of video games is that they have been contrasted with books. But he doesn't just say the comparison is unfair: he says that the comparison has been conducted unfairly. How does he make this argument? What are his examples? What general lessons might you be able to draw from his analysis of this specific case?
3. **connections** Imagine a conversation between Johnson and Marie Winn ("Television: The Plug-In Drug," p. 438). What might they have to say to each other about the evils and/or benefits of the media which are their subjects? Would Winn say the same things about video games as she says about television? Conversely, would Johnson say the same things about television that he says about video games?
4. Johnson writes, "You can't get much more conventional than the conventional wisdom that kids today would be better off spending more time reading books, and less time zoning out in front of their video games" (par. 1). Leaving aside the specifics of Johnson's argument,

reflect on the idea of conventional wisdom. That ideas are conventional, that is, widely held and largely unchallenged, can be taken to indicate two opposite things — that they are true because most people agree that they are true, or that they are false because most people simply assume they are true without thinking about them. What do you think of the idea of conventional wisdom? Are you more likely to trust it or distrust it? Why? Think of examples to support your answer.

MARTIN LUTHER KING JR.

Letter from Birmingham Jail

The foremost leader of the American civil rights movement of the 1950s and 1960s, Martin Luther King was born in Atlanta, Georgia, in 1929 and assassinated in Memphis, Tennessee, in 1968. He was an ordained minister with a Ph.D., a powerful preacher and speechmaker, and an author. A crusader against segregation in his role as organizer of the Montgomery, Alabama, bus boycott and head of the Southern Christian Leadership Conference, King advocated nonviolent resistance in the face of discrimination and violence. The steadfast dignity with which he pursued rights for African Americans earned him worldwide renown and a Nobel Peace Prize.

"Letter from Birmingham Jail" was written while King and hundreds of other protesters were under arrest for demonstrating in Birmingham, Alabama. It is a response to eight of his fellow clergymen who questioned his methods of protest even as they supported his ultimate aims. Note, as you read, the combination in his writing of the cool logic of his argument and his passionate sense of the injustice African Americans have suffered.

My Dear Fellow Clergymen:

While confined here in the Birmingham city jail, I came across your recent statement calling my present activities "unwise and untimely." Seldom do I pause to answer criticism of my work and ideas. If I sought to answer all the criticisms that cross my desk, my secretaries would have little time for anything other than such correspondence in the course of the day, and I would have no time for constructive work. But since I feel that you are men of genuine good will and that your criticisms are sincerely set forth, I want to try to answer your statement in what I hope will be patient and reasonable terms.

I think I should indicate why I am here in Birmingham, since you have been influenced by the view which argues against "outsiders coming in." I have the honor of serving as president of the Southern Christian Leadership Conference, an organization operating in every southern state, with headquarters in Atlanta, Georgia. We have some eighty-five affiliated organizations across the South, and one of them is the Alabama Christian Movement for Human Rights. Frequently we share staff, educational, and financial resources with our affiliates. Several months ago the affiliate here in Birmingham asked us to be on call to engage in a nonviolent direct-action program if such were deemed necessary. We readily consented, and when the hour came we lived up to our promise. So I, along with several members of my staff, am here because I was invited here. I am here because I have organizational ties here.

But more basically, I am in Birmingham because injustice is here. Just as the prophets of the eighth century B.C. left their villages and carried their "thus saith the Lord" far beyond the boundaries of their home towns, and just as the Apostle Paul left his village of Tarsus and carried the gospel of Jesus Christ to the far corners of the Greco-Roman world, so am I compelled to carry the gospel of freedom beyond my own home town. Like Paul, I must constantly respond to the Macedonian call for aid.

Moreover, I am cognizant of the interrelatedness of all communities and states. I cannot sit idly by in Atlanta and not be concerned about what happens in Birmingham. Injustice anywhere is a threat to justice everywhere. We are caught in an inescapable network of mutuality, tied in a single garment of destiny. Whatever affects one directly, affects all indirectly. Never again can we afford to live with the narrow, provincial "outside agitator" idea. Anyone who lives inside the United States can never be considered an outsider anywhere within its bounds.

You deplore the demonstrations taking place in Birmingham. 5
But your statement, I am sorry to say, fails to express a similar concern for the conditions that brought about the demonstrations. I am sure that none of you would want to rest content with the superficial kind of social analysis that deals merely with effects and does not grapple with underlying causes. It is unfortunate that demonstrations are taking place in Birmingham, but it is even more unfortunate that the city's white power structure left the Negro community with no alternative.

In any nonviolent campaign there are four basic steps: collection of the facts to determine whether injustices exist; negotiation; self-purification; and direct action. We have gone through all these steps in Birmingham. There can be no gainsaying the fact that racial injustice engulfs this community. Birmingham is probably the most thoroughly segregated city in the United States. Its ugly record of brutality is widely known. Negroes have experienced grossly unjust treatment in the courts. There have been more unsolved bombings of Negro homes and churches in Birmingham than in any other city in the nation. These are the hard, brutal facts of the case. On the basis of these conditions, Negro leaders sought to negotiate with the city fathers. But the latter consistently refused to engage in good-faith negotiation.

Then, last September, came the opportunity to talk with leaders of Birmingham's economic community. In the course of the negotiations, certain promises were made by the merchants — for example, to remove the stores' humiliating racial signs. On the basis of these promises, the Reverend Fred Shuttlesworth and the leaders of the Alabama Christian Movement for Human Rights agreed to a moratorium on all demonstrations. As the weeks and months went by, we realized that we were the victims of a broken promise. A few signs, briefly removed, returned; the others remained.

As in so many past experiences, our hopes had been blasted, and the shadow of deep disappointment settled upon us. We had no alternative except to prepare for direct action, whereby we would present our very bodies as a means of laying our case before the conscience of the local and the national community. Mindful of the difficulties involved, we decided to undertake a process of self-purification. We began a series of workshops on nonviolence, and we repeatedly asked ourselves: "Are you able to accept blows without retaliating?" "Are you able to endure the ordeal of jail?" We decided to schedule our direct-action program for the Easter season, realizing that except for Christmas, this is the main shopping period of the year. Knowing that a strong economic withdrawal program would be the by-product of direct action, we felt that this would be the best time to bring pressure to bear on the merchants for the needed change.

Then it occurred to us that Birmingham's mayoral election was coming up in March, and we speedily decided to postpone action until after election day. When we discovered that the Commissioner of Public Safety, Eugene "Bull" Connor, had piled up enough votes to be in the runoff, we decided again to postpone action until the day after the runoff so that the demonstrations could not be used to cloud the issues. Like many others, we wanted to see Mr. Connor defeated, and to this end we endured postponement after postponement. Having aided in this community need, we felt that our direct-action program could be delayed no longer.

10 You may well ask, "Why direct action? Why sit-ins, marches, and so forth? Isn't negotiation a better path?" You are quite right in calling for negotiation. Indeed, this is the very purpose of direct action. Nonviolent direct action seeks to create such a crisis and foster such a tension that a community which has constantly refused to negotiate is forced to confront the issue. It seeks so to dramatize the issue that it can no longer be ignored. My citing the creation of tension as part of the work of the nonviolent-resister may sound rather shocking. But I must confess that I am not afraid of the word "tension." I have earnestly opposed violent tension, but there is a type of constructive, nonviolent tension which is necessary for growth. Just as Socrates felt that it was necessary to create a tension in the mind so that individuals could rise from the bondage of myths and half-truths to the unfettered realm of creative analysis and objective appraisal, so must we see the need for nonviolent gadflies to create the kind of tension in society that will help men rise from the dark depths of prejudice and racism to the majestic heights of understanding and brotherhood.

The purpose of our direct-action program is to create a situation so crisis-packed that it will inevitably open the door to negotiation. I therefore concur with you in your call for negotiation. Too long has our beloved Southland been bogged down in a tragic effort to live in monologue rather than dialogue.

One of the basic points in your statement is that the action that I and my associates have taken in Birmingham is untimely. Some have asked: "Why didn't you give the new city administration time to act?" The only answer that I can give to this query is that the new Birmingham administration must be prodded about as much as the outgoing one, before it will act. We are sadly mistaken if we feel that the election of Albert Boutwell as mayor will bring the millennium to Birmingham. While Mr. Boutwell is a much more gentle person than Mr. Connor, they are both segregationists, dedicated to maintenance of the status quo. I have hoped that Mr. Boutwell will be reasonable enough to see the futility of massive resistance to desegregation. But he will not see this without pressure from devotees of civil rights. My friends, I must say to you that we have not made a single gain in civil rights without determined legal and nonviolent pressure. Lamentably, it is an historical fact that privileged groups seldom give up their privileges voluntarily. Individuals may see the moral light and voluntarily give up their unjust posture, but, as Reinhold Niebuhr has reminded us, groups tend to be more immoral than individuals.

We know through painful experience that freedom is never voluntarily given by the oppressor; it must be demanded by the oppressed. Frankly, I have yet to engage in a direct-action campaign that was "well timed" in the view of those who have not suffered unduly from the disease of segregation. For years now I have heard the word "Wait!" It rings in the ear of every Negro with piercing familiarity. This "Wait" has almost always meant "Never." We must come to see, with one of our distinguished jurists, that "justice too long delayed is justice denied."

We have waited for more than 340 years for our constitutional and God-given rights. The nations of Asia and Africa are moving with jet-like speed toward gaining political independence, but we still creep at horse-and-buggy pace toward gaining a cup of coffee at a lunch counter. Perhaps it is easy for those who have never felt the stinging darts of segregation to say, "Wait." But when you have seen vicious mobs lynch your mothers and fathers at will and drown your sisters and brothers at whim; when you have seen hate-filled policemen curse, kick, and even kill your black brothers and sisters; when you see the vast majority of your twenty million Negro brothers smothering in an airtight cage of poverty in the midst of an affluent society; when you suddenly find your tongue twisted and your speech stammering as you seek to explain to your six-year-old daughter why she can't go to the public amusement park that has just been advertised on television, and see tears welling up in her eyes when she is told that Funtown is closed to colored children, and see ominous clouds of inferiority beginning to form in her little mental sky, and see her beginning to distort her personality by developing an unconscious bitterness toward white people; when you have to concoct an answer for a five-year-old son who is asking, "Daddy, why do white people treat colored people so mean?"; when you take a cross-country drive and find it necessary to sleep night after night in the uncomfortable corners of your automobile because no motel will accept you; when you are humiliated day in and day out by nagging signs reading "white" and "colored"; when your first name becomes "nigger," your middle name becomes "boy" (however old you are) and your last name becomes "John," and your wife and mother are never given the respected title "Mrs."; when you are harried by day and haunted by night by the fact that you are a Negro, living constantly at tiptoe stance, never quite knowing what to expect next, and are plagued with inner fears and outer resentments; when you are forever fighting a degenerating sense of "nobodiness" — then you will understand why we find it difficult to wait. There comes a time when the cup of endurance runs over, and men are no longer willing to be plunged into the abyss of despair. I hope, sirs, you can understand our legitimate and unavoidable impatience.

You express a great deal of anxiety over our willingness to break 15
laws. This is certainly a legitimate concern. Since we so diligently urge people to obey the Supreme Court's decision of 1954 outlawing segregation in the public schools, at first glance it may seem rather paradoxical for us consciously to break laws. One may well ask: "How can you advocate breaking some laws and obeying others?" The answer lies in the fact that there are two types of laws: just and unjust. I would be the first to advocate obeying just laws. One has not only a legal but a moral responsibility to obey just laws. Conversely, one has a moral responsibility to disobey unjust laws. I would agree with St. Augustine that "an unjust law is no law at all."

Now, what is the difference between the two? How does one determine whether a law is just or unjust? A just law is a man-made code that squares with the moral law or the law of God. An unjust law is a code that is out of harmony with the moral law. To put it in the terms of St. Thomas Aquinas: An unjust law is a human law that is not rooted in eternal law and natural law. Any law that uplifts human personality is just. Any law that degrades human personality is unjust. All segregation statutes are unjust because segregation distorts the soul and damages the personality. It gives the segregator a false sense of superiority and the segregated a false sense of inferiority. Segregation, to use the terminology of the Jewish philosopher Martin Buber, substitutes an "I-it" relationship for an "I-thou" relationship and ends up relegating persons to the status of things. Hence segregation is not only politically, economically, and sociologically unsound, it is morally wrong and sinful. Paul Tillich has said that sin is separation. Is not segregation an existential expression of man's tragic separation, his awful estrangement, his terrible sinfulness? Thus it is that I can urge men to obey the 1954 decision of the Supreme Court, for it is morally right; and I can urge them to disobey segregation ordinances, for they are morally wrong.

Let us consider a more concrete example of just and unjust laws. An unjust law is a code that a numerical or power majority group compels a minority group to obey but does not make binding on itself. This is *difference* made legal. By the same token, a just law is a code that a majority compels a minority to follow and that it is willing to follow itself. This is *sameness* made legal.

Let me give another explanation. A law is unjust if it is inflicted on a minority that, as a result of being denied the right to vote, had no part in enacting or devising the law. Who can say that the legislature of Alabama which set up that state's segregation laws was democratically elected? Throughout Alabama all sorts of devious methods are used to prevent Negroes from becoming registered voters, and there are some counties in which, even though Negroes constitute a majority of the population, not a single Negro is registered. Can any law enacted under such circumstances be considered democratically structured?

Sometimes a law is just on its face and unjust in its application. For instance, I have been arrested on a charge of parading without a permit. Now, there is nothing wrong in having an ordinance which requires a permit for a parade. But such an ordinance becomes unjust when it is used to maintain segregation and to deny citizens the First-Amendment privilege of peaceful assembly and protest.

I hope you are able to see the distinction I am trying to point 20
out. In no sense do I advocate evading or defying the law, as would the rabid segregationist. That would lead to anarchy. One who breaks an unjust law must do so openly, lovingly, and with a willingness to accept the penalty. I submit that an individual who breaks a law that conscience tells him is unjust, and who willingly accepts the penalty of imprisonment in order to arouse the

conscience of the community over its injustice, is in reality expressing the highest respect for law.

Of course, there is nothing new about this kind of civil disobedience. It was evidenced sublimely in the refusal of Shadrach, Meshach, and Abednego to obey the laws of Nebuchadnezzar, on the ground that a higher moral law was at stake. It was practiced superbly by the early Christians, who were willing to face hungry lions and the excruciating pain of chopping blocks rather than submit to certain unjust laws of the Roman Empire. To a degree, academic freedom is a reality today because Socrates practiced civil disobedience. In our own nation, the Boston Tea Party represented a massive act of civil disobedience.

We should never forget that everything Adolf Hitler did in Germany was "legal" and everything the Hungarian freedom fighters did in Hungary was "illegal." It was "illegal" to aid and comfort a Jew in Hitler's Germany. Even so, I am sure that, had I lived in Germany at the time, I would have aided and comforted my Jewish brothers. If today I lived in a Communist country where certain principles dear to the Christian faith are suppressed, I would openly advocate disobeying that country's anti-religious laws.

I must make two honest confessions to you, my Christian and Jewish brothers. First, I must confess that over the past few years I have been gravely disappointed with the white moderate. I have almost reached the regrettable conclusion that the Negro's great stumbling block in his stride toward freedom is not the White Citizen's Counciler or the Ku Klux Klanner, but the white moderate, who is more devoted to "order" than to justice; who prefers a negative peace which is the absence of tension to a positive peace which is the presence of justice; who constantly says, "I agree with you in the goal you seek, but I cannot agree with your methods of direct action"; who paternalistically believes he can set the timetable for another man's freedom; who lives by a mythical concept of time and who constantly advises the Negro to wait for a "more convenient season." Shallow understanding from people of good will is more frustrating than absolute misunderstanding from people of ill will. Lukewarm acceptance is much more bewildering than outright rejection.

I had hoped that the white moderate would understand that law and order exist for the purpose of establishing justice and that when they fail in this purpose they become the dangerously structured dams that block the flow of social progress. I had hoped that the white moderate would understand that the present tension in the South is a necessary phase of the transition from an obnoxious negative peace, in which the Negro passively accepted his unjust plight, to a substantive and positive peace, in which all men will respect the dignity and worth of human personality. Actually, we who engage in nonviolent direct action are not the creators of tension. We merely bring to the surface the hidden tension that is already alive. We bring it out in the open, where it can be seen and dealt with. Like a boil that can never be cured so long as it is covered up but must be opened with all its ugliness to the natural medicines of air and light, injustice must be exposed, with all the tension its exposure creates, to the light of human conscience and the air of national opinion, before it can be cured.

In your statement you assert that our actions, even though 25
peaceful, must be condemned because they precipitate violence. But is this a logical assertion? Isn't this like condemning a robbed man because his possession of money precipitated the evil act of robbery? Isn't this like condemning Socrates because his unswerving commitment to truth and his philosophical inquiries precipitated the act by the misguided populace in which they made him drink hemlock? Isn't this like condemning Jesus because his unique God-consciousness and never-ceasing devotion to God's will precipitated the evil act of crucifixion? We must come to see that, as the federal courts have consistently affirmed, it is wrong to urge an individual to cease his efforts to gain his basic constitutional rights because the quest may precipitate violence. Society must protect the robbed and punish the robber.

I had also hoped that the white moderate would reject the myth concerning time in relation to the struggle for freedom. I have just received a letter from a white brother in Texas. He writes: "All Christians know that the colored people will receive equal rights eventually, but it is possible that you are in too great a religious hurry. It has taken Christianity almost two thousand years to accomplish what it has. The teachings of Christ take time to come to earth." Such an attitude stems from a tragic misconception of time, from the strangely irrational notion that there is something in the very flow of time that will inevitably cure all ills. Actually, time itself is neutral; it can be used either destructively or constructively. More and more I feel that the people of ill will have used time much more effectively than have the people of good will. We will have to repent in this generation not merely for the hateful words and actions of the bad people, but for the appalling silence of the good people. Human progress never rolls in on wheels of inevitability; it comes through the tireless efforts of men willing to be co-workers with God, and without this hard work, time itself becomes an ally of the forces of social stagnation. We must use time creatively, in the knowledge that the time is always ripe to do right. Now is the time to make real the promise of democracy and transform our pending national elegy into a creative psalm of brotherhood. Now is the time to lift our national policy from the quicksand of racial injustice to the solid rock of human dignity.

You speak of our activity in Birmingham as extreme. At first I was rather disappointed that fellow clergymen would see my nonviolent efforts as those of an extremist. I began thinking about the fact that I stand in the middle of two opposing forces in the Negro community. One is a force of complacency, made up in part of Negroes who, as a result of long years of oppression, are so drained of self-respect and a sense of "somebodiness" that they have adjusted to segregation; and in part of a few middle-class Negroes who, because of a degree of academic and economic security and because in some ways they profit by segregation, have become insensitive to the problems of the masses. The other force is one of bitterness and hatred, and it comes perilously close to advocating violence. It is expressed in the various black nationalist groups that are springing up across the nation, the largest and best-known being Elijah Muhammad's Muslim movement. Nourished by the Negro's frustration over the continued existence of racial discrimination, this movement is made up of people who have lost faith in America, who have absolutely repudiated Christianity, and who have concluded that the white man is an incorrigible "devil."

I have tried to stand between these two forces, saying that we need emulate neither the "do-nothingism" of the complacent nor the hatred and despair of the black nationalist. For there is the more excellent way of love and nonviolent protest. I am grateful to God that, through the influence of the Negro church, the way of nonviolence became an integral part of our struggle.

If this philosophy had not emerged, by now many streets of the South would, I am convinced, be flowing with blood. And I am further convinced that if our white brothers dismiss as "rabblerousers" and "outside agitators" those of us who employ nonviolent direct action, and if they refuse to support our nonviolent efforts, millions of Negroes will, out of frustration and despair, seek solace and security in black-nationalist ideologies — a development that would inevitably lead to a frightening racial nightmare.

Oppressed people cannot remain oppressed forever. The yearn- 30
ing for freedom eventually manifests itself, and that is what has happened to the American Negro. Something within has reminded him of his birthright of freedom, and something without has reminded him that it can be gained. Consciously or unconsciously, he has been caught up by the *Zeitgeist*, and with his black brothers of Africa and his brown and yellow brothers of Asia, South America, and the Caribbean, the United States Negro is moving with a sense of great urgency toward the promised land of racial justice. If one recognizes this vital urge that has engulfed the Negro community, one should readily understand why public demonstrations are taking place. The Negro has many pent-up resentments and latent frustrations, and he must release them. So let him march; let him make prayer pilgrimages to the city hall; let him go on freedom rides — and try to understand why he must do so. If his repressed emotions are not released in nonviolent ways, they will seek expression through violence; this is not a threat but a fact of history. So I have not said to my people, "Get rid of your discontent." Rather, I have tried to say that this normal and healthy discontent can be channeled into the creative outlet of nonviolent direct action. And now this approach is being termed extremist.

But though I was initially disappointed at being categorized as an extremist, as I continued to think about the matter I gradually gained a measure of satisfaction from the label. Was not Jesus an extremist for love: "Love your enemies, bless them that curse you, do good to them that hate you, and pray for them which despitefully use you, and persecute you." Was not Amos an extremist for justice: "Let justice roll down like waters and righteousness like an ever-flowing stream." Was not Paul an extremist for the Christian gospel: "I bear in my body the marks of the Lord Jesus." Was not Martin Luther an extremist: "Here I stand; I cannot do otherwise, so help me God." And John Bunyan: "I will stay in jail to the end of my days before I make a butchery of my conscience." And Abraham Lincoln: "This nation cannot survive half slave and half free." And Thomas Jefferson: "We hold these truths to be self-evident, that all men are created equal. . . ." So the question is not whether we will be extremists, but what kind of extremists we will be. Will we be extremists for hate or for love? Will we be extremists for the preservation of injustice or for the extension of justice? In that dramatic scene on Calvary's hill three men were crucified. We must never forget that all three were crucified for the same crime — the crime of extremism. Two were extremists for immorality, and thus fell below their environment. The other, Jesus Christ, was an extremist for love, truth, and goodness, and thereby rose above his environment. Perhaps the South, the nation, and the world are in dire need of creative extremists.

I had hoped that the white moderate would see this need. Perhaps I was too optimistic; perhaps I expected too much. I suppose I should have realized that few members of the oppressor race can understand the deep groans and passionate yearnings of the oppressed race, and still fewer have the vision to see that injustice must be rooted out by strong, persistent, and determined action. I am thankful, however, that some of our white brothers in the South have grasped the meaning of this social revolution and committed themselves to it. They are still all too few in quantity, but they are big in quality. Some — such as Ralph McGill, Lillian Smith, Harry Golden, James McBridge Dabbs, Ann Braden, and Sarah Patton Boyle — have written about our struggle in eloquent and prophetic terms. Others have marched with us down nameless streets of the South. They have languished in filthy, roach-infested jails, suffering the abuse and brutality of policemen who view them as "dirty nigger-lovers." Unlike so many of their moderate brothers and sisters, they have recognized the urgency of the moment and sensed the need for powerful "action" antidotes to combat the disease of segregation.

Let me take note of my other major disappointment. I have been so greatly disappointed with the white church and its leadership.

Of course, there are some notable exceptions. I am not unmindful of the fact that each of you has taken some significant stands on this issue. I commend you, Reverend Stallings, for your Christian stand on this past Sunday, in welcoming Negroes to your worship service on a nonsegregated basis. I commend the Catholic leaders of this state for integrating Spring Hill College several years ago.

But despite these notable exceptions, I must honestly reiterate that I have been disappointed with the church. I do not say this as one of those negative critics who can always find something wrong with the church. I say this as a minister of the gospel, who loves the church; who was nurtured in its bosom; who has been sustained by its spiritual blessings and who will remain true to it as long as the cord of life shall lengthen.

When I was suddenly catapulted into the leadership of the bus 35
protest in Montgomery, Alabama, a few years ago, I felt we would be supported by the white church. I felt that the white ministers, priests, and rabbis of the South would be among our strongest allies. Instead, some have been outright opponents, refusing to understand the freedom movement and misrepresenting its leaders; all too many others have been more cautious than courageous and have remained silent behind the anesthetizing security of stained-glass windows.

In spite of my shattered dreams, I came to Birmingham with the hope that the white religious leadership of this community would see the justice of our cause and, with deep moral concern, would serve as the channel through which our just grievances could reach the power structure. I had hoped that each of you would understand. But again I have been disappointed.

I have heard numerous southern religious leaders admonish their worshipers to comply with a desegregation decision because it is the law, but I have longed to hear white ministers declare: "Follow this decree because integration is morally right and because the Negro is your brother." In the midst of blatant injustices inflicted upon the Negro, I have watched white churchmen stand on the sideline and mouth pious irrelevancies and sanctimonious trivialities. In the midst of a mighty struggle to rid our nation of racial and economic injustice, I have heard many ministers say: "Those are social issues, with which the gospel has no real concern." And I have watched many churches commit themselves to a completely otherworldly religion which makes a strange, un-Biblical distinction between body and soul, between the sacred and the secular.

I have traveled the length and breadth of Alabama, Mississippi, and all the other southern states. On sweltering summer days and crisp autumn mornings I have looked at the South's beautiful churches with their lofty spires pointing heavenward. I have beheld the impressive outlines of her massive religious-education buildings. Over and over I have found myself asking: "What kind of people worship here? Who is their God? Where were their voices when the lips of Governor Barnett dripped with words of interposition and nullification? Where were they when Governor Wallace gave a clarion call for defiance and hatred? Where were their voices of support when bruised and weary Negro men and women decided to rise from the dark dungeons of complacency to the bright hills of creative protest?"

Yes, these questions are still in my mind. In deep disappointment I have wept over the laxity of the church. But be assured that my tears have been tears of love. There can be no deep disappointment where there is not deep love. Yes, I love the church. How could I do otherwise? I am in the rather unique position of being the son, the grandson, and the great-grandson of preachers. Yes, I see the church as the body of Christ. But, oh! How we have blemished and scarred that body through social neglect and through fear of being nonconformists.

There was a time when the church was very powerful — in the 40
time when the early Christians rejoiced at being deemed worthy to suffer for what they believed. In those days the church was not merely a thermometer that recorded the ideas and principles of popular opinion; it was a thermostat that transformed the mores of society. Whenever the early Christians entered a town, the people in power became disturbed and immediately sought to convict the Christians for being "disturbers of the peace" and "outside agitators." But the Christians pressed on, in the conviction that they were "a colony of heaven," called to obey God rather than man. Small in number, they were big in commitment. They were too God-intoxicated to be "astronomically intimidated." By their effort and example they brought an end to such ancient evils as infanticide and gladiatorial contests.

Things are different now. So often the contemporary church is a weak, ineffectual voice with an uncertain sound. So often it is an archdefender of the status quo. Far from being disturbed by the presence of the church, the power structure of the average community is consoled by the church's silent — and often even vocal — sanction of things as they are.

But the judgment of God is upon the church as never before. If today's church does not recapture the sacrificial spirit of the early church, it will lose its authenticity, forfeit the loyalty of millions, and be dismissed as an irrelevant social club with no meaning for the twentieth century. Every day I meet young people whose disappointment with the church has turned into outright disgust.

Perhaps I have once again been too optimistic. Is organized religion too inextricably bound to the status quo to save our nation and the world? Perhaps I must turn my faith to the inner spiritual church, the church within the church, as the true *ekklesia* and the hope of the world. But again I am thankful to God that some noble souls from the ranks of organized religion have broken loose from the paralyzing chains of conformity and joined us as active partners in the struggle for freedom. They have left their secure congregations and walked the streets of Albany, Georgia, with us. They have gone down the highways of the South on tortuous rides for freedom. Yes, they have gone to jail with us. Some have been dismissed from their churches, have lost the support of their bishops and fellow ministers. But they have acted in the faith that right defeated is stronger than evil triumphant. Their witness has been the spiritual salt that has preserved the true meaning of the gospel in these troubled times. They have carved a tunnel of hope through the dark mountain of disappointment.

I hope the church as a whole will meet the challenge of this decisive hour. But even if the church does not come to the aid of justice, I have no despair about the future. I have no fear about the outcome of our struggle in Birmingham, even if our motives are at present misunderstood. We will reach the goal of freedom in Birmingham and all over the nation, because the goal of America is freedom. Abused and scorned though we may be, our destiny is tied up with America's destiny. Before the pilgrims landed at Plymouth, we were here. Before the pen of Jefferson etched the majestic words of the Declaration of Independence across the pages of history, we were here. For more than two centuries our forebears labored in this country without wages: they made cotton king; they built the homes of their masters while suffering gross injustice and shameful humiliation — and yet out of a bottomless vitality they continued to thrive and develop. If the inexpressible cruelties of slavery could not stop us, the opposition we now face will surely fail. We will win our freedom because the sacred heritage of our nation and the eternal will of God are embodied in our echoing demands.

Before closing I feel impelled to mention one other point in 45
your statement that has troubled me profoundly. You warmly commended the Birmingham police force for keeping "order" and "preventing violence." I doubt that you would have so warmly commended the police force if you had seen its dogs sinking their teeth into unarmed, nonviolent Negroes. I doubt that you would so quickly commend the policemen if you were to observe their ugly and inhumane treatment of Negroes here in the city jail; if you were to watch them push and curse old Negro women and young Negro girls; if you were to see them slap and kick old Negro men and young boys; if you were to observe them, as they did on two occasions, refuse to give us food because we wanted to sing our grace together. I cannot join you in your praise of the Birmingham police department.

It is true that the police have exercised a degree of discipline in handling the demonstrators. In this sense they have conducted themselves rather "nonviolently" in public. But for what purpose? To preserve the evil system of segregation. Over the past few years I have consistently preached that nonviolence demands that the means we use must be as pure as the ends we seek. I have tried to make clear that it is wrong to use immoral means to attain moral ends. But now I must affirm that it is just as wrong, or perhaps even more so, to use moral means to preserve immoral ends. Perhaps Mr. Connor and his policemen have been rather nonviolent in public, as was Chief Pritchett in Albany, Georgia, but they have used the moral means of nonviolence to maintain the immoral end of racial injustice. As T. S. Eliot has said. "The last temptation is the greatest treason: To do the right deed for the wrong reason."

I wish you had commended the Negro sit-inners and demonstrators of Birmingham for their sublime courage, their willingness to suffer, and their amazing discipline in the midst of great provocation. One day the South will recognize its real heroes. They will be the James Merediths, with the noble sense of purpose that enables them to face jeering and hostile mobs, and with the agonizing loneliness that characterizes the life of the pioneer. They will be old, oppressed, battered Negro women, symbolized in a seventy-two-year-old woman in Montgomery, Alabama, who rose up with a sense of dignity and with her people decided not to ride segregated buses, and who responded with ungrammatical profundity to one who inquired about her weariness: "My feets is tired, but my soul is at rest." They will be the young high school and college students, the young ministers of the gospel and a host of their elders, courageously and nonviolently sitting in at lunch counters and willingly going to jail for conscience' sake. One day the South will know that when these disinherited children of God sat down at lunch counters, they were in reality standing up for what is best in the American dream and for the most sacred values in our Judaeo-Christian heritage, thereby bringing our nation back to those great wells of democracy which were dug deep by the founding fathers in their formulation of the Constitution and the Declaration of Independence.

Never before have I written so long a letter. I'm afraid it is much too long to take your precious time. I can assure you that it would have been much shorter if I had been writing from a comfortable desk, but what else can one do when he is alone in a narrow jail cell, other than write long letters, think long thoughts, and pray long prayers?

If I have said anything in this letter that overstates the truth and indicates an unreasonable impatience, I beg you to forgive me. If I have said anything that understates the truth and indicates my having a patience that allows me to settle for anything less than brotherhood, I beg God to forgive me.

I hope this letter finds you strong in the faith. I also hope that 50
circumstances will soon make it possible for me to meet each of you, not as an integrationist or a civil-rights leader but as a fellow clergyman and a Christian brother. Let us all hope that the dark clouds of racial prejudice will soon pass away and the deep fog of misunderstanding will be lifted from our fear-drenched communities, and in some not too distant tomorrow the radiant stars of love and brotherhood will shine over our great nation with all their scintillating beauty.

Yours for the cause of Peace and Brotherhood,
MARTIN LUTHER KING JR.

For Discussion and Writing

1. List the other historical movements to which King compares the civil rights movement. What is the purpose of including this information?
2. Describe what King does in the two sentences that make up his second-to-last paragraph (par. 49). How do these two variations on an apology sum up his approach to argument in this essay?
3. **connections** Compare King's understanding of race to Zora Neale Hurston's in "How It Feels to Be Colored Me" (p. 182). Be careful to note ways in which they agree as well as ways in which they disagree.
4. Pick a law people might break because they think it is wrong. If you might do so too, write an essay in which you defend your actions. If you would not, write an essay in which you argue against those who would. Consider the reasons King cites for his violations of the law.

MAXINE HONG KINGSTON

No Name Woman

Maxine Hong Kingston was born in Stockton, California, in 1940 to Chinese immigrant parents. She is a writer and academic known best for The Woman Warrior: Memoirs of a Girlhood among Ghosts *(1976), a mixture of history, autobiography, and fiction informed by the oral history and folktales she heard growing up in a tight-knit Chinese American neighborhood.* China Men *(1980),* Tripmaster Monkey: His Fake Book *(1989), and* The Fifth Book of Peace *(2003) continue Kingston's exploration of Chinese American life.*

"No Name Woman" is the first chapter of The Woman Warrior, *which has been hailed for the ways in which it weaves together a variety of genres and ways of understanding the world. Note, as you read this selection, the ways in which Kingston connects history to the story of her family.*

"You must not tell anyone," my mother said, "what I am about to tell you. In China your father had a sister who killed herself. She jumped into the family well. We say that your father has all brothers because it is as if she had never been born.

"In 1924 just a few days after our village celebrated seventeen hurry-up weddings — to make sure that every young man who went 'out on the road' would responsibly come home — your father and his brothers and your grandfather and his brothers and your aunt's new husband sailed for America, the Gold Mountain. It was your grandfather's last trip. Those lucky enough to get contracts waved good-bye from the decks. They fed and guarded the stowaways and helped them off in Cuba, New York, Bali, Hawaii. 'We'll meet in California next year,' they said. All of them sent money home.

"I remember looking at your aunt one day when she and I were dressing; I had not noticed before that she had such a protruding melon of a stomach. But I did not think, 'She's pregnant,' until she began to look like other pregnant women, her shirt pulling and the white tops of her black pants showing. She could not have been pregnant, you see, because her husband had been gone for years. No one said anything. We did not discuss it. In early summer she was ready to have the child, long after the time when it could have been possible.

"The village had also been counting. On the night the baby was to be born the villagers raided our house. Some were crying. Like a great saw, teeth strung with lights, files of people walked zigzag across our land, tearing the rice. Their lanterns doubled in the disturbed black water, which drained away through the broken bunds. As the villagers closed in, we could see that some of them, probably men and women we knew well, wore white masks. The people with long hair hung it over their faces. Women with short hair made it stand up on end. Some had tied white bands around their foreheads, arms, and legs.

5 "At first they threw mud and rocks at the house. Then they threw eggs and began slaughtering our stock. We could hear the animals scream their deaths — the roosters, the pigs, a last great roar from the ox. Familiar wild heads flared in our night windows; the villagers encircled us. Some of the faces stopped to peer at us, their eyes rushing like searchlights. The hands flattened against the panes, framed heads, and left red prints.

"The villagers broke in the front and the back doors at the same time, even though we had not locked the doors against them. Their knives dripped with the blood of our animals. They smeared blood on the doors and walls. One woman swung a chicken, whose throat she had slit, splattering blood in red arcs about her. We stood together in the middle of our house, in the family hall with the pictures and tables of the ancestors around us, and looked straight ahead.

"At that time the house had only two wings. When the men came back we would build two more to enclose our courtyard and a third one to begin a second courtyard. The villagers pushed through both wings, even your grandparents' rooms, to find your aunt's, which was also mine until the men returned. From this room a new wing for one of the younger families would grow. They ripped up her clothes and shoes and broke her combs, grinding them underfoot. They tore her work from the loom. They scattered the cooking fire and rolled the new weaving in it. We could hear them in the kitchen breaking our bowls and banging the pots. They overturned the great waist-high earthenware jugs; duck eggs, pickled fruits, vegetables burst out and mixed in acrid torrents. The old woman from the next field swept a broom through the air and loosed the spirits-of-the-broom over our heads. 'Pig.' 'Ghost.' 'Pig,' they sobbed and scolded while they ruined our house.

"When they left, they took sugar and oranges to bless themselves. They cut pieces from the dead animals. Some of them took bowls that were not broken and clothes that were not torn. Afterward we swept up the rice and sewed it back up into sacks. But the smells from the spilled preserves lasted. Your aunt gave birth in the pigsty that night. The next morning when I went up for the water, I found her and the baby plugging up the family well.

"Don't let your father know that I told you. He denies her. Now that you have started to menstruate, what happened to her could happen to you. Don't humiliate us. You wouldn't like to be forgotten as if you had never been born. The villagers are watchful."

Whenever she had to warn us about life, my mother told sto- 10
ries that ran like this one, a story to grow up on. She tested our strength to establish realities. Those in the emigrant generations who could not reassert brute survival died young and far from home. Those of us in the first American generations have had to figure out how the invisible world the emigrants built around our childhoods fit in solid America.

The emigrants confused the gods by diverting their curses, misleading them with crooked streets and false names. They must try to confuse their offspring as well, who, I suppose, threaten them in similar ways — always trying to get things straight, always trying to name the unspeakable. The Chinese I know hide their names; sojourners take new names when their lives change and guard their real names with silence.

Chinese-Americans, when you try to understand what things in you are Chinese, how do you separate what is peculiar to childhood, to poverty, insanities, one family, your mother who marked your growing with stories, from what is Chinese? What is Chinese tradition and what is the movies?

If I want to learn what clothes my aunt wore, whether flashy or ordinary, I would have to begin, "Remember Father's drowned-in-the-well sister?" I cannot ask that. My mother has told me once and for all the useful parts. She will add nothing unless powered by Necessity, a riverbank that guides her life. She plants vegetable gardens rather than lawns; she carries the odd-shaped tomatoes home from the fields and eats food left for the gods.

Whenever we did frivolous things, we used up energy; we flew high kites. We children came up off the ground over the melting cones our parents brought home from work and the American movie on New Years' Day — *Oh, You Beautiful Doll* with Betty Grable one year, and *She Wore a Yellow Ribbon* with John Wayne another year. After the one carnival ride each, we paid in guilt; our tired father counted his change on the dark walk home.

Adultery is extravagance. Could people who hatch their own 15
chicks and eat the embryos and the heads for delicacies and boil the feet in vinegar for party food, leaving only the gravel, eating even the gizzard lining — could such people engender a prodigal aunt? To be a woman, to have a daughter in starvation time was a waste enough. My aunt could not have been the lone romantic who gave up everything for sex. Women in the old China did not choose. Some man had commanded her to lie with him and be his secret evil. I wonder whether he masked himself when he joined the raid on her family.

Perhaps she encountered him in the fields or on the mountain where the daughters-in-law collected fuel. Or perhaps he first noticed her in the marketplace. He was not a stranger because the village housed no strangers. She had to have dealings with him other than sex. Perhaps he worked an adjoining field, or he sold her the cloth for the dress she sewed and wore. His demand must have surprised, then terrified her. She obeyed him; she always did as she was told.

When the family found a young man in the next village to be her husband, she stood tractably beside the best rooster, his proxy, and promised before they met that she would be his forever. She was lucky that he was her age and she would be the first wife, an advantage secure now. The night she first saw him, he had sex with her. Then he left for America. She had almost forgotten what he looked like. When she tried to envision him, she only saw the black and white face in the group photograph the men had had taken before leaving.

The other man was not, after all, much different from her husband. They both gave orders: she followed. "If you tell your family, I'll beat you. I'll kill you. Be here again next week." No

Resources for Teaching

A PORTABLE ANTHOLOGY

THIRD EDITION

Samuel Cohen

University of Missouri

Bedford/St. Martin's   Boston ◆ New York

5 4 3 2 1 0
f e d c b a

For information, write: Bedford/St. Martin's, 75 Arlington Street, Boston, MA 02116 (617-399-4000)

ISBN-10: 0-312-67543-7
ISBN-13: 978-0-312-67543-1

Preface

The materials in this Instructor's Manual are intended to provide you with guidance as you assign readings from *50 Essays: A Portable Anthology*. The sample syllabi present suggestions for ways to structure your course. Notes on each of the reading selections cover some of the reasoning behind the questions that follow the essays in the book and offer direction on further avenues of exploration. Since there are so many essays that have become staples of the composition classroom included in *50 Essays*, the materials that follow are only a few of the ways these selections can be taught. For suggestions on teaching our course through an emphasis on writing purpose, with paired essays or casebooks, or with a thematic, rhetorical, or chronological focus, consult the "Alternate Table of Contens" located at the front of *50 Essays*.

Contents

Preface iii

Sample Syllabi 1

SHERMAN ALEXIE, *The Joy of Reading and Writing: Superman and Me* 13
MAYA ANGELOU, *Graduation* 13
GLORIA ANZALDÚA, *How to Tame a Wild Tongue* 14
BARBARA LAZEAR ASCHER, *On Compassion* 14
JAMES BALDWIN, *Notes of a Native Son* 15
DAVE BARRY, *Turkeys in the Kitchen* 16
WILLIAM F. BUCKLEY JR., *Why Don't We Complain?* 16
RACHEL CARSON, *The Obligation to Endure* 17
JUDITH ORTIZ COFER, *The Myth of the Latin Woman: I Just Met a Girl Named María* 17
JARED DIAMOND, *The Ends of the World as We Know Them* 18
JOAN DIDION, *On Morality* 19
ANNIE DILLARD, *Seeing* 20
FREDERICK DOUGLASS, *Learning to Read and Write* 20
BARBARA EHRENREICH, *Serving in Florida* 21
LARS EIGHNER, *On Dumpster Diving* 22
STEPHANIE ERICSSON, *The Ways We Lie* 22
STEPHEN JAY GOULD, *Sex, Drugs, Disasters, and the Extinction of Dinosaurs* 23
LANGSTON HUGHES, *Salvation* 23
ZORA NEALE HURSTON, *How It Feels to Be Colored Me* 24
THOMAS JEFFERSON, *The Declaration of Independence* 25
STEVEN JOHNSON, *Games* 25
MARTIN LUTHER KING JR., *Letter from Birmingham Jail* 26
MAXINE HONG KINGSTON, *No Name Woman* 26
VERLYN KLINKENBORG, *Our Vanishing Night* 27
AUDRE LORDE, *The Fourth of July* 28

NANCY MAIRS, *On Being a Cripple* 28
MALCOLM X, *Learning to Read* 29
BILL MCKIBBEN, *Curbing Nature's Paparazzi* 29
N. SCOTT MOMADAY, *The Way to Rainy Mountain* 30
BHARATI MUKHERJEE, *Two Ways to Belong in America* 30
GEORGE ORWELL, *Shooting an Elephant* 31
PLATO, *Allegory of the Cave* 31
MICHAEL POLLAN, *What's Eating America* 32
RICHARD RODRIGUEZ, *Aria: Memoir of a Bilingual Childhood* 32
MIKE ROSE, *"I Just Wanna Be Average"* 33
SCOTT RUSSELL SANDERS, *The Men We Carry in Our Minds* 34
ERIC SCHLOSSER, *Kid Kustomers* 34
DAVID SEDARIS, *A Plague of Tics* 35
SUSAN SONTAG, *Regarding the Pain of Others* 35
ELIZABETH CADY STANTON, *Declaration of Sentiments and Resolutions* 36
BRENT STAPLES, *Just Walk on By: Black Men and Public Space* 36
JONATHAN SWIFT, *A Modest Proposal* 37
AMY TAN, *Mother Tongue* 37
HENRY DAVID THOREAU, *Where I Lived, and What I Lived For* 38
SOJOURNER TRUTH, *Ain't I a Woman?* 39
SARAH VOWELL, *Shooting Dad* 39
ALICE WALKER, *In Search of Our Mothers' Gardens* 40
E. B. WHITE, *Once More to the Lake* 40
MARIE WINN, *Television: The Plug-In Drug* 41
VIRGINIA WOOLF, *The Death of the Moth* 42

Sample Syllabi

Sample Syllabus by Rhetorical Mode

SAMUEL COHEN

Writing I

COURSE

To quote from the description of Writing I in the undergraduate bulletin: "This is an intensive course dealing with the organization and development of ideas in coherent, interesting, effective essays." My goal for this section of composition is to help you to improve your writing by helping you to work on these areas:

- the process of writing (invention, composition, revision);
- methods of writing (narration, description, process analysis, example, definition, classification, comparison/contrast, cause/effect, argument/persuasion);
- the larger elements of writing (structuring essays and paragraphs, using sources);
- the smaller elements of writing (spelling, grammar, syntax, style).

You will work on these areas by reading examples of good writing, by writing in and outside of class, and by planning, revising, and editing your writing with me and with your classmates. You will also be required to write a research paper, which will go through a number of stages of planning and revision. My hope is that by the end of the semester you will have produced a number of the bulletin-required "coherent, interesting, effective essays" and that you will have dealt with some important ideas about the world in the course of your reading and writing. The ultimate goal is that you will learn to enjoy writing and to excel at it, because no skill is more important or rewarding.

COURSE REQUIREMENTS

Attendance, etc. Mandatory. To quote again from the bulletin: "All students are required to attend every session of their courses. If a freshman or sophomore is absent in excess of twice the number of class sessions per week, the instructor must give the student a WU grade, which counts as an F. The instructor may give a junior or senior a WU grade (the equivalent of an F) for excessive absences. The WU grade may be given by the instructor at any time." Fifteen minutes late is absent, but it's still good to come even if you are late. Excuses are entertained and, if reasonable, accepted. It is always better to come to class without an assignment than to come at the end of class, or after class, with it. Eating in class is prohibited, as it is a distraction and class really isn't that long. Drinking is fine.

Assignments Reading and writing assignments are due at the beginning of class on the day under which they appear on the syllabus. Late assignments are penalized one full letter grade for each day they are late. All work must be handed in for the student to pass the class; this means that even if something is so late that it will earn no grade, it must be handed in. Again, exceptions will be made only for serious reasons.

Readings It is expected that you will come to class having done the reading assigned for that day. Note taking in the text (underlining, circling, annotating) is encouraged, as it makes you read more carefully and remember more accurately.

Postings You will be required to go online and post on Blackboard one question for further thought about the reading for the next class, by midnight of the day before that class meets. These posts are required but ungraded. Doing them will accomplish these goals: you will be more active readers because you will have to come up with a cogent question and you will learn to use Blackboard, which is valuable for computer literacy and for other courses that will require it.

Essays You will write an essay for six of the nine kinds of writing we will be covering this semester; three of these (narration, description, classification) will be revised. Essays should be typed, double-spaced, in a font no greater than 12 point, in black ink, with margins no greater than 1½ inches, and with nothing other than a staple or, if you have to, a paper clip fastening the pages together (in-class essays should be written in as legible a manner as possible on lined paper in blue or black ink, double-spaced, with decent margins). No essay should be shorter than three pages (in-class excepted).

Research Essay On an approved topic of your choosing. The process of writing the research essay will include a number of stages — coming up with a topic, gathering sources, drafting, revising. The essay must be at least five pages.

Portfolio Must be brought to class every meeting, and handed in the last day of class. Should contain all drafts of your formal essays, including your research paper, all of my comments (electronic submissions must be printed out, *with my* comments), and all revisions. Source notes and outline for research paper should also be included.

Presentations Each student will make two presentations: the first will be a few minutes leading a discussion of your question about the day's reading; the second will be a presentation of your research paper. Presentations are informal, but presenters should strive for clear and forceful expression of their ideas.

Workshops We will workshop our writing in a number of ways — individually or in pairs, small groups, or as a class — but the goal will always be to work with your classmates on your writing.

Conferences We will hold two required conferences in my office, for which you will sign up ahead of time. Any day during my office hours, in the hall, or on the sidewalk, if you can catch me are the times when we can hold nonrequired conferences whenever there's something you need to discuss. I am also available by e-mail.

Plagiarism From the college Web site: "Plagiarism is the act of presenting another person's ideas, research, or writings as your own. The following are some examples of plagiarism: Copying another person's actual words without the use of quotation marks and footnotes. Presenting another person's ideas or theories in your own words without acknowledging them. Using information that is not common knowledge without acknowledging the source. Failing to acknowledge collaborators on homework and laboratory assignments." For more on academic honesty, see the college Web site.

Grades and Standards

Your grade breaks down like this:

Six essays: 60%
Research essay: 20%

Presentations: 5%
Portfolio: 5%
Effort: 10%

The essays (revised versions, if more than one draft) are graded on ideas, clarity, style, and correctness. The presentations are graded on clarity of expression. The portfolio is graded on completeness and on evidence of improvement. Effort is graded on postings (which are ungraded but required), participation in class discussions and workshops, and general good humor. You can access your grades through Blackboard.

SCHEDULE (subject to change, as all things are)

Week 1

M Course introduction
Writing sample

W Writing sample review for style and correctness

Week 2

M *Narration*
50 Essays: George Orwell, "Shooting an Elephant," pp. 284–91
Handbook: "Getting Started and Finding a Focus"

W *Narration*
50 Essays: David Sedaris, "A Plague of Tics," pp. 359–72

Week 3

M *Handbook*: "Developing and Organizing Ideas"
Narration essay due

W College closed

Week 4

M College closed

W *Description*
50 Essays: Zora Neale Hurston, "How It Feels to Be Colored Me," pp. 182–86
Handbook: "Revising and Editing"
Narration essay workshop

Week 5

M *Description*
50 Essays: Virginia Woolf, "The Death of the Moth," pp. 448–51

Handbook: "Writing an Argument and Thinking Critically"
Narration essay revision due

W *Handbook*: "Top Ten Problems and Basic Grammar Review"
Description essay due

Week 6

M *Process analysis*
50 Essays: Frederick Douglass, "Learning to Read and Write," pp. 129–35
Handbook: "Research Basics"
Research essay workshop — topics

W *Process analysis*
50 Essays: Eighner, "On Dumpster Diving," pp. 146–58
Handbook: "Searching for Sources" "Evaluating Sources"
Description essay workshop

Week 7

M Conferences — research topic approval

W *Example*
50 Essays: Barbara Lazear Ascher, "On Compassion," pp. 46–49
Handbook: "The Five C's of Style"
Description essay revision due

Week 8

M *Example*
50 Essays: Thomas Jefferson, "The Declaration of Independence," pp. 187–95
Research essay source notes due

W Research essay workshop — sources

Week 9

M *Definition*
50 Essays: Gloria Anzaldúa, "How to Tame a Wild Tongue," pp. 33–45

W *Definition*
50 Essays: Scott Russell Sanders, "The Men We Carry in Our Minds," pp. 346–52

Week 10

M Research essay workshop

W *Classification*

50 Essays: Judith Ortiz Cofer, "The Myth of the Latin Woman: I Just Met a Girl Named María," pp. 91–97

Week 11

M *Classification*
50 Essays: Mike Rose, "'I Just Wanna Be Average,'" pp. 331–45

W Conferences — research sources and outline
Classification essay due

Week 12

M *Comparison/contrast*
50 Essays: James Baldwin, "Notes of a Native Son," pp. 50–71
Research paper draft due

W *Comparison/contrast*
50 Essays: Henry David Thoreau, "Where I Lived, and What I Lived For," pp. 403–09
In-class comparison/contrast essay

Week 13

M *Cause/effect*
50 Essays: Brent Staples, "Just Walk on By: Black Men and Public Space," pp. 383–86
Peer work on research essay
Classification essay revision due

W *Cause/effect*
50 Essays: Michael Pollan, "What's Eating America," pp. 300–306
In-class cause/effect essay

Week 14

M Research paper due

W *Argument/persuasion*
50 Essays: Martin Luther King Jr., "Letter from Birmingham Jail," pp. 203–20
Presentations

Week 15

M *Argument/persuasion*
50 Essays: Jonathan Swift, "A Modest Proposal," pp. 387–95

	In-class argument/persuasion essay
W	Presentations
	Portfolio due

Sample Syllabus by Theme

SCHEDULE

Week 1

M	Course introduction
	Writing sample
W	Writing sample review for style and correctness

Week 2

M	*Education*
	50 Essays: Sherman Alexie, "The Joy of Reading and Writing: Superman and Me," pp. 15–19
	Handbook: "Getting Started and Finding a Focus"
W	*Education*
	50 Essays: Frederick Douglass, "Learning to Read and Write," pp. 129–35

Week 3

M	*Handbook*: "Developing and Organizing Ideas"
	Education essay due
W	College closed

Week 4

M	College closed
W	*Identity*
	50 Essays: Gloria Anzaldúa, "How to Tame a Wild Tongue," pp. 33–45
	Handbook: "Revising and Editing"
	Education essay workshop

Week 5

M	*Identity*
	50 Essays: Nancy Mairs, "On Being a Cripple," pp. 244–56
	Handbook: "Writing an Argument and Thinking Critically"
	Education essay revision due

W *Handbook*: "Top Ten Problems and Basic Grammar Review"
Identity essay due

Week 6

M *Family*
50 Essays: Maxine Hong Kingston, "No Name Woman," pp. 221–33
Handbook: "Research Basics"
Research essay workshop — topics

W *Family*
50 Essays: Marie Winn, "Television: The Plug-In Drug," pp. 438–47
Identity essay workshop

Week 7

M Conferences — research topic approval

W *Gender*
50 Essays: Sojourner Truth, "Ain't I a Woman?" pp. 410–11
Handbook: "The Five C's of Style"
Identity essay revision due

Week 8

M *Gender*
50 Essays: Brent Staples, "Just Walk on By: Black Men and Public Space," pp. 383–86
Research essay source notes due

W Research essay workshop — sources

Week 9

M *Race and Culture*
50 Essays: James Baldwin, "Notes of a Native Son," pp. 50–71

W *Race and Culture*
50 Essays: Martin Luther King Jr., "Letter from Birmingham Jail," pp. 203–20

Week 10

M Research essay workshop

W *Reading, Writing, and Speaking*
50 Essays: Amy Tan, "Mother Tongue," pp. 396–402

Week 11

M *Reading, Writing, and Speaking*
50 Essays: Malcolm X, "Learning to Read," pp. 257–66

W Conferences — research sources and outline
Reading, Writing, and Speaking essay due

Week 12

M *Work and Class*
50 Essays: Barbara Ehrenreich, "Serving in Florida," pp. 136–45
Research paper draft due

W *Work and Class*
50 Essays: Mike Rose, "'I Just Wanna Be Average,'" pp. 331–45
In-class Work and Class essay due

Week 13

M *History and Politics*
50 Essays: Bharati Mukherjee, "Two Ways to Belong in America," pp. 280–83
Peer work on research essay
Reading, Writing, and Speaking

W *History and Politics*
50 Essays: Jonathan Swift, "A Modest Proposal," pp. 387–95
In-class History and Politics essay due

Week 14

M Research paper due

W *Ethics*
50 Essays: Joan Didion, "On Morality," pp. 106–11
Presentations

Week 15

M *Ethics*
50 Essays: Susan Sontag, "Regarding the Pain of Others," pp. 373–78
In-class Ethics essay due

W Presentations
Portfolio due

Sample Syllabus by Purpose

SCHEDULE

Week 1

M Course introduction
Writing sample

W Writing sample review for style and correctness

Week 2

M *Personal*
50 Essays: Sherman Alexie, "The Joy of Reading and Writing: Superman and Me," pp. 15–19
Handbook: "Getting Started and Finding a Focus"

W *Personal*
50 Essays: James Baldwin, "Notes of a Native Son," pp. 50–71

Week 3

M *Handbook*: "Developing and Organizing Ideas"
Personal essay group work

W College closed

Week 4

M College closed

W *Personal*
50 Essays: David Sedaris, "A Plague of Tics," pp. 359–72
Handbook: "Revising and Editing"
Personal essay due

Week 5

M *Personal*
50 Essays: Scott Russell Sanders, "The Men We Carry in Our Minds," pp. 346–52
Handbook: "Writing an Argument and Thinking Critically"
Personal essay workshop

W *Handbook*: "Top Ten Problems and Basic Grammar Review"
Personal essay revision due

Week 6

M *Personal*
50 Essays: Alice Walker, "In Search of Our Mothers' Gardens," pp. 420–30
Handbook: "Research Basics"
Research essay workshop — topics

W *Personal*
50 Essays: Zora Neale Hurston, "How It Feels to Be Colored Me," pp. 182–86

Week 7

M Conferences — research topic approval

W *Expository*
50 Essays: Barbara Lazear Ascher, "On Compassion," pp. 46–49
Handbook: "The Five C's of Style"
Expository essay group work

Week 8

M *Expository*
50 Essays: Sarah Vowell, "Shooting Dad," pp. 412–19
Research essay source notes due

W Research essay workshop — sources
Expository essay due

Week 9

M *Expository*
50 Essays: Lars Eighner, "On Dumpster Diving," pp. 146–58

W *Expository*
50 Essays: Bharati Mukherjee, "Two Ways to Belong in America," pp. 280–83
Expository essay workshop

Week 10

M Research essay workshop

W *Expository*
50 Essays: George Orwell, "Shooting an Elephant," pp. 284–91

Week 11

M *Expository*
50 Essays: Virginia Woolf, "The Death of the Moth," pp. 448–51

W Conferences — research sources and outline
Expository essay revision due

Week 12

M *Argumentative*
50 Essays: Bill McKibben, "Curbing Nature's Paparazzi," pp. 267–72
Research paper draft due

W *Argumentative*
50 Essays: Barbara Ehrenreich, "Serving in Florida," pp. 136–45
In-class argumentative essay

Week 13

M *Argumentative*
50 Essays: Martin Luther King Jr., "Letter from Birmingham Jail," pp. 203–20
Peer work on research essay

W *Argumentative*
50 Essays: Rachel Carson, "The Obligation to Endure," pp. 83–90
Argumentative essay workshop

Week 14

M Research paper due

W *Argumentative*
50 Essays: Elizabeth Cady Stanton, "Declaration of Sentiments and Resolutions," pp. 379–82
Presentations

Week 15

M *Argumentative*
50 Essays: Henry David Thoreau, "Where I Lived, and What I Lived For," pp. 403–9
Argumentative essay revision due

W Presentations
Portfolio due

Sherman Alexie

The Joy of Reading and Writing: Superman and Me

There's a moment in Alexie's story "This Is What It Means to Say Phoenix, Arizona" (1993) in which a boy from the reservation jumps off the roof of the tribal school and flies, for a second, before he hits the ground, breaking his arm. Afterward, the Indian boys hate him for his courage, but, Alexie writes, "One of his dreams came true for just a second, just enough to make it real." "The Joy of Reading and Writing: Superman and Me" can come alive for students if the courage-to-fly theme — as well as the hostility that such bravery can incur — is emphasized in the classroom. Highlighting the implications of heroism and life saving (Question 1) and the refusal to bow to peer pressure (Question 3) can make more immediate Alexie's story of coming to literacy. Another good theme to discuss is the effort it takes to make dreams come true, especially in a world hostile to them (Question 2). Asking students to write their own story, as Question 4 does, can help them think about the story from the outside a little bit, to pay attention to the generic conventions that shape the story and the reality that twists those conventions.

Maya Angelou

Graduation

James Baldwin wrote that *I Know Why the Caged Bird Sings* "liberates the reader into life simply because Maya Angelou confronts her own life with such a moving wonder, such a luminous dignity." The story Angelou tells here of her grade school graduation is a good example of what Baldwin saw in Angelou's work. She confronts a formative moment in her life with wonder at what the world could do to her people and writes with dignity how her people, guided by their poets — to "survive" and feel "a proud member of the wonderful, beautiful Negro race" (par. 61), as Gloria Anzaldúa in "How to Tame a Wild Tongue" (p. 33) felt a sense of Chicanos as a people when she first read published Chicano poetry (par. 29) — can take what the world dishes out (Question 3). The clash of her high expectations for herself and her classmates with the low expectations of the speaker, raised in Question 1 — "The white kids were going to have a chance to become Galileos and Madame Curies and Edisons and Gauguins, and our boys (the girls weren't even in on it) would try to be Jesse Owenses and Joe Louises" (par. 40), is echoed by the emotional clash of the young Angelou's excitement with her disappointment. While the mood mirrors this clash, moving from hopefulness to disappointment, Angelou carefully provides background information during the first part of the essay that prepares for the second (Question 2).

Angelou's reassertion of ethnic pride at the end of "Graduation" provides an opening into a discussion or writing exercise (Question 4) about the ways in which we react to disappointment. The moment when the tears are not wiped away would be one place to start.

Gloria Anzaldúa

How to Tame a Wild Tongue

Starting (with Question 1) by thinking about the different ways in which we could list the languages Anzaldúa says she speaks allows students to reflect on assumptions about language. Working from there to discuss the definitions she offers of language and of languages continues this process of uncovering assumptions, giving the class the chance to compare her definitions to their own (Question 2). It also affords students the opportunity to see effective use of definition in writing. Last, it offers a way into an essay whose fragmented construction gives students some trouble. Coming to an understanding of what Anzaldúa means by code switching and thinking about it more broadly and about the ways in which they have done it themselves (Question 4) allows students to extend the essay's understanding of identity and Americanness and apply it to other questions of identity. Comparing Anzaldúa's sense of her identity with Audre Lorde's in "The Fourth of July" (p. 239), on the other hand, will allow them to think about what happens when two aspects of individual identity are found to clash in others' eyes (Question 3).

Barbara Lazear Ascher

On Compassion

Ascher's use of example in "On Compassion" can be scrutinized to teach both example and argument and also to facilitate discussion of her thesis (Question 1). Imagining alternative examples she could have used

(Question 2) helps with both: thinking about other anecdotes she could have told makes it possible to think about how choice of example is everything in argumentation generally, and how it enables her argument that compassion is not inborn but comes from confronting misfortune daily (an argument that students can confront by thinking about their own experiences, as Question 4 asks). Likewise, Ascher's point of view could be seen to result in viewing the less fortunate from the outside, a view that leads to observations and conclusions different from those Lars Eighner makes in "On Dumpster Diving" (p. 146); while Ascher is concerned with how "we," the fortunate, deal with the discomfiting presence of the homeless, Eighner is concerned as much with what it's like to be homeless or hungry as he is with how others think of them (Question 3).

JAMES BALDWIN

Notes of a Native Son

Henry Louis Gates Jr. said the essays that make up "Notes of a Native Son" "articulated for the first time to white America what it meant to be American and a black American at the same time." While Baldwin was not the first to write about this — W. E. B. Du Bois did it in 1903 in *Souls of Black Folk*, in which he coined the term "double consciousness" — Baldwin described the "twoness" (to borrow Du Bois's term) of African American identity as well as anyone ever has. In "Notes of a Native Son" he does it especially well. Telling stories from his life that illustrate his experiences with his family and in the world (Question 1), Baldwin plumbs the depths of his anger and finds its source to be the source both of his father's bitterness and also of the difficulties in their relationship (Question 2). He also finds the strength to try to move past his father's anger, to realize, as he states at the end of the essay, that hatred "never failed to destroy the man who hated" (par. 45). A discussion of students' own experiences with anger can begin from these last paragraphs (Question 4). A discussion of the connections between anger and social criticism and change can also start there, from Baldwin's insistence on holding two ideas in mind, acceptance and fighting injustice (par. 46).

It is a useful exercise to ask students to analyze Baldwin's prose in itself and in comparison to the prose of another writer (Question 3). Martin Luther King Jr.'s "Letter from Birmingham Jail" (p. 203) provides an interesting comparison, as it shares with Baldwin's "Notes" elements of both a black church style and a cooler argument style, and also differs greatly. It is helpful to think of these differences in terms of genre, audience, and purpose.

Dave Barry

Turkeys in the Kitchen

Regardless of whether you find this essay funny, it provides a good opportunity to get students talking about the nature of humor generally and the humorous essay in particular. Barry's simple structure can be easily taken apart so that students can see the purpose of individual sentences, whether they are throwaway lines or steps building toward a larger humorous moment. Comparing "Turkeys in the Kitchen" to David Sedaris's "A Plague of Tics" (p. 359) can allow students the chance to differentiate between kinds of humor and to identify their own tastes (Question 3). Such a comparison may require a fair amount of leading by the hand by the instructor, as humor, while often thought of as an easy, low form, is hard to talk about. The sources of humor — embarrassment for oneself or others, schadenfreude, recognition, incongruity, wisdom — can be identified as the writers touch on them. An interesting exercise in reader-response criticism can come out of this essay as well: Barry's happy acceptance of his domestic inadequacy is certain to draw a variety of reactions (Question 2).

This exercise can also lead to a discussion about the activity of reaching general conclusions from particular observations (Questions 1 and 4). Rather than simply discussing the truth or falseness of particular stereotypes, the class can talk about how all kinds of thinking depend on generalizing and how most of the essays they write will depend on it too, in moving from particulars to a more general thesis.

William F. Buckley Jr.

Why Don't We Complain?

Taken in themselves, Buckley's stories of his failure to complain do not add up to much (Question 1). He puts these examples together in order to reflect on American political apathy, in a leap some readers might find too large. But the phenomenon on which he wishes us to focus — "our" failure to raise our voices — is one worth discussing, and this essay provides a springboard for doing so (Question 2). It also gives us the chance to think about point of view, to ask who the "we" Buckley speaks about and for is, exactly, as Barbara Lazear Ascher's "On Compassion" (p. 46) does (Question 3). And it can serve as an example of the uses of anecdote and example, whether you think it works or not — negative examples can be as instructive as positive ones.

While Buckley does not refer to his politics or any politics specifically, one kind of writing response the essay could lead to is one in which students are encouraged to think about their own politics (Question 4). What would they raise their voices in protest against, if they could? Do they believe in protest?

RACHEL CARSON

The Obligation to Endure

In response to Carson's *Silent Spring*, Monsanto published an article parodying Carson called "The Desolate Year," that imagined devastation wreaked by uncontrolled insects. It is important for students to see that Carson was not against all attempts to control insects but rather that, as Carson herself makes clear, she only wants insect control to be carried out in ways that are mindful of the damage it can do. Helping students to see exactly what Carson is against (Question 1) and exactly what knowledge she argues we pay attention to and act on (Question 2) should work toward this goal. Another important aspect of Carson's work is that it is not just about what we do or even what we know but about how we think, and about the connections between how people think and historical change. Reading her against Verlyn Klinkenborg ("Our Vanishing Night," p. 234), who also talks about the unintended consequences of changes made possible by modernity and calls for changes in the ways we think, should help highlight this aspect of Carson's work (Question 3). Thinking beyond Carson to current efforts to get people to change the way they live in part by getting them to change the way they think (Question 4) is another way to draw out this part of Carson.

JUDITH ORTIZ COFER

The Myth of the Latin Woman: I Just Met a Girl Named María

Cofer illustrates, with a few sharply drawn anecdotes, the way mainstream society takes stereotypes and attempts to imprint those outside the mainstream with them (Question 1). Cofer is told, in these moments, that she can be a sexy Latina, a waitress, but not a student at Oxford or a poet (Question 2). The contrast between the reason she is in the places she is when sung to or asked for coffee and the stereotypes of the Latina provide the power of these moments. The classifications made of her contrast with the classes into which she is actually placing herself. In pointing out these contrasts, Cofer tells us something about both the ways Latinas are classified and also the way we classify generally. Another way to approach the question of classification is through attention to what happens when people escape the constraints of their "category" as it is defined by others and, sometimes, by themselves. Read Cofer's treatment of becoming a writer, of the way it leads to confusion among those who think they know who she should be and what she should do for a living, with Alice Walker's thoughts in "In Search of Our Mothers' Gardens" (p. 420) about the creativity of African American women, and how that went unrecognized and mistaken for something else because of the rigidity of their categorization.

Any exercise that asks students to write about their own experience with classifying people can include reflection on the act of classifying itself (Question 4). They can take a critical stance on stereotyping by understanding Cofer's sense that Latinas are seen as "whore, domestic or criminal" (par. 14) and by seeing how they use the same myths in thinking about groups of people; they can then use this writing to think about the ways in which this kind of activity is difficult to avoid, and even to argue about current issues in which this question has been asked, such as the use of racial profiling by police and government intelligence agencies.

Jared Diamond

The Ends of the World as We Know Them

Save for one brief mention five paragraphs from the end of the essay, Diamond does not remind readers of the occasion with which he frames his thoughts on the history of the collapse of societies. It is worth reminding them, as Question 2 does, so that they keep in mind the essay's emphasis not just on reflection but on resolutions. In the reflection category, reviewing the major causes of these collapses (Question 1) will help students focus on what has happened in the past. Question 3 focuses further on reflection, asking them to reflect on reflection itself, a second-order kind of thinking that might be difficult for them to get at first but should prove interesting, raising questions about how the size and nature of the frame we put around history changes the picture of the past we get. Turning to resolution in Question 4, you can help your class think about how making a resolution is about turning from the past to the future — about looking at your past and deciding to try to make the future different. Thinking of Diamond's concluding questions about whether our ability to learn from the mistakes of the past means we actually will do so in this way — as the individual's decision to go to the gym more, or work harder, or be nicer, writ very, very large — may help them to see that this essay, and the situation that is its subject, are not just about what we can know but about the gap between knowledge and action.

Joan Didion

On Morality

Didion is an interesting figure, politically. A fifth-generation Sacramento native, Didion grew up with an inland northern California libertarian Republicanism, which over the course of her career she shed for positions more toward the left on the political spectrum, eventually becoming a critic of conservative administrations and policies. Her early essays (among them "On Morality") were sometimes met with harsh criticism for their take on various aspects of American cultural life. This is partly because of the complexity of her ideas and partly because of her desire to examine popularly held notions. Who could be against conscience? In going through this essay with students, it may help to provide some background on Didion's contemporary context, but it might be even more helpful to underline Didion's acknowledgement of the discomfort her line of questioning causes: as she writes, "Of course we would all like to 'believe' in something" (par. 9). Prepared for the reexamining of assumptions that Didion is really about, they can then turn to considering the difficulties not simply of knowing what's right (Question 3) or even of acting on that knowledge (Question 1) but of understanding the nature of rightness itself. Finally, it is important (as with all things) to give students the space to disagree with the author's message, once they understand it; as is usually the case, they can do this best with concrete examples (Question 4).

Annie Dillard

Seeing

One good way to teach this essay is to keep Dillard's sometimes abstract insights tied to a more (if not the most) concrete aspect of writing — description. In this way, students aren't just thinking about what Dillard is trying to say about the way what we see is shaped by what we expect to see and by what meaning we assign to the things we see — instead, they're thinking about these things in the context of Dillard's own descriptions of the things she sees, her own assigning of meaning. One way to do this is to start with Question 2 in order to help them see that the form of the essay is closely tied to its message. They can then turn to considering what Dillard values about vision (Question 1) and where she places the greater emphasis, in comparison to Susan Sontag in "Regarding the Pain of Others" (p. 373) — on the seer or the thing seen (Question 3) — having already seen how Dillard makes meaning out of what she sees and how she communicates that meaning through description. Asking them to apply Dillard's key insight to their own experience is in some ways the most difficult part of teaching this essay, but it can also be the most fruitful; while it is of course hard to understand how you most often see what you expect to see, if you can get students to understand the premise — and accept it — you can then get them to see where the notions that shape their vision come from.

Frederick Douglass

Learning to Read and Write

Like many *bildungsromane*, Douglass's autobiography is part *künstlerroman*, part *erziehungsroman.* While not a novel, of course, it is the story of Douglass's coming of age as a man and as a writer, and in particular of his education into not just the word but the world. Discussion of Douglass's story of his learning to read and write must take into account what else he learns (Question 1). It is also interesting to think about what is learned by others who play a part in this story — his mistress, his young friends, the Irishman he meets on the wharf (Question 2). Further, the comparison named in Question 3, of the world Douglass lived in and that which Malcolm X writes from in "Learning to Read" (p. 257), can teach students what Malcolm X himself learned — that he lived in a society that had not changed as much as it might have in what it thought about the education and literacy of minorities and the poor.

This piece offers an opportunity to reflect on the learning of painful truths (Question 4). This is a difficult opportunity to get students to seize, though, so it would not be a bad idea to start off this exercise with a class discussion or with directed small group work intended to help them begin to think about it.

Barbara Ehrenreich

Serving in Florida

Nickel and Dimed is a powerful book in part because of the way Ehrenreich takes us inside the daily lives of workers with whom many of us interact regularly but understand less than we think. This experience is powerful because it is about more than experience — we don't just smell the back hall of Jerry's, we are taught the economic reasons that a fully employed waitress needs to sleep in a parking lot. While Question 2 points students in the direction of these examples, it is important to help students see that the detailed stories Ehrenreich tells us are not simply meant to be emotionally affecting but also and especially to support an argument about the difficulties and inequities of wage work. Questions 1 and 4 focus on the position of Ehrenreich in relation to the lives she is describing; leading students to think about where she stands and how she "informs" on what she observes from that position can lead to some interesting ideas about where this kind of writing stands and also about where they stand when they think about this subject. Similarly, Question 3 asks them to think about thinking — to consider how Lars Eighner, in "On Dumpster Diving" (p. 146), and Ehrenreich do not just describe a situation, but explain it to argue against commonly held assumptions. While both writers allude to "what people think," instructors can further help students see what Eighner and Ehrenreich are responding to by talking about the preconceptions people outside these experiences have about them and about the people who live them.

LARS EIGHNER

On Dumpster Diving

Question 1 draws students' attention to Eighner's defining of the terms he uses, such as *scavenging, foraging,* even *Dumpster,* and can lead to a discussion about Eighner's purpose (par. 4). Why write about an activity most would rather ignore if not to get readers to think differently about it, to redefine it? Asking this kind of question can lead students both to examine our culture's ideas about poverty and hunger and also to think more generally about the relation between the way we define the terms we use and the way we think about things. Eighner's detailed analysis of the process of Dumpster diving, and the educated, thoughtful way in which he writes, can lead to the same kind of examinations (Question 2).

Questions 3 and 4 ask students to think about the way American culture values material things, in the context of another critic, Henry David Thoreau (in "Where I Lived, and What I Lived For," p. 403), and in the context of their own values. It might be instructive for students to compare Thoreau's voluntarily absenting himself from mainstream society to Eighner's forced withdrawal to the world of scavenging, and to think about how that might help determine the things they choose to criticize.

STEPHANIE ERICSSON

The Ways We Lie

Toward the close of "The Ways We Lie," Stephanie Ericsson asks, "How much do we tolerate before we become sick and tired of being sick and tired?" (par. 36). Ericsson's question asks when we will demand that truth be spoken not just to but by power. While the lies that pervade public discourse are not William F. Buckley Jr.'s concern in "Why Don't We Complain?" (p. 76), speaking up is, and in reading these two essays together students can see that Ericsson, more than simply anatomizing the ways we lie, is issuing a call to action (Question 3). Asking students to list the number and different kinds of lies Ericsson catalogs (Questions 1 and 2) will help them think about the meaning of the action of making such a thorough catalog — the sheer variety and volume of untruths says something about the ubiquity of lies in our lives.

Asking students to imagine a day without lying, as Question 4 does, can help them understand Ericsson's distinction between the lies we tell to keep things moving and lies of greater consequence.

Stephen Jay Gould

Sex, Drugs, Disasters, and the Extinction of Dinosaurs

Stephen Jay Gould's essays are not taught in writing classes so frequently because first-year college students love science. One of the reasons they are taught is because their structure is so transparent, the line of their argument so easy to follow. In other words, they are useful because of their method. If you are congenial to this sort of approach, talking about why you chose to have them read this essay can highlight a useable connection here: This essay is useful for writing instruction because its method of making its points is so clear, and this essay's main point is about method, namely, the scientific method. This is what Gould is "preaching" about (Question 3), and the value of the scientific method — the transparency, clarity, and usefulness of the proposing and testing and refuting of testable claims — is exemplified everywhere in the essay's clear laying out and testing of ideas (Question 1). That Gould is preaching makes for an interesting opportunity (especially in these times when science is being challenged in the political arena): ask your students to consider the use of science to make the case for action outside of science (Question 4). Noting the rhetorical moves made when writers use science to urge action might lead to spirited discussions about the different ways this happens every day in the world.

Langston Hughes

Salvation

In this very short, simple-seeming piece of writing, Hughes tells a complicated story. Asking the apparently simple question of what Hughes cried about that night (Question 1) can lead students to see that complexity — he cried, he writes, "because I couldn't bear to tell her that I had lied, that I had deceived everybody in the church, and I hadn't seen Jesus, and that now I didn't believe there was a Jesus any more, since he didn't come to help me" (par. 15). The power of this essay comes in part from this complexity; it also comes from the impact of this big moment coming at the end of such a short narrative, which might have seemed almost slight (Question 2).

The idea that Hughes had lied not just to his aunt but to the whole congregation is important to the essay because it underscores the connections between faith and communities of belief and because the publicness of the moment is integral to how it feels to Hughes and to what it makes him do. Reading "Salvation" with George Orwell's "Shooting an Elephant" (p. 284) can help students see this (Question 3). Asking students to write about their own experiences with family expectations (Question 4) — something they know a lot about — should help them think about Hughes's experience and also help them see how these kinds of experiences can be good material for writing.

Zora Neale Hurston

How It Feels to Be Colored Me

Asking students at the start, in Question 1, to identify the irony in Hurston's first sentence is meant to accustom them to Hurston's humor and to get them used to the idea that she is writing against received ideas and assumptions. As does Question 1, Question 2 asks students to pay attention not only to ideas but also to the way they are expressed, in this case, the creative ways in which she makes her points.

Hurston writes, "Someone is always at my elbow reminding me that I am the granddaughter of slaves. It fails to register depression with me. Slavery is sixty years in the past. The operation was successful and the patient is doing well, thank you" (par. 7). Questions 3 and 4 ask students to evaluate what Hurston proposes in place of the assumptions against which she writes, to think critically about her ideas on race and culture, some of which aroused vehement disagreement from her contemporaries and fellow African American artists.

Thomas Jefferson

The Declaration of Independence

In *A Summary View of the Rights of British America, Set Forth in Some Resolutions Intended for the Instruction of the Present Delegates of the People of Virginia Now in Convention* (1774), Jefferson offered King George III "the advice of your great American council." In the Declaration, Jefferson is not offering advice, or even pretending to; he is not even talking to the king any longer. Asking students to count the list of wrongs (Question 1) can lead them to think about Jefferson's purpose in constructing the Declaration in this way and so to think about the effect he wished it to have. Question 2 can help students see that the Declaration was written; while of course they know this already, it will have for many of them something of the feeling of the bible about it, as if it appeared in stone on mountaintop. Examining the changes the Declaration went through in revision should accomplish this goal and also reinforce the idea that it was written with a goal in mind other than offering advice.

Simply asking Question 3 may have the effect of connecting for students the British Empire that appears in George Orwell's India, in "Shooting an Elephant" (p. 284), and in America, an obvious fact when you think of it, but one not always recognized. Question 3 also gives students the chance to see criticisms of empire from the point of view of the colonized and the colonizer, and to examine the differences in these two colonial situations. Question 4 offers the opportunity to evaluate the Declaration not as a piece of writing but as a founding statement of America; it also offers the opportunity to do their own political writing, even to write in a Jeffersonian, declaratory style.

Steven Johnson

Games

Much of this essay is about comparisons, not just in those it makes (between books and video games, most importantly) but also in its analyses of the making of comparisons themselves (Question 2). Anything you can do to make the discussion move beyond the specifics of the subject (after nailing them down, as in Question 1) to the larger, metadiscussion of comparison itself will be good for students. It will help them think about how Johnson compares and contrasts and how they do it in their own writing, and also what comparison and contrast can be used for. Having them compare different arguments (Question 3) can also be helpful; putting them in dialogue with each other can help them compare arguments on different topics and see the parallels between the two discussions. Finally, pushing students to reflect on the idea of conventional wisdom can help them not only to grasp Johnson's point about it but also to think about one of the common curses of the first-year essay — the unreflective recourse to "common sense" we spend so much time trying to get them to push past.

Martin Luther King Jr.

Letter from Birmingham Jail

In drawing students' attention to the historical analogies King makes to biblical, ancient, and American Revolutionary instances of civil disobedience, Question 1 shows how King directly addresses his audience's concerns with his methods. If they agree with his cause as they surely agree with those causes, then how can they disagree with methods that are the same as theirs? Question 2 also asks students to consider not just King's points but his method of arguing them. In a neat bit of doubling, he doesn't really apologize for anything, but rather indicates that getting at the truth and achieving justice are his only goals. Question 4 asks students to work with both message and argument, coming down on one side of a hypothetical issue of civil disobedience and then arguing for or against it.

Question 3 asks a difficult question, which is to compare the views of King and Zora Neale Hurston (in "How It Feels to Be Colored Me," p. 182) on race. One place to start is the bag image with which Hurston closes her essay.

Maxine Hong Kingston

No Name Woman

Questions 1 and 2 can lead to a long discussion about audience, purpose, and the differences between reporting and imagining. To get to these, help students find moments where Kingston or her mother comment on stories or allude to the fact that they are telling stories — from the first line, her mother's "You must not tell anyone what I am about to tell you" to her own "Whenever she had to warn us about life, my mother told stories that ran like this one, a story to grow up on" (par. 10) and "I alone devote pages of paper to her" (par. 49). You can also ask them to notice the kinds of verb forms that Kingston uses when imaginatively filling in the gaps in her aunt's story — they may read right past the "mays" and "might haves," but will easily grasp what such words indicate when they are pointed out.

Comparison is one of the most important ways students learn to improve their writing. Whether they are comparing two different examples of published writing to each other or one example of published writing to their own writing, students learn not to be intimidated by finished products and not to sell their own work short. Questions 3 and 4 are both comparative, asking students in the first case to compare two different accounts of ancestral influence and in the second to compare their own account of a real or imagined family secret to Kingston's. These kinds of exercises can help make even as polished and accomplished a piece as "No Name Woman" accessible.

Verlyn Klinkenborg

Our Vanishing Night

"Our Vanishing Night" is one of those essays that makes readers see what they may not have noticed before, and use that new perception to think differently about something they may not have thought much about before. Helping students to notice how Klinkenborg makes his claim that humans have "occupied" the night sky (Question 1), in particular, his use of description (Question 2) — can help them see the interrelation of the different modes of writing we often separate to help us think about them. Klinkenborg is making an argument, to be sure, but it wouldn't work without his use of description (or, for that matter, without his use of narrative). What Klinkenborg uses description (and these other modes) for is to make them "take a second look at nature"; part of comparing (Question 3) this essay to Michael Pollan's "What's Eating America" (p. 300) can be looking at just how Pollan achieves the same effect. Question 4 can also be seen as an exercise connected to the idea that this is the kind of essay that makes readers look, and think, again, in that it asks them to look again at the most mundane aspects of their life, such as how much sleep they get and how much night light they live in, and reconsider them in scientific and historic contexts.

Audre Lorde

The Fourth of July

While Lorde's essay is on one level not particularly difficult, it repays special attention to its finely observed and carefully wrought writing. From the smaller units of expression, such as the repetition of words to increasing effect (Question 1), to the larger, like the repetition of the idea that she was leaving childhood in the first and last sentences, Lorde's essay adds up to much more than a summary can capture. Attention to pacing (Question 2) can be similarly rewarding. Question 1 can also lead into Question 3, since one of the ways in which graduation, education, and learning are figured are as a leaving of childhood. Question 4 asks students to pay careful attention to irony, a natural subject given the essay's use of irony from its title onward. While students might not always be confident about the term, they usually have a fine, nuanced grasp of irony and sometimes just need help parsing the different kinds; the discussion should pay dividends, as Lorde's use of irony so informs her handling of the essay's subject matter, including her deft use of tone.

Nancy Mairs

On Being a Cripple

From the opening image of the author fallen, clothed, onto a toilet seat, "On Being a Cripple" confronts not just our stereotypes about disability but our sensitivities about it. By eschewing the terms *disabled* and *handicapped*, Mairs confronts both stereotypes about what the disabled cannot do and also our unwillingness, when talking about disability, to confront what she calls the "widening . . . gap between word and reality" (par. 3). Asking students to make lists of things Mairs says she does well and things she says she is unable to do (Question 1), as asking them to look again at her comment about swaggering (Question 2), can help them see these two goals of her essay. Ask them (Question 3) also to compare Mairs's attitude toward labeling to David Sedaris's in "A Plague of Tics" (p. 359). With Question 4, these exercises can help students to see the importance of point of view to perception not just in essays about disability but in life — as so much of human experience can be seen as depending on the fact that things look different from different angles.

MALCOLM X

Learning to Read

Assigning "Learning to Read" along with Frederick Douglass's "Learning to Read and Write" (p. 129) is valuable not just because their life stories are historically connected but because both connect literacy with a coming to political awareness (Questions 1, 2, and 3). Having to teach himself his letters later in life (Question 1), as Douglass has to teach himself his, surreptitiously, Malcolm X, as he learns to read, also learns the power of the written word and the danger, to the powerful, of readers.

Question 4 broaches a difficult subject that is nonetheless worth discussing. Though it is tangential to "Learning to Read," Malcolm X makes a number of comments concerning the recovery of African history — as when he refers to Aesop (par. 23), Europe (par. 25), and Socrates (par. 40). An examination of these comments might lead to an interesting discussion (perhaps with a little background provided by the instructor) about the project of recovering histories — particularly the politics informing the debates over attempts to retell this history.

BILL McKIBBEN

Curbing Nature's Paparazzi

McKibben's essay is valuable in part because, like Verlyn Klinkenborg's "Our Vanishing Night" (p. 234), it impels readers to reexamine something they may have previously taken for granted. In this case, it asks readers to reconsider nature photography, to see it as something mediated rather than captured, something that is less transparent than it seems. This is valuable because it offers an example of writing that makes people see things as if for the first time. So it's good to get students to register the surprise, and to think about why that surprise might be less than comfortable (Question 1). It's also good to help them see that McKibben's use of the counterfactual is an example of one slightly unorthodox way to get people to see something they've seen a million times in a way they haven't seen it before (Question 2).

Putting McKibben and Steven Johnson ("Games," p. 196) in conversation (Question 3) might seem like asking apples to talk to oranges, but the discussion might be a fruitful one if the issues of the effects of method of content delivery and the relative importance of profit versus other things can be highlighted. While Question 4 might seem a bit out of the blue, the essay raises interesting questions about what practically can be done with the kind of eye-opening facts and resulting moral quandaries that McKibben brings to readers' attention, and so seem worthy of discussing.

N. Scott Momaday

The Way to Rainy Mountain

Reminding students that Momaday repeats the path of the migration of the Kiowa from Montana to Oklahoma (Question 1) reinforces the idea that the title's "Way to Rainy Mountain" is not just topographical but historical and cultural. It also can lead students to think about the way Momaday intertwines narratives and ask why he tells the three stories he tells — his people's, his grandmother's, and his own (Question 2). Question 3's comparison to Maxine Hong Kingston's "No Name Woman" (p. 221) also encourages students to think not just about the information conveyed in the essays but the style in which they tell their stories.

Question 4 can be a short writing exercise or can become a larger project, even a research paper, if conceived broadly enough. The variety of access that students may have to their family pasts requires broadening if this question is to become a research paper topic, but this can be done in creative ways that incorporate historical and cultural research and more personal kinds of narrative.

Bharati Mukherjee

Two Ways to Belong in America

Questions 1 and 2 can help students see that the two ways of belonging in America to which Mukherjee refers in the title and on which she focuses her essay are represented by her and her sister. They can also help them see the differences between the sisters — and so between these two ways of belonging as an immigrant. Question 1 in particular, in asking them to list qualities, behaviors, and beliefs, can also lead them to think about the connections between the three that both explain behavior and complicate our understandings of any situations in which identity and action are at play.

These questions can also help students see ways of writing about family in connection to larger ideas and phenomena. Similarly, Question 3's comparison to Annie Dillard's "Seeing" (p. 112) can show them ways in which different kinds of information and writing, from the personal to the academic, can be joined. Question 4 asks for more strictly personal writing, bringing the reading of the essay back to its interpersonal base and returning students to writing about that which they know best.

George Orwell

Shooting an Elephant

While "Shooting an Elephant" has become a classic essay, many students will not be familiar with the historical situation that explains the central action of the essay. While the essay (and its headnote) may supply this context, the first two questions can get students started thinking about why Orwell does what he does. They can also help them think about the significance of this anecdote for Orwell — about what this event told him about imperialism.

Question 3 gives students the opportunity to think about the ultimate underlying reasons some might cite but Orwell refutes for doing what he reports doing in this essay. Reading Orwell against Joan Didion ("On Morality," p. 106) lets them think about more than the "higher" moral reasons British imperialists might cite and Orwell might argue against: it also allows them to think about the idea of higher morality itself. Question 4 can be tweaked in this direction as well, if students are asked to consider not just what they would have done in Orwell's shoes but what they think of the very idea of moral imperatives.

Plato

Allegory of the Cave

Allegory, while it will be a new concept for many students, is not an especially difficult one. Asking them (Question 1) to list the elements of Plato's allegory and explain what they represent will help them to grasp the device and the uses to which it is put in "The Allegory of the Cave" (Question 2).

Questions 3 and 4 both bring what can at times seem a historically distant and abstract discussion into the modern world. Asking students to think about George Orwell's ("Shooting an Elephant," p. 284) thoughts about his situation in light of Plato's reflections on leadership (Question 3), like asking them to think about contemporary affairs in this same light, can help them to take Plato's lightness and darkness, silver and gold, and make them concrete.

Michael Pollan

What's Eating America

This essay, though clearly written, is complicated, and making sure students follow it (Question 1) is part of the challenge of teaching it. But this difficulty can also become a topic of discussion or writing itself: asking students to think, for example, about the nature of the connections Pollan makes — not just what the connections are but what about them makes them difficult — is a great way to understand this kind of argument and to think about what it takes to make it yourself. This attention to unintended consequences is also one of the essay's themes, so it is doubly useful to bring it up in the classroom. Students can then be asked (Question 3) to see this kind of argument made in other essays, like Rachel Carson's ("The Obligation to Endure," p. 83), and to think about where they see unintended consequences in their own experience or observations (Question 4).

Richard Rodriguez

Aria: Memoir of a Bilingual Childhood

Much of the specificity of Rodriguez's arguments comes from the descriptions of the way his parents spoke. Using his memories, Rodriguez bolsters his arguments against bilingual education not just with logic or general illustrations but with discussions of language use from his own life, replete with scenes and, of course, dialogue. When asked to discuss Rodriguez's argument themselves (Question 2), students will find it helpful to look at these specifics (Question 2).

Question 3 asks students to think about how anecdotes can be used as support for arguments — as Rodriguez uses stories to make his argument, Langston Hughes in "Salvation" (p. 179) uses narrative to make a less obviously polemical but no less important statement. Beyond asking them to analyze the use of narrative, though, this question can get them to think about the use of form, not just in their reading but in their own writing. Question 4 can be enriched by asking them, in their arguments for or against the position Rodriguez takes in his essay, to themselves use narratives taken from their own experiences or observations.

Mike Rose

"I Just Wanna Be Average"

"I Just Wanna Be Average" is relatively long and largely narrative in form. As a result, students may have a hard time picking Rose's arguments out of his stories. Asking them to list teachers by name and qualities will help them understand what Rose is trying to say by telling these stories (Question 1). One thing this listing will help them to see is that Rose is talking not just about the way we classify "good" and "bad" students but also about the way he classifies good and bad teachers (Question 2). Getting students to think about the teachers as part of the subject of this essay can help them see the relation between pedagogical philosophies and practices and "products" — how the way we classify and educate students guarantees, almost as self-fulfilling prophecy, that they will come out the way they do. Question 4 also provides an opportunity to think about the process in which they are engaged every day — not just from their side but from the front of the classroom. Reflecting on what has made them work hard and what makes other students work hard can help them move from specific recollections to general applications of educational philosophy (as does Question 3's comparison of responses to different kinds of "tracking").

Scott Russell Sanders

The Men We Carry in Our Minds

"The Men We Carry in Our Minds" poses an interesting set of challenges, some of them related. While Sanders's prose is not hard to follow, his point in this essay is not immediately apparent, and as it reveals itself readers must be attentive both to what he is saying about the world and what he is saying about his feelings about what he is saying. Is he a feminist? Does he share his friend's belief, stated in the essay's opening, about men being discredited for their oppression of women? The answers are not simple (Question 1). The challenge of untangling the essay's point as it slowly unwinds is not entirely separate from the nature of its subject matter, which Sanders argues is more complicated than people have often thought. Complicating feminism, then, by adding class to the equation, Sanders also complicates the way he writes (Question 4). Tracking how the argument unfolds, by analyzing how, for example, he uses examples (Question 2), can help students appreciate the complexity of this kind of writing (Question 3).

Eric Schlosser

Kid Kustomers

A great majority of the students reading this essay will have been born in the age of the Kid Kustomer. That is, they will not remember or have any experience of the time, "twenty-five years ago," when ads weren't so focused on children, and so they will have always been kid kustomers themselves. Helping them to understand this development, then, is especially important (Question 1), as is helping them to understand its effects on its targets (Question 2). Asking them to read Schlosser against Steven Johnson ("Games" p. 353) can help them see the judgment often implicit in Schlosser's account; while his writing is careful to avoid polemic, it's important that students not think he's got no opinion about these matters (or that, like Johnson, he is in favor of the modern development that is his subject), in part because this essay is a great example of the rhetorical power of withholding direct value statements. While Schlosser's primary focus is on the nature of advertising aimed at children and its effects, his essay also provides an excellent opportunity to get students to think about their own assumed notions of the nature of childhood (Question 4).

David Sedaris

A Plague of Tics

It's hard to write about humor. It's also hard to talk about it. "A Plague of Tics" offers a good opportunity for your students to do either or both. This is so in part because one of the things that's so hard to get a handle on when thinking about humor is just what makes things funny; systematic attempts have been made over the years, by such Borscht Belt regulars as Aristotle and Freud, but none have been entirely successful. Sedaris is a master humorist, and one whose work is coming to be taught more and more frequently because even in the lightest moments, he's not just trying to be something funny. Asking students to analyze his use of humor (Question 2) can help them see just how hard it is to put your finger on what makes something funny. It can also help them see how humor can be used to serious ends, such as Sedaris' reflection on disability (Question 1) and identity (Question 3). Asking students to reflect on their own experiences with the feeling of not being able to stop thinking about something (Question 4) can help them identify with a condition not many of them will have experienced in a way that does not diminish their recognition of its seriousness, just as Sedaris's use of humor to recount his experience does not.

Susan Sontag

Regarding the Pain of Others

Students may find it hard to get a handle on Sontag's essay, and that's okay. One of the pleasures of Sontag's writing is the way she handles ideas and connects them; her larger argument, if it can be pinned down, is often less important (Question 2). While instructors may not necessarily want students to use this aspect of Sontag's writing as a model, her ability to inspire further thought — to make readers think rather than to simply tell them what to think — can itself serve as inspiration to student writers to try to think harder and come up with ideas that make their own readers think. This goes for their analysis of her claims too: Students might not agree that photos have to shock (Question 1), or that text can never do what visual media do (Question 4), but they may be inspired to think further about these claims and about what larger beliefs or assumptions lay behind them (Question 3).

Elizabeth Cady Stanton

Declaration of Sentiments and Resolutions

Students may at first not think there is much to say about this document. Like the Declaration of Independence (p. 187), however, it is a carefully composed piece of writing, and the way it positions itself in relation to other documents, historical moments, and ideas is as interesting as the way it is worded. Question 1 helps students recognize the basic analogy Stanton draws between Revolution-era Americans and women of her time; a discussion of the specific parallels she sees would list not only the demand for change but also the catalog of wrongs and the assertion of rights. Question 3 can help students fully appreciate Stanton's use of the Declaration of Independence by asking them to put the two documents side by side. From the use of the structure (statement of justification, list of wrongs, demand of redress) to the echoing of language, students will recognize how much Stanton alludes to the original Declaration and should then be able to think further about the historical parallels she is pointing out as well as the careful way she distinguishes her declaration from it (Question 2). They should also be prepared to write their own latter-day declarations, perhaps even moving beyond mimicking the form to drawing historical parallels as well as pointing out differences between these earlier situations and the ones that are their subjects.

Brent Staples

Just Walk on By: Black Men and Public Space

"My first victim was a woman," "Just Walk on By" begins; the power of Staples's essay comes from moments like this in which he develops the paradoxes of his subject. From describing the gulf between his self-image and the way he is often perceived (Question 1) to relating the ways in which he avoids the danger of being seen as dangerous (Question 2), Staples draws attention to the fear many have of black men and the "alienation" (par. 5) and "rage" (par. 11) felt by them as a result. Question 3 asks students to recognize this result by comparing Staples's essay to James Baldwin's "Notes of a Native Son" (p. 50); an open-ended discussion of the similarities and differences between Staples's and Baldwin's responses and their historical situations can help students contextualize Staples's brief account of his experience.

Asking students to think about identification and sympathy can lead them to move beyond recognizing the content of Staples's essay to seeing its formal qualities (Question 4). It might be good to illustrate the importance of the point of view by beginning with the way the essay's opening plays with what the writer sees and how he is perceived and asking students to describe their reactions as they read.

Jonathan Swift

A Modest Proposal

"A Modest Proposal" presents a number of difficulties for the instructor, but they are worth slogging through and are, in fact, productive. The difficulty students have in understanding the complicated irony Swift employs here is exactly what makes the piece work, and so the process of negotiating that difficulty leads directly to an appreciation of Swift's message and his genius in communicating it. All four of these questions can help in this process, getting students to think about the apparent rationality of the proposal (Question 1), the contrast between the Projector's views and Swift's own (Question 2), and the value of indirection in making an argument in certain political and rhetorical situations (Question 3). Question 4 can help them break down the actual experience of reading the "Proposal" and help them see how Swift engineers their responses. Again, while assigning this essay will require more guidance from the instructor — providing historical context as well as explanations of the workings of irony — it is well worth it.

Amy Tan

Mother Tongue

When Amy Tan hears herself saying "Not waste money that way" (par. 4) to her mother, what she is hearing is her mother's English coming out of her mouth; this reminder that there are actual mothers behind the title phrase "mother tongue" is worth pointing out to students, as it will help them see what Tan is saying about language and about the point of view embedded in it (Questions 1 and 2). Question 4 can help students understand this idea by examining their own ways of speaking.

Tan's essay and Richard Rodriguez's "Aria: Memory of a Bilingual Childhood" (p. 307) make interesting reading next to each other. Both writers deal with what it's like as people and as writers (who are, of course, also people) to deal with divided linguistic legacies, with different home language and public language. And both pay a great deal of attention not just to what they think of the way their parents talk but to what the world thinks. Helping direct students to moments of publicness — to narrated scenes of walking down the street or in stores or other places of business — will help them see where the authors' thoughts are complicated by the perceptions of others.

Henry David Thoreau

Where I Lived, and What I Lived For

"I went to the woods because I wished to live deliberately" — so begins this excerpt from *Walden*. Thoreau's intention, as important as his decision to move to the woods and to live alone and be self-sufficient, is to live deliberately, to be self-conscious about the ways in which he spends his time on Earth. What this resolution allows — the chance to live differently than he had been and to reflect on that difference — is not secondary to the deliberate life, but at least depends on it. Encouraging students to see this excerpt in the context of Thoreau's decision to live deliberately can help them appreciate these reflections as more than armchair musings.

The question of what Thoreau means when he says "Simplify, simplify" (Question 1) can be best addressed by pointing students to paragraph 2, where this line appears and where he writes, "Our life is frittered away by detail." Students can approach Question 2 from this same angle, thinking about the way his attention to all of the busy "details" of normal life mounts its own argument on behalf of life in the woods. The comparison of this excerpt and E. B. White's "Once More to the Lake" (p. 431) comes up naturally, as it were, in their focus on nature; one way that this comparison can be facilitated is by asking students to connect White's intimation of mortality at the end of his essay with Thoreau's effort to "front only the essential facts of life, and see if I could not learn what it had to teach, and not, when I came to die, discover that I had not lived" (par. 1).

Question 4 asks students to conduct their own Thoreauvian analysis; it will be more successful if students are encouraged to think about their "improvement" in Thoreau's terms rather than in more general ones.

Sojourner Truth

Ain't I a Woman?

One good way to approach Truth's speech is to examine it as a speech. Such an approach will help students more readily think about its rhetorical context — a response to a previous speaker at a women's rights convention (Question 1) — and style, especially in comparison to the very different style of another public assertion of women's rights, Elizabeth Cady Stanton's "Declaration of Sentiments and Resolutions" (p. 379) (Question 3). Question 2 can also lead in to Question 3, as it highlights the use of examples that both pieces share, though they use them in very different ways.

Question 4 also asks students to consider "Ain't I Woman?" as a speech, especially in terms of the audience to whom it was delivered. It is not as if Truth makes it easy to ignore the context: "If the first woman God ever made was strong enough to turn the world upside down all alone, these . . . together ought to be able to turn it back and get it right side up again! And now they is asking to do it, the men better let them" (par. 5). Thinking about and re-creating that context can contribute to students' appreciation of this piece's rhetorical power and historical interest.

Sarah Vowell

Shooting Dad

Concentrating on rhetorical mode or thematic concern to the exclusion of the reading experience can slight the humor in "Shooting Dad." Instead, you might find a phenomenological approach especially fitting for reading this essay: helping students to recognize the humor gives them permission to think about humor as an appropriate subject for academic work, and it gives them the opportunity to connect humor to the other ways in which the essay works. Question 2, while it may elicit work with various levels of success, is worth assigning because it encourages students to focus analytically on a reading experience that more often is noticed and moved past. If you are aiming for a more substantial writing assignment, outside reading on the nature of humor might help.

Question 4 asks students to do something that some of them will find difficult; this is one question (among many in *50 Essays*) that would lend itself to group work. Students could help each other to come up with five examples and also to theorize about the nature of humor on that evidence, and you can go group-to-group to help them along.

Alice Walker

In Search of Our Mothers' Garden

Unlike some of the essays in this anthology, Walker's does not assume or pretend a pose of disinterestedness: "Therefore we must fearlessly pull out of ourselves and look at and identify with our lives the living creativity some of our great-grandmothers knew, even without 'knowing' it." The story Walker tells, and the argument she makes, are personal, and the essay is shaped by this. Like Scott Sanders's "The Men We Carry in Our Minds" (p. 346), the language is shaped by identification and emotion, not just logic, and the argument is bolstered by support drawn from personal experience (Question 3). Helping students to think about this essay — about the way it draws connections (Question 2), about the portrait it draws of Walker's female ancestors and those like them (Question 1) — through its personal frame can help them appreciate the way it is written. Asking students to draw from their own experience or personal observations may help them to think about the ways creativity expresses itself in more personal ways.

E. B. White

Once More to the Lake

Beginning by calling attention to White's diction can help students recognize from the start the quality of White's writing (Question 1). As is true with any great stylist, of course, the meaning of the work resides in the style, as does White's sense of the lake's immutability in his description of it (Question 2). Question 4, in asking students to borrow elements of White's descriptive style, asks them to do something all writers do, that is, mimic other writers they have read. This question also provides an always-useful opportunity to reinforce the difference between homage and plagiarism.

Question 3 asks students to consider the power of the evocation of death in the middle of scenes of placid or even lively nature. While White's is not just thematic but also central to the movement of the narrative, Bill McKibben's ("Curbing Nature's Paparazzi," p. 267) is less about revelation and more about what's hidden — the growing scarcity of animals pictured in such abundance. Both pieces uncover something that from one perspective is not visible but that can be become so with the right kind of attention; what they do with this suddenly visible thing, of course, is different, and students should be able to uncover that, given the opportunity.

Marie Winn

Television: The Plug-In Drug

A number of questions could be asked to help students follow Winn's fairly complicated essay about the deleterious effects of the television on family life; Question 1 is only one of them, and its answer could provide a place to begin answering Question 2, which asks students to make an outline of Winn's argument. Question 3 is at least as much about David Sedaris's "A Plague of Tics" (p. 359) as it is about Winn's essay. However, its attention to the latter essay may help highlight its own assumptions about families and about the typical life that is damaged by the presence of television.

Question 4 can prove an interesting research exercise, and could even become a research essay if students wanted to involve a number of subjects rather than only studying their own responses to television watching. Even if kept small scale, though, the exercise provides a fun way for students to test the truth of a general cultural argument against the personal experience of their very specific selves.

Virginia Woolf

The Death of the Moth

A common response to this essay runs along the lines of, "What's the big deal about the moth?" Helping students see the big questions behind Woolf's close observation of the small insect should not be too difficult, though. Once they have grasped the basic idea, helped by focusing their attention on the atmospheric shift in paragraph 5 (Question 1), students can begin to think about why Woolf chooses to contemplate mortality through such a small and short-lived creature. One way to help them do this — and a good way generally to help students think about why writers make the choices they do — is to ask them to imagine alternative choices, roads not taken. Focusing on the descriptive passages of the essay may help them see the power of the perceived difference in importance or significance between her immediate subject and her larger one (Question 2). A different tack is to remind them of a time when they might have experienced a similar thought in response to a similar sight (Question 4).

Question 3 asks students to compare "The Death of the Moth" and E. B. White's "Once More to the Lake" (p. 431), two classic essays by two master stylists. Focusing again on the use of description — in addition to helping students consider the variety of ways observations of nature can be used as springboards to deeper reflection — can help students appreciate how description, when used effectively, always seeks to leave a dominant impression in the service of a larger motive.

one talked sex, ever. And she might have separated the rapes from the rest of living if only she did not have to buy her oil from him or gather wood in the same forest. I want her fear to have lasted just as long as rape lasted so that the fear could have been contained. No drawn-out fear. But women at sex hazarded birth and hence lifetimes. The fear did not stop but permeated everywhere. She told the man, "I think I'm pregnant." He organized the raid against her.

On nights when my mother and father talked about their life back home, sometimes they mentioned an "outcast table" whose business they still seemed to be settling, their voices tight. In a commensal tradition, where food is precious, the powerful older people made wrongdoers eat alone. Instead of letting them start separate new lives like the Japanese, who could become samurais and geishas, the Chinese family, faces averted but eyes glowering sideways, hung on to the offenders and fed them leftovers. My aunt must have lived in the same house as my parents and eaten at an outcast table. My mother spoke about the raid as if she had seen it, when she and my aunt, a daughter-in-law to a different household, should not have been living together at all. Daughters-in-law lived with their husbands' parents, not their own; a synonym for marriage in Chinese is "taking a daughter-in-law." Her husband's parents could have sold her, mortgaged her, stoned her. But they had sent her back to her own mother and father, a mysterious act hinting at disgraces not told me. Perhaps they had thrown her out to deflect the avengers.

She was the only daughter; her four brothers went with her 20
father, husband, and uncles "out on the road" and for some years became western men. When the goods were divided among the family, three of the brothers took land, and the youngest, my father, chose an education. After my grandparents gave their daughter away to her husband's family, they had dispensed all the adventure and all the property. They expected her alone to keep the traditional ways, which her brothers, now among the barbarians, could fumble without detection. The heavy, deep-rooted women were to maintain the past against the flood, safe for returning. But the rare urge west had fixed upon our family, and so my aunt crossed boundaries not delineated in space.

The work of preservation demands that the feelings playing about in one's guts not be turned into action. Just watch their passing like cherry blossoms. But perhaps my aunt, my forerunner, caught in a slow life, let dreams grow and fade and after some months or years went toward what persisted. Fear at the enormities of the forbidden kept her desires delicate, wire and bone. She looked at a man because she liked the way the hair was tucked behind his ears, or she liked the question-mark line of a long torso curving at the shoulder and straight at the hip. For warm eyes or a soft voice or a slow walk — that's all — a few hairs, a line, a brightness, a sound, a pace, she gave up family. She offered us up for a charm that vanished with tiredness, a pigtail that didn't toss when the wind died. Why, the wrong lighting could erase the dearest thing about him.

It could very well have been, however, that my aunt did not take subtle enjoyment of her friend, but, a wild woman, kept rollicking company. Imagining her free with sex doesn't fit, though. I don't know any women like that, or men either. Unless I see her life branching into mine, she gives me no ancestral help.

To sustain her being in love, she often worked at herself in the mirror, guessing at the colors and shapes that would interest him, changing them frequently in order to hit on the right combination. She wanted to look back.

On a farm near the sea, a woman who tended her appearance reaped a reputation for eccentricity. All the married women blunt-cut their hair in flaps about their ears or pulled it back in tight buns. No nonsense. Neither style blew easily into heart-catching tangles. And at their weddings they displayed themselves in their long hair for the last time. "It brushed the back of my knees," my mother tells me. "It was braided, and even so, it brushed the backs of my knees."

At the mirror my aunt combed individuality into her bob. A 25
bun could have been contrived to escape into black streamers blowing in the wind or in quiet wisps about her face, but only the older women in our picture album wear buns. She brushed her hair back from her forehead, tucking the flaps behind her ears. She looped a piece of thread, knotted into a circle between her index fingers and thumbs, and ran the double strand across her forehead. When she closed her fingers as if she were making a pair of shadow geese bite, the string twisted together catching the little hairs. Then she pulled the thread away from her skin, ripping the hairs out neatly, her eyes watering from the needles of pain. Opening her fingers, she cleaned the thread, then rolled it

along her hairline and the tops of the eyebrows. My mother did the same to me and my sisters and herself. I used to believe that the expression "caught by the short hairs" meant a captive held with a depilatory string. It especially hurt at the temples, but my mother said we were lucky we didn't have to have our feet bound when we were seven. Sisters used to sit on their beds and cry together, she said, as their mothers or their slave removed the bandages for a few minutes each night and let the blood gush back into their veins. I hope that the man my aunt loved appreciated a smooth brow, that he wasn't just a tits-and-ass man.

Once my aunt found a freckle on her chin, at a spot that the almanac said predestined her for unhappiness. She dug it out with a hot needle and washed the wound with peroxide.

More attention to her looks than these pullings of hairs and pickings at spots would have caused gossip among the villagers. They owned work clothes and good clothes, and they wore good clothes for feasting the new seasons. But since a woman combing her hair hexes beginnings, my aunt rarely found an occasion to look her best. Women looked like great sea snails — the corded wood, babies, and laundry they carried were the whorls on their backs. The Chinese did not admire a bent back; goddesses and warriors stood straight. Still there must have been a marvelous freeing of beauty when a worker laid down her burden and stretched and arched.

Such commonplace loveliness, however, was not enough for my aunt. She dreamed of a lover for the fifteen days of New Year's, the time for families to exchange visits, money, and food. She plied her secret comb. And sure enough she cursed the year, the family, the village, and herself.

Even as her hair lured her imminent lover, many other men looked at her. Uncles, cousins, nephews, brothers would have looked, too, had they been home between journeys. Perhaps they had already been restraining their curiosity, and they left, fearful that their glances, like a field of nesting birds, might be startled and caught. Poverty hurt, and that was their first reason for leaving. But another, final reason for leaving the crowded house was the never-said.

She may have been unusually beloved, the precious only 30
daughter, spoiled and mirror-gazing because of the affection the family lavished on her. When her husband left, they welcomed

the chance to take her back from the in-laws; she could live like the little daughter for just a while longer. There are stories that my grandfather was different from other people, "crazy ever since the little Jap bayoneted him in the head." He used to put his naked penis on the dinner table, laughing. And one day he brought home a baby girl, wrapped up inside his brown western-style greatcoat. He had traded one of his sons, probably my father, the youngest, for her. My grandmother made him trade back. When he finally got a daughter of his own, he doted on her. They must have all loved her, except perhaps my father, the only brother who never went back to China, having once been traded for a girl.

Brothers and sisters, newly men and women, had to efface their sexual color and present plain miens. Disturbing hair and eyes, a smile like no other, threatened the ideal of five generations living under one roof. To focus blurs, people shouted face to face and yelled from room to room. The immigrants I know have loud voices, unmodulated to American tones even after years away from the village where they called their friendships out across the fields. I have not been able to stop my mother's screams in public libraries or over telephones. Walking erect (knees straight, toes pointed forward, not pigeon-toed, which is Chinese-feminine) and speaking in an inaudible voice, I have tried to turn myself American-feminine. Chinese communication was loud, public. Only sick people had to whisper. But at the dinner table, where the family members came nearest one another, no one could talk, not the outcasts nor any eaters. Every word that falls from the mouth is a coin lost. Silently they gave and accepted food with both hands. A preoccupied child who took his bowl with one hand got a sideways glare. A complete moment of total attention is due everyone alike. Children and lovers have no singularity here, but my aunt used a secret voice, a separate attentiveness.

She kept the man's name to herself throughout her labor and dying; she did not accuse him that he be punished with her. To save her inseminator's name she gave silent birth.

He may have been somebody in her own household, but intercourse with a man outside the family would have been no less abhorrent. All the village were kinsmen, and the titles shouted in loud country voices never let kinship be forgotten. Any man within visiting distance would have been neutralized as a lover — "brother," "younger brother," "older brother" — 115 relationship titles. Parents researched birth charts probably not so much to assure good fortune as to circumvent incest in a population that has but one hundred surnames. Everybody has eight million relatives. How useless then sexual mannerisms, how dangerous.

As if it came from an atavism deeper than fear, I used to add "brother" silently to boys' names. It hexed the boys, who would or would not ask me to dance, and made them less scary and as familiar and deserving of benevolence as girls.

But, of course, I hexed myself also — no dates. I should have 35
stood up, both arms waving, and shouted out across libraries, "Hey, you! Love me back." I had no idea, though, how to make attraction selective, how to control its direction and magnitude. If I made myself American-pretty so that the five or six Chinese boys in the class fell in love with me, everyone else — the Caucasian, Negro, and Japanese boys — would too. Sisterliness, dignified and honorable, made much more sense.

Attraction eludes control so stubbornly that whole societies designed to organize relationships among people cannot keep order, not even when they bind people to one another from childhood and raise them together. Among the very poor and the wealthy, brothers married their adopted sisters, like doves. Our family allowed some romance, paying adult brides' prices and providing dowries so that their sons and daughters could marry strangers. Marriage promises to turn strangers into friendly relatives — a nation of siblings.

In the village structure, spirits shimmered among the live creatures, balanced and held in equilibrium by time and land. But one human being flaring up into violence could open up a black hole, a maelstrom that pulled in the sky. The frightened villagers, who depended on one another to maintain the real, went to my aunt to show her a personal, physical representation of the break she made in the "roundness." Misallying couples snapped off the future, which was to be embodied in true offspring. The villagers punished her for acting as if she could have a private life, secret and apart from them.

If my aunt had betrayed the family at a time of large grain yields and peace, when many boys were born, and wings were being built on many houses, perhaps she might have escaped such severe punishment. But the men — hungry, greedy, tired of planting in dry soil, cuckolded — had been forced to leave the village in order to send food-money home. There were ghost plagues, bandit plagues, wars with the Japanese, floods. My Chinese brother and sister had died of an unknown sickness. Adultery, perhaps only a mistake during good times, became a crime when the village needed food.

The round moon cakes and round doorways, the round tables of graduated size that fit one roundness inside another, round windows and rice bowls — these talismans had lost their power to warn this family of the law: A family must be whole, faithfully keeping the descent line by having sons to feed the old and the dead who in turn look after the family. The villagers came to show my aunt and lover-in-hiding a broken house. The villagers were speeding up the circling of events because she was too short-sighted to see that her infidelity had already harmed the village, that waves of consequences would return unpredictably, sometimes in disguise, as now, to hurt her. This roundness had to be made coin-sized so that she would see its circumference: Punish her at the birth of her baby. Awaken her to the inexorable. People who refused fatalism because they could invent small resources insisted on culpability. Deny accidents and wrest fault from the stars.

After the villagers left, their lanterns now scattering in various 40
directions toward home, the family broke their silence and cursed her. "Aiaa, we're going to die. Death is coming. Death is coming. Look what you've done. You've killed us. Ghost! Dead Ghost! Ghost! You've never been born." She ran out into the fields, far enough from the house so that she could no longer hear their voices, and pressed herself against the earth, her own land no more. When she felt the birth coming, she thought that she had been hurt. Her body seized together. "They've hurt me too much," she thought. "This is gall, and it will kill me." With forehead and knees against the earth, her body convulsed and then relaxed. She turned on her back, lay on the ground. The black well of sky and stars went out and out forever; her body and her complexity seemed to disappear. She was one of the stars, a bright dot in blackness, without home, without a companion, in eternal cold and silence. An agoraphobia rose in her, speeding higher and higher, bigger and bigger; she would not be able to contain it; there would be no end to fear.

Flayed, unprotected against space, she felt pain return, focusing her body. This pain chilled her — a cold, steady kind of surface pain. Inside, spasmodically, the other pain, the pain of the child, heated her. For hours she lay on the ground, alternately body and space. Sometimes a vision of normal comfort obliterated reality: She saw the family in the evening gambling at the dinner table, the young people massaging their elders' backs. She saw them congratulating one another, high joy on the mornings the rice shoots came up. When these pictures burst, the stars drew yet further apart. Black space opened.

She got to her feet to fight better and remembered that old-fashioned women gave birth in their pigsties to fool the jealous, pain-dealing gods, who do not snatch piglets. Before the next spasms could stop her, she ran to the pigsty, each step a rushing out into emptiness. She climbed over the fence and knelt in the dirt. It was good to have a fence enclosing her, a tribal person alone.

Laboring, this woman who had carried her child as a foreign growth that sickened her every day, expelled it at last. She reached down to touch the hot, wet, moving mass, surely smaller than anything human, and could feel that it was human after all — fingers, toes, nails, nose. She pulled it up on to her belly, and it lay curled there, butt in the air, feet precisely tucked one under the other. She opened her loose shirt and buttoned the child inside. After resting, it squirmed and thrashed and she pushed it up to her breast. It turned its head this way and that until it found her nipple. There, it made little snuffling noises. She clenched her teeth at its preciousness, lovely as a young calf, a piglet, a little dog.

She may have gone to the pigsty as a last act of responsibility: She would protect this child as she had protected its father. It would look after her soul, leaving supplies on her grave. But how would this tiny child without family find her grave when there would be no marker for her anywhere, neither in the earth nor the family hall? No one would give her a family hall name. She had taken the child with her into the wastes. At its birth the two of them had felt the same raw pain of separation, a wound that only the family pressing tight could close. A child with no descent line would not soften her life but only trail after her, ghostlike, begging her to give it purpose. At dawn the villagers on their way to the fields would stand around the fence and look.

Full of milk, the little ghost slept. When it awoke, she hardened 45
her breasts against the milk that crying loosens. Toward morning she picked up the baby and walked to the well.

Carrying the baby to the well shows loving. Otherwise abandon it. Turn its face into the mud. Mothers who love their children take them along. It was probably a girl; there is some hope of forgiveness for boys.

"Don't tell anyone you had an aunt. Your father does not want to hear her name. She has never been born." I have believed that sex was unspeakable and words so strong and fathers so frail that "aunt" would do my father mysterious harm. I have thought that my family, having settled among immigrants who had also been their neighbors in the ancestral land, needed to clean their name, and a wrong word would incite the kinspeople even here. But there is more to this silence: They want me to participate in her punishment. And I have.

In the twenty years since I heard this story I have not asked for details nor said my aunt's name; I do not know it. People who comfort the dead can also chase after them to hurt them further — a reverse ancestor worship. The real punishment was not the raid swiftly inflicted by the villagers, but the family's deliberately forgetting her. Her betrayal so maddened them, they saw to it that she would suffer forever, even after death. Always hungry, always needing, she would have to beg food from other ghosts, snatch and steal it from those whose living descendants give them gifts. She would have to fight the ghosts massed at crossroads for the buns a few thoughtful citizens leave to decoy her away from village and home so that the ancestral spirits could feast unharassed. At peace, they could act like gods, not ghosts, their descent lines providing them with paper suits and dresses, spirit money, paper houses, paper automobiles, chicken, meat, and rice into eternity — essences delivered up in smoke and flames, steam and incense rising from each rice bowl. In an attempt to make the Chinese care for people outside the family, Chairman Mao encourages us now to give our paper replicas to the spirits of outstanding soldiers and workers, no matter whose ancestors they may be. My aunt remains forever hungry. Goods are not distributed evenly among the dead.

My aunt haunts me — her ghost drawn to me because now, after fifty years of neglect, I alone devote pages of paper to her, though not origamied into houses and clothes. I do not think she always means me well. I am telling on her, and she was a spite suicide, drowning herself in the drinking water. The Chinese are always very frightened of the drowned one, whose weeping ghost, wet hair hanging and skin bloated, waits silently by the water to pull down a substitute.

For Discussion and Writing

1. Compare the story about Kingston's aunt told by Kingston's mother to the stories Kingston herself tells. How are they different?
2. " 'You must not tell anyone . . . what I am about to tell you,' " Kingston's mother tells her at the essay's opening (par. 1). The rest of the essay, of course, is Kingston doing just that. Why does she do so?
3. **connections** In "In Search of Our Mothers' Gardens" (p. 420), Alice Walker writes, "Perhaps in more than Phillis Wheatley's biological life is her mother's signature made clear" (par. 50). Compare Kingston's claim that her aunt "haunts" her (par. 49) to Walker's idea of the "signature." What is the difference between these two scenarios of ancestral influence on individual identity?
4. Think about family secrets. Does yours have any, or can you imagine one? Write a semi- or wholly fictional account of your family secret. What might Kingston say about your account?

VERLYN KLINKENBORG

Our Vanishing Night

Most city skies have become virtually empty of stars.

Born in 1952 in Colorado and raised in Iowa and California, Verlyn Klinkenborg has a Ph.D. in English from Princeton University and has taught literature and creative writing at a number of colleges and universities. He is on the editorial board of the New York Times *and is the author of* Making Hay *(1986),* The Last Fine Time *(1991), and* The Rural Life *(2003). He has written for* The New Yorker, National Geographic, Harper's, *and many other magazines.*

"Our Vanishing Night," which first appeared in National Geographic, *shows Klinkenborg doing more than writing about the rural life he has captured so evocatively in his pieces for the* New York Times. *As you read, observe how he deftly incorporates history and science into his writing.*

If humans were truly at home under the light of the moon and stars, we would go in darkness happily, the midnight world as visible to us as it is to the vast number of nocturnal species on this planet. Instead, we are diurnal creatures, with eyes adapted to living in the sun's light. This is a basic evolutionary fact, even though most of us don't think of ourselves as diurnal beings any more than we think of ourselves as primates or mammals or Earthlings. Yet it's the only way to explain what we've done to the night: We've engineered it to receive us by filling it with light.

This kind of engineering is no different than damming a river. Its benefits come with consequences — called light pollution — whose effects scientists are only now beginning to study. Light pollution is largely the result of bad lighting design, which allows artificial light to shine outward and upward into the sky, where it's not wanted, instead of focusing it downward, where it is. Ill-designed lighting washes out the darkness of night and radically alters the light levels — and light rhythms — to which many forms of life, including ourselves, have adapted. Wherever human light spills into the natural world, some aspect of life — migration, reproduction, feeding — is affected.

For most of human history, the phrase "light pollution" would have made no sense. Imagine walking toward London on a moonlit night around 1800, when it was Earth's most populous city. Nearly a million people lived there, making do, as they always had, with candles and rushlights and torches and lanterns. Only a few houses were lit by gas, and there would be no public gaslights in the streets or squares for another seven years. From a few miles away, you would have been as likely to *smell* London as to see its dim collective glow.

Now most of humanity lives under intersecting domes of reflected, refracted light, of scattering rays from overlit cities and suburbs, from light-flooded highways and factories. Nearly all of nighttime Europe is a nebula of light, as is most of the United States and all of Japan. In the south Atlantic the glow from a single fishing fleet — squid fishermen luring their prey with metal halide lamps — can be seen from space, burning brighter, in fact, than Buenos Aires or Rio de Janeiro.

In most cities the sky looks as though it has been emptied of 5
stars, leaving behind a vacant haze that mirrors our fear of the dark and resembles the urban glow of dystopian science fiction. We've grown so used to this pervasive orange haze that the original glory of an unlit night — dark enough for the planet Venus to throw shadows on Earth — is wholly beyond our experience, beyond memory almost. And yet above the city's pale ceiling lies the rest of the universe, utterly undiminished by the light we waste — a bright shoal of stars and planets and galaxies, shining in seemingly infinite darkness.

We've lit up the night as if it were an unoccupied country, when nothing could be further from the truth. Among mammals alone, the number of nocturnal species is astonishing. Light is a powerful biological force, and on many species it acts as a magnet, a process being studied by researchers such as Travis Longcore and Catherine Rich, co-founders of the Los Angeles–based Urban Wildlands Group. The effect is so powerful that scientists speak of songbirds and seabirds being "captured" by searchlights on land or by the light from gas flares on marine oil platforms, circling and circling in the thousands until they drop. Migrating at night, birds are apt to collide with brightly lit tall buildings; immature birds on their first journey suffer disproportionately.

Insects, of course, cluster around streetlights, and feeding at those insect clusters is now ingrained in the lives of many bat species. In some Swiss valleys the European lesser horseshoe bat began to vanish after streetlights were installed, perhaps because those valleys were suddenly filled with light-feeding pipistrelle bats. Other nocturnal mammals — including desert rodents, fruit bats, opossums, and badgers — forage more cautiously under the permanent full moon of light pollution because they've become easier targets for predators.

Some birds — blackbirds and nightingales, among others — sing at unnatural hours in the presence of artificial light. Scientists have determined that long artificial days — and artificially short nights — induce early breeding in a wide range of birds. And because a longer day allows for longer feeding, it can also affect migration schedules. One population of Bewick's swans wintering in England put on fat more rapidly than usual, priming them to begin their Siberian migration early. The problem, of course, is that migration, like most other aspects of bird behavior, is a precisely timed biological behavior. Leaving early may mean arriving too soon for nesting conditions to be right.

Nesting sea turtles, which show a natural predisposition for dark beaches, find fewer and fewer of them to nest on. Their hatchlings, which gravitate toward the brighter, more reflective sea horizon, find themselves confused by artificial lighting behind the beach. In Florida alone, hatchling losses number in the hundreds of thousands every year. Frogs and toads living near brightly lit highways suffer nocturnal light levels that are as much as a million times brighter than normal, throwing nearly every aspect of their behavior out of joint, including their nighttime breeding choruses.

Of all the pollutions we face, light pollution is perhaps the most 10
easily remedied. Simple changes in lighting design and installation yield immediate changes in the amount of light spilled into the atmosphere and, often, immediate energy savings.

It was once thought that light pollution only affected astronomers, who need to see the night sky in all its glorious clarity. And, in fact, some of the earliest civic efforts to control light pollution — in Flagstaff, Arizona, half a century ago — were made to protect the view from Lowell Observatory, which sits high above that city. Flagstaff has tightened its regulations since then, and in 2001 it was declared the first International Dark Sky City. By now the effort to control light pollution has spread around the globe. More and more cities and even entire countries, such as the Czech Republic, have committed themselves to reducing unwanted glare.

Unlike astronomers, most of us may not need an undiminished view of the night sky for our work, but like most other creatures we do need darkness. Darkness is as essential to our biological welfare, to our internal clockwork, as light itself. The regular oscillation of waking and sleep in our lives — one of our circadian rhythms — is nothing less than a biological expression of the regular oscillation of light on Earth. So fundamental are these rhythms to our being that altering them is like altering gravity.

For the past century or so, we've been performing an open-ended experiment on ourselves, extending the day, shortening the night, and short-circuiting the human body's sensitive response to light. The consequences of our bright new world are more readily perceptible in less adaptable creatures living in the peripheral glow of our prosperity. But for humans, too, light pollution may take a biological toll. At least one new study has suggested a direct correlation between higher rates of breast cancer in women and the nighttime brightness of their neighborhoods.

In the end, humans are no less trapped by light pollution than the frogs in a pond near a brightly lit highway. Living in a glare of our own making, we have cut ourselves off from our evolutionary and cultural patrimony — the light of the stars and the rhythms of day and night. In a very real sense, light pollution causes us to lose sight of our true place in the universe, to forget the scale of our being, which is best measured against the dimensions of a deep night with the Milky Way — the edge of our galaxy — arching overhead.

For Discussion and Writing

1. "We've lit up the night as if it were an unoccupied country, when nothing could be further from the truth," Klinkenborg writes (par. 6). How have we done this? By what is the night occupied?
2. Klinkenborg makes an argument in "Our Vanishing Night," but he does so through the use of precise, evocative descriptions. Often these

descriptions are of phenomena readers may not have known about or realized. How do these kinds of descriptions help Klinkenborg to make his argument?

3. **connections** Michael Pollan, in "What's Eating America" (p. 300), argues that industrialized farmers need to "take a second look at nature" to understand how to grow crops without hurting the environment. Compare how Klinkenborg and Pollan, in making their arguments, make readers take a second look at nature.
4. Klinkenborg describes the shortening of the night and lighting up of the night sky as an experiment we've been performing on ourselves. Think about your own life in these terms, about the amount of sleep you get and the amount of night light you experience. Do you think the modern experiment with light pollution has had effects on you?

AUDRE LORDE

The Fourth of July

Audre Lorde (1934–1992) was a poet and nonfiction writer. Born in New York City to Caribbean immigrants, Lorde trained and worked as a librarian and became a widely published poet in the 1960s, when she also became politically active. Her poetry collections include The First Cities *(1968),* Cables to Rage *(1970), and* The Black Unicorn *(1978); her other books were memoir and political and social theory, including* The Cancer Journals *(1980) and* Zami: A New Spelling of My Name *(1982).*

"The Fourth of July" is a beautifully spare yet forceful piece of writing. In it, readers can see the anger that spurred much of Lorde's writing, whether about racism, as in this essay, or about sexism or homophobia, but they can also see the control with which Lorde expressed her ideas and the honesty with which she implicated herself and her family in her writing.

The first time I went to Washington, D.C., was on the edge of the summer when I was supposed to stop being a child. At least that's what they said to us all at graduation from the eighth grade. My sister Phyllis graduated at the same time from high school. I don't know what she was supposed to stop being. But as graduation presents for us both, the whole family took a Fourth of July trip to Washington, D.C., the fabled and famous capital of our country.

It was the first time I'd ever been on a railroad train during the day. When I was little, and we used to go to the Connecticut shore, we always went at night on the milk train, because it was cheaper.

Preparations were in the air around our house before school was even over. We packed for a week. There were two very large suitcases that my father carried, and a box filled with food. In fact, my first trip to Washington was a mobile feast; I started eating as soon as we were comfortably ensconced in our seats, and did not stop until somewhere after Philadelphia. I remember it was Philadelphia because I was disappointed not to have passed by the Liberty Bell.

My mother had roasted two chickens and cut them up into dainty bite-size pieces. She packed slices of brown bread and butter and green pepper and carrot sticks. There were little violently yellow iced cakes with scalloped edges called "marigolds," that came from Cushman's Bakery. There was a spice bun and rockcakes from Newton's, the West Indian bakery across Lenox Avenue from St. Mark's School, and iced tea in a wrapped mayonnaise jar. There were sweet pickles for us and dill pickles for my father, and peaches with the fuzz still on them, individually wrapped to keep them from bruising. And, for neatness, there were piles of napkins and a little tin box with a washcloth dampened with rosewater and glycerine for wiping sticky mouths.

I wanted to eat in the dining car because I had read all about 5
them, but my mother reminded me for the umpteenth time that dining car food always cost too much money and besides, you never could tell whose hands had been playing all over that food, nor where those same hands had been just before. My mother never mentioned that black people were not allowed into railroad dining cars headed south in 1947. As usual, whatever my mother did not like and could not change, she ignored. Perhaps it would go away, deprived of her attention.

I learned later that Phyllis's high school senior class trip had been to Washington, but the nuns had given her back her deposit in private, explaining to her that the class, all of whom were white, except Phyllis, would be staying in a hotel where Phyllis "would not be happy," meaning, Daddy explained to her, also in private, that they did not rent rooms to Negroes. "We will take you to Washington, ourselves," my father had avowed, "and not just for an overnight in some measly fleabag hotel."

American racism was a new and crushing reality that my parents had to deal with every day of their lives once they came to this country. They handled it as a private woe. My mother and father believed that they could best protect their children from the realities of race in America and the fact of American racism by never giving them name, much less discussing their nature. We were told we must never trust white people, but *why* was never explained, nor the nature of their ill will. Like so many other vital pieces of information in my childhood, I was supposed to know without being told. It always seemed like a very strange injunction coming from my mother, who looked so much like one of those people we were never supposed to trust. But something always warned me not to ask my mother why she wasn't white, and why Auntie Lillah and Auntie Etta weren't, even though they were all that same problematic color so different from my father and me, even from my sisters, who were somewhere in-between.

In Washington, D.C., we had one large room with two double beds and an extra cot for me. It was a back-street hotel that belonged to a friend of my father's who was in real estate, and I spent the whole next day after Mass squinting up at the Lincoln Memorial where Marian Anderson had sung after the D.A.R. refused to allow her to sing in their auditorium because she was black. Or because she was "Colored," my father said as he told us the story. Except that what he probably said was "Negro," because for his times, my father was quite progressive.

I was squinting because I was in that silent agony that characterized all of my childhood summers, from the time school let out in June to the end of July, brought about by my dilated and vulnerable eyes exposed to the summer brightness.

10 I viewed Julys through an agonizing corolla of dazzling whiteness and I always hated the Fourth of July, even before I came to realize the travesty such a celebration was for black people in this country.

My parents did not approve of sunglasses, nor of their expense.

I spent the afternoon squinting up at monuments to freedom and past presidencies and democracy, and wondering why the light and heat were both so much stronger in Washington, D.C., than back home in New York City. Even the pavement on the streets was a shade lighter in color than back home.

Late that Washington afternoon my family and I walked back down Pennsylvania Avenue. We were a proper caravan, mother bright and father brown, the three of us girls step-standards in-between. Moved by our historical surroundings and the heat of early evening, my father decreed yet another treat. He had a great sense of history, a flair for the quietly dramatic and the sense of specialness of an occasion and a trip.

"Shall we stop and have a little something to cool off, Lin?"

Two blocks away from our hotel, the family stopped for a dish 15
of vanilla ice cream at a Breyer's ice cream and soda fountain. Indoors, the soda fountain was dim and fan-cooled, deliciously relieving to my scorched eyes.

Corded and crisp and pinafored, the five of us seated ourselves one by one at the counter. There was I between my mother and father, and my two sisters on the other side of my mother. We settled ourselves along the white mottled marble counter, and when the waitress spoke at first no one understood what she was saying, and so the five of us just sat there.

The waitress moved along the line of us closer to my father and spoke again. "I said I kin give you to take out, but you can't eat here. Sorry." Then she dropped her eyes looking very embarrassed, and suddenly we heard what it was she was saying all at the same time, loud and clear.

Straight-backed and indignant, one by one, my family and I got down from the counter stools and turned around and marched out of the store, quiet and outraged, as if we had never been black before. No one would answer my emphatic questions with anything other than a guilty silence. "But we hadn't done anything!" This wasn't right or fair! Hadn't I written poems about Bataan and freedom and democracy for all?

My parents wouldn't speak of this injustice, not because they had contributed to it, but because they felt they should have anticipated it and avoided it. This made me even angrier. My fury was not going to be acknowledged by a like fury. Even my two sisters copied my parents' pretense that nothing unusual and anti-American had occurred. I was left to write my angry letter to the president of the United States all by myself, although my father did promise I could type it out on the office typewriter next week, after I showed it to him in my copybook diary.

The waitress was white, and the counter was white, and the ice 20
cream I never ate in Washington, D.C., that summer I left childhood was white, and the white heat and the white pavement and the white stone monuments of my first Washington summer made me sick to my stomach for the whole rest of that trip and it wasn't much of a graduation present after all.

For Discussion and Writing

1. What adjective does Lorde use six times in the essay's one-sentence final paragraph? Why do you think she chose to use it so many times?
2. Though Lorde says that the story she tells here really happened to her, it is as carefully constructed as any short story. One aspect of story construction she pays special attention to is setting things up in such a way that the dramatic moment will have its greatest impact. What is the dramatic moment in "The Fourth of July"? How does Lorde tell the story in a way that makes that moment especially effective?
3. **connections** Though the events that are related in "The Fourth of July" take place long after school is out and all the ceremonies have been held, it is significant that two graduations are mentioned. Compare the significance of graduation in Lorde's essay and Maya Angelou's "Graduation" (p. 20). How is each of these essays about education? How is each about the learning that happens outside of school, after the learning is ostensibly over?
4. Reflect on Lorde's use of irony in this essay. On one level, irony is simply when you say one thing but mean another, or when people in a narrative perceive a situation one way while readers know they're wrong; on another, deeper level, irony is about how things in the world are widely said to be one way when in fact they are not that way at all. How does Lorde use the surface ironies available to narrative — the ways in which things aren't what they seem — to write about the deeper ironies of American society?

NANCY MAIRS

On Being a Cripple

Born in 1943 in Long Beach, California, and raised north of Boston, Massachusetts, Nancy Mairs is a poet, essayist, and teacher. She has written memoirs and personal essays about women's issues, disability, and death in contemporary culture. In "On Being a Cripple," Mairs demonstrates the power of writing that confronts social issues through personal narrative as well as impersonal analysis. Starting with her blunt title, the piece offers an extended consideration of how we choose to name disability, and how that definition affects how we think about it. "I am not a disease," she writes (par. 23). Note other powerful moments in her essay when these two strands cross.

To escape is nothing. Not to escape is nothing. — LOUISE BOGAN

The other day I was thinking of writing an essay on being a cripple. I was thinking hard in one of the stalls of the women's room in my office building, as I was shoving my shirt into my jeans and tugging up my zipper. Preoccupied, I flushed, picked up my book bag, took my cane down from the hook, and unlatched the door. So many movements unbalanced me, and as I pulled the door open I fell over backward, landing fully clothed on the toilet seat with my legs splayed in front of me: the old beetle-on-its-back routine. Saturday afternoon, the building deserted, I was free to laugh aloud as I wriggled back to my feet, my voice bouncing off the yellowish tiles from all directions. Had anyone been there with me, I'd have been still and faint and hot with chagrin. I decided that it was high time to write the essay.

First, the matter of semantics. I am a cripple. I choose this word to name me. I choose from among several possibilities, the most common of which are "handicapped" and "disabled." I made the choice a number of years ago, without thinking, unaware of my motives for doing so. Even now, I'm not sure what those motives are, but I recognize that they are complex and not entirely flattering. People — crippled or not — wince at the word "cripple," as they do not at "handicapped" or "disabled." Perhaps I want them to wince. I want them to see me as a tough customer, one to whom the fates/gods/viruses have not been kind, but who can face the brutal truth of her existence squarely. As a cripple, I swagger.

But, to be fair to myself, a certain amount of honesty underlies my choice. "Cripple" seems to me a clean word, straightforward and precise. It has an honorable history, having made its first appearance in the Lindisfarne Gospel in the tenth century. As a lover of words, I like the accuracy with which it describes my condition: I have lost the full use of my limbs. "Disabled," by contrast, suggests any incapacity, physical or mental. And I certainly don't like "handicapped," which implies that I have deliberately been put at a disadvantage, by whom I can't imagine (my God is not a Handicapper General), in order to equalize chances in the great race of life. These words seem to me to be moving away from my condition, to be widening the gap between word and reality. Most remote is the recently coined euphemism "differently abled," which partakes of the same semantic hopefulness that transformed countries from "undeveloped" to "underdeveloped," then to "less developed," and finally to "developing" nations. People have continued to starve in those countries during the shift. Some realities do not obey the dictates of language.

Mine is one of them. Whatever you call me, I remain crippled. But I don't care what you call me, so long as it isn't "differently abled," which strikes me as pure verbal garbage designed, by its ability to describe anyone, to describe no one. I subscribe to George Orwell's thesis that "the slovenliness of our language makes it easier for us to have foolish thoughts." And I refuse to participate in the degeneration of the language to the extent that I deny that I have lost anything in the course of this calamitous disease; I refuse to pretend that the only differences between you and me are the various ordinary ones that distinguish any one person from another. But call me "disabled" or "handicapped" if you like. I have long since grown accustomed to them; and if they are vague, at least they hint at the truth. Moreover, I use them myself. Society is no readier to accept crippledness than to accept death, war, sex, sweat, or wrinkles. I would never refer to another person as a cripple. It is the word I use to name only myself.

I haven't always been crippled, a fact for which I am soundly 5
grateful. To be whole of limb is, I know from experience, infinitely more pleasant and useful than to be crippled; and if that knowledge leaves one open to bitterness at my loss, the physical soundness I once enjoyed (though I did not enjoy it half enough) is well worth the occasional stab of regret. Though never any good at sports, I was a normally active child and young adult. I climbed trees, played hopscotch, jumped rope, skated, swam, rode my bicycle, sailed. I despised team sports, spending some of the wretchedest afternoons of my life, sweaty and humiliated, behind a field-hockey stick and under a basketball hoop. I tramped alone for miles along the bridle paths that webbed the woods behind the house I grew up in. I swayed through countless dim hours in the arms of one man or another under the scattered shot of light from mirrored balls, and gyrated through countless more as Tab Hunter and Johnny Mathis gave way to the Rolling Stones, Creedence Clearwater Revival, Cream. I walked down the aisle. I pushed baby carriages, changed tires in the rain, marched for peace.

When I was twenty-eight I started to trip and drop things. What at first seemed my natural clumsiness soon became too pronounced to shrug off. I consulted a neurologist, who told me that I had a brain tumor. A battery of tests, increasingly disagreeable, revealed no tumor. About a year and a half later I developed a blurred spot in one eye. I had, at last, the episodes "disseminated in space and time" requisite for a diagnosis: multiple sclerosis. I have never been sorry for the doctor's initial misdiagnosis, however. For almost a week, until the negative results of the tests were in, I thought that I was going to die right away. Every day for the past nearly ten years, then, has been a kind of gift. I accept all gifts.

Multiple sclerosis is a chronic degenerative disease of the central nervous system, in which the myelin that sheathes the nerves is somehow eaten away and scar tissue forms in its place, interrupting the nerves' signals. During its course, which is unpredictable and uncontrollable, one may lose vision, hearing, speech, the ability to walk, control of bladder and/or bowels, strength in any or all extremities, sensitivity to touch, vibration, and/or pain, potency, coordination of movements — the list of possibilities is lengthy and, yes, horrifying. One may also lose one's sense of humor. That's the easiest to lose and the hardest to survive without.

In the past ten years, I have sustained some of these losses. Characteristic of MS are sudden attacks, called exacerbations, followed by remissions, and these I have not had. Instead, my disease has been slowly progressive. My left leg is now so weak that I walk with the aid of a brace and a cane; and for distances I use an Amigo, a variation on the electric wheelchair that looks rather like an electrified kiddie car. I no longer have much use of my left hand. Now my right side is weakening as well. I still have the blurred spot in my right eye. Overall, though, I've been lucky so far. My world has, of necessity, been circumscribed by my losses, but the terrain left me has been ample enough for me to continue many of the activities that absorb me: writing, teaching, raising children and cats and plants and snakes, reading, speaking publicly about MS and depression, even playing bridge with people patient and honorable enough to let me scatter cards every which way without sneaking a peek.

Lest I begin to sound like Pollyanna, however, let me say that I don't like having MS. I hate it. My life holds realities — harsh ones, some of them — that no right-minded human being ought to accept without grumbling. One of them is fatigue. I know of no one with MS who does not complain of bone-weariness; in a disease that presents an astonishing variety of symptoms, fatigue seems to be a common factor. I wake up in the morning feeling the way most people do at the end of a bad day, and I take it from there. As a result, I spend a lot of time *in extremis* and, impatient with limitation, I tend to ignore my fatigue until my body breaks down in some way and forces rest. Then I miss picnics, dinner parties, poetry readings, the brief visits of old friends from out of town. The offspring of a puritanical tradition of exceptional venerability, I cannot view these lapses without shame. My life often seems a series of small failures to do as I ought.

I lead, on the whole, an ordinary life, probably rather like the 10
one I would have led had I not had MS. I am lucky that my predilections were already solitary, sedentary, and bookish — unlike the world-famous French cellist I have read about, or the young woman I talked with one long afternoon who wanted only to be a jockey. I had just begun graduate school when I found out something was wrong with me, and I have remained, interminably, a

graduate student. Perhaps I would not have if I'd thought I had the stamina to return to a full-time job as a technical editor; but I've enjoyed my studies.

In addition to studying, I teach writing courses. I also teach medical students how to give neurological examinations. I pick up freelance editing jobs here and there. I have raised a foster son and sent him into the world, where he has made me two grand-babies, and I am still escorting my daughter and son through adolescence. I go to Mass every Saturday. I am a superb, if messy, cook. I am also an enthusiastic laundress, capable of sorting a hamper full of clothes into five subtly differentiated piles, but a terrible housekeeper. I can do italic writing and, in an emergency, bathe an oil-soaked cat. I play a fiendish game of Scrabble. When I have the time and the money, I like to sit on my front steps with my husband drinking Amaretto and smoking a cigar, as we imagine our counterparts in Leningrad and make sure that the sun gets down once more behind the sharp childish scrawl of the Tucson Mountains.

This lively plenty has its bleak complement, of course, in all the things I can no longer do. I will never run again, except in dreams, and one day I may have to write that I will never walk again. I like to go camping, but I can't follow George and the children along the trails that wander out of a campsite through the desert or into the mountains. In fact, even on the level I've learned never to check the weather or try to hold a coherent conversation: I need all my attention for my wayward feet. Of late, I have begun to catch myself wondering how people can propel themselves without canes. With only one usable hand, I have to select my clothing with care not so much for style as for ease of ingress and egress, and even so, dressing can be laborious. I can no longer do fine stitchery, pick up babies, play the piano, braid my hair. I am immobilized by acute attacks of depression, which may or may not be physiologically related to MS but are certainly its logical concomitant.

These two elements, the plenty and the privation, are never pure, nor are the delight and wretchedness that accompany them. Almost every pickle that I get into as a result of my weakness and clumsiness — and I get into plenty — is funny as well as maddening and sometimes painful. I recall one May afternoon when a friend and I were going out for a drink after finishing up at school.

As we were climbing into opposite sides of my car, chatting, I tripped and fell, flat and hard, onto the asphalt parking lot, my abrupt departure interrupting him in mid-sentence. "Where'd you go?" he called as he came around the back of the car to find me hauling myself up by the door frame. "Are you all right?" Yes, I told him, I was fine, just a bit rattly, and we drove off to find a shady patio and some beer. When I got home an hour or so later, my daughter greeted me with "What have you done to yourself?" I looked down. One elbow of my white turtleneck with the green froggies, one knee of my white trousers, one white kneesock were bloodsoaked. We peeled off the clothes and inspected the damage, which was nasty enough but not alarming. That part wasn't funny: The abrasions took a long time to heal, and one got a little infected. Even so, when I think of my friend talking earnestly, suddenly, to the hot thin air while I dropped from his view as though through a trap door, I find the image as silly as something from a Marx Brothers movie.

I may find it easier than other cripples to amuse myself because I live propped by the acceptance and the assistance and, sometimes, the amusement of those around me. Grocery clerks tear my checks out of my checkbook for me, and sales clerks find chairs to put into dressing rooms when I want to try on clothes. The people I work with make sure I teach at times when I am least likely to be fatigued, in places I can get to, with the materials I need. My students, with one anonymous exception (in an end-of-the-semester evaluation), have been unperturbed by my disability. Some even like it. One was immensely cheered by the information that I paint my own fingernails; she decided, she told me, that if I could go to such trouble over fine details, she could keep on writing essays. I suppose I became some sort of bright-fingered muse. She wrote good essays, too.

The most important struts in the framework of my existence, 15
of course, are my husband and children. Dismayingly few marriages survive the MS test, and why should they? Most twenty-two- and nineteen-year-olds, like George and me, can vow in clear conscience, after a childhood of chicken pox and summer colds, to keep one another in sickness and in health so long as they both shall live. Not many are equipped for catastrophe: the dismay, the depression, the extra work, the boredom that a degenerative disease can insinuate into a relationship. And our society, with

its emphasis on fun and its association of fun with physical performance, offers little encouragement for a whole spouse to stay with a crippled partner. Children experience similar stresses when faced with a crippled parent, and they are more helpless, since parents and children can't usually get divorced. They hate, of course, to be different from their peers, and the child whose mother is tacking down the aisle of a school auditorium packed with proud parents like a Cape Cod dinghy in a stiff breeze jolly well stands out in a crowd. Deprived of legal divorce, the child can at least deny the mother's disability, even her existence, forgetting to tell her about recitals and PTA meetings, refusing to accompany her to stores or church or the movies, never inviting friends to the house. Many do.

But I've been limping along for ten years now, and so far George and the children are still at my left elbow, holding tight. Anne and Matthew vacuum floors and dust furniture and haul trash and rake up dog droppings and button my cuffs and bake lasagna and Toll House cookies with just enough grumbling so I know that they don't have brain fever. And far from hiding me, they're forever dragging me by racks of fancy clothes or through teeming school corridors, or welcoming gaggles of friends while I'm wandering through the house in Anne's filmy pink babydoll pajamas. George generally calls before he brings someone home, but he does just as many dumb thankless chores as the children. And they all yell at me, laugh at some of my jokes, write me funny letters when we're apart — in short, treat me as an ordinary human being for whom they have some use. I think they like me. Unless they're faking. . . .

Faking. There's the rub. Tugging at the fringes of my consciousness always is the terror that people are kind to me only because I'm a cripple. My mother almost shattered me once, with that instinct mothers have — blind, I think, in this case, but unerring nonetheless — for striking blows along the fault-lines of their children's hearts, by telling me, in an attack on my selfishness, "We all have to make allowances for you, of course, because of the way you are." From the distance of a couple of years, I have to admit that I haven't any idea just what she meant, and I'm not sure that she knew either. She was awfully angry. But at the time, as the words thudded home, I felt my worst fear, suddenly realized. I could bear being called selfish: I am. But I couldn't bear the corroboration that those around me were doing in fact what I'd always suspected them of doing, professing fondness while silently putting up with me because of the way I am. A cripple. I've been a little cracked ever since.

Along with this fear that people are secretly accepting shoddy goods comes a relentless pressure to please — to prove myself worth the burdens I impose, I guess, or to build a substantial account of goodwill against which I may write drafts in times of need. Part of the pressure arises from social expectations. In our society, anyone who deviates from the norm had better find some way to compensate. Like fat people, who are expected to be jolly, cripples must bear their lot meekly and cheerfully. A grumpy cripple isn't playing by the rules. And much of pressure is self-generated. Early on I vowed that, if I had to have MS, by God I was going to do it well. This is a class act, ladies and gentlemen. No tears, no recriminations, no faint-heartedness.

One way and another, then, I wind up feeling like Tiny Tim, peering over the edge of the table at the Christmas goose, waving my crutch, piping down God's blessing on us all. Only sometimes I don't want to play Tiny Tim. I'd rather be Caliban, a most scurvy monster. Fortunately, at home no one much cares whether I'm a good cripple or a bad cripple as long as I make vichyssoise with fair regularity. One evening several years ago, Anne was reading at the dining-room table while I cooked dinner. As I opened a can of tomatoes, the can slipped in my left hand and juice spattered me and the counter with bloody spots. Fatigued and infuriated, I bellowed, "I'm so sick of being crippled!" Anne glanced at me over the top of her book. "There now," she said, "do you feel better?" "Yes," I said, "yes, I do." She went back to her reading. I felt better. That's about all the attention my scurviness ever gets.

Because I hate being crippled, I sometimes hate myself for 20
being a cripple. Over the years I have come to expect — even accept — attacks of violent self-loathing. Luckily, in general our society no longer connects deformity and disease directly with evil (though a charismatic once told me that I have MS because a devil is in me) and so I'm allowed to move largely at will, even among small children. But I'm not sure that this revision of attitude has been particularly helpful. Physical imperfection, even freed of moral disapprobation, still defies and violates the ideal, especially for women, whose confinement in their bodies as objects

of desire is far from over. Each age, of course, has its ideal, and I doubt that ours is any better or worse than any other. Today's ideal woman, who lives on the glossy pages of dozens of magazines, seems to be between the ages of eighteen and twenty-five; her hair has body, her teeth flash white, her breath smells minty, her underarms are dry; she has a career but is still a fabulous cook, especially of meals that take less than twenty minutes to prepare; she does not ordinarily appear to have a husband or children; she is trim and deeply tanned; she jogs, swims, plays tennis, rides a bicycle, sails, but does not bowl; she travels widely, even to out-of-the-way places like Finland and Samoa, always in the company of the ideal man, who possesses a nearly identical set of characteristics. There are a few exceptions. Though usually white and often blonde, she may be black, Hispanic, Asian, or Native American, so long as she is unusually sleek. She may be old, provided she is selling a laxative or is Lauren Bacall. If she is selling a detergent, she may be married and have a flock of strikingly messy children. But she is never a cripple.

Like many women I know, I have always had an uneasy relationship with my body. I was not a popular child, largely, I think now, because I was peculiar: intelligent, intense, moody, shy, given to unexpected actions and inexplicable notions and emotions. But as I entered adolescence, I believed myself unpopular because I was homely: my breasts too flat, my mouth too wide, my hips too narrow, my clothing never quite right in fit or style. I was not, in fact, particularly ugly, old photographs inform me, though I was well off the ideal; but I carried this sense of self-alienation with me into adulthood, where it regenerated in response to the depredations of MS. Even with my brace I walk with a limp so pronounced that, seeing myself on the videotape of a television program on the disabled, I couldn't believe that anything but an inchworm could make progress humping along like that. My shoulders droop and my pelvis thrusts forward as I try to balance myself upright, throwing my frame into a bony S. As a result of contractures, one shoulder is higher than the other and I carry one arm bent in front of me, the fingers curled into a claw. My left arm and leg have wasted into pipestems, and I try always to keep them covered. When I think about how my body must look to others, especially to men, to whom I have been trained to display myself, I feel ludicrous, even loathsome.

At my age, however, I don't spend much time thinking about my appearance. The burning egocentricity of adolescence, which assures one that all the world is looking all the time, has passed, thank God, and I'm generally too caught up in what I'm doing to step back, as I used to, and watch myself as though upon a stage. I'm also too old to believe in the accuracy of self-image. I know that I'm not a hideous crone, that in fact, when I'm rested, well dressed, and well made up, I look fine. The self-loathing I feel is neither physically nor intellectually substantial. What I hate is not me but a disease.

I am not a disease.

And a disease is not — at least not singlehandedly — going to determine who I am, though at first it seemed to be going to. Adjusting to a chronic incurable illness, I have moved through a process similar to that outlined by Elisabeth Kübler-Ross in *On Death and Dying*. The major difference — and it is far more significant than most people recognize — is that I can't be sure of the outcome, as the terminally ill cancer patient can. Research studies indicate that, with proper medical care, I may achieve a "normal" life span. And in our society, with its vision of death as the ultimate evil, worse even than decrepitude, the response to such news is, "Oh well, at least you're not going to *die*." Are there worse things than dying? I think that there may be.

25 I think of two women I know, both with MS, both enough older than I to have served me as models. One took to her bed several years ago and has been there ever since. Although she can sit in a high-backed wheelchair, because she is incontinent she refuses to go out at all, even though incontinence pants, which are readily available at any pharmacy, could protect her from embarrassment. Instead, she stays at home and insists that her husband, a small quiet man, a retired civil servant, stay there with her except for a quick weekly foray to the supermarket. The other woman, whose illness was diagnosed when she was eighteen, a nursing student engaged to a young doctor, finished her training, married her doctor, accompanied him to Germany when he was in the service, bore three sons and a daughter, now grown and gone. When she can, she travels with her husband; she plays bridge, embroiders, swims regularly; she works, like me, as a symptomatic-patient instructor of medical students in neurology. Guess which woman I hope to be.

At the beginning, I thought about having MS almost incessantly and because of the unpredictable course of the disease, my thoughts were always terrified. Each night I'd get into bed wondering whether I'd get out again the next morning, whether I'd be able to see, to speak, to hold a pen between my fingers. Knowing that the day might come when I'd be physically incapable of killing myself, I thought perhaps I ought to do so right away, while I still had the strength. Gradually I came to understand that the Nancy who might one day lie inert under a bedsheet, arms and legs paralyzed, unable to feed or bathe herself, unable to reach out for a gun, a bottle of pills, was not the Nancy I was at present, and that I could not presume to make decisions for that future Nancy, who might well not want in the least to die. Now the only provision I've made for the future Nancy is that when the time comes — and it is likely to come in the form of pneumonia, friend to the weak and the old — I am not to be treated with machines and medications. If she is unable to communicate by then, I hope she will be satisfied with these terms.

Thinking all the time about having MS grew tiresome and intrusive, especially in the large and tragic mode in which I was accustomed to considering my plight. Months and even years went by without catastrophe (at least without one related to MS), and really I was awfully busy, what with George and children and snakes and students and poems, and I hadn't the time, let alone the inclination, to devote myself to being a disease. Too, the richer my life became, the funnier it seemed, as though there were some connection between largesse and laughter, and so my tragic stance began to waver until, even with the aid of a brace and a cane, I couldn't hold it for very long at a time.

After several years I was satisfied with my adjustment. I had suffered my grief and fury and terror, I thought, but now I was at ease with my lot. Then one summer day I set out with George and the children across the desert for a vacation in California. Part way to Yuma I became aware that my right leg felt funny. "I think I've had an exacerbation," I told George. "What shall we do?" he asked. "I think we'd better get the hell to California," I said, "because I don't know whether I'll ever make it again." So we went on to San Diego and then to Orange, up the Pacific Coast Highway to Santa Cruz, across to Yosemite, down to Sequoia and Joshua Tree, and so back over the desert to home. It was a fine two-week trip, filled with friends and fair weather, and I wouldn't have missed it for the world, though I did in fact make it back to California two years later. Nor would there have been any point in missing it, since in MS, once the symptoms have appeared, the neurological damage has been done, and there's no way to predict or prevent that damage.

The incident spoiled my self-satisfaction, however. It renewed my grief and fury and terror, and I learned that one never finishes adjusting to MS. I don't know now why I thought one would. One does not, after all, finish adjusting to life, and MS is simply a fact of my life — not my favorite fact, of course — but as ordinary as my nose and my tropical fish and my yellow Mazda station wagon. It may at any time get worse, but no amount of worry, or anticipation can prepare me for a new loss. My life is a lesson in losses. I learn one at a time.

And I had best be patient in the learning, since I'll have to do it 30
like it or not. As any rock fan knows, you can't always get what you want. Particularly when you have MS. You can't, for example, get cured. In recent years researchers and the organizations that fund research have started to pay MS some attention even though it isn't fatal; perhaps they have begun to see that life is something other than a quantitative phenomenon, that one may be very much alive for a very long time in a life that isn't worth living. The researchers have made some progress toward understanding the mechanism of the disease: It may well be an autoimmune reaction triggered by a slow-acting virus. But they are nowhere near its prevention, control, or cure. And most of us want to be cured. Some, unable to accept incurability, grasp at one treatment after another, no matter how bizarre: megavitamin therapy, gluten-free diet, injections of cobra venom, hypothermal suits, lymphocytopharesis, hyperbaric chambers. Many treatments are probably harmless enough, but none are curative.

The absence of a cure often makes MS patients bitter toward their doctors. Doctors are, after all, the priests of modern society, the new shamans, whose business is to heal, and many an MS patient roves from one to another, searching for the "good" doctor who will make him well. Doctors too think of themselves as healers, and for this reason many have trouble dealing with MS patients, whose disease in its intransigence defeats their aims and mocks their skills. Too few doctors, it is true, treat their patients as whole human beings, but the reverse is also true. I have always tried to be gentle with my doctors, who often have more at stake in terms of ego than I do. I may be frustrated, maddened, depressed by the incurability of my disease, but I am not diminished by it, and they are. When I push myself up from my seat in the waiting room and stumble toward them, I incarnate the limitation of their powers. The least I can do is refuse to press on their tenderest spots.

This gentleness is part of the reason that I'm not sorry to be a cripple. I didn't have it before. Perhaps I'd have developed it anyway — how could I know such a thing? — and I wish I had more of it, but I'm glad of what I have. It has opened and enriched my life enormously, this sense that my frailty and need must be mirrored in others, that in searching for and shaping a stable core in a life wrenched by change and loss, change and loss, I must recognize the same process, under individual conditions, in the lives around me. I do not deprecate such knowledge, however I've come by it.

All the same, if a cure were found, would I take it? In a minute. I may be a cripple, but I'm only occasionally a loony and never a saint. Anyway, in my brand of theology God doesn't give bonus points for a limp. I'd take a cure; I just don't need one. A friend who also has MS startled me once by asking, "Do you ever say to yourself, 'Why me, Lord?'" "No, Michael, I don't," I told him, "because whenever I try, the only response I can think of is 'Why not?'" If I could make a cosmic deal, who would I put in my place? What in my life would I give up in exchange for sound limbs and a thrilling rush of energy? No one. Nothing. I might as well do the job myself. Now that I'm getting the hang of it.

For Discussion and Writing

1. Make two lists, one of Mairs's talents and one of the activities her MS makes difficult or impossible.
2. "As a cripple, I swagger," Mairs writes (par. 2). What does this mean? More generally, what is Mairs saying about her MS in this essay? How does this use of the word *cripple* help her say it?
3. **connections** Mairs rejects the labels "handicapped" and "disabled," preferring "crippled," even though many see it as offensive. How does her handling of her condition compare to David Sedaris's handling of his in "A Plague of Tics" (p. 359)? How does he label himself and his condition? Does he accept or eschew certain labels? Why?
4. Think about the way others see you and the way you see yourself. How would you correct their perception of you if it were possible?

MALCOLM X

Learning to Read

Malcolm Little, born in Omaha, Nebraska, in 1925, was reborn Malcolm X in his twenties while imprisoned for burglary. (He considered "Little" a slave name and chose the "X" to signify his lost African tribal name.) His conversion to Islam under the Nation of Islam and his rigorous self-education led him to a life of political activism marked by hatred, violence, and hope. For a time, as the foremost spokesman of the Nation of Islam, Malcolm preached a separatist philosophy with racist rhetoric; on breaking with the Nation of Islam and converting to orthodox Islam after a pilgrimage to Mecca, Malcolm again changed his name (to El-Hajj Malik El-Shabazz) and philosophy, moving closer to the integrationist goals of the mainstream civil rights movement. Not quite a year later, he was assassinated.

"Learning to Read" is an excerpt from The Autobiography of Malcolm X *(1965), which was written by Alex Haley from interviews completed shortly before Malcolm's death. While ghostwritten, Malcolm's fierce intelligence and passion are evident; it is easier to miss the sometimes surprising moments of humor, but look for them because they give a fuller sense of the man.*

It was because of my letters that I happened to stumble upon starting to acquire some kind of a homemade education.

I became increasingly frustrated at not being able to express what I wanted to convey in letters that I wrote, especially those to Mr. Elijah Muhammad. In the street, I had been the most articulate hustler out there — I had commanded attention when I said something. But now, trying to write simple English, I not only wasn't articulate, I wasn't even functional. How would I sound writing in slang, the way I would *say* it, something such as "Look, daddy, let me pull your coat about a cat, Elijah Muhammad —"

Many who today hear me somewhere in person, or on television, or those who read something I've said, will think I went to school far beyond the eighth grade. This impression is due entirely to my prison studies.

It had really begun back in the Charlestown Prison, when Bimbi first made me feel envy of his stock of knowledge. Bimbi had always taken charge of any conversation he was in, and I had tried to emulate him. But every book I picked up had few sentences which didn't contain anywhere from one to nearly all of the words that might as well have been in Chinese. When I just skipped those words, of course, I really ended up with little idea of what the book said. So I had come to the Norfolk Prison Colony still going through only book-reading motions. Pretty soon, I would have quit even these motions, unless I had received the motivation that I did.

I saw that the best thing I could do was get hold of a diction- 5
ary — to study, to learn some words. I was lucky enough to reason also that I should try to improve my penmanship. It was sad. I couldn't even write in a straight line. It was both ideas together that moved me to request a dictionary along with some tablets and pencils from the Norfolk Prison Colony school.

I spent two days just riffling uncertainly through the dictionary's pages. I'd never realized so many words existed! I didn't know *which* words I needed to learn. Finally, just to start some kind of action, I began copying.

In my slow, painstaking, ragged handwriting, I copied into my tablet everything printed on that first page, down to the punctuation marks.

I believe it took me a day. Then, aloud, I read back, to myself, everything I'd written on the tablet. Over and over, aloud, to myself, I read my own handwriting.

I woke up the next morning, thinking about those words — immensely proud to realize that not only had I written so much at one time, but I'd written words that I never knew were in the world. Moreover, with a little effort, I also could remember what many of these words meant. I reviewed the words whose meanings I didn't remember. Funny thing, from the dictionary first page right now, that "aardvark" springs to my mind. The dictionary had a picture of it, a long-tailed, long-eared, burrowing African mammal, which lives off termites caught by sticking out its tongue as an anteater does for ants.

10 I was so fascinated that I went on — I copied the dictionary's next page. And the same experience came when I studied that. With every succeeding page, I also learned of people and places and events from history. Actually the dictionary is like a miniature encyclopedia. Finally the dictionary's A section had filled a whole tablet — and I went on into the B's. That was the way I started copying what eventually became the entire dictionary. It went a lot faster after so much practice helped me to pick up handwriting speed. Between what I wrote in my tablet, and writing letters, during the rest of my time in prison I would guess I wrote a million words.

I suppose it was inevitable that as my word-base broadened, I could for the first time pick up a book and read and now begin to understand what the book was saying. Anyone who has read a great deal can imagine the new world that opened. Let me tell you something: from then until I left that prison, in every free moment I had, if I was not reading in the library, I was reading on my bunk. You couldn't have gotten me out of books with a wedge. Between Mr. Muhammad's teachings, my correspondence, my visitors — usually Ella and Reginald — and my reading of books, months passed without my even thinking about being imprisoned. In fact, up to then, I never had been so truly free in my life.

The Norfolk Prison Colony's library was in the school building. A variety of classes was taught there by instructors who came from such places as Harvard and Boston universities. The weekly debates between inmate teams were also held in the school building. You would be astonished to know how worked up convict debaters and audiences would get over subjects like "Should Babies Be Fed Milk?"

Available on the prison library's shelves were books on just about every general subject. Much of the big private collection that Parkhurst had willed to the prison was still in crates and boxes in the back of the library — thousands of old books. Some of them looked ancient: covers faded, old-time parchment-looking binding. Parkhurst, I've mentioned, seemed to have been principally interested in history and religion. He had the money and the special interest to have a lot of books that you wouldn't have in general circulation. Any college library would have been lucky to get that collection.

As you can imagine, especially in a prison where there was heavy emphasis on rehabilitation, an inmate was smiled upon if he demonstrated an unusually intense interest in books. There was a sizable number of well-read inmates, especially the popular debaters. Some were said by many to be practically walking encyclopedias. They were almost celebrities. No university would ask any student to devour literature as I did when this new world opened to me, of being able to read and *understand*.

I read more in my room than in the library itself. An inmate 15
who was known to read a lot could check out more than the permitted maximum number of books. I preferred reading in the total isolation of my own room.

When I had progressed to really serious reading, every night at about ten P.M. I would be outraged with the "lights out." It always seemed to catch me right in the middle of something engrossing.

Fortunately, right outside my door was a corridor light that cast a glow into my room. The glow was enough to read by, once my eyes adjusted to it. So when "lights out" came, I would sit on the floor where I could continue reading in that glow.

At one-hour intervals the night guards paced past every room. Each time I heard the approaching footsteps, I jumped into bed and feigned sleep. And as soon as the guard passed, I got back out of bed onto the floor area of that light-glow, where I would read for another fifty-eight minutes — until the guard approached again. That went on until three or four every morning. Three or four hours of sleep a night was enough for me. Often in the years in the streets I had slept less than that.

The teachings of Mr. Muhammad stressed how history had been "whitened" — when white men had written history books, the black man simply had been left out. Mr. Muhammad couldn't have said anything that would have struck me much harder. I had never forgotten how when my class, me and all of those whites, had studied seventh-grade United States history back in Mason, the history of the Negro had been covered in one paragraph, and the teacher had gotten a big laugh with his joke, "Negroes' feet are so big that when they walk, they leave a hole in the ground."

This is one reason why Mr. Muhammad's teachings spread so 20
swiftly all over the United States, among *all* Negroes, whether or not they became followers of Mr. Muhammad. The teachings ring

true — to every Negro. You can hardly show me a black adult in America — or a white one, for that matter — who knows from the history books anything like the truth about the black man's role. In my own case, once I heard of the "glorious history of the black man," I took special pains to hunt in the library for books that would inform me on details about black history.

I can remember accurately the very first set of books that really impressed me. I have since bought that set of books and have it at home for my children to read as they grow up. It's called *Wonders of the World*. It's full of pictures of archeological finds, statues that depict, usually, non-European people.

I found books like Will Durant's *Story of Civilization*. I read H. G. Wells' *Outline of History*. *Souls of Black Folk* by W. E. B. Du Bois gave me a glimpse into the black people's history before they came to this country. Carter G. Woodson's *Negro History* opened my eyes about black empires before the black slave was brought to the United States, and the early Negro struggles for freedom.

J. A. Rogers' three volumes of *Sex and Race* told about race-mixing before Christ's time; about Aesop being a black man who told fables; about Egypt's Pharaohs; about the great Coptic Christian Empires; about Ethiopia, the earth's oldest continuous black civilization, as China is the oldest continuous civilization.

Mr. Muhammad's teaching about how the white man had been created led me to *Findings in Genetics* by Gregor Mendel. (The dictionary's G section was where I had learned what "genetics" meant.) I really studied this book by the Austrian monk. Reading it over and over, especially certain sections, helped me to understand that if you started with a black man, a white man could be produced; but starting with a white man, you never could produce a black man — because the white gene is recessive. And since no one disputes that there was but one Original Man, the conclusion is clear.

25 During the last year or so, in the *New York Times*, Arnold Toynbee used the word "bleached" in describing the white man. (His words were: "White (i.e., bleached) human beings of North European origin. . . .") Toynbee also referred to the European geographic area as only a peninsula of Asia. He said there is no such thing as Europe. And if you look at the globe, you will see for yourself that America is only an extension of Asia. (But at the

same time Toynbee is among those who have helped to bleach history. He has written that Africa was the only continent that produced no history. He won't write that again. Every day now, the truth is coming to light.)

I never will forget how shocked I was when I began reading about slavery's total horror. It made such an impact upon me that it later became one of my favorite subjects when I became a minister of Mr. Muhammad's. The world's most monstrous crime, the sin and the blood on the white man's hands, are almost impossible to believe. Books like the one by Frederick Olmstead opened my eyes to the horrors suffered when the slave was landed in the United States. The European woman, Fannie Kimball, who had married a Southern white slaveowner, described how human beings were degraded. Of course I read *Uncle Tom's Cabin*. In fact, I believe that's the only novel I have ever read since I started serious reading.

Parkhurst's collection also contained some bound pamphlets of the Abolitionist Anti-Slavery Society of New England. I read descriptions of atrocities, saw those illustrations of black slave women tied up and flogged with whips; of black mothers watching their babies being dragged off, never to be seen by their mothers again; of dogs after slaves, and of the fugitive slave catchers, evil white men with whips and clubs and chains and guns. I read about the slave preacher Nat Turner, who put the fear of God into the white slavemaster. Nat Turner wasn't going around preaching pie-in-the-sky and "non-violent" freedom for the black man. There in Virginia one night in 1831, Nat and seven other slaves started out at his master's home and through the night they went from one plantation "big house" to the next, killing, until by the next morning 57 white people were dead and Nat had about 70 slaves following him. White people, terrified for their lives, fled from their homes, locked themselves up in public buildings, hid in the woods, and some even left the state. A small army of soldiers took two months to catch and hang Nat Turner. Somewhere I have read where Nat Turner's example is said to have inspired John Brown to invade Virginia and attack Harper's Ferry nearly thirty years later, with thirteen white men and five Negroes.

I read Herodotus, "the father of History," or, rather, I read about him. And I read the histories of various nations, which opened my eyes gradually, then wider and wider, to how the whole world's white men had indeed acted like devils, pillaging and raping and bleeding and draining the whole world's non-white people. I remember, for instance, books such as Will Durant's story of Oriental civilization, and Mahatma Gandhi's accounts of the struggle to drive the British out of India.

Book after book showed me how the white man had brought upon the world's black, brown, red, and yellow peoples every variety of the sufferings of exploitation. I saw how since the sixteenth century, the so-called "Christian trader" white man began to ply the seas in his lust for Asian and African empires, and plunder, and power. I read, I saw, how the white man never has gone among the non-white peoples bearing the Cross in the true manner and spirit of Christ's teachings — meek, humble, and Christ-like.

I perceived, as I read, how the collective white man had been 30
actually nothing but a piratical opportunist who used Faustian machinations to make his own Christianity his initial wedge in criminal conquests. First, always "religiously," he branded "heathen" and "pagan" labels upon ancient non-white cultures and civilizations. The stage thus set, he then turned upon his non-white victims his weapons of war.

I read how, entering India — half a *billion* deeply religious brown people — the British white man, by 1759, through promises, trickery, and manipulations, controlled much of India through Great Britain's East India Company. The parasitical British administration kept tentacling out to half of the subcontinent. In 1857, some of the desperate people of India finally mutinied — and, excepting the African slave trade, nowhere has history recorded any more unnecessary bestial and ruthless human carnage than the British suppression of the non-white Indian people.

Over 115 million African blacks — close to the 1930s population of the United States — were murdered or enslaved during the slave trade. And I read how when the slave market was glutted, the cannibalistic white powers of Europe next carved up, as their colonies, the richest areas of the black continent. And Europe's chancelleries for the next century played a chess game of naked exploitation and power from Cape Horn to Cairo.

Ten guards and the warden couldn't have torn me out of those books. Not even Elijah Muhammad could have been more eloquent than those books were in providing indisputable proof that the collective white man had acted like a devil in virtually every contact he had with the world's collective non-white man. I listen today to the radio, and watch television, and read the headlines about the collective white man's fear and tension concerning China. When the white man professes ignorance about why the Chinese hate him so, my mind can't help flashing back to what I read, there in prison, about how the blood forebears of this same white man raped China at a time when China was trusting and helpless. Those original white "Christian traders" sent into China millions of pounds of opium. By 1839, so many of the Chinese were addicts that China's desperate government destroyed twenty thousand chests of opium. The first Opium War was promptly declared by the white man. Imagine! Declaring *war* upon someone who objects to being narcotized! The Chinese were severely beaten, with Chinese-invented gunpowder.

The Treaty of Nanking made China pay the British white man for the destroyed opium; forced open China's major ports to British trade; forced China to abandon Hong Kong; fixed China's import tariffs so low that cheap British articles soon flooded in, maiming China's industrial development.

After a second Opium War, the Tientsin Treaties legalized the 35
ravaging opium trade, legalized a British-French-American control of China's customs. China tried delaying that Treaty's ratification; Peking was looted and burned.

"Kill the foreign white devils!" was the 1901 Chinese war cry in the Boxer Rebellion. Losing again, this time the Chinese were driven from Peking's choicest areas. The vicious, arrogant white man put up the famous signs, "Chinese and dogs not allowed."

Red China after World War II closed its doors to the Western white world. Massive Chinese agricultural, scientific, and industrial efforts are described in a book that *Life* magazine recently published. Some observers inside Red China have reported that the world never has known such a hate-white campaign as is now going on in this non-white country where, present birth-rates continuing, in fifty more years Chinese will be half the earth's population. And it seems that some Chinese chickens will soon come home to roost, with China's recent successful nuclear tests.

Let us face reality. We can see in the United Nations a new world order being shaped, along color lines — an alliance among the non-white nations. America's U.N. Ambassador Adlai Stevenson complained not long ago that in the United Nations "a skin game" was being played. He was right. He was facing reality. A "skin game" *is* being played. But Ambassador Stevenson sounded like Jesse James accusing the marshal of carrying a gun. Because who in the world's history ever has played a worse "skin game" than the white man?

Mr. Muhammad, to whom I was writing daily, had no idea of what a new world had opened up to me through my efforts to document his teachings in books.

When I discovered philosophy, I tried to touch all the landmarks 40
of philosophical development. Gradually, I read most of the old philosophers, Occidental and Oriental. The Oriental philosophers were the ones I came to prefer; finally, my impression was that most Occidental philosophy had largely been borrowed from the Oriental thinkers. Socrates, for instance, traveled in Egypt. Some sources even say that Socrates was initiated into some of the Egyptian mysteries. Obviously Socrates got some of his wisdom among the East's wise men.

I have often reflected upon the new vistas that reading opened to me. I knew right there in prison that reading had changed forever the course of my life. As I see it today, the ability to read awoke inside me some long dormant craving to be mentally alive. I certainly wasn't seeking any degree, the way a college confers a status symbol upon its students. My homemade education gave me, with every additional book that I read, a little bit more sensitivity to the deafness, dumbness, and blindness that was afflicting the black race in America. Not long ago, an English writer telephoned me from London, asking questions. One was, "What's your alma mater?" I told him, "Books." You will never catch me with a free fifteen minutes in which I'm not studying something I feel might be able to help the black man.

Yesterday I spoke in London, and both ways on the plane across the Atlantic I was studying a document about how the United Nations proposes to insure the human rights of the oppressed minorities of the world. The American black man is the world's most shameful case of minority oppression. What makes the black man think of himself as only an internal United States issue is just a catch-phrase, two words, "civil rights." How is the black man going to get "civil rights" before first he wins his *human* rights? If the American black man will start thinking about his *human* rights, and then start thinking of himself as part of one of the world's great peoples, he will see he has a case for the United Nations.

I can't think of a better case! Four hundred years of black blood and sweat invested here in America, and the white man still has the black man begging for what every immigrant fresh off the ship can take for granted the minute he walks down the gang-plank.

But I'm digressing. I told the Englishman that my alma mater was books, a good library. Every time I catch a plane, I have with me a book that I want to read — and that's a lot of books these days. If I weren't out here every day battling the white man, I could spend the rest of my life reading, just satisfying my curiosity — because you can hardly mention anything I'm not curious about. I don't think anybody ever got more out of going to prison than I did. In fact, prison enabled me to study far more intensively than I would have if my life had gone differently and I had attended some college. I imagine that one of the biggest troubles with colleges is there are too many distractions, too much panty-raiding, fraternities, and boola-boola and all of that. Where else but in a prison could I have attacked my ignorance by being able to study intensely sometimes as much as fifteen hours a day?

For Discussion and Writing

1. How did the process by which Malcolm learned to read differ from the typical way people learn to read?
2. In "Learning to Read," Malcolm tells us that he learned to read by teaching himself. What else did he teach himself while he taught himself to read?
3. **connections** What are the parallels between the ways Malcolm and Frederick Douglass, in "Learning to Read and Write" (p. 129), learned to read? What are the parallels and differences in the things they learned from their reading?
4. Though Malcolm changed many of his views after the time covered in this portion of his autobiography, the project of recovering African history remained important to him and remains important to this day to many African Americans. How do you react to his claims about African history?

BILL McKIBBEN

Curbing Nature's Paparazzi

Bill McKibben (b. 1960) is a writer and environmentalist. He started out at the New Yorker *but has also written for the* New York Times, *the* Atlantic Monthly, Harper's, *the* New York Review of Books, National Geographic, *and* Rolling Stone. *His many books include* The End of Nature *(1989), which helped popularize the notion of climate change;* The Age of Missing Information *(1992); and* Deep Economy: The Wealth of Communities and the Durable Future *(2007).*

"Curbing Nature's Paparazzi," which first appeared in Harper's, *is typical of much of McKibben's work in that it tries to understand its subject not as an isolated phenomenon but as the product of a number of forces and as part of an interconnected web of phenomena. It is also representative of McKibben's writing in that it not only analyzes and interprets but also advocates. One of the things to watch for as you read is the mix of these modes.*

The art of wildlife photography employs quite a few people scattered around the country. Filmmakers supply hour upon hour of video for PBS, the major networks, and cable channels. Still photographers take pictures for magazines, calendars, books, and advertisements, and they market countless trips for amateurs and aspiring professionals, teaching them the tricks of the trade. Their images do a lot of good: from Flipper and Jacques Cousteau to the mountain lion nuzzling her kit on your latest mailing from an environmental group, they've helped change how we see the wild. I've seen neighbors of mine, who had no use for wolves, begin to melt during a slide show about the creatures. It is no great exaggeration to say that dolphin-safe tuna flows directly from the barrel of a Canon, that without Kodak there'd be no Endangered Species Act.

But it's not a completely benign enterprise. In the wild, photographers often need to subtly harass wildlife to get their shots: to camp near watering holes, say, where their very presence may unnerve and scatter creatures. Worse, and less recognized, is a sort of conceptual problem. After a lifetime of exposure to nature shows and magazine photos, we arrive at the woods conditioned to expect splendor and are surprised when the parking lot does not contain a snarl of animals mating and killing one another. Because the only images we see are close-ups, we've lost much of our sense of the calm and quotidian beauty of the natural world, of the fact that animals are usually preoccupied with hiding or wandering around looking for food.

There is something frankly pornographic about the animal horror videos (*Fangs!*) marketed on late-night TV, and even about some of the shots you see in something as staid as *Natural History* magazine. Here is an emerald boa eating a parrot — the odds, according to the photographers I talked to, were "jillions to one" that it was a wild shot. Indeed, the photographer who took it boasted to *People* magazine about how, in order to get other dramatic shots, he'd spray-painted ferrets to convert them to the endangered blackfooted kind, and how he'd hoisted tame and declawed jaguars into tree branches for good shots, and starved piranhas so that they would attack with great ferocity. Another photographer took a game stab at defending the shot of the emerald boa munching the parrot: "It very graphically illustrates the relationship between higher and lower vertebrates," he said. So it does, but that's a little like saying that Miss September graphically illustrates the development of the mammary gland in *Homo sapiens*.

Even worse, perhaps, is the way the constant flow of images undercuts the sense that there's actually something wrong with the world. How can there really be a shortage of whooping cranes when you've seen a thousand images of them, seen ten times more images than there are actually whooping cranes left in the wild? We're rarely shown a photograph of the empty trees where there are no baboons anymore; whatever few baboons remain are dutifully pursued until they're captured on film, and even if all the captions are about their horrid plight, the essential message of the picture remains: baboons.

At this point we could — indeed we should — start talking about 5
a new ethic. People have tried, from time to time, to promul-

gate ethics for most of the arts, and nature photography is no exception. Photographer Daniel Dancer, writing recently in *Wild Earth* magazine, suggested using photos for advocacy purposes — shooting the clear-cut next to the forest, for instance. One editor envisions sending a photographer out to document, say, the hour-by-hour life of a snake rather than a young grizzly striking poses at a game farm. Reading and talking to such thinkers, though, it's easy to find a note of resignation — the deep suspicion that such rhetoric is not going to affect very quickly or very profoundly the marketplace in which photographers operate.

"A big problem we see is an editor who says, 'I want this kind of picture,' and then the word gets out," says Chuck Jonkel of the Wildlife Film Festival. "Editors will say, 'Give us a picture of a caribou running full tilt, and we'll give you $1,700.' Someone's going to hire a helicopter and run the shit out of the caribou to get that $1,700. I don't blame the photographer for that — I blame the editors." If one photographer or editor falters, chances are that there will be another to take his place. Dancer offers the wise advice of Wendell Berry that "one must begin in one's own life the private solutions that can only in turn become public solutions." That is so. But my work on environmental issues has made me wary of completely private solutions, for the momentum of our various tragedies makes the slow conversion of small parts of the society insufficient. Aren't we ethically impelled to also try to imagine ways that such private solutions might turn into public and widespread practice?

It's precisely for that reason that wildlife photography interests me so much. It's a small enough world that, at least for purposes of argument, you could postulate real changes. Suppose the eight or nine magazines that run most of the nature photos and the three or four top TV nature shows formed among them a cooperative, or clearinghouse, for wildlife images and announced that, up to a certain date, anyone could mail them as many slides or reels of film as they wished. *And after that date they wouldn't take any new submissions.* Then, when the editors of *Natural History* decided they needed some elephant photos, the staff of the cooperative agency could send over a wide array to choose from. For the fact is, there are already plenty of elephant photos in the world (when *Wildlife Conservation Magazine* was planning a piece on elephants a few years ago, its editors reviewed ten thousand slides).

And since most of the competing magazines and TV shows would belong to the cooperative, commercial pressure might diminish; no one else would have a two-inch-away close-up of the golden tamarind monkey either.

If some member of the consortium had a good reason for needing a new picture — if there were a new species or a new behavior that needed illustrating, or someone was needed to accompany a scientific expedition — then the cooperative could assign a photographer, along with strict instructions about conduct: about, say, how far away to stay from the animals. These measures might solve some of the ethical problems surrounding the industry's treatment of animals. It's also possible that such a cooperative agency could eventually begin to deal with the larger questions — for instance, over time, it could cull from its stock extreme close-ups and other kinds of photos that miseducate viewers about the natural world. It's the kind of place where a new ethic might *adhere*, might grow into something powerful.

Imagining institutions allows you to test the strength of the ethic on which they're based against very real and practical objections. In this case, the most obvious drawback is that the cooperative would put photographers out of work or force them to find new subjects, for if the agency worked as planned, it would need very few new wildlife photos annually. This potential clearinghouse for wildlife photos would announce, in effect: "We've got enough images now; we can recycle them more or less forever; please don't bother taking any more." And since negatives don't really degrade with use, that would be that. But this, we intuitively feel, is not fair. Who am I, or you, to tell someone else how he can or can't make a living?

It is an almost unknown thing in our society to say, "That's 10
enough." And it sounds especially heretical in any creative endeavor. The word "censorship" rises unbidden to one's lips. And even if you can convince yourself that it's not really censorship (it's not the government, after all; it's no more than some magazine telling you that it won't print your story for whatever damn reason; it's editing), even so, it seems repressive. It *is* repressive. It's the imposition of a new taboo. Consumers aren't supposed to have taboos; they're supposed to consume. And consume we do: not just goods and services but images, ideas, knowledge. Nothing is off-limits. So there's something a little creepy about saying,

"We'll be buying no new photos of wildebeests. We don't think it's a good idea to be taking them." Do we really want any new taboos?

As I've become more interested in environmental matters, I've thought a lot about these questions of restraint — about when one's curiosity or creative impulse can be bane as well as boon, about whether there are places where taboos once more make sense. The answers are easier to see when the questions concern things, not ideas. Clearly, for instance, we'd be better off environmentally if as a culture we frowned on automobiles, if we said that the freedom they afforded was not worth the cost in terms of global warming, suburban sprawl, and so forth. And a taboo against the next, ever-larger version of the Ford Explorer, even if it somehow developed, wouldn't seem a real threat to the human spirit.

But the debate about limiting ideas is one we're incapable of having, because we operate under the assumption that the limitation of creativity is repellent. We take as a given that we should find out everything we can, develop everything we can, photograph and write about everything we can, and then let the marketplace decide what to do with it. By definition, therefore, if it sells it is good. If we can clone animals, say, then we will; to suggest otherwise is to stand against not only free enterprise but also the free imagination. But in our blind defense of these things that seem "right," we may be short-circuiting the process of thinking things through as a culture, leaving ourselves no way to entertain the possibility of restraint.

And yet self-restraint is a uniquely human capacity, belonging as exclusively to us as flight belongs to the birds. It's the one gift no other creature possesses — even as a possibility.

For Discussion and Writing

1. Why would most readers of nature magazines (or watchers of nature television) be surprised to find that many of the images they encounter are staged or in some other way artificial? Why would they be bothered?
2. McKibben imagines a counterfactual, a thing that does not exist, to support his argument — "a photograph of the empty trees where there are no baboons anymore" (par. 4). What do you think of this move in

his argument, which is different from more standard moves in arguments — appeals to evidence, or logic, say? Is it effective? If not, why? If so, what makes it so?

3. **connections** Imagine a conversation in which McKibben and Steven Johnson ("Games," p. 196) engage each other on both of their subjects. What might Johnson say about McKibben's argument about the harmful conceptual effects of wildlife photography as it is now practiced? What might McKibben say about Johnson's citing the fact that video games now make more money than movies do?

4. McKibben proposes what he calls "a cooperative, or clearinghouse, for wildlife images" (par. 7). He goes on to outline some objections. What do you think of these? Do you think such a thing could work, especially now that all of these images are digital? If not, are your reasons logistical or political — that is, do you think it wouldn't work because of the objections he raises, or for more practical reasons?

N. SCOTT MOMADAY

The Way to Rainy Mountain

A poet, novelist, autobiographer, playwright, teacher, visual artist, and environmentalist, N. Scott Momaday is a foremost Native American voice. He was born in 1934 in Lawton, Oklahoma, and raised on a reservation in New Mexico. His first novel, House Made of Dawn *(1968), won a Pulitzer Prize, and his autobiographical* The Way to Rainy Mountain *(1969) is still widely read today. In 2007, Momaday was awarded the National Medal of Arts by then President George W. Bush.*

This excerpt from The Way to Rainy Mountain *demonstrates well Momaday's use of the Kiowa oral tradition. The folktales and legends lend both poetry and wisdom to Momaday's exploration of his family's past and his culture's history. As you read, consider how his identity is tied to the place where he was born and raised. How true is that for you?*

A single knoll rises out of the plain in Oklahoma, north and west of the Wichita Range. For my people, the Kiowas, it is an old landmark, and they gave it the name Rainy Mountain. The hardest weather in the world is there. Winter brings blizzards, hot tornadic winds arise in the spring, and in summer the prairie is an anvil's edge. The grass turns brittle and brown, and it cracks beneath your feet. There are green belts along the rivers and creeks, linear groves of hickory and pecan, willow and witch hazel. At a distance in July or August the steaming foliage seems almost to writhe in fire. Great green and yellow grasshoppers are everywhere in the tall grass, popping up like corn to sting the flesh, and tortoises crawl about on the red earth, going nowhere in the plenty of time. Loneliness is an aspect of the land. All things in the plain are isolate; there is no confusion of objects in the eye, but *one* hill or *one* tree or *one* man. To look upon that landscape in the early morning, with the sun at your back, is to lose the sense of proportion. Your imagination comes to life, and this, you think, is where Creation was begun.

I returned to Rainy Mountain in July. My grandmother had died in the spring, and I wanted to be at her grave. She had lived to be very old and at last infirm. Her only living daughter was with her when she died, and I was told that in death her face was that of a child.

I like to think of her as a child. When she was born, the Kiowas were living the last great moment of their history. For more than a hundred years they had controlled the open range from the Smoky Hill River to the Red, from the headwaters of the Canadian to the fork of the Arkansas and Cimarron. In alliance with the Comanches, they had ruled the whole of the southern Plains. War was their sacred business, and they were among the finest horsemen the world has ever known. But warfare for the Kiowas was preeminently a matter of disposition rather than of survival, and they never understood the grim, unrelenting advance of the U.S. Cavalry. When at last, divided and ill-provisioned, they were driven onto the Staked Plains in the cold rains of autumn, they fell into panic. In Palo Duro Canyon they abandoned their crucial stores to pillage and had nothing then but their lives. In order to save themselves, they surrendered to the soldiers at Fort Sill and were imprisoned in the old stone corral that now stands as a military museum. My grandmother was spared the humiliation of those high gray walls by eight or ten years, but she must have known from birth the affliction of defeat, the dark brooding of old warriors.

Her name was Aho, and she belonged to the last culture to evolve in North America. Her forebears came down from the high country in western Montana nearly three centuries ago. They were a mountain people, a mysterious tribe of hunters whose language has never been positively classified in any major group. In the late seventeenth century they began a long migration to the south and east. It was a journey toward the dawn, and it led to a golden age. Along the way the Kiowas were befriended by the Crows, who gave them the culture and religion of the Plains. They acquired horses, and their ancient nomadic spirit was suddenly free of the ground. They acquired Tai-me, the sacred Sun Dance doll, from that moment the object and symbol of their worship, and so shared in the divinity of the sun. Not least, they acquired the sense of destiny, therefore courage and pride. When they entered upon the southern Plains they had been transformed. No longer were they slaves to the simple necessity of survival; they were a lordly and dangerous society of fighters and thieves, hunters and priests of the sun. According to their origin myth, they entered the world through a hollow log. From one point of view, their migration was the fruit of an old prophecy, for indeed they emerged from a sunless world.

Although my grandmother lived out her long life in the shadow 5
of Rainy Mountain, the immense landscape of the continental interior lay like memory in her blood. She could tell of the Crows, whom she had never seen, and of the Black Hills, where she had never been. I wanted to see in reality what she had seen more perfectly in the mind's eye, and traveled fifteen hundred miles to begin my pilgrimage.

Yellowstone, it seemed to me, was the top of the world, a region of deep lakes and dark timber, canyons and waterfalls. But, beautiful as it is, one might have the sense of confinement there. The skyline in all directions is close at hand, the high wall of the woods and deep cleavages of shade. There is a perfect freedom in the mountains, but it belongs to the eagle and the elk, the badger and the bear. The Kiowas reckoned their stature by the distance they could see, and they were bent and blind in the wilderness.

Descending eastward, the highland meadows are a stairway to the plain. In July the inland slope of the Rockies is luxuriant with flax and buckwheat, stonecrop and larkspur. The earth unfolds and the limit of the land recedes. Clusters of trees, and animals grazing far in the distance, cause the vision to reach away and wonder to build upon the mind. The sun follows a longer course in the day, and the sky is immense beyond all comparison. The great billowing clouds that sail upon it are the shadows that move upon the grain like water, dividing light. Farther down, in the land of the Crows and Blackfeet, the plain is yellow. Sweet clover takes hold of the hills and bends upon itself to cover and seal the soil. There the Kiowas paused on their way; they had come to the place where they must change their lives. The sun is at home on the plains. Precisely there does it have the certain character of a god. When the Kiowas came to the land of the Crows, they could see the dark lees of the hills at dawn across the Bighorn River, the profusion of light on the grain shelves, the oldest deity ranging after the solstices. Not yet would they veer southward to the caldron of the land that lay below; they must wean their blood from the northern winter and hold the mountains a while longer in their view. They bore Tai-me in procession to the east.

A dark mist lay over the Black Hills, and the land was like iron. At the top of a ridge I caught sight of Devil's Tower upthrust against the gray sky as if in the birth of time the core of the earth had broken through its crust and the motion of the world was begun. There are things in nature that engender an awful quiet in the heart of man; Devil's Tower is one of them. Two centuries ago, because they could not do otherwise, the Kiowas made a legend at the base of the rock. My grandmother said:

> Eight children were there at play, seven sisters and their brother. Suddenly the boy was struck dumb; he trembled and began to run upon his hands and feet. His fingers became claws, and his body was covered with fur. Directly there was a bear where the boy had been. The sisters were terrified; they ran, and the bear after them. They came to the stump of a great tree, and the tree spoke to them. It bade them climb upon it, and as they did so it began to rise into the air. The bear came to kill them, but they were just beyond its reach. It reared against the tree and scored the bark all around with its claws. The seven sisters were borne into the sky, and they became the stars of the Big Dipper.

From that moment, and so long as the legend lives, the Kiowas have kinsmen in the night sky. Whatever they were in the mountains, they could be no more. However tenuous their well-being, however much they had suffered and would suffer again, they had found a way out of the wilderness.

My grandmother had a reverence for the sun, a holy regard that now is all but gone out of mankind. There was a wariness in her, and an ancient awe. She was a Christian in her later years, but she had come a long way about, and she never forgot her birthright. As a child she had been to the Sun Dances; she had taken part in those annual rites, and by them she had learned the restoration of her people in the presence of Tai-me. She was about seven when the last Kiowa Sun Dance was held in 1887 on the Washita River above Rainy Mountain Creek. The buffalo were gone. In order to consummate the ancient sacrifice — to impale the head of a buffalo bull upon the medicine tree — a delegation of old men journeyed into Texas, there to beg and barter for an animal from the Goodnight herd. She was ten when the Kiowas came together for the last time as a living Sun Dance culture.

They could find no buffalo; they had to hang an old hide from the sacred tree. Before the dance could begin, a company of soldiers rode out from Fort Sill under orders to disperse the tribe. Forbidden without cause the essential act of their faith, having seen the wild herds slaughtered and left to rot upon the ground, the Kiowas backed away forever from the medicine tree. That was July 20, 1890, at the great bend of the Washita. My grandmother was there. Without bitterness, and for as long as she lived, she bore a vision of deicide.

10 Now that I can have her only in memory, I see my grandmother in the several postures that were peculiar to her: standing at the wood stove on a winter morning and turning meat in a great iron skillet; sitting at the south window, bent above her beadwork, and afterwards, when her vision failed, looking down for a long time into the fold of her hands; going out upon a cane, very slowly as she did when the weight of age came upon her; praying. I remember her most often at prayer. She made long, rambling prayers out of suffering and hope, having seen many things. I was never sure that I had the right to hear, so exclusive were they of all mere custom and company. The last time I saw her she prayed standing by the side of her bed at night, naked to the waist, the light of a kerosene lamp moving upon her dark skin. Her long, black hair, always drawn and braided in the day, lay upon her shoulders and against her breasts like a shawl. I do not speak Kiowa, and I never understood her prayers, but there was something inherently sad in the sound, some merest hesitation upon the syllables of sorrow. She began in a high and descending pitch, exhausting her breath to silence; then again and again — and always the same intensity of effort, of something that is, and is not, like urgency in the human voice. Transported so in the dancing light among the shadows of her room, she seemed beyond the reach of time. But that was illusion; I think I knew then that I should not see her again.

Houses are like sentinels in the plain, old keepers of the weather watch. There, in a very little while, wood takes on the appearance of great age. All colors wear soon away in the wind and rain, and then the wood is burned gray and the grain appears and the nails turn red with rust. The windowpanes are black and opaque; you imagine there is nothing within, and indeed there are many ghosts, bones given up to the land. They stand here and there against the sky, and you approach them for a longer time than you expect. They belong in the distance; it is their domain.

Once there was a lot of sound in my grandmother's house, a lot of coming and going, feasting and talk. The summers there were full of excitement and reunion. The Kiowas are a summer people; they abide the cold and keep to themselves, but when the season turns and the land becomes warm and vital they cannot hold still; an old love of going returns upon them. The aged visitors who came to my grandmother's house when I was a child were made of lean and leather, and they bore themselves upright. They wore great black hats and bright ample shirts that shook in the wind. They rubbed fat upon their hair and wound their braids with strips of colored cloth. Some of them painted their faces and carried the scars of old and cherished enmities. They were an old council of warlords, come to remind and be reminded of who they were. Their wives and daughters served them well. The women might indulge themselves; gossip was at once the mark and compensation of their servitude. They made loud and elaborate talk among themselves, full of jest and gesture, fright and false alarm. They went abroad in fringed and flowered shawls, bright beadwork and German silver. They were at home in the kitchen, and they prepared meals that were banquets.

There were frequent prayer meetings, and great nocturnal feasts. When I was a child I played with my cousins outside, where the lamplight fell upon the ground and the singing of the old people rose up around us and carried away into the darkness. There were a lot of good things to eat, a lot of laughter and surprise. And afterwards, when the quiet returned, I lay down with my grandmother and could hear the frogs away by the river and feel the motion of the air.

Now there is a funeral silence in the rooms, the endless wake of some final word. The walls have closed in upon my grandmother's house. When I returned to it in mourning, I saw for the first time in my life how small it was. It was late at night, and there was a white moon, nearly full. I sat for a long time on the stone steps by the kitchen door. From there I could see out across the land; I could see the long row of trees by the creek, the low light upon the rolling plains, and the stars of the Big Dipper. Once I looked at the moon and caught sight of a strange thing. A cricket had perched upon the handrail, only a few inches away from me. My line of vision was such that the creature filled the moon like a fossil. It had gone there, I thought, to live and die, for there, of all places, was its small definition made whole and eternal. A warm wind rose up and purled like the longing within me.

The next morning I awoke at dawn and went out on the dirt 15
road to Rainy Mountain. It was already hot, and the grasshoppers began to fill the air. Still, it was early in the morning, and the birds sang out of the shadows. The long yellow grass on the mountain shone in the bright light, and a scissortail hied above the land. There, where it ought to be, at the end of a long and legendary way, was my grandmother's grave. Here and there on the dark stones were ancestral names. Looking back once, I saw the mountain and came away.

For Discussion and Writing

1. Where does Momaday's journey begin? Where does it end?
2. Momaday tells at least three stories in "The Way to Rainy Mountain" — his, his grandmother's, and that of the Kiowa people. Why does he tell them together?
3. **connections** Compare Momaday's telling of the past to Maxine Hong Kingston's in "No Name Woman" (p. 221). How do their styles differ, and how do those differences relate to their stories?
4. Do you have an older relative to whom you can talk about your family's past? If so, write the story of that past as far back as you can go; if not, fill in the blanks with your imagination.

BHARATI MUKHERJEE

Two Ways to Belong in America

Born in 1940 and raised in Calcutta, India, Bharati Mukherjee immigrated to the United States in 1961 and earned an M.F.A. and a Ph.D. in literature. Mukherjee is the author of several novels, including Tiger's Daughter *(1972),* Jasmine *(1989),* Desirable Daughters *(2002), and* The Tree Bride *(2004). She has also written short story collections, such as* The Middleman and Other Stories *(1988). She teaches literature and fiction writing at the University of California, Berkeley.*

"Two Ways to Belong in America" first appeared in the New York Times. *It was written to address a movement in Congress to take away government benefits from resident aliens. Like her fiction, though, it is about the issues that confront immigrants in America.*

This is a tale of two sisters from Calcutta, Mira and Bharati, who have lived in the United States for some 35 years, but who find themselves on different sides in the current debate over the status of immigrants. I am an American citizen and she is not. I am moved that thousands of long-term residents are finally taking the oath of citizenship. She is not.

Mira arrived in Detroit in 1960 to study child psychology and pre-school education. I followed her a year later to study creative writing at the University of Iowa. When we left India, we were almost identical in appearance and attitude. We dressed alike, in saris; we expressed identical views on politics, social issues, love, and marriage in the same Calcutta convent-school accent. We would endure our two years in America, secure our degrees, then return to India to marry the grooms of our father's choosing.

Instead, Mira married an Indian student in 1962 who was getting his business administration degree at Wayne State University. They soon acquired the labor certifications necessary for the green card of hassle-free residence and employment.

Mira still lives in Detroit, works in the Southfield, Mich., school system, and has become nationally recognized for her contributions in the fields of pre-school education and parent-teacher relationships. After 36 years as a legal immigrant in this country, she clings passionately to her Indian citizenship and hopes to go home to India when she retires.

5 In Iowa City in 1963, I married a fellow student, an American of Canadian parentage. Because of the accident of his North Dakota birth, I bypassed labor-certification requirements and the race-related "quota" system that favored the applicant's country of origin over his or her merit. I was prepared for (and even welcomed) the emotional strain that came with marrying outside my ethnic community. In 33 years of marriage, we have lived in every part of North America. By choosing a husband who was not my father's selection, I was opting for fluidity, self-invention, blue jeans, and T-shirts, and renouncing 3,000 years (at least) of caste-observant, "pure culture" marriage in the Mukherjee family. My books have often been read as unapologetic (and in some quarters overenthusiastic) texts for cultural and psychological "mongrelization." It's a word I celebrate.

Mira and I have stayed sisterly close by phone. In our regular Sunday morning conversations, we are unguardedly affectionate. I am her only blood relative on this continent. We expect to see each other through the looming crises of aging and ill health without being asked. Long before Vice President Gore's "Citizenship U.S.A." drive, we'd had our polite arguments over the ethics of retaining an overseas citizenship while expecting the permanent protection and economic benefits that come with living and working in America.

Like well-raised sisters, we never said what was really on our minds, but we probably pitied one another. She, for the lack of structure in my life, the erasure of Indianness, the absence of an unvarying daily core. I, for the narrowness of her perspective, her uninvolvement with the mythic depths or the superficial pop culture of this society. But, now, with the scapegoatings of "aliens" (documented or illegal) on the increase, and the targeting of long-term legal immigrants like Mira for new scrutiny and new self-consciousness, she and I find ourselves unable to maintain the same polite discretion. We were always unacknowledged adversaries, and we are now, more than ever, sisters.

"I feel used," Mira raged on the phone the other night. "I feel manipulated and discarded. This is such an unfair way to treat a person who was invited to stay and work here because of her talent. My employer went to the I.N.S. and petitioned for the labor certification. For over 30 years, I've invested my creativity and professional skills into the improvement of *this* country's preschool system. I've obeyed all the rules, I've paid my taxes, I love my work, I love my students, I love the friends I've made. How dare America now change its rules in midstream? If America wants to make new rules curtailing benefits of legal immigrants, they should apply only to immigrants who arrive after those rules are already in place."

To my ears, it sounded like the description of a long-enduring, comfortable yet loveless marriage, without risk or recklessness. Have we the right to demand, and to expect, that we be loved? (That, to me, is the subtext of the arguments by immigration advocates.) My sister is an expatriate, professionally generous and creative, socially courteous and gracious, and that's as far as her Americanization can go. She is here to maintain an identity, not to transform it.

I asked her if she would follow the example of others who have 10
decided to become citizens because of the anti-immigration bills in Congress. And here, she surprised me. "If America wants to play the manipulative game, I'll play it, too," she snapped. "I'll become a U.S. citizen for now, then change back to India when I'm ready to go home. I feel some kind of irrational attachment to India that I don't to America. Until all this hysteria against legal immigrants, I was totally happy. Having my green card meant I could visit any place in the world I wanted to and then come back to a job that's satisfying and that I do very well."

In one family, from two sisters alike as peas in a pod, there could not be a wider divergence of immigrant experience. America spoke to me — I married it — I embraced the demotion from expatriate aristocrat to immigrant nobody, surrendering those thousands of years of "pure culture," the saris, the delightfully accented English. She retained them all. Which of us is the freak?

Mira's voice, I realize, is the voice not just of the immigrant South Asian community but of an immigrant community of the millions who have stayed rooted in one job, one city, one house, one ancestral culture, one cuisine, for the entirety of their productive years. She speaks for greater numbers than I possibly can. Only the fluency of her English and the anger, rather than fear, born of confidence from her education, differentiate her from the seamstresses, the domestics, the technicians, the shop owners, the millions of hard-working but effectively silenced documented immigrants as well as their less fortunate "illegal" brothers and sisters.

Nearly 20 years ago, when I was living in my husband's ancestral homeland of Canada, I was always well-employed but never allowed to feel part of the local Quebec or larger Canadian society. Then, through a Green Paper that invited a national referendum on the unwanted side effects of "nontraditional" immigration, the government officially turned against its immigrant communities, particularly those from South Asia.

I felt then the same sense of betrayal that Mira feels now. I will never forget the pain of that sudden turning, and the casual racist outbursts the Green Paper elicited. That sense of betrayal had its desired effect and drove me, and thousands like me, from the country.

15 Mira and I differ, however, in the ways in which we hope to interact with the country that we have chosen to live in. She is happier to live in America as expatriate Indian than as an immigrant American. I need to feel like a part of the community I have adopted (as I tried to feel in Canada as well). I need to put roots down, to vote and make the difference that I can. The price that the immigrant willingly pays, and that the exile avoids, is the trauma of self-transformation.

For Discussion and Writing

1. Make a list of specific qualities, behaviors, and beliefs for each of the two sisters. What similarities and differences are evident?
2. Mukherjee spends much of this essay comparing herself to her sister. What larger comparison does this analysis support?
3. **connections** Mukherjee's essay contains a lot of background information (about politics and history), which she skillfully weaves into the story she tells about herself and her sister. Compare the way she incorporates information to the method used by Annie Dillard in "Seeing" (p. 112).
4. Think of a sibling or friend with whom you disagree vehemently over some issue or idea. Describe your arguments about it. Are they "polite," as Mukherjee says hers are with her sister?

GEORGE ORWELL

Shooting an Elephant

Born in India in 1903, Eric Blair was the son of an English civil servant in the British Raj, the rule of India by the British, as was his father. Educated in England, Blair was an Imperial policeman in India for five years but resigned and returned to England to pursue his dream of becoming a writer, complete with a pen name, George Orwell. Known best for his novels Animal Farm *(1945) and* 1984 *(1949), Orwell's political concerns were expressed in nonfiction as well, in works such as his chronicle of life among the poor,* Down and Out in Paris and London *(1933). Because of his stands against economic injustice and totalitarianism, Orwell remains an influential figure, as the adjectivization of his pen name shows —* Orwellian *has entered the vernacular as a term to describe the violence done to language and common sense by totalitarianism. "Shooting an Elephant" tells the story of a moment early in Orwell's life when his sense of injustice surfaced.*

In Moulmein, in Lower Burma, I was hated by large numbers of people — the only time in my life that I have been important enough for this to happen to me. I was sub-divisional police officer of the town, and in an aimless, petty kind of way anti-European feeling was very bitter. No one had the guts to raise a riot, but if a European woman went through the bazaars alone somebody would probably spit betel juice over her dress. As a police officer I was an obvious target and was baited whenever it seemed safe to do so. When a nimble Burman tripped me up on the football field and the referee (another Burman) looked the other way, the crowd yelled with hideous laughter. This happened more than once. In the end the sneering yellow faces of young men that met me everywhere, the insults hooted after me when I was at a safe distance, got badly on my nerves. The young Buddhist priests were the worst of all. There were several thousands of them in the town and none of them seemed to have anything to do except stand on street corners and jeer at Europeans.

All this was perplexing and upsetting. For at that time I had already made up my mind that imperialism was an evil thing and the sooner I chucked up my job and got out of it the better. Theoretically — and secretly, of course — I was all for the Burmese and all against their oppressors, the British. As for the job I was doing, I hated it more bitterly than I can perhaps make clear. In a job like that you see the dirty work of Empire at close quarters. The wretched prisoners huddling in the stinking cages of the lock-ups, the grey, cowed faces of the long-term convicts, the scarred buttocks of the men who had been flogged with bamboos — all these oppressed me with an intolerable sense of guilt. But I could get nothing into perspective. I was young and ill-educated and I had had to think out my problems in the utter silence that is imposed on every Englishman in the East. I did not even know that the British Empire is dying, still less did I know that it is a great deal better than the younger empires that are going to supplant it. All I knew was that I was stuck between my hatred of the empire I served and my rage against the evil-spirited little beasts who tried to make my job impossible. With one part of my mind I thought of the British Raj as an unbreakable tyranny, as something clamped down, in *saecula saeculorum* upon the will of prostrate peoples; with another part I thought that the greatest joy in the world would be to drive a bayonet into a Buddhist priest's guts. Feelings like these are the normal by-products of imperialism; ask any Anglo-Indian official, if you can catch him off duty.

One day something happened which in a roundabout way was enlightening. It was a tiny incident in itself, but it gave me a better glimpse than I had had before of the real nature of imperialism — the real motives for which despotic governments act. Early one morning the sub-inspector at a police station the other end of the town rang me up on the phone and said that an elephant was ravaging the bazaar. Would I please come and do something about it? I did not know what I could do, but I wanted to see what was happening and I got on to a pony and started out. I took my rifle, an old .44 Winchester and much too small to kill an elephant, but I thought the noise might be useful *in terrorem*. Various Burmans stopped me on the way and told me about the elephant's doings.

It was not, of course, a wild elephant, but a tame one which had gone "must." It had been chained up, as tame elephants always are when their attack of "must" is due, but on the previous night it had broken its chain and escaped. Its mahout, the only person who could manage it when it was in that state, had set out in pursuit, but had taken the wrong direction and was now twelve hours' journey away, and in the morning the elephant had suddenly reappeared in the town. The Burmese population had no weapons and were quite helpless against it. It had already destroyed somebody's bamboo hut, killed a cow and raided some fruit-stalls and devoured the stock; also it had met the municipal rubbish van and, when the driver jumped out and took to his heels, had turned the van over and inflicted violences upon it.

The Burmese sub-inspector and some Indian constables were waiting for me in the quarter where the elephant had been seen. It was a very poor quarter, a labyrinth of squalid bamboo huts, thatched with palm-leaf, winding all over a steep hillside. I remember that it was a cloudy, stuffy morning at the beginning of the rains. We began questioning the people as to where the elephant had gone and, as usual, failed to get any definite information. That is invariably the case in the East; a story always sounds clear enough at a distance, but the nearer you get to the scene of events the vaguer it becomes. Some of the people said that the elephant had gone in one direction, some said that he had gone in another, some professed not even to have heard of any elephant. I had almost made up my mind that the whole story was a pack of lies, when we heard yells a little distance away. There was a loud, scandalized cry of "Go away, child! Go away this instant!" and an old woman with a switch in her hand came round the corner of a hut, violently shooing away a crowd of naked children. Some more women followed, clicking their tongues and exclaiming; evidently there was something that the children ought not to have seen. I rounded the hut and saw a man's dead body sprawling in the mud. He was an Indian, a black Dravidian coolie, almost naked, and he could not have been dead many minutes. The people said that the elephant had come suddenly upon him round the corner of the hut, caught him with its trunk, put its foot on his back and ground him into the earth. This was the rainy season and the ground was soft, and his face had scored a trench a foot deep and a couple of yards long. He was lying on his belly with arms crucified and head sharply twisted to one side. His face was coated with mud, the eyes wide open, the teeth bared and grinning with an expression of unendurable agony. (Never tell me, by the way, that the dead look peaceful. Most of the corpses I have seen looked devilish.) The friction of the great beast's foot had stripped the skin from his back as neatly as one skins a rabbit. As soon as I saw the dead man I sent an orderly to a friend's house nearby to borrow an elephant rifle. I had already sent back the pony, not wanting it to go mad with fright and throw me if it smelt the elephant.

The orderly came back in a few minutes with a rifle and five 5
cartridges, and meanwhile some Burmans had arrived and told us that the elephant was in the paddy fields below, only a few hundred yards away. As I started forward practically the whole population of the quarter flocked out of the houses and followed me. They had seen the rifle and were all shouting excitedly that I was going to shoot the elephant. They had not shown much interest in the elephant when he was merely ravaging their homes, but it was different now that he was going to be shot. It was a bit of fun to them, as it would be to an English crowd; besides they wanted the meat. It made me vaguely uneasy. I had no intention of shooting the elephant — I had merely sent for the rifle to defend myself if necessary — and it is always unnerving to have a crowd following you. I marched down the hill, looking and feeling a fool, with the rifle over my shoulder and an ever-growing army of people jostling at my heels. At the bottom, when you got away from the huts, there was a metalled road and beyond that a miry waste of paddy fields a thousand yards across, not yet ploughed but soggy from the first rains and dotted with coarse grass. The elephant was standing eight yards from the road, his left side towards us. He took not the slightest notice of the crowd's approach. He was tearing up bunches of grass, beating them against his knees to clean them and stuffing them into his mouth.

I had halted on the road. As soon as I saw the elephant I knew with perfect certainty that I ought not to shoot him. It is a serious matter to shoot a working elephant — it is comparable to destroying a huge and costly piece of machinery — and obviously one ought not to do it if it can possibly be avoided. And at that distance, peacefully eating, the elephant looked no more dangerous than a cow. I thought then and I think now that his attack of "must" was already passing off; in which case he would merely wander harmlessly about until the mahout came back and caught him. Moreover, I did not in the least want to shoot him. I decided that I would watch him for a little while to make sure that he did not turn savage again, and then go home.

But at that moment I glanced round at the crowd that had followed me. It was an immense crowd, two thousand at the least and growing every minute. It blocked the road for a long distance on either side. I looked at the sea of yellow faces above the garish clothes — faces all happy and excited over this bit of fun, all certain that the elephant was going to be shot. They were watching me as they would watch a conjurer about to perform a trick. They did not like me, but with the magical rifle in my hands I was momentarily worth watching. And suddenly I realized that I should have to shoot the elephant after all. The people expected it of me and I had got to do it; I could feel their two thousand wills pressing me forward, irresistibly. And it was at this moment, as I stood there with the rifle in my hands, that I first grasped the hollowness, the futility of the white man's dominion in the East. Here was I, the white man with his gun, standing in front of the unarmed native crowd — seemingly the leading actor of the piece; but in reality I was only an absurd puppet pushed to and fro by the will of those yellow faces behind. I perceived in this moment that when the white man turns tyrant it is his own freedom that he destroys. He becomes a sort of hollow, posing dummy, the conventionalized figure of a sahib. For it is the condition of his rule that he shall spend his life in trying to impress the "natives," and so in every crisis he has got to do what the "natives" expect of him. He wears a mask, and his face grows to fit it. I had got to shoot the elephant. I had committed myself to doing it when I sent for the rifle. A sahib has got to act like a sahib; he has got to appear resolute, to know his own mind and do definite things. To come all that way, rifle in hand, with two thousand people marching at my heels, and then to trail feebly away, having done nothing — no, that was impossible. The crowd would laugh at me. And my whole life, every white man's life in the East, was one long struggle not to be laughed at.

But I did not want to shoot the elephant. I watched him beating his bunch of grass against his knees, with that preoccupied grandmotherly air that elephants have. It seemed to me that it would be murder to shoot him. At that age I was not squeamish about killing animals, but I had never shot an elephant and never wanted to. (Somehow it always seems worse to kill a *large* animal.) Besides, there was the beast's owner to be considered. Alive, the elephant was worth at least a hundred pounds; dead, he would only be worth the value of his tusks, five pounds, possibly. But I had got to act quickly. I turned to some experienced-looking Burmans who had been there when we arrived, and asked them how the elephant had been behaving. They all said the same thing: he took no notice of you if you left him alone, but he might charge if you went too close to him.

It was perfectly clear to me what I ought to do. I ought to walk up to within, say, twenty-five yards of the elephant and test his behavior. If he charged, I could shoot; if he took no notice of me, it would be safe to leave him until the mahout came back. But also I knew that I was going to do no such thing. I was a poor shot with a rifle and the ground was soft mud into which one would sink at every step. If the elephant charged and I missed him, I should have about as much chance as a toad under a steam-roller. But even then I was not thinking particularly of my own skin, only of the watchful yellow faces behind. For at that moment, with the crowd watching me, I was not afraid in the ordinary sense, as I would have been if I had been alone. A white man mustn't be frightened in front of "natives"; and so, in general, he isn't frightened. The sole thought in my mind was that if anything went wrong those two thousand Burmans would see me pursued, caught, trampled on and reduced to a grinning corpse like that Indian up the hill. And if that happened it was quite probable that some of them would laugh. That would never do. There was only one alternative. I shoved the cartridges into the magazine and lay down on the road to get a better aim.

The crowd grew very still, and a deep, low, happy sigh, as of 10
people who see the theater curtain go up at last, breathed from innumerable throats. They were going to have their bit of fun after all. The rifle was a beautiful German thing with cross-hair sights. I did not then know that in shooting an elephant one would shoot to cut an imaginary bar running from ear-hole to ear-hole. I ought, therefore, as the elephant was sideways on, to have aimed straight at his ear-hole; actually I aimed several inches in front of this, thinking the brain would be further forward.

When I pulled the trigger I did not hear the bang or feel the kick — one never does when a shot goes home — but I heard the devilish roar of glee that went up from the crowd. In that instant, in too short a time, one would have thought, even for the bullet to get there, a mysterious, terrible change had come over the elephant. He neither stirred nor fell, but every line of his body had altered. He looked suddenly stricken, shrunken, immensely old, as though the frightful impact of the bullet had paralyzed him without knocking him down. At last, after what seemed a long time — it might have been five seconds, I dare say — he sagged flabbily to his knees. His mouth slobbered. An enormous senility seemed to have settled upon him. One could have imagined him thousands of years old. I fired again into the same spot. At the second shot he did not collapse but climbed with desperate slowness to his feet and stood weakly upright, with legs sagging and head drooping. I fired a third time. That was the shot that did for him. You could see the agony of it jolt his whole body and knock the last remnant of strength from his legs. But in falling he seemed for a moment to rise, for as his hind legs collapsed beneath him he seemed to tower upward like a huge rock toppling, his trunk reaching skywards like a tree. He trumpeted, for the first and only time. And then down he came, his belly towards me, with a crash that seemed to shake the ground even where I lay.

I got up. The Burmans were already racing past me across the mud. It was obvious that the elephant would never rise again, but he was not dead. He was breathing very rhythmically with long rattling gasps, his great mound of a side painfully rising and falling. His mouth was wide open — I could see far down into caverns of pale pink throat. I waited a long time for him to die, but his breathing did not weaken. Finally I fired my two remaining shots into the spot where I thought his heart must be. The thick blood welled out of him like red velvet, but still he did not die. His body did not even jerk when the shots hit him, the tortured breathing continued without a pause. He was dying, very slowly and in great agony, but in some world remote from me where not even a bullet could damage him further. I felt that I had got to put an end to that dreadful noise. It seemed dreadful to see the great beast lying there, powerless to move and yet powerless to die, and not even to be able to finish him. I sent back for my small rifle and poured shot after shot into his heart and down his throat. They seemed to make no impression. The tortured gasps continued as steadily as the ticking of a clock.

In the end I could not stand it any longer and went away. I heard later that it took him half an hour to die. Burmans were bringing dahs and baskets even before I left, and I was told they had stripped his body almost to the bones by the afternoon.

Afterwards, of course, there were endless discussions about the shooting of the elephant. The owner was furious, but he was only an Indian and could do nothing. Besides, legally I had done the right thing, for a mad elephant has to be killed, like a mad dog, if its owner fails to control it. Among the Europeans opinion was divided. The older men said I was right, the younger men said it was a damn shame to shoot an elephant for killing a coolie, because an elephant was worth more than any damn Coringhee coolie. And afterwards I was very glad that the coolie had been killed; it put me legally in the right and it gave me a sufficient pretext for shooting the elephant. I often wondered whether any of the others grasped that I had done it solely to avoid looking a fool.

For Discussion and Writing

1. Why does Orwell shoot the elephant?
2. Orwell uses the anecdote of his shooting an elephant to illustrate his feelings about imperialism. What are those feelings, and how does the anecdote illustrate them?
3. **connections** Orwell calls what he is doing in Lower Burma "the dirty work of Empire" (par. 2), and judges his shooting of the elephant finally as the product of the conflicting motivations behind his position and empire itself. Read "Shooting an Elephant" through the lens of Joan Didion in "On Morality" (p. 106). What are the "higher" moral beliefs that imperialists claimed? In what ways does Orwell's essay refute these claims?
4. What would you have done if you had been in Orwell's place? Why?

PLATO

The Allegory of the Cave

Plato was born in 428 B.C.E. in Athens, Greece. He is known as a student of Socrates and teacher of Aristotle. Most of what we know about Socrates, in fact, comes from Plato's writings, many of which are constructed as philosophical dialogues between Socrates and his students. Plato is best known for the Republic, *a work of political philosophy based in metaphysics (which examines the nature of reality), ethics (the study of right conduct), and epistemology (the study of knowledge itself); as in his other works, he is not concerned only with how we should act but also with how we know, who we are, and what is true.*

"The Allegory of the Cave," taken from the Republic, *demonstrates this mixture of concerns in Plato's work. (An allegory is a representation — a story or image — that dramatizes abstract ideas.) As you read, note the ways in which his thoughts about politics are grounded in his understanding of the nature of human experience and knowledge.*

And now, I said, let me show in a figure how far our nature is enlightened or unenlightened: — Behold! human beings living in an underground den, which has a mouth open towards the light and reaching all along the den; here they have been from their childhood, and have their legs and necks chained so that they cannot move, and can only see before them, being prevented by the chains from turning round their heads. Above and behind them a fire is blazing at a distance, and between the fire and the prisoners there is a raised way; and you will see, if you look, a low wall built along the way, like the screen which marionette players have in front of them, over which they show the puppets.

I see.

And do you see, I said, men passing along the wall carrying all sorts of vessels, and statues and figures of animals made of wood and stone and various materials, which appear over the wall? Some of them are talking, others silent.

You have shown me a strange image, and they are strange prisoners.

Like ourselves, I replied; and they see only their own shadows, or the shadows of one another, which the fire throws on the opposite wall of the cave?

True, he said; how could they see anything but the shadows if they were never allowed to move their heads?

And of the objects which are being carried in like manner they would only see the shadows?

Yes, he said.

And if they were able to converse with one another, would they not suppose that they were naming what was actually before them?

Very true.

And suppose further that the prison had an echo which came from the other side, would they not be sure to fancy when one of the passers-by spoke that the voice which they heard came from the passing shadow?

No question, he replied.

To them, I said, the truth would be literally nothing but the shadows of the images.

That is certain.

And now look again, and see what will naturally follow if the prisoners are released and disabused of their error. At first, when any of them is liberated and compelled suddenly to stand up and turn his neck round and walk and look towards the light, he will suffer sharp pains; the glare will distress him, and he will be unable to see the realities of which in his former state he had seen the shadows; and then conceive someone saying to him, that what he saw before was an illusion, but that now, when he is approaching nearer to being and his eye is turned towards more real existence, he has a clearer vision — what will be his reply? And you may further imagine that his instructor is pointing to the objects as they pass and requiring him to name them, — will he not be perplexed? Will he not fancy that the shadows which he formerly saw are truer than the objects which are now shown to him?

Far truer.

And if he is compelled to look straight at the light, will he not have a pain in his eyes which will make him turn away to take refuge in the objects of vision which he can see, and which he will conceive to be in reality clearer than the things which are now being shown to him?

True, he said.

And suppose once more, that he is reluctantly dragged up a steep and rugged ascent, and held fast until he is forced into the presence of the sun himself, is he not likely to be pained and irritated? When he approaches the light his eyes will be dazzled, and he will not be able to see anything at all of what are now called realities.

Not all in a moment, he said.

He will require to grow accustomed to the sight of the upper world. And first he will see the shadows best, next the reflections of men and other objects in the water, and then the objects themselves; then he will gaze upon the light of the moon and the stars and the spangled heaven; and he will see the sky and the stars by night better than the sun or the light of the sun by day?

Certainly.

Last of all he will be able to see the sun, and not mere reflections of him in the water, but he will see him in his own proper place, and not in another; and he will contemplate him as he is.

Certainly.

He will then proceed to argue that this is he who gives the season and the years, and is the guardian of all that is in the visible world, and in a certain way the cause of all things which he and his fellows have been accustomed to behold?

Clearly, he said, he would first see the sun and then reason about him.

And when he remembered his old habitation, and the wisdom of the den and his fellow prisoners, do you not suppose that he would felicitate himself on the change, and pity them?

Certainly, he would.

And if they were in the habit of conferring honors among themselves on those who were quickest to observe the passing shadows and to remark which of them went before, and which followed after, and which were together; and who were therefore best able to draw conclusions as to the future, do you think that he would care for such honors and glories, or envy the possessors of them? Would he not say with Homer,

> Better to be the poor servant of a poor master,

and to endure anything, rather than think as they do and live after their manner?

Yes, he said, I think that he would rather suffer anything than entertain these false notions and live in this miserable manner.

Imagine once more, I said, such an one coming suddenly out of the sun to be replaced in his old situation; would he not be certain to have his eyes full of darkness?

To be sure, he said.

And if there were a contest, and he had to compete in measuring the shadows with the prisoners who had never moved out of the den, while his sight was still weak, and before his eyes had become steady (and the time which would be needed to acquire this new habit of sight might be very considerable), would he not be ridiculous? Men would say of him that up he went and down he came without his eyes; and that it was better not even to think of ascending; and if any one tried to loose another and lead him up to the light, let them only catch the offender, and they would put him to death.

No question, he said.

This entire allegory, I said, you may now append, dear Glaucon, to the previous argument; the prison house is the world of sight, the light of the fire is the sun, and you will not misapprehend me if you interpret the journey upwards to be the ascent of the soul into the intellectual world according to my poor belief, which, at your desire, I have expressed — whether rightly or wrongly God knows. But, whether true or false, my opinion is that in the world of knowledge the idea of good appears last of all, and is seen only with an effort; and, when seen, is also inferred to be the universal author of all things beautiful and right, parent of light and of the lord of light in this visible world, and the immediate source of reason and truth in the intellectual; and that this is the power upon which he who would act rationally either in public or private life must have his eye fixed.

I agree, he said, as far as I am able to understand you.

Moreover, I said, you must not wonder that those who attain to this beatific vision are unwilling to descend to human affairs; for their souls are ever hastening into the upper world where they desire to dwell; which desire of theirs is very natural, if our allegory may be trusted.

Yes, very natural.

And is there anything surprising in one who passes from divine contemplations to the evil state of man, misbehaving himself in a ridiculous manner; if, while his eyes are blinking and before he has become accustomed to the surrounding darkness, he is compelled to fight in courts of law, or in other places, about the images or the shadows of images of justice, and is endeavoring to meet the conceptions of those who have never yet seen absolute justice?

Anything but surprising, he replied. 40

Anyone who has common sense will remember that the bewilderments of the eyes are of two kinds, and arise from two causes, either from coming out of the light or from going into the light, which is true of the mind's eye, quite as much as of the bodily eye; and he who remembers this when he sees anyone whose vision is perplexed and weak, will not be too ready to laugh; he will first ask whether that soul of man has come out of the brighter life, and is unable to see because unaccustomed to the dark, or having turned from darkness to the day is dazzled by excess of light. And he will count the one happy in his condition and state of being, and he will pity the other; or, if he have a mind to laugh at the soul which comes from below into the light, there will be more reason in this than in the laugh which greets him who returns from above out of the light into the den.

That, he said, is a very just distinction.

But then, if I am right, certain professors of education must be wrong when they say that they can put a knowledge into the soul which was not there before, like sight into blind eyes.

They undoubtedly say this, he replied.

Whereas, our argument shows that the power and capacity of 45
learning exists in the soul already; and that just as the eye was unable to turn from darkness to light without the whole body, so too the instrument of knowledge can only by the movement of the whole soul be turned from the world of becoming into that of being, and learn by degrees to endure the sight of being, and of the brightest and best of being, or in other words, of the good.

Very true.

And must there not be some art which will effect conversion in the easiest and quickest manner; not implanting the faculty of sight, for that exists already, but has been turned in the wrong direction, and is looking away from the truth?

Yes, he said, such an art may be presumed.

And whereas the other so-called virtues of the soul seem to be akin to bodily qualities, for even when they are not originally innate they can be implanted later by habit and exercise, the virtue of wisdom more than anything else contains a divine element which always remains, and by this conversion is rendered useful and profitable; or, on the other hand, hurtful and useless. Did you never observe the narrow intelligence flashing from the keen eye of a clever rogue — how eager he is, how clearly his paltry soul sees the way to his end; he is the reverse of blind, but his keen eyesight is forced into the service of evil, and he is mischievous in proportion to his cleverness?

Very true, he said.

But what if there had been a circumcision of such natures in the days of their youth; and they had been severed from those sensual pleasures, such as eating and drinking, which, like leaden weights, were attached to them at their birth, and which drag them down and turn the vision of their souls upon the things that are below — if, I say, they had been released from these impediments and turned in the opposite direction, the very same faculty in them would have seen the truth as keenly as they see what their eyes are turned to now.

Very likely.

Yes, I said; and there is another thing which is likely, or rather a necessary inference from what has preceded, that neither the uneducated and uninformed of the truth, nor yet those who never make an end of their education, will be able ministers of State; not the former, because they have no single aim of duty which is the rule of all their actions, private as well as public; nor the latter, because they will not act at all except upon compulsion, fancying that they are already dwelling apart in the islands of the blessed.

Very true, he replied.

Then, I said, the business of us who are the founders of the State will be to compel the best minds to attain that knowledge which we have already shown to be the greatest of all — they must continue to ascend until they arrive at the good; but when they have ascended and seen enough we must not allow them to do as they do now.

What do you mean?

I mean that they remain in the upper world: but this must not be allowed; they must be made to descend again among the prisoners in the den, and partake of their labors and honors, whether they are worth having or not.

But is not this unjust? he said; ought we to give them a worse life, when they might have a better?

You have again forgotten, my friend, I said, the intention of the legislator, who did not aim at making any one class in the State happy above the rest; the happiness was to be in the whole State, and he held the citizens together by persuasion and necessity, making them benefactors of the State, and therefore benefactors of one another; to this end he created them, not to please themselves, but to be his instruments in binding up the State.

True, he said, I had forgotten.

Observe, Glaucon, that there will be no injustice in compelling our philosophers to have a care and providence of others; we shall explain to them that in other States, men of their class are not obliged to share in the toils of politics: and this is reasonable, for they grow up at their own sweet will, and the government would rather not have them. Being self-taught, they cannot be expected to show any gratitude for a culture which they have never received. But we have brought you into the world to be rulers of the hive, kings of yourselves and of the other citizens, and have educated you far better and more perfectly than they have been educated, and you are better able to share in the double duty. Wherefore each of you, when his turn comes, must go down to the general underground abode, and get the habit of seeing in the dark. When you have acquired the habit, you will see ten thousand times better than the inhabitants of the den, and you will know what the several images are, and what they represent, because you have seen the beautiful and just and good in their truth. And thus our State, which is also yours, will be a reality, and not a dream only, and will be administered in a spirit unlike that of other States, in which men fight with one another about shadows only and are distracted in the struggle for power, which in their eyes is a great good. Whereas the truth is that the State in which the rulers are most reluctant to govern is always the best and most quietly governed, and the State in which they are most eager, the worst.

Quite true, he replied.

And will our pupils, when they hear this, refuse to take their turn at the toils of State, when they are allowed to spend the greater part of their time with one another in the heavenly light?

Impossible, he answered; for they are just men, and the commands which we impose upon them are just; there can be no doubt that every one of them will take office as a stern necessity, and not after the fashion of our present rulers of State.

65 Yes, my friend, I said; and there lies the point. You must contrive for your future rulers another and a better life than that of a ruler, and then you may have a well-ordered State; for only in the State which offers this, will they rule who are truly rich, not in silver and gold, but in virtue and wisdom, which are the true blessings of life. Whereas if they go to the administration of public affairs, poor and hungering after their own private advantage, thinking that hence they are to snatch the chief good, order there can never be; for they will be fighting about office, and the civil and domestic broils which thus arise will be the ruin of the rulers themselves and of the whole State.

Most true, he replied.

And the only life which looks down upon the life of political ambition is that of true philosophy. Do you know of any other?

Indeed, I do not, he said.

For Discussion and Writing

1. What does the cave stand for in Plato's allegory? Make a list of the other elements in the allegory — chains, light, darkness, and so on — and explain what they represent.
2. Plato compares a number of things in this essay — the material world to the world of ideas, the life of the mind to the work of governing, silver and gold to virtue and wisdom. How does he use his comparisons to make his argument?
3. **connections** Though George Orwell, in "Shooting an Elephant" (p. 284), is a different kind of leader than the rulers in Plato's allegory, he is in a position of authority. Do you think there are points of connection between the two essays in this area? Can you consider Orwell's reflection on his actions, and the tangle of motivations behind them, in light of Plato's discussion of the potentially conflicting motivations of rulers?
4. Plato argues that working in public affairs and working for one's own private advantage cannot mix. How might contemporary politics bear out this assertion or contradict it?

MICHAEL POLLAN

What's Eating America

Corn is one of the plant kingdom's biggest successes.
That's not necessarily good for the United States.

Born in 1955, Michael Pollan is a journalist, professor of journalism, and activist who has focused much of his recent attention on food — how we produce it, how we eat it, how we think about it. His food books include The Omnivore's Dilemma: A Natural History of Four Meals *(2006),* In Defense of Food: An Eater's Manifesto *(2008), and* Food Rules: An Eater's Manual *(2009); other books include* The Botany of Desire: A Plant's-Eye View of the World *(2001);* A Place of My Own *(1997); and* Second Nature *(1991).*

"What's Eating America," originally published in Smithsonian *magazine, has many strengths, including the range of information on which Pollan draws and the skill with which he translates it for a popular venue. But the essay is especially good at drawing the reader in from the start. Reading the opening, pause and inspect the way in which it piques interest, implicates the reader, and intriguingly raises the key issues that will be Pollan's subject by approaching them from an oblique angle. Then, if you are having a corn-based snack while you read, try not to let it be ruined.*

Descendants of the Maya living in Mexico still sometimes refer to themselves as "the corn people." The phrase is not intended as metaphor. Rather, it's meant to acknowledge their abiding dependence on this miraculous grass, the staple of their diet for almost 9,000 years.

For an American like me, growing up linked to a very different food chain, yet one that is also rooted in corn, not to think of himself as a corn person suggests either a failure of imagination or a triumph of capitalism.

Or perhaps a little of both. For the great edifice of variety and choice that is an American supermarket rests on a remarkably narrow biological foundation: corn. It's not merely the feed that the steers and the chickens and the pigs and the turkeys ate; it's not just the source of the flour and the oil and the leavenings, the glycerides and coloring in the processed foods; it's not just sweetening the soft drinks or lending a shine to the magazine cover over by the checkout. The supermarket itself — the wallboard and joint compound, the linoleum and fiberglass and adhesives out of which the building itself has been built — is in no small measure a manifestation of corn.

There are some 45,000 items in the average American supermarket, and more than a quarter of them contain corn. At the same time, the food industry has done a good job of persuading us that the 45,000 different items or SKUs (stock keeping units) represent genuine variety rather than the clever rearrangements of molecules extracted from the same plant.

5 How this peculiar grass, native to Central America and unknown to the Old World before 1492, came to colonize so much of our land and bodies is one of the plant world's greatest success stories. I say the plant world's success story because it is no longer clear that corn's triumph is such a boon to the rest of the world.

At its most basic, the story of life on earth is the competition among species to capture and store as much energy as possible — either directly from the sun, in the case of plants, or, in the case of animals, by eating plants and plant eaters. The energy is stored in the form of carbon molecules and measured in calories: the calories we eat, whether in an ear of corn or a steak, represent packets of energy once captured by a plant. Few plants can manufacture quite as much organic matter (and calories) from the same quantities of sunlight and water and basic elements as corn.

The great turning point in the modern history of corn, which in turn marks a key turning point in the industrialization of our food, can be dated with some precision to the day in 1947 when the huge munitions plant at Muscle Shoals, Alabama, switched over from making explosives to making chemical fertilizer. After World War II, the government had found itself with a tremendous surplus of ammonium nitrate, the principal ingredient in the making of explosives. Ammonium nitrate also happens to be an excellent source of nitrogen for plants. Serious thought was given to spraying America's forests with the surplus chemical, to help the timber industry. But agronomists in the Department of

Agriculture had a better idea: spread the ammonium nitrate on farmland as fertilizer. The chemical fertilizer industry (along with that of pesticides, which are based on the poison gases developed for war) is the product of the government's effort to convert its war machine to peacetime purposes. As the Indian farmer activist Vandana Shiva says in her speeches, "We're still eating the left-overs of World War II."

F1 hybrid corn is the greediest of plants, consuming more fertilizer than any other crop. Though F1 hybrids were introduced in the 1930s, it wasn't until they made the acquaintance of chemical fertilizers in the 1950s that corn yields exploded. The discovery of synthetic nitrogen changed everything — not just for the corn plant and the farm, not just for the food system, but also for the way life on earth is conducted.

All life depends on nitrogen; it is the building block from which nature assembles amino acids, proteins and nucleic acid; the genetic information that orders and perpetuates life is written in nitrogen ink. But the supply of usable nitrogen on earth is limited. Although earth's atmosphere is about 80 percent nitrogen, all those atoms are tightly paired, nonreactive and therefore useless; the nineteenth-century chemist Justus von Liebig spoke of atmospheric nitrogen's "indifference to all other substances." To be of any value to plants and animals, these self-involved nitrogen atoms must be split and then joined to atoms of hydrogen.

Chemists call this process of taking atoms from the atmosphere 10
and combining them into molecules useful to living things "fixing" that element. Until a German Jewish chemist named Fritz Haber figured out how to turn this trick in 1909, all the usable nitrogen on earth had at one time been fixed by soil bacteria living on the roots of leguminous plants (such as peas or alfalfa or locust trees) or, less commonly, by the shock of electrical lightning, which can break nitrogen bonds in the air, releasing a light rain of fertility.

In his book *Enriching the Earth: Fritz Haber, Carl Bosch, and the Transformation of World Food Production*, Vaclav Smil pointed out that "there is no way to grow crops and human bodies without nitrogen." Before Haber's invention, the sheer amount of life earth could support — the size of crops and therefore the number of human bodies — was limited by the amount of nitrogen that bacteria and lightning could fix. By 1900, European scientists had recognized that unless a way was found to augment this naturally occurring nitrogen, the growth of the human population would soon grind to a very painful halt. The same recognition by Chinese scientists a few decades later is probably what compelled China's opening to the West: after Nixon's 1972 trip, the first major order the Chinese government placed was for 13 massive fertilizer factories. Without them, China would have starved.

This is why it may not be hyperbole to claim, as Smil does, that the Haber-Bosch process for fixing nitrogen (Bosch gets the credit for commercializing Haber's idea) is the most important invention of the twentieth century. He estimates that two of every five humans on earth today would not be alive if not for Fritz Haber's invention. We can easily imagine a world without computers or electricity, Smil points out, but without synthetic fertilizer billions of people would never have been born. Though, as these numbers suggest, humans may have struck a Faustian bargain with nature when Fritz Haber gave us the power to fix nitrogen.

Fritz Haber? No, I'd never heard of him either, even though he was awarded the Nobel Prize in 1918 for "improving the standards of agriculture and the well-being of mankind." But the reason for his obscurity has less to do with the importance of his work than an ugly twist of his biography, which recalls the dubious links between modern warfare and industrial agriculture: during World War I, Haber threw himself into the German war effort, and his chemistry kept alive Germany's hopes for victory, by allowing it to make bombs from synthetic nitrate. Later, Haber put his genius for chemistry to work developing poison gases — ammonia, then chlorine. (He subsequently developed Zyklon B, the gas used in Hitler's concentration camps.) His wife, a chemist sickened by her husband's contribution to the war effort, used his army pistol to kill herself; Haber died, broken and in flight from Nazi Germany, in a Basel hotel room in 1934.

His story has been all but written out of the twentieth century. But it embodies the paradoxes of science, the double edge to our manipulations of nature, the good and evil that can flow not only from the same man but from the same knowledge. Even Haber's agricultural benefaction has proved to be a decidedly mixed blessing.

When humankind acquired the power to fix nitrogen, the basis 15
of soil fertility shifted from a total reliance on the energy of the

sun to a new reliance on fossil fuel. That's because the Haber-Bosch process works by combining nitrogen and hydrogen gases under immense heat and pressure in the presence of a catalyst. The heat and pressure are supplied by prodigious amounts of electricity, and the hydrogen is supplied by oil, coal or, most commonly today, natural gas. True, these fossil fuels were created by the sun, billions of years ago, but they are not renewable in the same way that the fertility created by a legume nourished by sunlight is. (That nitrogen is fixed by a bacterium living on the roots of the legume, which trades a tiny drip of sugar for the nitrogen the plant needs.)

Liberated from the old biological constraints, the farm could now be managed on industrial principles, as a factory transforming inputs of raw material — chemical fertilizer — into outputs of corn. And corn adapted brilliantly to the new industrial regime, consuming prodigious quantities of fossil fuel energy and turning out ever more prodigious quantities of food energy. Growing corn, which from a biological perspective had always been a process of capturing sunlight to turn it into food, has in no small measure become a process of converting fossil fuels into food. More than half of all the synthetic nitrogen made today is applied to corn.

From the standpoint of industrial efficiency, it's too bad we can't simply drink petroleum directly, because there's a lot less energy in a bushel of corn (measured in calories) than there is in the half-gallon of oil required to produce it. Ecologically, this is a fabulously expensive way to produce food — but "ecologically" is no longer the operative standard. In the factory, time is money, and yield is everything.

One problem with factories, as opposed to biological systems, is that they tend to pollute. Hungry for fossil fuel as hybrid corn is, farmers still feed it far more than it can possibly eat, wasting most of the fertilizer they buy. And what happens to that synthetic nitrogen the plants don't take up? Some of it evaporates into the air, where it acidifies the rain and contributes to global warming. Some seeps down to the water table, whence it may come out of the tap. The nitrates in water bind to hemoglobin, compromising the blood's ability to carry oxygen to the brain. (I guess I was wrong to suggest we don't sip fossil fuels directly; sometimes we do.)

It has been less than a century since Fritz Haber's invention, yet already it has changed earth's ecology. More than half of the world's supply of usable nitrogen is now man-made. (Unless you grew up on organic food, most of the kilo or so of nitrogen in your body was fixed by the Haber-Bosch process.) "We have perturbed the global nitrogen cycle," Smil wrote, "more than any other, even carbon." The effects may be harder to predict than the effects of the global warming caused by our disturbance of the carbon cycle, but they are no less momentous.

The flood of synthetic nitrogen has fertilized not just the farm 20
fields but the forests and oceans, too, to the benefit of some species (corn and algae being two of the biggest beneficiaries) and to the detriment of countless others. The ultimate fate of the nitrates spread in Iowa or Indiana is to flow down the Mississippi into the Gulf of Mexico, where their deadly fertility poisons the marine ecosystem. The nitrogen tide stimulates the wild growth of algae, and the algae smother the fish, creating a "hypoxic," or dead, zone as big as New Jersey — and still growing. By fertilizing the world, we alter the planet's composition of species and shrink its biodiversity.

And yet, as organic farmers (who don't use synthetic fertilizer) prove every day, the sun still shines, plants and their bacterial associates still fix nitrogen, and farm animals still produce vast quantities of nitrogen in their "waste," so-called. It may take more work, but it's entirely possible to nourish the soil, and ourselves, without dumping so much nitrogen into the environment. The key to reducing our dependence on synthetic nitrogen is to build a more diversified agriculture — rotating crops and using animals to recycle nutrients on farms — and give up our vast, nitrogen-guzzling monocultures of corn. Especially as the price of fossil fuels climbs, even the world's most industrialized farmers will need to take a second look at how nature, and those who imitate her, go about creating fertility without diminishing our world.

For Discussion and Writing

1. Americans don't just grow corn to eat it on the cob. What else do we do with corn now?
2. Much of Pollan's argument consists of him connecting causes and effects — actions taken and the resulting, often unexpected consequences. How is this kind of explanation different from the explanation

of, say, how a car engine works, or the carbon cycle? What does Pollan use his cause-and-effect explanations for? How does he use them to make his larger argument?

3. **connections** Read Pollan's essay next to Rachel Carson's "The Obligation to Endure" (p. 83). While their subjects are very different, both write about the impact of humans on the natural world, and both touch on particular critical agricultural practices. How do their treatments of their subjects compare — their uses of tone, their conclusions?

4. Pollan writes, "The discovery of synthetic nitrogen changed everything — not just for the corn plant and the farm, not just for the food system, but also for the way life on earth is conducted" (par. 8). These changes were not foreseen or planned for when the decision was first made to use ammonium nitrate as a fertilizer. Can you think of another invention or advance that "changed everything" in ways it wasn't intended to?

RICHARD RODRIGUEZ

Aria: Memoir of a Bilingual Childhood

Born in 1944 in San Francisco to Mexican immigrants, and raised in Sacramento, California, Richard Rodriguez is a foremost and sometimes controversial Chicano voice. Best known for his memoir Hunger of Memory: The Education of Richard Rodriguez *(1982), Rodriguez was a literary scholar and teacher until leaving the profession and becoming a full-time essayist. He is now a columnist and editor for the Pacific News Service, a regular essayist for PBS's* NewsHour with Jim Lehrer, *and a contributor to numerous magazines and newspapers. His latest book,* Brown: The Last Discovery of America *(2002), continues his questioning of orthodoxy about race, identity, and politics in America.*

"Aria: Memoir of a Bilingual Childhood" is taken from Hunger of Memory. *That book cemented Rodriguez's controversial reputation because of its stands against bilingual education and affirmative action. Knowing these stands might be controversial, he takes them firmly: Of bilingual voters' ballots, Rodriguez writes, "It is not enough to say that these schemes are foolish and certainly doomed" (par. 61). As you read Aria, note other moments in which Rodriguez takes on ideas with which he disagrees.*

1

I remember to start with that day in Sacramento — a California now nearly thirty years past — when I first entered a classroom, able to understand some fifty stray English words.

The third of four children, I had been preceded to a neighborhood Roman Catholic school by an older brother and sister. But neither of them had revealed very much about their classroom experiences. Each afternoon they returned, as they left in the morning, always together, speaking in Spanish as they climbed the five steps of the porch. And their mysterious books, wrapped in shopping-bag paper, remained on the table next to the door, closed firmly behind them.

An accident of geography sent me to a school where all my classmates were white, many the children of doctors and lawyers and business executives. All my classmates certainly must have been uneasy on that first day of school — as most children are uneasy — to find themselves apart from their families in the first institution of their lives. But I was astonished.

The nun said, in a friendly but oddly impersonal voice, "Boys and girls, this is Richard Rodriguez." (I heard her sound out: *Rich-heard Road-ree-guess*.) It was the first time I had heard anyone name me in English. "Richard," the nun repeated more slowly, writing my name down in her black leather book. Quickly I turned to see my mother's face dissolve in a watery blur behind the pebbled glass door.

Many years later there is something called bilingual educa- 5
tion — a scheme proposed in the late 1960s by Hispanic-American social activists, later endorsed by a congressional vote. It is a program that seeks to permit non-English-speaking children, many from lower-class homes, to use their family language as the language of school. (Such is the goal its supporters announce.) I hear them and am forced to say no: It is not possible for a child — any child — ever to use his family's language in school. Not to understand this is to misunderstand the public uses of schooling and to trivialize the nature of intimate life — a family's "language."

Memory teaches me what I know of these matters; the boy reminds the adult. I was a bilingual child, a certain kind — socially disadvantaged — the son of working-class parents, both Mexican immigrants.

In the early years of my boyhood, my parents coped very well in America. My father had steady work. My mother managed at home. They were nobody's victims. Optimism and ambition led them to a house (our home) many blocks from the Mexican south side of town. We lived among *gringos* and only a block from the biggest, whitest houses. It never occurred to my parents that they couldn't live wherever they chose. Nor was the Sacramento of the fifties bent on teaching them a contrary lesson. My mother and father were more annoyed than intimidated by those two or three neighbors who tried initially to make us unwelcome. ("Keep your brats away from my sidewalk!") But despite all they achieved, perhaps because they had so much to achieve, any deep feeling of ease, the confidence of "belonging" in public was withheld from them both. They regarded the people at work, the faces in crowds, as very distant from us. They were the others, *los gringos*. That term was interchangeable in their speech with another, even more telling, *los americanos*.

I grew up in a house where the only regular guests were my relations. For one day, enormous families of relatives would visit and there would be so many people that the noise and the bodies would spill out to the backyard and front porch. Then, for weeks, no one came by. (It was usually a salesman who rang the doorbell.) Our house stood apart. A gaudy yellow in a row of white bungalows. We were the people with the noisy dog. The people who raised pigeons and chickens. We were the foreigners on the block. A few neighbors smiled and waved. We waved back. But no one in the family knew the names of the old couple who lived next door; until I was seven years old, I did not know the names of the kids who lived across the street.

In public, my father and mother spoke a hesitant, accented, not always grammatical English. And they would have to strain — their bodies tense — to catch the sense of what was rapidly said by *los gringos*. At home they spoke Spanish. The language of their Mexican past sounded in counterpoint to the English of public society. The words would come quickly, with ease. Conveyed through those sounds was the pleasing, soothing, consoling reminder of being at home.

10 During those years when I was first conscious of hearing, my mother and father addressed me only in Spanish; in Spanish I learned to reply. By contrast, English *(inglés)*, rarely heard in the house, was the language I came to associate with *gringos*. I learned my first words of English overhearing my parents speak to strangers. At five years of age, I knew just enough English for my mother to trust me on errands to stores one block away. No more.

I was a listening child, careful to hear the very different sounds of Spanish and English. Wide-eyed with hearing, I'd listen to sounds more than words. First, there were English *(gringo)* sounds. So many words were still unknown that when the butcher or the lady at the drugstore said something to me, exotic polysyllabic sounds would bloom in the midst of their sentences. Often, the speech of people in public seemed to me very loud, booming with confidence. The man behind the counter would literally ask, "What can I do for you?" But by being so firm and so clear, the sound of his voice said that he was a *gringo*; he belonged in public society.

I would also hear then the high nasal notes of middle-class American speech. The air stirred with sound. Sometimes, even now, when I have been traveling abroad for several weeks, I will hear what I heard as a boy. In hotel lobbies or airports, in Turkey or Brazil, some Americans will pass, and suddenly I will hear it again — the high sound of American voices. For a few seconds I will hear it with pleasure, for it is now the sound of *my* society — a reminder of home. But inevitably — already on the flight headed for home — the sound fades with repetition. I will be unable to hear it anymore.

When I was a boy, things were different. The accent of *los gringos* was never pleasing nor was it hard to hear. Crowds at Safeway or at bus stops would be noisy with sound. And I would be forced to edge away from the chirping chatter above me.

I was unable to hear my own sounds, but I knew very well that I spoke English poorly. My words could not stretch far enough to form complete thoughts. And the words I did speak I didn't know well enough to make into distinct sounds. (Listeners would usually lower their heads, better to hear what I was trying to say.) But it was one thing for *me* to speak English with difficulty. It was more troubling for me to hear my parents speak in public: their high-whining vowels and guttural consonants; their sentences that got stuck with "eh" and "ah" sounds; the confused syntax; the hesitant rhythm of sounds so different from the way *gringos* spoke. I'd notice, moreover, that my parents' voices were softer than those of *gringos* we'd meet.

15 I am tempted now to say that none of this mattered. In adulthood I am embarrassed by childhood fears. And, in a way, it didn't matter very much that my parents could not speak English with ease. Their linguistic difficulties had no serious consequences. My mother and father made themselves understood at the county hospital clinic and at government offices. And yet, in another way, it mattered very much — it was unsettling to hear my parents struggle with English. Hearing them, I'd grow nervous, my clutching trust in their protection and power weakened.

There were many times like the night at a brightly lit gasoline station (a blaring white memory) when I stood uneasily, hearing my father. He was talking to a teenaged attendant. I do not recall what they were saying, but I cannot forget the sounds my father made as he spoke. At one point his words slid together to form one word — sounds as confused as the threads of blue and green oil in the puddle next to my shoes. His voice rushed through what he had left to say. And, toward the end, reached falsetto notes, appealing to his listener's understanding. I looked away to the lights of passing automobiles. I tried not to hear anymore. But I heard only too well the calm, easy tones in the attendant's reply. Shortly afterward, walking toward home with my father, I shivered when he put his hand on my shoulder. The very first chance that I got, I evaded his grasp and ran on ahead into the dark, skipping with feigned boyish exuberance.

But then there was Spanish. *Español*: my family's language. *Español*: the language that seemed to me a private language. I'd hear strangers on the radio and in the Mexican Catholic church across town speaking in Spanish, but I couldn't really believe that Spanish was a public language, like English. Spanish speakers, rather, seemed related to me, for I sensed that we shared — through our language — the experience of feeling apart from *los gringos*. It was thus a ghetto Spanish that I heard and I spoke. Like those whose lives are bound by a barrio, I was reminded by Spanish of my separateness from *los otros, los gringos* in power. But more intensely than for most barrio children — because I did not live in a barrio — Spanish seemed to me the language of home. (Most days it was only at home that I'd hear it.) It became the language of joyful return.

A family member would say something to me and I would feel myself specially recognized. My parents would say something to me and I would feel embraced by the sounds of their words. Those sounds said: *I am speaking with ease in Spanish. I am addressing you in words I never use with* los gringos. *I recognize you as someone special, close, like no one outside. You belong with us. In the family.*

(Ricardo.)

At the age of five, six, well past the time when most other chil- 20
dren no longer easily notice the difference between sounds uttered at home and words spoken in public, I had a different experience.

I lived in a world magically compounded of sounds. I remained a child longer than most; I lingered too long, poised at the edge of language — often frightened by the sounds of *los gringos*, delighted by the sounds of Spanish at home. I shared with my family a language that was startlingly different from that used in the great city around us.

For me there were none of the gradations between public and private society so normal to a maturing child. Outside the house was public society; inside the house was private. Just opening or closing the screen door behind me was an important experience. I'd rarely leave home all alone or without reluctance. Walking down the sidewalk, under the canopy of tall trees, I'd warily notice the — suddenly — silent neighborhood kids who stood warily watching me. Nervously, I'd arrive at the grocery store to hear there the sounds of the *gringo* — foreign to me — reminding me that in this world so big, I was a foreigner. But then I'd return. Walking back toward our house, climbing the steps from the sidewalk, when the front door was open in summer, I'd hear voices beyond the screen door talking in Spanish. For a second or two, I'd stay, linger there, listening. Smiling, I'd hear my mother call out, saying in Spanish (words): "Is that you, Richard?" All the while her sounds would assure me: *You are home now; come closer; inside. With us.*

"*Sí,*" I'd reply.

Once more inside the house I would resume (assume) my place in the family. The sounds would dim, grow harder to hear. Once more at home, I would grow less aware of that fact. It required, however, no more than the blurt of the doorbell to alert me to listen to sounds all over again. The house would turn instantly still while my mother went to the door. I'd hear her hard English sounds. I'd wait to hear her voice return to soft-sounding Spanish, which assured me, as surely as did the clicking tongue of the lock on the door, that the stranger was gone.

Plainly, it is not healthy to hear such sounds so often. It is not healthy to distinguish public words from private sounds so easily. I remained cloistered by sounds, timid and shy in public, too dependent on voices at home. And yet it needs to be emphasized: I was an extremely happy child at home. I remember many nights when my father would come back from work, and I'd hear him call out to my mother in Spanish, sounding relieved. In Spanish, he'd sound light and free notes he never could manage in English. Some nights I'd jump up just at hearing his voice. With *mis hermanos* I would come running into the room where he was with my mother. Our laughing (so deep was the pleasure!) became screaming. Like others who know the pain of public alienation, we transformed the knowledge of our public separateness and made it consoling — the reminder of intimacy. Excited, we joined our voices in a celebration of sounds. *We are speaking now the way we never speak out in public. We are alone — together,* voices sounded, surrounded to tell me. Some nights, no one seemed willing to loosen the hold sounds had on us. At dinner, we invented new words. (Ours sounded Spanish, but made sense only to us.) We pieced together new words by taking, say, an English verb and giving it Spanish endings. My mother's instructions at bedtime would be lacquered with mock-urgent tones. Or a word like *sí* would become, in several notes, able to convey added measures of feeling. Tongues explored the edges of words, especially the fat vowels. And we happily sounded that military drum roll, the twirling roar of the Spanish *r*. Family language: my family's sounds. The voices of my parents and sisters and brother. Their voices insisting: *You belong here. We are family members. Related. Special to one another. Listen!* Voices singing and sighing, rising, straining, then surging, teeming with pleasure that burst syllables into fragments of laughter. At times it seemed there was steady quiet only when, from another room, the rustling whispers of my parents faded and I moved closer to sleep.

2

Supporters of bilingual education today imply that students like 25
me miss a great deal by not being taught in their family's language. What they seem not to recognize is that, as a socially disadvantaged child, I considered Spanish to be a private language. What I needed to learn in school was that I had the right — and the obligation — to speak the public language of *los gringos*. The odd truth is that my first-grade classmates could have become bilingual, in the conventional sense of that word, more easily than I. Had they been taught (as upper-middle-class children are often taught early) a second language like Spanish or French, they

could have regarded it simply as that: another public language. In my case such bilingualism could not have been so quickly achieved. What I did not believe was that I could speak a single public language.

Without question, it would have pleased me to hear my teachers address me in Spanish when I entered the classroom. I would have felt much less afraid. I would have trusted them and responded with ease. But I would have delayed — for how long postponed? — having to learn the language of public society. I would have evaded — and for how long could I have afforded to delay? — learning the great lesson of school, that I had a public identity.

Fortunately, my teachers were unsentimental about their responsibility. What they understood was that I needed to speak a public language. So their voices would search me out, asking me questions. Each time I'd hear them, I'd look up in surprise to see a nun's face frowning at me. I'd mumble, not really meaning to answer. The nun would persist, "Richard, stand up. Don't look at the floor. Speak up. Speak to the entire class, not just to me!" But I couldn't believe that the English language was mine to use. (In part, I did not want to believe it.) I continued to mumble. I resisted the teacher's demands. (Did I somehow suspect that once I learned public language my pleasing family life would be changed?) Silent, waiting for the bell to sound, I remained dazed, diffident, afraid.

Because I wrongly imagined that English was intrinsically a public language and Spanish an intrinsically private one, I easily noted the difference between classroom language and the language of home. At school, words were directed to a general audience of listeners. ("Boys and girls.") Words were meaningfully ordered. And the point was not self-expression alone but to make oneself understood by many others. The teacher quizzed: "Boys and girls, why do we use that word in this sentence? Could we think of a better word to use there? Would the sentence change its meaning if the words were differently arranged? And wasn't there a better way of saying much the same thing?" (I couldn't say. I wouldn't try to say.)

Three months. Five. Half a year passed. Unsmiling, ever watchful, my teachers noted my silence. They began to connect my behavior with the difficult progress my older sister and brother were making. Until one Saturday morning three nuns arrived at the house to talk to our parents. Stiffly, they sat on the blue living room sofa. From the doorway of another room, spying the visitors, I noted the incongruity — the clash of two worlds, the faces and voices of school intruding upon the familiar setting of home. I overheard one voice gently wondering, "Do your children speak only Spanish at home, Mrs. Rodriguez?" While another voice added, "That Richard especially seems so timid and shy."

That Rich-heard! 30

With great tact the visitors continued, "Is it possible for you and your husband to encourage your children to practice their English when they are home?" Of course, my parents complied. What would they not do for their children's well-being? And how could they have questioned the Church's authority which those women represented? In an instant, they agreed to give up the language (the sounds) that had revealed and accentuated our family's closeness. The moment after the visitors left, the change was observed. "*Ahora*, speak to us *en inglés*," my father and mother united to tell us.

At first, it seemed a kind of game. After dinner each night, the family gathered to practice "our" English. (It was still then *inglés*, a language foreign to us, so we felt drawn as strangers to it.) Laughing, we would try to define words we could not pronounce. We played with strange English sounds, often over-anglicizing our pronunciations. And we filled the smiling gaps of our sentences with familiar Spanish sounds. But that was cheating, somebody shouted. Everyone laughed. In school, meanwhile, like my brother and sister, I was required to attend a daily tutoring session. I needed a full year of special attention. I also needed my teachers to keep my attention from straying in class by calling out, *Rich-heard* — their English voices slowly prying loose my ties to my other name, its three notes, *Ri-car-do*. Most of all I needed to hear my mother and father speak to me in a moment of seriousness in broken — suddenly heartbreaking — English. The scene was inevitable: One Saturday morning I entered the kitchen where my parents were talking in Spanish. I did not realize that they were talking in Spanish however until, at the moment they saw me, I heard their voices change to speak English. Those *gringo* sounds they uttered startled me. Pushed me away. In that moment of trivial misunderstanding and profound insight, I felt my throat twisted by unsounded grief. I turned quickly and left the room. But I had no place to escape to with Spanish. (The spell was broken.) My brother and sisters were speaking English in another part of the house.

Again and again in the days following, increasingly angry, I was obliged to hear my mother and father: "Speak to us *en inglés*." *(Speak.)* Only then did I determine to learn classroom English. Weeks after, it happened: One day in school I raised my hand to volunteer an answer. I spoke out in a loud voice. And I did not think it remarkable when the entire class understood. That day, I moved very far from the disadvantaged child I had been only days earlier. The belief, the calming assurance that I belonged in public, had at last taken hold.

Shortly after, I stopped hearing the high and loud sounds of *los gringos*. A more and more confident speaker of English, I didn't trouble to listen to *how* strangers sounded, speaking to me. And there simply were too many English-speaking people in my day for me to hear American accents anymore. Conversations quickened. Listening to persons who sounded eccentrically pitched voices, I usually noted their sounds for an initial few seconds before I concentrated on *what* they were saying. Conversations became content-full. Transparent. Hearing someone's *tone* of voice — angry or questioning or sarcastic or happy or sad — I didn't distinguish it from the words it expressed. Sound and word were thus tightly wedded. At the end of a day, I was often bemused, always relieved, to realize how "silent," though crowded with words, my day in public had been. (This public silence measured and quickened the change in my life.)

35 At last, seven years old, I came to believe what had been technically true since my birth: I was an American citizen.

But the special feeling of closeness at home was diminished by then. Gone was the desperate, urgent, intense feeling of being at home; rare was the experience of feeling myself individualized by family intimates. We remained a loving family, but one greatly changed. No longer so close; no longer bound tight by the pleasing and troubling knowledge of our public separateness. Neither my older brother nor sister rushed home after school anymore. Nor did I. When I arrived home there would often be neighborhood kids in the house. Or the house would be empty of sounds.

Following the dramatic Americanization of their children, even my parents grew more publicly confident. Especially my mother.

She learned the names of all the people on our block. And she decided we needed to have a telephone installed in the house. My father continued to use the word *gringo*. But it was no longer charged with the old bitterness or distrust. (Stripped of any emotional content, the word simply became a name for those Americans not of Hispanic descent.) Hearing him, sometimes, I wasn't sure if he was pronouncing the Spanish word *gringo* or saying gringo in English.

Matching the silence I started hearing in public was a new quiet at home. The family's quiet was partly due to the fact that, as we children learned more and more English, we shared fewer and fewer words with our parents. Sentences needed to be spoken slowly when a child addressed his mother or father. (Often the parent wouldn't understand.) The child would need to repeat himself. (Still the parent misunderstood.) The young voice, frustrated, would end up saying, "Never mind" — the subject was closed. Dinners would be noisy with the clinking of knives and forks against dishes. My mother would smile softly between her remarks; my father at the other end of the table would chew and chew at his food, while he stared over the heads of his children.

My *mother!* My *father!* After English became my primary language, I no longer knew what words to use in addressing my parents. The old Spanish words (those tender accents of sound) I had used earlier — *mamá* and *papá* — I couldn't use anymore. They would have been too painful reminders of how much had changed in my life. On the other hand, the words I heard neighborhood kids call *their* parents seemed equally unsatisfactory. *Mother* and *Father; Ma, Papa, Pa, Dad, Pop* (how I hated the all-American sound of that last word especially) — all these terms I felt were unsuitable, not really terms of address for *my* parents. As a result, I never used them at home. Whenever I'd speak to my parents, I would try to get their attention with eye contact alone. In public conversations, I'd refer to "my parents" or "my mother and father."

My mother and father, for their part, responded differently, as 40
their children spoke to them less. She grew restless, seemed troubled and anxious at the scarcity of words exchanged in the house. It was she who would question me about my day when I came home from school. She smiled at small talk. She pried at the edges of my sentences to get me to say something more.

(What?) She'd join conversations she overheard, but her intrusions often stopped her children's talking. By contrast, my father seemed reconciled to the new quiet. Though his English improved somewhat, he retired into silence. At dinner he spoke very little. One night his children and even his wife helplessly giggled at his garbled English pronunciation of the Catholic Grace before Meals. Thereafter he made his wife recite the prayer at the start of each meal, even on formal occasions, when there were guests in the house. Hers became the public voice of the family. On official business, it was she, not my father, one would usually hear on the phone or in stores, talking to strangers. His children grew so accustomed to his silence that, years later, they would speak routinely of his shyness. (My mother would often try to explain: Both his parents died when he was eight. He was raised by an uncle who treated him like little more than a menial servant. He was never encouraged to speak. He grew up alone. A man of few words.) But my father was not shy, I realized, when I'd watch him speaking Spanish with relatives. Using Spanish, he was quickly effusive. Especially when talking with other men, his voice would spark, flicker, flare alive with sounds. In Spanish, he expressed ideas and feelings he rarely revealed in English. With firm Spanish sounds, he conveyed confidence and authority English would never allow him.

The silence at home, however, was finally more than a literal silence. Fewer words passed between parent and child, but more profound was the silence that resulted from my inattention to sounds. At about the time I no longer bothered to listen with care to the sounds of English in public, I grew careless about listening to the sounds family members made when they spoke. Most of the time I heard someone speaking at home and didn't distinguish his sounds from the words people uttered in public. I didn't even pay much attention to my parents' accented and ungrammatical speech. At least not at home. Only when I was with them in public would I grow alert to their accents. Though, even then, their sounds caused me less and less concern. For I was increasingly confident of my own public identity.

I would have been happier about my public success had I not sometimes recalled what it had been like earlier, when my family had conveyed its intimacy through a set of conveniently private sounds. Sometimes in public, hearing a stranger, I'd hark back to my past. A Mexican farmworker approached me downtown to ask directions to somewhere. "*¿Hijito . . . ?*" he said. And his voice summoned deep longing. Another time, standing beside my mother in the visiting room of a Carmelite convent, before the dense screen which rendered the nuns shadowy figures, I heard several Spanish-speaking nuns — their busy, singsong overlapping voices — assure us that yes, yes, we were remembered, all our family was remembered in their prayers. (Their voices echoed faraway family sounds.) Another day, a dark-faced old woman — her hand light on my shoulder — steadied herself against me as she boarded a bus. She murmured something I couldn't quite comprehend. Her Spanish voice came near, like the face of a never-before-seen relative in the instant before I was kissed. Her voice, like so many of the Spanish voices I'd hear in public, recalled the golden age of my youth. Hearing Spanish then, I continued to be a careful, if sad, listener to sounds. Hearing a Spanish-speaking family walking behind me, I turned to look. I smiled for an instant, before my glance found the Hispanic-looking faces of strangers in the crowd going by.

Today I hear bilingual educators say that children lose a degree of "individuality" by becoming assimilated into public society. (Bilingual schooling was popularized in the seventies, that decade when middle-class ethnics began to resist the process of assimilation — the American melting pot.) But the bilingualists simplistically scorn the value and necessity of assimilation. They do not seem to realize that there are *two* ways a person is individualized. So they do not realize that while one suffers a diminished sense of *private* individuality by becoming assimilated into public society, such assimilation makes possible the achievement of *public* individuality.

The bilingualists insist that a student should be reminded of his difference from others in mass society, his heritage. But they equate mere separateness with individuality. The fact is that only in private — with intimates — is separateness from the crowd a prerequisite for individuality. (An intimate draws me apart, tells me that I am unique, unlike all others.) In public, by contrast, full individuality is achieved, paradoxically, by those who are able to consider themselves members of the crowd. Thus it happened for me: Only when I was able to think of myself as an American, no longer an alien in *gringo* society, could I seek the rights and opportunities necessary for full public individuality. The social and political advantages I enjoy as a man result from the day that I came to believe that my name, indeed, is *Rich-heard Road-ree-guess*. It is true that my public society today is often impersonal. (My public society is usually mass society.) Yet despite the anonymity of the crowd and despite the fact that the individuality I achieve in public is often tenuous — because it depends on my being one in a crowd — I celebrate the day I acquired my new name. Those middle-class ethnics who scorn assimilation seem to me filled with decadent self-pity, obsessed by the burden of public life. Dangerously, they romanticize public separateness and they trivialize the dilemma of the socially disadvantaged.

45 My awkward childhood does not prove the necessity of bilingual education. My story discloses instead an essential myth of childhood — inevitable pain. If I rehearse here the changes in my private life after my Americanization, it is finally to emphasize the public gain. The loss implies the gain: The house I returned to each afternoon was quiet. Intimate sounds no longer rushed to the door to greet me. There were other noises inside. The telephone rang. Neighborhood kids ran past the door of the bedroom where I was reading my schoolbooks — covered with shopping-bag paper. Once I learned public language, it would never again be easy for me to hear intimate family voices. More and more of my day was spent hearing words. But that may only be a way of saying that the day I raised my hand in class and spoke loudly to an entire roomful of faces, my childhood started to end.

3

I grew up victim to a disabling confusion. As I grew fluent in English, I no longer could speak Spanish with confidence. I continued to understand spoken Spanish. And in high school, I learned how to read and write Spanish. But for many years I could not pronounce it. A powerful guilt blocked my spoken words; an essential glue was missing whenever I'd try to connect words to form sentences. I would be unable to break a barrier of sound, to speak freely. I would speak, or try to speak, Spanish, and I would manage to utter halting, hiccuping sounds that betrayed my unease.

When relatives and Spanish-speaking friends of my parents came to the house, my brother and sisters seemed reticent to use Spanish, but at least they managed to say a few necessary words before being excused. I never managed so gracefully. I was cursed with guilt. Each time I'd hear myself addressed in Spanish, I would be unable to respond with any success. I'd know the words I wanted to say, but I couldn't manage to say them. I would try to speak, but everything I said seemed to me horribly anglicized. My mouth would not form the words right. My jaw would tremble. After a phrase or two, I'd cough up a warm, silvery sound. And stop.

It surprised my listeners to hear me. They'd lower their heads, better to grasp what I was trying to say. They would repeat their questions in gentle, affectionate voices. But by then I would answer in English. No, no, they would say, we want you to speak to us in Spanish. *("... en español.")* But I couldn't do it. *Pocho* then they called me. Sometimes playfully, teasingly, using the tender diminutive — *mi pochito*. Sometimes not so playfully, mockingly, *Pocho*. (A Spanish dictionary defines that word as an adjective meaning "colorless" or "bland." But I heard it as a noun, naming the Mexican-American who, in becoming an American, forgets his native society.) *"¡Pocho!"* the lady in the Mexican food store muttered, shaking her head. I looked up to the counter where red and green peppers were strung like Christmas tree lights and saw the frowning face of the stranger. My mother laughed somewhere behind me. (She said that her children didn't want to practice "our Spanish" after they started going to school.) My mother's smiling voice made me suspect that the lady who faced me was not really angry at me. But, searching her face, I couldn't find the hint of a smile.

Embarrassed, my parents would regularly need to explain their children's inability to speak flowing Spanish during those years. My mother met the wrath of her brother, her only brother, when he came up from Mexico one summer with his family. He saw his nieces and nephews for the very first time. After listening to me, he looked away and said what a disgrace it was that I couldn't speak Spanish, *"su proprio idioma."* He made that remark to my mother; I noticed, however, that he stared at my father.

I clearly remember one other visitor from those years. A long- 50
time friend of my father from San Francisco would come to stay with us for several days in late August. He took great interest in

me after he realized that I couldn't answer his questions in Spanish. He would grab me as I started to leave the kitchen. He would ask me something. Usually he wouldn't bother to wait for my mumbled response. Knowingly, he'd murmur: "*¿Ay Pocho, Pocho, adónde vas?*" And he would press his thumbs into the upper part of my arms, making me squirm with currents of pain. Dumbly, I'd stand there, waiting for his wife to notice us, for her to call him off with a benign smile. I'd giggle, hoping to deflate the tension between us, pretending that I hadn't seen the glittering scorn in his glance.

I remember that man now, but seek no revenge in this telling. I recount such incidents only because they suggest the fierce power Spanish had for many people I met at home; the way Spanish was associated with closeness. Most of those people who called me a *pocho* could have spoken English to me. But they would not. They seemed to think that Spanish was the only language we could use, that Spanish alone permitted our close association. (Such persons are vulnerable always to the ghetto merchant and the politician who have learned the value of speaking their clients' family language to gain immediate trust.) For my part, I felt that I had somehow committed a sin of betrayal by learning English. But betrayal against whom? Not against visitors to the house exactly. No, I felt that I had betrayed my immediate family. I *knew* that my parents had encouraged me to learn English. I *knew* that I had turned to English only with angry reluctance. But once I spoke English with ease, I came to *feel* guilty. (This guilt defied logic.) I felt that I had shattered the intimate bond that had once held the family close. This original sin against my family told whenever anyone addressed me in Spanish and I responded, confounded.

But even during those years of guilt, I was coming to sense certain consoling truths about language and intimacy. I remember playing with a friend in the backyard one day, when my grandmother appeared at the window. Her face was stern with suspicion when she saw the boy (the *gringo*) I was with. In Spanish she called out to me, sounding the whistle of her ancient breath. My companion looked up and watched her intently as she lowered the window and moved, still visible, behind the light curtain, watching us both. He wanted to know what she had said. I started to tell him, to say — to translate her Spanish words into English. The problem was, however, that though I knew how to translate exactly *what* she had told me, I realized that any translation would distort the deepest meaning of her message: It had been directed only to me. This message of intimacy could never be translated because it was not *in* the words she had used but passed *through* them. So any translation would have seemed wrong; her words would have been stripped of an essential meaning. Finally, I decided not to tell my friend anything. I told him that I didn't hear all she had said.

This insight unfolded in time. Making more and more friends outside my house, I began to distinguish intimate voices speaking through *English*. I'd listen at times to a close friend's confidential tone or secretive whisper. Even more remarkable were those instances when, for no special reason apparently, I'd become conscious of the fact that my companion was speaking only to me. I'd marvel just hearing his voice. It was a stunning event: to be able to break through his words, to be able to hear this voice of the other, to realize that it was directed only to me. After such moments of intimacy outside the house, I began to trust hearing intimacy conveyed through my family's English. Voices at home at last punctured sad confusion. I'd hear myself addressed as an intimate at home once again. Such moments were never as raucous with sound as past times had been when we had had "private" Spanish to use. (Our English-sounding house was never to be as noisy as our Spanish-speaking house had been.) Intimate moments were usually soft moments of sound. My mother was in the dining room while I did my homework nearby. And she looked over at me. Smiled. Said something — her words said nothing very important. But her voice sounded to tell me *(We are together)* I was her son.

(Richard!)

Intimacy thus continued at home; intimacy was not stilled by 55
English. It is true that I would never forget the great change of my life, the diminished occasions of intimacy. But there would also be times when I sensed the deepest truth about language and intimacy: *Intimacy is not created by a particular language; it is created by intimates.* The great change in my life was not linguistic but social. If, after becoming a successful student, I no longer heard intimate voices as often as I had earlier, it was not because I spoke English rather than Spanish. It was because I used public language for most of the day. I moved easily at last, a citizen in a crowded city of words.

4

This boy became a man. In private now, alone, I brood over language and intimacy — the great themes of my past. In public I expect most of the faces I meet to be the faces of strangers. (How do you do?) If meetings are quick and impersonal, they have been efficiently managed. I rush past the sounds of voices attending only to the words addressed to me. Voices seem planed to an even surface of sound, soundless. A business associate speaks in a deep baritone, but I pass through the timbre to attend to his words. The crazy man who sells me a newspaper every night mumbles something crazy, but I have time only to pretend that I have heard him say hello. Accented versions of English make little impression on me. In the rush-hour crowd a Japanese tourist asks me a question, and I inch past his accent to concentrate on what he is saying. The Eastern European immigrant in a neighborhood delicatessen speaks to me through a marinade of sounds, but I respond to his words. I note for only a second the Texas accent of the telephone operator or the Mississippi accent of the man who lives in the apartment below me.

My city seems silent until some ghetto black teenagers board the bus I am on. Because I do not take their presence for granted, I listen to the sounds of their voices. Of all the accented versions of English I hear in a day, I hear theirs most intently. They are *the* sounds of the outsider. They annoy me for being loud — so self-sufficient and unconcerned by my presence. Yet for the same reason they seem to me glamorous. (A romantic gesture against public acceptance.) Listening to their shouted laughter, I realize my own quiet. Their voices enclose my isolation. I feel envious, envious of their brazen intimacy.

I warn myself away from such envy, however. I remember the black political activists who have argued in favor of using black English in schools. (Their argument varies only slightly from that made by foreign-language bilingualists.) I have heard "radical" linguists make the point that black English is a complex and intricate version of English. And I do not doubt it. But neither do I think that black English should be a language of public instruction. What makes black English inappropriate in classrooms is not something *in* the language. It is rather what lower-class speakers make of it. Just as Spanish would have been a dangerous language for me to have used at the start of my education, so black English would be a dangerous language to use in the schooling of teenagers for whom it reenforces feelings of public separateness.

This seems to me an obvious point. But one that needs to be made. In recent years there have been attempts to make the language of the alien public language. "Bilingual education, two ways to understand . . . ," television and radio commercials glibly announce. Proponents of bilingual education are careful to say that they want students to acquire good schooling. Their argument goes something like this: Children permitted to use their family language in school will not be so alienated and will be better able to match the progress of English-speaking children in the crucial first months of instruction. (Increasingly confident of their abilities, such children will be more inclined to apply themselves to their studies in the future.) But then the bilingualists claim another, very different goal. They say that children who use their family language in school will retain a sense of their individuality — their ethnic heritage and cultural ties. Supporters of bilingual education thus want it both ways. They propose bilingual schooling as a way of helping students acquire the skills of the classroom crucial for public success. But they likewise insist that bilingual instruction will give students a sense of their identity apart from the public.

Behind this screen there gleams an astonishing promise: One 60
can become a public person while still remaining a private person. At the very same time one can be both! There need be no tension between the self in the crowd and the self apart from the crowd! Who would not want to believe such an idea? Who can be surprised that the scheme has won the support of many middle-class Americans? If the barrio or ghetto child can retain his separateness even while being publicly educated, then it is almost possible to believe that there is no private cost to be paid for public success. Such is the consolation offered by any of the current bilingual schemes. Consider, for example, the bilingual voters' ballot. In some American cities one can cast a ballot printed in several languages. Such a document implies that a person can exercise that most public of rights — the right to vote — while still keeping apart, unassimilated from public life.

It is not enough to say that these schemes are foolish and certainly doomed. Middle-class supporters of public bilingualism toy with the confusion of those Americans who cannot speak standard English as well as they can. Bilingual enthusiasts, moreover, sin against intimacy. An Hispanic-American writer tells me, "I will never give up my family language; I would as soon give up my soul." Thus he holds to his chest a skein of words, as though it were the source of his family ties. He credits to language what he should credit to family members. A convenient mistake. For as long as he holds on to words, he can ignore how much else has changed in his life.

It has happened before. In earlier decades, persons newly successful and ambitious for social mobility similarly seized upon certain "family words." Working-class men attempting political power took to calling one another "brother." By so doing they escaped oppressive public isolation and were able to unite with many others like themselves. But they paid a price for this union. It was a public union they forged. The word they coined to address one another could never be the sound *(brother)* exchanged by two in intimate greeting. In the union hall the word "brother" became a vague metaphor; with repetition a weak echo of the intimate sound. Context forced the change. Context could not be overruled. Context will always guard the realm of the intimate from public misuse.

Today nonwhite Americans call "brother" to strangers. And white feminists refer to their mass union of "sisters." And white middle-class teenagers continue to prove the importance of context as they try to ignore it. They seize upon the idioms of the black ghetto. But their attempt to appropriate such expressions invariably changes the words. As it becomes a public expression, the ghetto idiom loses its sound — its message of public separateness and strident intimacy. It becomes with public repetition a series of words, increasingly lifeless.

The mystery remains: intimate utterance. The communication of intimacy passes through the word to enliven its sound. But it cannot be held by the word. Cannot be clutched or ever quoted. It is too fluid. It depends not on word but on person.

My grandmother! 65

She stood among my other relations mocking me when I no longer spoke Spanish. *"Pocho,"* she said. But then it made no difference. (She'd laugh.) Our relationship continued. Language was never its source. She was a woman in her eighties during the first decade of my life. A mysterious woman to me, my only living grandparent. A woman of Mexico. The woman in long black dresses that reached down to her shoes. My one relative who spoke no word of English. She had no interest in *gringo* society. She remained completely aloof from the public. Protected by her daughters. Protected even by me when we went to Safeway together and I acted as her translator. Eccentric woman. Soft. Hard.

When my family visited my aunt's house in San Francisco, my grandmother searched for me among my many cousins. She'd chase them away. Pinching her granddaughters, she'd warn them all away from me. Then she'd take me to her room, where she had prepared for my coming. There would be a chair next to the bed. A dusty jellied candy nearby. And a copy of *Life en Español* for me to examine. "There," she'd say. I'd sit there content. A boy of eight. *Pocho*. Her favorite. I'd sift through the pictures of earthquake-destroyed Latin American cities and blond-wigged Mexican movie stars. And all the while I'd listen to the sound of my grandmother's voice. She'd pace round the room, searching through closets and drawers, telling me stories of her life. Her past. They were stories so familiar to me that I couldn't remember the first time I'd heard them. I'd look up sometimes to listen. Other times she'd look over at me. But she never seemed to expect a response. Sometimes I'd smile or nod. (I understood exactly what she was saying.) But it never seemed to matter to her one way or another. It was enough I was there. The words she spoke were almost irrelevant to that fact — the sounds she made. Content.

The mystery remained: intimate utterance.

I learn little about language and intimacy listening to those social activists who propose using one's family language in public life. Listening to songs on the radio, or hearing a great voice at the opera, or overhearing the woman downstairs singing to herself at an open window, I learn much more. Singers celebrate the human voice. Their lyrics are words. But animated by voice those words are subsumed into sounds. I listen with excitement as the words yield their enormous power to sound — though the words are never totally obliterated. In most songs the drama or tension results from the fact that the singer moves between word (sense) and note (song). At one moment the song simply "says" something. At another moment the voice stretches out the words — the heart cannot contain! — and the voice moves toward pure sound. Words take flight.

Singing out words, the singer suggests an experience of sound 70
most intensely mine at intimate moments. Literally, most songs are about love. (Lost love; celebrations of loving; pleas.) By simply being occasions when sound escapes word, however, songs put me in mind of the most intimate moments of my life.

Finally, among all types of song, it is the song created by lyric poets that I find most compelling. There is no other public occasion of sound so important for me. Written poems exist on a page, at first glance, as a mere collection of words. And yet, despite this, without musical accompaniment, the poet leads me to hear the sounds of the words that I read. As song, the poem passes between sound and sense, never belonging for long to one realm or the other. As public artifact, the poem can never duplicate intimate sound. But by imitating such sound, the poem helps me recall the intimate times of my life. I read in my room — alone — and grow conscious of being alone, sounding my voice, in search of another. The poem serves then as a memory device. It forces remembrance. And refreshes. It reminds me of the possibility of escaping public words, the possibility that awaits me in meeting the intimate.

The poems I read are not nonsense poems. But I read them for reasons which, I imagine, are similar to those that make children play with meaningless rhyme. I have watched them before: I have noticed the way children create private languages to keep away the adult; I have heard their chanting riddles that go nowhere in logic but harken back to some kingdom of sound; I have watched them listen to intricate nonsense rhymes, and I have noted their wonder. I was never such a child. Until I was six years old, I remained in a magical realm of sound. I didn't need to remember that realm because it was present to me. But then the screen door shut behind me as I left home for school. At last I began my movement toward words. On the other side of initial sadness would come the realization that intimacy cannot be held. With time would come the knowledge that intimacy must finally pass.

I would dishonor those I have loved and those I love now to claim anything else. I would dishonor our closeness by holding on to a particular language and calling it my family language. Intimacy is not trapped within words. It passes through words. It passes. The truth is that intimates leave the room. Doors close. Faces move away from the window. Time passes. Voices recede into the dark. Death finally quiets the voice. And there is no way to deny it. No way to stand in the crowd, uttering one's family language.

The last time I saw my grandmother I was nine years old. I can tell you some of the things she said to me as I stood by her bed. I cannot, however, quote the message of intimacy she conveyed with her voice. She laughed, holding my hand. Her voice illumined disjointed memories as it passed them again. She remembered her husband, his green eyes, the magic name of Narciso. His early death. She remembered the farm in Mexico. The eucalyptus nearby. (Its scent, she remembered, like incense.) She remembered the family cow, the bell round its neck heard miles away. A dog. She remembered working as a seamstress. How she'd leave her daughters and son for long hours to go into Guadalajara to work. And how my mother would come running toward her in the sun — her bright yellow dress — to see her return. *"Mmmaaammmmáááá,"* the old lady mimicked her daughter (my mother) to her son. She laughed. There was the snap of a cough. An aunt came into the room and told me it was time I should leave. "You can see her tomorrow," she promised. And so I kissed my grandmother's cracked face. And the last thing I saw was her thin, oddly youthful thigh, as my aunt rearranged the sheet on the bed.

At the funeral parlor a few days after, I knelt with my relatives 75
during the rosary. Among their voices but silent, I traced, then lost, the sounds of individual aunts in the surge of the common prayer. And I heard at that moment what I have since heard often again — the sounds the women in my family make when they are praying in sadness. When I went up to look at my grandmother, I saw her through the haze of a veil draped over the open lid of the casket. Her face appeared calm — but distant and unyielding to love. It was not the face I remembered seeing most often. It was the face she made in public when the clerk at Safeway asked her some question and I would have to respond. It was her public face the mortician had designed with his dubious art.

For Discussion and Writing

1. What are the two educational philosophies Rodriguez describes?
2. Much of Rodriguez's essay is spent comparing the Spanish his parents spoke at home to the English they spoke outside it, "the language of their Mexican past" to "the English of public society" (par. 9). What is the point of including this material? How do these comparisons support his argument?
3. **connections** Rodriguez creates many moments where his point is illustrated in narrative — for example, the moment in school when he first hears his name in English (par. 4), and how the threat to his familial and cultural identity is represented in his seeing his mother's face "dissolve in a watery blur behind the pebbled glass door" (par. 4). Find similar moments in Langston Hughes's "Salvation" (p. 179). How do those moments add to Hughes's larger concern?
4. Do you agree with Rodriguez or with those who support bilingual education? Why?

MIKE ROSE

"I Just Wanna Be Average"

Born in 1944 to Italian immigrants and raised in South Central Los Angeles, Mike Rose is a professor of education at UCLA and an advocate for the democratization of the university and for creative teaching. His Lives on the Boundary: The Struggles and Achievements of America's Underprepared *(1989) investigated remedial education, and* Possible Lives: The Promise of Public Education in America *(1995) was the product of four years of research into teaching in America.*

"I Just Wanna Be Average," taken from Lives on the Boundary, *examines learning, knowledge, and expectations and is drawn from Rose's own experiences in school. Of knowledge, Rose writes, "It enabled me to do things in the world" (par. 37) — an idea at once simple and profound. Consider, as you read, the kinds of things that your education has allowed you to do. What else do you need to learn to "do things in the world"?*

It took two buses to get to Our Lady of Mercy. The first started deep in South Los Angeles and caught me at midpoint. The second drifted through neighborhoods with trees, parks, big lawns, and lots of flowers. The rides were long but were livened up by a group of South L.A. veterans whose parents also thought that Hope had set up shop in the west end of the county. There was Christy Biggars, who, at sixteen, was dealing and was, according to rumor, a pimp as well. There were Bill Cobb and Johnny Gonzales, grease-pencil artists extraordinaire, who left Nembutal-enhanced swirls of "Cobb" and "Johnny" on the corrugated walls of the bus. And then there was Tyrrell Wilson. Tyrrell was the coolest kid I knew. He ran the dozens like a metric halfback, laid down a rap that outrhymed and outpointed Cobb, whose rap was good but not great — the curse of a moderately soulful kid trapped in white skin. But it was Cobb who would sneak a radio onto the bus, and thus underwrote his patter with Little Richard, Fats

Domino, Chuck Berry, the Coasters, and Ernie K. Doe's mother-in-law, an awful woman who was "sent from down below." And so it was that Christy and Cobb and Johnny G. and Tyrrell and I and assorted others picked up along the way passed our days in the back of the bus, a funny mix brought together by geography and parental desire.

Entrance to school brings with it forms and releases and assessments. Mercy relied on a series of tests, mostly the Stanford-Binet, for placement, and somehow the results of my tests got confused with those of another student named Rose. The other Rose apparently didn't do very well, for I was placed in the vocational track, a euphemism for the bottom level. Neither I nor my parents realized what this meant. We had no sense that Business Math, Typing, and English–Level D were dead ends. The current spate of reports on the schools criticizes parents for not involving themselves in the education of their children. But how would someone like Tommy Rose, with his two years of Italian schooling, know what to ask? And what sort of pressure could an exhausted waitress apply? The error went undetected, and I remained in the vocational track for two years. What a place.

My homeroom was supervised by Brother Dill, a troubled and unstable man who also taught freshman English. When his class drifted away from him, which was often, his voice would rise in paranoid accusations, and occasionally he would lose control and shake or smack us. I hadn't been there two months when one of his brisk, face-turning slaps had my glasses sliding down the aisle. Physical education was also pretty harsh. Our teacher was a stubby ex-lineman who had played old-time pro ball in the Midwest. He routinely had us grabbing our ankles to receive his stinging paddle across our butts. He did that, he said, to make men of us. "Rose," he bellowed on our first encounter; me standing geeky in line in my baggy shorts. " 'Rose'? What the hell kind of name is that?"

"Italian, sir," I squeaked.

"Italian! Ho. Rose, do you know the sound a bag of shit makes 5
when it hits the wall?"

"No, sir."

"Wop!"

Sophomore English was taught by Mr. Mitropetros. He was a large, bejeweled man who managed the parking lot at the Shrine

Auditorium. He would crow and preen and list for us the stars he'd brushed against. We'd ask questions and glance knowingly and snicker, and all that fueled the poor guy to brag some more. Parking cars was his night job. He had little training in English, so his lesson plan for his day work had us reading the district's required text, *Julius Caesar,* aloud for the semester. We'd finished the play way before the twenty weeks was up, so he'd have us switch parts again and again and start again: Dave Snyder, the fastest guy at Mercy, muscling through Caesar to the breathless squeals of Calpurnia, as interpreted by Steve Fusco, a surfer who owned the school's most envied paneled wagon. Week ten and Dave and Steve would take on new roles, as would we all, and render a water-logged Cassius and a Brutus that are beyond my powers of description.

Spanish I — taken in the second year — fell into the hands of a new recruit. Mr. Montez was a tiny man, slight, five foot six at the most, soft-spoken and delicate. Spanish was a particularly rowdy class, and Mr. Montez was as prepared for it as a doily maker at a hammer throw. He would tap his pencil to a room in which Steve Fusco was propelling spitballs from his heavy lips, in which Mike Dweetz was taunting Billy Hawk, a half-Indian, half-Spanish, reed-thin, quietly explosive boy. The vocational track at Our Lady of Mercy mixed kids traveling in from South L.A. with South Bay surfers and a few Slavs and Chicanos from the harbors of San Pedro. This was a dangerous miscellany: surfers and hodads and South-Central blacks all ablaze to the metronomic tapping of Hector Montez's pencil.

One day Billy lost it. Out of the corner of my eye I saw him 10
strike out with his right arm and catch Dweetz across the neck. Quick as a spasm, Dweetz was out of his seat, scattering desks, cracking Billy on the side of the head, right behind the eye. Snyder and Fusco and others broke it up, but the room felt hot and close and naked. Mr. Montez's tenuous authority was finally ripped to shreds, and I think everyone felt a little strange about that. The charade was over, and when it came down to it, I don't think any of the kids really wanted it to end this way. They had pushed and pushed and bullied their way into a freedom that both scared and embarrassed them.

Students will float to the mark you set. I and the others in the vocational classes were bobbing in pretty shallow water. Vocational education has aimed at increasing the economic opportunities of students who do not do well in our schools. Some serious programs succeed in doing that, and through exceptional teachers — like Mr. Gross in *Horace's Compromise* — students learn to develop hypotheses and troubleshoot, reason through a problem, and communicate effectively — the true job skills. The vocational track, however, is most often a place for those who are just not making it, a dumping ground for the disaffected. There were a few teachers who worked hard at education; young Brother Slattery, for example, combined a stern voice with weekly quizzes to try to pass along to us a skeletal outline of world history. But mostly the teachers had no idea of how to engage the imaginations of us kids who were scuttling along at the bottom of the pond.

And the teachers would have needed some inventiveness, for none of us was groomed for the classroom. It wasn't just that I didn't know things — didn't know how to simplify algebraic fractions, couldn't identify different kinds of clauses, bungled Spanish translations — but that I had developed various faulty and inadequate ways of doing algebra and making sense of Spanish. Worse yet, the years of defensive tuning out in elementary school had given me a way to escape quickly while seeming at least half alert. During my time in Voc. Ed., I developed further into a mediocre student and a somnambulant problem solver, and that affected the subjects I did have the wherewithal to handle: I detested Shakespeare; I got bored with history. My attention flitted here and there. I fooled around in class and read my books indifferently — the intellectual equivalent of playing with your food. I did what I had to do to get by, and I did it with half a mind.

But I did learn things about people and eventually came into my own socially. I liked the guys in Voc. Ed. Growing up where I did, I understood and admired physical prowess, and there was an abundance of muscle here. There was Dave Snyder, a sprinter and halfback of true quality. Dave's ability and his quick wit gave him a natural appeal, and he was welcome in any clique, though he always kept a little independent. He enjoyed acting the fool and could care less about studies, but he possessed a certain maturity and never caused the faculty much trouble. It was a testament to his independence that he included me among his friends — I eventually went out for track, but I was no jock.

Owing to the Latin alphabet and a dearth of *R*s and *S*s, Snyder sat behind Rose, and we started exchanging one-liners and became friends.

There was Ted Richard, a much-touted Little League pitcher. He was chunky and had a baby face and came to Our Lady of Mercy as a seasoned street fighter. Ted was quick to laugh and he had a loud, jolly laugh, but when he got angry he'd smile a little smile, the kind that simply raises the corner of the mouth a quarter of an inch. For those who knew, it was an eerie signal. Those who didn't found themselves in big trouble, for Ted was very quick. He loved to carry on what we would come to call philosophical discussions: What is courage? Does God exist? He also loved words, enjoyed picking up big ones like *salubrious* and *equivocal* and using them in our conversations — laughing at himself as the word hit a chuckhole rolling off his tongue. Ted didn't do all that well in school — baseball and parties and testing the courage he'd speculated about took up his time. His textbooks were *Argosy* and *Field and Stream*, whatever newspapers he'd find on the bus stop — from the *Daily Worker* to pornography — conversations with uncles or hobos or businessmen he'd meet in a coffee shop, *The Old Man and the Sea*. With hindsight, I can see that Ted was developing into one of those rough-hewn intellectuals whose sources are a mix of the learned and the apocryphal, whose discussions are both assured and sad.

And then there was Ken Harvey. Ken was good-looking in a 15
puffy way and had a full and oily ducktail and was a car enthusiast . . . a hodad. One day in religion class, he said the sentence that turned out to be one of the most memorable of the hundreds of thousands I heard in those Voc. Ed. years. We were talking about the parable of the talents, about achievement, working hard, doing the best you can do, blah-blah-blah, when the teacher called on the restive Ken Harvey for an opinion. Ken thought about it, but just for a second, and said (with studied, minimal affect), "I just wanna be average." That woke me up. Average? Who wants to be average? Then the athletes chimed in with the clichés that make you want to laryngectomize them, and the exchange became a platitudinous melee. At the time, I thought Ken's assertion was stupid, and I wrote him off. But his sentence has stayed with me all these years, and I think I am finally coming to understand it.

Ken Harvey was gasping for air. School can be a tremendously disorienting place. No matter how bad the school, you're going to encounter notions that don't fit with the assumptions and beliefs that you grew up with — maybe you'll hear these dissonant notions from teachers, maybe from the other students, and maybe you'll read them. You'll also be thrown in with all kinds of kids from all kinds of backgrounds, and that can be unsettling — this is especially true in places of rich ethnic and linguistic mix, like the L.A. basin. You'll see a handful of students far excel you in courses that sound exotic and that are only in the curriculum of the elite: French, physics, trigonometry. And all this is happening while you're trying to shape an identity, your body is changing, and your emotions are running wild. If you're a working-class kid in the vocational track, the options you'll have to deal with this will be constrained in certain ways: you're defined by your school as "slow"; you're placed in a curriculum that isn't designed to liberate you but to occupy you, or, if you're lucky, train you, though the training is for work the society does not esteem; other students are picking up the cues from your school and your curriculum and interacting with you in particular ways. If you're a kid like Ted Richard, you turn your back on all this and let your mind roam where it may. But youngsters like Ted are rare. What Ken and so many others do is protect themselves from such suffocating madness by taking on with a vengeance the identity implied in the vocational track. Reject the confusion and frustration by openly defining yourself as the Common Joe. Champion the average. Rely on your own good sense. Fuck this bullshit. Bullshit, of course, is everything you — and the others — fear is beyond you: books, essays, tests, academic scrambling, complexity, scientific reasoning, philosophical inquiry.

The tragedy is that you have to twist the knife in your own gray matter to make this defense work. You'll have to shut down, have to reject intellectual stimuli or diffuse them with sarcasm, have to cultivate stupidity, have to convert boredom from a malady into a way of confronting the world. Keep your vocabulary simple, act stoned when you're not or act more stoned than you are, flaunt ignorance, materialize your dreams. It is a powerful and effective defense — it neutralizes the insult and the frustration of being a vocational kid and, when perfected, it drives teachers up the wall, a delightful secondary effect. But like all strong magic, it exacts a price.

My own deliverance from the Voc. Ed. world began with sophomore biology. Every student, college prep to vocational, had to take biology, and unlike the other courses, the same person taught all sections. When teaching the vocational group, Brother Clint probably slowed down a bit or omitted a little of the fundamental biochemistry, but he used the same book and more or less the same syllabus across the board. If one class got tough, he could get tougher. He was young and powerful and very handsome, and looks and physical strength were high currency. No one gave him any trouble.

I was pretty bad at the dissecting table, but the lectures and the textbook were interesting: plastic overlays that, with each turned page, peeled away skin, then veins and muscle, then organs, down to the very bones that Brother Clint, pointer in hand, would tap out on our hanging skeleton. Dave Snyder was in big trouble, for the study of life — versus the living of it — was sticking in his craw. We worked out a code for our multiple-choice exams. He'd poke me in the back: once for the answer under *A*, twice for *B*, and so on; and when he'd hit the right one, I'd look up to the ceiling as though I were lost in thought. Poke: cytoplasm. Poke, poke: methane. Poke, poke, poke: William Harvey. Poke, poke, poke, poke: islets of Langerhans. This didn't work out perfectly, but Dave passed the course, and I mastered the dreamy look of a guy on a record jacket. And something else happened. Brother Clint puzzled over this Voc. Ed. kid who was racking up 98s and 99s on his tests. He checked the school's records and discovered the error. He recommended that I begin my junior year in the College Prep program. According to all I've read since, such a shift, as one report put it, is virtually impossible. Kids at that level rarely cross tracks. The telling thing is how chancy both my placement into and exit from Voc. Ed. was; neither I nor my parents had anything to do with it. I lived in one world during spring semester, and when I came back to school in the fall, I was living in another.

Switching to College Prep was a mixed blessing. I was an 20
erratic student. I was undisciplined. And I hadn't caught onto the rules of the game: why work hard in a class that didn't grab my

fancy? I was also hopelessly behind in math. Chemistry was hard; toying with my chemistry set years before hadn't prepared me for the chemist's equations. Fortunately, the priest who taught both chemistry and second-year algebra was also the school's athletic director. Membership on the track team covered me; I knew I wouldn't get lower than a C. U.S. history was taught pretty well, and I did okay. But civics was taken over by a football coach who had trouble reading the textbook aloud — and reading aloud was the centerpiece of his pedagogy. College Prep at Mercy was certainly an improvement over the vocational program — at least it carried some status — but the social science curriculum was weak, and the mathematics and physical sciences were simply beyond me. I had a miserable quantitative background and ended up copying some assignments and finessing the rest as best I could. Let me try to explain how it feels to see again and again material you should once have learned but didn't.

You are given a problem. It requires you to simplify algebraic fractions or to multiply expressions containing square roots. You know this is pretty basic material because you've seen it for years. Once a teacher took some time with you, and you learned how to carry out these operations. Simple versions, anyway. But that was a year or two or more in the past, and these are more complex versions, and now you're not sure. And this, you keep telling yourself, is ninth- or even eighth-grade stuff.

Next it's a word problem. This is also old hat. The basic elements are as familiar as story characters: trains speeding so many miles per hour or shadows of buildings angling so many degrees. Maybe you know enough, have sat through enough explanations, to be able to begin setting up the problem: "If one train is going this fast . . ." or "This shadow is really one line of a triangle. . . ." Then: "Let's see . . ." "How did Jones do this?" "Hmmmm." "No." "No, that won't work." Your attention wavers. You wonder about other things: a football game, a dance, that cute new checker at the market. You try to focus on the problem again. You scribble on paper for a while, but the tension wins out and your attention flits elsewhere. You crumple the paper and begin daydreaming to ease the frustration.

The particulars will vary, but in essence this is what a number of students go through, especially those in so-called remedial classes. They open their textbooks and see once again the familiar and impenetrable formulas and diagrams and terms that have stumped them for years. There is no excitement here. *No* excitement. Regardless of what the teacher says, this is not a new challenge. There is, rather, embarrassment and frustration and, not surprisingly, some anger in being reminded once again of long-standing inadequacies. No wonder so many students finally attribute their difficulties to something inborn, organic: "That part of my brain just doesn't work." Given the troubling histories many of these students have, it's miraculous that any of them can lift the shroud of hopelessness sufficiently to make deliverance from these classes possible.

Through this entire period, my father's health was deteriorating with cruel momentum. His arteriosclerosis progressed to the point where a simple nick on his shin wouldn't heal. Eventually it ulcerated and widened. Lou Minton would come by daily to change the dressing. We tried renting an oscillating bed — which we placed in the front room — to force blood through the constricted arteries in my father's legs. The bed hummed through the night, moving in place to ward off the inevitable. The ulcer continued to spread, and the doctors finally had to amputate. My grandfather had lost his leg in a stockyard accident. Now my father too was crippled. His convalescence was slow but steady, and the doctors placed him in the Santa Monica Rehabilitation Center, a sun-bleached building that opened out onto the warm spray of the Pacific. The place gave him some strength and some color and some training in walking with an artificial leg. He did pretty well for a year or so until he slipped and broke his hip. He was confined to a wheelchair after that, and the confinement contributed to the diminishing of his body and spirit.

I am holding a picture of him. He is sitting in his wheelchair 25
and smiling at the camera. The smile appears forced, unsteady, seems to quaver, though it is frozen in silver nitrate. He is in his mid-sixties and looks eighty. Late in my junior year, he had a stroke and never came out of the resulting coma. After that, I would see him only in dreams, and to this day that is how I join him. Sometimes the dreams are sad and grisly and primal: my father lying in a bed soaked with his suppuration, holding me, rocking me. But sometimes the dreams bring him back to me

healthy: him talking to me on an empty street, or buying some pictures to decorate our old house, or transformed somehow into someone strong and adept with tools and the physical.

Jack MacFarland couldn't have come into my life at a better time. My father was dead, and I had logged up too many years of scholastic indifference. Mr. MacFarland had a master's degree from Columbia and decided, at twenty-six, to find a little school and teach his heart out. He never took any credentialing courses, couldn't bear to, he said, so he had to find employment in a private system. He ended up at Our Lady of Mercy teaching five sections of senior English. He was a beatnik who was born too late. His teeth were stained, he tucked his sorry tie in between the third and fourth buttons of his shirt, and his pants were chronically wrinkled. At first, we couldn't believe this guy, thought he slept in his car. But within no time, he had us so startled with work that we didn't much worry about where he slept or if he slept at all. We wrote three or four essays a month. We read a book every two to three weeks, starting with the *Iliad* and ending up with Hemingway. He gave us a quiz on the reading every other day. He brought a prep school curriculum to Mercy High.

MacFarland's lectures were crafted, and as he delivered them he would pace the room jiggling a piece of chalk in his cupped hand, using it to scribble on the board the names of all the writers and philosophers and plays and novels he was weaving into his discussion. He asked questions often, raised everything from Zeno's paradox to the repeated last line of Frost's "Stopping by Woods on a Snowy Evening." He slowly and carefully built up our knowledge of Western intellectual history — with facts, with connections, with speculations. We learned about Greek philosophy, about Dante, the Elizabethan worldview, the Age of Reason, existentialism. He analyzed poems with us, had us reading sections from John Ciardi's *How Does a Poem Mean?*, making a potentially difficult book accessible with his own explanations. We gave oral reports on poems Ciardi didn't cover. We imitated the styles of Conrad, Hemingway, and *Time* magazine. We wrote and talked, wrote and talked. The man immersed us in language.

Even MacFarland's barbs were literary. If Jim Fitzsimmons, hung over and irritable, tried to smart-ass him, he'd rejoin with a flourish that would spark the indomitable Skip Madison — who'd lost his front teeth in a hapless tackle — to flick his tongue through the gap and opine, "good chop," drawing out the single "o" in stinging indictment. Jack MacFarland, this tobacco-stained intellectual, brandished linguistic weapons of a kind I hadn't encountered before. Here was this *egghead,* for God's sake, keeping some pretty difficult people in line. And from what I heard, Mike Dweetz and Steve Fusco and all the notorious Voc. Ed. crowd settled down as well when MacFarland took the podium. Though a lot of guys groused in the schoolyard, it just seemed that giving trouble to this particular teacher was a silly thing to do. Tomfoolery, not to mention assault, had no place in the world he was trying to create for us, and instinctively everyone knew that. If nothing else, we all recognized MacFarland's considerable intelligence and respected the hours he put into his work. It came to this: the troublemaker would look foolish rather than daring. Even Jim Fitzsimmons was reading *On the Road* and turning his incipient alcoholism to literary ends.

There were some lives that were already beyond Jack MacFarland's ministrations, but mine was not. I started reading again as I hadn't since elementary school. I would go into our gloomy little bedroom or sit at the dinner table while, on the television, Danny McShane was paralyzing Mr. Moto with the atomic drop, and work slowly back through *Heart of Darkness,* trying to catch the words in Conrad's sentences. I certainly was not MacFarland's best student; most of the other guys in College Prep, even my fellow slackers, had better backgrounds than I did. But I worked very hard, for MacFarland had hooked me. He tapped my old interest in reading and creating stories. He gave me a way to feel special by using my mind. And he provided a role model that wasn't shaped on physical prowess alone, and something inside me that I wasn't quite aware of responded to that. Jack MacFarland established a literacy club, to borrow a phrase of Frank Smith's, and invited me — invited all of us — to join.

30 There's been a good deal of research and speculation suggesting that the acknowledgment of school performance with extrinsic rewards — smiling faces, stars, numbers, grades — diminishes the intrinsic satisfaction children experience by engaging in reading or writing or problem solving. While it's certainly true that we've created an educational system that encourages our best and brightest to become cynical grade collectors and, in general, have developed an obsession with evaluation and assessment, I must

tell you that venal though it may have been, I loved getting good grades from MacFarland. I now know how subjective grades can be, but then they came tucked in the back of essays like bits of scientific data, some sort of spectroscopic readout that said, objectively and publicly, that I had made something of value. I suppose I'd been mediocre for too long and enjoyed a public redefinition. And I suppose the workings of my mind, such as they were, had been private for too long. My linguistic play moved into the world; . . . these papers with their circled, red B-pluses and A-minuses linked my mind to something outside it. I carried them around like a club emblem.

One day in the December of my senior year, Mr. MacFarland asked me where I was going to go to college. I hadn't thought much about it. Many of the students I teach today spent their last year in high school with a physics text in one hand and the Stanford catalog in the other, but I wasn't even aware of what "entrance requirements" were. My folks would say that they wanted me to go to college and be a doctor, but I don't know how seriously I ever took that; it seemed a sweet thing to say, a bit of supportive family chatter, like telling a gangly daughter she's graceful. The reality of higher education wasn't in my scheme of things: no one in the family had gone to college; only two of my uncles had completed high school. I figured I'd get a night job and go to the local junior college because I knew that Snyder and Company were going there to play ball. But I hadn't even prepared for that. When I finally said, "I don't know," MacFarland looked down at me — I was seated in his office — and said, "Listen, you can write."

My grades stank. I had A's in biology and a handful of B's in a few English and social science classes. All the rest were C's — or worse. MacFarland said I would do well in his class and laid down the law about doing well in the others. Still, the record for my first three years wouldn't have been acceptable to any four-year school. To nobody's surprise, I was turned down flat by USC and UCLA. But Jack MacFarland was on the case. He had received his bachelor's degree from Loyola University, so he made calls to old professors and talked to somebody in admissions and wrote me a strong letter. Loyola finally accepted me as a probationary student. I would be on trial for the first year, and if I did okay, I would be granted regular status. MacFarland also intervened to get me a loan, for I could never have afforded a private college without it.

Four more years of religion classes and four more years of boys at one school, girls at another. But at least I was going to college. Amazing.

In my last semester of high school, I elected a special English course fashioned by Mr. MacFarland, and it was through this elective that there arose at Mercy a fledgling literati. Art Mitz, the editor of the school newspaper and a very smart guy, was the kingpin. He was joined by me and by Mark Dever, a quiet boy who wrote beautifully and who would die before he was forty. MacFarland occasionally invited us to his apartment, and those visits became the high point of our apprenticeship: we'd clamp on our training wheels and drive to his salon.

He lived in a cramped and cluttered place near the airport, tucked away in the kind of building that architectural critic Reyner Banham calls a *dingbat*. Books were all over: stacked, piled, tossed, and crated, underlined and dog eared, well worn and new. Cigarette ashes crusted with coffee in saucers or spilling over the sides of motel ashtrays. The little bedroom had, along two of its walls, bricks and boards loaded with notes, magazines, and oversized books. The kitchen joined the living room, and there was a stack of German newspapers under the sink. I had never seen anything like it: a great flophouse of language furnished by City Lights and Café le Metro. I read every title. I flipped through paperbacks and scanned jackets and memorized names: Gogol, *Finnegans Wake*, Djuna Barnes, Jackson Pollock, *A Coney Island of the Mind*, F. O. Matthiessen's *American Renaissance*, all sorts of Freud, *Troubled Sleep*, Man Ray, *The Education of Henry Adams*, Richard Wright, *Film as Art*, William Butler Yeats, Marguerite Duras, *Redburn, A Season in Hell, Kapital*. On the cover of Alain-Fournier's *The Wanderer* was an Edward Gorey drawing of a young man on a road winding into dark trees. By the hotplate sat a strange Kafka novel called *Amerika*, in which an adolescent hero crosses the Atlantic to find the Nature Theater of Oklahoma. Art and Mark would be talking about a movie or the school newspaper, and I would be consuming my English teacher's library. It was heady stuff. I felt like a Pop Warner athlete on steroids.

Art, Mark, and I would buy stogies and triangulate from Mac- 35
Farland's apartment to the Cinema, which now shows X-rated films but was then L.A.'s premier art theater, and then to the musty Cherokee Bookstore in Hollywood to hobnob with beatnik

homosexuals — smoking, drinking bourbon and coffee, and trying out awkward phrases we'd gleaned from our mentor's bookshelves. I was happy and precocious and a little scared as well, for Hollywood Boulevard was thick with a kind of decadence that was foreign to the South Side. After the Cherokee, we would head back to the security of MacFarland's apartment, slaphappy with hipness.

Let me be the first to admit that there was a good deal of adolescent passion in this embrace of the avant-garde: self-absorption, sexually charged pedantry, an elevation of the odd and abandoned. Still it was a time during which I absorbed an awful lot of information: long lists of titles, images from expressionist paintings, new wave shibboleths, snippets of philosophy, and names that read like Steve Fusco's misspellings — Goethe, Nietzsche, Kierkegaard. Now this is hardly the stuff of deep understanding. But it was an introduction, a phrase book, a Baedeker to a vocabulary of ideas, and it felt good at the time to know all these words. With hindsight I realize how layered and important that knowledge was.

It enabled me to do things in the world. I could browse bohemian bookstores in far-off, mysterious Hollywood; I could go to the Cinema and see events through the lenses of European directors; and, most of all, I could share an evening, talk that talk, with Jack MacFarland, the man I most admired at the time. Knowledge was becoming a bonding agent. Within a year or two, the persona of the disaffected hipster would prove too cynical, too alienated to last. But for a time it was new and exciting: it provided a critical perspective on society, and it allowed me to act as though I were living beyond the limiting boundaries of South Vermont.

For Discussion and Writing

1. List the different teachers Rose writes about in this essay, adding a sentence to each name describing his significance for Rose.
2. This essay is from Rose's powerful book *Lives on the Boundary*. What boundaries does Rose write about here? What acts of classification do these boundaries serve?
3. **connections** Rose is put on the vocational track accidentally and remains there for two years because his parents are unequipped to help him. Compare his responses to his experience to those of Maya

Angelou in "Graduation" (p. 20), whose "classification" may not be accidental but certainly is unfair.

4. "Students will float to the mark you set," Rose writes (par. 11). Write about a time in your life when this was true of you, and reflect more generally on your life as a student. Have you found that your educational experiences thus far have pushed you to exceed what you originally thought was possible? What kinds of motivation are built into our educational system? Has traditional motivation (such as getting good grades) worked for you? What kind of an educational system might motivate *all* students?

SCOTT RUSSELL SANDERS

The Men We Carry in Our Minds

Scott Russell Sanders, born in 1945, is a professor of literature and creative writing at Indiana University and a prolific essayist and fiction writer. He has published numerous essay and short story collections, novels, and children's books. His work is often concerned with environmental and other social issues, family, and writing itself, as in Hunting for Hope: A Father's Journeys *(1998), a collection of essays inspired by a camping trip with his son, and his latest,* A Conservationist Manifesto *(2009).*

In this essay, originally published in the Milkweed Chronicle *in 1984, Sanders writes about social class and gender equality, and about the way his ideas about class and gender are the product of his perceptions of the men he saw in his childhood. As you read, look out for the way Sanders uses classification and description to develop his argument.*

This must be a hard time for women," I say to my friend Anneke. "They have so many paths to choose from, and so many voices calling them."

"I think it's a lot harder for men," she replies.

"How do you figure that?"

"The women I know feel excited, innocent, like crusaders in a just cause. The men I know are eaten up with guilt."

We are sitting at the kitchen table drinking sassafras tea, our 5
hands wrapped around the mugs because this April morning is cool and drizzly. "Like a Dutch morning," Anneke told me earlier. She is Dutch herself, a writer and midwife and peacemaker, with the round face and sad eyes of a woman in a Vermeer painting who might be waiting for the rain to stop, for a door to open. She leans over to sniff a sprig of lilac, pale lavender, that rises from a vase of cobalt blue.

"Women feel such pressure to be everything, do everything," I say. "Career, kids, art, politics. Have their babies and get back to the office a week later. It's as if they're trying to overcome a million years' worth of evolution in one lifetime."

"But we help one another. We don't try to lumber on alone, like so many wounded grizzly bears, the way men do." Anneke sips her tea. I gave her the mug with owls on it, for wisdom. "And we have this deep-down sense that we're in the *right* — we've been held back, passed over, used — while men feel they're in the wrong. Men are the ones who've been discredited, who have to search their souls."

I search my soul. I discover guilty feelings aplenty — toward the poor, the Vietnamese, Native Americans, the whales, an endless list of debts — a guilt in each case that is as bright and unambiguous as a neon sign. But toward women I feel something more confused, a snarl of shame, envy, wary tenderness, and amazement. This muddle troubles me. To hide my unease I say, "You're right, it's tough being a man these days."

"Don't laugh," Anneke frowns at me, mournful-eyed, through the sassafras steam. "I wouldn't be a man for anything. It's much easier being the victim. All the victim has to do is break free. The persecutor has to live with his past."

How deep is that past? I find myself wondering after Anneke 10
has left. How much of an inheritance do I have to throw off? Is it just the beliefs I breathed in as a child? Do I have to scour memory back through father and grandfather? Through St. Paul? Beyond Stonehenge and into the twilit caves? I'm convinced the past we must contend with is deeper even than speech. When I think back on my childhood, on how I learned to see men and women, I have a sense of ancient, dizzying depths. The back roads of Tennessee and Ohio where I grew up were probably closer, in their sexual patterns, to the campsites of Stone Age hunters than to the genderless cities of the future into which we are rushing.

The first men, besides my father, I remember seeing were black convicts and white guards, in the cottonfield across the road from our farm on the outskirts of Memphis. I must have been three or four. The prisoners wore dingy gray-and-black zebra suits, heavy as canvas, sodden with sweat. Hatless, stooped, they chopped weeds in the fierce heat, row after row, breathing the acrid dust of boll-weevil poison. The overseers wore dazzling white shirts and broad shadowy hats. The oiled barrels of their shotguns flashed in the sunlight. Their faces in memory are utterly blank. Of course those men, white and black, have become for me an emblem of racial hatred. But they have also come to stand for the twin poles of my early vision of manhood — the brute toiling animal and the boss.

When I was a boy, the men I knew labored with their bodies. They were marginal farmers, just scraping by, or welders, steelworkers, carpenters; they swept floors, dug ditches, mined coal, or drove trucks, their forearms ropy with muscle; they trained horses, stoked furnaces, built tires, stood on assembly lines wrestling parts onto cars and refrigerators. They got up before light, worked all day long whatever the weather, and when they came home at night they looked as though somebody had been whipping them. In the evenings and on weekends they worked on their own places, tilling gardens that were lumpy with clay, fixing broken-down cars, hammering on houses that were always too drafty, too leaky, too small.

The bodies of the men I knew were twisted and maimed in ways visible and invisible. The nails of their hands were black and split, the hands tattooed with scars. Some had lost fingers. Heavy lifting had given many of them finicky backs and guts weak from hernias. Racing against conveyor belts had given them ulcers. Their ankles and knees ached from years of standing on concrete. Anyone who had worked for long around machines was hard of hearing. They squinted, and the skin of their faces was creased like the leather of old work gloves. There were times, studying them, when I dreaded growing up. Most of them coughed, from dust or cigarettes, and most of them drank cheap wine or whiskey, so their eyes looked bloodshot and bruised. The fathers of my friends always seemed older than the mothers. Men wore out sooner. Only women lived into old age.

As a boy I also knew another sort of men, who did not sweat and break down like mules. They were soldiers, and so far as I could tell they scarcely worked at all. During my early school years we lived on a military base, an arsenal in Ohio, and every day I saw GIs in the guardshacks, on the stoops of barracks, at the wheels of olive drab Chevrolets. The chief fact of their lives was boredom. Long after I left the Arsenal I came to recognize the sour smell the soldiers gave off as that of souls in limbo. They were all waiting — for wars, for transfers, for leaves, for promotions, for the end of their hitch — like so many braves waiting for the hunt to begin. Unlike the warriors of older tribes, however, they would have no say about when the battle would start or how it would be waged. Their waiting was broken only when they practiced for war. They fired guns at targets, drove tanks across the churned-up fields of the military reservation, set off bombs in the wrecks of old fighter planes. I knew this was all play. But I also felt certain that when the hour for killing arrived, they would kill. When the real shooting started, many of them would die. This was what soldiers were *for,* just as a hammer was for driving nails.

Warriors and toilers: those seemed, in my boyhood vision, to 15
be the chief destinies for men. They weren't the only destinies, as I learned from having a few male teachers, from reading books, and from watching television. But the men on television — the politicians, the astronauts, the generals, the savvy lawyers, the philosophical doctors, the bosses who gave orders to both soldiers and laborers — seemed as remote and unreal to me as the figures in tapestries. I could no more imagine growing up to become one of these cool, potent creatures than I could imagine becoming a prince.

A nearer and more hopeful example was that of my father, who had escaped from a red-dirt farm to a tire factory, and from the assembly line to the front office. Eventually he dressed in a white shirt and tie. He carried himself as if he had been born to work with his mind. But his body, remembering the earlier years of slogging work, began to give out on him in his fifties, and it quit on him entirely before he turned sixty-five. Even such a partial escape from man's fate as he had accomplished did not seem possible for most of the boys I knew. They joined the Army, stood in line for jobs in the smoky plants, helped build highways. They were bound to work as their fathers had worked, killing themselves or preparing to kill others.

A scholarship enabled me not only to attend college, a rare enough feat in my circle, but even to study in a university meant for the children of the rich. Here I met for the first time young men who had assumed from birth that they would lead lives of comfort and power. And for the first time I met women who told me that men were guilty of having kept all the joys and privileges of the earth for themselves. I was baffled. What privileges? What joys? I thought about the maimed, dismal lives of most of the men back home. What had they stolen from their wives and daughters? The right to go five days a week, twelve months a year, for thirty or forty years to a steel mill or a coal mine? The right to drop bombs and die in war? The right to feel every leak in the roof, every gap in the fence, every cough in the engine, as a wound they must mend? The right to feel, when the lay-off comes or the plant shuts down, not only afraid but ashamed?

I was slow to understand the deep grievances of women. This was because, as a boy, I had envied them. Before college, the only people I had ever known who were interested in art or music or literature, the only ones who read books, the only ones who ever seemed to enjoy a sense of ease and grace were the mothers and daughters. Like the menfolk, they fretted about money, they scrimped and made-do. But, when the pay stopped coming in, they were not the ones who had failed. Nor did they have to go to war, and that seemed to me a blessed fact. By comparison with the narrow, ironclad days of fathers, there was an expansiveness, I thought, in the days of mothers. They went to see neighbors, to shop in town, to run errands at school, at the library, at church. No doubt, had I looked harder at their lives, I would have envied them less. It was not my fate to become a woman, so it was easier for me to see the graces. Few of them held jobs outside the home, and those who did filled thankless roles as clerks and waitresses. I didn't see, then, what a prison a house could be, since houses seemed to me brighter, handsomer places than any factory. I did not realize — because such things were never spoken of — how often women suffered from men's bullying. I did learn about the wretchedness of abandoned wives, single mothers, widows; but I also learned about the wretchedness of lone men. Even then I could see how exhausting it was for a mother to cater all day to the needs of young children. But if I had been asked, as a boy, to choose between tending a baby and tending a machine, I think I would have chosen the baby. (Having now tended both, I know I would choose the baby.)

So I was baffled when the women at college accused me and my sex of having cornered the world's pleasures. I think something like my bafflement has been felt by other boys (and by girls as well) who grew up in dirt-poor farm country, in mining country, in black ghettos, in Hispanic barrios, in the shadows of factories, in Third World nations — any place where the fate of men is as grim and bleak as the fate of women. Toilers and warriors. I realize now how ancient these identities are, how deep the tug they exert on men, the undertow of a thousand generations. The miseries I saw, as a boy, in the lives of nearly all men I continue to see in the lives of many — the body-breaking toil, the tedium, the call to be tough, the humiliating powerlessness, the battle for a living and for territory.

When the women I met at college thought about the joys and 20
privileges of men, they did not carry in their minds the sort of men I had known in my childhood. They thought of their fathers, who were bankers, physicians, architects, stockbrokers, the big wheels of the big cities. These fathers rode the train to work or drove cars that cost more than any of my childhood houses. They were attended from morning to night by female helpers, wives and nurses and secretaries. They were never laid off, never short of cash at month's end, never lined up for welfare. These fathers made decisions that mattered. They ran the world.

The daughters of such men wanted to share in this power, this glory. So did I. They yearned for a say over their future, for jobs worthy of their abilities, for the right to live at peace, unmolested, whole. Yes, I thought, yes yes. The difference between me and these daughters was that they saw me, because of my sex, as destined from birth to become like their fathers, and therefore as an enemy to their desires. But I knew better. I wasn't an enemy, in fact or in feeling. I was an ally. If I had known, then, how to tell them so, would they have believed me? Would they now?

For Discussion and Writing

1. Why does Sanders see himself as an ally of the women he met in college? Against whom were they allied? Why did they not see him as an ally?
2. Sanders uses a number of examples to illustrate the idea that we all carry different models of manhood in our minds. Make an annotated list of Sanders's examples, including the characteristics of each model and what they have meant to Sanders.
3. **connections** Of the characters who were professional men that he saw on television when he was a kid, Sanders writes, "I could no more imagine growing up to become one of these cool, potent creatures

than I could imagine becoming a prince" (par. 5). Compare Sanders's account of class identity to Mike Rose's in "I Just Wanna Be Average" (p. 331). How does each deal with personal expectations as well as the world's?

4. Sanders complicates (without refuting) the standard feminist take on gender, voiced by his friend at the beginning of his essay, by adding in the element of class. Toni Morrison wrote an essay in the early 1970s called "What the Black Woman Thinks of Women's Lib" that similarly complicated feminism, in this case by considering not just gender but also race (as Alice Walker also does regarding Virginia Woolf's arguments about women writers in "In Search of Our Mothers' Gardens," p. 420). What do you think of these arguments? Do you think complicating a social critique strengthens or weakens it? Why?

ERIC SCHLOSSER

Kid Kustomers

Eric Schlosser, born in 1959 and raised in New York City and Los Angeles, is a journalist and writer who is a correspondent for the Atlantic Monthly *and has also written for the* New Yorker, *the* Nation, Vanity Fair, *and* Rolling Stone. *His book* Fast Food Nation *(2001) was adapted into a 2006 film and brought increased attention to the fast-food industry. He was also involved in the making of* Food, Inc., *a 2009 documentary.*

"Kid Kustomers" is an incisive account of the way Madison Avenue has found some eyeballs to attract to their clients' products. One of the things to appreciate about this essay is the way it showcases Schlosser's ability to make a scathing indictment without being polemical. As you read, note how Schlosser lays out the facts without appearing to editorialize — how he judges without seeming to be judgmental.

Twenty-five years ago, only a handful of American companies directed their marketing at children — Disney, McDonald's, candy makers, toy makers, manufacturers of breakfast cereal. Today children are being targeted by phone companies, oil companies, and automobile companies as well as clothing stores and restaurant chains. The explosion in children's advertising occurred during the 1980s. Many working parents, feeling guilty about spending less time with their kids, started spending more money on them. One marketing expert has called the 1980s "the decade of the child consumer." After largely ignoring children for years, Madison Avenue began to scrutinize and pursue them. Major ad agencies now have children's divisions, and a variety of marketing firms focus solely on kids. These groups tend to have sweet-sounding names: Small Talk, Kid Connection, Kid2Kid, the Gepetto Group, Just Kids, Inc. At least three industry publications — *Youth Market Alert*, *Selling to Kids*, and *Marketing to Kids Report* — cover the latest ad campaigns and market research. The growth in children's advertising has been driven by efforts to increase not just current, but also future, consumption. Hoping that nostalgic childhood memories of a brand will lead to a lifetime of purchases, companies now plan "cradle-to-grave" advertising strategies. They have come to believe what Ray Kroc and Walt Disney realized long ago — a person's "brand loyalty" may begin as early as the age of two. Indeed, market research has found that children often recognize a brand logo before they can recognize their own name.

The discontinued Joe Camel ad campaign, which used a hip cartoon character to sell cigarettes, showed how easily children can be influenced by the right corporate mascot. A 1991 study published in the *Journal of the American Medical Association* found that nearly all of America's six-year-olds could identify Joe Camel, who was just as familiar to them as Mickey Mouse. Another study found that one-third of the cigarettes illegally sold to minors were Camels. More recently, a marketing firm conducted a survey in shopping malls across the country, asking children to describe their favorite TV ads. According to the CME KidCom Ad Traction Study II, released at the 1999 Kids' Marketing Conference in San Antonio, Texas, the Taco Bell commercials featuring a talking chihuahua were the most popular fast food ads. The kids in the survey also liked Pepsi and Nike commercials, but their favorite television ad was for Budweiser.

The bulk of the advertising directed at children today has an immediate goal. "It's not just getting kids to whine," one marketer explained in *Selling to Kids*, "it's giving them a specific reason to ask for the product." Years ago sociologist Vance Packard described children as "surrogate salesmen" who had to persuade other people, usually their parents, to buy what they wanted. Marketers now use different terms to explain the intended response to their ads — such as "leverage," "the nudge factor," "pester power." The aim of most children's advertising is straightforward: Get kids to nag their parents and nag them well.

James U. McNeal, a professor of marketing at Texas A&M University, is considered America's leading authority on marketing to children. In his book *Kids As Customers* (1992), McNeal provides marketers with a thorough analysis of "children's requesting styles and appeals." He classifies juvenile nagging tactics into seven major categories. A *pleading* nag is one accompanied by repetitions of words like "please" or "mom, mom, mom." A *persistent* nag involves constant requests for the coveted product and may include the phrase "I'm gonna ask just one more time." *Forceful* nags are extremely pushy and may include subtle threats, like "Well, then, I'll go and ask Dad." *Demonstrative* nags are the most high-risk, often characterized by full-blown tantrums in public places, breath-holding, tears, a refusal to leave the store. *Sugar-coated* nags promise affection in return for a purchase and may rely on seemingly heartfelt declarations like "You're the best dad in the world." *Threatening* nags are youthful forms of blackmail, vows of eternal hatred and of running away if something isn't bought. *Pity* nags claim the child will be heartbroken, teased, or socially stunted if the parent refuses to buy a certain item. "All of these appeals and styles may be used in combination," McNeal's research has discovered, "but kids tend to stick to one or two of each that proved most effective . . . for their own parents."

McNeal never advocates turning children into screaming, 5
breath-holding monsters. He has been studying "Kid Kustomers" for more than thirty years and believes in a more traditional marketing approach. "The key is getting children to see a firm . . . in much the same way as [they see] mom or dad, grandma or grandpa," McNeal argues. "Likewise, if a company can ally itself with universal values such as patriotism, national defense, and good health, it is likely to nurture belief in it among children."

Before trying to affect children's behavior, advertisers have to learn about their tastes. Today's market researchers not only conduct surveys of children in shopping malls, they also organize focus groups for kids as young as two or three. They analyze children's artwork, hire children to run focus groups, stage slumber parties and then question children into the night. They send cultural anthropologists into homes, stores, fast food restaurants, and other places where kids like to gather, quietly and surreptitiously observing the behavior of prospective customers. They study the academic literature on child development, seeking insights from the work of theorists such as Erik Erikson and Jean Piaget. They study the fantasy lives of young children; they apply the findings in advertisements and product designs.

Dan S. Acuff — the president of Youth Market System Consulting and the author of *What Kids Buy and Why* (1997) — stresses the importance of dream research. Studies suggest that until the age of six, roughly 80 percent of children's dreams are about animals. Rounded, soft creatures like Barney, Disney's animated characters, and the Teletubbies therefore have an obvious appeal to young children. The Character Lab, a division of Youth Market System Consulting, uses a proprietary technique called Character Appeal Quadrant Analysis to help companies develop new mascots. The technique purports to create imaginary characters who perfectly fit the targeted age group's level of cognitive and neurological development.

Children's clubs have for years been considered an effective means of targeting ads and collecting demographic information; the clubs appeal to a child's fundamental need for status and belonging. Disney's Mickey Mouse Club, formed in 1930, was one of the trailblazers. During the 1980s and 1990s, children's clubs proliferated, as corporations used them to solicit the names, addresses, zip codes, and personal comments of young customers. "Marketing messages sent through a club not only can be personalized," James McNeal advises, "they can be tailored for a certain age or geographical group." A well-designed and well-run children's club can be extremely good for business. According to one Burger King executive, the creation of a Burger King Kids Club in 1991 increased the sales of children's meals as much as 300 percent.

The Internet has become another powerful tool for assembling data about children. In 1998 a federal investigation of Web sites aimed at children found that 89 percent requested personal information from kids; only 1 percent required that children obtain parental approval before supplying the information. A character on the McDonald's Web site told children that Ronald McDonald was "the ultimate authority in everything." The site encouraged kids to send Ronald an e-mail revealing their favorite menu item at McDonald's, their favorite book, their favorite sports team — and their name. Fast food Web sites no longer ask children to provide personal information without first gaining parental approval; to do so is now a violation of federal law, thanks to the Children's Online Privacy Protection Act, which took effect in April of 2000.

10 Despite the growing importance of the Internet, television remains the primary medium for children's advertising. The effects of these TV ads have long been a subject of controversy. In 1978, the Federal Trade Commission (FTC) tried to ban all television

ads directed at children seven years old or younger. Many studies had found that young children often could not tell the difference between television programming and television advertising. They also could not comprehend the real purpose of commercials and trusted that advertising claims were true. Michael Pertschuk, the head of the FTC, argued that children need to be shielded from advertising that preys upon their immaturity. "They cannot protect themselves," he said, "against adults who exploit their present-mindedness."

The FTC's proposed ban was supported by the American Academy of Pediatrics, the National Congress of Parents and Teachers, the Consumers Union, and the Child Welfare League, among others. But it was attacked by the National Association of Broadcasters, the Toy Manufacturers of America, and the Association of National Advertisers. The industry groups lobbied Congress to prevent any restrictions on children's ads and sued in federal court to block Pertschuk from participating in future FTC meetings on the subject. In April of 1981, three months after the inauguration of President Ronald Reagan, an FTC staff report argued that a ban on ads aimed at children would be impractical, effectively killing the proposal. "We are delighted by the FTC's reasonable recommendation," said the head of the National Association of Broadcasters.

The Saturday-morning children's ads that caused angry debates twenty years ago now seem almost quaint. Far from being banned, TV advertising aimed at kids is now broadcast twenty-four hours a day, closed-captioned and in stereo. Nickelodeon, the Disney Channel, the Cartoon Network, and the other children's cable networks are now responsible for about 80 percent of all television viewing by kids. None of these networks existed before 1979. The typical American child now spends about twenty-one hours a week watching television — roughly one and a half months of TV every year. That does not include the time children spend in front of a screen watching videos, playing video games, or using the computer. Outside of school, the typical American child spends more time watching television than doing any other activity except sleeping. During the course of a year, he or she watches more than thirty thousand TV commercials. Even the nation's youngest children are watching a great deal of television. About one-quarter of American children between the ages of two and five have a TV in their room.

For Discussion and Writing

1. Why was the 1980s "the decade of the child consumer"?
2. Schlosser connects the turning of children into customers to a number of factors. What are the causes for the growth of the child market, and how does Schlosser connect these causes and effects? Thinking outside of this essay, what further effects do you imagine might be caused by this growth?
3. **connections** Compare Schlosser's approach to youth marketing to Steven Johnson's treatment of video games in "Games" (p. 196). How does each author feel about his subject? Can you imagine what each might say about the other's subject? Would Johnson see something valuable in the exposure of children to advertising? Would Schlosser criticize video games?
4. Many readers will be disturbed by the notions that children often recognize brand logos before their own name and that dream research is used in child-focused marketing. Why do you think this is? Do you find these things disturbing? Why or why not?

DAVID SEDARIS

A Plague of Tics

Born in 1956 in Johnson City, New York, David Sedaris grew up in Raleigh, North Carolina. He is a playwright (in collaboration with his sister Amy) and an essayist whose work has been featured regularly on National Public Radio and in collections such as Me Talk Pretty One Day *(2000),* Dress Your Family in Corduroy and Denim *(2004), and* When You Are Engulfed in Flames *(2008). Sedaris's work tends toward the satiric, but even the most wickedly pointed of his pieces are marked by an ironic stance that includes the author among those humans whose folly must be satirized. This insistence on turning his satiric eye on himself is evident in "A Plague of Tics," taken from* Naked *(1997), in which he recounts — with humor and vivid detail — the obsessive-compulsive behaviors that afflicted him from elementary school through college.*

When the teacher asked if she might visit with my mother, I touched my nose eight times to the surface of my desk.

"May I take that as a 'yes'?" she asked.

According to her calculations, I had left my chair twenty-eight times that day. "You're up and down like a flea. I turn my back for two minutes and there you are with your tongue pressed against that light switch. Maybe they do that where you come from, but here in my classroom we don't leave our seats and lick things whenever we please. That is Miss Chestnut's light switch, and she likes to keep it dry. Would you like me to come over to your house and put my tongue on *your* light switches? Well, would you?"

I tried to picture her in action, but my shoe was calling. *Take me off*, it whispered. *Tap my heel against your forehead three times. Do it now, quick, no one will notice.*

"Well?" Miss Chestnut raised her faint, penciled eyebrows. "I'm 5
asking you a question. Would you or would you not want me licking the light switches in your house?"

I slipped off my shoe, pretending to examine the imprint on the heel.

"You're going to hit yourself over the head with that shoe, aren't you?"

It wasn't "hitting," it was tapping; but still, how had she known what I was about to do?

"Heel marks all over your forehead," she said, answering my silent question.

"You should take a look in the mirror sometime. Shoes are 10
dirty things. We wear them on our feet to protect ourselves against the soil. It's not healthy to hit ourselves over the head with shoes, is it?"

I guessed that it was not.

"Guess? This is not a game to be guessed at. I don't 'guess' that it's dangerous to run into traffic with a paper sack over my head. There's no guesswork involved. These things are facts, not riddles." She sat at her desk, continuing her lecture as she penned a brief letter. "I'd like to have a word with your mother. You do have one, don't you? I'm assuming you weren't raised by animals. Is she blind, your mother? Can she see the way you behave, or do you reserve your antics exclusively for Miss Chestnut?" She handed me the folded slip of paper. "You may go now, and on your way out the door I'm asking you please not to bathe my light switch with your germ-ridden tongue. It's had a long day; we both have."

It was a short distance from the school to our rented house, no more than six hundred and thirty-seven steps, and on a good day I could make the trip in an hour, pausing every few feet to tongue a mailbox or touch whichever single leaf or blade of grass demanded my attention. If I were to lose count of my steps, I'd have to return to the school and begin again. "Back so soon?" the janitor would ask. "You just can't get enough of this place, can you?"

He had it all wrong. I wanted to be at home more than anything, it was getting there that was the problem. I might touch the telephone pole at step three hundred and fourteen and then, fifteen paces later, worry that I hadn't touched it in exactly the right spot. It needed to be touched again. I'd let my mind wander for one brief moment and then doubt had set in, causing me to question not just the telephone pole but also the lawn ornament back at step two hundred and nineteen. I'd have to go back and lick that concrete mushroom one more time, hoping its guardian wouldn't once again rush from her house shouting, "Get your face out of my toadstool!" It might be raining or maybe I had to go to the bathroom, but running home was not an option. This was a long and complicated process that demanded an oppressive attention to detail. It wasn't that I enjoyed pressing my nose against the scalding hood of a parked car — pleasure had nothing to do with it. A person *had* to do these things because nothing was worse than the anguish of not doing them. Bypass that mailbox and my brain would never for one moment let me forget it. I might be sitting at the dinner table, daring myself not to think about it, and the thought would revisit my mind. *Don't think about it.* But it would already be too late and I knew then exactly what I had to do. Excusing myself to go to the bathroom, I'd walk out the front door and return to that mailbox, not just touching but jabbing, practically pounding on the thing because I thought I hated it so much. What I really hated, of course, was my mind. There must have been an off switch somewhere, but I was damned if I could find it.

I didn't remember things being this way back north. Our family 15
had been transferred from Endicott, New York, to Raleigh, North Carolina. That was the word used by the people at IBM, *transferred.* A new home was under construction, but until it was finished we were confined to a rental property built to resemble a plantation house. The building sat in a treeless, balding yard, its white columns promising a majesty the interior failed to deliver. The front door opened onto a dark, narrow hallway lined with bedrooms not much larger than the mattresses that furnished them. Our kitchen was located on the second floor, alongside the living room, its picture window offering a view of the cinder-block wall built to hold back the tide of mud generated by the neighboring dirt mound.

"Our own little corner of hell," my mother said, fanning herself with one of the shingles littering the front yard.

Depressing as it was, arriving at the front stoop of the house meant that I had completed the first leg of that bitter-tasting journey to my bedroom. Once home I would touch the front door seven times with each elbow, a task made more difficult if there was someone else around. "Why don't you try the knob," my sister Lisa would say. "That's what the rest of us do, and it seems to work for us." Inside the house there were switches and doorstops to be acknowledged. My bedroom was right there off the hallway, but first I had business to tend to. After kissing the fourth, eighth, and twelfth carpeted stair, I wiped the cat hair off my lips and proceeded to the kitchen, where I was commanded to stroke the burners of the stove, press my nose against the refrigerator door, and arrange the percolator, toaster, and blender into a straight row. After making my rounds of the living room, it was time to kneel beside the banister and blindly jab a butter knife in the direction of my favorite electrical socket. There were bulbs to lick and bathroom faucets to test before finally I was free to enter my bedroom, where I would carefully align the objects on my dresser, lick the corners of my metal desk, and lie upon my bed, rocking back and forth and thinking of what an odd woman she was, my third-grade teacher, Miss Chestnut. Why come here and lick my switches when she never used the one she had? Maybe she was drunk.

Her note had asked if she might visit our home in order to discuss what she referred to as my "special problems."

"Have you been leaving your seat to lick the light switch?" my mother asked. She placed the letter upon the table and lit a cigarette.

"Once or twice," I said. 20

"Once or twice what? Every half hour? Every ten minutes?"

"I don't know," I lied. "Who's counting?"

"Well, your goddamned math teacher, for one. That's her *job*, to count. What, do you think she's not going to notice?"

"Notice what?" It never failed to amaze me that people might notice these things. Because my actions were so intensely private, I had always assumed they were somehow invisible. When cornered, I demanded that the witness had been mistaken.

"What do you mean, 'notice what?' I got a phone call just this 25
afternoon from that lady up the street, that Mrs. Keening, the one with the twins. She says she caught you in her front yard, down on your hands and knees kissing the evening edition of her newspaper."

"I wasn't kissing it. I was just trying to read the headline."

"And you had to get that close? Maybe we need to get you some stronger glasses."

"Well, maybe we do," I said.

"And I suppose this Miss . . ." My mother unfolded the letter and studied the signature. "This Miss Chestnut is mistaken, too? Is that what you're trying to tell me? Maybe she has you confused with the other boy who leaves his seat to lick the pencil sharpener or touch the flag or whatever the hell it is you do the moment her back is turned?"

"That's very likely," I said. "She's old. There are spots on her 30
hands."

"How many?" my mother asked.

On the afternoon that Miss Chestnut arrived for her visit, I was in my bedroom, rocking. Unlike the obsessive counting and touching, rocking was not a mandatory duty but a voluntary and highly pleasurable exercise. It was my hobby, and there was nothing else I would rather do. The point was not to rock oneself to sleep: This was not a step toward some greater goal. It was the goal itself. The perpetual movement freed my mind, allowing me to mull things over and construct elaborately detailed fantasies. Toss in a radio, and I was content to rock until three or four o'clock in the morning, listening to the hit parade and discovering that each and every song was about me. I might have to listen two or three hundred times to the same song, but sooner or later its private message would reveal itself. Because it was pleasant and relaxing, my rocking was bound to be tripped up, most often by my brain, which refused to allow me more than ten consecutive minutes of happiness. At the opening chords of my current favorite song, a voice would whisper, *Shouldn't you be upstairs making sure there are really one hundred and fourteen peppercorns left in that small ceramic jar? And, hey, while you're up there, you might want to check the iron and make sure it's not setting fire to the baby's bedroom*. The list of demands would grow by the moment. *What about that television antenna? Is it still set into that perfect* V, *or has one of your sisters destroyed its integrity. You know, I was just wondering how tightly the lid is screwed onto that mayonnaise jar. Let's have a look, shall we?*

I would be just on the edge of truly enjoying myself, this close to breaking the song's complex code, when my thoughts would get in the way. The trick was to bide my time until the record was no longer my favorite, to wait until it had slipped from its number-one position on the charts and fool my mind into believing I no longer cared.

I was coming to terms with "The Shadow of Your Smile" when Miss Chestnut arrived. She rang the bell, and I cracked open my bedroom door, watching as my mother invited her in.

"You'll have to forgive me for these boxes." My mother flicked 35
her cigarette out the door and into the littered yard. "They're filled with crap, every last one of them, but God forbid we throw anything away. Oh no, we can't do that! My husband's saved it all: every last Green Stamp and coupon, every outgrown bathing suit and scrap of linoleum, it's all right here along with the rocks and knotted sticks he swears look just like his old department head or associate district manager or some goddamned thing." She mopped at her forehead with a wadded paper towel. "Anyway, to hell with it. You look like I need a drink, scotch all right?"

Miss Chestnut's eyes brightened. "I really shouldn't but, oh, why not?" She followed my mother up the stairs. "Just a drop with ice, no water."

I tried rocking in bed, but the sound of laughter drew me to the top of the landing, where from my vantage point behind an oversized wardrobe box, I watched the two women discuss my behavior.

"Oh, you mean the touching," my mother said. She studied the ashtray that sat before her on the table, narrowing her eyes much like a cat catching sight of a squirrel. Her look of fixed concentration suggested that nothing else mattered. Time had stopped, and she was deaf to the sounds of the rattling fan and my sisters' squabbling out in the driveway. She opened her mouth just slightly, running her tongue over her upper lip, and then she inched forward, her index finger prodding the ashtray as though it were a sleeping thing she was trying to wake. I had never seen myself in action, but a sharp, stinging sense of recognition told me that my mother's impersonation had been accurate.

"Priceless!" Miss Chestnut laughed, clasping her hands in delight. "Oh, that's very good, you've captured him perfectly. Bravo, I give you an A-plus."

"God only knows where he gets it from," my mother said. "He's 40
probably down in his room right this minute, counting his eyelashes or gnawing at the pulls on his dresser. One, two o'clock in the morning and he'll still be at it, rattling around the house to poke the laundry hamper or press his face against the refrigerator

door. The kid's wound too tight, but he'll come out of it. So, what do you say, another scotch, Katherine?"

Now she was Katherine. Another few drinks and she'd probably be joining us for our summer vacation. How easy it was for adults to bond over a second round of cocktails. I returned to my bed, cranking up the radio so as not to be distracted by the sound of their cackling. Because Miss Chestnut was here in my home, I knew it was only a matter of time before the voices would order me to enter the kitchen and make a spectacle of myself. Maybe I'd have to suck on the broom handle or stand on the table to touch the overhead light fixture, but whatever was demanded of me, I had no choice but to do it. The song that played on the radio posed no challenge whatsoever, the lyric as clear as if I'd written it myself. "Well, I think I'm going out of my head," the man sang, "yes, I think I'm going out of my head."

Following Miss Chestnut's visit, my father attempted to cure me with a series of threats. "You touch your nose to that windshield one more time and I'll guarantee you'll wish you hadn't," he said driving home from the grocery store with a lapful of rejected, out-of-state coupons. It was virtually impossible for me to ride in the passenger seat of a car and not press my nose against the windshield, and now that the activity had been forbidden, I wanted it more than anything. I tried closing my eyes, hoping that might eliminate my desire, but found myself thinking that perhaps *he* was the one who should close his eyes. So what if I wanted to touch my nose to the windshield? Who was it hurting? Why was it that he could repeatedly worry his change and bite his lower lip without the threat of punishment? My mother smoked and Miss Chestnut massaged her waist twenty, thirty times a day — and here *I* couldn't press my nose against the windshield of a car? I opened my eyes, defiant, but when he caught me moving toward my target, my father slammed on the brakes.

"You like that, did you?" He handed me a golf towel to wipe the blood from my nose. "Did you like the feel of that?"

Like was too feeble for what I felt. I loved it. If mashed with the right amount of force, a blow to the nose can be positively narcotic. Touching objects satisfied a mental itch, but the task involved a great deal of movement: run upstairs, cross the room, remove a shoe. I soon found those same urges could be fulfilled within the confines of my own body. Punching myself in the nose was a good place to start, but the practice was dropped when I began rolling my eyes deep in their sockets, an exercise that produced quick jolts of dull, intoxicating pain.

"I know exactly what you're talking about," my mother said to 45
Mrs. Shatz, my visiting fourth-grade teacher. "The eyes rolling every which way, it's like talking to a slot machine. Hopefully, one day he'll pay off, but until then, what do you say we have ourselves another glass of wine?"

"Hey, sport," my father said, "if you're trying to get a good look at the contents of your skull, I can tell you right now that you're wasting your time. There's nothing there to look at, and these report cards prove it."

He was right. I had my nose pressed to the door, the carpet, and the windshield but not, apparently, to the grindstone. School held no interest whatsoever. I spent my days waiting to return to the dark bedroom of our new house, where I could roll my eyes, listen to the radio, and rock in peace.

I took to violently shaking my head, startled by the feel of my brain slamming against the confines of my skull. It felt so good and took so little time; just a few quick jerks and I was satisfied for up to forty-five seconds at a time.

"Have a seat and let me get you something cool to drink." My mother would leave my fifth- and then my sixth-grade teachers standing in the breakfast nook while she stepped into the kitchen to crack open a tray of ice. "I'm guessing you're here about the head-shaking, am I right?" she'd shout. "That's my boy, all right, no flies on him." She suggested my teachers interpret my jerking head as a nod of agreement. "That's what I do, and now I've got him washing the dishes for the next five years. I ask, he yanks his head, and it's settled. Do me a favor, though, and just don't hold him after five o'clock. I need him at home to straighten up and make the beds before his father gets home."

This was part of my mother's act. She played the ringleader, 50
blowing the whistle and charming the crowd with her jokes and exaggerated stories. When company came, she often pretended to forget the names of her six children. "Hey, George, or Agnes, whatever your name is, how about running into the bedroom and finding my cigarette lighter." She noticed my tics and habits but

was never shamed or seriously bothered by any of them. Her observations would be collected and delivered as part of a routine that bore little resemblance to our lives.

"It's a real stretch, but I'm betting you're here about the tiny voices," she said, offering a glass of sherry to my visiting seventh-grade teacher. "I'm thinking of either taking him to an exorcist or buying him a doll so he can bring home some money as a ventriloquist."

It had come out of nowhere, my desperate urge to summon high-pitched noises from the back of my throat. These were not words, but sounds that satisfied an urge I'd never before realized. The sounds were delivered not in my voice but in that of a thimble-sized, temperamental diva clinging to the base of my uvula. "Eeeeeeeee — ummmmmmmmmmmm — ahhhh — ahhh — meeeeeeee." I was a host to these wailings but lacked the ability to control them. When I cried out in class, the teachers would turn from their blackboards with increasingly troubled expressions. "Is someone rubbing a balloon? Who's making that noise?"

I tried making up excuses, but everything sounded implausible. "There's a bee living in my throat." Or "If I don't exercise my vocal cords every three minutes, there's a good chance I'll never swallow again." The noise-making didn't replace any of my earlier habits, it was just another addition to what had become a freakish collection of tics. Worse than the constant yelps and twitchings was the fear that tomorrow might bring something even worse, that I would wake up with the urge to jerk other people's heads. I might go for days without rolling my eyes, but it would all come back the moment my father said, "See, I knew you could quit if you just put your mind to it. Now, if you can just keep your head still and stop making those noises, you'll be set."

Set for what? I wondered. Often while rocking, I would imagine my career as a movie star. There I was attending the premiere beneath a floodlit sky, a satin scarf tied just so around my throat. I understood that most actors probably didn't interrupt a love scene to press their noses against the camera or wail a quick "Eeeeeee — ahhhhhhh" during a dramatic monologue, but in my case the world would be willing to make an exception. "This is a moving and touching film," the papers would report. "An electrifying, eye-popping performance that has audiences squealing and the critics nodding, 'Oscar, Oscar, Oscar.' "

I'd like to think that some of my nervous habits faded during 55
high school, but my class pictures tell a different story. "Draw in the missing eyeballs and this one might not be so bad," my mother would say. In group shots I was easily identified as the blur in the back row. For a time I thought that if I accompanied my habits with an outlandish wardrobe, I might be viewed as eccentric rather than just plain retarded. I was wrong. Only a confirmed idiot would wander the halls of my high school dressed in a floor-length caftan; as for the countless medallions that hung from around my neck, I might as well have worn a cowbell. They clanged and jangled with every jerk of my head, calling attention when without them I might have passed unnoticed. My oversized glasses did nothing but provide a clearer view of my rolling, twitching eyes, and the clunky platform shoes left lumps when used to discreetly tap my forehead. I was a mess.

I could be wrong, but according to my calculations, I got exactly fourteen minutes of sleep during my entire first year of college. I'd always had my own bedroom, a meticulously clean and well-ordered place where I could practice my habits in private. Now I would have a roommate, some complete stranger spoiling my routine with his God-given right to exist. The idea was mortifying, and I arrived at the university in full tilt.

"The doctors tell me that if I knock it around hard enough, there's a good chance the brain tumor will shrink to the point where they won't have to operate," I said the first time my roommate caught me jerking my head. "Meanwhile, these other specialists have me doing these eye exercises to strengthen what they call the 'corneal fibers,' whatever that means. They've got me coming and going, but what can you do, right? Anyway, you go ahead and settle in. I think I'll just test this electrical socket with a butter knife and re-arrange a few of the items on my dresser. Eeeee-sy does it. That's what I always s-ahhhhhhh."

It was hard enough coming up with excuses, but the real agony came when I was forced to give up rocking.

"Give it a rest, Romeo," my roommate moaned the first night he heard my bedsprings creak. He thought I was masturbating, and while I wanted to set the record straight, something told me I wouldn't score any points by telling him that I was simply rocking in bed, just like any other eighteen-year-old college student. It was torture to lie there doing nothing. Even with a portable radio and earphones, there was no point listening to music unless I could sway back and forth with my head on a pillow. Rocking is basically dancing in a horizontal position, and it allowed me to practice in private what I detested in public. With my jerking head, rolling eyes, and rapid stabbing gestures, I might have been a sensation if I'd left my bed and put my tics to work on the dance floor. I should have told my roommate that I was an epileptic and left it at that. He might have charged across the room every so often to ram a Popsicle stick down my throat, but so what? I was used to picking splinters out of my tongue. *What,* I wondered, *was an average person expected to do while stretched out in a darkened room?* It felt pointless to lie there motionless and imagine a brighter life. Squinting across the cramped, cinder-block cell, I realized that an entire lifetime of wishful thinking had gotten me no further than this. There would be no cheering crowds or esteemed movie directors shouting into their bullhorns. I might have to take this harsh reality lying down, but while attempting to do so, couldn't I rock back and forth just a little bit?

60 Having memorized my roommate's course schedule, I took to rushing back to the room between classes, rocking in fitful spurts but never really enjoying it for fear he might return at any moment. Perhaps he might feel ill or decide to cut class at the last minute. I'd hear his key in the door and jump up from my bed, mashing down my wadded hair and grabbing one of the textbooks I kept on my prop table. "I'm just studying for that pottery test," I'd say. "That's all I've been up to, just sitting in this chair reading about the history of jugs." Hard as I tried, it always wound up sounding as if I were guilty of something secretive or perverse. *He* never acted in the least bit embarrassed when caught listening to one of his many heavy-metal albums, a practice far more shameful than anything I have yet to imagine. There was no other solution: I had to think of a way to get rid of this guy.

His biggest weakness appeared to be his girlfriend, whose photograph he had tacked in a place of honor above the stereo. They'd been dating since tenth grade, and while he had gone off to college, she'd stayed behind to attend a two-year nursing school in their hometown. A history of listening to Top 40 radio had left me with a ridiculous and clichéd notion of love. I had never entertained the feeling myself but knew that it meant never having to say you're sorry. It was a many-splendored thing. Love was a rose *and* a hammer. Both blind and all-seeing, it made the world go round.

My roommate thought that he and his girlfriend were strong enough to make it through the month without seeing each other, but I wasn't so sure. "I don't know that I'd trust her around all those doctors," I said. "Love fades when left untended, especially in a hospital environment. Absence might make the heart grow fonder, but love is a two-way street. Think about it."

When my roommate went out of town, I would spend the entire weekend rocking in bed and fantasizing about his tragic car accident. I envisioned him wrapped tight as a mummy, his arms and legs suspended by pulleys. "Time is a great healer," his mother would say, packing the last of his albums into a milk crate. "Two years of bed rest and he'll be as good as new. Once he gets out of the hospital, I figure I'll set him up in the living room. He likes it there."

Sometimes I would allow him to leave in one piece, imagining his joining the army or marrying his girlfriend and moving someplace warm and sunny, like Peru or Ethiopia. The important thing was that he leave this room and never come back. I'd get rid of him and then move on to the next person, and the one after that, until it was just me, rocking and jerking in private.

Two months into the semester, my roommate broke up with his 65
girlfriend. "And I'm going to spend every day and night sitting right here in this room until I figure out where I went wrong." He dabbed his moist eyes with the sleeve of his flannel shirt. "You and me, little buddy. It's just you and me and Jethro Tull from here on out. Say, what's with your head? The old tumor acting up again?"

"College is the best thing that can ever happen to you," my father used to say, and he was right, for it was there that I discovered drugs, drinking, and smoking. I'm unsure of the scientific aspects, but for some reason, my nervous habits faded about the same time I took up with cigarettes. Maybe it was coincidental or perhaps the tics retreated in the face of an adversary that, despite its health risks, is much more socially acceptable than crying out in tiny voices. Were I not smoking, I'd probably be on some sort of medication that would cost the same amount of money but deny me the accoutrements: the lighters I can thoughtlessly open and close, the ashtrays that provide me with a legitimate reason to leave my chair, and the cigarettes that calm me down while giving me something to do with my hands and mouth. It's as if I had been born to smoke, and until I realized it, my limbs were left to search for some alternative. Everything's fine as long as I know there's a cigarette in my immediate future. The people who ask me not to smoke in their cars have no idea what they're in for.

"Remember when you used to roll your eyes?" my sisters ask. "Remember the time you shook your head so hard, your glasses fell into the barbeque pit?"

At their mention I sometimes attempt to revisit my former tics and habits. Returning to my apartment late at night, I'll dare myself to press my nose against the doorknob or roll my eyes to achieve that once-satisfying ache. Maybe I'll start counting the napkins sandwiched in their plastic holder, but the exercise lacks its old urgency and I soon lose interest. I would no sooner rock in bed than play "Up, Up, and Away" sixty times straight on my record player. I could easily listen to something else an equal number of times while seated in a rocking chair, but the earlier, bedridden method fails to comfort me, as I've forgotten the code, the twitching trick needed to decipher the lyrics to that particular song. I remember only that at one time the story involved the citizens of Raleigh, North Carolina, being herded into a test balloon of my own design and making. It was rigged to explode once it reached the city limits, but the passengers were unaware of that fact. The sun shone on their faces as they lifted their heads toward the bright blue sky, giddy with excitement.

"Beautiful balloon!" they all said, gripping the handrails and climbing the staircase to their fiery destiny. "Wouldn't you like to ride?"

"Sorry, folks," I'd say, pressing my nose against the surface of 70
my ticket booth. "But I've got other duties."

For Discussion and Writing

1. Compose a list of Sedaris's tics and try to establish some general rules that make them tics and not more acceptable repeated motions, like his mother's smoking or his teacher's waist massaging.
2. As is apparent when he reads his work on the radio, Sedaris is a master storyteller. One of the things that makes his stories so effective is the way he uses humor. His essays are rarely simply funny; as is the

case with "A Plague of Tics," he uses humor in combination with other elements, to various effects — for example, as contrast or relief. List five funny moments in this essay. In what context do they appear? How do they interact with their contexts? What do you think Sedaris was trying to do with humor in each of these instances?

3. **connections** Sedaris is concerned as much, if not more, with what others think of his behaviors as with what he thinks of them. Compare Sedaris' account of the way his identity depends on how others see him to Judith Ortiz Cofer's in "The Myth of the Latin Woman: I Just Met a Girl Named María" (p. 91). How do the issues with which they are concerned, and the way they react to how they are perceived, compare?
4. "*Don't think about it,*" Sedaris tells himself when he is young. But he is unable not to obsess over his compulsions — as he says, "There must have been an off switch somewhere, but I was damned if I could find it" (par. 14). Reflect on moments in your life when you have been unable to not think about something — something that happened to you, something you did, something you are looking forward to or fearful of. When have you wished you had an off switch? What do you think it means that people are not able to simply turn their minds off?

SUSAN SONTAG

Regarding the Pain of Others

Susan Sontag (1933–2004) was an intellectual who ranged widely, writing about subjects including photography, the AIDS epidemic, and literary theory. She was also a novelist, playwright, and filmmaker. Her nonfiction books include Against Interpretation *(1966),* On Photography *(1977),* Illness as Metaphor *(1978), and* Regarding the Pain of Others *(2003); her novels include* The Volcano Lover *(1992) and* In America *(2000). "Regarding the Pain of Others," drawn from the book of the same title, demonstrates two of Sontag's greatest interests, aesthetics and politics, as much of her work has done — whether she is studying the impact of photographs of atrocity or the impact of language on the way we think about disease, Sontag's work is concerned with the way representation informs the way people think about the world. Keep an eye out as you read for the ways in which Sontag brings these two interests together here.*

Often something looks, or is felt to look, "better" in a photograph. Indeed, it is one of the functions of photography to improve the normal appearance of things. (Hence, one is always disappointed by a photograph that is not flattering.) Beautifying is one classic operation of the camera, and it tends to bleach out a moral response to what is shown. Uglifying, showing something at its worst, is a more modern function: didactic, it invites an active response. For photographs to accuse, and possibly to alter conduct, they must shock.

An example: A few years ago, the public health authorities in Canada, where it had been estimated that smoking kills 45,000 people a year, decided to supplement the warning printed on every pack of cigarettes with a shock photograph — of cancerous lungs, or a stroke-clotted brain, or a damaged heart, or a bloody mouth in acute periodontal distress. A pack with such a picture accompanying the warning about the deleterious effects of smoking would be 60 times more likely to inspire smokers to quit, a research study had somehow calculated, than a pack with only the verbal warning.

Let's assume this is true. Still one might wonder, for how long? Does shock have term limits? Right now the smokers of Canada are recoiling in disgust, if they do look at these pictures. Will those smoking five years from now still be upset? Shock can become familiar. Shock can wear off. Even if it doesn't, one can *not* look. People have means to defend themselves against what is upsetting — in this instance, unpleasant information for those wishing to continue to smoke. This seems normal, that is, adaptive. As one can become habituated to horror in real life, one can become habituated to the horror of certain images.

Yet there are cases where repeated exposure to what shocks, saddens, appalls does not use up a full-hearted response. Habituation is not automatic, for images (portable, insertable) obey different rules than real life. Representations of the Crucifixion do not become banal to believers, if they really are believers. This is even more true of staged representations. Performances of *Chushingura*, probably the best-known narrative in all of Japanese culture, can be counted on to make a Japanese audience sob when Lord Asano admires the beauty of the cherry blossoms on his way to where he must commit seppuku — sob each time, no matter how often they have followed the story (as a Kabuki or Bunraku play, as a film); the *ta'ziyah* drama of the betrayal and murder of Imam Hussayn does not cease to bring an Iranian audience to tears no matter how many times they have seen the martyrdom enacted. On the contrary. They weep, in part, because they have seen it many times. People want to weep. Pathos, in the form of a narrative, does not wear out.

But do people want to be horrified? Probably not. Still, there 5
are pictures whose power does not abate, in part because one cannot look at them often. Pictures of the ruin of faces that will always testify to a great iniquity survived, at a cost: the faces of horribly disfigured First World War veterans who survived the inferno of the trenches; the faces melted and thickened with scar tissue of survivors of the American atomic bombs dropped on Hiroshima and Nagasaki; the faces cleft by machete blows of Tutsi survivors of the genocidal rampage launched by the Hutus in Rwanda — is it correct to say that people get *used* to these?

Indeed, the very notion of atrocity, of war crime, is associated with the expectation of photographic evidence. Such evidence is, usually, of something posthumous: the remains, as it were — the mounds of skulls in Pol Pot's Cambodia, the mass graves in Guatemala and El Salvador, Bosnia and Kosovo. And this posthumous reality is often the keenest of summations. As Hannah Arendt pointed out soon after the end of the Second World War, all the photographs and newsreels of the concentration camps are misleading because they show the camps at the moment the Allied troops marched in. What makes the images unbearable — the piles of corpses, the skeletal survivors — was not at all typical for the camps, which, when they were functioning, exterminated their inmates systematically (by gas, not starvation and illness), then immediately cremated them. And photographs echo photographs: It was inevitable that the photographs of emaciated Bosnian prisoners at Omarska, the Serb death camp created in northern Bosnia in 1992, would recall memories of the photographs taken in the Nazi death camps in 1945.

Photographs of atrocity illustrate as well as corroborate. Bypassing disputes about exactly how many were killed (numbers are often inflated at first), the photograph gives the indelible sample. The illustrative function of photographs leaves opinions, prejudices, fantasies, misinformation untouched. The information that many fewer Palestinians died in the assault on Jenin than had been claimed by Palestinian officials (as the Israelis had said all along) made much less impact than the pictures of the razed center of the refugee camp. And, of course, atrocities that are not secured in our minds by well-known photographic images, or of which we simply have had very few images — the total extermination of the Herero people in Namibia decreed by the German colonial administration in 1904; the Japanese onslaught in China, notably the massacre of nearly 400,000 and the rape of 80,000 Chinese in December 1937, the so-called Rape of Nanking; the rape of some 130,000 women and girls (10,000 of whom committed suicide) by victorious Soviet soldiers unleashed by their commanding officers in Berlin in 1945 — seem more remote. These are memories that few have cared to claim.

The familiarity of certain photographs builds our sense of the present and immediate past. Photographs lay down routes of reference, and serve as totems of causes: Sentiment is more likely to crystalize around a photograph than around a verbal slogan. And photographs help construct — and revise — our sense of a more distant past, with the posthumous shocks engineered by the circulation of hitherto unknown photographs. Photographs that everyone recognizes are now a constituent part of what a society chooses to think about, or declares that it has chosen to think about. It calls these ideas "memories," and that is, over the long run, a fiction. Strictly speaking, there is no such thing as collective memory — part of the same family of spurious notions as collective guilt. But there is collective instruction.

All memory is individual, unreproducible — it dies with each person. What is called collective memory is not a remembering but a stipulating: that *this* is important, and this is the story of how it happened, with the pictures that lock the story in our minds. Ideologies create substantiating archives of images, representative images, which encapsulate common ideas of significance and trigger predictable thoughts, feelings. Poster-ready photographs — the mushroom cloud of an A-bomb test, Martin Luther King, Jr., speaking at the Lincoln Memorial in Washington, D.C., the astronaut on the moon — are the visual equivalent of sound bites. They commemorate, in no less blunt fashion than postage stamps, Important Historical Moments; indeed, the triumphalist ones (the picture of the A-bomb excepted) become postage stamps. Fortunately, there is no one signature picture of the Nazi death camps.

As art has been redefined during a century of modernism as 10
whatever is destined to be enshrined in some kind of museum, so it is now the destiny of many photographic troves to be exhibited and preserved in museum-like institutions. Among such archives of horror, the photographs of genocide have undergone the greatest institutional development. The point of creating public repositories for these and other relics is to ensure that the crimes they depict will continue to figure in people's consciousness. This is called remembering, but in fact it is a good deal more than that.

The memory museum in its current proliferation is a product of a way of thinking about, and mourning, the destruction of European Jewry in the 1930s and 1940s, which came to institutional fruition in Yad Vashem in Jerusalem, the Holocaust Memorial Museum in Washington, D.C., and the Jewish Museum in Berlin. Photographs and other memorabilia of the Shoah have been committed to a perpetual recirculation, to ensure that what they show will be remembered. Photographs of the suffering and martyrdom of a people are more than reminders of death, of failure, of victimization. They invoke the miracle of survival. To aim at the perpetuation of memories means, inevitably, that one has undertaken the task of continually renewing, of creating, memories — aided, above all, by the impress of iconic photographs. People want to be able to visit — and refresh — their memories. Now many victim peoples want a memory museum, a temple that houses a comprehensive, chronologically organized, illustrated narrative of their sufferings. Armenians, for example, have long been clamoring for a museum in Washington to institutionalize the memory of the genocide of Armenian people by the Ottoman Turks. But why is there not already, in the nation's capital, which happens to be a city whose population is overwhelmingly African American, a Museum of the History of Slavery? Indeed, there is no Museum of the History of Slavery — the whole story, starting with the slave trade in Africa itself, not just selected parts, such as the Underground Railroad — anywhere in the United States. This, it seems, is a memory judged too dangerous to social stability to activate and to create. The Holocaust Memorial Museum and the future Armenian Genocide Museum and Memorial are about events that didn't happen in America, so the memory-work doesn't risk rousing an embittered domestic population against authority. To have a museum chronicling the great crime that was African slavery in the United States of America would be to acknowledge that the evil was *here.* Americans prefer to picture the evil that was *there,* and from which the United States — a unique nation, one without any certifiably wicked leaders throughout its entire history — is exempt. That this country, like every other country, has its tragic past does not sit well with the founding, and still all-powerful, belief in American exceptionalism. The national consensus on American history as a history of progress is a new setting for distressing photographs — one that focuses our attention on wrongs, both here and elsewhere, for which America sees itself as the solution or cure.

For Discussion and Writing

1. What does Sontag say photographs have to be able to do to have an impact on people's consciences and behavior?
2. While "Regarding the Pain of Others" has certain analytic points to make about the way photographs of atrocity work on viewers, it is hard to say from this excerpt that she is arguing one central point;

even the title's first word points to an exploration rather than an argument. However, she does make a number of claims. How does she make them? What kind of evidence does she use to support them? And how does she connect these different claims?

3. **connections** Though William F. Buckley Jr. (in "Why Don't We Complain?," p. 76) and Sontag are writing about very different kinds of phenomena (and are very different kinds of writers), both are concerned with the reasons people are and are not roused to action by events. Compare the way they think and write about their concerns. Why do people act or not act in each of these essays? Why? What might the nature of these authors' concerns say about them?

4. Sontag writes of the power of narrative to escape habituation (par. 4), but then, after offering a short but powerful list of twentieth-century atrocities (par. 7), Sontag claims that photographs are more powerful than words (par. 8). In effect, Sontag's own narrative of atrocities follows her first claim but contradicts her second. Do you think stories, fictional and nonfictional, can attest just as powerfully to atrocity as photographs can? Why or why not? Can you think of any examples?

ELIZABETH CADY STANTON

Declaration of Sentiments and Resolutions

Born in 1815 in Johnstown, New York, Elizabeth Cady Stanton was a leader of the American women's rights movement of the mid- and late-nineteenth century. An organizer of the Seneca Falls, New York, convention in 1848, she was active in trying to obtain for women the right to vote, to divorce, and to be equal to men under the law. Active also in abolition, Stanton lectured widely on women's suffrage and edited a weekly newspaper focusing on women's rights issues.

*The "Declaration of Sentiments and Resolutions" was produced at Seneca Falls by Stanton and others. When Mary Wollstonecraft wrote her own women's rights document in 1792, she alluded to the "Vindication of the Rights of Man," a defense of the French Revolution, by calling it "Vindication of the Rights of Woman." As you read the Seneca Falls declaration, think about its parallels to the American Declaration of Independence (**p. 187**) and think about why Stanton decided not to use the word* independence *in the document.*

When, in the course of human events, it becomes necessary for one portion of the family of man to assume among the people of the earth a position different from that which they have hitherto occupied, but one to which the laws of nature and of nature's God entitle them, a decent respect to the opinions of mankind requires that they should declare the causes that impel them to such a course.

We hold these truths to be self-evident: that all men and women are created equal; that they are endowed by their Creator with certain inalienable rights; that among these are life, liberty, and the pursuit of happiness; that to secure these rights governments are instituted, deriving their just powers from the consent of the governed. Whenever any form of government becomes destructive of these ends, it is the right of those who suffer from it to refuse allegiance to it, and to insist upon the institution of a new government, laying its foundation on such principles, and organizing its powers in such form, as to them shall seem most likely to effect their safety and happiness. Prudence indeed, will dictate that governments long established should not be changed for light and transient causes; and accordingly all experience hath shown that mankind are more disposed to suffer, while evils are sufferable, than to right themselves by abolishing the forms to which they were accustomed. But when a long train of abuses and usurpations, pursuing invariably the same object evinces a design to reduce them under absolute despotism, it is their duty to throw off such government, and to provide new guards for their future security. Such has been the patient sufferance of the women under this government, and such is now the necessity which constrains them to demand the equal station to which they are entitled.

The history of mankind is a history of repeated injuries and usurpations on the part of man toward woman, having in direct object the establishment of an absolute tyranny over her. To prove this, let facts be submitted to a candid world.

He has never permitted her to exercise her inalienable right to the elective franchise.

He has compelled her to submit to laws, in the formation of 5
which she had no voice.

He has withheld from her rights which are given to the most ignorant and degraded men — both natives and foreigners.

Having deprived her of this first right of a citizen, the elective franchise, thereby leaving her without representation in the halls of legislation, he has oppressed her on all sides.

He has made her, if married, in the eye of the law, civilly dead.

He has taken from her all right in property, even to the wages she earns.

He has made her, morally, an irresponsible being, as she can 10
commit many crimes with impunity, provided they be done in the presence of her husband. In the covenant of marriage, she is compelled to promise obedience to her husband, he becoming, to all intents and purposes, her master — the law giving him power to deprive her of her liberty, and to administer chastisement.

He has so framed the laws of divorce, as to what shall be the proper causes, and in case of separation, to whom the guardianship of the children shall be given, as to be wholly regardless of the happiness of women — the law, in all cases, going upon a false supposition of the supremacy of man, and giving all power into his hands.

After depriving her of all rights as a married woman, if single, and the owner of property, he has taxed her to support a government which recognizes her only when her property can be made profitable to it.

He has monopolized nearly all the profitable employments, and from those she is permitted to follow, she receives but a scanty remuneration. He closes against her all the avenues to wealth and distinction which he considers most honorable to himself. As a teacher of theology, medicine, or law, she is not known.

He has denied her the facilities for obtaining a thorough education, all colleges being closed against her.

He allows her in Church, as well as State, but a subordinate 15
position, claiming Apostolic authority for her exclusion from the ministry, and, with some exceptions, from any public participation in the affairs of the Church.

He has created a false public sentiment by giving to the world a different code of morals for men and women, by which moral delinquencies which exclude women from society, are not only tolerated, but deemed of little account in man.

He has usurped the prerogative of Jehovah himself, claiming it as his right to assign for her a sphere of action, when that belongs to her conscience and to her God.

He has endeavored, in every way that he could, to destroy her confidence in her own powers, to lessen her self-respect, and to make her willing to lead a dependent and abject life.

Now, in view of this entire disfranchisement of one-half the people of this country, their social and religious degradation — in view of the unjust laws above mentioned, and because women do feel themselves aggrieved, oppressed, and fraudulently deprived of their most sacred rights, we insist that they have immediate admission to all the rights and privileges which belong to them as citizens of the United States.

In entering upon the great work before us, we anticipate no 20
small amount of misconception, misrepresentation, and ridicule; but we shall use every instrumentality within our power to effect our object. We shall employ agents, circulate tracts, petition the

State and National legislatures, and endeavor to enlist the pulpit and the press in our behalf. We hope this Convention will be followed by a series of Conventions embracing every part of the country.

For Discussion and Writing

1. What is the analogy Stanton sets up between Revolution-era Americans and women of her time?
2. Read Stanton's argument through her title: Why does she declare sentiments and resolutions? (Start by defining both terms.) How does she get from the former to the latter?
3. **connections** Compare Stanton's declaration to Thomas Jefferson's declaration (p. 187). How does she use both the form and the historical significance of the original text to make her point?
4. What group today could write a declaration akin to Jefferson's and Stanton's? Write its declaration, playing off of these earlier declarations.

BRENT STAPLES

Just Walk on By: Black Men and Public Space

Brent Staples, born in 1951 in Chester, Pennsylvania, has a doctorate in psychology and has taught, but he has built a career as a reporter and columnist. He is on the editorial board of the New York Times *where he writes on education, culture, and politics. He has also contributed to* Ms., Harper's, *and other magazines. Staples's memoir,* Parallel Time: Growing Up in Black and White *(1994), tells the story of his youth and that of his younger brother, whose violent life followed a very different path.*

"Just Walk on By" originally appeared in Ms. *As you read, think about why this piece might be appropriate for a publication intended primarily for women.*

My first victim was a woman — white, well dressed, probably in her early twenties. I came upon her late one evening on a deserted street in Hyde Park, a relatively affluent neighborhood in an otherwise mean, impoverished section of Chicago. As I swung onto the avenue behind her, there seemed to be a discreet, uninflammatory distance between us. Not so. She cast back a worried glance. To her, the youngish black man — a broad six feet two inches with a beard and billowing hair, both hands shoved into the pockets of a bulky military jacket — seemed menacingly close. After a few more quick glimpses, she picked up her pace and was soon running in earnest. Within seconds she disappeared into a cross street.

That was more than a decade ago, I was twenty-two years old, a graduate student newly arrived at the University of Chicago. It was in the echo of that terrified woman's footfalls that I first began to know the unwieldy inheritance I'd come into — the ability to alter public space in ugly ways. It was clear that she thought herself the quarry of a mugger, a rapist, or worse. Suffering a bout of insomnia, however, I was stalking sleep, not defenseless wayfarers. As a softy who is scarcely able to take a knife to a raw chicken — let alone hold one to a person's throat — I was surprised, embarrassed, and dismayed all at once. Her flight made me feel like an accomplice in tyranny. It also made it clear that I was indistinguishable from the muggers who occasionally seeped into the area from the surrounding ghetto. That first encounter, and those that followed, signified that a vast, unnerving gulf lay between nighttime pedestrians — particularly women — and me. And I soon gathered that being perceived as dangerous is a hazard in itself. I only needed to turn a corner into a dicey situation, or crowd some frightened, armed person in a foyer somewhere, or make an errant move after being pulled over by a policeman. Where fear and weapons meet — and they often do in urban America — there is always the possibility of death.

In that first year, my first away from my hometown, I was to become thoroughly familiar with the language of fear. At dark, shadowy intersections, I could cross in front of a car stopped at a traffic light and elicit the *thunk, thunk, thunk, thunk* of the driver — black, white, male, or female — hammering down the door locks. On less traveled streets after dark, I grew accustomed to but never comfortable with people crossing to the other side of the street rather than pass me. Then there were the standard unpleasantries with policemen, doormen, bouncers, cabdrivers, and others whose business it is to screen out troublesome individuals *before* there is any nastiness.

I moved to New York nearly two years ago and I have remained an avid night walker. In central Manhattan, the near-constant crowd cover minimizes tense one-on-one street encounters. Elsewhere — in SoHo, for example, where sidewalks are narrow and tightly spaced buildings shut out the sky — things can get very taut indeed.

After dark, on the warrenlike streets of Brooklyn where I live, 5
I often see women who fear the worst from me. They seem to have set their faces on neutral, and with their purse straps strung across their chests bandolier-style, they forge ahead as though bracing themselves against being tackled. I understand, of course, that the danger they perceive is not a hallucination. Women are particularly vulnerable to street violence, and young black males are drastically overrepresented among the perpetrators of that

violence. Yet these truths are no solace against the kind of alienation that comes of being ever the suspect, a fearsome entity with whom pedestrians avoid making eye contact.

It is not altogether clear to me how I reached the ripe old age of twenty-two without being conscious of the lethality nighttime pedestrians attributed to me. Perhaps it was because in Chester, Pennsylvania, the small, angry industrial town where I came of age in the 1960s, I was scarcely noticeable against a backdrop of gang warfare, street knifings, and murders. I grew up one of the good boys, had perhaps a half-dozen fistfights. In retrospect, my shyness of combat has clear sources.

As a boy, I saw countless tough guys locked away; I have since buried several, too. They were babies, really — a teenage cousin, a brother of twenty-two, a childhood friend in his mid-twenties — all gone down in episodes of bravado played out in the streets. I came to doubt the virtues of intimidation early on. I chose, perhaps unconsciously, to remain a shadow — timid, but a survivor.

The fearsomeness mistakenly attributed to me in public places often has a perilous flavor. The most frightening of these confusions occurred in the late 1970s and early 1980s, when I worked as a journalist in Chicago. One day, rushing into the office of a magazine I was writing for with a deadline story in hand, I was mistaken for a burglar. The office manager called security and, with an ad hoc posse, pursued me through the labyrinthine halls, nearly to my editor's door. I had no way of proving who I was. I could only move briskly toward the company of someone who knew me.

Another time I was on assignment for a local paper and killing time before an interview. I entered a jewelry store on the city's affluent Near North Side. The proprietor excused herself and returned with an enormous red Doberman pinscher straining at the end of a leash. She stood, the dog extended toward me, silent to my questions, her eyes bulging nearly out of her head. I took a cursory look around, nodded, and bade her good night.

Relatively speaking, however, I never fared as badly as another 10
black male journalist. He went to nearby Waukegan, Illinois, a couple of summers ago to work on a story about a murderer who was born there. Mistaking the reporter for the killer, police officers hauled him from his car at gunpoint and but for his press credentials would probably have tried to book him. Such episodes are not uncommon. Black men trade tales like this all the time.

Over the years, I learned to smother the rage I felt at so often being taken for a criminal. Not to do so would surely have led to madness. I now take precautions to make myself less threatening. I move about with care, particularly late in the evening. I give a wide berth to nervous people on subway platforms during the wee hours, particularly when I have exchanged business clothes for jeans. If I happen to be entering a building behind some people who appear skittish, I may walk by, letting them clear the lobby before I return, so as not to seem to be following them. I have been calm and extremely congenial on those rare occasions when I've been pulled over by the police.

And on late-evening constitutionals I employ what has proved to be an excellent tension-reducing measure: I whistle melodies from Beethoven and Vivaldi and the more popular classical composers. Even steely New Yorkers hunching toward nighttime destinations seem to relax, and occasionally they even join in the tune. Virtually everybody seems to sense that a mugger wouldn't be warbling bright, sunny selections from Vivaldi's *Four Seasons*. It is my equivalent of the cowbell that hikers wear when they know they are in bear country.

For Discussion and Writing

1. How does Staples describe himself? How is he sometimes seen by others?
2. Staples begins his essay by discussing the effect of his presence on another person. However, others' reactions to his presence affect him in return, and he spends much of the essay explaining the emotional and practical effects he experiences as a consequence of his interactions. How is the complication and paradox of these situations expressed by the last sentence about Staples's whistling classical music being the "equivalent of the cowbell that hikers wear when they know they are in bear country" (par. 12)?
3. **connections** Compare Staples's reaction to race-inflected encounters to James Baldwin's reaction to the encounter in the restaurant in "Notes of a Native Son" (p. 50). What might the differences tell us about the individuals and their respective times?
4. The person with whom you find yourself identifying in a story sometimes depends on your own identity. With whom did you identify at the start of Staples's essay, and how did it affect your reading of the full piece?

JONATHAN SWIFT

A Modest Proposal

Born in 1667 in Ireland and raised there by English parents, Jonathan Swift was dean of St. Patrick's Cathedral in Dublin and a prolific poet, satirist, and pamphleteer. While he is best known today for his satiric novel Gulliver's Travels *(1726) and for "A Modest Proposal," his political pamphlets and essays on behalf of Irish causes had great impact and are themselves masterpieces of political irony. Swift's work is thought by some to reveal a misanthropic, skeptical, and hopeless heart, but there always exists in his writing the possibility of alternatives, the hope for improvement. In "A Modest Proposal," Swift writes, "Therefore I repeat, let no man talk to me of these and the like expedients, till he has at least some glimpse of hope that there will be ever some hearty and sincere attempt to put them in practice" (par. 30). As you read this essay and try to tease out Swift's messages, keep this idea in mind.*

In 1729, when "A Modest Proposal" was published, years of drought were exacerbated by a crop failure that caused thousands of Irish to starve to death, and this suffering was essentially ignored by English landowners. "A Modest Proposal" is Swift's response to this tragedy.

It is a melancholy object to those who walk through this great town or travel in the country, when they see the streets, the roads, and cabin doors, crowded with beggars of the female sex, followed by three, four, or six children, all in rags and importuning every passenger for an alms. These mothers instead of being able to work for their honest livelihood, are forced to employ all their time in strolling to beg sustenance for their helpless infants: who as they grow up either turn thieves for want of work, or leave their dear native country to fight for the pretender in Spain, or sell themselves to the Barbadoes.

I think it is agreed by all parties that this prodigious number of children in the arms, or on the backs, or at the heels of their mothers, and frequently of their fathers, is in the present deplorable state of the kingdom a very great additional grievance; and, therefore, whoever could find out a fair, cheap, and easy method of making these children sound, useful members of the commonwealth, would deserve so well of the public as to have his statute set up for a preserver of the nation.

But my intention is very far from being confined to provide only for the children of professed beggars; it is of a much greater extent, and shall take in the whole number of infants at a certain age who are born of parents in effect as little able to support them as those who demand our charity in the streets.

As to my own part, having turned my thoughts for many years upon this important subject, and maturely weighed the several schemes of our projectors, I have always found them grossly mistaken in their computation. It is true, a child just dropped from its dam may be supported by her milk for a solar year, with little other nourishment; at most not above the value of 2s., which the mother may certainly get, or the value in scraps, by her lawful occupation of begging; and it is exactly at one year old that I propose to provide for them in such a manner as instead of being a charge upon their parents or the parish, or wanting food and raiment for the rest of their lives, they shall on the contrary contribute to the feeding, and partly to the clothing, of many thousands.

There is likewise another great advantage in my scheme, that 5
it will prevent those voluntary abortions, and that horrid practice of women murdering their bastard children, alas! too frequent among us! sacrificing the poor innocent babes I doubt more to avoid the expense than the shame, which would move tears and pity in the most savage and inhuman breast.

The number of souls in this kingdom being usually reckoned one million and a half, of these I calculate there may be about 200,000 couple whose wives are breeders; from which number I subtract 30,000 couple who are able to maintain their own children (although I apprehend there cannot be so many, under the present distress of the kingdom); but this being granted, there will remain 170,000 breeders. I again subtract 50,000 for those women who miscarry, or whose children die by accident or disease within the year. There only remain 120,000 children of poor parents annually born. The question therefore is, how this number shall be reared and provided for? which, as I have already said, under the present situation of affairs, is utterly impossible by all the methods hitherto proposed. For we can neither employ them in handicraft of agriculture; we neither build houses (I mean in the country) nor cultivate land; they can very seldom pick up a livelihood by stealing, till they arrive at six years old, except where they are of towardly parts, although I confess they learn the rudiments much earlier; during which time they can, however, be properly looked upon only as probationers; as I have been informed by a principal gentleman in the county of Cavan, who protested to me that he never knew above one or two instances under the age of six, even in a part of the kingdom so renowned for the quickest proficiency in that art.

I am assured by our merchants, that a boy or a girl before twelve years old is no salable commodity; and even when they come to this age they will not yield above 3£. or 3£. 2s. 6d. at most on the exchange; which cannot turn to account either to the parents or kingdom, the charge of nutriment and rags having been at least four times that value.

I shall now therefore humbly propose my own thoughts, which I hope will not be liable to the least objection.

I have been assured by a very knowing American of my acquaintance in London, that a young healthy child well nursed is at a year old a most delicious, nourishing, and wholesome food, whether stewed, roasted, baked, or broiled; and I make no doubt that it will equally serve in a fricassee or a ragout.

I do therefore humbly offer it to public consideration that of 10
the 120,000 children already computed, 20,000 may be reserved for breed, whereof only one-fourth part to be males; which is more than we allow to sheep, black cattle, or swine; and my reason is, that these children are seldom the fruits of marriage, a circumstance not much regarded by our savages; therefore one male will be sufficient to serve four females. That the remaining 100,000 may, at a year old, be offered in sale to the persons of quality and fortune through the kingdom; always advising the mother to let them suck plentifully in the last month, so as to render them plump and fat for a good table. A child will make two dishes at an entertainment for friends; and when the family dines alone, the fore and hind quarter will make a reasonable dish, and seasoned with a little pepper or salt will be very good boiled on the fourth day, especially in winter.

I have reckoned upon a medium that a child just born will weigh 12 pounds, and in a solar year, if tolerably nursed, will increase to 28 pounds.

I grant this food will be somewhat dear, and therefore very proper for landlords, who, as they have already devoured most of the parents, seem to have the best title to the children.

Infants' flesh will be in season throughout the year, but more plentiful in March, and a little before and after: for we are told by a grave author, an eminent French physician, that fish being a prolific diet, there are more children born in Roman Catholic countries about nine months after Lent than at any other season; therefore, reckoning a year after Lent, the markets will be more glutted than usual, because the number of popish infants is at least three to one in this kingdom: and therefore it will have one other collateral advantage, by lessening the number of papists among us.

I have already computed the charge of nursing a beggar's child (in which list I reckon all cottagers, laborers, and four-fifths of the farmers) to be about 2s. per annum, rags included; and I believe no gentleman would repine to give 10s. for the carcass of a good fat child, which, as I have said, will make four dishes of excellent nutritive meat, when he has only some particular friend or his own family to dine with him. Thus the squire will learn to be a good landlord, and grow popular among the tenants; the mother will have 8s. net profit, and be fit for work till she produces another child.

Those who are more thrifty (as I must confess the times 15
require) may flay the carcass; the skin of which artificially dressed will make admirable gloves for ladies, and summer boots for fine gentlemen.

As to our city of Dublin, shambles may be appointed for this purpose in the most convenient parts of it, and butchers we may be assured will not be wanting: although I rather recommend buying the children alive, and dressing them hot from the knife as we do roasting pigs.

A very worthy person, a true lover of his country, and whose virtues I highly esteem, was lately pleased in discoursing on this matter to offer a refinement upon my scheme. He said that many gentlemen of this kingdom, having of late destroyed their deer, he conceived that the want of venison might be well supplied by the bodies of young lads and maidens, not exceeding fourteen years of age nor under twelve; so great a number of both sexes in every country being now ready to starve for want of work and service; and these to be disposed of by their parents, if alive, or otherwise by their nearest relations. But with due deference to so excellent a friend and so deserving a patriot, I cannot be altogether in his sentiments; for as to the males, my American acquaintance assured me from frequent experience that their flesh was generally tough and lean, like that of our schoolboys by continual exercise, and their taste disagreeable; and to fatten them would not answer the charge. Then as to the females, it would, I think, with humble submission be a loss to the public, because they soon would become breeders themselves: and besides, it is not improbable that some scrupulous people might be apt to censure such a practice (although indeed very unjustly), as a little bordering upon cruelty; which, I confess, has always been with me the strongest objection against any project, how well soever intended.

But in order to justify my friend, he confessed that this expedient was put into his head by the famous Psalmanazar, a native of the island Formosa, who came from thence to London about twenty years ago: and in conversation told my friend, that in his country when any young person happened to be put to death, the executioner sold the carcass to persons of quality as a prime dainty; and that in his time the body of a plump girl of fifteen, who was crucified for an attempt to poison the emperor, was sold to his imperial majesty's prime minister of state, and other great mandarins of the court, in joints from the gibbet, at 400 crowns. Neither indeed can I deny, that if the same use were made of several plump young girls in this town, who without one single groat to their fortunes cannot stir abroad without a chair, and appear at the playhouse and assemblies in foreign fineries which they never will pay for, the kingdom would not be the worse.

Some persons of a desponding spirit are in great concern about the vast number of poor people, who are aged, diseased, or maimed, and I have been desired to employ my thoughts what course may be taken to ease the nation of so grievous an encumbrance. But I am not in the least pain upon that matter, because it is very well known that they are every day dying and rotting by cold and famine, and filth and vermin, as fast as can be reasonably expected. And as to the young laborers, they are now in as hopeful condition: They cannot get work, and consequently pine away for want of nourishment, to a degree that if at any time they are accidentally hired to common labor, they have not strength to perform it; and thus the country and themselves are happily delivered from the evils to come.

I have too long digressed, and therefore shall return to my sub- 20
ject. I think the advantages by the proposal which I have made are obvious and many, as well as of the highest importance.

For first, as I have already observed, it would greatly lessen the number of papists, with whom we are yearly overrun, being the principal breeders of the nation as well as our most dangerous enemies; and who stay at home on purpose to deliver the kingdom to the Pretender, hoping to take their advantage by the absence of so many good Protestants, who have chosen rather to leave their country than stay at home and pay tithes against their conscience to an Episcopal curate.

Secondly, The poor tenants will have something valuable of their own, which by law may be made liable to distress and help to pay their landlord's rent, their corn and cattle being already seized, and money a thing unknown.

Thirdly, Whereas the maintenance of 100,000 children from two years old and upward, cannot be computed at less that 10s. a-piece per annum, the nation's stock will be thereby increased £50,000 per annum, beside the profit of a new dish introduced to the tables of all gentlemen of fortune in the kingdom who have any refinement in taste. And the money will circulate among ourselves, the goods being entirely of our own growth and manufacture.

Fourthly, The constant breeders beside the gain of 8s. sterling per annum by the sale of their children, will be rid of the charge of maintaining them after the first year.

Fifthly, This food would likewise bring great custom to taverns, 25
where the vintners will certainly be so prudent as to procure the best receipts for dressing it to perfection, and consequently have their houses frequented by all the fine gentlemen, who justly value themselves upon their knowledge in good eating; and a skilful cook who understands how to oblige his guests, will contrive to make it as expensive as they please.

Sixthly, This would be a great inducement to marriage, which all wise nations have either encouraged by rewards or enforced by laws and penalties. It would increase the care and tenderness of mothers toward their children, when they were sure of a settlement for life to the poor babes, provided in some sort by the public, to their annual profit instead of expense. We should see an honest emulation among the married women, which of them would bring the fattest child to the market. Men would become as fond of their wives during the time of their pregnancy as they are now of their mares in foal, their cows in calf, their sows when they are ready to farrow; nor offer to beat or kick them (as is too frequent a practice) for fear of a miscarriage.

Many other advantages might be enumerated. For instance, the addition of some thousand carcasses in our exportation of barreled beef, the propagation of swine's flesh, and improvement in the art of making good bacon, so much wanted among us by the great destruction of pigs, too frequent at our table; which are no way comparable in taste or magnificence to a well-grown, fat, yearling child, which roasted whole will make a considerable figure at a lord mayor's feast or any other public entertainment. But this and many others I omit, being studious of brevity.

Supposing that 1,000 families in this city would be constant customers for infants' flesh, besides others who might have it at merry-meetings, particularly at weddings and christenings, I compute that Dublin would take off annually about 20,000 carcasses; and the rest of the kingdom (where probably they will be sold somewhat cheaper) the remaining 80,000.

I can think of no one objection that will possibly be raised against this proposal unless it should be urged that the number of people will be thereby much lessened in the kingdom. This I freely own, and it was indeed one principal design in offering it to the world. I desire the reader will observe, that I calculate my remedy for this one individual kingdom of Ireland and for no other that ever was, is, or I think ever can be upon earth. Therefore let no man talk to me of other expedients: of taxing our absentees at 5s. a pound: of using neither clothes nor household furniture except what is of our own growth and manufacture: of utterly rejecting the materials and instruments that promote foreign luxury: of curing the expensiveness of pride, vanity, idleness, and gaming in our women: of introducing a vein of parsimony, prudence, and temperance: of learning to love our country, in the want of which we differ even from Laplanders and the inhabitants of Topinamboo: of quitting our animosities and factions, nor acting any longer like the Jews, who were murdering one another at the very moment their city was taken: of being a little cautious not to sell our country and conscience for nothing: of teaching landlords to have at least one degree of mercy toward their tenants: lastly, of putting a spirit of honesty, industry, and skill into our shopkeepers; who, if a resolution could now be taken to buy only our native goods, would immediately unite to cheat and exact upon us in the price the measure, and the goodness, nor could ever yet be brought to make one fair proposal of just dealing, though often and earnestly invited to it.

Therefore I repeat, let no man talk to me of these and the like 30
expedients, till he has at least some glimpse of hope that there will be ever some hearty and sincere attempt to put them in practice.

But as to myself, having been wearied out for many years with offering vain, idle, visionary thoughts, and at length utterly despairing of success, I fortunately fell upon this proposal; which, as it is wholly new, so it has something solid and real, of no expense and little trouble, full in our own power, and whereby we can incur no danger in disobliging England. For this kind of commodity will not bear exportation, the flesh being of too tender a consistence to admit a long continuance in salt, although perhaps I could name a country which would be glad to eat up our whole nation without it.

After all, I am not so violently bent upon my own opinion as to reject any offer proposed by wise men, which shall be found equally innocent, cheap, easy, and effectual. But before something of that kind shall be advanced in contradiction to my scheme, and offering a better, I desire the author or authors will be pleased maturely to consider two points. First, as things now stand, how they will be able to find food and raiment for 100,000 useless mouths and backs. And secondly, there being a round million of creatures in human figure throughout this kingdom, whose subsistence put into a common stock would leave them in debt 2,000,000£. sterling, adding those who are beggars by profession to the bulk of farmers, cottagers, and laborers, with the wives and children who are beggars in effect; I desire those politicians who dislike my overture, and may perhaps be so bold as to attempt an answer, that they will first ask the parents of these mortals, whether they would not at this day think it a great happiness to have been sold for food at a year old in the manner I prescribe, and thereby have avoided such a perpetual scene of misfortunes as they have since gone through by the oppression of landlords, the impossibility of paying rent without money or trade, the want of common sustenance, with neither house nor clothes to cover them from the inclemencies of the weather, and the most inevitable prospect of entailing the like or greater miseries upon their breed for ever.

I profess, in the sincerity of my heart, that I have not the least personal interest in endeavoring to promote this necessary work, having no other motive than the public good of my country, by advancing our trade, providing for infants, relieving the poor, and giving some pleasure to the rich. I have no children by which I can propose to get a single penny; the youngest being nine years old, and my wife past childbearing.

For Discussion and Writing

1. List the ways in which the proposal is presented that make it appear rational.
2. If there exists a "typical" method for making an argument, Swift's method here is not it. What is the real point Swift is arguing, and how does it relate to the apparent point the speaker makes?
3. **connections** Swift's use of a persona — here, the "projector" who makes this proposal — involves the use of irony to make a political point, while Thomas Jefferson's Declaration of Independence (p. 187) is straightforward. Why might these texts' differing strategies be appropriate for their political goals?
4. Write a short response to "A Modest Proposal" focusing on the experience of reading it. How do your responses — to the beginning, to the moment when the proposal is laid out, to the handling of objections — change?

AMY TAN

Mother Tongue

Amy Tan, born in 1952, was raised in northern California. Formerly a business writer, Tan is now a novelist. She is best known for her first book, The Joy Luck Club *(1989), but has also written* The Kitchen God's Wife *(1991),* The Hundred Secret Senses *(1995),* The Bonesetter's Daughter *(2001), and* Saving Fish from Drowning *(2005). Her fiction grows out of her experiences as the child of Chinese immigrants growing up and living in American culture.*

In "Mother Tongue," Tan describes the variety of Englishes she uses. In doing so, she addresses the connections between languages and cultures, but in her writing she also demonstrates what she says about herself in the essay: "I am a writer. And by that definition, I am someone who has always loved language" (par. 2).

I am not a scholar of English or literature. I cannot give you much more than personal opinions on the English language and its variations in this country or others.

I am a writer. And by that definition, I am someone who has always loved language. I am fascinated by language in daily life. I spend a great deal of my time thinking about the power of language — the way it can evoke an emotion, a visual image, a complex idea, or a simple truth. Language is the tool of my trade. And I use them all — all the Englishes I grew up with.

Recently, I was made keenly aware of the different Englishes I do use. I was giving a talk to a large group of people, the same talk I had already given to half a dozen other groups. The nature of the talk was about my writing, my life, and my book, *The Joy Luck Club*. The talk was going along well enough, until I remembered one major difference that made the whole talk sound wrong. My mother was in the room. And it was perhaps the first time she had heard me give a lengthy speech, using the kind of English I have never used with her. I was saying things like "The intersection of memory upon imagination" and "There is an aspect of my fiction that relates to thus-and-thus" — a speech filled with carefully wrought grammatical phrases, burdened, it suddenly seemed to me, with nominalized forms, past perfect tenses, conditional phrases, all the forms of standard English that I had learned in school and through books, the forms of English I did not use at home with my mother.

Just last week, I was walking down the street with my mother, and I again found myself conscious of the English I was using, the English I do use with her. We were talking about the price of new and used furniture and I heard myself saying this: "Not waste money that way." My husband was with us as well, and he didn't notice any switch in my English. And then I realized why. It's because over the twenty years we've been together I've often used that same kind of English with him, and sometimes he even uses it with me. It has become our language of intimacy, a different sort of English that relates to family talk, the language I grew up with.

5 So you'll have some idea of what this family talk I heard sounds like, I'll quote what my mother said during a recent conversation which I videotaped and then transcribed. During this conversation, my mother was talking about a political gangster in Shanghai who had the same last name as her family's, Du, and how the gangster in his early years wanted to be adopted by her family, which was rich by comparison. Later, the gangster became more powerful, far richer than my mother's family, and one day showed up at my mother's wedding to pay his respects. Here's what she said in part:

"Du Yusong having business like fruit stand. Like off the street kind. He is Du like Du Zong — but not Tsung-ming Island people. The local people call putong, the river east side, he belong to that side local people. That man want to ask Du Zong father take him in like become own family. Du Zong father wasn't look down on him, but didn't take seriously, until that man big like become a mafia. Now important person, very hard to inviting him. Chinese way, came only to show respect, don't stay for dinner. Respect for making big celebration, he shows up. Mean gives lots of respect. Chinese custom. Chinese social life that way. If too important won't have to stay too long. He come to my wedding. I didn't see, I heard it. I gone to boy's side, they have YMCA dinner. Chinese age I was nineteen."

You should know that my mother's expressive command of English belies how much she actually understands. She reads the *Forbes* report, listens to *Wall Street Week*, converses daily with her stockbroker, reads all of Shirley MacLaine's books with ease — all kinds of things I can't begin to understand. Yet some of my friends tell me they understand 50 percent of what my mother says. Some say they understand 80 to 90 percent. Some say they understand none of it, as if she were speaking pure Chinese. But to me, my mother's English is perfectly clear, perfectly natural. It's my mother tongue. Her language, as I hear it, is vivid, direct, full of observation and imagery. That was the language that helped shape the way I saw things, expressed things, made sense of the world.

Lately, I've been giving more thought to the kind of English my mother speaks. Like others, I have described it to people as "broken" or "fractured" English. But I wince when I say that. It has always bothered me that I can think of no other way to describe it other than "broken," as if it were damaged and needed to be fixed, as if it lacked a certain wholeness and soundness. I've heard other terms used, "limited English," for example. But they seem just as bad, as if everything is limited, including people's perceptions of the limited English speaker.

I know this for a fact, because when I was growing up, my mother's "limited" English limited *my* perception of her. I was ashamed of her English. I believed that her English reflected the quality of what she had to say. That is, because she expressed them imperfectly her thoughts were imperfect. And I had plenty of empirical evidence to support me: the fact that people in department stores, at banks, and at restaurants did not take her seriously, did not give her good service, pretended not to understand her, or even acted as if they did not hear her.

10 My mother has long realized the limitations of her English as well. When I was fifteen, she used to have me call people on the phone to pretend I was she. In this guise, I was forced to ask for information or even to complain and yell at people who had been rude to her. One time it was a call to her stockbroker in New York. She had cashed out her small portfolio and it just so happened we were going to go to New York the next week, our very first trip outside California. I had to get on the phone and say in an adolescent voice that was not very convincing, "This is Mrs. Tan."

And my mother was standing in the back whispering loudly, "Why he don't send me check, already two weeks late. So mad he lie to me, losing me money."

And then I said in perfect English, "Yes, I'm getting rather concerned. You had agreed to send the check two weeks ago, but it hasn't arrived."

Then she began to talk more loudly. "What he want, I come to New York tell him front of his boss, you cheating me?" And I was trying to calm her down, make her be quiet, while telling the stockbroker, "I can't tolerate any more excuses. If I don't receive the check immediately, I am going to have to speak to your manager when I'm in New York next week." And sure enough, the following week there we were in front of this astonished stockbroker, and I was sitting there red-faced and quiet, and my mother, the real Mrs. Tan, was shouting at his boss in her impeccable broken English.

We used a similar routine just five days ago, for a situation that was far less humorous. My mother had gone to the hospital for an appointment, to find out about a benign brain tumor a CAT scan had revealed a month ago. She said she had spoken very good English, her best English, no mistakes. Still, she said, the hospital did not apologize when they said they had lost the CAT scan and she had come for nothing. She said they did not seem to have any sympathy when she told them she was anxious to know the exact diagnosis, since her husband and son had both died of brain tumors. She said they would not give her any more information until the next time and she would have to make another appointment for that. So she said she would not leave until the doctor called her daughter. She wouldn't budge. And when the doctor finally called her daughter, me, who spoke in perfect English — lo and behold — we had assurances the CAT scan would be found, promises that a conference call on Monday would be held, and apologies for any suffering my mother had gone through for a most regrettable mistake.

15 I think my mother's English almost had an effect on limiting my possibilities in life as well. Sociologists and linguists probably will tell you that a person's developing language skills are more influenced by peers. But I do think that the language spoken in the family, especially in immigrant families which are more insular, plays a large role in shaping the language of the child. And I

believe that it affected my results on achievement tests, IQ tests, and the SAT. While my English skills were never judged as poor, compared to math, English could not be considered my strong suit. In grade school I did moderately well, getting perhaps B's, sometimes B-pluses, in English and scoring perhaps in the sixtieth or seventieth percentile on achievement tests. But those scores were not good enough to override the opinion that my true abilities lay in math and science, because in those areas I achieved A's and scored in the ninetieth percentile or higher.

This was understandable. Math is precise; there is only one correct answer. Whereas, for me at least, the answers on English tests were always a judgment call, a matter of opinion and personal experience. Those tests were constructed around items like fill-in-the-blank sentence completion, such as "Even though Tom was ____, Mary thought he was ____." And the correct answer always seemed to be the most bland combinations of thoughts, for example, "Even though Tom was shy, Mary thought he was charming," with the grammatical structure "even though" limiting the correct answer to some sort of semantic opposites, so you wouldn't get answers like, "Even though Tom was foolish, Mary thought he was ridiculous." Well, according to my mother, there were very few limitations as to what Tom could have been and what Mary might have thought of him. So I never did well on tests like that.

The same was true with word analogies, pairs of words in which you were supposed to find some sort of logical, semantic relationship — for example, "*Sunset* is to *nightfall* as ____ is to ____." And here you would be presented with a list of four possible pairs, one of which showed the same kind of relationship: *red* is to *stoplight, bus* is to *arrival, chills* is to *fever, yawn* is to *boring*. Well, I could never think that way. I knew what the tests were asking, but I could not block out of my mind the images already created by the first pair, "*sunset* is to *nightfall*" — and I would see a burst of colors against a darkening sky, the moon rising, the lowering of a curtain of stars. And all the other pairs of words — red, bus, stoplight, boring — just threw up a mass of confusing images, making it impossible for me to sort out something as logical as saying: "A sunset precedes nightfall" is the same as "a chill precedes a fever." The only way I would have gotten that answer right would have been to imagine an associative situation, for example, my being disobedient and staying out past sunset, catching a chill at night, which turns into feverish pneumonia as punishment, which indeed did happen to me.

I have been thinking about all this lately, about my mother's English, about achievement tests. Because lately I've been asked, as a writer, why there are not more Asian Americans represented in American literature. Why are there few Asian Americans enrolled in creative writing programs? Why do so many Chinese students go into engineering? Well, these are broad sociological questions I can't begin to answer. But I have noticed in surveys — in fact, just last week — that Asian students, as a whole, always do significantly better on math achievement tests than in English. And this makes me think that there are other Asian-American students whose English spoken in the home might also be described as "broken" or "limited." And perhaps they also have teachers who are steering them away from writing and into math and science, which is what happened to me.

Fortunately, I happen to be rebellious in nature and enjoy the challenge of disproving assumptions made about me. I became an English major my first year in college, after being enrolled as pre-med. I started writing nonfiction as a freelancer the week after I was told by my former boss that writing was my worst skill and I should hone my talents toward account management.

But it wasn't until 1985 that I finally began to write fiction. And 20
at first I wrote using what I thought to be wittily crafted sentences, sentences that would finally prove I had mastery over the English language. Here's an example from the first draft of a story that later made its way into *The Joy Luck Club*, but without this line: "That was my mental quandary in its nascent state." A terrible line, which I can barely pronounce.

Fortunately, for reasons I won't get into today, I later decided I should envision a reader for the stories I would write. And the reader I decided upon was my mother, because these were stories about mothers. So with this reader in mind — and in fact she did read my early drafts — I began to write stories using all the Englishes I grew up with: the English I spoke to my mother, which for lack of a better term might be described as "simple"; the English she used with me, which for lack of a better term might be described as "broken"; my translation of her Chinese, which could certainly be described as "watered down"; and what I imagined to be her translation of her Chinese if she could speak in perfect English, her internal language, and for that I sought to preserve the essence, but neither an English nor a Chinese structure. I wanted to capture what language ability tests can never reveal: her intent, her passion, her imagery, the rhythms of her speech, and the nature of her thoughts.

Apart from what any critic had to say about my writing, I knew I had succeeded where it counted when my mother finished reading my book and gave me her verdict: "So easy to read."

For Discussion and Writing

1. List the different Englishes Tan describes, defining each.
2. Of her mother's English, Tan writes, "That was the language that helped shape the way I saw things, expressed things, made sense of the world" (par. 7). How was the effect of her mother's English positive, and how was it negative?
3. **connections** Richard Rodriguez, in "Aria: Memory of a Bilingual Childhood" (p. 307), expresses a complicated set of feelings about his linguistic inheritances and what they mean to him and to the world around him. Compare his feelings to Tan's as expressed in "Mother Tongue." How does each deal with the way the world thinks of their language(s)?
4. Do you use different Englishes yourself? Even if English is your sole language, consider how your use of it changes depending on circumstances and audience. Write an essay in which you describe the different ways you speak and the meaning of these differences.

HENRY DAVID THOREAU

Where I Lived, and What I Lived For

Henry David Thoreau was born in 1817 and raised in Concord, Massachusetts, living there for most of his life. Along with Ralph Waldo Emerson, Thoreau was one of the most important thinkers of his time in America and is still widely read today. Walden *(1854), the work for which he is best known, is drawn from the journal he kept during his two-year-long stay in a cabin on Walden Pond. In* Walden, *Thoreau explores his interests in naturalism, individualism, and self-sufficiency. He is also remembered for his essay "Civil Disobedience" (1849), an early, influential statement of this tactic of protest later practiced by Mahatma Gandhi and, under the leadership of Martin Luther King Jr., many in the civil rights movement.*

"Where I Lived, and What I Lived For" is taken from Walden. *In it, Thoreau makes the argument for his going to live in the woods. Writing about* Walden, *scholars have pointed out that Thoreau was not particularly deep in the woods and that he was regularly visited and supplied with, among other things, pies. As you read, consider how this influences your acceptance of what he has to say.*

I went to the woods because I wished to live deliberately, to front only the essential facts of life, and see if I could not learn what it had to teach, and not, when I came to die, discover that I had not lived. I did not wish to live what was not life, living is so dear; nor did I wish to practice resignation, unless it was quite necessary. I wanted to live deep and suck out all the marrow of life, to live so sturdily and Spartan-like as to put to rout all that was not life, to cut a broad swath and shave close, to drive life into a corner, and reduce it to its lowest terms, and, if it proved to be mean, why then to get the whole and genuine meanness of it, and publish its meanness to the world; or if it were sublime, to know it by experience, and be able to give a true account of it in my next excursion.

For most men, it appears to me, are in a strange uncertainty about it, whether it is of the devil or of God, and have *somewhat hastily* concluded that it is the chief end of man here to "glorify God and enjoy him forever."

Still we live meanly, like ants; though the fable tells us that we were long ago changed into men; like pygmies we fight with cranes; it is error upon error, and clout upon clout, and our best virtue has for its occasion a superfluous and evitable wretchedness. Our life is frittered away by detail. An honest man has hardly need to count more than his ten fingers, or in extreme cases he may add his ten toes, and lump the rest. Simplicity, simplicity, simplicity! I say, let your affairs be as two or three, and not a hundred or a thousand; instead of a million count half a dozen, and keep your accounts on your thumb-nail. In the midst of this chopping sea of civilized life, such are the clouds and storms and quicksands and thousand-and-one items to be allowed for, that a man has to live, if he would not founder and go to the bottom and not make his port at all, by dead reckoning, and he must be a great calculator indeed who succeeds. Simplify, simplify. Instead of three meals a day, if it be necessary eat but one; instead of a hundred dishes, five; and reduce other things in proportion. Our life is like a German Confederacy, made up of petty states, with its boundary forever fluctuating, so that even a German cannot tell you how it is bounded at any moment. The nation itself, with all its so-called internal improvements, which, by the way are all external and superficial, is just such an unwieldy and overgrown establishment, cluttered with furniture and tripped up by its own traps, ruined by luxury and heedless expense, by want of calculation and a worthy aim, as the million households in the lands; and the only cure for it, as for them, is in a rigid economy, a stern and more than Spartan simplicity of life and elevation of purpose. It lives too fast. Men think that it is essential that the *Nation* have commerce, and export ice, and talk through a telegraph, and ride thirty miles an hour, without a doubt, whether *they* do or not; but whether we should live like baboons or like men, is a little uncertain. If we do not get our sleepers, and forge rails, and devote days and nights to the work, but go to tinkering upon our *lives* to improve *them*, who will build railroads? And if railroads are not built, how shall we get to heaven in season? But if we stay at home and mind our business, who will want railroads? We do not ride on the railroad; it rides upon us. Did you ever think what those sleepers are that underlie the railroad? Each one is a man, an Irishman, or a Yankee man. The rails are laid on them, and they are covered with sand, and the cars run smoothly over them. They are sound sleepers, I assure you. And every few years a new lot is laid down and run over, so that, if some have the pleasure of riding on a rail, others have the misfortune to be ridden upon. And when they run over a man that is walking in his sleep, a supernumerary sleeper in the wrong position, and wake him up, they suddenly stop the cars, and make a hue and cry about it, as if this were an exception. I am glad to know that it takes a gang of men for every five miles to keep the sleepers down and level in their beds as it is, for this is a sign that they may sometimes get up again.

Why should we live with such hurry and waste of life? We are determined to be starved before we are hungry. Men say that a stitch in time saves nine, and so they take a thousand stitches today to save nine tomorrow. As for *work*, we haven't any of any consequence. We have the Saint Vitus' dance, and cannot possibly keep our heads still. If I should only give a few pulls at the parish bell-rope, as for a fire, that is, without setting the bell, there is hardly a man on his farm in the outskirts of Concord, notwithstanding that press of engagements which was his excuse so many times this morning, nor a boy, nor a woman, I might almost say, but would foresake all and follow that sound, not mainly to save property from the flames, but, if we will confess the truth, much more to see it burn, since burn it must, and we, be it known, did not set it on fire — or to see it put out, and have a hand in it, if that is done as handsomely; yes, even if it were the parish church itself. Hardly a man takes a half-hour's nap after dinner, but when he wakes he holds up his head and asks, "What's the news?" as if the rest of mankind had stood his sentinels. Some give directions to be waked every half-hour, doubtless for no other purpose; and then, to pay for it, they tell what they have dreamed. After a night's sleep the news is as indispensable as the breakfast. "Pray tell me anything new that has happened to a man anywhere on this globe" — and he reads it over his coffee and rolls, that a man has had his eyes gouged out this morning on the Wachito River; never dreaming the while that he lives in the dark unfathomed mammoth cave of this world, and has but the rudiment of an eye himself.

For my part, I could easily do without the post-office. I think that there are very few important communications made through it. To speak critically, I never received more than one or two letters in my life — I wrote this some years ago — that were worth the postage. The penny-post is, commonly, an institution through which you seriously offer a man that penny for his thoughts which is so often safely offered in jest. And I am sure that I never read any memorable news in a newspaper. If we read of one man robbed, or murdered, or killed by accident, or one house burned, or one vessel wrecked or one steamboat blown up, or one cow run over on the Western Railroad, or one mad dog killed, or one lot of grasshoppers in the winter — we never need read of another. One is enough. If you are acquainted with the principle, what do you care for a myriad instances and applications? To a philosopher all *news*, as it is called, is gossip, and they who edit and read it are old women over their tea. Yet not a few are greedy after this gossip. There was such a rush, as I hear, the other day at one of the offices to learn the foreign news by the last arrival, that several large squares of plate glass belonging to the establishment were broken by the pressure — news which I seriously think a ready wit might write a twelvemonth, or twelve years, beforehand with sufficient accuracy. As for Spain, for instance, if you know how to throw in Don Carlos and the Infanta, and Don Pedro and Seville and Granada, from time to time in the right proportions — they may have changed the names a little since I saw the papers — and serve up a bullfight when other entertainments fail, it will be true to the letter, and give us as good an idea of the exact state or ruin of things in Spain as the most succinct and lucid reports under this head in the newspapers; and as for England, almost the last significant scrap of news from that quarter was the revolution of 1649; and if you have learned the history of her crops for an average year, you never need attend to that thing again, unless your speculations are of a merely pecuniary character. If one may judge who rarely looks into the newspapers, nothing new does ever happen in foreign parts, a French revolution not excepted.

What news! how much more important to know what that is 5
which was never old! "Kieou-he-yu (great dignitary of the state of Wei) sent a man to Khoung-tseu to know his news. Khoung-tseu caused the messenger to be seated near him, and questioned him in these terms: What is your master doing? The messenger

answered with respect: My master desires to diminish the number of his faults, but he cannot come to the end of them. The messenger being gone, the philosopher remarked: What a worthy messenger! What a worthy messenger!" The preacher, instead of vexing the ears of drowsy farmers on their day of rest at the end of the week — for Sunday is the fit conclusion of an ill-spent week, and not the fresh and brave beginning of a new one — with this one other draggle-tail of a sermon, should shout with thundering voice, "Pause! Avast! Why so seeming fast, but deadly slow?"

Shams and delusions are esteemed for soundless truths, while reality is fabulous. If men would steadily observe realities only, and not allow themselves to be deluded, life, to compare it with such things as we know, would be like a fairy tale and the Arabian Nights' Entertainments. If we respected only what is inevitable and has a right to be, music and poetry would resound along the streets. When we are unhurried and wise, we perceive that only great and worthy things have any permanent and absolute existence, that petty fears and petty pleasures are but the shadow of the reality. This is always exhilarating and sublime. By closing the eyes and slumbering, and consenting to be deceived by shows, men establish and confirm their daily life of routine and habit everywhere, which still is built on purely illusory foundations. Children, who play life, discern its true law and relations more clearly than men, who fail to live it worthily, but who think that they are wiser by experience, that is, by failure. I have read in a Hindoo book, that "there was a king's son, who, being expelled in infancy from his native city, was brought up by a forester, and, growing up to maturity in that state, imagined himself to belong to the barbarous race with which he lived. One of his father's ministers having discovered him, revealed to him what he was, and the misconception of his character was removed, and he knew himself to be a prince. So soul," continues the Hindoo philosopher, "from the circumstances in which it is placed, mistakes its own character, until the truth is revealed to it by some holy teacher and then it knows itself to be *Brahme*." I perceive that we inhabitants of New England live this mean life that we do because our vision does not penetrate the surface of things. We think that that *is* which *appears* to be. If a man should walk through this town and see only the reality, where, think you, would the "Mill-dam" go to? If he should give us an account of the realities he beheld there, we should not recognize the place in his description. Look at the meetinghouse, or a courthouse, or a jail, or a shop, or a dwelling-house, and say what that thing really is before a true gaze, and they would all go to pieces in your account of them. Men esteem truth remote, in the outskirts of the system, behind the farthest star, before Adam and after the last man. In eternity there is indeed something true and sublime. But all these times and places and occasions are now and here. God himself culminates in the present moment, and will never be more divine in the lapse of all the ages. And we are enabled to apprehend at all what is sublime and noble only by the perpetual instilling and drenching of the reality that surrounds us. The universe constantly and obediently answers to our conceptions; whether we travel fast or slow, the track is laid for us. Let us spend our lives in conceiving then. The poet or the artist never yet had so fair and noble a design but some of his posterity at least could accomplish it.

Let us spend one day as deliberately as Nature, and not be thrown off the track by every nutshell and mosquito's wing that falls on the rails. Let us rise early and fast, or breakfast, gently and without perturbation; let company come and let company go, let the bells ring and the children cry — determined to make a day of it. Why should we knock under and go with the stream? Let us not be upset and overwhelmed in that terrible rapid and whirlpool called a dinner, situated in the meridian shallows. Weather this danger and you are safe, for the rest of the way is downhill. With unrelaxed nerves, with morning vigor, sail by it, looking another way, tied to the mast like Ulysses. If the engine whistles, let it whistle till it is hoarse for its pains. If the bell rings, why should we run? We will consider what kind of music they are like. Let us settle ourselves and work and wedge our feet downward through the mud and slush of opinion, and prejudice, and tradition, and delusion, and appearance, that alluvion which covers the globe, through Paris and London, through New York and Boston and Concord, through Church and State, through poetry and philosophy and religion, till we come to a hard bottom and rocks in place, which we can call *reality*, and say, This is, and no mistake; and then begin, having a *point d'appui*, below freshet and frost and fire, a place where you might found a wall or a state, or set a lamppost safely, or perhaps a gauge, not a Nilometer, but a Realometer, that future ages might know how deep a freshet of shams and appearances had gathered from time to time. If you stand right fronting and face to face to a fact, you will see the sun glimmer on both its surfaces, as if it were a cimeter, and feel its sweet edge dividing you through the heart and marrow, and so you will happily conclude your mortal career. Be it life or death, we crave only reality. If we are really dying, let us hear the rattle in our throats and feel cold in the extremities; if we are alive, let us go about our business.

Time is but the stream I go afishing in. I drink at it; but while I drink I see the sandy bottom and detect how shallow it is. Its thin current slides away but eternity remains. I would drink deeper; fish in the sky, whose bottom is pebbly with stars. I cannot count one. I know not the first letter of the alphabet. I have always been regretting that I was not as wise as the day I was born. The intellect is a cleaver; it discerns and rifts its way into the secret of things. I do not wish to be any more busy with my hands than is necessary. My head is hands and feet. I feel all my best faculties concentrated in it. My instinct tells me that my head is an organ for burrowing, as some creatures use their snout and fore paws, and with it I would mine and burrow my way through these hills. I think that the richest vein is somewhere hereabouts; so by the divining-rod and thin rising vapors, I judge; and here I will begin to mine.

For Discussion and Writing

1. What exactly is Thoreau recommending when he writes, "Simplify, simplify" (par. 2)?
2. Thoreau compares his life in the woods to normal daily life in towns and cities, but spends much more time describing the latter than he does describing the former. Why might he have chosen to do this?
3. **connections** Compare Thoreau's account of his time in the woods to E. B. White's in "Once More to the Lake" (p. 431). While these pieces of writing are very different in terms of style, audience, and purpose, how might their conclusions be related?
4. "We do not ride on the railroad; it rides upon us," Thoreau writes (par. 2). Name an "improvement" in contemporary life that is supposed to represent progress but that you think has had a negative impact overall. Describe its impact. Has it had any benefits?

SOJOURNER TRUTH

Ain't I a Woman?

Born Isabella Baumfree in Ulster County, New York, around 1797, Sojourner Truth, as she later renamed herself, was freed from slavery in 1827 when New York State emancipated the slaves within its borders. She renamed herself following a religious experience and began a career as a traveling preacher arguing for abolition and women's rights. "Ain't I a Woman?" is the title given a speech Truth delivered at a women's rights convention in 1851 that was later transcribed and published. There are several different accounts of Truth's speech; the one reprinted here appeared in The History of Woman Suffrage, *edited by Elizabeth Cady Stanton and Susan B. Anthony. Recent scholarship has questioned the accuracy of the most often reprinted versions (including this one). Regardless, "Ain't I a Woman?" remains a model of a short, powerful, extemporaneous speech. As you read, imagine the impact it may have had on its audience. How do you think listeners reacted?*

Well, children, where there is so much racket there must be something out of kilter. I think that 'twixt the negroes of the South and the women of the North, all talking about rights, the white men will be in a fix pretty soon. But what's all this here talking about?

That man over there says that women need to be helped into carriages, and lifted over ditches, and to have the best place everywhere. Nobody ever helps me into carriages, or over mud-puddles, or gives me any best place! And ain't I a woman? Look at me! Look at my arm! I have ploughed and planted, and gathered into barns, and no man could head me! And ain't I a woman? I could work as much and eat as much as a man — when I could get it — and bear the lash as well! And ain't I a woman? I have borne thirteen children, and seen them most all sold off to slavery, and when I cried out with my mother's grief, none but Jesus heard me! And ain't I a woman?

Then they talk about this thing in the head; what's this they call it? [Intellect, someone whispers.] That's it, honey. What's that got to do with women's rights or negro's rights? If my cup won't hold but a pint, and yours holds a quart, wouldn't you be man not to let me have my little half-measure full?

Then that little man in black there, he says women can't have as much rights as men, 'cause Christ wasn't a woman! Where did your Christ come from? Where did your Christ come from? From God and a woman! Man had nothing to do with Him.

If the first woman God ever made was strong enough to turn 5
the world upside down all alone, these women together ought to be able to turn it back, and get it right side up again! And now they is asking to do it, the men better let them.

Obliged to you for hearing me, and now old Sojourner ain't got nothing more to say.

For Discussion and Writing

1. To whom and to what is Truth responding?
2. Truth's argument takes the form of examples. What are they examples of, and what point do they help her make?
3. **connections** Compare Truth's argument for women's rights to Elizabeth Cady Stanton's in "Declaration of Sentiments and Resolutions" (p. 379). How is each of their very different styles effective?
4. Imagine you were in the audience when Truth delivered this speech in 1851. What perceptions of her might you have had, and how might what she said have countered them?

SARAH VOWELL

Shooting Dad

Born in Oklahoma in 1969 and raised both there and in Montana, Sarah Vowell is a writer of books and radio pieces. Her work has appeared on public radio, in particular on the Public Radio International show This American Life, *in periodicals such as* GQ, Spin, *and* Esquire, *and in a number of books, including* Radio On: A Listener's Diary *(1996),* Take the Cannoli: Stories from the New World *(2000),* Partly Cloudy Patriot *(2002),* Assassination Vacation *(2005), and* The Wordy Shipmates *(2008).*

Vowell first delivered "Shooting Dad" as a radio essay on This American Life *(in slightly different form). As you read the print version, think about voice, about the distinctive quality of the way a writer writes — the words she chooses and the way she combines them, the way images and phrases and rhythms are employed. Reading Vowell's piece, the origin of the writing term* voice *— from the Old French and Latin words for* speech *— is clear.*

If you were passing by the house where I grew up during my teenage years and it happened to be before Election Day, you wouldn't have needed to come inside to see that it was a house divided. You could have looked at the Democratic campaign poster in the upstairs window and the Republican one in the downstairs window and seen our home for the Civil War battleground it was. I'm not saying who was the Democrat or who was the Republican — my father or I — but I will tell you that I have never subscribed to *Guns & Ammo*, that I did not plaster the family vehicle with National Rifle Association stickers, and that hunter's orange was never my color.

About the only thing my father and I agree on is the Constitution, though I'm partial to the First Amendment, while he's always favored the Second.

I am a gunsmith's daughter. I like to call my parents' house, located on a quiet residential street in Bozeman, Montana, the United States of Firearms. Guns were everywhere: the so-called pretty ones like the circa 1850 walnut muzzleloader hanging on the wall, Dad's clients' fixer-uppers leaning into corners, an entire rack right next to the TV. I had to move revolvers out of my way to make room for a bowl of Rice Krispies on the kitchen table.

I was eleven when we moved into that Bozeman house. We had never lived in town before, and this was a college town at that. We came from Oklahoma — a dusty little Muskogee County nowhere called Braggs. My parents' property there included an orchard, a horse pasture, and a couple of acres of woods. I knew our lives had changed one morning not long after we moved to Montana when, during breakfast, my father heard a noise and jumped out of his chair. Grabbing a BB gun, he rushed out the front door. Standing in the yard, he started shooting at crows. My mother sprinted after him screaming, "Pat, you might ought to check, but I don't think they do that up here!" From the look on his face, she might as well have told him that his American citizenship had been revoked. He shook his head, mumbling, "Why, shooting crows is a national pastime, like baseball and apple pie." Personally, I preferred baseball and apple pie. I looked up at those crows flying away and thought, I'm going to like it here.

Dad and I started bickering in earnest when I was fourteen, 5
after the 1984 Democratic National Convention. I was so excited when Walter Mondale chose Geraldine Ferraro as his running mate that I taped the front page of the newspaper with her picture on it to the refrigerator door. But there was some sort of mysterious gravity surge in the kitchen. Somehow, that picture ended up in the trash all the way across the room.

Nowadays, I giggle when Dad calls me on Election Day to cheerfully inform me that he has once again canceled out my vote, but I was not always so mature. There were times when I found the fact that he was a gunsmith horrifying. And just *weird*. All he ever cared about were guns. All I ever cared about was art. There were years and years when he hid out by himself in the garage making rifle barrels and I holed up in my room reading Allen Ginsberg poems, and we were incapable of having a conversation that didn't end in an argument.

Our house was partitioned off into territories. While the kitchen and the living room were well within the DMZ,° the respective work spaces governed by my father and me were jealously guarded totalitarian states in which each of us declared ourselves dictator. Dad's shop was a messy disaster area, a labyrinth of lathes. Its walls were hung with the mounted antlers of deer he'd bagged, forming a makeshift museum of death. The available flat surfaces were buried under a million scraps of paper on which he sketched his mechanical inventions in blue ballpoint pen. And the floor, carpeted with spiky metal shavings, was a tetanus shot waiting to happen. My domain was the cramped, cold space known as the music room. It was also a messy disaster area, an obstacle course of musical instruments — piano, trumpet, baritone horn, valve trombone, various percussion doodads (bells!), and recorders. A framed portrait of the French composer Claude Debussy was nailed to the wall. The available flat surfaces were buried under piles of staff paper, on which I penciled in the pompous orchestra music given titles like "Prelude to the Green Door" (named after an O. Henry short story by the way, not the watershed porn flick *Behind the Green Door*) I started writing in junior high.

It has been my experience that in order to impress potential suitors, skip the teen Debussy anecdotes and stick with the always attention-getting line "My dad makes guns." Though it won't cause the guy to like me any better, it will make him handle the inevitable breakup with diplomacy — just in case I happen to have any loaded family heirlooms lying around the house.

But the fact is, I have only shot a gun once and once was plenty. My twin sister, Amy, and I were six years old — six — when Dad decided that it was high time we learned how to shoot. Amy remembers the day he handed us the gun for the first time differently. She liked it.

Amy shared our father's enthusiasm for firearms and the quick- 10
draw cowboy mythology surrounding them. I tended to daydream through Dad's activities — the car trip to Dodge City's Boot Hill, his beloved John Wayne Westerns on TV. My sister, on the other hand, turned into Rooster Cogburn Jr., devouring Duke movies with Dad. In fact, she named her teddy bear Duke, hung a colos-

DMZ: Demilitarized zone, an area where military forces and operations are prohibited. [Ed.]

sal John Wayne portrait next to her bed, and took to wearing one of those John Wayne shirts that button on the side. So when Dad led us out to the backyard when we were six and, to Amy's delight, put the gun in her hand, she says she felt it meant that Daddy trusted us and that he thought of us as "big girls."

But I remember holding the pistol only made me feel small. It was so heavy in my hand. I stretched out my arm and pointed it away and winced. It was a very long time before I had the nerve to pull the trigger and I was so scared I had to close my eyes. It felt like it just went off by itself, as if I had no say in the matter, as if the gun just had this *need*. The sound it made was as big as God. It kicked little me back to the ground like a bully, like a foe. It hurt. I don't know if I dropped it or just handed it back over to my dad, but I do know that I never wanted to touch another one again. And, because I believed in the devil, I did what my mother told me to do every time I felt an evil presence. I looked at the smoke and whispered under my breath, "Satan, I rebuke thee."

It's not like I'm saying I was traumatized. It's more like I was decided. Guns: Not For Me. Luckily, both my parents grew up in exasperating households where children were considered puppets and/or slaves. My mom and dad were hell-bent on letting my sister and me make our own choices. So if I decided that I didn't want my father's little death sticks to kick me to the ground again, that was fine with him. He would go hunting with my sister, who started calling herself "the loneliest twin in history" because of my reluctance to engage in family activities.

Of course, the fact that I was allowed to voice my opinions did not mean that my father would silence his own. Some things were said during the Reagan administration that cannot be taken back. Let's just say that I blamed Dad for nuclear proliferation and Contra aid. He believed that if I had my way, all the guns would be confiscated and it would take the commies about fifteen minutes to parachute in and assume control.

We're older now, my dad and I. The older I get, the more I'm interested in becoming a better daughter. First on my list: Figure out the whole gun thing.

Not long ago, my dad finished his most elaborate tool of death 15
yet. A cannon. He built a nineteenth-century cannon. From scratch. It took two years.

My father's cannon is a smaller replica of a cannon called the Big Horn Gun in front of Bozeman's Pioneer Museum. The barrel of the original has been filled with concrete ever since some high school kids in the '50s pointed it at the school across the street and shot out its windows one night as a prank. According to Dad's historical source, a man known to scholars as A Guy at the Museum, the cannon was brought to Bozeman around 1870, and was used by local white merchants to fire at the Sioux and Cheyenne Indians who blocked their trade access to the East in 1874.

"Bozeman was founded on greed," Dad says. The courthouse cannon, he continues, "definitely killed Indians. The merchants filled it full of nuts, bolts, and chopped-up horseshoes. Sitting Bull could have been part of these engagements. They definitely ticked off the Indians, because a couple of years later, Custer wanders into them at Little Bighorn. The Bozeman merchants were out to cause trouble. They left fresh baked bread with cyanide in it on the trail to poison a few Indians."

Because my father's sarcastic American history yarns rarely go on for long before he trots out some nefarious ancestor of ours — I come from a long line of moonshiners, Confederate soldiers, murderers, even Democrats — he cracks that the merchants hired some "community-minded Southern soldiers from North Texas." These soldiers had, like my great-great-grandfather John Vowell, fought under pro-slavery guerrilla William C. Quantrill. Quantrill is most famous for riding into Lawrence, Kansas, in 1863 flying a black flag and commanding his men pharaohlike to "kill every male and burn down every house."

"John Vowell," Dad says, "had a little rep for killing people." And since he abandoned my great-grandfather Charles, whose mother died giving birth to him in 1870, and wasn't seen again until 1912, Dad doesn't rule out the possibility that John Vowell could have been one of the hired guns on the Bozeman Trail. So the cannon isn't just another gun to my dad. It's a map of all his obsessions — firearms, certainly, but also American history and family history, subjects he's never bothered separating from each other.

After tooling a million guns, after inventing and building a rifle 20
barrel boring machine, after setting up that complicated shop filed with lathes and blueing tanks and outmoded blacksmithing tools, the cannon is his most ambitious project ever. I thought

that if I was ever going to understand the ballistic bee in his bonnet, this was my chance. It was the biggest gun he ever made and I could experience it and spend time with it with the added bonus of not having to actually pull the trigger myself.

I called Dad and said that I wanted to come to Montana and watch him shoot off the cannon. He was immediately suspicious. But I had never taken much interest in his work before and he would take what he could get. He loaded the cannon into the back of his truck and we drove up into the Bridger Mountains. I was a little worried that the National Forest Service would object to us lobbing fiery balls of metal onto its property. Dad laughed, assuring me that "you cannot shoot fireworks, but this is considered a fire*arm*."

It is a small cannon, about as long as a baseball bat and as wide as a coffee can. But it's heavy — 110 pounds. We park near the side of the hill. Dad takes his gunpowder and other tools out of this adorable wooden box on which he has stenciled "PAT G. VOWELL CANNONWORKS." Cannonworks: So that's what NRA members call a metal-strewn garage.

Dad plunges his homemade bullets into the barrel, points it at an embankment just to be safe, and lights the fuse. When the fuse is lit, it resembles a cartoon. So does the sound, which warrants Ben Day dot° words along the lines of *ker-pow!* There's so much Fourth of July smoke everywhere I feel compelled to sing the national anthem.

I've given this a lot of thought — how to convey the giddiness I felt when the cannon shot off. But there isn't a sophisticated way to say this. It's just really, really cool. My dad thought so, too.

25 Sometimes, I put together stories about the more eccentric corners of the American experience for public radio. So I happen to have my tape recorder with me, and I've never seen levels like these. Every time the cannon goes off, the delicate needles which keep track of the sound quality lurch into the bad, red zone so fast and so hard I'm surprised they don't break.

The cannon was so loud and so painful, I had to touch my head to make sure my skull hadn't cracked open. One thing that my

Ben Day dots: Colored ink dots used in a printing technique that creates vivid colors. They are often used in comics to intensify the depiction of actions and sounds. [Ed.]

dad and I share is that we're both a little hard of hearing — me from Aerosmith, him from gunsmith.

He lights the fuse again. The bullet knocks over the log he was aiming at. I instantly utter a sentence I never in my entire life thought I would say. I tell him, "Good shot, Dad."

Just as I'm wondering what's coming over me, two hikers walk by. Apparently, they have never seen a man set off a homemade cannon in the middle of the wilderness while his daughter holds a foot-long microphone up into the air recording its terrorist boom. One hiker gives me a puzzled look and asks, "So you work for the radio and that's your dad?"

Dad shoots the cannon again so that they can see how it works. The other hiker says, "That's quite the machine you got there." But he isn't talking about the cannon. He's talking about my tape recorder and my microphone — which is called a *shotgun* mike. I stare back at him, then I look over at my father's cannon, then down at my microphone, and I think, Oh. My. God. My dad and I are the same person. We're both smart-alecky loners with goofy projects and weird equipment. And since this whole target practice outing was my idea, I was no longer his adversary. I was his accomplice. What's worse, I was liking it.

I haven't changed my mind about guns. I can get behind the 30
cannon because it is a completely ceremonial object. It's unwieldy and impractical, just like everything else I care about. Try to rob a convenience store with this 110-pound Saturday night special, you'd still be dragging it in the door Sunday afternoon.

I love noise. As a music fan, I'm always waiting for that moment in a song when something just flies out of it and explodes in the air. My dad is a one-man garage band, the kind of rock 'n' roller who slaves away at his art for no reason other than to make his own sound. My dad is an artist — a pretty driven, idiosyncratic one, too. He's got his last *Gesamtkunstwerk*° all planned out. It's a performance piece. We're all in it — my mom, the loneliest twin in history, and me.

When my father dies, take a wild guess what he wants done with his ashes. Here's a hint: It requires a cannon.

Gesamtkunstwerk: "Total artwork," a work that encompasses different branches of art (German). [Ed.]

"You guys are going to love this," he smirks, eyeballing the cannon. "You get to drag this thing up on top of the Gravellies on opening day of hunting season. And looking off at Sphinx Mountain, you get to put me in little paper bags. I can take my last hunting trip on opening morning."

I'll do it, too. I will have my father's body burned into ashes. I will pack these ashes into paper bags. I will go to the mountains with my mother, my sister, and the cannon. I will plunge his remains into the barrel and point it into a hill so that he doesn't take anyone with him. I will light the fuse. But I will not cover my ears. Because when I blow what used to be my dad into the earth, I want it to hurt.

For Discussion and Writing

1. What rights do the First and Second Amendments to the Constitution aim to protect? Why does it make sense that Vowell's favorite is the First, while her father's is the Second?
2. As befits someone who often performs her work on the radio, Vowell is a master storyteller; she has to grab listeners' attention and keep it from wandering to the cooking or the road or the many other distractions with which the radio has to compete. How does she do it? Analyze one of the stories Vowell tells in "Shooting Dad" — for example, the story of the crow-shooting incident or the story of the first and only time she shot a gun — and think about how the way she tells it keeps the reader interested.
3. **connections** While "Shooting Dad" is very funny, it is also about, among other things, a particular dynamic in families. What happens when family members disagree about politics or religion or other fundamental beliefs is complicated, and can sometimes test the relationships between the parties who find themselves in disagreement. Compare Bharati Mukherjee's "Two Ways to Belong in America" (p. 280) to Vowell's essay on these terms. How do the people in each disagree? How do they deal with the fact of their disagreement?
4. Part of the appeal of Vowell's work is its humor. Humor is a notoriously hard thing to analyze: we know when we find something funny because we laugh, out loud or to ourselves, but we have a harder time explaining why something *is* funny. Pick five different moments when you laughed aloud or to yourself at something in Vowell's essay, and try to explain what it was that was funny about each moment. Then see if you can come up with a hypothesis, generalizing from these specific moments, about what makes things funny.

ALICE WALKER

In Search of Our Mothers' Gardens

Alice Walker was born in 1944 in Eatonton, Georgia. She is a widely read novelist whose work The Color Purple *(1982), which won a Pulitzer Prize, was made into a film, and is the work for which she is best known. She has written poetry and short story collections as well as a number of other novels and essay collections, including* In Search of Our Mothers' Gardens *(1983). In all of her work, Walker is concerned with African American history and the production of art, families, and individual identity out of that history.*

"In Search of Our Mothers' Gardens" is taken from a collection with the same name. As many personal essays do, "Our Mothers' Gardens" weaves together stories drawn from the author's life and reflections on larger questions and truths about life inspired by the experiences recounted in the stories. As you read, look out for the techniques Walker uses to connect these two strands.

> I described her own nature and temperament. Told how they needed a larger life for their expression. . . . I pointed out that in lieu of proper channels, her emotions had overflowed into paths that dissipated them. I talked, beautifully I thought, about an art that would be born, an art that would open the way for women the likes of her. I asked her to hope, and build up an inner life against the coming of that day. . . . I sang, with a strange quiver in my voice, a promise song.
>
> — "Avey," JEAN TOOMER, *Cane*
> *The poet speaking to a prostitute*
> *who falls asleep while he's talking*

When the poet Jean Toomer walked through the South in the early twenties, he discovered a curious thing: Black women whose spirituality was so intense, so deep, so *unconscious,* they were themselves unaware of the richness they held. They stumbled blindly through their lives: creatures so abused and mutilated in body, so dimmed and confused by pain, that they considered themselves unworthy even of hope. In the selfless abstractions their bodies became to the men who used them, they became more than "sexual objects," more even than mere women: they became "Saints." Instead of being perceived as whole persons, their bodies became shrines: what was thought to be their minds became temples suitable for worship. These crazy Saints stared out at the world, wildly, like lunatics — or quietly, like suicides; and the "God" that was in their gaze was as mute as a great stone.

Who were these Saints? These crazy, loony, pitiful women?

Some of them, without a doubt, were our mothers and grandmothers.

In the still heat of the post-Reconstruction South, this is how they seemed to Jean Toomer: exquisite butterflies trapped in an evil honey, toiling away their lives in an era, a century, that did not acknowledge them, except as "the *mule* of the world." They dreamed dreams that no one knew — not even themselves, in any coherent fashion — and saw visions no one could understand. They wandered or sat about the countryside crooning lullabies to ghosts, and drawing the mother of Christ in charcoal on courthouse walls.

5 They forced their minds to desert their bodies and their striving spirits sought to rise, like frail whirlwinds from the hard red clay. And when those frail whirlwinds fell, in scattered particles, upon the ground, no one mourned. Instead, men lit candles to celebrate the emptiness that remained, as people do who enter a beautiful but vacant space to resurrect a God.

Our mothers and grandmothers, some of them: moving to music not yet written. And they waited.

They waited for a day when the unknown thing that was in them would be made known; but guessed, somehow in their darkness, that on the day of their revelation they would be long dead. Therefore to Toomer they walked, and even ran, in slow motion. For they were going nowhere immediate, and the future was not yet within their grasp. And men took our mothers and grandmothers, "but got no pleasure from it." So complex was their passion and their calm.

To Toomer, they lay vacant and fallow as autumn fields, with harvest time never in sight: and he saw them enter loveless marriages, without joy; and become prostitutes, without resistance; and become mothers of children, without fulfillment.

For these grandmothers and mothers of ours were not Saints, but Artists; driven to a numb and bleeding madness by the springs of creativity in them for which there was no release. They were Creators, who lived lives of spiritual waste, because they were so rich in spirituality — which is the basis of Art — that the strain of enduring their unused and unwanted talent drove them insane. Throwing away this spirituality was their pathetic attempt to lighten the soul to a weight their work-worn, sexually abused bodies could bear.

What did it mean for a Black woman to be an artist in our 10
grandmothers' time? In our great-grandmothers' day? It is a question with an answer cruel enough to stop the blood.

Did you have a genius of a great-great-grandmother who died under some ignorant and depraved white overseer's lash? Or was she required to bake biscuits for a lazy backwater tramp, when she cried out in her soul to paint watercolors of sunsets, or the rain falling on the green and peaceful pasturelands? Or was her body broken and forced to bear children (who were more often than not sold away from her) — eight, ten, fifteen, twenty children — when her one joy was the thought of modeling heroic figures of rebellion, in stone or clay?

How was the creativity of the Black woman kept alive, year after year and century after century, when for most of the years Black people have been in America, it was a punishable crime for a Black person to read or write? And the freedom to paint, to sculpt, to expand the mind with action did not exist. Consider, if you can bear to imagine it, what might have been the result if singing, too, had been forbidden by law. Listen to the voices of Bessie Smith, Billie Holiday, Nina Simone, Roberta Flack, and Aretha Franklin, among others, and imagine those voices muzzled for life. Then you may begin to comprehend the lives of our "crazy," "Sainted" mothers and grandmothers. The agony of the lives of women who might have been Poets, Novelists, Essayists, and Short-Story Writers (over a period of centuries), who died with their real gifts stifled within them.

And, if this were the end of the story, we would have cause to cry out in my paraphrase of Okot p'Bitek's great poem:

O, my clanswoman
Let us all cry together!
Come,
Let us mourn the death of our mother,
The death of a Queen
The ash that was produced
By a great fire!
O, this homestead is utterly dead
Close the gates
With *lacari* thorns,
For our mother
The creator of the Stool is lost!
And all the young men
Have perished in the wilderness!

But this is not the end of the story, for all the young women — our mothers and grandmothers, *ourselves* — have not perished in the wilderness. And if we ask ourselves why, and search for and find the answer, we will know beyond all efforts to erase it from our minds, just exactly who, and of what, we Black American women are.

15 One example, perhaps the most pathetic, most misunderstood one, can provide a backdrop for our mothers' work: Phillis Wheatley, a slave in the 1700s.

Virginia Woolf, in her book *A Room of One's Own*, wrote that in order for a woman to write fiction she must have two things, certainly: a room of her own (with key and lock) and enough money to support herself.

What then are we to make of Phillis Wheatley, a slave, who owned not even herself? This sickly, frail Black girl who required a servant of her own at times — her health was so precarious — and who, had she been white, would have been easily considered the intellectual superior of all the women and most of the men in the society of her day.

Virginia Woolf wrote further, speaking of course not of our Phillis, that "any woman born with a great gift in the sixteenth century [insert "eighteenth century," insert "Black woman," insert "born or made a slave"] would certainly have gone crazed, shot herself, or ended her days in some lonely cottage outside the village, half witch, half wizard [insert "Saint"], feared and mocked at. For it needs little skill and psychology to be sure that a highly gifted girl who had tried to use her gift of poetry would have been so thwarted and hindered by contrary instincts [add "chains, guns, the lash, the ownership of one's body by someone else, submission to an alien religion"], that she must have lost her health and sanity to a certainty."

The key words, as they relate to Phillis, are "contrary instincts." For when we read the poetry of Phillis Wheatley — as when we read the novels of Nella Larsen or the oddly false-sounding autobiography of that freest of all Black women writers, Zora Hurston — evidence of "contrary instincts" is everywhere. Her loyalties were completely divided, as was, without question, her mind.

But how could this be otherwise? Captured at seven, a slave of 20
wealthy, doting whites who instilled in her the "savagery" of the Africa they "rescued" her from . . . one wonders if she was even able to remember her homeland as she had known it, or as it really was.

Yet, because she did try to use her gift for poetry in a world that made her a slave, she was "so thwarted and hindered by . . . contrary instincts, that she . . . lost her health. . . ." In the last years of her brief life, burdened not only with the need to express her gift but also with a penniless, friendless "freedom" and several small children for whom she was forced to do strenuous work to feed, she lost her health, certainly. Suffering from malnutrition and neglect and who knows what mental agonies, Phillis Wheatley died.

So torn by "contrary instincts" was Black, kidnapped, enslaved Phillis that her description of "the Goddess" — as she poetically called the Liberty she did not have — is ironically, cruelly humorous. And, in fact, has held Phillis up to ridicule for more than a century. It is usually read prior to hanging Phillis's memory as that of a fool. She wrote:

> The Goddess comes, she moves divinely fair,
> Olive and laurel binds her *golden* hair.
> Wherever shines this native of the skies,
> Unnumber'd charms and recent graces rise. [My italics]

It is obvious that Phillis, the slave, combed the "Goddess's" hair every morning; prior, perhaps, to bringing in the milk, or fixing her mistress's lunch. She took her imagery from the one thing she saw elevated above all others.

With the benefit of hindsight we ask, "How could she?"

But at last, Phillis, we understand. No more snickering when 25
your stiff, struggling, ambivalent lines are forced on us. We know now that you were not an idiot or a traitor; only a sickly little Black girl, snatched from your home and country and made a slave; a woman who still struggled to sing the song that was your gift, although in a land of barbarians who praised you for your bewildered tongue. It is not so much what you sang, as that you kept alive, in so many of our ancestors, *the notion of song*.

Black women are called, in the folklore that so aptly identifies one's status in society, "the *mule* of the world," because we have been handed the burdens that everyone else — *everyone* else — refused to carry. We have also been called "Matriarchs," "Superwomen," and "Mean and Evil Bitches." Not to mention "Castraters" and "Sapphire's Mama." When we have pleaded for understanding, our character has been distorted; when we have asked for simple caring, we have been handed empty inspirational appellations, then stuck in the farthest corner. When we have asked for love, we have been given children. In short, even our plainer gifts, our labors of fidelity and love, have been knocked down our throats. To be an artist and a Black woman, even today, lowers our status in many respects, rather than raises it: and yet, artists we will be.

Therefore we must fearlessly pull out of ourselves and look at and identify with our lives the living creativity some of our great-grandmothers were not allowed to know. I stress *some* of them because it is well known that the majority of our great-grandmothers knew, even without "knowing" it, the reality of their spirituality, even if they didn't recognize it beyond what happened in the singing at church — and they never had any intention of giving it up.

How they did it — those millions of Black women who were not Phillis Wheatley, or Lucy Terry or Frances Harper or Zora Hurston or Nella Larsen or Bessie Smith; or Elizabeth Catlett, or Katherine Dunham, either — brings me to the title of this essay, "In Search of Our Mothers' Gardens," which is a personal account that is yet shared, in its theme and its meaning, by all of us. I found, while thinking about the far-reaching world of the creative Black woman, that often the truest answer to a question that really matters can be found very close.

* * *

In the late 1920s my mother ran away from home to marry my father. Marriage, if not running away, was expected of seventeen-year-old girls. By the time she was twenty, she had two children and was pregnant with a third. Five children later, I was born. And this is how I came to know my mother: she seemed a large, soft, loving-eyed woman who was rarely impatient in our home. Her quick, violent temper was on view only a few times a year, when she battled with the white landlord who had the misfortune to suggest to her that her children did not need to go to school.

She made all the clothes we wore, even my brothers' overalls. 30
She made all the towels and sheets we used. She spent the summers canning vegetables and fruits. She spent the winter evenings making quilts enough to cover all our beds.

During the "working" day, she labored beside — not behind — my father in the fields. Her day began before sunup, and did not end until late at night. There was never a moment for her to sit down, undisturbed, to unravel her own private thoughts; never a time free from interruption — by work or the noisy inquiries of her many children. And yet, it is to my mother — and all our mothers who were not famous — that I went in search of the secret of what has fed that muzzled and often mutilated, but vibrant, creative spirit that the Black woman has inherited, and that pops out in wild and unlikely places to this day.

But when, you will ask, did my overworked mother have time to know or care about feeding the creative spirit?

The answer is so simple that many of us have spent years discovering it. We have constantly looked high, when we should have looked high — and low.

For example: in the Smithsonian Institution in Washington, D.C., there hangs a quilt unlike any other in the world. In fanciful, inspired, and yet simple and identifiable figures, it portrays the story of the Crucifixion. It is considered rare, beyond price. Though it follows no known pattern of quiltmaking, and though it is made of bits and pieces of worthless rags, it is obviously the work of a person of powerful imagination and deep spiritual feeling. Below this quilt I saw a note that says it was made by "an anonymous Black woman in Alabama, a hundred years ago."

If we could locate this "anonymous" Black woman from Ala- 35
bama, she would turn out to be one of our grandmothers — an

artist who left her mark in the only materials she could afford, and in the only medium her position in society allowed her to use.

As Virginia Woolf wrote further, in *A Room of One's Own:*

> Yet genius of a sort must have existed among women as it must have existed among the working class. [Change this to "slaves" and "the wives and daughters of sharecroppers."] Now and again an Emily Brontë or a Robert Burns [change this to "a Zora Hurston or a Richard Wright"] blazes out and proves its presence. But certainly it never got itself on to paper. When, however, one reads of a witch being ducked, of a woman possessed by devils [or "Sainthood"], of a wise woman selling herbs [or root workers], or even a very remarkable man who had a mother, then I think we are on the track of a lost novelist, a suppressed poet, or some mute and inglorious Jane Austen. . . . Indeed, I would venture to guess that Anon, who wrote so many poems without signing them, was often a woman. . . .

And so our mothers and grandmothers have, more often than not anonymously, handed on the creative spark, the seed of the flower they themselves never hoped to see: or like a sealed letter they could not plainly read.

And so it is, certainly, with my own mother. Unlike "Ma" Rainey's songs, which retained their creator's name even while blasting forth from Bessie Smith's mouth, no song or poem will bear my mother's name. Yet so many of the stories that I write, that we all write, are my mother's stories. Only recently did I fully realize this: that through years of listening to my mother's stories of her life, I have absorbed not only the stories themselves, but something of the manner in which she spoke, something of the urgency that involves the knowledge that her stories — like her life — must be recorded. It is probably for this reason that so much of what I have written is about characters whose counterparts in real life are so much older than I am.

But the telling of these stories, which came from my mother's lips as naturally as breathing, was not the only way my mother showed herself as an artist. For stories, too, were subject to being distracted, to dying without conclusion. Dinners must be started, and cotton must be gathered before the big rains. The artist that was and is my mother showed itself to me only after many years. This is what I finally noticed:

Like Mem, a character in *The Third Life of Grange Copeland*, 40
my mother adorned with flowers whatever shabby house we were

forced to live in. And not just your typical straggly country stand of zinnias, either. She planted ambitious gardens — and still does — with over fifty different varieties of plants that bloom profusely from early March until late November. Before she left home for the fields, she watered her flowers, chopped up the grass, and laid out new beds. When she returned from the fields she might divide clumps of bulbs, dig a cold pit, uproot and replant roses, or prune branches from her taller bushes or trees — until night came and it was too dark to see.

Whatever she planted grew as if by magic, and her fame as a grower of flowers spread over three counties. Because of her creativity with her flowers, even my memories of poverty are seen through a screen of blooms — sunflowers, petunias, roses, dahlias, forsythia, spirea, delphiniums, verbena . . . and so on.

And I remember people coming to my mother's yard to be given cuttings from her flowers; I hear again the praise showered on her because whatever rocky soil she landed on, she turned into a garden. A garden so brilliant with colors, so original in its design, so magnificent with life and creativity, that to this day people drive by our house in Georgia — perfect strangers and imperfect strangers — and ask to stand or walk among my mother's art.

I notice that it is only when my mother is working in her flowers that she is radiant, almost to the point of being invisible — except as Creator: hand and eye. She is involved in work her soul must have. Ordering the universe in the image of her personal conception of Beauty.

Her face, as she prepares the Art that is her gift, is a legacy of respect she leaves to me, for all that illuminates and cherishes life. She has handed down respect for the possibilities — and the will to grasp them.

For her, so hindered and intruded upon in so many ways, being 45
an artist has still been a daily part of her life. This ability to hold on, even in very simple ways, is work Black women have done for a very long time.

This poem is not enough, but it is something, for the woman who literally covered the holes in our walls with sunflowers:

They were women then
My mama's generation
Husky of voice — Stout of

Step
With fists as well as
Hands
How they battered down
Doors
And ironed
Starched white
Shirts
How they led
Armies
Headragged Generals
Across mined
Fields
Booby-trapped
Kitchens
To discover books
Desks
A place for us
How they knew what we
Must know
Without knowing a page
Of it
Themselves.

Guided by my heritage of a love of beauty and a respect for strength — in search of my mother's garden, I found my own.

And perhaps in Africa over two hundred years ago, there was just such a mother; perhaps she painted vivid and daring decorations in oranges and yellows and greens on the walls of her hut; perhaps she sang — in a voice like Roberta Flack's — *sweetly* over the compounds of her village; perhaps she wove the most stunning mats or told the most ingenious stories of all the village storytellers. Perhaps she was herself a poet — though only her daughter's name is signed to the poems that we know.

Perhaps Phillis Wheatley's mother was also an artist.

Perhaps in more than Phillis Wheatley's biological life is her 50
mother's signature made clear.

For Discussion and Writing

1. Why are the women who are Walker's subject the way they are?
2. Walker asks, "How was the creativity of Black women kept alive, year after year and century after century, when for most of the years Black

people have been in America it was a punishable crime for a Black person to read or write?" (par. 12). How does she answer her question? And, in answering this question, how does she draw a line of cause and effect that begins and ends with two things normally not thought of as directly connected in this way?

3. **connections** Compare the men who Scott Russell Sanders calls his "inheritance" in "The Men We Carry in Our Minds" (p. 346) to the "mothers and grandmothers" (par. 9) Walker connects to Jean Toomer's women. How are they similar? How are they different? How does thinking about them effect each author?
4. Walker paints a powerful picture of her mother's creative output. Can you think of a family member or friend or more distant connection who has a similar creative outlet? Try to describe it — what is made, the making of it, and the person as she or he is doing the making — in a manner that captures the ways in which this activity is about more than itself.

E. B. WHITE

Once More to the Lake

Born in Mount Vernon, New York, in 1899, E. B. White was an editor, essayist, and writer of children's books. He is identified in some circles as the writer of sketches, poems, editorials, and essays for the young New Yorker *magazine and in others as the author of the children's books* Stuart Little *(1945) and* Charlotte's Web *(1952). He is also known for his revision of William Strunk Jr.'s,* The Elements of Style *(1959).*

White's involvement with The Elements of Style *highlights what is for many the most important element of his writing — his style. As you read "Once More to the Lake," look for telling details in his descriptions and take note of the kinds of words he chooses.*

One summer, along about 1904, my father rented a camp on a lake in Maine and took us all there for the month of August. We all got ringworm from some kittens and had to rub Pond's Extract on our arms and legs night and morning, and my father rolled over in a canoe with all his clothes on; but outside of that the vacation was a success and from then on none of us ever thought there was any place in the world like that lake in Maine. We returned summer after summer — always on August 1 for one month. I have since become a salt-water man, but sometimes in summer there are days when the restlessness of the tides and the fearful cold of the sea water and the incessant wind that blows across the afternoon and into the evening make me wish for the placidity of a lake in the woods. A few weeks ago this feeling got so strong I bought myself a couple of bass hooks and a spinner and returned to the lake where we used to go, for a week's fishing and to revisit old haunts.

I took along my son, who had never had any fresh water up his nose and who had seen lily pads only from train windows. On the journey over to the lake I began to wonder what it would be like.

I wondered how time would have marred this unique, this holy spot — the coves and streams, the hills that the sun set behind, the camps and the paths behind the camps. I was sure that the tarred road would have found it out, and I wondered in what other ways it would be desolated. It is strange how much you can remember about places like that once you allow your mind to return into the grooves that lead back. You remember one thing, and that suddenly reminds you of another thing. I guess I remembered clearest of all the early mornings, when the lake was cool and motionless, remembered how the bedroom smelled of the lumber it was made of and of the wet woods whose scent entered through the screen. The partitions in the camp were thin and did not extend clear to the top of the rooms, and as I was always the first up I would dress softly so as not to wake the others, and sneak out into the sweet outdoors and start out in the canoe, keeping close along the shore in the long shadows of the pines. I remembered being very careful never to rub my paddle against the gunwale for fear of disturbing the stillness of the cathedral.

The lake had never been what you would call a wild lake. There were cottages sprinkled around the shores, and it was in farming country although the shores of the lake were quite heavily wooded. Some of the cottages were owned by nearby farmers, and you would live at the shore and eat your meals at the farmhouse. That's what our family did. But although it wasn't wild, it was a fairly large and undisturbed lake and there were places in it that, to a child at least, seemed infinitely remote and primeval.

I was right about the tar: it led to within half a mile of the shore. But when I got back there, with my boy and we settled into a camp near a farmhouse and into the kind of summertime I had known, I could tell that it was going to be pretty much the same as it had been before — I knew it, lying in bed the first morning, smelling the bedroom and hearing the boy sneak quietly out and go off along the shore in a boat. I began to sustain the illusion that he was I, and therefore, by simple transposition, that I was my father. This sensation persisted, kept cropping up all the time we were there. It was not an entirely new feeling, but in this setting it grew much stronger. I seemed to be living a dual existence. I would be in the middle of some simple act, I would be picking up a bait box or laying down a table fork, or I would be saying something, and suddenly it would be not I but my father who was saying the words or making the gesture. It gave me a creepy sensation.

We went fishing the next morning. I felt the same damp moss 5
covering the worms in the bait can, and saw the dragonfly alight on the tip of my rod as it hovered a few inches from the surface of the water. It was the arrival of this fly that convinced me beyond any doubt that everything was as it always had been, that the years were a mirage and that there had been no years. The small waves were the same, chucking the rowboat under the chin as we fished at anchor, and the boat was the same boat, the same color green and the ribs broken in the same places, and under the floorboards the same fresh-water leavings and débris — the dead helgramite, the wisps of moss, the rusty discarded fishhook, the dried blood from yesterday's catch. We stared silently at the tips of our rods, at the dragonflies that came and went. I lowered the tip of mine into the water, tentatively, pensively dislodging the fly, which darted two feet away, poised, darted two feet back, and came to rest again a little farther up the rod. There had been no years between the ducking of this dragonfly and the other one — the one that was part of memory. I looked at the boy, who was silently watching his fly, and it was my hands that held his rod, my eyes watching. I felt dizzy and didn't know which rod I was at the end of.

We caught two bass, hauling them in briskly as though they were mackerel, pulling them over the side of the boat in a businesslike manner without any landing net, and stunning them with a blow on the back of the head. When we got back for a swim before lunch, the lake was exactly where we had left it, the same number of inches from the dock, and there was only the merest suggestion of a breeze. This seemed an utterly enchanted sea, this lake you could leave to its own devices for a few hours and come back to, and find that it had not stirred, this constant and trustworthy body of water. In the shallows, the dark, water-soaked sticks and twigs, smooth and old, were undulating in clusters on the bottom against the clean ribbed sand, and the track of the mussel was plain. A school of minnows swam by, each minnow with its small individual shadow, doubling the attendance, so clear and sharp in the sunlight. Some of the other campers were in swimming, along the shore, one of them with a cake of soap, and the water felt thin and clear and unsubstantial. Over the years there had been this person with the cake of soap, this cultist, and here he was. There had been no years.

Up to the farmhouse to dinner through the teeming, dusty field, the road under our sneakers was only a two-track road. The middle track was missing, the one with the marks of the hooves and the splotches of dried, flaky manure. There had always been three tracks to choose from in choosing which track to walk in; now the choice was narrowed down to two. For a moment I missed terribly the middle alternative. But the way led past the tennis court, and something about the way it lay there in the sun reassured me; the tape had loosened along the backline, the alleys were green with plantains and other weeds, and the net (installed in June and removed in September) sagged in the dry noon, and the whole place steamed with midday heat and hunger and emptiness. There was a choice of pie for dessert, and one was blueberry and one was apple, and the waitresses were the same country girls, there having been no passage of time, only the illusion of it as in a dropped curtain — the waitresses were still fifteen; their hair had been washed, that was the only difference — they had been to the movies and seen the pretty girls with the clean hair.

Summertime, oh, summertime, pattern of life indelible, the fade-proof lake, the woods unshatterable, the pasture with the sweetfern and the juniper forever and ever, summer without end; this was the background, and the life along the shore was the design, the cottagers with their innocent and tranquil design, their tiny docks with the flagpole and the American flag floating against the white clouds in the blue sky, the little paths over the roots of the trees leading from camp to camp and the paths leading back to the outhouses and the can of lime for sprinkling, and at the souvenir counters at the store the miniature birchbark canoes and the postcards that showed things looking a little better than they looked. This was the American family at play, escaping the city heat, wondering whether the newcomers in the camp at the head of the cove were "common" or "nice," wondering whether it was true that the people who drove up for Sunday dinner at the farmhouse were turned away because there wasn't enough chicken.

It seemed to me, as I kept remembering all this, that those times and those summers had been infinitely precious and worth saving. There had been jollity and peace and goodness. The arriving (at the beginning of August) had been so big a business in itself, at the railway station the farm wagon drawn up, the first smell of the pine-laden air, the first glimpse of the smiling farmer, and the great importance of the trunks and your father's enormous authority in such matters, and the feel of the wagon under you for the long ten-mile haul, and at the top of the last long hill catching the first view of the lake after eleven months of not seeing this cherished body of water. The shouts and cries of the other campers when they saw you, and the trunks to be unpacked, to give up their rich burden. (Arriving was less exciting nowadays, when you sneaked up in your car and parked it under a tree near the camp and took out the bags and in five minutes it was all over, no fuss, no loud wonderful fuss about trunks.)

Peace and goodness and jollity. The only thing that was wrong 10
now, really, was the sound of the place, an unfamiliar nervous sound of the outboard motors. This was the note that jarred, the one thing that would sometimes break the illusion and set the years moving. In those other summertimes all motors were inboard; and when they were at a little distance, the noise they made was a sedative, an ingredient of summer sleep. They were one-cylinder and two-cylinder engines, and some were make-and-break and some were jump-spark, but they all made a sleepy sound across the lake. The one-lungers throbbed and fluttered, and the twin-cylinder ones purred and purred, and that was a quiet sound, too. But now the campers all had outboards. In the daytime, in the hot mornings, these motors made a petulant, irritable sound; at night, in the still evening when the afterglow lit the water, they whined about one's ears like mosquitoes. My boy loved our rented outboard, and his great desire was to achieve single-handed mastery over it, and authority, and he soon learned the trick of choking it a little (but not too much), and the adjustment of the needle valve. Watching him I would remember the things you could do with the old one-cylinder engine with the heavy flywheel, how you could have it eating out of your hand if you got really close to it spiritually. Motorboats in those days didn't have clutches, and you would make a landing by shutting off the motor at the proper time and coasting in with a dead rudder. But there was a way of reversing them, if you learned the trick, by cutting the switch and putting it on again exactly on the final dying revolution of the flywheel, so that it would kick back against compression and begin reversing. Approaching a dock in a strong following breeze, it was difficult to slow up sufficiently by the ordinary coasting method, and if a boy felt he had complete mastery over his motor, he was tempted to keep it running beyond its time and then reverse it a

few feet from the dock. It took a cool nerve, because if you threw the switch a twentieth of a second too soon you would catch the flywheel when it still had speed enough to go up past center, and the boat would leap ahead, charging bull-fashion at the dock.

We had a good week at the camp. The bass were biting well and the sun shone endlessly, day after day. We would be tired at night and lie down in the accumulated heat of the little bedrooms after the long hot day and the breeze would stir almost imperceptibly outside and the smell of the swamp drift in through the rusty screens. Sleep would come easily and in the morning the red squirrel would be on the roof, tapping out his gay routine. I kept remembering everything, lying in bed in the mornings — the small steamboat that had a long rounded stern like the lip of a Ubangi, and how quietly she ran on the moonlight sails, when the older boys played their mandolins and the girls sang and we ate doughnuts dipped in sugar, and how sweet the music was on the water in the shining night, and what it had felt like to think about girls then. After breakfast we would go up to the store and the things were in the same place — the minnows in a bottle, the plugs and spinners disarranged and pawed over by the youngsters from the boys' camp, the Fig Newtons and the Beeman's gum. Outside, the road was tarred and cars stood in front of the store. Inside, all was just as it had always been, except there was more Coca-Cola and not so much Moxie and root beer and birch beer and sarsaparilla. We would walk out with the bottle of pop apiece and sometimes the pop would backfire up our noses and hurt. We explored the streams, quietly, where the turtles slid off the sunny logs and dug their way into the soft bottom; and we lay on the town wharf and fed worms to the tame bass. Everywhere we went I had trouble making out which was I, the one walking at my side, the one walking in my pants.

One afternoon while we were there at that lake a thunderstorm came up. It was like the revival of an old melodrama that I had seen long ago with childish awe. The second-act climax of the drama of the electrical disturbance over a lake in America had not changed in any important respect. This was the big scene, still the big scene. The whole thing was so familiar, the first feeling of oppression and heat and a general air around camp of not wanting to go very far away. In midafternoon (it was all the same) a curious darkening of the sky, and a lull in everything that had made life tick; and then the way the boats suddenly swung the other way at their moorings with the coming of a breeze out of the new quarter, and the premonitory rumble. Then the kettle drum, then the snare, then the bass drum and cymbals, then crackling light against the dark, and the gods grinning and licking their chops in the hills. Afterward the calm, the rain steadily rustling in the calm lake, the return of light and hope and spirits, and the campers running out in joy and relief to go swimming in the rain, their bright cries perpetuating the deathless joke about how they were getting simply drenched, and the children screaming with delight at the new sensation of bathing in the rain, and the joke about getting drenched linking the generations in a strong indestructible chain. And the comedian who waded in carrying an umbrella.

When the others went swimming, my son said he was going in, too. He pulled his dripping trunks from the line where they had hung all through the shower and wrung them out. Languidly, and with no thought of going in, I watched him, his hard little body, skinny and bare, saw him wince slightly as he pulled up around his vitals the small, soggy, icy garment. As he buckled the swollen belt, suddenly my groin felt the chill of death.

For Discussion and Writing

1. Why does White describe the lake as "fade-proof" and the woods as "unshatterable" (par. 8)?
2. White uses description to give a fairly simple story great richness. Note and explain the effectiveness of five descriptive moments in the essay.
3. **connections** White's account of his trip turns suddenly to thoughts of mortality. Readers who have been enjoying a placid description of nature and peaceful human activity are generally unprepared for the "chill of death" (par. 13) that grips the essay at its end. Compare this evoking of the unexpected to Bill McKibben's attention to endangerment and extinction in "Curbing Nature's Paparazzi" (p. 267). How does each writer use this surprise? What does each want us to think about?
4. Describe a childhood trip you remember well. Try to borrow descriptive devices from White.

MARIE WINN

Television: The Plug-In Drug

Marie Winn was born in 1936 in Prague, in what is now the Czech Republic, and raised in New York City. She is an author and a translator of Czech writers such as Vaclav Havel, playwright and president of the Czech Republic (1993–2003). The Plug-In Drug: Television, Children, and the Family *(1977, revised 2002) was the first in a series of books by Winn about family in modern society; this excerpt is taken from that book. As you read, follow her sophisticated argument closely.*

Not much more than fifty years after the introduction of television into American society, the medium has become so deeply ingrained in daily life that in many states the TV set has attained the rank of a legal necessity, safe from repossession in case of debt along with clothes and cooking utensils. Only in the early years after television's introduction did writers and commentators have sufficient perspective to separate the activity of watching television from the actual content it offers the viewer. In those days writers frequently discussed the effects of television on family life. However, a curious myopia afflicted those first observers: almost without exception they regarded television as a favorable, beneficial, indeed, wondrous influence upon the family.

"Television is going to be a real asset in every home where there are children," predicted a writer in 1949.

"Television will take over your way of living and change your children's habits, but this change can be a wonderful improvement," claimed another commentator.

"No survey's needed, of course, to establish that television has brought the family together in one room," wrote *The New York Times*'s television critic in 1949.

The early articles about television were almost invariably 5
accompanied by a photograph or illustration showing a family

cozily sitting together before the television set, Sis on Mom's lap, Buddy perched on the arm of Dad's chair, Dad with his arm around Mom's shoulder. Who could have guessed that twenty or so years later Mom would be watching a drama in the kitchen, the kids would be looking at cartoons in their room, while Dad would be taking in the ball game in the living room?

Of course television sets were enormously expensive when they first came on the market. The idea that by the year 2000 more than three quarters of all American families would own two or more sets would have seemed preposterous. The splintering of the multiple-set family was something the early writers did not foresee. Nor did anyone imagine the number of hours children would eventually devote to television, the changes television would effect upon child-rearing methods, the increasing domination of family schedules by children's viewing requirements — in short, the power of television to dominate family life.

As children's consumption of the new medium increased together with parental concern about the possible effects of so much television viewing, a steady refrain helped soothe and reassure anxious parents. "Television always enters a pattern of influences that already exist: the home, the peer group, the school, the church and culture generally," wrote the authors of an early and influential study of television's effects on children. In other words, if the child's home life is all right, parents need not worry about the effects of too much television watching.

But television did not merely influence the child; it deeply influenced that "pattern of influences" everyone hoped would ameliorate the new medium's effects. Home and family life have changed in important ways since the advent of television. The peer group has become television-oriented, and much of the time children spend together is occupied by television viewing. Culture generally has been transformed by television. Participation in church and community activities has diminished, with television a primary cause of this change. Therefore it is improper to assign to television the subsidiary role its many apologists insist it plays. Television is not merely one of a number of important influences upon today's child. Through the changes it has made in family life, television emerges as *the* important influence in children's lives today.

THE QUALITY OF LIFE

Television's contribution to family life has been an equivocal one. For while it has, indeed, kept the members of the family from dispersing, it has not served to bring them together. By its domination of the time families spend together, it destroys the special quality that distinguishes one family from another, a quality that depends to a great extent on what a family does, what special rituals, games, recurrent jokes, familiar songs, and shared activities it accumulates.

Yet parents have accepted a television-dominated family life 10
so completely that they cannot see how the medium is involved in whatever problems they might be having. A first-grade teacher reports:

> I have one child in the group who's an only child. I wanted to find out more about her family life because this little girl was quite isolated from the group, didn't make friends, so I talked to her mother. Well, they don't have time to do anything in the evening, the mother said. The parents come home after picking up the child at the baby-sitter's. Then the mother fixes dinner while the child watches TV. Then they have dinner and the child goes to bed. I said to this mother, "Well, couldn't she help you fix dinner? That would be a nice time for the two of you to talk," and the mother said, "Oh, but I'd hate to have her miss *Zoom*. It's such a good program!"

Several decades ago a writer and mother of two boys aged three and seven described her family's television schedule in a newspaper article. Though some of the programs her kids watched then have changed, the situation she describes remains the same for great numbers of families today:

> We were in the midst of a full-scale War. Every day was a new battle and every program was a major skirmish. We agreed it was a bad scene all around and were ready to enter diplomatic negotiations. . . . In principle we have agreed on 2½ hours of TV a day, *Sesame Street, Electric Company* (with dinner gobbled up in between) and two half-hour shows between 7 and 8:30 which enables the grown-ups to eat in peace and prevents the two boys from destroying one another. Their pre-bedtime choice is dreadful, because, as Josh recently admitted, "There's nothing much on I really like." So . . . it's *What's My Line* or *To Tell the Truth*. . . . Clearly there is a need for first-rate children's shows at this time. . . .

Consider the “family life” described here: Presumably the father comes home from work during the *Sesame Street–Electric Company* stint. The children are either watching television, gobbling their dinner, or both. While the parents eat their dinner in peaceful privacy, the children watch another hour of television. Then there is only a half-hour left before bedtime, just enough time for baths, getting pajamas on, brushing teeth, and so on. The children’s evening is regimented with an almost military precision. They watch their favorite programs, and when there is “nothing much on I really like,” they watch whatever else is on — because *watching* is the important thing. Their mother does not see anything amiss with watching programs just for the sake of watching; she only wishes there were some first-rate children’s shows on at those times.

Without conjuring up fantasies of bygone eras with family games and long, leisurely meals, the question arises: Isn’t there a better family life available than this dismal, mechanized arrangement of children watching television for however long is allowed them, evening after evening?

Of course, families today still do things together at times: go camping in the summer, go to the zoo on a nice Sunday, take various trips and expeditions. But their ordinary daily life together is diminished — those hours of sitting around at the dinner table, the spontaneous taking up of an activity, the little games invented by children on the spur of the moment when there is nothing else to do, the scribbling, the chatting, and even the quarreling, all the things that form the fabric of a family, that define a childhood. Instead, the children have their regular schedule of television programs and bedtime, and the parents have their peaceful dinner together.

15 The author of the quoted newspaper article notes that “keeping a family sane means mediating between the needs of both children and adults.” But surely the needs of the adults in that family were being better met than the needs of the children. The kids were effectively shunted away and rendered untroublesome, while their parents enjoyed a life as undemanding as that of any childless couple. In reality, it is those very demands that young children make upon a family that lead to growth, and it is the way parents respond to those demands that builds the relationships

upon which the future of the family depends. If the family does not accumulate its backlog of shared experiences, shared everyday experiences that occur and recur and change and develop, then it is not likely to survive as anything other than a caretaking institution.

FAMILY RITUALS

Ritual is defined by sociologists as "that part of family life that the family likes about itself, is proud of and wants formally to continue." Another text notes that "the development of a ritual by a family is an index of the common interest of its members in the family as a group."

What has happened to family rituals, those regular, dependable, recurrent happenings that give members of a family a feeling of belonging to a home rather than living in it merely for the sake of convenience, those experiences that act as the adhesive of family unity far more than any material advantages?

Mealtime rituals, going-to-bed rituals, illness rituals, holiday rituals — how many of these have survived the inroads of the television set?

A young woman who grew up near Chicago reminisces about her childhood and gives an idea of the effects of television upon family rituals:

> As a child I had millions of relatives around — my parents both come from relatively large families. My father had nine brothers and sisters. And so every holiday there was this great swoop-down of aunts, uncles, and millions of cousins. I just remember how wonderful it used to be. The cousins would come and everyone would play and ultimately, after dinner, all the women would be in the front of the house, drinking coffee and talking, all the men would be in the back of the house, drinking and smoking, and all the kids would be all over the place, playing hide and seek. Christmas time was particularly nice because everyone always brought all their toys and games. Our house had a couple of rooms with go-through closets, so there were always kids running in a great circle route. I remember it was just wonderful.
>
> And then all of a sudden one year I remember becoming suddenly aware of how different everything had become. The kids were no longer playing Monopoly or Clue or the other games we used to play together. It was because we had a television set which had been turned on for a football game. All of that socializing that had gone on previously had

> ended. Now everyone was sitting in front of the television set, on a holiday, at a family party! I remember being stunned by how awful that was. Somehow the television had become more attractive.

As families have come to spend more and more of their time 20
together engaged in the single activity of television watching, those rituals and pastimes that once gave family life its special quality have become more and more uncommon. Not since prehistoric times, when cave families hunted, gathered, ate, and slept, with little time remaining to accumulate a culture of any significance, have families been reduced to such a sameness.

REAL PEOPLE

The relationships of family members to each other are affected by television's powerful competition in both obvious and subtle ways. For surely the hours that children spend in a one-way relationship with television people, an involvement that allows for no communication or interaction, must have some effect on their relationships with real-life people.

Studies show the importance of eye-to-eye contact, for instance, in real-life relationships, and indicate that the nature of one's eye-contact patterns, whether one looks another squarely in the eye or looks to the side or shifts one's gaze from side to side, may play a significant role in one's success or failure in human relationships. But no eye contact is possible in the child-television relationship, although in certain children's programs people purport to speak directly to the child and the camera fosters this illusion by focusing directly upon the person being filmed. How might such a distortion affect a child's development of trust, of openness, of an ability to relate well to *real* people?

Bruno Bettelheim suggested an answer:

> Children who have been taught, or conditioned, to listen passively most of the day to the warm verbal communications coming from the TV screen, to the deep emotional appeal of the so-called TV personality, are often unable to respond to real persons because they arouse so much less feeling than the skilled actor. Worse, they lose the ability to learn from reality because life experiences are much more complicated than the ones they see on the screen. . . .

A teacher makes a similar observation about her personal viewing experiences:

> I have trouble mobilizing myself and dealing with real people after watching a few hours of television. It's just hard to make that transition from watching television to a real relationship. I suppose it's because there was no effort necessary while I was watching, and dealing with real people always requires a bit of effort. Imagine, then, how much harder it might be to do the same thing for a small child, particularly one who watches a lot of television every day.

But more obviously damaging to family relationships is the 25
elimination of opportunities to talk and converse, or to argue, to air grievances between parents and children and brothers and sisters. Families frequently use television to avoid confronting their problems, problems that will not go away if they are ignored but will only fester and become less easily resolvable as time goes on.

A mother reports:

> I find myself, with three children, wanting to turn on the TV set when they're fighting. I really have to struggle not to do it because I feel that's telling them this is the solution to the quarrel — but it's so tempting that I often do it.

A family therapist discusses the use of television as an avoidance mechanism:

> In a family I know the father comes home from work and turns on the television set. The children come and watch with him and the wife serves them their meal in front of the set. He then goes and takes a shower, or works on the car or something. She then goes and has her own dinner in front of the television set. It's a symptom of a deeper-rooted problem, sure. But it would help them all to get rid of the set. It would be far easier to work on what the symptom really means without the television. The television simply encourages a double avoidance of each other. They'd find out more quickly what was going on if they weren't able to hide behind the TV. Things wouldn't necessarily be better, of course, but they wouldn't be anesthetized.

A number of research studies done when television was a relatively new medium demonstrated that television interfered with family activities and the formation of family relationships. One survey showed that 78 percent of the respondents indicated no conversation taking place during viewing except at specified times such as commercials. The study noted: "The television atmosphere in most households is one of quiet absorption on the part of family members who are present. The nature of the family social life during a program could be described as 'parallel' rather than interactive, and the set does seem to dominate family life when it is on." Thirty-six percent of the respondents in another study indicated that television viewing was the only family activity participated in during the week.

The situation has only worsened during the intervening decades. When the studies were made, the great majority of American families had only one television set. Though the family may have spent more time watching TV in those early days, at least they were all together while they watched. Today the vast majority of all families have two or more sets, and nearly a third of all children live in homes with four or more TVs. The most telling statistic: almost 60 percent of all families watch television during meals, and not necessarily at the same TV set. When do they talk about what they did that day? When do they make plans, exchange views, share jokes, tell about their triumphs or little disasters? When do they get to be a real family?

UNDERMINING THE FAMILY

Of course television has not been the only factor in the decline of 30
family life in America. The steadily rising divorce rate, the increase in the number of working mothers, the trends towards people moving far away from home, the breakdown of neighborhoods and communities — all these have seriously affected the family.

Obviously the sources of family breakdown do not necessarily come from the family itself, but from the circumstances in which the family finds itself and the way of life imposed upon it by those circumstances. As Urie Bronfenbrenner has suggested:

> When those circumstances and the way of life they generate undermine relationships of trust and emotional security between family members, when they make it difficult for parents to care for, educate and enjoy their children, when there is no support or recognition from the outside world for one's role as a parent and when time spent with one's family means frustration of career, personal fulfillment and peace of mind, then the development of the child is adversely affected.

Certainly television is not the single destroyer of American family life. But the medium's dominant role in the family serves to anesthetize parents into accepting their family's diminished state and prevents them from struggling to regain some of the richness the family once possessed.

One research study alone seems to contradict the idea that television has a negative impact on family life. In their important book *Television and the Quality of Life*, sociologists Robert Kubey and Mihaly Csikszentmihalyi observe that the heaviest viewers of TV among their subjects were "no less likely to spend time with their families" than the lightest viewers. Moreover, those heavy viewers reported feeling happier, more relaxed, and satisfied when watching TV with their families than light viewers did. Based on these reports, the researchers reached the conclusion that "television viewing harmonizes with family life."

Using the same data, however, the researchers made another observation about the heavy and light viewers: ". . . families that spend substantial portions of their time together watching television are likely to experience greater percentages of their family time feeling relatively passive and unchallenged compared with families who spend small proportions of their time watching TV."

At first glance the two observations seem at odds: the heavier 35
viewers feel happy and satisfied, yet their family time is more passive and unchallenging — less satisfying in reality. But when one considers the nature of the television experience, the contradiction vanishes. Surely it stands to reason that the television experience is instrumental in preventing viewers from recognizing its dulling effects, much as a mind-altering drug might do.

In spite of everything, the American family muddles on, dimly aware that something is amiss but distracted from an understanding of its plight by an endless stream of television images. As family ties grow weaker and vaguer, as children's lives become more separate from their parents', as parents' educational role in their children's lives is taken over by the media, the school, and the peer group, family life becomes increasingly more unsatisfying for both parents and children. All that seems to be left is love, an abstraction that family members know is necessary but find great difficulty giving to each other since the traditional opportunities for expressing it within the family have been reduced or eliminated.

For Discussion and Writing

1. What does the change in the price of television sets from their invention to today have to do with Winn's essay?
2. Winn's thesis is fairly straightforward — television keeps family members from being as close as they might be — but the way she argues it is complicated. Outline her argument, noting the ways in which television impedes closeness.
3. **connections** Winn titles her last section "Undermining the Family." Compare her description of the American family, and what's lost when it succumbs to television, to David Sedaris's account of his family in "A Plague of Tics" (p. 359). Does he idealize family? Is his picture dark? Is love, which Winn believes the contemporary American family under the thrall of television has a hard time expressing, present in Sedaris's family? How does it express itself?
4. Keep a journal of your television viewing habits and your mental and emotional state during and after your viewing. Review your journal and select a time period. How did you feel, and how did you relate to others?

VIRGINIA WOOLF

The Death of the Moth

Born Adeline Virginia Stephen in London in 1882, Virginia Woolf is one of the most important writers not just of her time but of all literary history. A modernist, Woolf, along with contemporaries such as James Joyce, T. S. Eliot, Ezra Pound, and Gertrude Stein, revolutionized literature by inventing new forms that explored the rich inner lives of their subjects. She is known especially for the novels Mrs. Dalloway *(1925) and* To the Lighthouse *(1927), but also for the nonfiction and feminist* A Room of One's Own *(1929).*

"The Death of the Moth" was published in The Death of the Moth and Other Essays *(1942) after Woolf's suicide. While the essay should and does stand on its own, how might what we know about Woolf's life and death color the way we read this piece?*

Moths that fly by day are not properly to be called moths; they do not excite that pleasant sense of dark autumn nights and ivy-blossom which the commonest yellow-underwing asleep in the shadow of the curtain never fails to rouse in us. They are hybrid creatures, neither gay like butterflies nor somber like their own species. Nevertheless the present specimen, with his narrow hay-colored wings, fringed with a tassel of the same color, seemed to be content with life. It was a pleasant morning, mid-September, mild, benignant, yet with a keener breath than that of the summer months. The plough was already scoring the field opposite the window, and where the share had been, the earth was pressed flat and gleamed with moisture. Such vigor came rolling in from the fields and the down beyond that it was difficult to keep the eyes strictly turned upon the book. The rooks too were keeping one of their annual festivities; soaring round the tree tops until it looked as if a vast net with thousands of black knots in it had been cast up into the air; which, after a few moments sank slowly down upon the trees until every twig seemed to have a knot at the end of it. Then, suddenly, the net would be thrown into the air again in a wider circle this time, with the utmost clamor and vociferation, as though to be thrown into the air and settle slowly down upon the tree tops were a tremendously exciting experience.

The same energy which inspired the rooks, the ploughmen, the horses, and even, it seemed, the lean bare-backed downs, sent the moth fluttering from side to side of his square of the window-pane. One could not help watching him. One was, indeed, conscious of a queer feeling of pity for him. The possibilities of pleasure seemed that morning so enormous and so various that to have only a moth's part in life, and a day moth's at that, appeared a hard fate, and his zest in enjoying his meager opportunities to the full, pathetic. He flew vigorously to one corner of his compartment, and, after waiting there a second, flew across to the other. What remained for him but to fly to a third corner and then to a fourth? That was all he could do, in spite of the size of the downs, the width of the sky, the far-off smoke of houses, and the romantic voice, now and then, of a steamer out at sea. What he could do he did. Watching him, it seemed as if a fiber, very thin but pure, of the enormous energy of the world had been thrust into his frail and diminutive body. As often as he crossed the pane, I could fancy that a thread of vital light became visible. He was little or nothing but life.

Yet, because he was so small, and so simple a form of the energy that was rolling in at the open window and driving its way through so many narrow and intricate corridors in my own brain and in those of other human beings, there was something marvellous as well as pathetic about him. It was as if someone had taken a tiny bead of pure life and decking it as lightly as possible with down and feathers, had set it dancing and zig-zagging to show us the true nature of life. Thus displayed one could not get over the strangeness of it. One is apt to forget all about life, seeing it humped and bossed and garnished and cumbered so that it has to move with the greatest circumspection and dignity. Again, the thought of all that life might have been had he been born in any other shape caused one to view his simple activities with a kind of pity.

After a time, tired by his dancing apparently, he settled on the window ledge in the sun, and, the queer spectacle being at an end, I forgot about him. Then, looking up, my eye was caught by him.

He was trying to resume his dancing, but seemed either so stiff or so awkward that he could only flutter to the bottom of the window-pane; and when he tried to fly across it he failed. Being intent on other matters I watched these futile attempts for a time without thinking, unconsciously waiting for him to resume his flight, as one waits for a machine, that has stopped momentarily, to start again without considering the reason of its failure. After perhaps a seventh attempt he slipped from the wooden ledge and fell, fluttering his wings, on to his back on the window sill. The helplessness of his attitude roused me. It flashed upon me that he was in difficulties; he could no longer raise himself; his legs struggled vainly. But, as I stretched out a pencil, meaning to help him to right himself, it came over me that the failure and awkwardness were the approach of death. I laid the pencil down again.

The legs agitated themselves once more. I looked as if for the 5
enemy against which he struggled. I looked out of doors. What had happened there? Presumably it was midday, and work in the fields had stopped. Stillness and quiet had replaced the previous animation. The birds had taken themselves off to feed in the brooks. The horses stood still. Yet the power was there all the same, massed outside indifferent, impersonal, not attending to anything in particular. Somehow it was opposed to the little hay-colored moth. It was useless to try to do anything. One could only watch the extraordinary efforts made by those tiny legs against an oncoming doom which could, had it chosen, have submerged an entire city, not merely a city, but masses of human beings; nothing, I knew, had any chance against death. Nevertheless after a pause of exhaustion the legs fluttered again. It was superb this last protest, and so frantic that he succeeded at last in righting himself. One's sympathies, of course, were all on the side of life. Also, when there was nobody to care or to know, this gigantic effort on the part of an insignificant little moth, against a power of such magnitude, to retain what no one else valued or desired to keep, moved one strangely. Again, somehow, one saw life, a pure bead. I lifted the pencil again, useless though I knew it to be. But even as I did so, the unmistakable tokens of death showed themselves. The body relaxed, and instantly grew stiff. The struggle was over. The insignificant little creature now knew death. As I looked at the dead moth, this minute wayside triumph of so great

a force over so mean an antagonist filled me with wonder. Just as life had been strange a few minutes before, so death was now as strange. The moth having righted himself now lay most decently and uncomplainingly composed. O yes, he seemed to say, death is stronger than I am.

For Discussion and Writing

1. What is the connection Woolf makes between the moth and the other things she sees outside her window?
2. When thinking about such large subjects as life and death, why does Woolf take as her immediate subject such a small creature? Reread the essay with that question in mind, focusing on the most descriptive passages, and try to answer by imagining alternative ways she might have written it.
3. **connections** Both Woolf's "The Death of the Moth" and E. B. White's "Once More to the Lake" (p. 431) deal with nature and contemplate death. How are their descriptions and the themes they develop from those descriptions different?
4. Remember a time when you saw an animal die or saw a recently dead animal. What did it make you think of?

Documentation Guide

Engaging with the work of others is an important part of academic writing. When writing formal essays about the works in *50 Essays*, or when you refer in your writing to other outside sources, you need to acknowledge these sources. When you summarize, paraphrase, or quote outside sources in your writing, it is crucial that you properly acknowledge them. It is important for two reasons. First, it demonstrates that you are joining the intellectual discussion, writing not just about your own ideas and out of your own experience but in conversation with the ideas and experiences of others. Second, it is your ethical responsibility to acknowledge when the words and ideas that appear in your work do not originate with you; if you don't, you will be guilty of plagiarism, a serious academic offense carrying serious consequences and also an act of dishonesty.

Documentation is the word for the activity of acknowledging sources. There are different systems or styles of documentation; the style most often used in English and the humanities is that recommended by the Modern Language Association (MLA). Below are some examples of the most common kinds of documentation in MLA style; consult the *MLA Handbook for Writers of Research Papers*, seventh edition, at http://mla.org/style, and Diana Hacker's *Research and Documentation Online* at http://www.hackerhandbooks.com/resdoc/ for additional information and models.

MLA PARENTHETICAL CITATIONS

MLA style is fairly simple. When you need to cite a source, you do so in a parenthetical in-text citation. Rather than use footnotes or endnotes, you insert, before the period at the end of the sentence, a parenthetical reference that lets readers know the source and, usually, where in the source the particular material can be found. If the source is clear from the sentence itself, you need only include a page number in parentheses; if the source is not clear, including the author's name along with the page number will be enough to allow the reader to find the source in the list of works cited, which you will include at the end of your essay (guidelines for which follow this section). Below are some examples of the most common kinds of parenthetical citations. There are a number of exceptions to these general rules; you'll find these below too.

ONE AUTHOR

The Emigrants begins: "At the end of September 1970, shortly before I took up my position in Norwich, I drove out to Hingham with Clara in search of somewhere to live" (Sebald 3).

TWO OR THREE AUTHORS

According to the Enlightenment, "thinking is the creation of unified, scientific order and the derivation of factual knowledge from principles" (Horkheimer and Adorno 83).

FOUR OR MORE AUTHORS

As one letter to the editor of an intellectual journal put it: "Eighteen months later, the CIA is still stonewalling" (Blakey et al. 65).

UNKNOWN AUTHOR

Of the avian flu, a recent editorial states: "Nobody has the foggiest idea whether a pandemic will arrive in the near future or how severe one might be, but federal officials argue, persuasively, that we have to brace ourselves for the worst" ("Vaccine Capacity" A22).

SOURCE WITHOUT PAGE NUMBERS

As a recent article on the Web periodical *Inside Higher Education* explains, in many federal agencies, "it is standard practice for external groups to formally ask officials to begin a process to review a specific rule or set of rules" (Lederman).

INDIRECT SOURCE

In his autobiography, Ford wrote, "If I'm remembered, it will probably be for healing the land" (qtd. in Patterson 94).

MLA LIST OF WORKS CITED

The works cited list is the place where your reader can go to find out more information about the sources cited in your parenthetical citations. Follow these guidelines for the format for this list, which should be given its own page or pages: It should be organized alphabetically by author's last name or first major word in the title; it should be double-spaced; each entry should begin at the left margin; and the second (and all following) lines of an entry should be indented one tab (or five spaces, or one half inch).

Books

ONE AUTHOR

Cohen, Samuel. *After the End of History: American Fiction in the 1990s.* Iowa City: U of Iowa P, 2009. Print.

TWO OR THREE AUTHORS

Mohlenbrock, Robert H., and Paul M. Thomson, Jr. *Flowering Plants: Smartweeds to Hazelnuts.* 2nd ed. Carbondale: Southern Illinois UP, 2009. Print.

FOUR OR MORE AUTHORS

Gordin, Seth, et al. *Do More Great Work: Stop the Busywork. Start the Work That Matters.* New York: Workman, 2010. Print.

TWO OR MORE BOOKS BY THE SAME AUTHOR

Menand, Louis. *The Marketplace of Ideas: Reform and Resistance in the American University.* New York: Norton, 2010. Print.

---. *The Metaphysical Club: A Story of Ideas in America.* New York: Farrar, 2001. Print.

BOOK WITH AN EDITOR

Woolf, Virginia. *Mrs. Dalloway*. Ed. Mark Hussey. Fort Washington: Harvest, 2005. Print.

WORK IN AN ANTHOLOGY

Hughes, Langston. "Salvation." *50 Essays*. Ed. Samuel Cohen. 3rd ed. Boston: Bedford, 2011. 179–81. Print.

MULTIVOLUME WORK

Knellwolf, Christa, and Christopher Norris, eds. *The Cambridge History of Literary Criticism*. 9 vols. Cambridge: Cambridge UP, 1900–2000. Print.

EDITION OTHER THAN THE FIRST

Dostoevsky, Fyodor. *The Brothers Karamazov*. Ed. Susan McReynolds. 2nd ed. New York: Norton, 2010. Print.

Periodicals

ARTICLE IN A JOURNAL

Gray, W. Russel. "Jimmying the Back Door of Literature: Dashiell Hammett's Blue-Collar Modernism." *Popular Culture* 41.5 (2008): 762–83. Print.

ARTICLE IN A MONTHLY MAGAZINE

Jones, Tim. "Desperation Theology." *Harper's* Mar. 2010: 16–18. Print.

ARTICLE IN A WEEKLY MAGAZINE

Baker, William F. "How to Save the News." *Nation* 12 Oct. 2009: 11. Print.

ARTICLE IN A NEWSPAPER

Wheatcroft, Geoffrey. "Why Orwell Endures." *New York Times* 14 Feb. 2010, New England ed.: 27. Print.

EDITORIAL OR LETTER TO THE EDITOR

Rouchka, Megan. Letter. *Columbia Missourian* 4 May 2006: A7. Print.

Electronic Sources

ENTIRE WEB SITE

The Smoking Gun. Turner Sports and Entertainment Digital Network, 2010. Web. 19 Feb. 2010.

SHORT WORK FROM A WEB SITE

"What Is MLA Style?" *Modern Language Association.* Mod. Lang. Assn., 13 Jan. 2009. Web. 17 Apr. 2009.

WORK FROM A SUBSCRIPTION SERVICE

Kuhnhenn, James. "Frist Facing Difficulties in Final Year of Senate." *Chattanooga Times Free Press* 13 Nov. 2005: A7. *LexisNexis Academic.* Web. 21 Mar. 2006.

ONLINE BOOK

Lewis, Sinclair. *Babbitt.* New York: Harcourt, 1922. *Bartleby.com: Great Books Online.* Web. 19 Feb. 2010.

ARTICLE IN AN ONLINE PERIODICAL

Reis, Rick. "Keeping It Simple." *Inside Higher Education* 19 Feb. 2010. Web. 19 Feb. 2010.

CD-ROM

Nimchinsky, Howard, and Jocelyn Camp. *Art of Literature.* New York: Longman, 2005. CD-ROM.

E-MAIL

Munk, Jonathan. "Re: Interplanetary Funksmen, Ahoy." Message to the author. 18 Jan. 2006. E-mail.

Other Sources

ADVERTISEMENT

LG. Advertisement. *Vanity Fair* Aug. 2009: 43–46. Print.

INTERVIEW

Gates, Henry Louis. Interview by Stephen Colbert. *The Colbert Report*. Comedy Central. 4 Feb. 2010. Television.

GOVERNMENT DOCUMENT

United States. Dept. of Education. "Saving Education Jobs and Promoting Reform." *ED.gov.* US Dept. of Educ., 19 Feb. 2010. Web. 22 Feb. 2010.

FILM, VIDEO, OR DVD

Soderbergh, Steven, dir. *The Informant!* Perf. Matt Damon. Warner Bros., 18 Sept. 2009. DVD.

TELEVISION OR RADIO PROGRAM

"Somewhere Out There." *This American Life.* Narr. Ira Glass. Natl. Public Radio. KBIA, Columbia, 15 Jan. 2010. Radio.

Glossary of Writing Terms

Allusion A reference to an artistic work, person, place, or event about which readers are assumed to already know. The relevance of the reference is also not usually explained: Readers are assumed to understand the connection between the writer's subject and the thing referred to. As a result of these assumptions, allusion is an economical way of making a point, as it crams a lot of information into a few words. When Judith Ortiz Cofer, in "The Myth of the Latin Woman: I Just Met a Girl Named Maria" (p. 91), refers to popular songs (as she does in her title, to a song from the musical *West Side Story*), she is making allusions — assuming that we will be familiar with her references and that we will understand the connections she is trying to make between popular songs and stereotypes.

Analogy An extended comparison. An analogy explains features of one thing by reference to features shared with something more commonly known and understood. In "Curbing Nature's Paparazzi" (p. 267), Bill McKibben makes his analogy plain in his title. His subject — the practice of wildlife photography — is likened to the actions of celebrity-stalking photographers, and the analogy expresses his argument that wildlife photographers "harass" (par. 2) the animals whose pictures they sell in much the same way that paparazzi harass movie stars.

Argument Writing that attempts to prove a point through reasoning. Argument presses its case by using logic and by supporting its logic with examples and **evidence**. When Elizabeth Cady Stanton, in "Declaration of Sentiments and Resolutions" (p. 379), argues for the rights of women by listing wrongs done them, she introduces her list like this: "The history of mankind is a history of repeated injuries and usurpations on the part of man toward woman, having in direct object the establishment of an absolute tyranny over her. To prove this, let facts be submitted to a candid world" (par. 3). Making a **claim** and then making the transition to supporting examples, Cady's writing is argument.

Audience As actors have audiences who can see and hear them, writers have readers. Having a sense of audience is important in writing because we write differently depending on who we think will be reading our work. If the audience is specific, we write in such a way that will appeal to a small group; if it is general, we write in such a way that as many people as possible will listen to, and be able to hear, what we have to say. It is especially easy to see considerations of audience in speeches, as in Sojourner Truth's "Ain't I a Woman?" (p. 410), and in public documents such as Thomas Jefferson's Declaration of Independence (p. 187), but it can also be seen in works in which writers are trying to explain their experiences to readers who might not have had such experiences themselves, as in Brent Staples's "Just Walk on By: Black Men and Public Space" (p. 383).

Cause and effect Analysis of events or situations in which reasons are sought and effects are considered. Writers tracing the chain of events leading to a present situation or arguing the consequences of a future decision are doing cause and effect writing. Marie Winn's "Television: The Plug-In Drug" (p. 438) is an argument about the effects of television watching on families, as is clear in this sentence from the middle of the essay: "But more obviously damaging to family relationships is the elimination of opportunities to talk and converse, or to argue, to air grievances between parents and children and brothers and sisters" (par. 25).

Claim What an argument tries to prove. Often called a **thesis**. Steven Johnson's claim in "Games" (p. 196), **paraphrased**, is that video games are bad for children. To support this thesis, he makes claims about the growth of what he calls "nonliterary popular culture" and the complementary set of skills this nonliterary popular culture develops in children.

Classification and division The sorting out of elements into classes or groups, or the separation of something into its parts. Classification and division are used when a writer wants to break something down into its elements or group a number of things in order to analyze them. When Mike Rose talks about different kinds of teachers and students in " 'I Just Wanna Be Average' " (p. 331), he is classifying; when Amy Tan in "Mother Tongue" (p. 396) breaks down her language use into the various Englishes she uses, she is dividing.

Cliché An old, tired expression that writers should avoid like the plague. "Like the plague" is an example of cliché. When drafting and especially when revising, writers scan their work for words and phrases that have that less-than-fresh feeling and strike them out. "Like the plague," for example, can be replaced with a new, concrete image, which "like the plague" must have been at one time (closer to the time of the plague itself, perhaps). The uniqueness of a writer's voice comes in part from the words chosen. Using well-worn, often-chosen phrases can be thought of, then, as a lost opportunity.

Comparison and contrast Examination of similarities and differences. One usually but not always appears with the other. Bharati Mukherjee's "Two Ways to Belong in America" (p. 280) shows in its first sentence that differences often arise between similar things, and so that comparison and contrast often go together: "This is a tale of two sisters from Calcutta, Mira and Bharati, who have lived in the United States for some 35 years, but who find themselves on different sides in the current debate over the status of immigrants" (par. 1).

Conclusion The ending of an **essay**, which should bring the writer's point home in a few sentences or even a **paragraph** or two. Good conclusions do more than repeat a **thesis**, and they can even sometimes point the way to extensions of the thesis, but they should not introduce entirely new thoughts. Conclusions can also be funny, as when Swift, at the end of "A Modest Proposal" (p. 387), insists he has no personal interest at stake in his **ironic** proposal that the people of Ireland eat their infants as, in his words, "I have no children by which I can propose to get a single penny; the youngest being nine years old, and my wife past childbearing" (par. 33).

Definition Explanation of the nature of a word, thing, or idea. **Essays** that define may use many other kinds of writing, such as **description**, **exposition**, and **narration**. Definition essays often are really redefinition essays: They attempt to make us understand something we thought we already understood. When Nancy Mairs writes, in "On Being a Cripple" (p. 244), "As a cripple, I swagger" (par. 2), she is embracing a label that others have tried not to use and she is redefining what it means.

Description Depiction through sensory evidence. Description is not just visual: It can use details of touch, smell, taste, and hearing. These concrete details can support a specific **argument**, give the reader a sense of immediacy, or establish a mood. Description, while tied to the concrete, can also use **metaphor**, as when Richard Rodriguez writes in "Aria: Memoir of a Bilingual Childhood" (p. 307), "At one point his words slid together to form one word — sounds as confused as the threads of blue and green oil in the puddle next to my shoes" (par. 16).

Diction Word choice. Can be characterized in terms of level of formality (formal or informal), concreteness (specific or abstract), and other choices that reflect a level appropriate to the writer's subject and **audience**. Diction is a central vehicle by which a writer makes her meaning clear, and it is a major element of a writer's style as well, and so of her tone. "The Declaration of Independence" (p. 187) is an excellent example of careful word choice. In this important document, Thomas Jefferson had to make every word count, and in his choice of words, some repeated, such as *equal*, *usurpations*, *tyrant*, and *independent*, Jefferson made his meaning very clear indeed.

Draft An unfinished **essay**. A draft may have a **conclusion**, but it has not been completely revised, edited, and proofread. When still in the draft stage, writers can rethink not just the structure of their essay but their ideas as well.

Essay A short nonfiction piece of writing. A writer should present one main idea in an essay. There are different kinds of essay — scholarly and personal, formal and informal — and many that mix these different kinds of writing.

Evidence The facts that support an **argument**. Evidence takes different forms depending on the kind of writing in which it appears, but it generally is concrete, agreed-on information that can be pointed to as example or proof. In "Serving in Florida" (p. 135), Barbara Ehrenreich supports the narrative of her experiences living as a low-income worker with both a detailed survey of the living conditions of her coworkers and statistical support gleaned from research. Ehrenreich's argument is strengthened by inclusion of these different kinds of evidence.

Exemplification Providing specific instances in support of general ideas. In "On Compassion" (p. 46), Barbara Lazear Ascher tells a number of anecdotes that serve as examples of encounters between the less fortunate and those who offer help.

Exposition Writing that explains. Rather than showing, as in **narrative**, exposition tells. A majority of **essays** contain some exposition because they need to convey information, give background, or tell how events occurred or processes work. Lars Eighner uses exposition in "On Dumpster Diving" (p. 146) to explain who scavenges from Dumpsters, how they do it, how things in Dumpsters get there, and many other things related to Dumpster diving.

Fallacy A logical error. Fallacies weaken an argument. They include the making of false choices, the false assigning of cause (as in saying that because something happened after something else, the first event caused the second), the making of false generalizations, and many others. Martin Luther King Jr., in his argument against criticisms made of him, in "Letter from Birmingham Jail" (p. 223), exposes a number of these fallacies in arguments made by his critics.

Introduction The beginning of an **essay**; it should generally state a writer's main point. An introduction can include a **thesis statement** and can even begin to develop the **thesis**, but it can also simply pose a question, the answer to which will be the essay's thesis, or it can begin with a **story**, out of which the thesis will come. William F. Buckley Jr.'s "Why Don't We Complain?" (p. 76) is a good example of this kind of introduction.

Irony Verbal irony is writing that says one thing while it means something else, often the opposite of what it says (sarcasm is one form of verbal irony). The difference between literal meaning and implicit meaning is often used to suggest the difference between what a situation or person seems or pretends to be and what it or he really is. This use of irony is the reason irony often appears in satirical writing (writing that mocks a situation or idea). Jonathan Swift's "A Modest Proposal" (p. 387) is entirely ironic; the difficulty lies in figuring out what meaning Swift intends, since the literal meaning is certainly not his message. When something occurs that is counter to what is expected (what people often refer to when they say something is ironic), it is sometimes called situational irony. An example of this latter form of irony can be seen in the conclusion of Langston Hughes's "Salvation" (p. 179).

Metaphor Metaphor can be understood as a figure of speech (a nonliteral use of language) that says one thing *is* another or, in the form of simile, as a figure of speech that says one thing is *like* another. In both cases, the writer is trying to explain one thing by means of comparing it to another, more familiar thing. One example of the metaphor that makes a comparison by saying one thing is another comes from E. B. White's "Once More to the Lake" (p. 431): "It took a cool nerve, because if you threw the switch a twentieth of a second too soon you would catch the flywheel when it still had speed enough to go up past center, and the boat would leap ahead, charging bull-fashion at the dock" (par. 10). Note that this metaphor does not say explicitly that the boat is a bull; rather it says that the boat would *leap* and *charge bull-fashion*.

Narration Telling a **story**, or giving an account of an event. Narration is a part of many different kinds of writing. Writers often tell an anecdote, or short narrative often told to make a point, as support for an **argument**. Some **essays** are almost entirely narration, but usually the events of the story lead to some kind of **conclusion**. George Orwell's "Shooting an Elephant" (p. 284) is largely narration and leads him to a very specific conclusion, as can be seen when he writes, of the story he tells, "It was a tiny incident in itself, but it gave me a better glimpse than I had had before of the real nature of imperialism — the real motives for which despotic governments act" (par. 3).

Paragraph A series of sentences, set off by an initial indentation or a blank line, that develop a main idea. Paragraphs often have **topic sentences** that state that main idea, followed by sentences that offer support.

Paraphrase A rephrasing of a section of a work into one's own words. A paraphrase is different from a **summary** in that it includes the details of a work and so is of similar length to the original; a paraphrase is similar to a summary in that both attempt to give some sense of another work without using its words.

Plagiarism Using another person's words or ideas in one's own work, without acknowledgment.

Point of view The angle from which a writer sees his or her subject. No matter how objective or impartial a writer claims to be, he or she is always writing from a point of view influenced by age, race, gender, and economic and social status, to name just a few factors. In the personal essay "How It Feels to Be Colored Me" (p. 182) Zora Neale Hurston acknowledges writing from her own point of view.

Prewriting Writing that happens before drafting. Prewriting is an early stage in the writing process during which writers brainstorm, come up with topics and theses, and begin to work on ways to develop them.

Process analysis Explaining how to do something, how others do it, or how certain things occur. Often process analysis supports another aim — to make a point or to tell one's own **story**, for example. When Malcolm X tells the story of his self-education in "Learning to Read" (p. 257), for example, he explains the process he went through to teach himself to read and also describes how he learned about the history of Africa and African Americans.

Quotation The inclusion of the words of another in one's own work, indicated by surrounding quotation marks. Used to convey a sense of the person who wrote or spoke those words, or to reproduce a phrase or sentence or more that perfectly captures some meaning the writer wishes also to convey, or to borrow some authority from an expert or eyewitness. Gloria Anzaldúa's "How to Tame a Wild Tongue" (p. 33) demonstrates a number of uses of quotation.

Revision The stage in the process of writing after a first **draft** is written when writers reexamine their work and try to improve it. This improvement consists of more than editing and proofreading — it also includes reevaluating the structure, the supporting **evidence**, the **thesis**, and even the topic. All good writers revise their work.

Rhetoric The effective use of language; also, the study of effective language use. The term can also be used negatively, as when it is said that a particular argument is really just using rhetoric, that is, using words persuasively (perhaps by making emotional appeals) without actually making a solid **argument**.

Story A **narrative**. The term is used in a number of different senses — to indicate a narrative within a nonfiction piece, to label a news article in a newspaper or magazine, or to name the genre of short fiction. Many, perhaps most, effective essays tell some kind of story.

Style The way a writer writes. Any of the choices writers make while writing — about **diction**, sentence length, structure, rhythm, and figures of speech — that make their work sound like them. The **tone** of a particular work can be due in part to a writer's style. James Baldwin is known for his distinctive style, one aspect of which is the mixing of formal, sometimes biblical, language and an everyday, conversational style, as in this sentence from "Notes of a Native Son" (p. 50): "I had declined to believe in that apocalypse which had been central to my father's vision; very well, life seemed to be saying, here is something that will certainly pass for an apocalypse until the real thing comes along" (par. 2).

Summary A condensation, in one's own words, of a work. Summaries consist of the main points of the work; supporting points, examples, and other kinds of support are left out.

Synthesis The use of outside sources to gather information and opinions, in order to develop ideas, amass evidence, and support arguments. Synthesis enables writers to do more than simply express their opinion — it enables them to enter the conversation about their topic already being held in the wider world. It also allows them to complicate their ideas, to see more than one side, and to marshal information and logical arguments in the service of their position.

Thesis The main idea in a piece of writing, which the work is trying to argue or explore. Also sometimes known as the **claim**, a term which also has a more specific meaning related to argumentation. The thesis can be explicit, as in essays that make an argument (as in Stephen Jay Gould's "Sex, Drugs, Disasters, and the Extinction of Dinosaurs," p. 169), or implicit or even secondary, as in some narrative essays (as in Maya Angelou's "Graduation," p. 20).

Thesis statement A sentence or group of sentences, usually appearing early in a piece of writing, that announce the thesis. The thesis statement often states plainly what the work as a whole is to be about, but it can take many forms, as in the following from Stephanie Ericsson's "The Ways We Lie" (p. 159), in which she makes an assertion and follows with a question: "We lie. We all do. We exaggerate, we minimize, we avoid confrontation, we spare people's feelings, we conveniently forget, we keep secrets, we justify lying to the big-guy institutions. Like most people, I indulge in small falsehoods and still think of myself as an honest person. Sure I lie, but it doesn't hurt anything. Or does it?" (par. 3).

Tone Attitude toward subject, readers, and even the writer and work itself; also sometimes mood or atmosphere more generally. Achieved through **style** as well as content. In his indictment of King George III in the Declaration of Independence (p. 187), Thomas Jefferson writes, "He has abdicated Government here, by declaring us out of his Protection and waging War against us. He has plundered our seas, ravaged our Coasts, burnt our towns, and destroyed the lives of our people" (pars. 20–21). His tone in this passage comes from his choice of words, the shape of his sentences, and his imagery.

Topic sentence The sentence in which the writer states a **paragraph**'s main idea. The topic sentence often appears at or near the beginning of the paragraph. When Gloria Anzaldúa in "How to Tame a Wild Tongue" (p. 33) begins a paragraph, "Chicanos, after 250 years of Spanish/Anglo colonization, have developed significant differences in the Spanish we speak" (par. 18), we should suspect the rest of the paragraph will develop that idea, perhaps with examples of these differences (and we would be right).

Transitions The connective tissue among sentences, ideas, and **paragraphs**. Transitions help readers follow writers through their ideas and see the connections among the parts of an **argument** or the relation between scenes in a **narrative**. Through the use of transitional words *(therefore, nonetheless, then)*, phrases *(on the other hand, as a result, in the same way)*, effects (such as repetition or parallel sentence structures), and even whole paragraphs, good writers include signposts to show readers the direction the argument or story is going. Nancy Mairs in "On Being a Cripple" (p. 244) begins many of her paragraphs with transitions that help readers follow the line of her thought. Some examples: "Lest I begin to sound like Polyanna, however, let me say that I don't like having MS" (par. 9); "Along with this fear that people are secretly accepting shoddy goods comes a relentless pressure to please" (par. 18); "This gentleness is part of the reason that I'm not sorry to be a cripple" (par. 32).

Acknowledgments (continued)

Sherman Alexie, "The Joy of Reading and Writing: Superman and Me," from *The Most Wonderful Books*, edited by Michael Dorris and Emilie Buchwald. Copyright © 1997 by Sherman Alexie. Published by Milkweed Editions. Reprinted with permission of Nancy Stauffer Associates on behalf of the author.

Maya Angelou, "Graduation." Copyright © 1969 and renewed 1997 by Maya Angelou, from *I Know why the Caged Bird Sings* by Maya Angelou. Used by permission of Random House, Inc.

Gloria Anzaldúa, "How to Tame a Wild Tongue," from *Borderlands: La Frontera: The New Mestiza*. Copyright © 1987, 1999 by Gloria Anzaldúa. Reproduced by permission of Aunt Lute Books.

Barbara Lazear Ascher, "On Compassion," from *The Habit of Loving* by Barbara Lazear Ascher. Copyright © 1986, 1987, 1989 by Barbara Lazear Ascher. Used by permission of Random House, Inc.

James Baldwin, excerpt from *Notes of a Native Son* by James Baldwin, pp. 85–114. Copyright © 1955, renewed 1983, by James Baldwin. Reprinted by permission of Beacon Press, Boston.

Dave Barry, "Turkeys in the Kitchen," first published in *The Miami Herald*, Feb. 2, 1986. Copyright © Dave Barry. Reprinted with permission. All rights reserved.

William F. Buckley Jr., "Why Don't We Complain?" from *Rumbles Left and Right* by William F. Buckley Jr. Copyright © 1960, 1963 by William F. Buckley Jr. First published in Esquire, 1960. Used by permission of the Wallace Literary Agency, Inc.

Rachel Carson, "The Obligation to Endure," from *Silent Spring* by Rachel Carson. Copyright © 1962 by Rachel L. Carson, renewed 1990 by Roger Christie. Reprinted by permission of Houghton Mifflin Harcourt Publishing Company. All rights reserved.

Judith Ortiz Cofer, "The Myth of the Latin Woman: I Just Met a Girl Named María," from *The Latin Deli: Prose and Poetry* by Judith Ortiz Cofer. Copyright © 1993 by Judith Ortiz Cofer. Reprinted by permission of The University of Georgia Press.

Jared Diamond, "The Ends of the World as We Know Them," from *The New York Times*, January 1, 2005. Copyright © 2005 by New York Times. Reproduced by permission.

Joan Didion, "On Morality," from *Slouching Toward Bethlehem* by Joan Didion. Copyright © 1966, 1968, renewed 1996 by Joan Didion. © 1968 by Farrar, Straus and Giroux, LLC.

Annie Dillard, "Seeing" (pp. 14–34) from *Pilgrim at Tinker Creek* by Annie Dillard. Copyright © 1974 by Annie Dillard. Reprinted by permission of HarperCollins Publishers.

Frederick Douglass, "Learning to Read and Write," from *Narrative of the Life of an American Slave*, Anti-Slavery Office, Boston, 1845.

Barbara Ehrenreich, "Serving in Florida," from *Nickel and Dimed: On (Not) Getting By in America* by Barbara Ehrenreich. Copyright © 2001 by Barbara Ehrenreich. Reprinted by permission of Henry Holt and Company, LLC.

Lars Eighner, "On Dumpster Diving," from *Travels with Lizbeth: Three Years on the Road and on the Streets* by Lars Eighner. Copyright © 1993 by Lars Eighner. Reprinted by permission of St. Martin's Press, LLC.

1978 by Sonia Pitt-Rivers. Reprinted by permission of Houghton Mifflin Harcourt Publishing Company.

Plato, from "The Allegory of the Cave," in *Dialogues of Plato* translated by Benjamin Jowett, The Colonial Press, 1899.

Michael Pollan, "What's Eating America," from *Smithsonian Magazine*, July 2006. Copyright © 2006 by Michael Pollan. Reprinted by permission of International Creative Management, Inc.

Richard Rodriguez, "Aria: Memoir of a Bilingual Childhood," from *Hunger of Memory: The Education of Richard Rodriguez* by Richard Rodriguez. Reprinted by permission of David R. Godine, Publisher, Inc. Copyright © 1982 by Richard Rodriguez.

Mike Rose, "I Just Wanna Be Average," excerpt from Chapter 2, pp. 24–47 in *Lives on the Boundary: The Struggles and Achievements of America's Underprepared* by Mike Rose. Copyright © 1989 by Mike Rose. Reprinted with permission of The Free Press, a Division of Simon & Schuster Inc. All rights reserved.

Scott Russell Sanders, "The Men We Carry in Our Minds." Copyright © 1984 by Scott Russell Sanders; first appeared in *Milkweed Chronicle*; collected in the author's *The Paradise of Bombs* (Boston: Beacon Press, 1993); reprinted by permission of the author.

Eric Schlosser, "Kid Kustomers," from *Fast Food Nation: The Dark Side of the All-American Meal* by Eric Schlosser. Copyright © 2001 by Eric Schlosser. Reprinted by permission of Houghton Mifflin Company. All rights reserved.

David Sedaris, "A Plague of Tics," from *Naked* by David Sedaris. Copyright © 1997 by David Sedaris. By permission of Little, Brown and Company.

Susan Sontag, excerpt from *Regarding the Pain of Others* by Susan Sontag. Copyright © 2003 by Susan Sontag. Reprinted by permission of Farrar, Straus and Giroux, LLC.

Elizabeth Cady Stanton, *The Declaration of Sentiments*, 1848.

Brent Staples, "Just Walk on By: Black Men and Public Space." Copyright © 1986 by Brent Staples. Reprinted by permission of the author.

Jonathan Swift, from *A Modest Proposal*, 1729.

Amy Tan, "Mother Tongue," first appeared in *The Threepenny Review*. Copyright © 1990 by Amy Tan. Reprinted with the permission of the author and the Sandra Dijkstra Literary Agency.

Henry David Thoreau, "Where I Lived, and What I Lived For," from *Walden: On Life in the Woods*, Boston, 1854.

Sojourner Truth (Isabella Baumfree), "Ain't I a Woman?" 1851.

Sarah Vowell, "Shooting Dad" (pp. 15–24). Reprinted with the permission of Simon & Schuster, Inc., from *Take the Cannoli* by Sarah Vowell. Copyright © 2000 by Sarah Vowell. All rights reserved.

Alice Walker, "In Search of Our Mother's Gardens," from *In Search of Our Mother's Gardens: Womanist Prose*, including "Women" from *Revolutionary Petunias & Other Poems* by Alice Walker. Copyright © 1974 by Alice Walker. Reprinted by permission of Houghton Mifflin Harcourt Publishing Company.

E. B. White, "Once More to the Lake," from *One Man's Meat* by E. B. White. Copyright © 1941 by E. B. White. Reprinted by permission of Tilbury House, Publishers, Gardiner, Maine.

Marie Winn, "Family Life," from *The Plug-In Drug*, revised and updated 25th Anniversary Edition by Marie Winn. Copyright © 1977, 1985, 2002 by Marie Winn Miller. Used by permission of Viking Penguin, a division of Penguin Group (USA) Inc.

Virginia Woolf, "The Death of the Moth," from *The Death of the Moth and Other Essays* by Virginia Woolf. Copyright © 1942 by Houghton Mifflin Harcourt Publishing Company and renewed 1970 by Majorie T. Parsons, Executrix. Reprinted by permission of Houghton Mifflin Harcourt Publishing Company.

Index of Authors and Titles

Alexie, Sherman, *The Joy of Reading and Writing: Superman and Me*, 15
Allegory of the Cave, The (Plato), 292
Angelou, Maya, *Graduation*, 20
Anzaldúa, Gloria, *How to Tame a Wild Tongue*, 33
Ain't I a Woman? (Truth), 410
Aria: Memoir of a Bilingual Childhood (Rodriguez), 307
Ascher, Barbara Lazear, *On Compassion*, 46

Baldwin, James, *Notes of a Native Son*, 50
Barry, Dave, *Turkeys in the Kitchen*, 72
Buckley, William F., Jr., *Why Don't We Complain?*, 76

Carson, Rachel, *The Obligation to Endure*, 83
Cofer, Judith Ortiz, *The Myth of the Latin Woman: I Just Met a Girl Named María*, 91
Curbing Nature's Paparazzi (McKibben), 267

Death of the Moth, The (Woolf), 448
Declaration of Independence, The (Jefferson), 187
Declaration of Sentiments and Resolutions (Stanton), 379
Diamond, Jared, *The Ends of the World as We Know Them*, 98
Didion, Joan, *On Morality*, 106
Dillard, Annie, *Seeing*, 112
Douglass, Frederick, *Learning to Read and Write*, 129

Ehrenreich, Barbara, *Serving in Florida*, 136
Eighner, Lars, *On Dumpster Diving*, 146
Ends of the World as We Know Them, The (Diamond), 98
Ericsson, Stephanie, *The Ways We Lie*, 159

Fourth of July, The (Lorde), 239

Games (Johnson), 196
Gould, Stephen Jay, *Sex, Drugs, Disasters, and the Extinction of Dinosaurs*, 169
Graduation (Angelou), 20

How It Feels to Be Colored Me (Hurston), 182
How to Tame a Wild Tongue (Anzaldúa), 33
Hughes, Langston, *Salvation*, 179
Hurston, Zora Neale, *How It Feels to Be Colored Me*, 182

"I Just Wanna Be Average" (Rose), 331
In Search of Our Mothers' Gardens (Walker), 420

Jefferson, Thomas, *The Declaration of Independence*, 187
Johnson, Steven, *Games*, 196

Joy of Reading and Writing: Superman and Me, The (Alexie), 15
Just Walk on By: Black Men and Public Space (Staples), 383

Kid Kustomers (Schlosser), 353
King, Martin Luther, Jr., *Letter from Birmingham Jail*, 203
Kingston, Maxine Hong, *No Name Woman*, 221
Klinkenborg, Verlyn, *Our Vanishing Night*, 234

Learning to Read (Malcolm X), 257
Learning to Read and Write (Douglass), 129
Letter from Birmingham Jail (King), 203
Lorde, Audre, *The Fourth of July*, 239

Mairs, Nancy, *On Being a Cripple*, 244
Malcolm X, *Learning to Read*, 257
McKibben, Bill, *Curbing Nature's Paparazzi*, 267
Men We Carry in Our Minds, The (Sanders), 346
Modest Proposal, A (Swift), 387
Momaday, N. Scott, *The Way to Rainy Mountain*, 273
Mother Tongue (Tan), 396
Mukherjee, Bharati, *Two Ways to Belong in America*, 280
Myth of the Latin Woman: I Just Met a Girl Named María, The (Ortiz Cofer), 91

No Name Woman (Kingston), 221
Notes of a Native Son (Baldwin), 50

Obligation to Endure, The (Carson), 83
On Being a Cripple (Mairs), 244
On Compassion (Ascher), 46
On Dumpster Diving (Eighner), 146
On Morality (Didion), 106
Once More to the Lake (White), 431
Our Vanishing Night (Klinkenborg), 234

Orwell, George, *Shooting an Elephant*, 284

Plato, *The Allegory of the Cave*, 292
Plague of Tics, A (Sedaris), 359
Pollan, Michael, *What's Eating America*, 300

Regarding the Pain of Others (Sontag), 373
Rodriguez, Richard, *Aria: Memoir of a Bilingual Childhood*, 307
Rose, Mike, *"I Just Wanna Be Average,"* 331

Said, Edward, *Clashing Civilizations?*, 365
Salvation (Hughes), 179
Sanders, Scott Russell, *The Men We Carry in Our Minds*, 346
Schlosser, Eric, *Kid Kustomers*, 353
Sedaris, David, *A Plague of Tics*, 359
Seeing (Dillard), 112
Serving in Florida (Ehrenreich), 136
Sex, Drugs, Disasters, and the Extinction of Dinosaurs (Gould), 169
Shooting an Elephant (Orwell), 284
Shooting Dad (Vowell), 412
Sontag, Susan, *Regarding the Pain of Others*, 373
Stanton, Elizabeth Cady, *Declaration of Sentiments and Resolutions*, 379
Staples, Brent, *Just Walk on By: Black Men and Public Space*, 383
Swift, Jonathan, *A Modest Proposal*, 387

Tan, Amy, *Mother Tongue*, 396
Television: The Plug-In Drug (Winn), 438
Thoreau, Henry David, *Where I Lived, and What I Lived For*, 403
Truth, Sojourner, *Ain't I a Woman?*, 410
Turkeys in the Kitchen (Barry), 72
Two Ways to Belong in America (Mukherjee), 280

Vowell, Sarah, *Shooting Dad*, 412

Walker, Alice, *In Search of Our Mothers' Gardens*, 420
Way to Rainy Mountain, The (Momaday), 273
Ways We Lie, The (Ericsson), 159
What's Eating American (Pollan), 300
Where I Lived, and What I Lived For (Thoreau), 403
White, E. B., *Once More to the Lake*, 431
Why Don't We Complain? (Buckley), 76
Winn, Marie, *Television: The Plug-In Drug*, 438
Woolf, Virginia, *The Death of the Moth*, 448